The
Winn L. Rosch
PC Upgrade Bible

Winn L. Rosch

*with illustrations by
Bruce Sanders*

Brady Publishing

New York London Toronto Sydney Tokyo Singapore

Brady Publishing

Published by Brady Publishing
A division of Simon & Schuster, Inc.
15 Columbus Circle
New York, NY 10023

Manufactured in the United States of America

10 9 8 7 6 5 4 3 2

ISBN: 0-13-932252-3

The illustrations in this book were first published in *PC Sources* and are used with permission.

Dedication

To C.E.R. wherever you are.

CONTENTS

1. INTRODUCTION   1

   Why Upgrade   5
   Developing a Plan   7
   Setting a Goal   8
      Running Particular Applications   8
      Achieving Better Performance   9
      Adding More Mass Storage   11
      Getting More Colors and Sharper Images   12
      Improving Power Reserves   13
      Exchanging Information with Other PCs   13
      Building Backup Security   14
   Determining the Bottlenecks   14
   Selecting an Upgrade   16
   Installing the Upgrade   17
   Why Not to Upgrade   18
      An Upgraded Computer Is an Old Computer   18
      Your PC Is Already Too Powerful   19
      Upgrades Lack Status   19
      Fear of Failure   19

2. SYSTEM BOTTLENECKS 21

    The Misleading Megahertz 23
    Bottleneck Causes, Effects, and Cures 26
        Microprocessor Bottlenecks 26
        Bus Bottleneck 29
        Memory Bottlenecks 31
        Disk Bottlenecks 33
        Display Bottlenecks 35
        Printing Bottlenecks 36
        Network Bottlenecks 37
        Human Bottlenecks 38
    Locating the Bottlenecks 40
        Verifying Processing Bottlenecks 40
        Checking Your Disk 41
        Determining Display Delays 41
        Checking for External Delays 42
        Checking the Human Interface 43
    Scientific Determination of Bottlenecks 44
    Recommendations for Specific Applications 45
        Word Processors 45
        Databases 46
        Spreadsheets 46
        Computer-aided Design 47
        Application Development 48
        OS/2 48
        Microsoft Windows 49

3. AVOIDING THE UPGRADE 51

    Simple Disk Speed-ups 53
        DOS Buffers 54
        Build a RAM Disk 59
        Use DOS FASTOPEN 61
        Trim Your Search Path 63
        Defragment Your Disk 64
        Softward-based Disk Caching 67
    Increasing Disk Capacity 71

Find Lost Clusters   71
Archive Inactive Files   72
Compress Data Bound for Disk   74
Improving Memory Speed   76
Extended Versus Expanded Memory   77
Trimming Wait States   78
Maximizing Memory   79
Improving Display Performance   81
Video Speed-up Programs   82
Video Shadowing   83
Display List Drivers   84
Printer Spooling   84
Keyboard Quickeners   85
Navigational Speed   86
Keyboard Macros   86

4.   MICROPROCESSOR UPGRADES   89

Chip Choice   92
The 8088 Family   92
The 8086 Family   94
The 80286 Family   95
The 80386 Family   96
The 80486 Family   100
Which Chip to Pick   101
Microprocessor Upgrade Alternatives   103
Increasing Clock Speed   103
Adding Memory Management   105
Memory Tricks   106
Trimming Wait States   107
Interleaving Memory   109
Expanding Cache Memory   109
Replacing Your Entire PC   110
Microprocessor Upgrade Method   111
Replacing Your Microprocessor   112
Turbo Boards   115
Replacement Motherboards   118
What You Can Keep   120

Choosing a Motherboard   120
Proprietary Upgrades   124
Step by Step Upgrade Guides   125
Microprocessor Replacement   125
Turbo Board Upgrades   127
System Board Upgrades   130

5. COPROCESSORS   135

Coprocessor Fundamentals   138
Applications That Benefit   140
Coprocessor History   143
Coprocessor Communications   145
I/O Mapping   146
Memory Mapping   147
Intel Architecture   149
The 8087   150
The 287   151
The 387   155
387-compatible Chips   157
Cyrix Corporation   157
Integrated Information Technology   160
ULSI   161
Weitek Corporation   161
The 487   163
Making the Upgrade   164
Finding the Right Chip   164
System Preparation   166
Preparing a Coprocessor   167
Chip Orientation   168
Coprocessor System Set-up   172

6. MEMORY   175

Memory Addressing   178
Program Limits   179
Operating System Limits   180

Microprocessor Limits   181
Architectural Limits   181
Types of Memory   182
Conventional Memory   183
Expanded Memory   186
Extended Memory   190
Cache Memory   190
Choosing a Memory Type   193
Application Considerations   193
Performance Considerations   194
Hardware Considerations   195
Selecting Memory Chips and Modules   199
Packaging   200
Capacity   202
Technology   205
Speed   207
Chip and Memory Module Installation   209
Preparing Chips   210
Which Sockets?   212
Chip Orientation   213
Plugging in Modules   215
Inspect Your Work   218
System Set-up   219

7.   HARD DISK UPGRADES   221

The Hard Disk as a System   224
Interface Designs   226
Device-level Interfaces   229
System-level Interfaces   231
Hard Disk Controllers and Host Adapter Issues   234
Capacity Issues   244
Disk Size and Form Factor   246
Hard Disk Arrays   249
Performance Issues   251
Access Time   252
Caching Concerns   253
Data Transfer Rate   254

Hard Disk Reliability   255
Choosing a Vendor   258
Evaluating Costs   259
Upgrade Method   262
Mechanical Installation   263
Cable Connections   265
Software Set-up   269
   System Configuration   270
   Low-level Formatting   270
   Disk Partitioning   271
   DOS Formatting   272
   Restoring Files   272

8.   FLOPPY DISK UPGRADES   273

Floppy Standards   275
Floppy Drive Compatibility   277
Floppy Disk Compatibility   279
DOS Considerations   281
PC Compatibility Issues   283
Laptop Compatibility Issues   289
Improving Compatibility   290
   Software Drivers   291
   Floppy Controller Upgrade   294
   Adding a New BIOS   296
Physical Considerations   298
   Internal Versus External Installation 298
   Mounting Hardware   299
   Floppy Drive Cables   301
Connecting Cables   302
Upgrade Mechanics   305
PS/2 Considerations   309
Final Steps   311

9.   OPTICAL DISK DRIVES   313

Three Optical Technologies   317
CD ROM Background   320
   CD ROM Media   322

CD ROM Players   323
CD ROM Standards   326
WORM Drives   327
WORM Systems   329
WORM Applications   331
Rewritable Optical Disks   332
Dye-polymer Storage   332
Phase-change Storage   333
Magneto-optical Storage   333
How Magneto-optical Drives Work   335
The Magneto-optical Drawback   337
Magneto-optical Media Considerations   339
Magneto-optical Standards   340
MO Cartridges   342
Magneto-optical Applications   343
Optical Drive Installation   344

10.   ADDING PORTS AND MODEMS   351

Serial Ports   354
Parallel Ports   357
Ports Addresses   358
Port Connectors   361
Shopping for Port Adapters   362
Port Preparation   363
Port Installation   366
Modems   370
Modem Function and Purpose   371
Modem Standards   373
Other Modem Considerations   380
Choosing Between Internal and External Modems   384
Fas Modems   387
Fax Background   389
The PC-to-fax Connection   390
Selecting a Fax Modem   391
Modem Support Issues   393

Preinstallation Considerations 395
Modem Installation 398

11. GRAPHICS: ADAPTERS, MONITORS AND INPUT DEVICES 403

Display Adapters 406
Resolution Issues 408
Color Issues 410
Performance Issues 413
Bus Width 414
BIOS Issues 415
Graphics Coprocessors and Coprocessed Adapters 416
Graphics Languages 417
Coprocessor Chips 419
Monitor Matching 420
Frequencies 420
Signal Type 422
Color Capability 424
One or Two Displays 424
Connections and Connectors 425
Installing Display Adapters 427
Monitors 429
Selecting a Monitor 430
Scanning Range 430
Input Type 433
Required Frequencies 434
Autosizing 436
Monitor Controls 437
Sharpness Versus Resolution 439
Convergence 443
Monitor Bandwidth 444
Interlacing 446
Monitor Colors and Phosphors 447
Monitor Brightness 450
Tilt-swivel Base 452
Monitor Connections 452

Input Devices   455
Keyboards   455
Mice   457
   Motion Detection   458
   Mouse Buttons   459
   Mouse Protocols   459
   Mouse Interfaces   460
   Mouse Resolution   461
   Mouse Installation   462
Trackballs   465
   Trackball Installation   467
Digitizing Tablets   469
   Digitizing Tablet Differences   470
     Size   471
     Resolution and Accuracy   471
     Speed   472
     Proximity   472
     Software and Emulations   472
     Cursors and Pens   472
     Templates   474
     Technology   474
     Ergonomics   474
   Digitizer Installation   475
Scanners   476
   Scanner Types   478
   Color Versus Grey Scale   480
   Optical Character Recognition   482
   Scanner Connections   484
   Scanner Installation   488

12.   TAPE SYSTEMS   491

Backup Philosophy   496
Backup Alternatives   498
Types of Tape Systems   501
   Nine-track Tape   501
   3480 Cartridges   503
   DC6000-style Cartridges   504

DC2000-style Cartridges   506
DC1000 Cartridges   509
Data Cassettes   509
Video-based Tape Backup Systems   510
Digital Audio Tape Systems   512
Choosing a Backup System   513
Backup Software Considerations   515
Media Considerations   516
Practical Backup Systems   517
Shopping for a Tape Drive   520
Physical Installation Considerations   521
Installing DC2000 Drives in PS/2s   522
Installing DC2000 Drives in $3\frac{1}{2}$-inch Bays   524
Installing DC6000 Drives   525
Cabling Concerns   528

13. POWER SUPPLIES AND BACKUP SYSTEMS 531

The Purpose of the Power Supply   534
Power Supply Upgrade Facts and Dangers   535
What a Power Supply Does   536
How Much Power You Need   537
Power Supply Connections   539
Physical Considerations   540
Removing Old Power Supplies   542
Installing a New Power Supply   545
Backup Power Systems   549
Standby Power Supplies   550
Uninterruptible Power Supplies   551
Internal Battery Supplies   552
Backup Power Strategies   553
State-saving Software   555
Backup Power Supply Ratings   556
Power   557
Energy   558
Buying a Backup Power Supply   559
External Backup Supplies   559
Internal Backup Supplies   561

Installing an External Backup Power Supply   562
Installing an Internal Backup Power Supply   563

APPENDICES   567

A.   Dealing With Your PC's Case   569
     Removing the Cover   572
     Fitting Expansion Boards   576
     Affixing the Cover   579
     The Case for Case Screws   580

B.   Drive Installation   583
     PC Disk Drives   585
     XT Disk Drives   586
     AT Disk Drives   587
     AT-compatible Disk Drives   589
     PS/2 Disk Drives   590

C.   The PC Toolkit   591
     Screwdrivers   594
     Phillips Screwdrivers   594
     Nutdrivers   595
     Torx Screwdrivers   595
     Long-nosed Pliers   596
     Chip Removal Tools   597

D.   Understanding SCSI   599
     Cabling   603
     Terminations   604
     Identification   606

INDEX   609

Acknowledgments

Every book has a story behind it as well as inside it. This book began with a lunch with Burton Gabriel of Brady Publishing who, supportive from the start, coaxed, cajoled, and coerced each chapter from the black, mysterious cave of my mind into the black, mysterious cave of the publishing house.

Much of the material that appears on these pages was developed from a regular feature called Upgrade Clinic that appears each month in *PC Sources* magazine. The people there were indispensible in drawing both truth and coherence from the material that was submitted to them.

I owe thanks to everyone at *PC Sources*. My first contact with the magazine came even before it had a name. A trio of foresighted and farsighted executives—Philip Korsant, Jim Stafford, and Jeff Ballowe—conjured up the idea of *PC Sources* from the maelstrom called computer publishing and, despite their decades of publishing experience, solicited my suggestions for creating the magazine.

The Upgrade Clinic itself was originally conceived by *PC Sources* editor-in-chief Peter McKie, who has guided the magazine for the entirety of its successful existence.

Peter also deserves thanks for bringing me together with Bruce Sanders, whose paintings illustrate the Upgrade Clinic in several languages and whose drawings in this book will assist you through the upgrade process. Without Bruce, the Upgrade Clinic would never be so readable and helpful. And without Bruce, the world might suffer an oversupply of Key Lime pie

Thanks are also due to Molly Faust, the *PC Sources* editor who made sense out of my scribblings (removing the typos, misspellings, and jokes that neither she nor I fully understood) and to Teri Robinson who took over the Upgrade Clinic from Molly in mid-1991.

Last but hardly least is Tom Dillon of Brady Publishing who had the dubious honor or bringing order from confusion, then instilling the book with a fresh sense of chaos.

In all, it's been well over a year since Burt and I had that fateful lunch—a long, troubling, tiring year. But above all the trials and hardships of preparing this book (and the Upgrade Clinics along the way), one thing sticks in my mind. Next time it's Burt's turn to buy.

Winn L. Rosch

Limits of Liability and Disclaimer of Warranty

The author and publisher of this book have used their best efforts in preparing this book and the programs contained in it. These effort include the development, research, and testing of the theories and programs to determine their effectiveness. The author and publisher make no warranty of any kind, expressed or implied, with regard to these programs or the documentation contained in this book. The author and publisher shall not be liable in any event for incidental or consequential damages in connection with, or arising out of, the furnishing, performance, or use of these programs.

All brand and product names mentioned herein are trademarks or registered trademarks of their respective holders.

1.

INTRODUCTION

Upgrading your PC is easy, quick, and will give you greater confidence in using your PC. To make a successful upgrade, however, you must carefully plan what you're going to do. In making your plans, you may discover that an upgrade is not the right solution for your system.

Imagine stretching your sedan into a Greyhound Landcruiser when you want to take a bevy of friends to the Big Game. Or goosing up the microwave to nuke through dinner in double-time. Make one of these changes in ten-minutes time, equipped with only a screwdriver and enough common sense to switch off the electricity before you start, and you'll begin to get the idea of the magnitude of change you can make by upgrading your computer, as well as how easy and simple the chore can be.

No other modern tool or toy can be upgraded as easily or as well as a personal computer. You can take the oldest IBM PC and in half an hour upgrade it into the equivalent of the fastest, most capable computers on sale. You can increase its speed by a factor of 20 or more. You can add megabytes to its memory. You can speed up its hard disk access by a factor of five, increase mass storage capacity by 30-fold, add bright new graphics, fax capabilities, tape backup—all in the time of a coffee-break.

The best part of making a PC upgrade is that you can do it yourself. No particular skills are required other than the ability to follow step-by-step instructions—like cooking a soufflé but without the worry of whether it will fall. Take just a little care and you're practically guaranteed success. Luck is not an issue. Neither are mechanical ability or computer knowledge. In fact, you'll probably gain a little of both (and maybe some luck—and a lot of self-assurance) in making an upgrade yourself.

Don't think of making an upgrade to your computer as something unusual or exotic. Personal computers aren't just upgradable. They are *designed* to be upgraded. No dangerous voltages are loose inside a PC when the top of its case is removed, even if you should forget to switch off the power or pull the plug. Expansion slots lie waiting the addition of new peripherals in nearly every machine. Each slot is designed to make the effort of adding an expansion board minimal. At most, you need to twist a screwdriver a couple of times. In fact, in IBM's latest PS/2 computers, all you need when adding a board or even a disk drive is a finger and opposable thumb—standard human equipment. Cables are keyed so you can't plug them in wrong. Everything is so easy that even your computer dealer can handle everything. There's no reason you can't, too.

Of course, all this simplicity and ease begs an important question: Why is a book on upgrading your PC necessary at all, if even the most craven misanthrope can handle the task blindfolded with one arm tied behind his back and fighting a severe head wind? The answers are several.

As with anything you do, upgrading your system is easiest the second time through. Anything improves with practice—riding a bicycle, building a bookcase, sipping Scotch. The first time is always a learning experience. You learn the tricks and the subtleties as you go along.

In making the first upgrade to your PC with the help of this book, you'll learn enough to become an expert in your own right. This book will provide the guidance you need to decipher how things come apart and fit together again, what parts go where, which corners you can cut, which details demand your particular attention. Having an expert at your side will make everything go more smoothly. The expert can give you hints about the small, less obvious choices you can make that may have big consequences on how easily your upgrade project goes. Instead of discovering secrets too late, the arm-side expert can warn you before you waste time and have to trace back through several steps all over again. Just a little hint—like to attach the cables to a disk drive *before* you screw it into place—can save you skinned knuckles and apologies to your spouse for the new and exotic language to which you expose your offspring.

Moreover, you'll find that the hard part of making an upgrade to your PC—the part you dread and fear as beyond your capabilities, the most time-consuming and trying part—is not the actual mechanical work of installing peripherals. Rather, the toughest part of any upgrade is the brainwork, making the decision about what to upgrade and which particular product to use.

More than a matter of armchair speculation, to make the right decision you have to analyze your computer system and the software you run to determine where you face bottlenecks. You have to find the weak links that determine the strength of your data processing chain, the slowest parts of your computer that ultimately limit its top speed. Identifying the bottlenecks will help you make the most cost-effective upgrade to your computer.

You also have to consider among the thousands of products that want to burrow into your computer and budget. If you want a better hard disk drive, you've got to consider a wide variety of issues from its interface to its access time, even the brand you want to buy. These matters are hardly trivial. An unwise choice will add unnecessary expenses. It could even slow your system down or leave you with a worthless hunk of hardware.

Fortunately, as confusing as all the issues are, they are not an insurmountable challenge to sort through. With a little background and understanding—the information provided by this book—you can determine the best upgrade strategy by simply observing how your PC works. Finding the right product then becomes a matter of matching features to your needs.

The big secret is knowing what to look for, how things work (and work together), and, finally, how to install your upgrade. In truth, most people do more worrying about upgrades than work installing them. With a little knowledge, which this book will magnanimously provide, you can smooth out the effort. The chore of upgrading will become, at worst, a learning experience. More likely, it will be a mere ten-minute pause that stretches between ordinary work and performance computing.

Why Upgrade

Just because you *can* do something doesn't mean that you should. You could drive at 100 miles per hour down a bumpy, curvy residential street, but the risks involved—to yourself and others—dictate that you drive more wisely. Likewise, you could mortgage your house to make the down payment on a mainframe computer if you wanted to make the ultimate upgrade.

The entire reason, goal, and purpose for upgrading can be summed in a single word: MORE. An upgrade will give you more of what you bought a computer for in the first place. More speed so you can accomplish more in your workday. More memory so you can handle bigger programs and truly huge blocks of data. More features, like built-in fax capabilities and the ability to run several applications at the same time, switching between them on the fly.

Getting more done in less time with a more useful tool, an upgraded computer.

Certainly you have other opportunities to get more done in your workday. You could buy a newer, faster computer. Or you could hire someone to do your work for you. Both alternatives have a lot to recommend them, and both suffer from a singular disadvantage: They are more expensive, probably much more expensive, than simply upgrading the PC you have today.

While an upgrade won't give you a single, overall solution that will speed up every aspect of your work, the upgrade can break through the one barrier that's holding the rest of your PC back. Making such a selective upgrade is the most cost-effective way of getting better performance.

Another reason to upgrade is the cost of your dreams. Almost everyone would like to have the fastest, most powerful computer available. Few individuals can afford such heavyweight hardware. Even the most munificent corporate budget may be strained by the expenses involved, particularly should you want to acquire all that power in one piece.

Making upgrades will let you ease your way into greater power. Instead of gouging your purse for a new microprocessor, new memory, a new hard disk, and a new display system at once, you can add what you need as you require it or as you can afford it. For example, you can add a larger, faster hard disk today to accommodate a growing database. Then, a month or a year later you can upgrade your microprocessor to give you more speed in processing the information that you've stored.

Another reason to upgrade is to keep up with developing technology. Display systems represent an area where this consideration is particularly important. As display standards have improved, monitors have become sharper, more colorful, and just plain easier on your eyes. You may be able to live with the lethargic processing of an antique PC, but to use any but the best display system is courting bifocals or worse. More recent monitors are also safer. For example, concern is growing about whether extremely lowfrequency magnetic fields—commonly called ELF—are a health hazard. Many of the latest computer monitors have been redesigned to minimize such fields. Upgrading your display system to take advantage of one of these products could be the best preventive medicine that you can buy.

Developing a Plan

Before considering any upgrade, you need to have a plan. You have to have a definite goal in mind. That goal will determine what part of your system you need to upgrade—or whether you have a more cost-effective alternative to making a change. Upgrading just because you think you should is both foolish and wasteful. You could invest thousands of dollars on your PC—more than the cost of a new computer—and get improvements in your actual productivity that are too small to be measured. Without a good idea of what you want to accomplish, you cannot determine what you need to upgrade. You won't know what the bottlenecks in your system are and the best way to sidestep them.

Your plan will involve four distinct steps. First, you will set your goal: Decide what your upgrade is to accomplish. Do you need more speed to make answers snap on your screen or more capacity to hold your burgeoning database? Do you need faster answers in statistical calculations? Do you want to take advantages of the advanced features of the latest microprocessors? Do you just want to make your PC better? Do you want to make the entire upgrade immediately or stagger the cost over several months?

Next you'll have to analyze your system to see exactly what stands between you and your goal. Your system may suffer from one or more bottlenecks, constituents of your computer that are unable to keep up with the rest of its circuitry. While part of your PC may be idling along, unchallenged by any task that you give it, some other part may be panting and straining every time you press a key. Upgrading the idling part will only give the new part more time to idle in. Upgrade the part of your system that's most strained, and its performance can leap ahead.

When you plan your upgrade, you'll also have to face the biggest constraint of all: your budget. You need to determine how much you want to spend, how much you can afford, and how much of an upgrade actually makes sense. Sometimes a hardware upgrade is *not* the most cost-effective change you can make—new software or a new computer system can make more financial sense.

Once you've determined what you want to upgrade, you've got to select the best product to fit your needs. For example, if you determine that your system would benefit most from a new hard disk, you have to consider how large the capacity of a new drive must be, what kind of interface it uses, how much performance it delivers, even how physically large it is. You need to consider what manufacturer supplies the product you want and where to buy it—from your local dealer, from a parts distributor, or from a mail order vendor.

Finally comes the part most people associate with upgrading: Installing the product inside your computer. From many aspects, this is the easiest of the upgrade chores. It should take a fraction of the time of making your upgrade plans. It's also the most satisfying. Making the upgrade will give you confidence and reassure you that you can still outsmart—and smarten up—your computer. Making the upgrade yourself proves that you're still in control.

Setting a Goal

Your first approach to upgrading your PC should be the same as for starting out any new project. You must set a goal for yourself. Determine from the outset what you want to accomplish. After all, if you don't have a goal, you can never know when (or whether) you've achieved it. Having a target that you can aim for will make the entire upgrading process easier. It will also simplify your decision-making along the way.

More importantly, if you can't set a goal, then you shouldn't be thinking about an upgrade at all. You will just be throwing money at your computer. You're not likely to accomplish anything but making yourself poorer and your computer unnecessarily complex.

Only *you* can determine what exactly your goal is. An incomplete list of some of the goals you might aim for is given in the checklist on page 20. In addition, you might have your own, private goal in making an upgrade—for example, you might make the successful completion of your upgrade as a rite of your passage into the contemporary age of personal computing. The more pragmatic goals you might set your sights on include the following:

Running Particular Applications

Many programs have particular hardware requirements without which they will not run on your PC. Other programs need to take advantage of particular hardware features to develop their full power. For example, you cannot run the latest versions of AutoDesk Corporation's AutoCAD design program without equipping your computer with a math coprocessor. Moving to a graphical operating environment like Microsoft's Windows or OS/2 Presentation Manager requires your computer to have a graphical display system. Versions of OS/2 later than 2.0 won't work unless you have a 386 or 486 microprocessor in your computer; programs like Windows and Quarterdeck Office Systems' DESQview won't deliver their full power without one of those more advanced microprocessors. And the biggest, more powerful programs are almost all extremely memory hungry. Even DOS, starting with Version 5.0, needs memory in excess of the 640K that was the maximum sold with most systems until just a few years ago. To get the most from any of the latest software, you'll have to upgrade your system with a massive dose of random access memory.

Sometimes a particular application area demands a hardware feature that your PC lacks. For example, information retrieval applications nowadays are leaning toward a reliance on optical-based storage systems such as CD ROM. Adding a CD ROM drive to your PC will help you snare the information you need with on-line speed.

Typically, a simple upgrade will satisfy the special needs of most programs—and do it for a lot less than the cost of a new computer. If all your system lacks is a single feature to bring your favorite advanced application to life, you've got a clear-cut upgrade goal, one that will probably be the least expensive way to run your application.

Achieving Better Performance

The biggest difference between the latest personal computers and those of ten years ago is *speed*. Today you can buy a machine that cost the same as the first IBM PC did back in 1981, but runs between 25 and 100 times faster! That makes the latest computer hardware a great bargain—and older systems annoyingly slow. But you can upgrade your old PC to the same performance level for less than the cost—maybe a small fraction of the cost—of a new machine. That makes the upgrade an even bigger bargain.

But achieving a noticable speed increase is not as straightforward as it would seem. In PCs, speed is not a singular thing. There are several aspects to system performance, and each can be individually upgraded.

When most people compare the speeds of computers, they talk about microprocessor performance—how quickly the brains of the computer can solve a given problem. They bandy around terms like clock rates, megahertz, MIPS (millions of instructions per second), and megaflops (millions of floating-point operations per second) as if they know what the terms mean (and as if the terms have some absolute meaning in themselves). But computer performance isn't a simple numbers game. Getting better numbers doesn't always mean your work will get done faster.

Nevertheless, a faster, more powerful microprocessor will help your PC carry out some operations quicker. It will be able to calculate numbers in spreadsheets with less waiting, find and replace text in documents faster, even respond to your commands with greater snap.

But in sorting through database records, loading large graphic images, and copying big files, you may see a substantially larger speed increase by upgrading your hard disk drive. The hard disk in your computer determines its mass storage speed. (If you don't have a hard disk, your first upgrade should be to add one. No contemporary computer is complete without one.)

If you use your computer for a lot of high-level mathematics—computing statistics, carrying out complex formulae, generating engineering drawings—adding a math coprocessor may boost its speed even more than a new microprocessor. Math coprocessors carry out some complex functions hundreds of times faster than ordinary microprocessors do.

Most people hardly strain the microprocessors in their computers. The chores they have to do are trivial compared to the power of even a simple 16-bit microprocessor chip. But they still appreciate one aspect of having a faster computer because such machines *respond* faster. The people who use those quicker systems *feel* like they are working faster, and that gives them the idea that they are getting more done. A snappier system may be enough encouragement so that they do, in fact, accomplish more.

Most of the apparent speed of a computer is determined by its display system. The faster the display system can put images on your monitor, the quicker your computer seems. Adding an improved display adapter (the board that generates the signals to operate your monitor) can thus give the most satisfying of performance increases to your computer.

This acceleration often is more than a mirage, however. A high-performance graphic coprocessor can actually make the rest of the computer work quicker, too, by offloading much of the work that's required to create an on-screen image. A quick display can thus deliver both the illusion and reality of performance computing.

Adding More Mass Storage

Many applications require truly huge amounts of disk storage. Some software is sneaky, starting with minimal demands on your system, then growing and growing until you need dozens, even hundreds of megabytes. Even if you don't have a particular application that's a mass storage spendthrift, your everyday use of your PC can easily spin off so many files that soon the hard disk, which once was adequate, is bumping against its capacity limit.

When the IBM PC XT was introduced in 1983, its ten megabytes was revolutionary, more capacity than anyone could imaginably need—at least for the first ten minutes of operation of the machine. Today, the most popular hard disk size is approaching 100 megabytes, and even casual PC users worry about filling them up.

If your PC has less than 20 megabytes of hard disk, you're already a candidate for an upgrade. If less than about 20 percent of your present hard disk's space remains unused, you should probably be thinking about an upgrade, too. Should the PC you're responsible for be a file server, every time you add a new user you should carefully consider whether now is the time to upgrade. It probably is.

Mass storage upgrades are becoming increasingly complicated, from the standpoint of planning on the availability of a number of new mass storage devices. While once your choice was merely among different hard disks, you now can select between fixed-media and removable-media hard disks, optically enhanced floppy disk storage (so-called floptical drives), high-density, flexible-media magnetic cartridge drives (primarily Iomega Corporation's Bernoulli Box), Write-Once Read-Many times optical disk drives

(WORM drives), and rewritable magneto-optical (MO) disks drives. Each of these drive types has its own strengths and shortcomings in particular applications.

Getting More Colors and Sharper Images

All the hottest new applications for PCs (some of which have already begun to cool off) involve graphics: desktop publishing; graphical user interfaces (GUIs), such as Windows and OS/2; presentation preparation; interactive video; and multimedia systems. All of these applications—as well as many others at the edge of the microcomputer mainstream, such as Computer-aided Design and Drafting—benefit from a better display systems. After all, graphic systems are designed to convey information more efficiently through visual communication. The more information that can be displayed and the more easily it can be distinguished, the better these systems work.

A sharper display system—one with higher resolution—puts more detail and thus more information on the screen. It can help you to make fine distinctions—instead of seeing a blob on screen that makes you think you're watching a Grade B movie, you'll know your mouse is pointing to the icon of one of your disk drives.

Higher resolution is great, but getting realistic images also requires color—and the more the better. Old-fashioned CGA (Color Graphics Adapter, IBM's first display system capable of putting graphics as well as text on PC monitor screens) systems offer a spectrum of 16 hues, which creates a world with the construction paper colors and the same rough, jarring transitions between them. You get red or green and little in between. The 64 colors of EGA (Enhanced Graphics Adapter) and 256 of VGA (Video Gate Array) give some improvement, but still pale in comparison with the variety of reality, which offers a nearly infinite range of hues. Even if you have the artistic abilities of a Neanderthal, you can probably distinguish a million different shades. Mimicking reality—or just coming close—takes hundreds of thousands of color choices.

Having a range of hues will also make images appear sharper at a given resolution level. That's why television, which has resolution hardly on par with a primitive PC's CGA display system, can look sharper than a good VGA image.

But upgrading to a graphics adapter with higher resolution and a wider color spectrum can be more healthful, too. The less you have to strain to see what your PC is trying to tell you, the clearer the images it generates, the happier your eyes will be. If you've ever awakened in the morning with an eyestrain headache gnawing at the back of your ocular sockets, you'll certainly appreciate that a sharper display system can be well worth its price.

Improving Power Reserves

Certainly all PCs are designed to be expandable, but some are more expandable than others. With some systems, the first thing that you run short of will likely be electricity. This problem is suffered most severely by owners of the original IBM PC, which had power reserves only describable as paltry. Other systems, too, suffer from such electrical inadequacies. Upgrading to a new power supply will give such systems a new lease on life—or at least the capability to be upgraded to something not quite so obsolete. In fact, many upgrades for systems with marginal power reserves will require that you make a power supply upgrade at the same time.

Exchanging Information with Other PCs

Just as no man (or person) is an island, PCs shouldn't be peninsulas with a single linkage to other computers around them. Oftentimes you'll want to exchange files with friends, coworkers, and cohorts. If you and they don't have a floppy disk drive format in common, you may find exchanging files about as simple as converting Confederate currency. By adding a second (or third, or whatever) floppy disk drive, you can give your PC the swapping abilities of a Middle Eastern bazaar.

Some of the latest programs require that you have a high-density drive just to get started. For example, applications delivered on high-density floppy disks require that your system have a high-density drive to read them. With the growing popularity of graphics, the ordinary floppy is proving to be an inadequate exchange medium. A single graphic file may require more bytes than even the biggest floppy drive makes available, leaving you to living with the vagaries of DOS's BACKUP program to split the data among several disks. Upgrading to a tape drive with a standard data format or an optical drive (and your coworkers doing likewise) can give you the ability to exchange megabytes as easily as floppies exchange illicit software.

Building Backup Security

While your computer can put megabytes of data on-line, it can also put what could be your most valuable possession on the line. The digital data that you've spent years amassing are vulnerable to every quirk of fate. Lightning, stupid mistakes, and even the well-meaning but ill-informed meddling of helpful friends and spouses can wipe out every byte stored on a hard disk in a fraction of a second.

Your first—and, typically, only—line of defense is a backup system. High-density floppies, high-technology removable disk media, and tape catridges all afford you the luxury and security of keeping several copies of your valuable files. Upgrading your system to work with one of these media can be your best hedge against disaster. You can keep not one but several copies of your most important records (even your least important ones, should you choose) to guard against thieves liberating your PC, fires in your home or office, even comets colliding head-on with your computer.

You can also add to the security of your system and its data by insuring that it can keep running when the utility that supplies your home or office with electricity fails. Adding a standby power system can eliminate the system crashes and loss of your work-in-progress that inevitably follows a power failure.

Determining the Bottlenecks

Of all the reasons to upgrade, speed is the most satisfying and probably the one that leads most people to add to the native endowment of their PCs. Should improving the performance of your system be your goal in making an upgrade, the next step in your planning process is determining what you want to upgrade, where you need better performance.

For most people, the goal is to get the most possible from their computer. The most effective speedup is, of course, the one that offers the greatest gain with the least pain in the purse. That, in turn, means breaking the bottlenecks that constrict the performance of your PC. In other words, to make the most effective upgrade, you have to determine which part of your computer is the slowest link in the chain of performance processing. If your system is held back by a slow hard disk, even the fastest microprocessor upgrade will yield a disappointing improvement. If you can make your system more responsive by simply upgrading its display adapter, you may save the thousands-of-dollars cost of a new system board or an entirely new PC.

The challenge in finding system bottlenecks is that they are not the same in every PC. Not only will the bottleneck vary with computer model, the performance constraints also depend on the options and peripherals connected to the PC, as well as the applications that are being run. A word processor, for example, faces entirely different potential bottlenecks than does a database. In fact, the principal factor in determining where bottlenecks arise is often not the computer but you, its operator. What you do with your PC will be the greatest influence on what part of the system most holds back performance. You have your own personal demands and you set your own performance criteria. You can optimize your PC to do one thing well or you can make it best at juggling a dozen applications at once, switching between them instantly at your demand.

Finding bottlenecks is thus a multistep process. You have to examine how you work with your PC and what you do with it. Then, you need to determine which part of your PC you stress most when you use it. Finally, you have to verify whether that part is actually constraining the performance of the system or whether something else has caused the burden to shift elsewhere.

Odds are, you can answer—or make a guess that comes close to the correct answer—most of those questions with just a few moments of thought. If you want to be absolutely sure, a few tests or a bit of careful observation may suffice to confirm your suspicions.

Armed with that knowledge, you can make an intelligent choice about what part of your PC to upgrade. And you face what is perhaps the most difficult part of any upgrade process: Determining which of the thousands of upgrade components of a particular type will be the optimum for making the upgrade you want.

Selecting an Upgrade

Even the most obnoxious and foul-smelling witches' brew doesn't have the variety of evil constituents that get mixed into the typical buying decision. The nastiest of all is the budget. After all, if you didn't have to worry about the cost of making an upgrade, you probably have the financial wherewithal to simply chuck your old computer and buy the latest and greatest for your desktop every time you flip to a new page in your DayRunner. Real people face real budget constraints, however, and those limits set a cap on what can even be considered in a computer upgrade. When you enter the kind of store with aisles of glitz and glitter that can only mean a direct assault on your wallet, the salesman's first question is how much you were thinking of spending. You should have an answer for him set in your own mind before you even start looking for an upgrade.

The next concern to dump into the cauldron is the level of performance you need to achieve to make your upgrade worthwhile. You may want a speedy 16-bit interface from a graphic adapter or a 15-millisecond average access time from a hard disk. Match your needs with your budget and see if any products can simultaneously conform with each. Three hundred dollars, for example, might not buy much of a hard disk (sorry) but does open a wide range of top-performing VGA display adapters to you.

Once you know you have a choice, you have to find the best choice—the product that gives you the most for your money, both today and tomorrow. You could have your choice of a dozen disk drives in the 100-megabyte range, all with access speeds that make your current drive as peppy as a sloth with a thyroid deficiency. You face a hard decision because you need to consider every aspect of every product—not just the numbers that appear on the specification sheet, but the intangibles, like the manufacturer's and dealer's reputation, services offered, and the length of the warranty. After all, the cheapest video board may not seem like such a great buy if it starts turning the brightest colors into greyish pastels the day after its one-week warranty runs dry.

Finding the one product that's right for your upgrade won't be easy, but after you finish this book you'll know what to look for, what's important and what's not. You can write out a check with confidence—or read the numbers off your plastic bank card if you're more cautious and want to add more weight to your negotiating position should your choice not deliver on its promises. Then, after you bring your prize back from your dealer or United Parcel Service delivers it to your door, you're ready for the easiest part (and the most feared part) of every upgrade—installing it.

Installing the Upgrade

The actual mechanical work of putting a new peripheral inside your PC is nothing to be feared. It's a job that requires minimal intellectual involvement. In fact, a 12-year-old or even a computer dealer can do it.

In fact, if you buy your upgrade from a local dealer, having the dealer do the installation for you can be a real bonus. Odds are your dealer will have had experience installing other upgrades, so he's learned the hard way how to do everything. (And he's probably learned how easy it is, so he won't mind spending the few minutes that installing your upgrade will take—but that may be his secret.) The dealer can also relieve your worries about making the upgrade yourself. When your dealer does the work, you need not fear that an errant slip of the screwdriver will short something out, bring down the local power grid, and cause the power company's nuclear reactor to overload and melt down. You shift responsibility to the dealer's hands. And in the unlikely case that your upgrade doesn't work the first time it's switched on, your dealer can probably quickly diagnose its ills or substitute an identical upgrade to get you going.

The best reason for not making an upgrade yourself is that you can often get someone else to do it for you. All it takes is the right persuasion. Dangle the dollars of a big purchase in front of your dealer, and he might not want to let a few minutes' effort stand in the way of consummating the deal. Or pull rank on one of the underlings of your company, hinting at the magic word "layoff" that might occur if your system doesn't get upgraded. Or add a few extra dollars to the allowance (or mall shopping budget) of your teenage daughter should she take care of the dirty work for you.

Even if you cannot blackmail or otherwise coerce your dealer or some other unsuspecting soul into making your upgrade for you, installation will still be the easiest part of your upgrade. You've got a great deal of incentive to do it yourself—such as the great deals that are available through mail order vendors. They pass along to you at least some of their savings in not needing to spend their time holding your hand and a screwdriver.

There's a spectrum to do-it-yourself jobs like making a computer upgrade. Some, like changing the oil in your car, involve so many concerns that today tip the balance in the other direction, having someone else do the labor for you. Changing oil is dirty work and time-consuming if that's all you want to do (buy the oil, change your clothes, jack up the car) and leaves you with loose ends—like all that oil to dispose in an environmentally safe way. At the other end of the spectrum is installing a toaster. You wouldn't think of hiring a handyman to come in simply to slide its plug into an electrical outlet. In the vast scheme of do-it-yourself things, the computer upgrade comes closer to the toaster than the oil change. You don't even have to change clothes. Moreover, whatever you pull out of your PC you can put on the shelf as a spare or find someone to take off your hands to recycle into his own system.

Why Not to Upgrade

Every story has at least two sides, and the upgrade saga is no different. While an upgrade can bring many benefits, it's not a panacea. In some cases you may be better off *not* upgrading your PC and either sticking with what you've got or swallowing hard and buying an entirely new system.

You have several down-to-earth reasons not to make an upgrade to your computer system. Most of these arguments make sense, but most will be overruled by your own particular needs, beliefs, and budget.

An Upgraded Computer Is an Old Computer

Upgrading a computer still leaves you with the same old computer you have before the upgrade. Certainly part of it will be brand new—the part that you upgraded—but everything else will be the same old stuff. And that can mean everything from just plain ugly to a disaster waiting to happen. Mechanical components like floppy disks suffer with age and slowly wear out. They also become obsolete as new, higher-density storage media are introduced. Buy a new computer and new disk drives will come with it. Upgrade your old machine, and you still have your same old floppy drives.

Of course, no one and nothing forces you to keep your old floppy drives after you make an upgrade. Adding a new drive only adds about $50 to the total cost of any other upgrade. Moreover, your old drive may have a lot of life left in it. You probably don't use it continuously. In fact, if you have a hard disk, you may only use your floppy for copying over new programs from their distribution disks and backing up.

Your PC Is Already Too Powerful

Another reason not to make an upgrade is that you may not be taking advantage of all the power that's already packed inside your PC in its present configuration. If you're not bumping against the performance limits of your PC, you don't need to change anything. Some applications, for example, don't strain even the slowest computers. Upgrading the performance of such a system won't help you accomplish more.

Upgrades Lack Status

If you own a PC simply for the status it affords, upgrading may yield no real benefit. Upgrading the system won't impress your friends and cow your competitors like buying a shiny new machine will. Of course, you may impress your coworkers with your PC prowess if you make an upgrade yourself. Then again, you could achieve the same effect just by telling them you've made the upgrade. If they're that easily impressed, they'll never know whether you've made a change or not.

Fear of Failure

You also face the chance of failure in making your upgrade. You may attach the wires wrong to your new system board and sear its silicon into a series of short circuits, ruining both your efforts and your budget. One false move, and several thousand dollars of investment will deliver no return.

Fortunately, your chance of failure is fleetingly small—at least if you heed the advice in this volume. Most of the connections you need to make are designed so that you can't err. Cables won't plug into the wrong places because the connectors are keyed so they only fit where they are meant to go. In most cases, you can't even plug something in backwards. Even should you go out of your way to hook things up wrong, in most cases the only problem you'll create is an unworking computer, one that can be revived just by taking it apart and putting it back together right. Disasters can happen, but they are also preventable.

Upgrades happen, too. If you want more from your system, you'll find them to be unavoidable.

1. **Run particular applications**
   Application may require:
   Specific microprocessor feature (286 for multitasking)
   Coprocessor (for AutoCAD, etc.)
   Specific amount of memory
   Hard disk (massive graphics application, database)
   Graphics coprocessor
   CD ROM (for information retrieval)
2. **Better system performance**
   Faster microprocessor
   Quicker hard disk
   Graphic coprocessor
   Math coprocessor
   Disk cache
   Faster video board
3. **More and sharper colors**
   Upgrade from monchrome for ordinary graphics
   Wider color range for better presentations
   True colors for photographic quality results
4. **More reserves in your system's power supply**
   Upgrade old PC to handle hard disk
   More power for new system board or peripherals
   Replace power supply with quieter one
   Replace power supply with better cooling
5. **A need to exchange information in a specific way**
   Specific floppy disk format (31/2 inch)
   Tape cartridge drive for exchanging megabytes
   Optical disk storage for wide-range distribution
6. **Backup security**
   Floppies for low capital cost, less convenience
   Higher cost tape with greater convenience
   WORM storage for permanent archives

2.

SYSTEM BOTTLENECKS

If you want to upgrade your system to improve its performance, the first thing you have to do is identify where it's slowing down and what's the cause of the slowdown. This chapter will help you find the factors holding back the performance of your system—the bottlenecks—and the ultimate limits on what it can do—the brick wall.

Brick walls abound in athletics, art, engineering, even your PC. In any endeavor you inevitably reach a plateau—a top marathon time, a creative style—that no amount of work or practice seems to lift you above. Then, one day with a flash of insight and inspiration, supplemented by a lot of hard work, you break through. By taking a new approach you easily put yourself ahead of the best you've done before.

Inside your PC, a similar brick wall may stand between you and measurably improved system performance. It could be erected around any of the many subsystems that make up your PC. For example, that masonry might be built of mighty blocks of megahertz, the measure of the speed of your system's microprocessor. A slow microprocessor carries out almost every one of your PCs functions more slowly than a chip run at a higher megahertz rate.

The Misleading Megahertz

Alas, the megahertz of your system's microprocessor doesn't tell the entire story. If some other peripheral is running into a brick wall, adding a faster microprocessor to your system won't appreciably improve its performance, notwithstanding all the advertised claims for the latest multimegahertz monster PCs and the babblings of misguided computer connoisseurs (primarily those who bought the monster machines) about microprocessor speed.

Adding a faster microprocessor to a system with another performance brick wall will just make the microprocessor spend more of its time waiting. Instead of getting twice the speed by doubling the megahertz of your system, you may simply get double the waiting.

The brick walls faced by systems can be subtle, too. If your system is constrained by the speed of its disk but you add a faster microprocessor instead, it may look faster. The quicker chip will flash messages on the screen with greater dispatch. Instead of requiring one-fifteenth second to fully paint a screen, the quicker chip may do the job in one-thirtieth of a second. You can easily tell the difference. But when you run the application for which you normally use your computer, the laggardly disk will still take its toll. A ten-minute database sort may still take nearly ten minutes. But if you don't time the same operation before and after your misdirected upgrade, you won't know you've spent a lot of money for nought. The quicker screen changes will make you think you're ahead in the game. In truth, your new, fast microprocessor may be doing double the waiting, leaving you exactly where you started. Okay, not exactly—your bank account will stand diminished by your expenditure for the new microprocessor.

In many cases, adding a more powerful microprocessor is the last upgrade to consider. So forget megahertz. Speed ratings represent only the top end of any computer's abilities—the rate they run downhill with a tailwind kicking up and the emergency brake tossed out the window. Few computers actually operate under the ideal conditions that make megahertz their performance limit. Instead, some other bottleneck chokes system throughput well below your PC's capacity. Moreover, a microprocessor upgrade is one of the more expensive improvements you can make to a computer. The best way to upgrade your microprocessor—replacing your old system board—is the electronic equivalent of stuffing a new computer in your old case. If something else is holding back your existing microprocessor, you can probably break the bottleneck more cheaply and effectively to make your programs zip ahead with blinding speed.

Many of the other system bottlenecks are well known. A few, however, are obscure and seem only tangentially related to system performance. If you want to get the best value for your computer investment, you can't afford to ignore any of the potential candidates, no matter how offbeat they seem.

Perhaps the most common of these other bottlenecks is your PC's hard disk. Disks are designed to handle the same data as your system's microprocessor, but they suffer a major handicap. The information that the microprocessor works with is electronic, and the chip processes it electronically at lightning speed (literally). Disks, on the other hand, are mechanical, and they move data mechanically, suffering all the handicaps enforced by the laws of physics. The spin of the disk itself must be finite and modest or it would fly apart from centrifugal stress. The mechanism that reads and writes the data on the disk must shuffle back and forth at a lazy rate imposed by inertia. In the simple act of finding a byte of data needed in a calculation, the disk may be a thousand times slower than the microprocessor. In moving large blocks of data in and out of storage, however, disks are better matched to microprocessors. In some systems, particularly older ones that seem to have microprocessors chipped from flint rather than grown from silicon, disks are actually quicker than the microprocessor. But in today's quickest computers, disk definitely lag behind, delivering data at one-tenth the rate that they could be used. A slow disk means your microprocessor will spend a large fraction of its time waiting.

Another performance-robbing bottleneck can arise in your PC's display system. Your computer could create a screen full of multicolored graphics, then have to spend its time waiting while your display adapter sorts out the pattern of pixels for your monitor to display. Or your system could idly spin its wheels waiting for memory to catch up with its operations. Dial the phone, and your modem may slow everything down to its Touch-Tone rate.

Like a bottleneck on the freeway, this invisible congestion is like an island of stalled traffic—the slowly creeping parking lot on the parkway—that separates high-speed territories. Clear up the jam, and traffic will flow more freely, and you get where you want to go faster—without having to violate the megahertz speed limit.

Which of these bottlenecks affects or afflicts you depends not only on your computer but also on the software that you run on it. If you can identify the one that plagues your system, you may be able to notch up its performance for a fraction of the cost of a faster PC.

Finding these bottlenecks is not as easy as it sounds, however. You can't just look up the make and model of your PC in some chart and point your finger at its slowest part. Bottlenecks don't arise out of hardware alone. They are a result of an interaction between your computer's circuitry and the application software that you run. Some programs stretch your system's microprocessor to the limits, demanding every last megahertz they can lay their greedy digits upon. Others leave the system's brain as idle as a bureaucrat's daytime hours. Like the traffic jam, you can't see the cause of a computer bottleneck till you get out of your vehicle and crane your neck.

Bottleneck Causes, Effects, and Cures

Performance bottlenecks have no single cause. They arise in different parts of your PC in a number of different ways. Some result from poor component choices that took place when your system was being designed. Some result from the special demands of particular applications that just cannot be fulfilled by ordinary, general-purpose hardware. Some simply result from your using your PC.

Poor component choice is perhaps the easiest to diagnose and improve—and the existence of which seems least justifiable. You would expect the manufacturer of your PC would give you the best possible components that would work perfectly with one another. That's rarely the case, however. Oftentimes the manufacturer had no choice. Even the quickest hard disk can't keep up with the best of today's microprocessors.

Sometimes, though, the reason for the mismatch is more mundane. Performance costs a premium, whether it be in entire PCs or just their components. To trim the original price of your computer, its manufacturer may have slighted you in the choice of componentry—slower RAM chips, a cheaper hard disk. Or the technology might have just not been available. The introduction of cached hard disk controllers lagged behind the development of computers that could benefit from them by several years.

When starting your search-and-destroy mission for system bottlenecks, it's best to know what you're looking for. You should understand how bottlenecks arise in the various components within your PC. Such an understanding will make both identifying them easier and the proper corrective procedure almost obvious. The following is a guide to the causes of most system bottlenecks and the effects that they have on the operation of your PC:

Microprocessor Bottlenecks

In truth, the microprocessor in a PC is more like the bottle itself rather than a bottleneck. The microprocessor does all the work, and it sets the pace for the rest of the computer. The microprocessor thus determines the ultimate speed limit for anything that your PC does.

Typically, other bottlenecks choke your system long before the shortcomings of the microprocessor enforce their limits. Microprocessor performance has taken great leaps, improving on the order of 5,000 percent in the last decade. Other parts of computer systems have been hard-pressed to keep up. Hard disk access speeds, for example, have increased by about a factor of five, disk data transfer rates somewhat less.

Even so, the microprocessor in your computer can still be the single most important factor holding back its performance. Tasks can be processor-bound, unable to accelerate no matter what improvement you make to the rest of your system. The types of problems the first computers were designed to solve—calculations—are most likely to run into this limit. Not that computers haven't gotten better at calculating, we've just demanded the solution of ever-tougher problems—and more of them. The math in engineering calculations, scientific data analysis, even the geometric equations needed to deduce the image to be displayed on your monitor screen, all stress the abilities of your system's microprocessor.

The sheer amount of work to be done certainly is one root of microprocessor-imposed limits. The microprocessor itself is, too. The Intel-architecture microprocessors that IBM-standard PCs are based upon also contribute to this bottleneck. The chips just aren't very good at math.

These microprocessors are the equivalent of four-function calculators squeezed onto a silicon wafer. (In fact, the first hand-held calculators were based on the predecessors of these garden-variety microprocessors.) The only mathematical functions included in their instruction sets—the repertory of commands that the microprocessor knows how to carry out—allow for only addition, subtraction, multiplication, and division. The great majority of commands in their instruction sets are for more general-purpose operations, such as manipulating individual data bits, comparing values of bytes and strings of characters, and following the steps of computer program. The tough math problems, like calculating a sine or tangent function, are approximated by repeatedly carrying out simple arithmetic commands. Figuring a sine value might, for example, take tens of thousands of rudimentary steps. A relatively simple problem, like plotting the path of a squiggle on the monitor screen, can easily take millions of calculations. Suddenly even a microprocessor that can handle millions of instructions per second strains, and system response is correspondingly slow.

The technical strategies for breaking through this kind of bottleneck are two: Make the microprocessor quicker about carrying out its appointed tasks or make the microprocessor more efficient at evaluating transcendental and other high-level math functions. Both strategies are possible in making practical PC upgrades.

In a few cases, you can actually make the microprocessor that's already in your PC run faster. But most microprocessors are designed to operate at a manufacturer-designated maximum speed and most computer-makers exploit the top speeds of the solid-state components they put in their PCs. In fact, less-reputable manufacturers may actually operate chips at speeds in excess of their ratings, sacrificing reliability. When a chip is already running at its top speed, you can't (or at least shouldn't) push it faster.

The more practical alternative is to upgrade the microprocessor to one that can handle higher speeds and then take advantage of those speeds. Just popping out a microprocessor and putting another in its stead is not workable because the other chips that support your system's microprocessor also have maximum speed ratings and they must also run at the same speed as the microprocessor. You can, however, swap out all the speed-determining circuitry in your system in a single swipe by replacing its system board. Alternately, you can plug a new microprocessor and its support circuitry into an expansion slot. These strategies are discussed in Chapter 4, *Microprocessor Upgrades*.

While you can't saw off the top of a microprocessor and tinker with its insides to make it more efficient, you can easily augment its math abilities by adding a numeric coprocessor (or "floating-point unit") to your system. Because of practical production and pricing concerns, Intel sliced many of its microprocessors in half. One-half is the general-purpose microprocessor that your PC is based upon. The other half, the numeric coprocessor, was optimized for all those transcendental operations. The two halves were meant to work together, but in the early days of microprocessors they were not cost-effective to produce as a single chip. The resulting piece of silicon would have been too big to be affordable and would offer benefits only to people needing transcendental functions. Only with the introduction of the 486 were these functions finally mated back together.

If you don't have a coprocessor in your PC and the work you do involves transcendentals, the coprocessor is the quickest, most useful (though hardly least expensive) upgrade you can make. Chapter 5, *Coprocessors*, tells you how.

Bus Bottlenecks

Other bottlenecks in your PC result from slow sections of your system not being able to keep up with its microprocessor. While the microprocessor might be able to perform more calculations, the rest of the PC can't supply data to it fast enough. The microprocessor must wait for the rest of the system to catch up. The problem is that peripherals can't find or create the data before the microprocessor yearns for more. Or the problem could be a bottleneck in the delivery system—peripherals produce the data to run your PC but can't transfer them to the microprocessor at the speed required.

Because most applications that you're likely to run on your PC involve data that must come from somewhere and go somewhere, rather than staying strictly within the microprocessor, the transfer of information can be a significant performance limit. The more the microprocessor needs to access information, the more constraining the data-transfer bottleneck becomes.

In most PCs, that delivery system is the expansion bus. The bus gives the microprocessor access to expansion board circuitry and all the peripherals connected to it, including input/output ports, the monitor (through display memory), the hard and floppy disks, sometimes even expansion memory. In these systems the speed at which information is transferred across the bus *could* be a bottleneck.

In traditional PCs—those that use the XT or AT expansion bus rather than innovations such as Micro Channel Architecture and EISA (Enhanced Industry Standard Architecture)—the microprocessor takes regal command of system operation and expects that the rest of your PC's circuitry will serve its needs exactly when it wants them to. When the microprocessor needs a particular byte of data—whether from memory, disk, or keyboard—it will single-mindedly wait until those data are dished up to it. The rest of the system comes to a halt without the microprocessor telling it what to do.

The support circuitry around the microprocessor serves these obstinate, single-minded demands without delay because the circuitry is designed to match microprocessor speed and always be instantly ready when a request is made. But when the microprocessor or the support circuitry has to send out for data (or send data out), it waits patiently for it as if it were ordering a home-delivery pizza. Eventually the order will come, but invariably it arrives later than it was wanted. The processor cools its heels instead of its dinner.

Most of these requests are made through the system's input/output (I/O) bus, which roughly corresponds to your PC's expansion bus where peripherals plug into your system. The speed at which information is moved across the expansion bus is controlled by two principal factors: the clock frequency of the bus and the number of bits of data that can be transferred in each clock cycle. In most high-performance computers, the bus operates at frequencies that are much lower than the clock speed of the microprocessor, perhaps one-quarter its speed. While microprocessors tick along at 33 megahertz and faster, the clock speed of the buses of most PCs is slower. The maximum clock frequency of the buses of most conventional PCs is eight megahertz because higher speeds are incompatible with the vast majority of expansion boards. That's automatically factor-of-four bottleneck when compared to top microprocessor speeds.

But the conventional AT expansion bus has another failing. The AT bus provides only a 16-bit connection with peripherals, half of the data-handling capacity of today's 32-bit microprocessors. This can slow the movement of data by another factor of two. As a result, when a program makes use of the input/output bus to any great extent, the bus speed, rather than the microprocessor speed, limits system performance. Such applications are called input/output-bound or I/O-bound.

That's the easy story. But other factors often have a greater influence on bus performance. One of them is the microprocessor itself. In conventional systems, the microprocessor is charged with the responsibility for controlling the movement of each byte across the bus. That in itself can be a speed limit because the overhead associated with each byte transferred can be many clock cycles. When printing, for example, moving a single byte across the expansion bus can require 500 to 1,000 separate microprocessor operations. This overhead can swamp all the other factors constraining bus performance, making the bus bottleneck actually a microprocessor constraint—but one that's best solved by improved bus technology rather than a new microprocessor.

The trick is to break the linkage between the microprocessor and the bus, putting some other component in control rather than the microprocessor. A technique called *bus mastering* does exactly that. When an expansion board needs to shift data, the board itself is permitted to take control, becoming the master in control of the bus, and taking over responsibility from the microprocessor. Special circuitry can be designed into the bus master that's actually faster at transferring data than is the general-purpose microprocessor. Moreover, while the bus master is doing the data transfer work, it's possible for the system microprocessor to engage in another task. With such a design, your PC could do two things at once.

The only way around bus bottlenecks is to replace one expansion bus with another that's faster and provides more features. The likely replacement candidates are Micro Channel Architecture and Enhanced Industry Standard Architecture (EISA). Adding either one to your system will require replacing its system board with a new one that uses the better bus (if you can find such a replacement system board). Instructions for such a replacement are given in Chapter IV as part of microprocessor upgrades.

Even though the bus is slower than the microprocessor, things connected to the bus drag down performance even further. Most PC peripherals are hard pressed to even achieve the data transfer rate of the 16-bit AT expansion bus, let alone the rates allowed by EISA or Micro Channel Systems. Such peripherals are also I/O bound, but by the peripherals themselves rather than the expansion bus. They require a different speed-up strategy—replacing the slow peripheral.

Memory Bottlenecks

Memory is generally considered to be an extension to the microprocessor. The two are intimately connected—nearly everything that the microprocessor does involves memory. But your system's microprocessor and its memory are not necessarily optimally matched and the memory in the machine can be a bottleneck on the path to better performance.

Memory bottlenecks arise because all memory is not the same. Memory varies in how it is connected to the microprocessor and how fast it can operate. A bad connection or slow chips will stand in the way of quicker operation of your PC.

In old-fashioned PCs, memory chips were connected almost directly to the microprocessor. Only a few support chips stood in the way of a direct connection. With such an arrangement, the memory was essentially an extension of the microprocessor. It reacted at the same speed as the chip and held back nothing. Even when memory was relegated to the expansion bus, instead of being nestled next to the microprocessor on the system board, performance impact was minimal. After all, in early machines the bus operated at the same clock speed as the microprocessor.

Fast 286-based PCs and all 386-based and more powerful machines pushed the microprocessor clock well beyond the rate that the expansion bus could reliably operate. Consequently, when memory was dropped into an expansion slot in one of these machines, it was guaranteed to hit throughput hard, slowing the system every time memory was accessed. The only way around this problem is to avoid using the slow expansion bus for memory expansion. Because system boards are physically limited in the number of memory chips that they can accommodate, computer manufacturers devised special proprietary expansion boards for memory that operated at microprocessor speed. For top performance, these slots, rather than normal expansion slots, must be used for memory expansion.

Not all memory chips are able to operate at the same high clock speeds as the fastest microprocessors. In fact, the most common dynamic RAM chips lag far behind microprocessors. While some exotic strategies have been used to better match these slow chips to fast microprocessors, these are far from perfect. Some systems allow you to improve this match by adding memory cache boards—blocks of high-speed memory that insulate the microprocessor from slower RAM. The larger the memory cache, the better the performance you can expect from your system. Adding a memory cache to a system with support for it will help bring the system up to its potential. You'll find other memory optimization strategies discussed in Chapter 4, while memory caching is considered along with microprocessor upgrades in Chapter 4.

Disk Bottlenecks

Hard disk systems are notorious for the delays they add when you want to access information. Most of the sluggishness in the response of disk system can be attributed to the mechanical basis of disk storage.

Unlike solid-state memory such as your system's RAM, all disks impose a slight delay period (called latency) while they spin around to find the byte the system requires. The read/write head hangs over the disk, and the disk itself must spin each bit into position under the head. On the average, the desired bit will be half a revolution of the disk away. At the nearly standard hard disk spin rate of 3,600 revolutions per minute, that works out to be about 13 milliseconds, compared to the microseconds that are required to find a bit in solid-state memory.

In addition, the hard disk causes more waiting as its head in the disk drive skitters laterally across the disk to zero in on the specific track that contains the needed information. This delay, called the *average access time* of the disk, may range from a dozen to a hundred milliseconds compared, again, to the microsecond-level access time of solid-state memory. At best, then, locating a byte on disk will typically be about a thousand times slower than finding it in electronic memory.

As a result, on applications that require repeated access to random disk information, disk access delays can swamp other aspects of system performance. Your system's microprocessor could be racing along, executing millions of instructions per second. Then it bumps into a command to read from the hard disk. Sparks fly from its brakes as the system grinds to a halt and waits, patiently, until the disk drive responds. Thousands of instructions might have been carried out in the same length of time. Instead, your system whiles away your investment in a faster microprocessor.

Just finding the data is not enough, however. Once the sluggard disk head finally locates the information that your microprocessor needs, the disk drive still needs to transfer the data back from disk platter to microprocessor. Most disk are linked to their system hosts through the expansion bus, and they suffer all the constraints imposed by the bus. Worse yet, the disk signals have to traverse an even slower data link, the hard disk interface. While the fastest of today's interfaces can accelerate up to a transfer rate of about 2.5

megabytes per second (the raw rate of the 20MHz ESDI hard disk drive and some SCSI and IDE drives), even the slow AT expansion bus can move information nearly three times as fast, eight megabytes per second. Your system microprocessor, on the other hand, may be able to handle information 16 times quicker than the bus, 50 times quicker than the hard disk. The result is that the performance of your system is constrained by the disk when loading large programs or retrieving and saving big files.

Note that the disk transfer rate bottleneck is lodged squarely in the disk subsystem, rather than in the expansion bus. A faster bus, by itself, won't speed up the disk data transfer performance.

One way to speed up your PC's disk system is simply to get a faster disk. Cut the average access time of your hard disk system in half by upgrading to a twice-as-quick hard disk, and you'll cut your waiting time nearly in half. You can gain similar improvements by making your upgrade to a hard disk that uses an advanced interface with a higher data transfer rate.

Some applications lend themselves to another form of disk acceleration, *disk caching* (not to be confused with *memory caching*, discussed earlier). The disk cache is a block of solid-state RAM that dynamically duplicates some of the contents of the disk. If your system's microprocessor requires disk-based data that are duplicated in the disk cache, the disk cache can deliver them at RAM speed rather than the mechanical speed of the disk drive. The speed-up can be dramatic, potentially a thousandfold improvement.

One of the principal differences between different disk caches is how they get information from disk to RAM. Typically, the faster cache is the smarter one, the one that can anticipate the data you'll need, making its judgments from your past information requirements.

Two types of disk caches have found favor in PCs. *Software caches* are simply programs that run in the background on your PC and appropriate a block of your system's extended or expanded memory for data storage. Software caches are inexpensive, generally easy to install, and easy to use. Sometimes, however, they show compatibility problems with some programs. Software caches are discussed in Chapter 3, along with other speed-up strategies that don't require a hardware investment.

Hardware caches are usually built into so-called caching disk controllers. These expansion boards use their own RAM dedicated to storing disk information and, typically, a microprocessor to manage the disk cache and keep the most-often-demanded data in the cache. Caching disk controllers tend to be expensive because of their need for large blocks of RAM, but can be very effective in agreeable applications. Caching controllers are discussed along with hard disks in Chapter 7.

Display Bottlenecks

One unexpected bottleneck is your PC's display system. You might think that your monitor merely reflects what your PC is actually accomplishing. In truth, it may be slowing everything else down.

The image on the monitor has to come from somewhere, and its origins lie deep inside your programs and PC. Using conventional display systems—monochrome, CGA, EGA, or VGA—your PC's microprocessor is charged with determining, one by one, exactly which pixels on the screen light up and, in color systems, what hue each has. Even with the primitive CGA display system, that's over 125,000 dots to control. The display can change up to 60 times a second, and the microprocessor must manage it all—while juggling everything else it has to do, from running the bus to executing programs.

The problem is compounded because to put any image on your monitor, your PC must route the data through its input/output bus. That means more bus-control instructions. And when squeezing data through its eight-bit interface on the way to the screen, an interface may add dozens of wait states to your microprocessor. Worse, putting characters on the screen and moving them is a complex process involving many layers of software instructions, piled on by both your system's BIOS (Basic Input/Output System) and DOS, which together force your microprocessor to grind through an arm's length list of code to display each character. That's more work and more waiting.

The killer is that the video slowdown is the most visible of the ills that can afflict your PC. Even when it takes a fraction of a second longer to paint an image on the screen, you'll notice it. When the characters start popping on the screen as if they were fired by a machine gun stuck in molasses, you'll very quickly get the idea that your PC isn't running as fast as it could.

Almost every program uses your PC's display system, but different applications put different demands on it. Text-based programs take the least work. They minimize the amount of data that must be manipulated, limiting it to 4,000 characters and attributes per screen. Graphics programs (and text-based programs that run in graphics mode, such as those that run within Microsoft Windows), take a very heavy toll on your system's processing time. Heavy-duty graphics—including desktop publishing, computer-aided drafting, and presentation graphics—require the most from your system and are most apt to slog down in the display system bottleneck. Your system's performance when running these applications is likely to be limited by your display system or the combination of display system and microprocessor.

Several different approaches can help speed up your screen displays and your system as well. You can substitute optimized display instructions for the laggardly commands in your BIOS or a display list driver for CAD programs, as noted in Chapter 3. Or you can install a new display adapter with a wider interface (for faster operation). Best of all, some of the most graphics-intensive applications will benefit most from a graphic coprocessor that will not only give you sharper images but will also take a load off your microprocessor and expansion bus. Graphics coprocessors are discussed along with other display adapters in Chapter 11.

Printing Bottlenecks

Printers suffer an overhead affliction similar to that of graphic displays, but printers compound the problem with their own physical limitations. In a PC, moving a single character to your printer using the system's built-in BIOS instructions can take a series of 500 separate commands. Multiply that by the amount of information on a full page of bit-mapped, laser-printed graphics, and the entire processing capacity of a chip (such as a 286) is quickly used up.

As with hard disks, printers are mechanical devices and they suffer from mechanical delays. For example, most printers can deal with data only as fast as they can pound, burn, or blaze it on paper, as slow as one- to ten-thousandth (1/1,000th to 1/10,000th) the rate your computer can generate them. When you turn your computer loose on a print job, it will waste the vast majority of its processing power just waiting for your printer to catch up with it.

Any application that makes you sit and watch an unchanging screen while your printer dodders along likely suffers from a printing bottleneck. A faster printer is the most straightforward cure and probably the most wasteful.

Software can often free up your microprocessor for other tasks while data are slowly reeled out to your printer. A print spooler utility divides your system's time between printing and other applications so you think you can do two things at once with your system. But software-based print spoolers don't do anything about the overhead required by printing instructions. Moreover, they add their own penalty because the time required to manage the spooler is stolen from whatever other application you want to run.

Hardware solutions are more satisfactory and just plain faster. An external print buffer, often packaged as part of a printer-sharing device, can make your printer look almost electronically fast to your PC. A properly designed buffer will accept data output from your PC as fast as it can be ushered out to your printer port. If you have an advanced expansion bus in your PC, you can also cut the microprocessor overhead required in printing by upgrading to a bus master printer adapter. These upgrade options are discussed in Chapter 3.

Network Bottlenecks

Networks typically compound the performance problems of your PC simply because information shared on the network is handled by at least two PCs on its way to being used. For example, should you need a specific record from the corporate database, you'll have to wait while a command to retrieve that record is sent from your PC through the network to its server. Then the hard disk in the server has to search out the record (imposing its average access delays) and copies the record to the server's network adapter—through the server's expansion bus. Then the record has to travel down the network line, which operates at a fraction of the speed of the typical system board expansion bus, perhaps waiting along the way for other network traffic to clear. Finally, when it arrives back in your PC, the record has to traverse the expansion bus once again from the network adapter to your microprocessor. Any one of these steps holds a potential bottleneck.

Far and away the slowest part of any network is usually the wiring linking the nodes together or to the server. Except for fiber optics, which today is little used in connecting individual nodes, all network wiring schemes operate at transfer rates that are a fraction of even system board bus speeds. Ethernet has a peak transfer rate of 1.25 megabytes per second, but cannot sustain lengthy transfers at that rate across an active network line. The bus speed of ordinary AT-style computers is more than four times faster.

Moving up to a faster network architecture is usually impractical. In most cases, it requires a complete rewiring of the entire network facility. But network performance can be improved by taking advantage of individual PC upgrades on the nodes and servers in the network. You can work around the wiring bottleneck itself by changing your usage strategies on your PCs, primarily in cutting back network traffic by keeping more tasks within the node instead of reaching out across the network line.

Human Bottlenecks

The most nagging of bottlenecks in the day-to-day operation of most PCs is the one over which you have the most control, and yet it is the one that holds the least potential for improvement: YOU. Okay, you can join a church, volunteer your services to aid the underprivileged in Africa or Appalachia, take night courses in Precambrian philosophy, or improve yourself in innumerable ways. But your fate will still be in your own hands when you use your PC. Your typing, your decisions about each keystroke and each dash of the mouse, the thoughts that surge and course and curse through your mind, all slow down your PC more than would the anchor of an XT hard disk or a video system left over from Lee De Forest's vacuum tube experiments. Most of the time, in most applications when the patience of your PC is being tried, the system is waiting not for memory or the disk to respond, but for your lightest touch at the keyboard. You press a key and maybe a million circuits swing into action, evaluating your latest message—that one, a single meaningful character that bounces into the keyboard buffer. For a fraction of a second, your computer is filled with electronic excitement classically described as a Chinese fire drill. Then, as quick as this flurry of activity began, the character is recognized, the computer determines whether it needs to carry out some advanced action, and more likely than not, the system falls back into a semiconductor slumber like a cat, quietly awaiting the next disturbance to its nap.

More than just a matter of typing in keystrokes to enter numbers or words, when you use some word processor or spreadsheet applications the performance of your system is limited by how fast you can move the cursor from the left of the screen to the right or from the top to the bottom. Lean on the cursor key and see how long it takes to move between cells or paragraphs. Each repeat of the keystroke comes at a predefined interval that can be devilishly long when you're at the bottom left cell and want to be at the top right. Although you might be able to make movements more quickly using a mouse, the delays are still substantial compared to the possible performance of your computer's microprocessor. You still may spend a fraction of a second on that one simple movement, a period in which your microprocessor might have carried out a million instructions.

Breaking through the bottleneck at the human interface can be a ticklish job. Caffeine may quicken your reactions, but it will never get you up to electronic speed. You can try to think faster and, eventually, you can learn to type faster, but there are a few better ways of broadening the bottlenecks even if you can't break through entirely.

Software can help speed up repetitive tasks. Write a macro and you can run through your weekly analyses with Lotus 1-2-3 at superhuman speeds. Macros—as well as style sheets, canned paragraphs, and letters—help, too, for speeding up text entry and printing with your word processor. You can also speed up the response of your keyboard or send your mouse ballistic. While these tricks (and others in the next chapter) will never get you exactly in step with the fleet thoughts of your PC, they'll help you get more done, faster. And that is, of course, what you bought your PC for. To get the most from your investment in your computer, you have to break through all the bottlenecks—including your own.

Locating the Bottlenecks

Before you can uncap a system bottleneck, you've got to identify it, to find out what computer demon is holding up the job. The identification is always timeconsuming, and there's often little evidence to go by (other than your computer not being as fast as you want it to be). It's sort of like identifying the perpetrator from fingerprints left after a snowball fight. The process takes time, observation, insight—and more than a little inspired guess work. Fortunately, even if you rely on an enlightened guess, you can often achieve remarkable success. Alternately, you can round up all the suspects and start the paper rolling through the polygraph, questioning them all until the scientific instrument points to the prime suspect. Similarly, you can be absolutely sure where the bottlenecks are by scientifically monitoring the operation of your programs using special software tools.

No matter what method you elect to locate your system's bottlenecks, the starting place is the same: your applications. Determine which programs you use most, the one for which faster operation will benefit you most.

Consider how that application uses your PC. You need to know what the primary program you use is doing and what system resources it requires—and how you use the program. What follows are several tests and observations you can make to help find where the bottlenecks in your PC may lurk.

Verifying Processing Bottlenecks

To determine whether your PC is plagued by a processing bottleneck, start by checking the response of your system using the software you normally run. If, after you press a keystroke that initiates a recalculation or computation, you can then play a round of golf or build an addition on your house before an answer appears, you have a good indication the program is drawing upon the microprocessor power in your system. If your system doesn't do anything else while performing the calculation—the display doesn't change and the disk activity light does not come on—you almost certainly have an application that's limited by processor performance.

Often, however, other forces conspire to slow your system down. In many cases, they may have more of an effect that your system's microprocessor. Only after you eliminate them all can you be sure that you're suffering from a processor bottleneck.

Checking Your Disk

The first to check for is the disk bottleneck. Some statistical packages may require reading data from disk, and language compilers may constantly require access to disk-based libraries. This disk access often can be the major cause of your interminable waiting. To find out for sure, watch the red drive lights on your hard disk drive. (If you don't have a hard disk, that in itself is a system bottleneck that needs attention before anything else!) If the drive light flashes on and off more than occasionally—perhaps so often and fast that it appears to be continuously, though dimly lit—your disk is likely one of the big bottlenecks in your system.

Other types of software programs are notorious for their disk use and should prompt you to begin your search for bottlenecks with a look at the drive light.

In general, any application that is based on a common database package—like dBase, r:Base, Paradox, or Oracle—will almost always be more disk intensive than processor intensive. Any application that creates or manages fat files stuffed with more than a few dozen kilobytes, including graphics and desktop publishing programs, will likely clog in the disk bottlenecks.

Determining Display Delays

Some bottlenecks are not restricted to a single class of software or the given operating mode. In particular, laggardly output can drag down the performance of nearly any applications. In many cases, a problem in slow system response—you press a key and your system delays before carrying out your command—can be attributed to your display system rather than the processor or disk.

Depending on how your program uses your display, your computer's video system can strangle execution speed in two ways, each with its own different cure. Watching what your software does when the screen changes will help you select the right microelectronic miracle drug.

If characters appear on your monitor screen one at a time or one line at a time, other than in response to your typing them in at the keyboard, the program you are running likely uses DOS and your computer's BIOS in generating its display. Such programs are constrained by software overhead and will respond to add-on speed-up software. On the other hand, graphics programs and those that can display screens of data as a single, simultaneously appearing block, typically sidestep DOS and the BIOS by writing directly to video memory. These programs are slowed by the video hardware in your system and may require a new display adapter hardware.

Checking for External Delays

Applications that rely on external system peripherals for a major part of their function can face bottlenecks both inside and outside of your computer. Printers can handle only a few dozen to a few thousand characters per second, while computers deal with millions. Characters wanting to fly out your parallel port get bottled up waiting for your printer to peck its way through those characters preceding them. On the other hand, some print jobs, particularly those that involve heavy-duty full-page graphics, draw upon all your PC's power to generate on-paper images.

To get the idea of how much faster your print jobs will finish by breaking the printer bottleneck—and whether enhancing printer performance will benefit your system—note the time it takes the program you most often use to print to a *file*. Compare that figure to the time it takes to create hard copy directly on the *printer*. The difference is a good indication of the improvement you can expect from a good printer performance enhancement.

Modem performance can be perplexing to new and even some experienced PC users. What many people blame on a slow computer at either end of the connection more often results from a slow modem connection. Finding out whether the computer or the modem is causing your hair to grey while you wait for a screen update is simply a matter of watching. If you're forced to stare helplessly at your monitor screen while characters pop on-screen one at a time, you're waiting for your modem. If, however, you wait during periods in which nothing appears on the screen—for instance, during a search or while the remote system pores through your mail—the computer at the far end of the modem connection is the cause of the delay. A faster modem can't eliminate those delays.

Checking the Human Interface

Although the class of software you run is a rough guide to the slow spots in your system, how you use your programs also affects where bottlenecks will appear. For example, databases are only bottled up during sorts and other reporting functions. Many database operations, such as input and revision, usually won't strain your disk system much—they are limited by how fast you can press keys to enter data or make commands.

In fact, any application that requires you to type in vast amounts of data—be it a mailing list or other database, spreadsheet, statistical analysis, or word processor—at some time or another will be limited by your fingers on the keyboard. Other times, however, these same keyboard-intensive applications may demand other system facilities. For example, you might use a word processor just to search for key words, paste together boilerplate paragraphs, or check spelling. Instead of the keyboard, your disk might then be limiting by the performance of your system. Instead of being keyboard-bound, your system may put your disk into action as the machine scans for obscure words. What you do most with your system will determine where shattering the bottleneck will be most effective.

Here are a few simple rules: If you use your computer chiefly to type in original materials—that is, you deal in data input—you and your fingers are the likely bottleneck. Typing lessons, practice, or hiring a pair of faster hands are your best hope for hyping throughput. If you edit more than input, the keyboard could still be holding you back, particularly if you press a lot of cursor keys. However, speed-up software or an alternate input device (mouse, trackball, or digitizing tablet) may help accelerate your thoughts. If you use your software merely to read or pull large blocks of data together, don't blame the keyboard for keeping you in low gear.

Scientific Determination of Bottlenecks

If casual but informed observation still leaves you guessing where your system bottlenecks are, you can try some tests to determine their location for sure.

For example, many people take the manufacturer's word on system performance. They get a 33 MHz system but don't know that it will add 20 wait states to each video access and four or five wait states to every memory access on the bus. Without a benchmark or measure, or another system to put side by side to compare, you have no real way to judge how your system is performing unless it's something very, very noticeable.

One commercial program, Personal Measure (from Spirit of Performance, Harvard, Massachusetts), is designed to do exactly that. When run in the background, this inexpensive program monitors the operation of any application you select and will give you a graphic display as well as printed reports of the time spent using your microprocessor, disk, keyboard, printer, and auxiliary ports. One look and you can tell exactly where the bottlenecks are.

Benchmarking programs will help you identify the slower components in your system, although they cannot actually locate the hardware-software interactions that cause true bottlenecks. Nevertheless, if you find a slow hard disk or display system in your otherwise fast computer, you know a likely candidate for hiking its speed. A number of such programs are available, many for free.

Pre-eminent among these are *PC Magazine*'s PC Lab Benchmark Utilities, available at no cost (other than line and connection charges) through PC MagNet, a Ziffnet service on CompuServe, or by mail request from PC Labs. (To reach PC MagNet, dial up CompuServe, log in, and type GO MAGNET.) Most local bulletin board services (BBS) also make PC Labs Benchmarks available along with other, similar performance-measuring software. Some local bulletin boards offer a dozen or more benchmarking programs, including the tests used by the no-longer-published *PC Tech Journal* and *Infoworld*.

The leading commercial benchmarking application is Power Meter (published by DiagSoft, Inc., Scotts Valley, California). This package includes a full set of tests for every aspect of system performance. One of its features, its database for managing your evaluation results, is particularly helpful in comparing systems to find bottlenecks.

Although identifying system slowdowns sounds complex, you can probably sort through the candidates in less than an hour, even faster and more certainly with the aid of this specialized software. The short time you spend in your search will reap you a large reward. Once you uncap the bottleneck and break through the brick wall between you and better performance, your system will be more responsive, and you'll get more done in every minute you use it. Your PC just may become fun to work with again.

Recommendations for Specific Applications

Word Processors

Word processors, such as WordPerfect, are mostly used as data entry programs. You press the keys on your keyboard to enter letters and words into documents. Most of what you do is thus limited by your own, very human typing limitations. Even the slowest 8088-based computers are fast enough to keep pace with your keystrokes. If all you do is type, then think finger exercises instead of system upgrades.

But today's word processors do more than just accept your keystrokes. Previewing documents takes processor and display horsepower to put all those dots on the screen. Graphics-based word processors (for instance, those that run under the Windows operating environment—Lotus Ami and Microsoft Word for Windows) take substantially more power than traditional text-based programs. You'll need more than 8088 power just to get them running, and a faster microprocessor will help make these programs more responsive. A faster display system will help improve the response time of graphics-based word processors.

Fast hard disks are generally unnecessary for word processing. However, several situations benefit from a faster disk drive. If you use Windows or another multitasking environment and have little memory or often shift between applications, a fast disk may add some snap. A disk with a higher transfer time will also aid in loading and saving large files. Spelling checks and spooled print operations can also benefit from a faster disk.

Databases

Databases, such as dBase III or IV, are the pre-eminent example of disk-intensive programs. A typical database sort causes more activity than a fire in a popcorn factory. The sort sends the disk head hopping every which way across the disk platter, making a hard disk drive with a low average access time best.

Of course, most people don't sort their databases a dozen times a day. Most database activity is merely data entry, and that suffers the same old human interface plague. Drugs might seem to be the only way to improve speed, but they're likely to decrease accuracy and increase the chances you'll end up in the hoosegow. You can get by with a slow PC for data entry. It may even work for sorting if you do it only occasionally and don't mind spending your afternoon shopping or fishing while your computer completes its job.

The one upgrade you're likely to need with a database is a bigger hard disk to accommodate the ever-growing raft of records you'll generate. Bigger disks also tend to be faster, so you'll take care of your sorting slowdowns at the same time. One rule of thumb is to buy a hard disk roughly twice as large as you think you'll need, so you'll run out of capacity after a few weeks rather than immediately.

Spreadsheets

Spreadsheets, such as Lotus 1-2-3, too, tend to occupy their time waiting for you to enter data. After all, you've got to get information into those cells sometime.

But spreadsheets recalculate, too, and every time they do, you end up waiting. A faster microprocessor will cut the time you spend waiting for those recalculations—and just about everything else you do with the spreadsheet. Or you can just tell your spreadsheet to recalculate on command rather than on the fly (if, of course, it gives you that option).

Because spreadsheets so often deal with numbers, you may be tempted to get a numeric coprocessor to help boost performance. Sometimes that helps, but often it does not. Most of the calculations performed with spreadsheets tend to be accounting functions, and that means simple arithmetic. Numeric coprocessors don't speed arithmetic. However, if you use your spreadsheet for more intensive calculations that use transcendental functions, such as analysis or loan amortization, a coprocessor can help out.

Some spreadsheets benefit more from numeric coprocessors than others. Borland International's Quattro Pro takes advantage of coprocessor power. If you use it, adding a coprocessor will reap you rewards in every operation. Current versions of Lotus 1-2-3 have much less coprocessor reliance, so expect performance to increase only on complex calculations. Microsoft Excel falls between the two. Because of its Windows foundation, however, Excel stands to gain the most from a faster microprocessor.

Computer-aided Design

Drafting and drawing programs, such as AutoCAD, tax your PC the most. They are number-intensive applications that tap the power of nearly every part of your computer. Most need so much horsepower they require that you install a numeric coprocessor just to load the program. A faster microprocessor will, of course, help out, too. In fact, most CAD users want the fastest possible microprocessor.

You'll also want to upgrade to as much memory as you can afford so that you can handle the largest possible drawings. Many CAD programs have threshold memory values. Although the programs will operate with less RAM (often by using virtual memory, substituting disk space for RAM), once you reach a certain level of RAM, performance improves dramatically. That's why CAD programs often have listed minimum and recommended memories. You'll want at least the recommended amount.

CAD programs are also display-intensive. After all, you have to see your work—and in as much detail as possible. Most people want the sharpest possible displays with their CAD programs. And they also want display speed. Updating on-screen images is often the most time-consuming part of using a CAD program. All of these display needs add up to one thing—a graphic coprocessor board. Adding a graphic coprocessor display board can often speed up CAD programs more than stepping up to the next most powerful microprocessor.

Because CAD programs naturally create huge files, fast disks can benefit them, too, particularly disks with high data transfer rates. You'll also want a large capacity to store all those files.

In other words, if you plan on using CAD, you'll want the most powerful upgrades of every type for your PC. If you have to buy one piece at a time, get the display system first, then the disk, then the microprocessor. Besides, by the time you get ready to buy a new microprocessor, a faster one will probably have come out.

Application Development

If you write software, you probably know what you need—the biggest, best, and most powerful computer. Compiling programs is a microprocessor-intensive task.

If you've been writing software for a while, you probably know all the tricks, like putting your compiler and libraries on a fast solid-state RAM disk. If you do that, you'll probably want as much memory as possible in your PC to allow for the largest possible disk (or at least one large enough to contain your language files). If you prefer to work from a hard disk or are forced to because of the size of the libraries involved, you'll want to upgrade to a hard disk drive with a low average access time. Your compiler will be digging for data from what you've written, and to the compiler your writing will look random, indeed.

OS/2

Operating systems by themselves don't use up much in the way of system resources. After all, the operating system itself is supposed to be invisible, something that gets your programs going and serves their needs, but nothing you want to deal with all the time.

That said, the applications that run under OS/2 are designed to be more powerful than those made for DOS (if not, then no one would switch to OS/2—which may explain a lot). A more powerful microprocessor would seem de rigueur.

Just to get OS/2 off the ground you'll need at least a 286 microprocessor for Versions through 1.4 and a 386 for Versions 2.0 or later. You'll also need memory, two megabytes for Version 1.3, and four megabytes for other versions. If you can afford more, you'll get better response, particularly when you engage in multitasking. Although you may not need a larger, faster hard disk, the High Performance File System of OS/2 Versions 1.2 and later will help you take advantage of greater capacity.

Microsoft Windows

Getting the most out of the latest versions of Microsoft Windows requires at least a 386 microprocessor and as much memory as possible. While the operating environment may work with as little as 640K and an 8088, getting its true power will require megabytes and megahertz. Figure four megabytes and 20 megahertz as the best trade-off between performance and cost.

3.

AVOIDING THE UPGRADE

Odds are you're not even squeezing all the performance possible out of your computer in its existing configuration. A few simple tricks can help you get more speed from your system without a hardware upgrade, either as an interim solution or a way of sidestepping a real upgrade until your finanaces look more favorable.

Even when the performance of your system is bottled up by one of its consitituent parts that can't keep up, you can still use a few tricks to eke more speed from it. You can even gain more disk space without a hard disk replacement. In fact, you might be so delighted with the improvement you can make—often without cost—that you might just postpone your upgrade. At least for a few minutes.

None of these tricks require that you install expensive new hardware in your system. Many of them require no more than taking advantage of all the features built into DOS. Others require no more than checking to be sure that you've set up your system to gain the most speed. Most of these hints and tricks will cost you nothing. Others require commercial software, but the benefits they bring makes their cost seem insignificant when compared to the expense of a hardware upgrade.

Simple Disk Speed-ups

Inadequate disk performance is such a nagging problem that whole classes of software and entire industries have been created to fight it. Consequently, a huge array of hardware or software products are available to break the disk bottleneck. The software solutions are quick and easy, although most require that you have substantial extra memory in your system.

Start off by taking advantage of all the facilities DOS offers. Almost as a free bonus with DOS, you get several utilities that can help you boost the performance of your system. You can also take time to reorganize your disk structure to get better performance from your system by making it easier for DOS to work with. Most of these tips and tricks concentrate on breaking through the disk bottleneck. After all, DOS is a *Disk* Operating System.

Each of the tricks that you can do with DOS offers its own benefits, and none are mutually exclusive. You can get the most from your system without spending more for an upgrade by taking advantage of them all.

Three of these tricks involve programs included with DOS that you must specifically load to bring to life. These are the BUFFERS statement made in your CONFIG.SYS file, the VDISK disk emulator that's also loaded through CONFIG.SYS, and FASTOPEN, which should be loaded through your AUTOEXEC.BAT file.

These two files are special in that DOS examines them every time you boot up your system. CONFIG.SYS holds device drivers and system options that stay resident in memory as extensions to DOS. AUTOEXEC.BAT is a special batch file that runs programs that you select at boot-up time.

DOS Buffers

Perhaps the simplest speed-up offered by DOS is its file buffers. Under the DOS definition, a buffer is part of your system's RAM that's devoted to storing additional information read from or written to your system's disks. As DOS reads information from your disk, it stores the data in RAM at the same time as it passes the information along to your program. If your program needs that information again, then DOS can quickly read the data directly from the buffer memory instead of waiting for the disk to catch up. In writing, buffers work exactly the same way. When DOS writes something to disk, it also preserves a copy in its buffers, ready to be read back instantly should your program need to take another look.

DOS always stores the most recently read or written data in its buffers. Once the buffers are filled, it discards the oldest data as it reads or writes something new. Thus, the buffers are kept fresh with all the latest information.

Since DOS 4.0 was introduced, DOS also include secondary buffers or *look-ahead buffers*. They add a twist to ordinary buffers by continuing to read a file after finishing delivery of the part of the file that a program wants. The next second of the file is kept waiting in the look-ahead buffer, ready to be delivered to your program at RAM speed.

Buffers are assigned in sector-size blocks, each holding 512 bytes. Because each buffer requires a bit of system overhead, each one steals from 528 bytes to over 532 bytes (depending on your DOS version and whom you believe) away from the DOS memory that's otherwise available to DOS applications. The more buffers DOS uses, the more likely that information that it needs will be located in them—and, of course, the more memory you'll have to devote to buffering. If you use a DOS version older than 4.0, you'll have to carve this buffer memory from the memory that's otherwise available for running your DOS applications. DOS 5.0 and later will automatically use RAM from the 64K above the one-megabyte real-mode memory range (which Microsoft calls the High Memory Area) if you have a 286-, 386-, or 486-based PC and the rest of DOS loads into HMA. (If you don't have any RAM in the HMA, DOS 5.0 will use conventional memory for itself and its buffers.) That way, memory won't be taken away from your DOS programs for buffering, although you'll still lose some RAM that might otherwise be usable by your system.

DOS 4.0 allows you to move buffers into expanded (EMS) memory, if you have enough EMS installed in your system. To use EMS memory with BUFFERS under Version 4.0 of DOS, you have to add a switch, /X, to the BUFFERS statement in your CONFIG.SYS file.

You can specify how much memory you want DOS to devote to buffering using the BUFFERS statement in CONFIG.SYS. The statement is easy to use. With DOS versions previous to 4.0, you simply indicate the number of sector-size buffers you want to assign following an equals sign after the BUFFERS statement itself. You can specify anywhere from 1 to 99 buffers, which will steal from 528 to 52,272 bytes from other purposes. A typical BUFFERS statement would look like this:

BUFFERS = 20

Later versions of DOS allow you to specify both normal buffers and look-ahead buffers. Just add the number of look-ahead buffers after the primary buffer number, using a comma as a separator. For example, the following command would install 30 conventional buffers and 8 look-ahead buffers:

BUFFERS = 30,8

To make DOS 4.0 use expanded memory for its buffers, you would modify this command to read:

BUFFERS = 30,8 /X

Buffers do the most good with applications that randomly access your disk drives, applications such as databases. Programs that read and write large files to disk won't benefit much at all because, as they course through a large file, they will constantly be reading new data from disk, updating the buffers, and discarding old data. By the time you go back to read or write the file again, most of it will have been discarded from the buffers. The largest file that can totally fit inside DOS-based buffers is one accommodated when using the BUFFERS = 99 statement (about 50K bytes), not very big at all in today's world of bit-image graphic files.

The largest number of buffers is rarely the best number to use, however. With a large number, like 99, DOS will spend more time searching for what it wants in the buffers than it will take to access a moderate-performance hard disk. Consequently, a moderate number of buffers—such as the 20 given in the example above—is usually considered the optimum number.

There is no one perfect number of buffers to use in all situations because the optimum number varies with the applications that you use and how you use them. Microsoft makes its own recommendations, based on the size of your hard disk, as listed in Table 3.1. Remember, however, these numbers are not golden. In some situations, other figures may work better. The only way to determine the best figure is by trial and error. Consequently most people stick with 20 to 30 buffers.

Table 3.1 **Microsoft's Recommended Number of Buffers**

Size of Your Hard Disk	Buffers to Use	Memory Penalty (Approximate)
5MB to 39MB	20	10,640
40 MB to 79MB	30	15,960
80 MB to 119MB	40	21,280
Larger than 120MB	50	26,600

The penalty for not including a BUFFERS statement in your CONFIG.SYS files also varies with the version of DOS that you use. Early versions of DOS defaulted to a small number of buffers, so adding a moderate number to your CONFIG.SYS file made a big difference. Since DOS Version 3.3, however, the number of buffers

DOS assigned by default has varied with the equipment in your system. If you have a PC with less than 128K of RAM and only 360K floppy disk drives, DOS will automatically assign you a measly two buffers. If you have the same paltry memory, but upgrade to a larger floppy disk drive (720K, 1.2M, 1.44M, or 2.88M capacity), DOS will add in an extra buffer.

Memory makes a bigger difference, however. If your system has more than 128K, but no more than 256K, DOS will assign five buffers. If your system has more than 256K, but not more than 512K, you'll get ten buffers. With more than 512K of RAM, DOS automatically assigns 15 buffers, very close to the preferred compromise. Table 3.2 summarizes the default number of buffers that current DOS versions (4.0 and later) use.

Table 3.2 **Default Buffer Settings Under DOS 4 and DOS 5**

System Configuration RAM	Disk drive	Default Buffers	Memory Penalty
Less than 128K	360K	2	Effectively none
Less than 128K	720K or larger	3	Effectively none
128K to 255K	any	5	2672
256K to 511K	any	10	5328
512K to 630K	any	15	7984

Note: The look-ahead buffer always defaults to one

Most PCs today have the DOS maximum memory of 640K, often more. For these systems, the BUFFERS = 20 statement isn't going to make a lot of difference in how your system operates. However, you can tweak the number of buffers to get slightly better random access performance from your disk.

There are situations in which you'll definitely want to use a BUFFERS = statement—but to reduce the automatic allotment that DOS assigns you. The pre-eminent case is when you add a third-party disk caching program to your system. A good disk cache can augment the speed of your disk system substantially more than loading your PC with all the buffers DOS allows (99). But while buffers are good and caches are better, using them both together is a waste. Since disk caching is just a more intelligent form of buffers, you're stacking two layers of work to accomplish one job. You might see a little extra benefit, but it probably won't be worth the work. It's like taking money from one pocket, putting it in another, then pulling it out again to pay for a newspaper. The extra movement doesn't add anything to the transaction but time—it takes longer to shift your attention and coins to an extra pocket. Similarly, moving bytes from disk to buffers to cache to memory (or disk to cache to buffers to memory) takes one step more than is necessary. The two end steps are necessary and the cache more efficient, so the buffers should be the first to go.

The basic rule is to minimize the number of buffers your system uses when you have a cache available. Many programs advise that you simply eliminate the BUFFERS statement from your CONFIG.SYS file when you use a hardware- or software-based disk cache. But you may still be stuck with 15 buffers if you have a system with a reasonable RAM endowment. The better alternative is to specify a minimal number of buffers, say two.

If you're operating from a RAM disk (like the DOS VDISK or RAMDrive program) for a substantial amount of the work that you do, buffers won't do much good, either. Again, you're already using fast RAM to handle your disk information, so buffers become an additional RAM step, slowing things down instead of speeding them up. When you work exclusively from a RAM disk, you'll want to minimize the number of buffers you assign with an explicit BUFFERS statement. If you work from both a RAM disk and a physical disk, you'll probably want to set up a compromise value—and the default of 15 offered by DOS isn't such a bad place to start (and finish).

The only other time you may want to reduce your buffers statement (but not necessarily eliminate it entirely) is when you use memory-hungry programs that need every byte you have. Remember, the more buffers you specify, the fewer bytes of DOS memory that will be available for your applications. A really memory-hungry application might not run if you have a substantial number of buffers. If you encounter such an insufficiency, reduce the number of buffers in your CONFIG.SYS until the greedy application agrees to run.

The symptoms of insufficient memory are difficult to ignore. Some programs warn you in a straightforward manner when your system lacks sufficient RAM to get the program running. They may send you a self-explanatory error message such as "Insufficient Memory." Some applications, however, merely jam up when loading in a system with insufficient RAM. Typically, you'll hear a flurry of head movement from your hard disk with nothing appearing on your screen but a flashing hyphen prompt. After a while, the disk activity stops—the program has loaded all of itself it could into your PC's RAM—but nothing else happens. The flashing prompt continues to flash, but no program appears and no amount of frantic key-pressing will return your system to life.

Build a RAM Disk

A RAM disk is sometimes called a *disk emulator* or *virtual disk*. It's simply a block of RAM that is made to act like a disk drive by a special program called a driver. Of course, a RAM disk isn't a real disk, and that's its biggest benefit. Because its storage is made entirely from fast solid-state memory, a RAM disk has RAM speed—it can be as fast as your system's microprocessor. There's no waiting for mechanical delays or transfer times. But being RAM, a RAM disk also holds a couple of disadvantages. One, it's volatile. When you switch off your PC, your RAM disk and its entire contents irrevocably vanish. Two, it requires RAM, sometimes prodigious amounts. You trade some RAM that could be used by some applications for additional speed on others.

That trade-off can yield big benefits, however. Programs that need repeated access to a single file or range of files run like lightning rolling on ball bearings. People who regularly compile and link programs or check the spelling of documents often copy their libraries and dictionaries to RAM disk to minimize the waiting time for disk access. In that nothing new is ever created on the RAM disk using this strategy, the volatility of the storage is not a problem. Should a power failure wipe out the contents of the RAM disk, the same library files can be quickly copied back into place.

In all versions of DOS since 2.0, a RAM disk driver has been included as standard equipment. Earlier versions of DOS used the driver VDISK.SYS, while more recent versions (including DOS 5.0) use a new program called RAMDRIVE.SYS. Either one loads as a device driver in your system's CONFIG.SYS file. For years, nearly every new AT system had a VDISK-driven RAM disk. The reason was that VDISK was just about the only program that could take advantage of the extended memory those systems offered. It can also use ordinary DOS memory, but that's in such short supply in most systems these days, few people hack out a hunk for RAM disk use. RAMDRIVE.SYS can use conventional, extended, or expanded memory.

Because RAM disks could take advantage of otherwise worthless memory, they initially became very popular. Since then, they have become less desirable for several reasons. Disk caching programs offer nearly the same speed-up without the need to set up a RAM disk or copy files to it. New software and advanced microprocessors (like the 386 and 486) are able to take advantage of extended memory, appropriating the RAM disk range for more practical purposes. Programs and libraries have also become so large and demand so much RAM disk space that few people are willing to give it all up. Moreover, too many people have suffered through power failures and lost every trace of their work that they had stored on RAM disk, while hard disk-based programs would have left at least a single backup version behind.

Nevertheless, a RAM disk can still be useful if you have an application that matches its virtues. Typically, you'll want to create an entire system revolving around the RAM disk. Along with the commands necessary for bringing the RAM disk to life, you'll also want to put instructions in your AUTOEXEC.BAT file to copy the files you'll use to your RAM disk automatically when you boot up. You'll also have to install those programs to use the drive letter assigned to your RAM disk, rather than the physical disk on which they are stored.

To create a RAM disk, you load the VDISK.SYS or RAM-DRIVE.SYS driver using the DEVICE= statement in your system's CONFIG.SYS file. Both VDISK and RAMDRIVE allows several options to be included on the line that loads the driver.

For VDISK, these options include the number of directory entries allowed on the RAM disk, the sector size of the RAM disk, and the total size of the RAM disk. Of these, only the last will be a major concern when setting up your RAM disk. You specify the RAM disk size by including the option B= (or the words Buffer Size=) followed by the RAM disk size in kilobytes. In its current incarnation, VDISK can create RAM disks ranging from 64K to 4mb in size, providing your system has sufficient RAM to accommodate it. The only other important option is /E, which tells VDISK to use extended memory for creating its RAM disk.

The command to create a 360K RAM disk in extended memory would look like this:

```
DEVICE = VDISK.SYS  B = 360  /E
```

Once VDISK is loaded, it stays in memory until you reboot your system. Consequently, you'll want to carefully consider how much memory to assign to it, lest you not be able to load programs later on.

RAMDRIVE.SYS works similarly. After the driver name on the command line, you specify the disk size you want to create (in kilobytes); the sector size (if you want something other than 512 bytes, the only other valid values being 128 and 256 bytes), and the number of entries possible in the disk's root directory, from 2 to 1024. The default is 64. In addition, the /e option indicates you want your RAMDRIVE to use *extended* memory; /a indicates to use *expanded* memory.

A typical RAMDRIVE entry in your CONFIG.SYS file to create a one-megabyte RAM disk in expanded memory would look like this:

```
DEVICE = RAMDRIVE.SYS  1024  /a
```

You could also specify a two-megabyte RAM drive in extended memory with 256-byte sectors and 512 directory entries with this entry:

```
DEVICE = RAMDRIVE.SYS  2048  128  512  /e
```

Use DOS FASTOPEN

DOS is not the smartest operating system in the whole wide world. In fact, it has a tendency to be quite forgetful. For example, when you give DOS a command to load a program, it must search for the file that you want even if it has carried out that same search just a few seconds earlier. Even if you give DOS a hint in finding a file by explicitly telling it in which subdirectory the file is located, DOS must read down the directory tree, opening each subdirectory to see how to get to the next one down, until it finally finds the program that you want and locates it on the disk. Even when you give the same command twice back to back, DOS goes through this same search, a creature of habit rather than an inspired worker.

You can add a bit of inspiration to DOS using its FASTOPEN command, which has been available in all versions of DOS since 3.0. FASTOPEN tells DOS to remember where it found files so that it can find them again—quickly—without stepping through the tedious search yet one more time.

A FASTOPEN command applies only to one hard disk drive. If you keep programs or regularly used files on more than one disk drive, you'll need to issue the FASTOPEN command for each disk you want to accelerate. To indicate which hard disk drive you want FASTOPEN to work with, you need to specify the drive letter (followed by a mandatory colon) after the command name.

FASTOPEN gives you one option, a choice of the number of directory entries or files to remember. As with the BUFFERS command, FASTOPEN has a set capacity. Once its memory is full, it dumps the least recently used directory entry from its memory, replacing it with the most recently accessed directory entry. You can set the number of file names that FASTOPEN remembers between 10 and 99. (These figures are not quite as arbitrary as they look—FASTOPEN can only read two-digit numbers. Even with FASTOPEN, DOS isn't very bright.) If you don't specify a number, FASTOPEN defaults to memorizing 34 directory entries (in DOS 3.3).

To buffer the default number of directory entries, type FAS-TOPEN followed by the letter of the disk drive to which you want the command to apply. For example, to make FASTOPEN work with drive D:, you would type this:

FASTOPEN D:

To specify the number of directory entries for FASTOPEN to memorize, append an "equals" sign after the drive to which you want FASTOPEN to work, and follow that by the number. For example, the command to remember the 45 most recent file accesses on drive C: would look like this:

FASTOPEN C:=45

The optimum number to use with FASTOPEN depends on how you use your hard disk. You can experiment to determine a value that works best. But you'll probably find that the default value will serve you well.

The FASTOPEN command can be given like any other DOS instruction on the command line or, better, it can be included in your AUTOEXEC.BAT file so that it leaps into action as soon as you boot your PC.

Trim Your Search Path

Speeding up your disk often is not a matter of adding to your system, but organizing what you have. DOS's tree-structured directory system is the primary case in point. One of the great conveniences of the later versions of DOS is its ability to search through multiple paths on your disks to find the programs that you want to run and even the files needed by programs. By nesting subdirectories, you can organize your disk logically so you can easily remember where each of your files is.

While the tree-structured directory system used by DOS versions since 2.0 are a great way of organizing your hard disk, they can also slow down the performance of the system. To find the starting cluster of a file (which is where DOS must always start reading a file), DOS needs to read through each layer of all the subdirectories along the way to find the file. This research can involve lots of head movement on your disk drive when a file is buried deeply, such as several layers of subdirectories down. That means your disk drive read/write head must scamper from track to track—and with each leap it incurrs a performance penalty statistically equal to the average access time of the drive. Five subdirectories and five leaps of a 40 millisecond drive will impose a delay of 200 milliseconds, a noticeable and bothersome one-fifth second wait. Obviously, if you want to take advantage of all the speed your hard disk has to offer, you'll want to be sure that your most-often-used files are nearest the root direectory.

There's another complication. DOS is able to find devices, including disk partitions, that are given their own drive letter faster than it can dig down into subdirectories. While DOS must search for subdirectories, it remembers where each root directory of each disk is. Hence, if you organize your files by partitioning (using FDISK) rather than using subdirectories (using MKDIR), you can speed access to them, trimming those hundreds-of-milliseconds waits. Note that using the SUBST command to give drive letter designations to subdirectories will not enhance disk speed because, although the process is invisible to you, DOS still must search through the SUBST-ed subdirectories despite their drive letter designations.

The subdirectory slowdown illustrates a sad fact: Nearly everything you do to enhance the convenience of using your hard disk will slow down its performance. One particular case in point is the PATH command, through which you tell DOS where to look for programs it cannot find in the current directory. Whenever you ask DOS to run a program and it cannot find it in the current directory, it searches through all the directory and subdirectory names listed in the last PATH command you gave it.

Obviously, the fewer alternate paths you specify, the less time it will take DOS to zero in on the program that you want (or give you the message that the program cannot be found). If you must specify more than one directory in a PATH command, put your most-often-used programs in the first directory specified. Better yet, specify disks instead of directories. Best of all, keep your most-often-used commands on a high-speed RAM disk emulator (like DOS's VDISK) and list the RAM disk first in your PATH command. Never put a floppy disk in your search path. Floppies are not only slow but you stand the good chance of not having the right disk in your drive. Should that happen, DOS will triumphantly announce "File Not Found" (or "Drive Not Ready" if you have no disk in the drive), wasting even more of your time. This problem is particularly annoying when you mistype a command and have to wait for DOS to exhaust all its path options before issuing an error message.

Defragment Your Disk

Every time you use your hard disk, it gets a little slower—slightly, almost imperceptibly, but slower nevertheless. This sluggishness is nothing mechanical, but is caused by an interaction between software—specifically DOS—and the head actuator (the mechanism that moves the read/write head of your disk drive). It's not really a problem, but an artifact of how your disk is organized and files are managed by DOS.

The source of this age-induced disk speed degradation is DOS's method of packing files onto disk. Because DOS was written when capacity was more important than speed, it tries to pack files on disk as stingily as possible by dividing them in clusters, and squeezing them as tightly as it can, cheek-by-jowl, with nary a space between.

Unlike files that vary in length, these clusters are interchangeable units of a standard size (from 512 to 8096 bytes, depending only on disk type, format, and DOS version). The contents of a single file may be spread among dozens or hundreds of these clusters, each one located anywhere on the disk and not necessarily physically near any of the other clusters in the file.

With earlier versions of DOS, a simple rule governs which clusters are assigned to each file. The first available cluster, the one nearest the beginning of the disk, is always the next one used. Thus, on a new disk, clusters are picked one after another, and all the clusters in a file are contiguous.

When a file is erased, its clusters are freed for reuse. These newly freed clusters, being closer to the beginning of the disk, will be the first ones chosen when the next file is written to disk. In effect, DOS first fills in the holes left by the erased file. As a result, the clusters of new files may be scattered all over the disk.

More recent versions of DOS first work to the end of the disk before trying to squeeze new data in clusters that were previously erased. But once it has written to the entire disk once, even newer DOS versions try to squeeze data into freed-up clusters scattered across the disk.

When you read or write to a file, DOS automatically and invisibly strings all of the clusters together using a map of disk space called the *file allocation table* or *FAT*. No matter how scattered over your disk the individual clusters of a file may be, you—and your software—only see a single file no matter how the clusters are scattered.

Although simple for DOS, this cluster sorting is a nightmare for the disk drive. The read/write head must jump all over the disk to shuttle between the scattered clusters. Every head motion wastes time, and the more scattered the clusters are, the slower the drive will perform.

By reorganizing your disk to optimize the interactions of DOS and the head actuator, you can make your system perform substantially faster, so much faster that you'll be able see the difference when you load programs or files. Programs that carry out the necessary reorganization are called *disk optimizers, disk defragmenters,* or (as Microsoft prefers) *disk compactors.* Although Microsoft recognizes the value of optimizing your disk, no version of DOS provides one. Fortunately, what DOS misses the aftermarket supplies in profusion. A number of special-purpose programs are available for disk optimization, and most hard disk utility packages also include such a program. Alternately, you can defragment your disk's files using your hard disk backup system (streaming tape, cartridge disk, or even floppy disk) to back up and restore all of your hard disk files.

The latter alternative is cheaper (if you already have the backup hardware) and has a side benefit that may save you a lot of pulled-out hair and profanity if disaster strikes later on. It guarantees that you'll have at least one backup copy of your disk files that you might never have otherwise made. The former method of defragmentation—using a commercial program—is easier, faster, and thus somewhat safer.

If you opt for the backup technique, the first step is to make a backup copy of your hard disk, which can be restored file-by-file (rather than as a disk image) using your normal backup system. Even the DOS BACKUP utility and floppy disks, though time-consuming, can be effective. Remember to have a stack of formatted disks (which need not be blank) ready when you use BACKUP.

Just to be safe, you may want to make two backups (particularly if you use the DOS BACKUP program) because the next optional (but recommended) step—reformatting your hard disk—can be frightening when you have megabytes on the line.

The formatting process gives DOS an effectively new disk to write your files back to by wiping the disk clean (and, of course, wiping out your original files). Reformatting may incidentally save you from some future disasters by spotting disk clusters that may have gone bad since you put the drive into service.

Although all disks deteriorate and develop bad clusters as they age (from magnetic decay or from small, unnoticed head crashes), DOS only checks for bad clusters when the disk is formatted. Consequently, sometimes your important data may be written to a cluster that has gone bad since formatting, and those data are forever lost. (This occurs principally with programs that bypass DOS's disk-writing safeguards to gain extra speed.) Reformatting your disk again when you optimize it finds such deteriorated clusters and flags them so that your data won't be trusted to them.

Once your hard disk is reformatted, the next step in optimization by backing up is to restore all your files to it using your backup system's file-by-file restoration option. During the restoration process, all files will be copied back to your disk so that their clusters are contiguous.

An alternative method for reorganizing scattered clusters is to use one of the commercial programs expressly designed for that purpose. Most disk utility packages (for instance, Central Point Software's PC Tools and Symantec's Norton Utilities) include disk optimizing features. These programs work by temporarily copying data from one area of the disk to another, freeing up a contiguous area of free clusters, and copying the data back to the newly freed clusters. At least one copy of your data is always safely recorded on the disk, so you don't risk losing anything if the power fails or the system crashes during the optimization process. They are easy to use—you just type a command at the DOS prompt or make a menu selection—and they automatically run to completion without your intervention. In fact, these programs are generally safe enough you can start one just before you leave work and come in the next day to an optimized disk.

Software-based Disk Caching

The most effective acceleration you can give your hard or floppy disk is a software disk cache. While adding buffers through CON-FIG.SYS will give your system a discernable boost in disk speed, a software disk cache will make a dramatic improvement. With an effective disk cache, neither you nor your program could tell the difference between your laggardly old XT hard disk and the fastest, most expensive modern high-speed drive. Either will operate at nearly the speed of a RAM disk emulator.

An effective disk cache almost entirely isolates your PC from the mechanical bottleneck of your hard disk. As with DOS buffers, the disk cache reads data from disk and stores them in fast RAM. Unlike buffers, the disk cache has a memory management scheme that attempts to anticipate the disk data your programs will need next. Although the algorithms used by most disk caches are proprietary, most combine reading ahead from your disk, knowing that after you read one cluster from a file, you're most likely to read the next one. They also retain the data that you've most recently accessed, in the belief that you'll need it again. Each different disk cache has its own balance of such memory-allocation strategies.

The best part about disk caching software is that it's cheap. Many computer manufacturers include disk caching programs with the PCs that sell. For example, both the latest IBM PS/2s and Compaq computers include disk caching programs. Windows and MS DOS versions later than 5.0 includes their own caches, too. Called SPEEDISK.SYS, the Windows-and-DOS disk cache can be automatically installed as part of the Windows or DOS installation procedure or installed manually in your CONFIG.SYS file. Morever, SPEEDISK.SYS has sufficient built-in intelligence that it shares memory with the EMS used by other programs.

Commercial disk caching programs, such as Flash (from Software Matters, Inc., Indianapolis, Indiana), and Super PC-Kwik (from Multisoft Corporation, Beaverton, Oregon), offer more performance potential. One reason is that they are based on better algorithms. More importantly, they can cache write operations, while the free disk caching programs generally only speed up read operations. Caching write operations is particularly valuable with floppy disk drives—you can save a file to floppy and immediately go on to another job while the disk cache slowly copies your file to the slowly spinning floppy disk. But caching disk write operations is problematic because vital data are vulnerable for the period between the time your program attempts to write to your disk—and the disk cache intercepts the data—and when the disk cache finally copies the data onto disk. Should you switch off your PC during this period or should your power fail, the data will be lost, even though you and your program will think that they have been safely written to disk.

Disk caches that handle write operations do attempt to minimize the danger period. Generally, a disk cache will only wait until your disk is no longer busy to carry out the write operation. Usually the disk cache has an override that ensures the disk cache will never wait too long before protecting the safety of your data to be written. Even so, when you use a disk cache that takes care of write operations, you should never switch off your PC immediately after you've saved a file.

The biggest shortcoming of the software disk cache is that it steals memory from your system that could otherwise be used by your applications. Some programs try to mitigate the damages. For example, Windows' SPEEDISK and the latest versions of PC-Kwik dynamically share cache memory with the EMS needs of other programs, shifting memory from one purpose to the other as it is requires, helping to minimize the memory impact of the disk cache. Disk caching software also requires a slice of your microprocessor's performance to manage its memory operations, but this typically has only a slight impact on the overall speed of your system (which it more than made up for by the quicker disk work won by using the disk cache).

Upgrading to a hardware disk cache in the form of a caching hard disk controller will eliminate these derogatory effects on your system. But hardware disk caches add extra expense instead. They need not only their own, dedicated RAM (which cannot be shared with applications as EMS memory), but also their own caching controllers (often microprocessors) and support circuitry.

Software disk caches hold the potential of operating faster than the more expensive hardware disk caches. The software disk cache operates in your system's memory, so it can keep up with your PC's microprocessor no matter what type of microprocessor it is or what speed it operates at. Hardware disk caches, in general, are connected to your system through its expansion bus and consequently suffer from the bus-speed bottleneck.

Both hardware and software disk caches can lead to compatibility problems. Some hardware-caching disk controllers have proved themselves incompatibile with popular disk utility programs (at least older versions of these programs). The hardware used by the disk cache prevents the utilities from getting the direct control of the disk that they require. This problem is disappearing as caching disk controllers become more popular and program writers adapt their products to match.

Software disk caches may also demonstrate incompatibilities with some applications. For example, early versions of software disk caches did not follow the XMS standard that has emerged for managing extended memory. As a result, these older caching programs would interfere with other software that attempted to use extended memory. The introduction of Windows 3.0 brought this problem to a head, and most disk cache writers have adapted to the new standards. However, some programs still may interact with disk cache software (particularly older versions) in weird ways. In that such incompatibilities are difficult to predict, trial and error is the only way of finding them. You'll minimize such problems by sticking to the latest versions of the commercial disk caching programs.

Once you've located such an incompatibility, you may be able to avoid it by disabling the disk cache or unloading the disk cache from memory when you use that application. Not all software disk caches can be disabled (check before you buy) nor can all disk caches be unloaded from memory. In fact, no disk cache that is installed through your CONFIG.SYS file can be unloaded from memory—at least easily. You might be able to unload it with a hammer, but your PC might not work so well afterwards. When you shop for a software disk cache, be sure that it can be both disabled and unloaded from memory when the applications you want to run demand it.

The most important factor in determining the performance of a software disk cache is the amount of memory available to the cache. While a small disk cache, on the order of 64 kilobytes, may improve the response of your PC, really benefiting from a disk caching program requires huge amounts of RAM. In other words, you should devote as much of your system's memory to your disk cache as you can—megabytes if you have them. For example, if your system has an extra 384K—the balance of the RAM in a one-megabyte system that's not directly accessible to DOS—a software disk cache is an excellent way of putting that RAM to work. If you want the best possible disk performance and you don't have megabytes to spare, consider a memory upgrade to get it. And if you plan on running Windows, by all means use a disk cache that can share RAM with the EMS that Windows uses (such as SPEEDISK.SYS and Super PC-Kwik, as previously mentioned) so that you get the most out of your system's available memory.

Most software disk caching programs give you a choice of the memory that you want to use for running them—DOS, expanded, or extended RAM. Never use DOS memory if you can avoid it. Extended memory is usually the best choice, particularly if you use a software EMS emulator (sometimes called a *LIMulator*) to add expanded memory to your system. It just doesn't make sense to use two layers of memory management when one will do. You'll also want to make sure that you use memory that operates at full microprocessor speed—avoid using expansion memory boards in PCs with clock speeds in excess of eight megahertz. If the memory used by your software disk cache runs slower than your microprocessor, your entire system will have to slow down every time you access your disk. (Disk accesses will probably still be faster than without a disk cache, but neither the disk cache nor the rest of your system will operate at its full speed potential.)

Increasing Disk Capacity

Speed is not the only reason you might want to upgrade your hard disk. You might need extra capacity.

The easiest, cheapest, and fastest way to get more disk space is to be a savage housekeeper—use a hatchet instead of a broom. Hack off without remorse all the files you don't regularly use. Blast away all those backup files that pollute your hard disk as insidiously as mosquitoes in swamp water. Trim away those temporary files left by big programs when you inelegantly exit from them with a system reboot. Bump off every unnecessary byte.

Of course, you've already done that. Or you don't want to do it because you like the convenience and security of having everything there on disk, available instantly whenever you need it. Or you know that those backup files are there for a reason, and you want the reassurance that they give. Whatever the reason for preserving what you have, you can still squeeze more space from your disk.

Find Lost Clusters

Sometimes even the best programs go wrong. They may create temporary files while they operate and delete them when they are done, but sometimes the files don't get completely deleted. While the offending name is removed from your disk's directory, the clusters used by the files may not be freed for reuse. Early versions of programs and odd combinations of software sometimes create this problem. Unfortunately, the evil process and its results are almost entirely invisible. You may never know that anything is wrong, yet space on your disk will disappear at an alarming rate. The problem is that your disk develops a number of *lost clusters*, unused space that DOS cannot use because it thinks (erroneously) that the space is actually allocated to files. Lost clusters subtract from the capacity of your disk without bringing you any benefit.

The best way to detect lost files is with the CHKDSK utility supplied with DOS. Among the other statistics it derives from your disk is the number, if any, of lost clusters and the capacity they consume.

If CHKDSK actually finds lost clusters, it warns ominously that its /F option was not used and asks whether to convert the lost clusters into files. Without the use of the /F (for Fix) option, CHKDSK just reports on what it finds on the disk; even if you choose to convert lost clusters into files, nothing on your disk changes. CHKDSK only reports what would happen should it make the conversion.

If you run CHKDSK and discover lost clusters, the only thing you need to do is use the /F option, typing the following command at the DOS prompt (assuming that you're logged into the drive you want to check and the CHKDSK program is located within the reach of your current search path):

CHKDSK /F

When CHKDSK asks, tell it to convert the lost chains into files. The result will be one or more (maybe hundreds) of strangely named new files in your root directory, starting with FILE0000.CHK, with the number incremented for each subsequent file. You can then examine the contents of these files using any editor you have handy to see if they contain any data you want. You can even use the DOS TYPE command if you don't mind seeing a strange, hesitant display accompanied by beeps as your system attempts to echo control codes as well as text.

Once you're satisfied you have no need for the recovered files, delete them. The space they occupied—the lost clusters—will then be freed for use by other programs. In extreme cases, tens of megabytes of new file space may become available on your disk.

Archive Inactive Files

The information stored in disk files can be arranged in any of a number of different formats—at times it seems that every application uses its own. If you've tried to exchange files between word processors, you know the frustration of it—a letter written using one word processor, when opened by another, turns into a collection of smiley faces, musical notes, and playing card suits. While some standard file formats have arisen in some application areas (dBase files, Lotus 1-2-3 files, and so on), all of these file formats have one thing in common—none is optimized to pack information on your disk as efficiently as possible. In fact, disk files are often like boxes of cereal—even when they are full, you pay for a lot of air space inside.

Just as you could squeeze the air out of the cereal box, you can squeeze the wasted space out of your files. And the amount of air you can remove makes the cereal companies look like paragons of generosity. Some files can be reduced to ten percent of their original size without losing the sense of their contents.

The trick to pumping out the air is called *file compression*, and it can be accomplished in a number of different ways. For example, the letters of the alphabet are typically stored one per byte in ASCII code on your hard disk. But all the letters of the alphabet, in upper- and lowercase, all the numbers, and all the normally used punctuation marks use fewer than half of the 256 different byte codes available in ASCII. A file compression program can squeeze two characters in every ASCII byte and cut the space needed by a text file in half. Spreadsheets are even more wasteful in disk space, often filling up sector upon sector with the contents of unused spreadsheet cells. Graphics files, too, are ripe for compression because most of them consist of byte after byte specifying individual pixels that will appear on screen. When the background of a drawing, that stretches across hundreds of contiguous bytes, is entirely in one color, it can be compressed to two or three code characters— one indicating the color and another or two listing how many bytes to repeat. Hundreds of bytes of a file could be reduced to just a few.

Several commercial file compression programs are available that use techniques similar to these and others devised by their programmers often given colorful names such as squeezing, crunching, and imploding. Of course, the name of the technique doesn't matter as long as it works, and as long as it can be undone to restore the compressed files to their original condition.

You need to be able to reverse the file compression process because compression changes the data format of the file—and thus renders the file unusable by the application that created it. The compressed files become *archive files*. And like paper archives, they are accessible only after a fashion. Accessing a paper archive means searching out some long-lost file cabinet, one possibly guarded by the last remaining Civil War veteran, carefully pulling open the rusted drawer, and gingerly lifting out the papers, hoping they don't turn to dust. Archive files are somewhat less trouble—you only need to extract them before you can use them with your program again. But the file archiving and recovery process involves several manual steps—running a program to make the archive, storing the archive (and eliminating the redundant and disk-space-wasting original), and extracting the file to use it again. If you're only keeping files to have them and not to use them regularly, file archiving can make a lot of sense for saving disk space despite the bother. If you need to use a file often, however, don't bother archiving it.

Minimizing the bother means making the compression and extraction processes as quick as possible. File compression programs have made great strides in the last few years, so a typical 386 computer can compress hundreds of kilobytes in a few seconds. File archiving programs also differ in their compression efficiency. Some pack data more tightly than others, sometimes (but hardly always) with a sacrifice of speed.

The best part of file archiving software is that some of the best programs for doing it are available free or as shareware (programs that you can test for free and only need to pay for if you decide that you want to use them). These programs are generally available on computer bulletin boards. Two of the most highly regarded shareware programs are ARC from System Enhancement Associates and PKZip from PKWare.

If you decide to use file archiving software, you should take one precaution. Make several backups of the software that does the file extraction. If you lose it, all your archived data will be inaccessible. Losing the file extraction program is like having a jail cell slam closed behind you while the key is in your other jeans at home in the wash.

Compress Data Bound for Disk

Some file compression schemes eliminate the most bothersome part of file archiving programs—the need to manually compress files before storing them and extract the same files before using them again. True file compression systems work in real time, compressing files as your programs store them on disk. They work invisibly in the background. You might never know that they are working except for the file space that they save—or at least so their publishers will contend.

These compression programs work by intercepting the data that are being sent to your disk for storage, compressing the data, then sending the compressed data back on their way to the disk. The intermediate processing step can be carried out through software or through a hardware upgrade (for example, special circuitry to handle the file compression can be built into your hard disk controller). These software compression schemes are less expensive, but they can slow down disk reading and writing operation because of the extra, nontrivial overhead they impose. The best hardware compression schemes are fast enough that full disk speed is maintained. On the other hand, disk copying operations may be speeded up because compressed files are smaller and require copying fewer bytes. (During the copy process, the compression programs step aside so they don't waste time uncompressing what they will just compress again.) Disk backups will also be quicker, at least with backup programs that don't have their own data compression schemes built in.

One downside of file compression is that it puts you data on your disks in a nonstandard format. You can't exchange it with coworkers and friends unless they, too, use the same compression system. (Some systems give you the option of not compressing data that's bound for floppy disks so that you can still readily exchange floppies with friends who don't have a data compression system.) The compressed format also can be worrisome if you don't have explicit faith in the software. (What if it makes a mistake in automatically extracting your files—will you lose contact with all your files on disk?) On the other hand, compression can act as a simple security system. Even if someone steals your hard disk, they won't be easily able to read through your confidential files when they are in nonstandard, compressed form.

The available file compression programs work in a variety of ways. A few are specific for certain file types. For example, Font-Space from Isogon Corporation is designed solely to compress fonts that you download to your printer every time you boot up your PC (or at print time). SQZ Plus from Symantec Corporation works to shrink Lotus 1-2-3 files.

General purpose compression programs generally use one of two *modus operandi*. Some, such as Cubit from SoftLogic Solutions work directly with data bound for disk, offering you the option of compressing them or leaving them untouched. When you later want to use the compressed file, it automatically uncompresses the file as it is read. It leaves its own, special signature on compressed files to determine whether they need decompression later. Other compression programs create a new virtual drive that holds only compressed files, the virtual drive carved out of space on an existing drive in such a way it looks like just another large (sometimes really large) file to DOS. Whenever you write something from the new virtual drive, it is automatically compressed. When you read from the virtual drive, the data are decompressed before being passed on to DOS or your applications. The files on the rest of your disks are left untouched and uncompressed. Squish Plus from Sundog Software and Stacker from Stac Electronics operate in this way. The choice between these operating methods is chiefly one of personal preference. Choose a program that works most like the way that you do.

Improving Memory Speed

While you can't make the memory in your PC run faster, you can make sure that it is running at its maximum possible speed. The speed of memory in your system is determined by the clock that drives your microprocessor, the configuration of the memory, and the operating limits of the solid-state memory chips themselves. While any of those factors can be altered with hardware upgrades, such changes are inevitably expensive.

Sometimes, however, you may not be taking advantage of all the performance potential that's built into your system. By making a slight change in how you work with memory or how you set it up, you may be able to coax somewhat more speed from what you have without investing in hardware changes.

Extended Versus Expanded Memory

The first place to look is at the kind of memory you have installed in your system. All PCs start with DOS memory, the basic memory that comes with your system and stretches upward to 640K. Beyond that range, in most systems you have your choice of using extended memory or expanded memory (EMS). The only exceptions are PCs based on the original 8088 microprocessor and those closely related to it: the 8086, 80C86, NEC V20, and NEC V30. Because of the limited addressability of these chips, they can be augmented only with expanded memory, which must take the form of a special expanded memory board that slides into an expansion slot.

Systems based on the 286 and more recent microprocessors have the option of using extended or expanded memory. The latter can be created using special EMS boards in expansion slots or through using EMS emulation software to change extended memory into expanded memory. Some programs, particularly those designed for the 386 and new microprocessors, also have the capability of using extended or expanded memory. Which you choose can affect the performance of your system. If you've made the wrong choice, correcting it can give you a modest performance boost without the cost of an upgrade.

The simple rule is to use extended memory with any programs that will accommodate it. As noted concerning the VDISK disk emulator above, using emulated expanded memory with programs that can use extended memory makes no sense because it results in the use of two redundant layers of memory management. In 286 systems, expanded memory emulation often means copying large (64-kilobyte) blocks of data from one area of memory to another to simulate the switching of memory banks. The overhead of this operation makes these expanded memory simulators particularly slow. Use them only when you need to run a specific program that's worth sacrificing performance.

Note that IBM's 286-based Micro Channel PS/2s have their own bank-switching abilities that eliminate this overhead when using expanded memory emulators. Extended or expanded memory will usually deliver equivalent speed in those systems.

The makers of some early Micro Channel memory expansion boards add another twist. A few such boards were designed to operate as expanded memory boards and came with special driver software that emulated extended memory. Because of this emulation, these boards delivered abysmally slow extended memory performance that should be avoided whenever possible. If you have a Micro Channel expansion board that uses an "extended memory emulator," try using the product only to provide expanded memory, avoiding its emulated extended memory whenever possible.

Another exception to the extended-memory rule is in PCs that have EMS memory boards in expansion slots, as well as matching microprocessor clock and expansion bus speeds. In these systems, and these systems only, expanded memory can actually perform faster than extended because the bank switching that's built into EMS memory boards can move a block of memory instantly.

Trimming Wait States

The only way to truly increase the memory performance of today's highest-speed PCs is to augment their memory caches with more high-speed cache memory—an expensive hardware upgrade. Sometimes you can improve memory performance by eliminating unneeded memory wait states that have been accidentally programmed in.

The chipsets used by a large number of 386- and some 286- and 486-based computers make the number of memory wait states programmable. Using either a utility supplied with these systems or built into their BIOS code, the number of wait states imposed per clock cycle can be altered. If your system is not set to use the optimum number, reducing this setting will improve performance. Some systems provide hardware jumpers to alter the number of wait states used.

The process of altering wait states through your PC's set-up procedure is very risky. If you lower the number of wait states too far, your system may not operate—even to let you switch the number of wait states back to a workable value. In other words, you can get yourself into big trouble monkeying around with the number of wait states used by your system. Before you begin, ensure that your system provides some means of resetting itself to its factory default settings. For example, some systems instruct you to move a jumper from one position to another to totally reset the machine. If you cannot find a means for resetting your PC back to its factory defaults, do not toy with its wait state settings.

When the wait states used by your system are set by hardware jumpers, you have fewer worries. If your PC won't work after you change the setting, you can always change it back to get it going again.

To be on the safe side, before you attempt any alterations to your system's hardware or software set-up, write down all the current set-up values so you can assure yourself of being able to restore them manually. Taking a little time before you begin will save you worries, headaches, and telephone calls when you try to put all the pieces back together again when something goes awry.

To alter the number of wait states in systems that support the changing of wait states through set-up, you'll only need to enter your PC's advanced set-up menu. (If your system doesn't have such a menu in its set-up system, you probably can't change its wait state setting through software.) Among the options available to you may be *wait states*. For more speed, reduce the number that's listed there. Zero wait states is as fast as any system can go.

The settings for hardware jumpers in systems that use them are usually given in the instruction manual of the machine or system board upon which the machine is based. You're most likely to find the settings given in an appendix.

Going the other direction—slowing your system down by adding wait states—is not at all dangerous. If the world is spinning too quickly for you, just add another wait state to your PC's present settings. You can also find programs to slow down your system on most bulletin boards. These programs work by adding wait states or their equivalent to your system. You'll find them particularly handy when you try to run an old game on a new computer and, after a blur of beeps and screen activity, the game ends before you can even touch the keyboard.

Maximizing Memory

The only way to get more memory in your system is to add more memory. But you can squeeze more useful memory from the RAM you have and, perhaps, forestall the inevitable memory upgrade. By managing your system's memory, you can make your PC behave as if it had more RAM at its disposal.

Your goal is to bring memory-hogging programs under control. While you can't trim the RAM required by king-size applications, you can cut down the contention among other programs and features for the memory you have.

One place to begin is with taming your *terminate-and-stay-resident (TSR)* programs. Using a TSR management program, you can load and remove your favorite TSR utilities from memory as needed, freeing up RAM for other applications. Some TSR programs also have their own abilities to remove themselves from memory. Typically, they require you to run the TSR program again with a special command-line option to pop them out of memory. There is one restriction to unloading TSR programs in this way—you must remove the utilities in the reverse order from which they were loaded.

TSR management programs unify the unloading process so that you don't have to type a half-dozen different commands to clear out your RAM. They allow you to load TSRs when you need them and dump them when you don't. In particular, when you want to run a gargantuan application, you can free up nearly all of your system's 640K for the program by ejecting the TSRs. Of course, you won't be able to run TSRs while the gargantuan application is running—but at least it will run. Later you can pop your TSRs back into place by loading them as you normally would.

TSR managers face the same restriction as unloading utilities individually. You can never remove a TSR that was loaded into memory before another one that's still resident. It's like a stack of dishes, only turned upside-down—you can't pull one out from the middle without making the whole stack crash down. In practical application, this limitation means that if you want to unload one TSR, you'll also have to dump any other TSRs you've loaded since that one. The moral is to be careful about the order that you load your TSRs. Not only do you need to worry about which ones must be loaded in which order to work, you want to take advantage of whatever flexibility that remains to prioritize your utilities. Load the more expendable utilities later.

Another way of managing TSR utilities is to use a *virtual memory* system, that is, a program that will allow you to spool your TSRs to disk by making part of your hard disk appear like added RAM. Memory management programs with virtual memory capabilities not only give you more control over your TSR software, they take over control from the TSR. Under their management, TSRs stay out of normal DOS memory except when you want to use them—even though they still act like they are memory-resident. Press a key, and the memory manager finds the TSR, puts it back into memory, and brings it to life. Once you exit the TSR, the memory management program puts the TSR away on disk (or in expanded or extended memory, should you system have some of either). Instead of letting a TSR program hog up DOS memory, the memory manager shifts it out of the way until you need the program. Of course, the shuffle adds a little time and slows the instant response of pop-up programs, but that can be a small price to pay for an extra 100K or more for your other applications. Two programs that will handle these memory management tasks are Headroom from Helix Software and Extra from Delta Technology International.

These programs, like any TSR manager, can't move everything out of DOS memory. Software drivers, RAM disks, or continuously running utilities like screen blanking programs need to stay in conventional memory because they are always working. Move them to disk and the applications will halt, likely stopping your system at the same time. The only way to cut the memory used by drivers and other continuously running programs is to fine-tune your system. For example, some drivers (such as caches and RAM disk emulators) allow you to select the amount of RAM they use. You can trim what you give them to the minimum that allows them to work to gain RAM for other applications. Similarly, you can judiciously reduce some of your DOS options—for example, the number of buffers, files, and environment size set in CONFIG.SYS—to gain a few extra bytes or a few kilobytes. Although those seem like paltry sums, they can make the difference between running the latest version of Lotus 1-2-3 and sitting around staring at a blank screen.

Improving Display Performance

Today's top-performing applications write directly to video memory. That is, they merely transfer bytes from your system's normal RAM to the video memory in your display adapter. This transfer is limited by the performance of your system's input/output bus.

The vast majority of programs rely on DOS or BIOS firmware to put characters on the screen rather than writing directly to memory. These applications are limited by both the bus bottleneck and the overhead imposed in the extra instructions. A further complication is that the BIOS video instructions are often held in ROM, which in most systems is substantially slower than system RAM. Several strategies and software utilities can help you avoid some of these slowdowns.

Video Speed-up Programs

The most visible improvement you can make in your PC is accelerating its display performance. A snappier screen makes a snappier, more responsive PC. But you don't have to go to the expense of upgrading your display system to get faster displays. By attacking the weaknesses in the way programs use your display system, you can make great improvements in display speed without an equally great investment in an upgrade.

The place to begin improving your display system is with your system's BIOS. DOS and many applications use routines in your PC's BIOS to put text and graphics on the screen. In the original design of the PC, the BIOS was supposed to be the primary connection between software and your PC hardware. But the BIOS routines are conservatively written to be easy to use and compatible with the widest range of programs. They are decidedly not written to be compatible with impatient human beings. Worse, DOS provides its own display routines that programmers can use, routines that dip down and use the BIOS code, adding a second layer of overhead (and second insult) to display speed. Many programmers have, in frustration, bypassed both the DOS and BIOS display routines to write bytes directly to video memory (the chips on your display adapter card), giving their systems a discernable speed boost. But many, many applications stick by the rules and write video with BIOS or DOS routines.

For these programs, as well as DOS, a little magic is available—software that alters the BIOS codes to kick in the display adrenalin. Altering your system's BIOS may sound like a drastic step—perhaps something that in level of difficulty is between brain surgery and building a nuclear plant—but it can be accomplished quickly and easily. A TSR program can intercept the interrupts used by the DOS and BIOS routines and substitute lean, mean, and high-speed display code. Pre-eminent among these programs is the screen portion of PC-Kwik Power Pak from Multisoft. It will add new snap to your video displays as well as a screen review feature. With applications that use DOS video routines, PC-Kwik Power Pak can actually make a bigger difference than shifting to a 16-bit video board. But it will benefit any system, including those with high-speed display adapters.

Video Shadowing

One of the most pernicious display bottlenecks is actually a memory problem. Programs that use BIOS routines must, of course, access the memory holding the code for those routines. In most systems, that code is stored in ROM memory. And ROM is notoriously slow. Accessing ROM adds extra wait states to the microprocessor. Moreover, most 32-bit systems use 16-bit ROM memory, slowing the routines stored there to half-speed.

The 386 and later microprocessors have built-in abilities to remap memory. That is, software can convince the chips to look at different memory locations than those indicated by applications for data that those applications need. When DOS or software attempts to read a BIOS routine, memory remapping allows the request to be redirected to some other memory location.

A technique called *video shadowing* copies the BIOS routines from slow ROM memory into fast RAM, then redirects the system (DOS and all programs) to look in RAM when it needs video routines. Shadowing can speed up display routines by a factor of two or more. Many of the latest high-performance computers have built-in ROM shadowing capabilities. That is, they automatically copy the code in slow ROM memory to fast RAM to speed up execution.

As with replacement TSR video routines, video shadowing runs from within the fastest RAM in your system. In that way, they are redundant. In fact, if you use speed-booting replacement video routines, you should avoid using video shadowing. The RAM memory that's allocated to shadowing will be wasted because the display routines copied in the shadowing process will be bypassed like any other BIOS display routines by the speed-up program. This is one case where the advantage of two acceleration methods do not add up. Combining them only results in wasted RAM.

Display List Drivers

With Computer-Aided Design programs, the actual work putting an image on your monitor screen is easy compared with the process of producing the image. The CAD program must compute exactly which dots on the screen to illuminate by mathematically calculating every line and curve to be drawn. While an image in video memory can be flashed on the screen in one-sixtieth of a second, filling the video memory with the image can take several minutes or more.

Every time the screen changes, the CAD program must calculate every dot all over again, a process called *regeneration* because the image is built up from its very beginnings, from the formless void as in Genesis. Regens are often the most time-consuming part of using a CAD program.

With *AutoCAD* from AutoDesk Corporation it is possible to side-step the regeneration process in many cases by using a *display list driver*. This add-on program remembers all the calculations that were done to generate a screen and regurgitates them to redraw the screen when it becomes necessary. With all the calculation time saved, updating the screen becomes a much faster process, often cut from minutes to seconds.

Adding a display list driver to AutoCAD is no more difficult than installing the driver needed to match any other display system to the drafting program. The driver is executed before AutoCAD is run. The AutoCAD program itself is set up to use its ADI display method. Many recent VGA boards include their own display list drivers to accelerate AutoCAD performance. A general purpose AutoCAD display list driver is available from Vermont Microsystems under the name AutoMate.

Printer Spooling

Too many PCs turn themselves and you into vegetables when they print. Once you issue the print command to your database or spreadsheet, your computer single-mindedly concentrates on shifting characters from its memory onto paper. Printers, being mechanical devices, can rarely keep up with the rate that your PC could spew out data. As a result, when printing, your PC must constantly wait while your printer laboriously pecks away. Meanwhile, you're stuck watching an immutable screen while the whole chore drags along. You could regain control of your PC from a print job more quickly if you could dump all the data out of your computer at its speed rather than the printer's. That way your PC never has to wait for the printer to catch up.

A device that accepts data from your PC as fast as it can be generated then doles the data out to your printer at its speed is called a printer *spooler* or printer buffer. The spooler can be a separate hardware upgrade or a software program.

The software solutions are the least expensive, particularly since the programs that you need are usually free. Nearly every memory expansion board at one time or another included a "free" bonus printer spooler. Some operating systems (such as OS/2 and *Unix*) and some operating environments (such as Windows) and many applications (particularly word processors) also include spoolers as standard equipment. Spoolers are also available on most computer bulletin board systems.

Software spoolers have an advantage over the hardware variety because they can acquire data as fast as your applications generate them, while data bound for hardware buffers must first squeeze through a communications port. But software spoolers can consume prodigious amounts of your PC's microprocessor power—and lots of disk or RAM if you let them. In 8088 machines, for example, a spooler will slow down your system to a fraction of its normal speed, sometime making it take agonizing seconds from the press of a key to a character appearing on the screen. While 286, 386, and 486 computers take less of a hit because they have greater performance reserves, the slowdown may still be noticeable. Nevertheless, when the choice is doing nothing while printing and working more slowly than usual, low speed can come up the big winner.

Note that adding a print spooler will not speed up the rate at which your printouts are finished nor will you gain back control of your PC instantaneously. Processing files for printing still takes time.

Keyboard Quickeners

The toughest bottleneck to beat is one that lies not in the electronic realm but human. While you can't do anything to quicken your thoughts, you can do something about communicating them to your PC faster. Without changing either your keyboard or adding more hardware (such as a mouse or track ball), you can boost the speed you can interact with your computer. You can make improvements in two places; navigating through menus and applications and keying in data.

Navigational Speed

Applications that require you to repeatedly press the cursor keys to move around in an editing display are particularly amenable to acceleration. By increasing the typematic rate—the speed at which a key that's held down squirts out a series of characters to your PC—you can make the cursor fly through applications. A faster cursor will accelerate the rate at which you can choose words and characters for editing or race through a data input template.

Some programs, notably Microsoft Windows, have their own built-in keyboard quickeners. Or you can buy a quickener as part of a generalized speed-up utility package. The keyboard-enhancer in Multisoft's PC-Kwik Power Pak is particularly useful.

Some computers don't require software keyboard quickeners at all. Instead, they may have built-in facilities for altering the keyboard's built-in typematic rate, often making it part of your system's set-up procedure (check your owner's manual). Several keyboard speed-up programs are also in the public domain and available on local electronic bulletin board services.

Keyboard Macros

Much of the typing that you do at your PC's keyboard is likely repeated time and again. For example, every letter you type probably has an address block at the top and your name at the bottom. Or you may issue a series of commands every time you use your PC to collect your E-mail, open a spreadsheet, and pull in the latest update from the corporate database. It's foolish for you to have to type these same words and commands over and over again when a device with a better memory than your own—your PC—could do the work for you.

A macro is a facility that allows your PC to read, write, or process a predefined sequence of text or data when given a simple command. A *keyboard macro* simulates the keystroke you type at your keyboard. The keyboard macro sends letters to your PC and the application it's running as if you had typed them in directly. The keyboard macro can send blocks of text to your word processor, commands to DOS, or data to a spreadsheet exactly as if you had typed it all.

Versions of DOS more recent than 5.0 include a rudimentary keystroke macro program called DOSKEY. It allows you to recycle old command lines and save strings of characters for later reuse.

Commercial keyboard macro programs go farther and are easier to use. Most include a simplified way of defining your macros called *learn mode*. To create a macro, you hit a hot-key combination—the keys you will later press to cause the macro to send keystrokes to your computer—and then you just type the sequence of keystrokes you want the macro to remember. Pressing a special key stops the learn mode and causes the macro to remember everything. Thereafter, each time you hit the hot-key, the macro will dutifully echo your previous keystrokes. You can save all the macros you make to disk so you can later read them back into memory without having to go through the learning process all over again.

The macro program itself is a terminate-and-stay-resident utility that lodges itself in your computer's memory every time you execute it. Although the program permanently remembers the macros you type by storing them on disk, it will typically keep them in RAM once you start the macro program running. Consequently, the macro steals not only enough memory to hold its own code, but also enough RAM to store the output of all the macro commands.

Most more powerful programs and operating environments like Quarterdeck Office Systems' DESQview have their own, built-in macros that minimize the need for external keyboard macros. Consequently, keyboard macro programs have has fallen from favor over the last few years and many products have been discontinued. The advent of DOSKEY as part of DOS will likely accelerate this trend. Nevertheless, keyboard macros remain useful should you want to automate lesser programs that lack built-in macro support.

4.

MICROPROCESSOR UPGRADES

The most radical change you can make in your PC is upgrading its microprocessor. The benefits are processing speed, the capability of handling greater amounts of memory, better abilities to make use of that memory, and entrée to new environments and operating systems. But a microprocessor upgrade can be costly. And while not difficult, tinkering with your system's innermost circuits can be worrisome.

Quite simply, the best way to get more out of your PC is to put more inside it—and the most dramatic addition you can make is a new microprocessor. The operation is essentially a brain transplant and the results are exactly what you should expect, a complete change in the personality of your system. Whereas it may have been lazy or at least lackadaisical in the past, a new brain will make a willing and speedy worker. Where your system once shirked from such towering tasks as running multiple programs at the same time, with a new personality it can juggle programs like plates or bowling pins and won't gasp at the sight of the stack of floppy disks holding a complete UNIX package. The transformation will be from woebegone to whippersnapper and it needn't take more than an hour of your time.

Although changing microprocessors can dramatically improve the performance of your system, it's not just a matter of speed, however. Your computer's microprocessor doesn't just do all the work, it also determines what work will get done. With a particularly propitious pick of microprocessors, you can take advantage of today's utilities that expand the amount of memory available to your DOS applications (and the new versions of DOS that do likewise). Thanks to the advanced memory handling capabilities of the latest microprocessors, you can stretch the addressing range of DOS and move memory-resident drivers and utilities out of the way of your programs. Moreover, the repertory of programs that your PC can handle will expand to embrace nearly everything available, including powerful 386-specific applications such as AutoCAD 386 and Paradox 386.

The best part about upgrading the microprocessor in your PC is that you can do it yourself with a lot less trouble and danger than changing a light switch or baking a casserole. If you know which way to spin a screwdriver and have managed to slide an expansion board into your PC without eliciting the sort of fireworks that would make Captain Kirk cringe, you can handle the job. Even the most difficult microprocessor upgrades can be completed in under an hour. The only tough part is deciding what microprocessor to install and which of the available upgrade methods to use.

Chip Choice

The first decision you must make—which microprocessor to upgrade to—might seem to be the easiest. Like every other PC owner in the universe, you probably want the kind of secret superchip that mainframe computer-makers have suppressed for fear of wiping out their sales, something along the lines of the long-awaited 500 MHz 80986, only faster. Unfortunately, while neither your imagination nor desires have no bounds, your budget probably does. The monetary limit and the current state of technology form a harsh reality that will limit your microprocessor choices to something more mundane.

Still, the range available to you is wide and the differences between chips dramatic. To help you get acquainted with the choices available to you, here is a brief chipography of the microprocessors currently compatible with the IBM standard.

The 8088 Family

This is the chip that ignited the fireworks of the PC revolution. In today's world of chrythanthemum shells and aerial bombs, the 8088 has all the bang of a soaked cap gun. In fact, on a scale of microprocessor performance from 1 to 100, with a 33 MHz 486 at the top, the 8088 rates almost exactly a 1. This scale is not arbitrary. A well-designed 486 can easily process data 100 times faster than an 8088.

Different models of 8088 chip are available with a number of maximum operating speeds. The fastest 8088 that's widely available runs as about 10 MHz, about twice as fast as the standard microprocessor in IBM PCs and XTs, which are throttled back to 4.77 MHz. But clock speeds of different microprocessor families are not directly comparable. The actual processing speed of a microprocessor is dependent on a number of factors, of which clock speed is only one. Each chip architecture also has an efficiency factor that roughly equates to the number of clock cycles required to carry out a single instruction. Various chip instructions can require from 1 to over 100 clock cycles to be carried out. Moreover, microprocessors also differ in the number of data bits that they can handle at a time. A chip that can process 32 bits at a time can carry out some operations four times faster than one limited to eight bits at a time, all else being equal. The greater bit-width of a chip also enables the chip to acquire instructions and data more quickly. When all those factors are taken into consideration, the 8088 pales in comparison to newer chips. For example, its direct descendent, the 80286 microprocessor, runs between four and five times faster than an 8088 at the same clock speed. In other words, the 8088 is not a microprocessor anyone would upgrade *to* but it is certainly a chip anyone would want to upgrade *from*.

The 8088 also serves as a starting point to compare to other microprocessors in its family, those that use Intel's architecture. All microprocessors in this cohort are defined by three characteristics—the bit-width of its internal registers (which carry out all of the microprocessor's instructions and calculations); the bit-width of the data lines used for acquiring data and instructions; and the number of address lines that determine the maximum memory that the chip can handle.

Inside, the 8088 chip has four principal registers that are 16 bits wide. It connections with the outside world are limited to a width of eight bits. Because the 8088 has 20 addressing lines, it can directly address a maximum of one megabyte of memory (that is, 2^{20} bytes of memory).

Because DOS was written to run on the 8088 series of microprocessors, DOS itself confines itself to the addressing limits of the 8088. To retain compatibility with 8088 microprocessors, DOS never attempts to address more than one megabyte of memory. In fact, some programs take advantage of the one-megabyte addressing limit and wrap addresses "around" the limit, knowing that when the limit is exceeded, the 8088 starts counting again from the beginning.

The more familiar 640K DOS limit is a result of IBM reserving the last 384K of the 8088's addressing range for fixed internal functions of the original PC. Because IBM didn't want programs interfering with these functions, a line was drawn at 640K that programs weren't allowed to cross.

The 8088 family also includes a few close relatives to the original, such as a low-power version, the 80C88. Except for the semiconductor technology used for fabricating the chips, the 8088 and 80C88 have essentially the same capabilities. Low-power Complimentary Metal Oxide Semiconductor (CMOS) construction makes the 80C88 consume much less power (and contributes the "C" in the name).

The V20 microprocessor is a clone of the 8088 made by NEC. It has the same register width, data path, and addressing limits of the 8088. However, the internal structure of the V20 is somewhat more efficient than the 8088, resulting in slightly better performance on *some* applications.

The 8086 Family

The 8088 microprocessor is actually an offshoot of another chip, the 8086. The difference between the two is simply that the 8088 has an eight-bit connection with external data, while the 8086 has a 16-bit connection. The 8088 was derived from the 8086 to reduce costs. At the time the 8088 was developed, microprocessor supporting circuits that used eight-bit data paths were substantially less expensive than those that used 16-bit paths. Consequently, using the 8088 allow computer manufacturers to cut costs.

Internally, the 8088 and 8086 use exactly the same register structure with four principal 16-bit general-purpose registers. The two chips also have the same 20-bit addressing ability. They also use exactly the same instruction sets. Consequently, the 8088 and 8086 will run exactly the same software. But because of their differing number of data connections, they are not pin-for-pin compatible. You cannot substitute one for the other.

The wider external connection of the 8086 means that it can read and write to memory and peripherals somewhat faster than the 8088. It can approach (but never really reach) a twofold performance improvement over the 8088 when the two chips operate at the same clock speeds. The performance improvement was sufficient so that some manufacturers once offered 8086 upgrades for 8088 systems. Most (if not all) of these have been discontinued, not only because of the modest speed gain but also because the 8086 is limited to only one megabyte of memory handling. It cannot run the protected-mode programs or operating systems that have become so popular today. In other words, the 8086 has changed from an 8088 upgrade to a chip that itself needs to be upgraded.

As with the 8088, the 8086 is available in a low-power version. NEC also offers its own clone of the 8086 called the V30. Another Intel chip, the 80186, is essentially an 8086 with some of its required external support chips grafted into its silicon. Except if you have the barest minimum—and most aged—PC, you won't want to consider any of these as candidates for your next upgrade.

The 80286 Family

In the early 1980s, Intel created the 80286 (now shortened in general use to simply the 286) as its *tour de force*. The new chip offered substantially greater inner efficiency than the 8086 predecessor and broke asunder the older chip's memory-handling barrier. This was to be the chip that would revolutionize how personal computers worked.

And the 286 did change computers, but not in the way expected. The 286 was chosen first by IBM for its powerful Personal Computer AT, which set the standard in the industry for future PCs, a standard that's only now wavering. But the 286 proved only a part of that new standard, and not a necessary part. The AT hardly exploited the full potential of the 286. The problem wasn't the machine, however, but DOS. The design work on the 286 was started before DOS dominated the entire world of personal computers. The 286 was made to be the powerhouse behind a new operating system. Unfortunately, not only was the world way behind DOS, but no new operating systems were delivered for the 286 for three years (and it—OS/2—had a chilly initial reception indeed). The 286 was stuck running DOS, which it did, quickly. But its memory-handling was hardly tapped because DOS couldn't do the tapping.

In a major break with the past, the 286 was designed to operate in two different, mutually exclusive modes. In *real mode* it emulates the 8086 but runs substantially faster. As with the 8086, it has 16-bit internal registers and 16-bit data connections. Although the 286 has 24 address lines (allowing it to directly address 16 megabytes of RAM) in real mode, the chip is constrained to addressing one megabyte of RAM.

The other operating mode of the 286 is *protected mode*. There are two chief distinctions of protected mode—it allows all 16 megabytes that the chip can address to be used by programs, and it allows several programs to run at the same time in this memory, protected from one another so that they don't interfere with each other. However, the 24-bit addressing of protected mode and the 16-bit addressing used by DOS don't mix. DOS cannot run in protected mode. Worse, the design of the 286 envisioned real mode only as a springboard to leap into protected mode. Once all that memory was available, the design engineers of the 286 believed, no one would want to go back to the confines of real mode. So the switch between real and protected modes was designed as a one-way street. The 286 could not switch modes at will. The 286 must boot up in real mode, and in most cases that's where it stays, running DOS applications.

The 286 has been termed "brain dead" by any number of industry commentators. The 286's persistent vegetative state was caused by the accident of DOS becoming popular and its incompatibility with DOS. But the 286 doesn't have a flat EEG. Its mind functions fine at a primitive—that is, DOS—level. It can run DOS applications at high speeds, particularly in its 20 MHz versions. But its brain death means that's about all it can do for your DOS applications. It can only run one at a time, and it can only let them touch addresses within the first megabytes of its memory range. If all you want to do is run DOS, the 286 will do it handily. It will also manage some versions of Novell Netware, UNIX and OS/2. But if you have higher aspirations, consider the 286 (and its low-power CMOS twin, the 80C286) another chip to upgrade from rather than to.

The 80386 Family

Large corporations learn from their mistakes, and the 80386 family of microprocessors—now termed simply the 386 family—is proof of the learning experience at Intel. Instead of ignoring DOS, the 386 embraces it. Not only does the 386 excel at running DOS quickly, it can run multiple DOS programs simultaneously.

This multitasking facility results from a third operating mode that Intel added to the 386, *Virtual 8086 Mode*. As with the 286, the 386 has both real and protected modes. The two modes operate exactly as they do in the 286 (to assure backward compatibility) with the exception that the 386 can switch back and forth between real and protected modes without difficulty or calamity. The new mode called *Virtual 8086 Mode* allows the 386 to divide up the memory available to it into areas that each operate like an 8086 microprocessor running in real mode. These memory areas are isolated from one another so that errant code from one cannot interfere with another. As with an actual 8086, the 386 can address up to one megabyte of RAM in each of these memory areas, providing of course that there's sufficient RAM in the system to allocate one megabyte to each area. The result of this architectural design is that an individual DOS program can run in each memory area as if it were in its own computer. In fact, each division of the memory of the 386 behaves exactly like a separate computer, allowing not just a single program but a full regiment of TSR programs and drivers to operate in each area as if the 386 were actually multiple PCs.

Virtual 8086 Mode is the key feature required by DOS multitasking systems like DESQview, Windows, PC MOS/386, and VM/386, as well as for OS/2 Versions 2.0 and later. If you want to do multitasking with DOS applications, you'll require at least a 386 microprocessor.

But Virtual 8086 Mode isn't the only reason you'll want to make the 386 your minimum microprocessor choice. The 386 also has built-in advanced memory management features. Among these, it is able to remap memory through its own internal hardware. Remapping allows the 386 to alter the logical address at which it recognizes physical memory. In other words, the 386 can be told to call RAM that's physically connected at location A0000(Hex) as if it were at 0A000(Hex). Memory remapping allows the 386 to trick programs. In particular, programs that must run at certain absolute addresses can be fooled into running elsewhere. This bit of prestidigitation allows computers to shadow their ROM memory for added speed. While some 286 computers allow ROM shadowing, they require this feature to be implemented in external memory management circuitry. Memory remapping also allows 386 computers to relocate drivers and TSR programs out of the DOS 640K addressing range and into high memory. This memory managing ability is required to take advantage of all the power of the latest versions of Windows as well as DOS Versions 5.0 and later.

The 386 also incorporates dramatic improvements, the value of which will only become apparent in the long run. The addressing range of the 386 was extended to a full 32 bits, putting up to four gigabytes of memory within its direct reach. The 386 can also address virtual memory—RAM that's simulated by disk memory—up to four trillion bytes of virtual RAM.

In addition, the 386 is a full 32-bit microprocessor. Its wide registers give it the capability of running applications twice as fast as the 16-bit 286. However, this performance advantage is not meaningful when you're only running DOS programs. DOS was written as a 16-bit operating system and its code uses only 16-bit instructions. When operating at the same clock speed, the 386 executes DOS applications at about the same rate as a 286 (some 286-based systems actually earn a performance edge over the 386 when running DOS). However, Intel makes 386 chips that run substantially higher clock speeds than do 286 chips, giving the 386 the performance lead on DOS.

Beyond DOS, there's no comparison between the 286 and 386. When given a program that uses true 32-bit instructions, the 386 will make the 286 look like it's standing still. In fact, the 286 will have to stand still because it cannot run programs that are based on the 386's 32-bit instuctions. Programs recoded with 32-bit instructions often run twice as fast (or faster) on 386 PCs than their 16-bit equivalents running on 286 computers. As more and more applications and operating systems are written using the 386's native 32-bit instruction set, you'll have even more reason to upgrade to the 386.

Your 386 upgrade choices are actually twofold, the *386DX* and *386SX*. The 386DX is the original 386 under a new name, a full 32-bit chip in all ways—32-bit registers, 32-bit addressing, and 32-bit input/output data path. The 386SX is a more recent down-market version of the original 386. It cuts the input/output data path in half to 16 bits while retaining the same 32-bit addressing and 32 internal registers of the 386DX. While the narrow data path reduces some of the speed capabilities of the 386SX, it also adds an important benefit. The 386SX works with 16-bit peripherals, which are in general less expensive than 32-bit parts. The 386SX is thus designed as an alternative for computer manufacturers that allows them to build less expensive machines.

The 386SX recognizes the same 32-bit instruction set as the 386DX, and it operates in the same three modes—real, protected, and virtual 8086. Consequently, the 386SX will run any program written for the 386DX and lesser microprocessors.

The 386SX is often compared to the 286 because both chips interface with 16-bit peripherals. But important differences separate the two chips. The 286 cannot run 386 applications. The 286 cannot run DOS multitasking operating environments. The 286 cannot in itself remap memory but requires external circuitry to do so. And while the two chips may approach the same performance on DOS applications (when operating at the same clock speed, of course), the 386SX will run 32-bit applications faster than the 286 can run their 16-bit equivalents.

Another later addition to the 386 family is the *386SL*, a chip with the same internal architecture as the other 386s but using a different circuit technology and design goal. The 386SL was created to be an energy skinflint, conserving power in a variety of ways to allow laptop and notebook PCs to run as close as possible to forever on a single charge. As far as application programs are concerned, the 386SL is just another 386. Everything that runs on a 386—from the tiniest utilities to memory-management programs to exotic, high-power graphics bombshells that use 32-bit instructions—will happily execute in a 386SL. But the 386SL is not a chip to plan an upgrade around. To computer hardware, the 386SL is an unusual beast, more a set of chips than a single microprocessor. And taking advantage of its unique energy management abilities requires special computer designs. You've little reason to try to squeeze more from the watts in your PC—the power demands of the support circuits and peripherals in desktop PCs are many times greater than those of the microprocessor. Switching chips won't make much of a dent in the overall consumption of your system. While the 386SL will give your PC the same program-running abilities as any other chip in the 386 family, the 386SX is a much lower-cost way to achieve that goal. The 386SL just doesn't make sense as an upgrade.

When you have a choice of upgrading to a 386DX or 386SX, all else being equal, the 386DX is the hands-down choice. It's the bigger, faster chip. The 386DX is available in higher-speed ratings than the 386SX. The 386DX is also the more expensive. A 386SX chip costs much less than a 386DX (perhaps hundreds of dollars), so when you count your coins as carefully as children on a field trip, the 386SX can come out the winner. The only disadvantage to choosing the 386SX to 386DX is speed. There is no difference in the applications that the two chips will run or their advanced features.

The 80486 Family

Intel's 80486, colloquially the *486*, is both a slimmed down and beefed up version of the 386. It's slimmed down in that its circuitry has been made more efficient. It can carry out many operations 15 to 25 percent faster than a 386 running at the same clock speed. At the same time, it has been beefed up by building in its own modest (four kilobyte) memory cache and a math coprocessor. The price of the chip, too, has been beefed up to match—the cost of a 486 hovers close to that of a 386DX with a matching 387DX math coprocessor.

Because it is at heart a 386, the 486 will run most of the same programs that the 386 will. The few exceptions are the work of clever programmers who attempted to modify the contents of the system's cache and unwittingly thwarted the 486's ability to keep the contents of memory and its internal cache congruent. The result makes itself dramatically known—incompatible programs crash. Note that the number of such incompatible programs was tiny to begin with and has steadily decreased to insignificant as programmers have had their transgressions pointed out to them.

Beyond these few, all programs, all multitasking operating environments, and all operating systems that run on 386 chips will run on the 486. The two chips understand the same 32-bit (as well as 16-bit and eight-bit) instructions, have the same three operating modes, and the same memory-handling abilities. Programs like AutoCAD that require a Intel-style math coprocessor will also run on systems equipped solely with a 486 microprocessor.

The 486 family is bifurcated like that of the 386, but in a different way. Just as the 386DX has its own, underpriviledged sibling, the high-end chip, now dubbed the *486DX*, has its own poor relation, the *486SX*. The difference between the two 486 chips is not the bus connection, however. Both the 486DX and 486SX are full-blown 32-bit chips. Rather, the 486SX is stripped of the built-in numeric coprocessor of the 486DX. In that many applications don't take advantage of the coprocessor in the 486DX, the 486SX can be quite useful, delivering streamlined 486 performance but at a more affordable price.

At first, the favorable pricing of the 486SX was believed by some to be the result of clever marketing—Intel was thought to be selling 486DX chips in which the coprocessor was defective (termed "floor-sweepings" by some) as 486SXs. Today, however, Intel runs a separate production line for the 486SX, making it a true chip in its own right.

In that the 486 family includes today's premiere microprocessors, you probably are eyeing them as likely candidates to upgrade to. But if you already have a PC equipped with a 386DX or 386SX chip, the most that a 486 will buy you is speed. Unlike the big step between a 286 and 386 that brings a multitude of advanced features, the step between the 386 and 486 is modest. Unless there is a great gulf in processor speeds between the 386 you have and the 486 you want, you stand to gain nothing from the upgrade. The 486 won't open new software opportunities to your system. On the other hand, at the same clock speed a 486 can process information substantially faster than a 386, at times doubling the older chips throughput. Select the 486DX if you want the ultimate in performance. The 486SX delivers equivalent speed on all applications except those that require extensive number crunching (say, serving a network). But if you just want to take advantage of advanced memory management, run Windows in Enhanced mode, or use programs written with 32-bit code, the 386DX or 386SX is likely a more economical choice. In other words, while a 486 may be wonderful, most people will find a 386 is to be good enough.

Which Chip to Pick

When you decide to upgrade your PC's microprocessor, the initial temptation is to get the most powerful chip available. Indeed, you'll get the most dramatic increase in power if you slide a 50MHz 80486 motherboard replacement into your old XT chassis. But the cost of moving to a top-of-the-line microprocessor upgrade can be staggering. An 80486 microprocessor alone, without its necessary support circuitry, can cost in the vicinity of $750. A full 486 motherboard may cost more than an entire 386 system complete with a new hard disk drive! Moreover, when you put a high-power microprocessor in your old system, it's likely to suffer from the laggardly abilities of the older disks and expansion boards that are already in your system. Upgrade them to match the new microprocessor and you can easily exceed the cost of a new computer. In most cases, the highest of the high end is not a wise choice for upgrading.

On the other hand, if you try to slide by on the cheap you may end up wasting most of your upgrade investment—the payoff won't justify the payout. For example, the relatively inexpensive move from the 8088 inside an PC or XT to the AT-level with an 286 microprocessor is probably not a wise move today. While you will gain three to ten times more speed, as well as the potential ability to run early versions of OS/2, your system will still lack all the 386 features that make power users drool. Your system will still be limited to addressing 16 megabytes of RAM (that's okay for today, but it may soon prove too little). And even with a 286 upgrade, you PC will still lack the memory abilities needed to take advantage of today's truly advanced applications that can run several standard DOS programs at the same time.

The best price-to-features compromise for older computers based on 8088, 8086, and 286 microprocessors is upgrading to the 386SX microprocessor. While the SX chip delivers only slightly better overall speed than an 286 operating at the same clock rate, it will endow your PC with the ability to run any 80386-specific application. You'll gain the advanced memory-mapping capabilities of the 386 family which, among other things, will allow you to relocate terminate-and-stay-resident programs out of DOS's nominal 640K and give you more memory for your regular programs. You'll gain the 386's virtual 8086 mode that supports true multitasking. And your newly enhanced system will understand the 32-bit 80386 instructions of high-powered programs like AutoCAD 386.

The cost of a 386SX upgrade may be $100–200 more than a 286, primarily as a result of the price differential charged by Intel for the chips. For what you get, the difference is well worth it. Moreover, if you move from a 286 to a 386SX, you probably won't need an entire new set of peripherals to get most of the new chip's benefits.

Should you want uncompromising high performance and have a budget to match, you'll find upgrades that equal the abilities of the best complete computer systems you can buy today. You don't have to stop with just a 486. You can buy some upgrade products that will take you into the realm of *Reduced Instruction Set Computing*, usually abbreviated as *RISC*. While RISC-based microprocessors won't run DOS, they can run more powerful operating systems—in particular Unix. Today you can upgrade your system to include an Intel i860 RISC microprocessor as easily as moving to a new 286 or 386.

Microprocessor Upgrade Alternatives

As compelling as microprocessor upgrades are, if your upgrade goals are more modest or more specific than just getting a whole bunch of features that you're not sure what to do with, you'll find a few more compelling alternatives. You can make a number of upgrade moves that may be more cost-effective in reaching a particular goal in particular systems. For example, when you want to eke as much performance as possible from your venerable IBM AT with a six megahertz clock speed, but don't want to go to the trouble and expense of changing its microprocessor, you just may be able to up its speed about 25 percent just by changing the crystal that controls its microprocessor clock. Or if you want to gain extra DOS memory for your programs by relocating drivers and TSR utilities to high memory, you may be able to add new memory management abilities to your old 286 with a simple plug-in board. Or, when you compute the cost of an upgrade with all the improvements you really want, you may find that the price is awfully close to the cost of a new PC. In such a situation, you may find it more cost-effective and more useful to keep your old computer as is and simply buy an entirely new (and more powerful) PC to complement it.

Increasing Clock Speed

A very few special computers allow you to eke an extra bit of extra performance without making major changes to the microprocessor or the rest of the machine. All you need to do is kick the existing microprocessor into high gear by increasing its clock frequency. The clock determines how quickly the computer computes, so the faster the clock, the faster the system will perform.

The very first ATs that IBM sold operated at a clock frequency of six megahertz. That speed limit appears to be artificially imposed because the computer's circuitry is capable of handling higher speeds. Some people believe that the original AT was purposely slowed from its potential top speed to avoid competing with the more powerful and more expensive computers that IBM offered. In fact, the schematic diagrams of the original AT in some IBM Technical Reference manuals indicate a speed not of six but eight megahertz.

These original ATs and a very few AT-clones can be sped up by increasing their clock speeds. The speed of the system clock is determined by a crystal, by exchanging their speed-determining crystals with those that operate at a higher speed. This strategy does not apply to newer ATs that are set by the factory to operate at eight megahertz because these machines are limited by their BIOS software as well as their crystals. When these newer ATs boot up, their test routines peek out and examine the system clock speed and prevent the computer from completing the boot process if their speed is altered from the factory spec. For a while, some companies offered kits to let you tip-toe past these speed restrictions. The kits held back the speed of the clock during the boot-up process, then unleashed performance once the system had finished its speed check. Unfortunately, after IBM halted production on the AT line, the market for these products dried up and they are difficult, if not impossible, to find today.

AT-compatible computers are rarely likely candidates for crystal swapping because they are generally designed, manufactured, and sold with their circuits operating at their maximum speed potentials. For example, the memory chips in such computers generally cannot operate much faster than the speed at which the system is sold. Any increase in clock speed will decrease the reliability of these systems.

If you have a six megahertz AT and want to increase its speed to eight megahertz (a safe upgrade) or higher (upgrades of dubious reliability), you'll first have to locate a source of crystals. It may be as near as your local Radio Shack store. You need to select a speed-determining crystal that oscillates at twice the frequency at which you want your system to run because the circuitry of your AT automatically slices the crystal frequency in half. In other words, the crystal in your six-megahertz AT runs at 12 megahertz and you'll want to upgrade to a sixteen-megahertz crystal to get an eight-megahertz AT. The speed-determining crystal in ATs is a small silver can that measures less than an inch wide and high. It's vaguely rectangular in shape, with the narrow sides rounded. In ATs, it is located near the rear of the system board just to the left of the power supply when looking back from the front of the computer. Compatible computers may locate the crystal anywhere on the system board, but the crystal generally will have the same size and shape as that used by IBM. The AT crystal is mounted in a socket, so you should be able to simply pull it out and slide a replacement in its stead.

Note that the leads from the original AT crystal are thick and some replacement crystals use very thin leads that make poor contact with the IBM crystal socket. In such cases, you can bend the leads over double before sliding the crystal into its socket to make a better connection.

PCs, XTs, and computers based on 8088 microprocessor compatible with them are *not* likely candidates for crystal acceleration. While the AT design uses separate crystals to control the speed of the microprocessor clock, the time of day clock, and other functions, all frequencies in PCs and XTs are controlled by a single crystal. Change the crystal, and the speed of everything will change. In particular, the system clock will take off and make the days really fly by. For your academic interest, the crystals in these computers are generally rated at three times the microprocessor speed, about 14.3 megahertz, and are marked as such. Look but don't touch—or you'll be sorry you did.

Adding Memory Management

Many people are happy with the performance that they get from their 286-based computers, but are frustrated by RAM cram. That is, they run so many TSR programs and software drivers that they end up with little room left for running their favorite applications. Although they start out with a full quota of 640K, they can quickly fill up enough of it with pop-up programs, network drivers, and other features so that even programs that demand 512K or less won't run. The easy thing to do is to stop using all that memory-hogging software or use a memory-management program that allows you to pry the programs out of RAM when you need to run a big application. Then again, you won't run into memory problems if you don't turn on your computer, either.

A more satisfactory (and functional) solution is to add memory-management abilities to the 286. The only impediment to this upgrade is that it requires modifications to your PC's circuitry—and that's nothing to be taken lightly. However, the ALL ChargeCard from ALL Computing and similar products provide all the necessary add-on circuitry on a small circuit board that plugs in between your system's microprocessor and its socket. Special software is supplied with the board for handling the actual relocation of your TSRs and driver software.

On the positive side, installing a ChargeCard is relatively simple—at least for those who don't mind tinkering and tampering with the microprocessor in their system. First you must remove your system's 286 microprocessor from its system board. Next you plug the chip into the socket waiting for it on the ChargeCard. Finally you need only plug the entire resulting assembly back into the microprocessor socket on the system board of your PC.

This process is complicated by reality, however. Rarely can you just reach in and pull out your system's microprocessor. Typically you'll need to remove many—if not all—expansion boards from your system to gain access to the microprocessor. And once you get a good look at the socket you may discover to your dismay that all 286 microprocessors are not the same. The chips are available in three physically different packages, and you must match the ChargeCard you want to use to the type of chip package it is supposed to work with. Be sure the salesman knows what kind of computer you want to install a ChargeCard in so you get the right adapters.

Moreover, the ChargeCard is not a panacea. For example, it does not change the performance of your 286, so you'll only gain enhanced memory ability with the ChargeCard. But the real downside of the ChargeCard is that it is expensive—you can probably buy a fully equipped 386SX system board for the price of the ChargeCard. Of course, you'll still need the software to remap your programs, but a 386SX will probably improve the overall performance of your system, too. Choose the ChargeCard and similar memory-mapping enhancements for their ease of installation. For performance and compatibility, you'll want to use an alternate microprocessor upgrade method.

Memory Tricks

Another way of squeezing more performance from an existing computer and microprocessor is to speed up its memory. Most microprocessor operations involve memory in one way or another—bytes have to be loaded into the microprocessor's registers from memory before they can be worked upon, and they have to be dumped back into memory when the calculations are done.

Only the calculations themselves—once the data are in the microprocessor's registers—are free from the influence of memory. Consequently, reducing the time required to access memory can accelerate the overall performance of your system much as would a faster microprocessor.

The three memory tricks that have the greatest influence on the overall performance of your system are wait states, memory interleaving, and caching. Where you can take advantage of these performance gains depends on the design of your PC. Not all systems allow the number of wait states to be changed, use memory interleaving, or have expandable caches. In fact, the last two features are usually available only in 386-based PC and more powerful machines. Some 286s have programmable wait states. But older 8088-based computers can't benefit from these strategies at all.

Trimming Wait States. Most dynamic RAM chips—the kind that are least expensive—cannot keep up with the speeds of today's fastest microprocessors, so PCs are designed to add wait states when memory is accessed. That is, the microprocessor waits for one or more clock cycles between memory accesses. The number of clock cycles that it waits—the wait states—is not a function of the microprocessor or memory but is part of the design of the computer. And some computer designs make this number flexible. As noted in Chapter III, you can alter it relatively easily.

In PCs that allow user-configurable wait states, one of three methods of control may be used: software, hardware, and automatic. Software control relies on the use of software to change a register in the chipset used to implement the computer's electronics. Hardware systems use a jumper or DIP switch setting to achieve the same result. Automatic systems sense the maximum operating speed of the memory that's installed inside them and adjust their wait states to match.

In their most common form, the software wait state settings are achieved as part of the system's advanced set-up procedure. Normally you confront a simplified set-up menu after you run a disk-based program or elicit the set-up routines in your PC's memory by striking the appropriate keys. You should be familiar with the procedure from the first time you switched your computer on—it asked for the correct time and date as well as the type of disks you had installed. Every time your system's battery gets low (and often at random times of your system's own choosing) you're confronted with a need to deal with this menu.

Some systems offer an adjunct to this menu, typically called *advanced set-up*. This procedure allows you to select more intimate operating parameters, such as EMS simulation and the shadowing of BIOS and video memory. Among the selections often available is the number of system wait states. As simply as striking a couple of keys, you can trim the number of wait states used by your PC from 2 to 1 or zero. But don't do it—at least before preparing for the worst. Selecting too few wait states will make your PC operate erratically, if at all. If you choose too low, as soon as your system tries to boot up it will bump squarely into a memory error. You don't pass "Go," and you may end up forfeiting $200 to your dealer to jump start your PC again. You get yourself into a situation like building a rocket-based race car, besting the land speed record, then coming to the end of the track and discovering that you forgot to install brakes on the car—and you don't know where to find the controls for the parachute.

Most computer manufacturers have anticipated your transgressions. Typically a system with software set-up will provide some means of making the system revert back to its factory settings should your adjustments go awry. For example, you may have to move a jumper from one position to another or simply ground a specific terminal as the computer boots up. Before you tinker with wait states—or any other advanced set-up paramenter—be certain you know how to undo any possible damage. Familiarize yourself with the means your system offers to reset itself to its factory defaults. Only then should you venture cautiously (and with enough spare time to work your way through potential problems) should you attempt to adjust wait state settings through software.

Your worries are fewer with hardware set-up of system wait states. All you need do is look up in your computer's manual (or the system board manual that some vendors substitute) for the proper jumper settings. Move the jumper to the number of wait states you want to try. And when your system doesn't work, move it back.

Normally your system won't work when you adjust its wait state values to a lower figure. The manufacturer has already made your system as fast as it thinks your PC's memory will allow. However, you can always upgrade your system to faster memory, and then trimming the number of wait states may be provident. Chapter 6 discusses upgrading your PC's memory.

Interleaving Memory. One way that many computer makers reduce the number of wait states that your system's microprocessor must endure is by interleaving memory. That is, they divide the RAM of your system into two or more banks, then they interleave the data in the memory such that every other byte is in one bank and the alternate bytes in the other. When the microprocessor goes to fetch sequential bytes, it first accesses one bank, then the other. While one bank is being accessed, the other can be refreshed so that on the next memory request the microprocessor can address that bank without wait states. Although interleaving saves waiting only on sequential transfers and every other random transfer (the odds are 50 percent that the next byte will be in the other bank when transfers are made at random), it can substantially reduce the waiting.

The only problem with memory interleaving is that it requires two or more banks to work properly. In 32-bit systems, that can be a lot of memory, more than many manufacturers want to make standard equipment. Consequently a number of PCs that support interleaving don't deliver it in their base configurations. They have to be enhanced with a second memory bank to bring the feature to life. Adding more memory to such a PC will not only give you more room for running your programs, but can also accelerate its performance.

The best way to determine whether your system supports interleaving and whether the feature is actually used in your system as it is currently configured is to check its instruction manual under "memory." You could also query the manufacturer's customer service department.

Expanding Cache Memory. In some systems the cache memory that helps match a fast microprocessor to slower RAM chips can be expanded. A number of manufacturers have incorporated expandable or scalable caches in their systems so that they can be sold at a low price with a small endowment of expensive cache memory and later enhanced with more cache. The larger the cache, the greater the likelihood of making a cache "hit" on each memory request and the lower the effective number of wait states suffered by the system.

Adding cache memory depends on the design adopted by the computer's manufacturer. Sometimes you add cache chips in exactly that form, loose chips, that install like any other chips, as discussed in Chapter 6. Other systems put their add-on caches on special proprietary boards that just plug into place. Compaq's Deskpros and Systempros, as well as IBM's PS/2s Models 90 and 95, are examples.

Caches require special high-speed static RAM chips. Ordinary RAM won't work. These static RAM chips are often quite expensive and more difficult to acquire than regular RAM chips. Some memory dealers don't carry them or don't stock the particular type of chip that might be needed by your PC. In that case, you'll be stuck buying what you need from the manufacturer of your PC or the dealer that sold it to you—and you'll have to pay the price they ask. And that can be steep. For example, the special board that adds up to 512K of high-speed static RAM IBM's Models 90 and 95 originally listed for about $2,500. Big caches for high-end Compaq computers were originally pegged at $2,999 to $3,999. These enhancements should be regarded as the final step to take when you absolutely have to eke the most possible performance from your PC without regard to cost.

Replacing Your Entire PC

However compelling the idea, upgrading a microprocessor is not for everyone. Certainly the idea of upgrading is compelling, and price is probably the part of the microprocessor upgrade that proves most inviting. An upgrade appears substantially less expensive than the alternative—buying an entirely new PC—when you want better performance and advanced features. But the economics of upgrading may not be as straightforward as you first think. A microprocessor upgrade will only improve a portion of your system, while a new PC may bring multiple improvements.

For example, the allure of upgrading your microprocessor may be that you won't have to write off your investment in the hard disk you've already got in your PC. But retaining your old disk can be a mistake—it may not be up to the speed needs of your new microprocessor (or even your old one). You could upgrade your disk at the same time you switch microprocessors, but that can up the upgrade cost considerably. Moreover, your upgrade requirements might not stop at a microprocessor and disk. Opting for an entirely new PC can also bring a multitude of other benefits, such as new floppy disk drives, a faster, sharper video system, and a heftier power supply.

That's the principal problem when upgrading your microprocessor. After you've finished you're still left with one computer system—albeit a better one—and you also have a microprocessor and its associated circuitry left over, neither of which will likely have any value to you. Choosing a new system instead will leave you with two PCs—one that you can use as a spare, hand down to someone else in your business or at home, or sell off (for a trivial price) to recover your investment in new hardware.

A microprocessor upgrade is not an alternative to a new computer. Rather, the upgrade should be viewed as a means of breaking through a rather particular bottleneck or as a way of adding specific features to the system you already have. The upgrade can be effective, but the miracles it will work are not in league with those made with a new machine.

Microprocessor Upgrade Method

Finding a microprocessor upgrade that's accessible to your system is the thorny side of the process. What you really want to do is too often impossible—you can almost never pull out one microprocessor and slide another in its place. When you want to exchange microprocessors, you're likely to also have to change a substantial amount of the circuitry of your PC. In most cases that will mean switching a complete assembly of one kind or another. For example, you can plug an accelerator (or "turbo") board into an expansion slot, adding not only a new microprocessor but a slot full of support electronics.

Although the various upgrade avenues require differing degrees of effort to install, deciding among the alternative upgrade strategies is more than a simple matter of how you install the hardware. You've got to balance factors that include the degree of performance improvement you expect, the smoothness with which your system will operate, the skill required in making the transplant, and the bottom line—the cost of the upgrade, whether you can afford it, and whether it's even worth your investment. The challenge is to sort through the alternatives to find the one that delivers the best combination of features and performance to suit your needs and budget.

Traditionally, you have your choice of four principal directions to take in making a microprocessor upgrade—simply switching microprocessors, adding a turbo board, replacing your system's entire motherboard, and opting for a proprietary upgrade scheme. This last choice is available only should the maker of your PC be one of the growing number of manufacturers that offers its own upgrades for the systems they sell. It will generally be a variation (a more expensive one) on one of the other three upgrade methods.

The first of these choices is far and away the most logical but, because of the limited interchangeabilty of microprocessors, the one with the smallest benefits and the least application. Turbo boards are favored by many people because they sometimes make the microprocessor upgrade a little more challenging than adding another expansion board to your system. You may be able to merely plug in a turbo board and blast through programs double-time—in theory, at least. The replacement motherboard is generally considered the most radical, the most difficult (it really isn't, as you will see), and the most worthwhile. The proprietary upgrade is undoubtedly the best strategy, but relatively few systems can reap its rewards.

Replacing Your Microprocessor

When you want to upgrade your microprocessor, the straightforward thing to do would be to pull out your old chip and plug in a new one. Unfortunately, this strategy is rarely available. Only the earliest of PCs can benefit from the direct microprocessor replacement strategy because different microprocessor types are, in general, not directly interchangeable. You cannot pull the 8088 out of your XT and slide a 486 in its place. The reason is compatibility. The powerful 486 is not only physically incompatible with the 8088 (even their black plastic packages are shaped differently), but also the two chips are electrically distinct and require different signals to operate. After all, you can hardly expect to take advantage of a 32-bit microprocesor if your PC only has a data channel capable of handling eight bits. Other microprocessor chips within the Intel family suffer similar cross-incompatibilities.

Only the oldest of PCs are candidates for the direct microprocessor replacement because only they are based on chips that have higher-performance equivalents. Only the Intel 8088 and 8086 microprocessors have direct substitutes that deliver greater performance. (Certainly you can find higher performance versions of the microprocessor already in your PC—such as a 33 MHz 386 to replace a 16 MHz version, but remember that the system board clock and not the chip sets the speed at which your system operates. The extra potential of a chip with a higher speed rating will be wasted in a slower PC.) The replacements for the Intel 8088 and 8086 chips are made by an entirely different manufacturer, NEC. That company's V20 and V30 microprocessors were engineered to duplicate the function of two Intel chips. The V20 mimics the 8088; the V30, the 8086. Having the benefit of hindsight and reverse engineering, NEC was able to design its chips to calculate somewhat faster than the Intel forebears at the same clock speed.

The amount of performance increase you'll get from one of these direct chip transplants varies with the kind of work that you do on your PC. At best—downhill with a tailwind—you might see a 30 percent improvement. Typically, you can expect a performance increase of about 10 percent. The only reason such a modest gain is worthwhile is that the upgrade cost itself is minimal—figure spending under $10 for a replacement chip. There's nothing else to worry about.

While NEC does make similar replacements for other microprocessors, the chips have been tied in legal knots by Intel's efforts to prevent their sale. Intel believes that NEC chips infringe on its patents. Consequently, the other NEC chips are difficult (if not impossible) to find.

While no direct plug-in replacement microprocessors are available for 286 or newer Intel chips, a few manufacturers have adapted a more powerful chip—the 386SX—to fit 286 sockets. Because the 80386SX is reasonably close enough electrically to the 286, all that's needed is a small amount of extra circuitry to convert the signals used by the SX to match those found in a 286 socket.

Several companies now offer plug-in assemblies that mate a 386SX microprocessor to 286 sockets. Included among these makers is Intel Corporation, adding legitimacy to this upgrade strategy.

The various products demonstrate philosophical differences. Some boards opt for the simple treatment, aiming only to bring the advanced features of the 386 (these include the ability to handle faster 32-bit instructions, advanced memory management, and the virtual 8086 mode that makes DOS multitasking possible) to 286-based PCs. With some upgrade products performance improvements are modest in 8 MHz AT-style systems and negligible in faster computers. Other boards start with those benefits and add some degree of performance enhancement. They speed up the 386SX and add cache memory to it, thus minimizing the drag imposed by the slower memory already installed in your system.

While, in theory, any of these boards should be able to fit into any 286-based PC, there is a major complication. Not all 286 microprocessors are the same. These versatile chips are available in a number of different housings, each of which requires a different kind of socket. Because a plug-in 386SX board plugs into your 286 socket, the kind of socket you have is important when you order this kind of upgrade. You should specify the make and model of your computer when you order a 386SX board to ensure mechanical compatibility. Alternately, should your vendor never have heard of your particular brand of computer, you can describe the kind of microprocessor you have. The three principal cases for 286 microprocessors are the *Pin-Grid Array (PGA)*, the *Leadless Chip Carrier (LCC)*, and the *Plastic Leadless Chip Carrier (PLCC)*.

When viewed installed in its socket, the PGA looks like a dark grey square of epoxy. No socket is visible except in side view because the chip completely overhangs it. When pried out of its socket, the PGA chip has two parallel rows of gold pins parallel to each of its edges on its bottom side. The LCC chip is a black square in a plastic socket, typically held in place by a wire at one edge. If you look at the slight gap between the edge of the chip and the socket, you won't see any connecting pins. If you pry up the wire and pop the chip from the socket, you'll see that its contacts are flat traces of gold that are flat against the bottom face of the chip. The PLCC has silvery pins folded around its perimeter. When the chip is in its socket, you can see these pins in the gap between chip and socket. Out of the socket, the leads run around the edge of the chip and curl underneath.

Choosing a microprocessor replacement is thus quite simple. First, you are limited in your choice of upgrades (and whether you can make the upgrade at all) by the microprocessor that your system was designed around. The prime motivation for replacing an 8088 or 8086 is that it costs so little you have virtually nothing to lose. The process is entirely reversable, so if you don't like the results, you can plug your old microprocessor back in. Upgrading your 286 to a 386SX will give you all those wonderful 386 features, but it may not be a cost-effective strategy considering the prices of 386-based motherboards today. Choose the plug-in 386SX only if you want to minimize the effort involved in your upgrade or you fear the worst from your own mechanical efforts.

Turbo Boards

The logical place to put any upgrade for your system is in its expansion slots. That's what the slots are designed for. Turbo boards do exactly that. They put a new microprocessor on an expansion board so that you can install a microprocessor upgrade as easily as you can add a serial port. At least sometimes. Other times, they require more work than a microprocessor upgrade. Turbo boards actually come in two styles, the coprocessor board and the microprocessor replacement, and they differ in the results they deliver and the mechanical skill required to put them to work.

The coprocessor is the purest form of turbo board. It earns its name from how it works, cooperating with the microprocessor already in your PC instead of replacing it. The coprocessor takes over all the tough work—the calculation and computations—and uses your PC's original microprocessor as a slave to handle your system's video display, hard disk, and other peripherals.

The coprocessor has three important benefits. It's easy to install. It's the classic expansion board. You just slide the coprocessor into any vacant expansion slot, run some software, and go to work at higher speed. Coprocessors include their own memory, so they are not limited by the slow RAM chips that may be in your PC. In most cases, the coprocessor board doesn't even care how much memory you've already installed in your PC. And because you don't remove your original microprocessor when you install the coprocessor-style turbo board, you can always retreat back to using the old chip by running a program or pulling the board from its slot when your software proves persnickety or the coprocessor (heaven forbid) fails.

On the other hand, the coprocessor-style turbo board has some severe drawbacks. Because it connects to your system through expansion slot, it suffers from all the shortcomings and limitations of your PC's expansion bus—and then some. Not only does the bus connection limit the performance of the board when accessing the memory on your motherboard, it also adds additional handicaps in communicating with other expansion boards. Traditional PC designs—those machines not built with advanced expansion buses like Micro Channel and EISA—simply don't expect to be controlled by a microprocessor in an expansion slot, and throw all sorts of roadblocks in its general direction. Video and disk performance cannot be any better than your PC delivered before the upgrade and often is worse with noticeably jumpy video displays. (Advanced bus coprocessor turbo boards, on the other hand, sidestep the roadblocks and often deliver excellent performance.) Coprocessor turbo boards are also relatively expensive because each one is essentially a complete computer built onto an expansion board. The coprocessor board duplicates many of the functions (such as memory) already in your PC. For these and other reasons, coprocessor-style turbo boards are becoming as rare on the market as absinthe, buggy-whips, and affordable housing.

The other kind of turbo board, the microprocessor replacement, exchanges its installation ease for a performance improvement. Besides fitting into an expansion slot, this form of turbo board exudes a tentacle-like connecting cable that latches onto the socket belonging to your system's original microprocessor. You have to pop out the microprocessor and replace it with the connecting cable and, through it, the turbo board. (See Figure 4.1)

By usurping your old microprocessor's socket, this kind of turbo board can take direct control of your PC. That means smoother operation. In many cases, it also means that the turbo board handicaps itself because it must make do with the circuits that are already installed on your motherboard, among them memory that probably was challenged to keep up with your pokey old microprocessor. Better quality replacement-processor turbo boards avoid the restrictions of your system's old circuitry by including onboard memory caches or their own RAM memory. Fast, on-board RAM means that

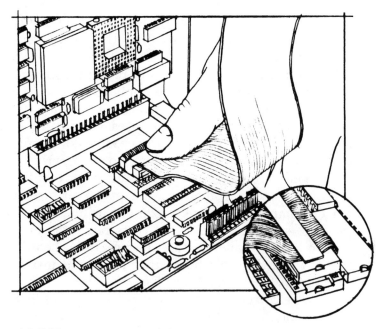

Figure 4.1 With microprocesor replacement turbo boards, the most critical step is plugging the board into the socket that held your old microprocessor. Be sure the notch on the cable connector lines up with the notch on the socket and be careful not to bend any connector pins.

the turbo board never needs to stoop to the slow speed of motherboard memory.

Although replacement-processor turbo boards are expansion board and they do slide into expansion slots, they really aren't as easy to install as most people suppose. The installation job may require removing all other expansion boards from inside your PC in order to gain enough room to get at the microprocessor socket. You also need to install the plug on the turbo board's cable very carefully into the waiting microprocessor socket—one bent lead and your PC won't work. As with 386SX boards, you'll also have to make sure that the turbo board you choose will mate with the socket of your microprocessor, be it PGA, LCC, or PLCC. Once the board and cable are in place, you must then painstakingly bend and fold the wide, flat connection cable inside your computer (easier said than done) so that it doesn't get in the way of expansion boards.

Turbo boards also often require extensive software set-up and support. To make them work properly, most turbo boards require software drivers that need to be installed in your system's CON-FIG.SYS file. As with all memory-resident software, these drivers can have odd effects on some applications—and you never know what will happen until it does. These software drivers also steal some memory for their own purposes, cutting into what is available to your programs. And, of course, you've got to properly install the drivers to make the entire system work properly.

The killer for any turbo board—the factor that has skewered the industry—is cost. In that the state-of-the-art turbo board is essentially a complete computer system board that you slide into an expansion slot, the turbo board costs nearly as much as an entire system board to manufacture. In fact, turbo board often cost *more* than an entire system board that you could install in your PC to upgrade its microprocessor. The advantage of the turbo board is thus its perceived (but often not actual) ease of installation and its reversability. Most of your PC is unchanged by the installation of a turbo board, so you can more readily restore your system to its old configuration when your best-laid plans go awry. Although it seems foolish that one of the better selling points of a technology is the facility with which you can avoid using it, such is the case of the turbo board.

All that said, a turbo board can make a significant improvement in the throughput of your PC. Although adding a 386-based turbo board won't push your PC into the same performance realm as a new computer, it will significantly increase your system's processing speed. More importantly, it can give your system all the features of a 386 microprocessor, which, for most people, are even more important than raw speed.

Replacement Motherboards

The chief installation difficulty with replacing your system's micro-processor or adding a replacement-style turbo board is that you often end up disassembling your PC to get access to what you need to enhance the machine. You may need to pull out all the expansion boards. In some cases, you'll have to pull out your system board to gain access to chips when they are hidden under the drive bays. Once you have the system board out, it's no more effort to replace the board than it is to reinstall the old one. Replacing your entire motherboard can be less dangerous than a microprocessor replacement or replacement-processor turbo board because you never need to deal with the delicate pins on integrated circuits or loose chips that are particularly prone to damage from static electricity. In fact, replacing your entire motherboard is a more elegant solution than a turbo board from both the software and firmware standpoint. A new motherboard simply takes over and runs like any other computer. You won't need new software drivers, as most turbo boards require. Moreover, installing a motherboard is hardly the dreadful task most folks fear. In many systems the entire motherboard replacement involves only removing about two screws and a few cables.

New motherboards are surprisingly inexpensive, too. They are apt to cost less than a turbo board even though they should be more expensive to make. Although motherboards in general require more materials and components than turbo boards, there is more competition among motherboard makers, which has driven down prices. In fact, motherboards are probably the biggest bargains available in the personal computer industry. That makes them an excellent microprocessor upgrade choice.

If you want to upgrade your 8088-based XT to a full 16-bit 286, you'll only have to spend about $100 for a new motherboard plus the cost of memory. Upgrading to a 386SX should cost about $300. Nothing else you can add to your PC will enhance performance so much for so little.

But microprocessor performance might not be the only or best reason to add a new motherboard to your system. A new motherboard can update the technology used in your computer, making it more reliable in addition to faster. Moreover, a new motherboard could bring other benefits, such as a new expansion bus like EISA. By exchanging one board you can conquer two major system bottlenecks—microprocessor and bus performance.

The downside to the motherboard replacement is that it makes your old computer into a new one, one that has its own idiosyncracies. You'll have to relearn the personality of your machine should you swap its motherboard. For example, if you pull the system board out of an IBM computer and replace it with another maker's product, you won't have an IBM machine any more. It won't run the IBM BASIC interpreter because it no longer has an IBM BIOS, and your IBM dealer may refuse to service the machine. Your old set-up and configuration utilities may not work on your PC after the upgrade. The software will simply think that you have an entirely new machine. Fortunately, most motherboards come equipped with all the set-up software that they normally need.

What You Can Keep. In most cases, little of what's on your present motherboard can be reused on its replacement. You generally won't be able to move your old BIOS and memory to the new motherboard. The BIOS is likely not to work and even if it does it may become the roadblock in the way of better performance. For example, the BIOS of the PC and XT uses only an eight-bit data path. The ROM chips themselves won't work if you slide them into sockets designed to be addressed 16 bits at a time like an AT's ROM sockets. But not to worry—almost every system board comes with its own BIOS chips already installed. Most also come with exactly the set-up software you'll need, either on disk or written into their ROM.

When upgrading to a new motherboard, you won't want to move memory from your old board to the new one, either. Your old memory is likely not going to be able to keep up with a faster microprocessor. Moreover, it probably won't even work on the new motherboard. Your old chips are likely the wrong capacity and technology to be used in a new motherboard. The latest motherboards use *Single In-Line Memory Modules* (*SIMMs*) rather than individual integrated circuits for memory. Those that use individual RAM chips usually prefer those chips with one megabyte or greater capacity. The chips on your old PC or XT held no more than 64 kilobytes. Additionally, new computers use page-mode memory chips to cut wait states, while PCs and XTs use linear addressing. Fortunately, your memory losses in making a motherboard upgrade are generally minimal. Typically you'll lose about 640K of RAM, about $25 worth, because that's about all most old motherboards hold.

Choosing a Motherboard. There's nothing esoteric about choosing the right motherboard to upgrade your PC. It's as straightforward and confusing as selecting a computer. Most of your concerns are identical—microprocessor, power, memory abilities.

You should look for exactly the same features you'd want in a new PC.

The only other concern is that the new motherboard actually fit into the case that you have. For the most part, that's easy because most motherboards are made in standard sizes. The two pre-eminent sizes match the dimensions of the motherboard of the IBM XT and the IBM AT. Most standard-size computers used motherboards of one of these two sizes. If you're not sure what size the motherboard in your current system might be, take out a ruler and measure it. Get a replacement of the same dimensions.

XT and PC systems boards are nearly the same size, but there is a complication. The expansion slots in PCs and some very early compatible computers are spaced at increments of 1.0 inch. XT, AT, and later expansion slots are spaced at 0.8-inch increments. If you try to put an XT-size motherboard in a PC chassis, the slots on the motherboard and the cut-outs on the rear of the chassis won't properly line up. Moreover, the locations of the screwholes that secure the motherboard to the chassis are slightly different for PC and XT motherboards. Most replacement board makers avoid this problem by drilling enough holes in their boards that mice might mistake them for cheese. These extra holes accommodate PC, XT, and even AT mounting arrangements and hardware. (See Figure 4.2.)

A few motherboards are available that use the PC spacing for their expansion slots. These are usually more expensive. So much more expensive, you will likely be better off buying a new XT-size case and moving everything from your PC's case into the new case. Use this strategy and you'll also get more expansion slots along with the new microprocessor.

Computer cases from vendors other than IBM may be more difficult to match with new motherboards when you are upgrading. For instance, Compaq Deskpros use a different mounting scheme than IBM products. Replacement motherboards designed for IBM computers won't fit into Compaq cases. Fortunately, one company, Hauppauge Computer Works, makes high-performance replacement motherboards for Compaq Deskpros. Alas, the proliferation of small-chassis computers make finding a replacement motherboard even more difficult. With these machines you usually have to either improvise on the case with a hacksaw and drill or choose some other form of microprocessor upgrade.

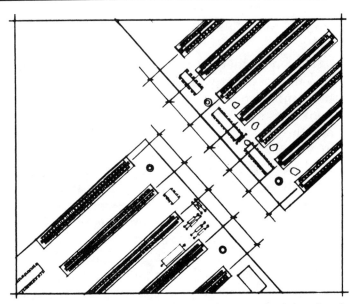

Figure 4.2 When upgrading your system board, it is critical that the slot spacing of your new board match the old. Expansion slots in PCs and some compatibles are spaced at one inch increments; XTs and newer computers use 0.8 inch spacing.

If the motherboard in the computer you want to upgrade is not a standard size, you can usually adopt the same strategy as with fitting XT products to PC hardware. Get a case along with your motherboard and move all your old peripherals into the new case. You may also need a new power supply. All told, $100 is a small penalty for the new features you'll get.

Most motherboards are designed to use exactly the same mounting hardware that IBM used for its motherboards, and most aftermarket cases use the same mounting strategy. That means only two screws are required to hold the board in place. All the necessary holes are predrilled.

On all official IBM products and many compatibles you also have to tangle with spacers in addition to the screws. That's good news because the spacers simply pop into place on the motherboard and let you slide the board into position inside the chassis. It's bad because you may have to move the spacers from your old motherboard onto the new board. It can be more than a minor bother. In theory, you can squeeze the space out by pinching its wings with a long-nosed pliers, then push the spacer out of its hole in the board (see Step 3 on page 130). Often, however, the spacers refuse to come off intact, leaving you with pieces that won't do much good in holding your new motherboard in place. You will be much happier with a motherboard that includes all the necessary spacers with it. You may even want to buy new spacers from the vendor who sells you your new motherboard. At least ask about them.

Some compatibles don't use spacers. Worse, some computers, while they have enough room for a standard-size motherboard, don't use the same spacing as IBM chose for its motherboard mounting holes. Should you be surprised by such a problem, you have two choices. You can either buy a new case or modify your own case to accept the hole spacing of your new motherboard. This modification involves drilling holes in the proper places in the chassis of your old computer. Make too many mistakes and you'll have to buy a new case, anyway.

Memory is important when considering a new motherboard for your PC, both in amount delivered on any product and how it can be expanded. Many motherboards are advertised at low prices with 0K, that is, no memory. Be sure to factor in the cost of adding memory chips or SIMMs to those boards when comparing them to products already stuffed with RAM.

More memory on the motherboard—or the capability of accommodating more memory—is better. Motherboard memory is typically the least expensive to add in and usually the fastest you can add to your system. Consequently, it pays to fit the most you can on the motherboard itself.

Be sure to consider how much memory the system can accommodate. Most 286, 386, and 486 systems can take advantage of 16 megabytes, the addressing limit on the AT expansion bus. Newer motherboards with advanced expansion buses may accommodate even more. If you're looking far into the future, you'll want all the memory capability you can get.

When the memory expansion of a motherboard requires a proprietary memory board, check its availability when you order the motherboard. Sometimes manufacturers rush their motherboards to the market and only later (if ever) produce the memory expansion boards that they need. Most of the time you're best off buying a memory expansion board without memory at the same time you buy your motherboard. That way your opportunity for memory expansion is not dependent on a board maker that may go out of business.

Remember, too, that all memory is not created equal. While Chapter 6 discusses all the types at length, for purposes of buying a motherboard you should be aware that several type of memory can be used on a motherboard—and those different types vary in expense and availability. The least expensive memory comes as standard dynamic RAM chips, which come in several speed ratings. The faster the memory your new motherboard requires (measured in nanoseconds, the lower the number of nanoseconds the faster), the more it is likely to cost. A growing number of memory boards require page-mode memory chips, which can be more expensive and more difficult to find than standard DRAM chips, but they will also add extra speed to your system. The important thing is to find out what kind of memory your system requires, particularly when you want to order expansion memory at the same time you buy your new system board.

Upgrading your system's microprocessor can be the most cost-effective means of wringing more power and greater capabilities from your PC, particularly when you've identified your old microprocessor as the principal bottleneck in your PC. Performance is the chief reason most people are attracted to upgrading. A faster microprocessor means that your system can carry out many of its functions quicker, and that means that graphics are snappier, you can zip through programs, blast through compilers, and end up spending less of your time waiting for your computer to catch up with you.

Proprietary Upgrades

Proprietary microprocessor upgrades combine the advantage of the installation ease of a pure turbo board with the smooth integration of the replacement motherboard. Their only disadvantages are limited availability—not all manufacturers and PCs support proprietary upgrades—and expense. There's little competition for proprietary products, so manufacturers charge what the market will bear, which can be a surprisingly high price. Double the cost of a similar but more generic upgrade is more the rule than the exception.

Exactly what proprietary upgrade options are available depends on the computer you have. Some computers, like early Zenith machines, had most of their critical circuitry installed on special expansion boards that could be easily replaced. One expansion board held the microprocessor and its support circuitry, and often memory, too. Swapping this one board for one newer and faster would be the equivalent of replacing an entire system board but without most of the hassle. Other manufacturers adapted similar strategies but different mounting hardware. In its PowerVEISA systems, Advanced Logic Research puts its microprocessor and cache circuitry on similar small daughter cards. IBM opts for a "Power Platform" that fits flat atop the system motherboard in its PS/2 Model 70, while using a Zenith-like major expansion board for the microprocessor circuitry of its Models 90 and 95. Tandon puts the microprocessor in a plug-in cartridge that doesn't even require you to open the case to replace.

Because the choice of proprietary upgrades is limited—few manufacturers even offer them, and those that do give only a few limited choices—your choice of power ranges is limited. You can follow only the upgrade trail broken by the system's maker. On the other hand, you are assured of compatibility with the hardware that you have. And that's the biggest recommendation of proprietary upgrades.

No matter which microprocessor or means of upgrading you choose, you'll sure to end up with a better performing system at far less cost than buying a new PC. You'll not only extend the life of your investment in your computer but you'll also have more of life to enjoy yourself. Your upgraded PC will get the job done faster so you can have more time for other things.

Step by Step Upgrade Guides

Microprocessor Replacement

When you want to upgrade the 8088 or 8086 microprocessor in your PC with a V20 or V30 chip, you need to be able to indentify the chip you want to replace. Both the 8088 and 8086 microprocessor are packaged in *40-pin Dual In-Line Pin* (*DIP*) cases, usually made from black epoxy. In systems that use 8088s or 8086s, the microprocessor is usually the largest (or one of the largest) integrated circuit in the computer, measuring about two inches long and eight-tenths of an inch wide. Once you locate this big, black chip, you can verify that it's the microprocessor by the pale grey silk-screen lettering on top of it. Amid all the code numbers, you'll find the important "8088" or "8086" listed, usually with a prefix of a few letters and a suffix of one or two.

Some systems impiously hide the microprocessor underneath the disk drive bays or other importune location that makes microprocessor replacement much more of a challenge. The only sure way to do the job when the chip is so inaccessible is to remove the system motherboard, replace the chip, then reinstall the motherboard. If you're going to all that trouble, you might as well spend a few extra dollars and replace the whole system board. The only way to tell where the microprocessor resides, is to open your system and look. You may want to take a preliminary glance before investing in a new chip.

Once you're assured that you can gain access to the microprocessor, you're ready to begin. Start by switching off your PC if you haven't already done so. To be safe, you'll also want to unplug the power cable from your system so it doesn't accidentally get switched on.

Next, pull off the cover of your system's case if you don't already have your PC open. Once you're inside, you'll want to gain access to your microprocessor by removing all the expansion boards that cover the chip. On general principles—the desire to avoid scratched and bloodied fingers—you may want to remove them all so there's nothing to get in the way.

Take out a pad and pen and draw a sketch of the general vicinity of where the microprocessor is located. Your goal will be to mark down the orientation of the existing microprocessor, noting whether its notched end points toward the front or back of your PC or its right or left side. Once you're sure you won't forget the orientation of the chip, remove your old microprocessor. Special tools, called *chip pullers*, are available to make the job easier. In a pinch, you can use a blank card retaining bracket from an expansion slot as a level. Put the short end of its L-shape under one edge of the chip and pry slightly up. Move the bracket to the opposite edge of the chip, and pry up. Alternate ends of the chip, prying a bit at a time until the chip comes free. You can then pick up the chip, being careful not to touch its leads (if you can avoid it) so you don't risk damaging the chip. You may need to plug it back in sometime.

Before you go further, you should also prepare your new microprocessor for the socket by bending its leads to be perpendicular to the body of the chip. Grasp the chip by its ends and press down on a hard surface such as a tabletop, and force the leads of the chip from being splayed slightly out to exactly square with the chip.

Once the leads on the new chip are ready, position the chip in the socket, ensuring that the orientation of its notch matches that of your old microprocessor. Refer to the sketch you made earlier. Ensure that all 40 leads (legs) of the new chip are exactly lined up with the holes that they match. Then press the chip straight down into its socket. Now inspect your work and ensure that all the leads go into their holes and do not fold under the chip or slide outside the socket.

Only after you're sure that all the leads are properly in their holes, you can begin reassembling your PC. Start by putting your expansion boards back into their sockets. Then reconnect all cables to your PC including the power cable. Switch your PC on and verify that it works properly.

Only after you're certain that your system is operating properly, turn it off and replace the cover. Your upgrade is finished.

Turbo Board Upgrades

Adding a coprocessor turbo board is handled exactly like adding any other expansion board—open your PC, scope out an empty slot, slide the board into it, and button everything back together.

Replacement microprocessor boards take more work. The first step is to open up your PC and survey the territory. Of course, don't forget to switch off your PC and disconnect the power cord for safety's sake. See the Appendix for case-opening instructions.

Once you're inside, locate your system's microprocessor because you'll be replacing it. Determine which expansion board—even one that's currently occupied—is nearest the microprocessor. Just as you would in replacing the microprocessor with a new chip, take out a pad and pen and sketch the general vicinity of where the

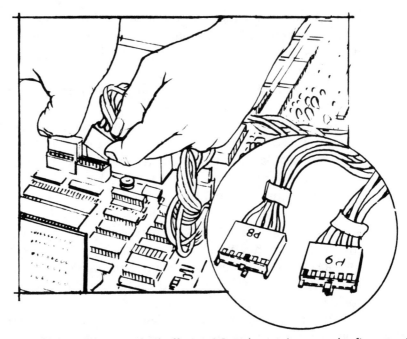

Step 1 After you have switched off your PC and open its case, the first step in upgrading your system board is to disconnect all cables from your old board. When you remove the power supply cables, as shown here, be sure to write down which went where.

microprocessor is located so that you have a record of the orientation of the old chip.

Once you're sure you won't forget the orientation of the chip, commit yourself to the upgrade by removing your old microprocessor. Again, a chip puller is the best tool to use, but a blank card-retaining bracket will serve as well. You can work PGA-packaged chips up by putting the short end of its L-shape under one edge of the chip and prying slightly up, then moving the bracket to the opposite edge of the chip and prying up again. Alternate ends of the chip, prying a bit at a time until the chip comes free. PLCC chips can be pried out with a thin screwdriver. LCC chips require you to remove the retaining wire at the top of the socket, freeing either a coverplate, heatsink, or the back of the chip itself. You can lift out the chip once it's free. Be careful not to touch the leads or the gold connectors pads on the chip because nearly all replace-

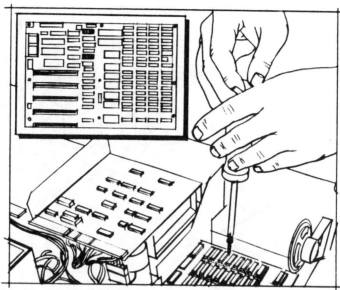

Step 2 Next, remove the two or so screws that hold the system board in place. To make reasonably easier, draw yourself a map and mark which holes the screws went into.

ment microprocessor turbo boards require that you plug the old chip into the turbo board itself.

Next, plug one end of the turbo board's adapter cable into the vacant microprocessor socket. Position the the connector on the cable above the microprocessor socket, ensuring that the orientation of the connector matches that of your old microprocessor. (That's what the sketch you made earlier is for.) Once you're sure that all the leads of the connector are properly lined up with the holes they match, press the connector down into place. Inspect your work and ensure that all the leads go into their holes and do not fold under the connector or sneak outside the edge of the socket.

If the turbo board you have requires it, plug your old microprocessor into the socket waiting on the board. If you plan to install a coprocessor on the board, do so now, too.

Now you're ready to slide the turbo board into the expansion slot you've chosen for it. Here you'll have to use your judgment—check to see whether it will be easier to plug the other end of the adapter cable into the turbo board before, during, or after you seat the turbo

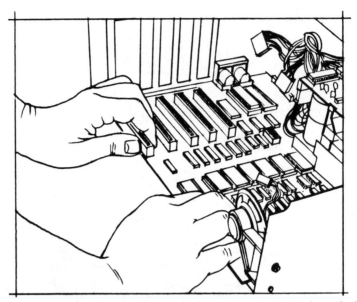

Step 3 To remove the system board from the chassis, slide the board about one inch to the left. It will then pivot up and out. If your old system board was secured by three or more screws, it may simply lift out after you've removed the screws.

board in its socket. Once you've made up your mind, act on your decision, sliding the board into place and plugging in the other end of the adapter cable.

While your PC's case is still open, reconnect all cables to your PC including the power cable. Switch your PC on and verify that the system boots. Then install the turbo board software and check the complete operation of the board. Once you've assured yourself that your system is operating properly, turn it off and replace the cover. Your turbo upgrade is finished.

System Board Upgrades

Before you begin to replace your system board, ensure that you have adequate working room. You're going to need a place to put all the expansion boards from your system and a convenient place to put your old system board.

Start the upgrade operation by switching off your PC. Unplug all cables connected to your system, power, and signal. If you doubt

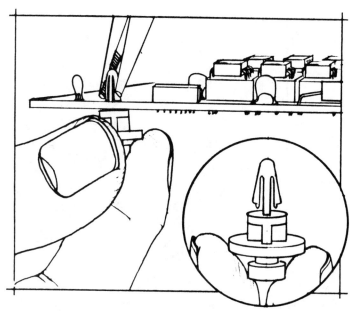

Step 4 Remove the spacers from your old system board and re-insert them in the identical positions in the new board. The spacers used in IBM and many compatible computers can be removed by squeezing their "wings" together with long-nosed pliers and pushing them out. They will snap directly back into the new board.

your memory, make a note of where each cable went. You can even use pieces of masking tape to label each cable and matching connector so you won't have any doubts about what goes where when you reassemble your system. Next, pull off the cover of your system's case if you don't already have your PC open.

Remove all expansion boards from inside your PC. Again, make a note of which ones went where so you can duplicate your old arrangement with your new system board.

Now disconnect all cables attached to your old motherboard. Typically these will include two power supply cables, a speaker cable, and, on newer machines, one or more cables for the system lock, backup battery, and turbo or reset switch. Check over the board twice to assure that you haven't missed anything.

Next, remove all the screws holding the motherboard in place. You'll be surprised at how few there are. PCs and XTs, for instance, only have two.

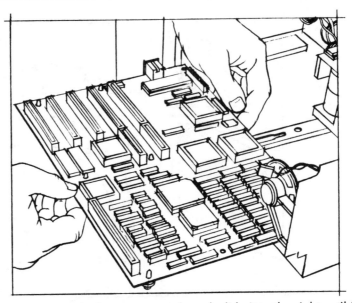

Step 5 When you put in the new system board, slide it to the right until it is approximately in place. When it is about one inch left of its final position, insure the bottoms of the spacers have engaged the slots in the bottom of the chassis. Slide the board the rest of the way, screw it down, replace the cables, and you're done.

When the screws are out, the system board will be loose inside the case, but not free. Slide the old motherboard to the left about one inch until you can move it no further. This releases the standoffs or spacers that hold the board in place.

The board is now free. Lift it out of your PC while you continue moving it to the left.

Once you have the old board out of your system, play vulture. Recycle whatever parts you can. For example, remove the spacers or standoffs that were used for mounting the old motherboard. Pinch the top of each spacer with long-nosed pliers and push it down through the hole it is installed it. Make a note of which holes in the board had screws and from which you removed spacers.

Transfer the hardware you removed from the old board to your new replacement. Snap the spacers into the holes in the same locations on the replacement motherboard.

Put the replacement motherboard in approximately the position your old motherboard stopped moving to the left when you removed it. Ensure that it fits down flat, parallel to the bottom of the case so that the spacers properly engage in their matching slots in the chassis. Then slide the new motherboard to the right until its stops and the screw holes in the board line up with those in the chassis of your PC.

Replace the screws, the cables, and the expansion board you removed from your system. Reassemble the case, plug in all cables, and switch on your system to verify that your new motherboard works. If your system successfully boots, replace the cover on your PC and you're finished with one of the most effective upgrades you can make.

5.

COPROCESSORS

Adding a numeric coprocessor to your PC is truly the easiest upgrade you can make, but one that benefits only certain applications. To do the job right, you've got to match the right chip to your needs and your PC. This chapter tells you how to accomplish both.

If any part of a PC sounds like the proverbial free lunch, it is the coprocessor. Believe its advocates, and you'll see the coprocessor as the perfect upgrade product. It costs next to nothing and can boost the performance of your PC by a factor of 1,000 or more. In other words, the coprocessor is a better buzz than a fresh hot cup of coffee on a gloomy Monday morn.

The negativist, of course, sees the coprocessor quite differently. To him not only does the coprocessor not reach the great heights of its promise but the shortfall approaches the fatal. Coprocessors can be prohibitively expensive, yet they won't benefit most applications at all. In comparison, the purchase of the Brooklyn Bridge sounds like an astute investment.

The reality is somewhere in between. A numeric coprocessor does exactly what it is designed to do, speed up mathematic operations. For the right system and the right application, the coprocessor does represent an economical accelerator—sometimes a mandatory addition to your system. Although you won't see the thousandfold speed improvement of which the coprocessor advocates speak, you may see a two to ten times increase in favorable situations. But the important consideration to remember is that you've got to match the chip to your needs to make it worthwhile as an upgrade.

If that's not complicated enough, today we have to add one further complication. While once there was only one true coprocessor that you could add to your PC, today the coprocessor marketplace is quickly becoming crowded. Instead of a single chip choice, today you have a choice of many. At least six different vendors—Advanced Micro Devices, Cyrix Corporation, Integrated Information Technology, Intel Corporation, ULSI/Specialty Development Corporation, and Weitek Corporation—currently offer chips that will plug into various PCs and accelerate their performance on some math-intensive tasks. The odds of picking the best one at random from this sextet are even worse than those against winning at Three-Card Monte.

On the other hand, a math coprocessor is the easiest upgrade you can make to your PC. You simply plug it in. The only worrisome part is orienting the chip properly in the waiting socket. The whole operation takes but a few minutes. In that willing applications might run twice as fast, it can be the most economical upgrade you can make. But you should know whether the program you regularly use will benefit from the addition of a coprocessor before you lay down your cash to benefit some predatory chip-maker.

Coprocessor Fundamentals

The concept of a coprocessor is straightforward. A coprocessor is simply something that works in cooperation with your PC's microprocessor. The goal is performance won by greater efficiency through specialization and division of labor—the electronic equivalent of a miniature Industrial Revolution. To divide the labor, the coprocessor takes charge of some particular task normally relegated to the general purpose microprocessor, relieving the main chip of some of its load. At the same time, the coprocessor is a specialist, designed to handle one particular task. In sacrificing the need to be all things to all software, it can be trimmed down to the bare essentials required to perform its task most efficiently.

Math coprocessors, which are also termed *numeric* coprocessors and *floating-point* units (or *FPUs*), specialize in manipulating numbers. In particular, they are designed to handle all the complex functions that gave you nightmares while you were daydreaming in high school: long division, trignometric functions, roots, and logarithms. These operations yield floating-point numbers, the type that math coprocessors are most adept at handling.

Floating-point describes a way of *expressing* numbers. At that, a floating-point number is not a mathematically defined class of numbers like integer, rational, and real numbers. Rather, a floating-point number can represent (or approximate) any of these. The essence of floating-point numbers—and how they got their name—is that the decimal point floats between a predefined number of significant digits rather than being fixed in place the way ordinary dollar values always have two decimal places.

Mathematically speaking, a floating-point number has three parts: a *sign*, which indicates whether the number is greater or less than zero; a *significant*—sometimes called a *mantissa*—which comprises all the digits that are mathematically meaningful; and an *exponent*, which determines the order of magnitude of the significant, essentially the location to which the decimal point floats. Think of a floating-point number as one represented by scientific notation, the compact way of expressing tiny and huge numbers you learned (or were supposed to learn) in high school. But where scientists are apt to deal in base ten—the exponents in scientific notation are powers of ten—math coprocessors think of floating-point numbers digitally in base two, all ones and zeros in powers of two.

In carrying out complex mathematic operations on floating-point numbers, the math coprocessor works in much the same way as a general purpose microprocessor. Using digital logic, it processes patterns of bits containing information (the floating-point numbers) under the control of other bit-patterns making up instructions. These operations are carried out in registers, special internal memory areas inside the coprocessor.

To make a computation, the math coprocessor first loads one of the numbers that it is to work upon into one of its registers, then loads the second number into another register. Next it reads the program instruction that tells the chip what particular operation it should carry out on the two numbers. The instruction starts another, miniature computer program running inside the coprocessor chip, and that program causes the circuitry of the coprocessor to actually calculate the desired answer. The entire set of programs inside the math coprocessor that respond to the various instructions that the chip understands are called its *microcode*, just as in an ordinary microprocessor.

Once a result has been calculated, getting the answer out of the coprocessor requires the execution of another instruction. Alternately, the next instruction can make the coprocessor carry out another operation on the results of the first.

General purpose microprocessors operate exactly the same way—load values, read instructions, and execute microcode. The math coprocessor earns its speed advantage over microprocessors in handling floating-point numbers because its command set includes high-level mathematic operations and because it has more internal circuitry devoted to carrying out those instructions. For example, a general purpose microprocessor can compute an irrational root, but it might have to execute a loop of simple instructions hundreds of times to come up with the answer, performing hundreds of iterations of integer math. The coprocessor solves the same problem with a single instruction.

Certainly a microprocessor could be designed so that it could carry out all of the complex instructions handled by a math coprocessor. The Intel 486DX microprocessor does exactly that. In effect, the 486DX combines a general purpose processor and a numeric processor on a single slab of silicon. In other microprocessors (including the low cost 486SX implementation) the coprocessor exists as a separate element for reasons tied to the standardization of floating-point calculations and the technology of integrated circuits.

Applications That Benefit

Before you even begin to consider which microprocessor you should add to your PC or whether you should add it, you need to know whether a math coprocessor will do you any good at all. If you don't need a specialist, you shouldn't hire one. After all, you wouldn't pay a thousand-dollar consulting fee to a brain surgeon if you have an aspirin-size headache.

When the manufacturers of math coprocessors talk about performance gains their products can give you, they usually trot out one or another special benchmark programs that they have written. Run the program and before your very eyes, you'll see performance race ahead as if you've severed the anchor chain. But should you try to run an actual application, you'll see that the benefits of a math coprocessor can be as elusive as catching a glimpse of Comet Kahoutek. Most programs that you are apt to run won't gain any extra speed at all from the addition of a math coprocessor.

The explanation is elementary—most programs simply don't use the complex math operations at which coprocessors excel. Even the number-crunching that most business people use their PCs for— the arithmetic of spreadsheet-based accounting—benefits little, if at all, from using a math coprocessor. The only chores that really stand to benefit from a coprocessor are those that are computationally intense, applications used in chores like statistics, engineering, and graphics.

If you do have a program that uses the advanced math that is the lifeblood of a numeric coprocessor, you'll probably discover that the performance improvement won by adding the chip won't be nearly as great as that demonstrated by the benchmarks written by the coprocessor providers. Coprocessor benchmarks are designed to give the chip a real workout, allowing no time for the chip to catch its breath. The benchmarks are nothing but wall-to-wall math problems. And the coprocessor loves the challenge, racing through at blinding speed.

Normal applications, however, are typically only lightly sprinkled with high-level math problems. Most of the time the typical application program is involved in input/output operations—waiting for keystrokes, moving data around, putting numbers on the screen. The coprocessor can't help with I/O, so the potential of the math chip is hardly tapped. It just sits around, waiting for its next assignment.

Exactly how big an improvement that you can expect in performance varies with the specific application that you run. For example, some spreadsheets benefit more than others. Compare the three best-selling spreadsheets running with and without coprocessor help, and you'll see widely divergent results. Lotus 1-2-3 Version 2.2 benefits the least, Quattro Pro Version 1.1 gains the most. Excel 2.1d falls in the middle.

The reason, according to the software publishers, is that Quattro is more explicitly designed to take advantage of a math coprocessor. The program checks for the existence of the auxiliary chip and when it finds one, the program switches over to code specially written to take advantage of the powerful coprocessor command set. Versions of Lotus 1-2-3 available in 1991 simply didn't put their full faith in coprocessors, probably because the programs weren't designed for tasks that would really take advantage of coprocessing.

The exact amount of acceleration also depends on what the spreadsheet is doing. Simple bookkeeping involves little more than adding and subtracting, which a coprocessor won't help at all. Adding a coprocessor will not significantly change performance on such applications. Should you use your spreadsheet more as a database to store, retrieve, and sort data, you can expect a similar lack of acceleration from a coprocessor. Disk operations aren't aided at all by adding the chip. While sorting may involve information processing, for the most part it involves instructions to compare strings that are not affected by the presence of a coprocessor.

Only when spreadsheets are called upon to calculate arrays of irrational numbers and trignometric functions—the type of tasks that might be involved in statistical analysis and engineering—does the availability of a coprocessor began to prove its value. On the average, you can expect about a threefold improvement in recalculation time with such chores once you take system overhead into account.

Beyond spreadsheets, the performance increase you can expect from a coprocessor is still dependent on the math functions required. To gain any performance improvement from a coprocessor, you must have a need for transcendental functions. Typical accounting programs have no need for calculating transcendentals—unless, perhaps, you're planning for the hereafter. Engineering and scientific chores are those most likely to require transcendentals. The stranger the symbols look in the math you want to do—sines, cosines, derivatives, integrals, logarithms, exponents—the more likely the coprocessor will help.

Computer-aided design programs all benefit from the addition of a math coprocessor, but the advantage gained varies with the operation carried out. Loading images and screen regenerations can be handled in about half the time when a coprocessor is available. Hidden-line removal benefits only a little more than 10 percent.

Of course, no matter the application, normal data entry performance won't change at all with the addition of a math coprocessor. Nor will the speed of standard DOS operations.

That's not to say that math coprocessors are over-rated time- (and cash-) wasters. If you have a job that can take advantage of one, there's no more cost-effective power-boost you can give your PC. If your application requires a coprocessor to work at all (as does AutoDesk Corporation's AutoCAD, for example) the coprocessor will be a necessity. But if you concentrate more on word processing, bookkeeping, or building and sorting databases, you'll be better off saving your shekels for some other system speed-up strategy.

Coprocessor History

In order to understand the relationship between the various available math coprocessors and why you might need a coprocessor at all, you need to understand a bit of the history of the technology. Coprocessors weren't a sudden inspiration to some obscure design engineer. Rather, they were a solution to a problem brought about by using precise digital technology to find answers for questions that arose in an irrational world.

In the mid-1970s there were no math coprocessors as they are known today. Computers were all mainframes and minicomputers. They all did floating-point operations and, oddly enough, they all came up with different answers. Not that they added two and two and deduced different results. Rather, when they calculated irrational numbers and rounded them, the last few decimal places varied, depending on what make and model of computer did the calculating. The problem was, of course, that real-world irrational numbers like *pi* have an infinite number of decimal places and computer memories are finite. Irrational answers can only be approximations, and different computers used various methods of approximating and rounding irrational numbers.

Scientists weren't really thrilled to have the results of their calculations vary with the hardware on which they were computed, so the Institute of Electrical and Electronic Engineers (the IEEE) formed an industry committee to develop standards for floating-point calculations.

At the same time the IEEE was standardizing, Intel Corporation was developing a successor to its successful 8080 and 8085 microprocessors and decided that it should develop a hardware implementation of the IEEE floating-point standard as part of that microprocessor program. Not that Intel foresaw the tremendous demand for personal computers that would develop. Rather, they saw the new microprocessor chips as finding use in things like robotic and numeric-control applications—commanding lathes, grinders, and milling equipment in machine shops and factories. The advanced math capabilities of a silicon-based implementation of the IEEE floating-point would be a boon to the design of such equipment.

The IEEE floating-point unit was first conceived as part of a microprocessor, but practical matters stood between that idea and reality. The microprocessor that Intel was working on eventually would become the 8086, the immediate predecessor of the 8088 that served as the foundation of the IBM PC. At the time the 8086 chip was being developed, in the years before its introduction in 1978, creating an integrated circuit was a much more exotic process than it is today. The size and number of components that could be grown and etched onto a wafer of silicon limited the complexity of possible (or at least affordable) integrated circuits. Ordinary microprocessors like the 8086 were the most complex circuits ever designed up to that time.

One of the rules of chip-making is that the larger the chip, the more likely it was (and is) to contain some defect that would make it unusable. Yet manufacturers cannot arbitrarily make chips smaller, because the state of the art in silicon fabrication constrains how small the details of a chip that can be practically manufactured can be. If the chip layout is too small, it will more likely suffer manufacturing defects, reducing the yield of the manufacturing process so that producing the chip is uneconomical. For example, the smallest possible details in the 8086 microprocessor measured five to ten microns across. Today chips are made with details as fine as one micron.

Together, the rule and the limit conspired to put an effective lid on the complexity of the new 8086 chip. Adding the IEEE floating-point circuitry to it would have far exceeded the level of complexity permitted by the technology of the times. Moreover, there was little incentive to try. Coprocessors for the 8080 and Z80 chips that were popular in the rudimentary desktop computers available at the time were unavailable. Hobbyists were only beginning to figure out what to do with the normal functions of those microprocessors. They had no conception of what to do with a coprocessor. And, just as today, most applications didn't need or couldn't use a floating-point processor that followed the evolving IEEE standard.

Weighing all these considerations, Intel elected not to include the IEEE processor as part of the 8086 or any other microprocessor chip. Instead, the circuitry was relegated to a separate element, which eventually was produced as a commercial product in 1980—the 8087 math coprocessor. In historic perspective, the 8087 was to become only the first product in a family of IEEE floating-point processors. As microprocessor technology developed, the 8087 was first updated to keep up. When Intel come up with the 80286 microprocessor, the 8087 was revamped into the initial incarnation of the 80287 (more familiarly, the 287) coprocessor. Later, the internal circuitry of the 8087 and 287 was redesigned to create the more efficient 80387 (or 387). Finally, technology reached a point at which it become practical to incorporate the IEEE circuitry on the same piece of silicon as the regular microprocessor circuitry, achieving the original floating-point design goal. The all-in-one chip that resulted with the first 486. And for people who bought the 486SX and discovered that a coprocessor was necessary after all, Intel reworked the 386 circuitry into a new chip, the 487SX.

Coprocessor Communications

No matter the part number or speed, all Intel math coprocessors share the same architectural elements. Except in the case of the 486, the Intel design makes a math coprocessor a separate piece of hardware that's nevertheless logically integral to the main microprocessor. And even the 486 devotes a dedicated area of its silicon to coprocessor functions. In operation, however, the math coprocessor is seen by programs as part of the main microprocessor. In fact, with Intel systems the only thing that changes when you add a math coprocessor to your system is that the microprocessor understands a wider repertory of commands, and these commands elicit answers to mathematic questions at great speed.

Because the coprocessor works with its microprocessor host, the two chips must communicate in some manner to exchange data and instructions. There are, in fact, two ways of linking microprocessor and coprocessor chips together that have been realized in commercial products. Some coprocessor chips link to the main microprocessor through a direct connection of input and output ports through which they send and receive data and instructions. Other coprocessors use a memory range to exchange data and instructions with the main microprocessor. The first type of coprocessor, which includes the Intel coprocessor family, are often termed *I/O-mapped coprocessors*. The second type, termed *memory-mapped coprocessors*, are more exotic chips that are less often encountered.

Besides all the math coprocessors made by Intel, all chips that claim compatibility with the Intel coprocessor chips use I/O-mapped technology. Included among these chips are the Cyrix 83D87, IIT 387, ULSI 83C87, and the various 287 chips from numerous manufacturers. The pre-eminent example of memory-mapped math coprocessors are those made by Weitek Corporation, the 1167 multichip platform as well as the 3167 and the 4167 single-chip implementations. Another alternative math coprocessor contender, the Cyrix EMC87, has characteristics of both of these types of coprocessor. This Cyrix chip works both as a I/O-mapped chip for compatibility with software written for the Intel 387, yet can accelerate to memory-mapped speed with applications written especially for it.

I/O Mapping

In the Intel I/O-mapped design, both the microprocessor and the coprocessor are connected to the data lines that carry information—program instructions as well as the data that they work on—inside your PC. Normally, the main microprocessor executes all of the instructions in most computer programs. Certain instructions are recognized by the math coprocessor as its own, however, and it can calculate them out directly.

In a way, the Intel I/O-mapped math coprocessor is like a leech, a parasite that cannot live without the microprocessor it clings to. Only the microprocessor has circuitry to control your PC's address lines to find information. Consequently, proper operation of the coprocessor requires careful coordination of its work with that of the main microprocessor. The effort of the two chips are kept together through a direct hardware link up—wires connecting the two chips—that are electrically controlled through input/output ports. These ports are internal to the two chips and, unlike the I/O ports used by your PC's peripherals, cannot be accessed directly by you.

Both the main microprocessor and the coprocessor have their own registers (in which all calculations take place) and internal control circuitry. As a result, the two chips can operate somewhat independently and simultaneously. That is, while your math coprocessor is wrestling with a particularly difficult problem, the microprocessor could do something else.

In theory, this design could add a degree of parallel processing to your PC. In reality, it often does not. Most programs send the math chip scurrying off in search of an answer and leave the microprocessor to wait until the results are found. A few applications, on the other hand—Borland's Quattro Pro being one example, take advantage of this parallel-processing capability. By carefully hand-coding assembly language routines, Borland was able to achieve a high degree of parallel processing when a coprocessor is present. That's why Quattro Pro will show a greater performance increase when a coprocessor is present than will most other spreadsheets.

Memory Mapping

Memory-mapped microprocessors communicate with your programs and microprocessor by using memory addresses as mailboxes. A small range of addresses (typically a 4K page) in far off paragraphs of your system's RAM—well above the 16 megabytes that most 386-based computers can use for physical RAM, but within the four-gigabyte addressing range of the microprocessor—is cordoned off for such communications. (All available memory-mapped coprocessors are design to work with 386 and more powerful microprocessors.) The microprocessor pushes instructions for the coprocessor to one group of addresses and data to be worked on to other addresses. The coprocessor gathers up the data and instructions, carries out the appropriate operations, and responds with its results in the same manner. No actual RAM chips are installed at the memory locations used for these communications. Rather, the memory for holding the commands and data are part of the coprocessor's circuitry.

One obvious requirement of the memory-mapped design is that the coprocessor chip must have access to the address lines used by the microprocessor. In that I/O-mapped coprocessors have no need for this address information, address lines are not available at coprocessor sockets designed for 387 chips. Memory-mapped coprocessors thus require larger sockets with more pins to accommodate all the address lines they need access to. That's why memory-mapped coprocessors have sockets the size of those used by 386 microprocessors, while 387 sockets are smaller. These special sockets for memory-mapped coprocessors are termed *EMC* sockets because they use an *Extended Math Coprocessor* interface. (It's quite possible that other uses for these sockets might be found beyond coprocessing. Any advanced function required direct memory addressing could take advantage of a memory-mapped coprocessor socket.)

Because of the additional address-decoding logic they require, memory-mapped coprocessors are inherently more complex than I/O-mapped chips. They are more difficult to design and make, and generally more expensive than equivalent (if there is such a thing) I/O-mapped chips. However, because the manufacturer's mark-up represents a huge percentage of the price of a coprocessor (chips that at one time sold for $1,000 cost $20 to make—now both figures are lower) this added cost may or may not appear in the actual price of the product.

In theory, a memory-mapped coprocessor can be faster than an I/O-mapped chip because the exchange of commands and data through memory is quicker than through the I/O route. While I/O-mapped chips must move instructions and data in separate operations over several clock cycles, memory-mapped chips can acquire all the data and instructions they need in a single operation. Even during calculations, the memory-mapped coprocessor can be quicker. Once the information to be processed has been loaded into its memory range, the memory-mapped coprocessor is on its own. It carries out its operations without further consultation with its microprocessor host. The I/O-mapped coprocessor requires more hand-holding. The main microprocessor first must read the instruction for the coprocessor, then poke the data into the proper port to get it to the coprocessor.

The big disadvantage of the memory-mapped coprocessor is that the interface has not been standardized. Each memory-mapped coprocessor family has its own commands and uses its own distinct address range. For example, while the Cyrix ECM87 and Weitek 3167 plug into the same socket, the two chips are completely incompatible and each is unable to execute programs written for the other chip. Hence, in order to take advantage of the coprocessor, programs must know the secrets particular to each coprocessor. Consequently, each memory-mapped math coprocessor requires its own version of a particular application. That need creates a huge burden for the software publisher, who must distribute a profusion of similar but incompatible programs should he or she want to take advantage of any available coprocessor. Few programs actually have such built-in support for any memory-mapped math coprocessor, let alone support for more than one family.

The sad fact is that while memory-mapped math coprocessors can be quicker, they don't often offer a speed advantage simply because most programs can't use them. Memory-mapped coprocessors are only an effective solution if you rely heavily in your everyday work on a single application and that application has specific support for the memory-mapped coprocessor that you chose.

Intel Architecture

The I/O-mapped coprocessors in the Intel family each share some common traits. Beyond the 8-, 16-, and 32-bit registers of microprocessors that you're used to dealing with, the Intel-style coprocessors work with 80-bit registers.

Eighty bits seems somewhat arbitrary in a computer world that's based on powers of two and a steady doubling of register size, from 8 to 16 to 32 to 64 bits. But 80-bit registers are exactly the right size to accommodate 64 bits of significant with 15 bits left over to hold an exponent value and an extra bit for the sign of the number held in the register.

The registers in Intel coprocessors are not limited to this single data format, however. They can calculate on 32-, 64-, or 80-bit floating point numbers, 32- or 64-bit integers, and 18-digit *binary coded decimal (BCD)* numbers as well. (Binary Coded Decimal numbers simply use a specific four-bit digital code to represent each of the decimal digits between zero and nine.)

Each Intel chip has eight of these 80-bit registers in which to perform their calculations. Instructions in your programs tell the math chip what format of numbers to work on and how. The only real difference is the form in which the math chip delivers its results to the microprocessor when it's done. All calculations are carried out using the full 80-bits of the chip's registers, unlike Intel microprocessors, which can independently manipulate its registers in byte-wide pieces.

The eight 80-bit registers in an Intel coprocessor also differ from those in a microprocessor in the way they are addressed. Commands for individual microprocessor registers are directly routed to the appropriate register as if sent by a switchboard. Coprocessor registers are arranged in a stack, sort of an elevator system. Values are pushed onto the stack, and with each new number the old one goes down one level. Stack machines are generally regarded as lean and mean computers. Their design is more austere and streamlined, which helps them run more quickly.

In the original design of Intel's first coprocessor, the company's engineers had the foresight to divide the chip's circuitry into two functional elements: a *bus interface unit* and a *floating-point unit*. The former links the chip to the rest of the system in which it is installed (the microprocessor in particular) and the latter performs the actual calculations. This division of labor allows chip designers great flexibility that Intel has exploited in improving its original coprocessors. Each part of the coprocessor can be upgraded as the need arises and technology develops. This step-by-step improvement method has allowed Intel to match coprocessors to microprocessor much more quickly than would have otherwise been possible.

The 8087

The 8087 was Intel's first IEEE floating-point unit, designed as a complement for its 8086 microprocessor. Although the two chips were conceived as a unified whole, the math coprocessor was not released until 1970, two years after the microprocessor it supported. Difficulty in designing the 8087 led to this lag. The 8087 just was not easy to make. In fact, according to Intel, the 8087 was the most complex large-scale integrated circuit ever produced at the time of its introduction. It adds a full 68 machine language instructions to the repertory of the 8086/8087 system.

The 8087 fits into a 40-pin DIP socket that provides the chip with the same addressing and data handling abilities of the chips it was to match, including 20 address lines. While 8087 can accept data from a 16-bit bus, it can also step backwards without modification and connect up with the eight-bit bus of the 8088. The 8087 automatically adapts itself to eight-bit operation as necessary. Besides the 8086 and its eight-bit cousin, the 8088, the 8087 math coprocessor can also operate in conjunction with the other Intel microprocessors that are derived from the 8086. These include the 80186 and 80188.

The 8087 is designed to operate at the same speed as its host microprocessor and ordinarily shares the same clock frequency with its microprocessor cohort. Intel still offers three models of 8087 chip, each of which is rated at a different operating speeds. The best match for IBM PCs and its compatible computers that run at 4.77 MHz is the 5 MHz 8087. Versions of the 8087 that operate at eight and ten megahertz are also available. The nomenclature describing these chips is somewhat odd, however. A chip labeled with nothing more than a plain *8087* operates at system clock speeds up to five megahertz. A chip bearing the identification *8087-2* operates at speed up to eight megahertz; and the *8087-1* operates at up to ten megahertz.

As with other chips, the speed rating defines the maximum rated operating speed of the chip and does not necessarily affect the speed at which the chip will operate (or how fast it can calculate). That speed is set by the clock inside the computer host. You can plug an 8087 into a system that calls for a chip with a lower speed rating, but you should never try to skimp by adding a slower 8087 than your system calls for. In other words, using a ten megahertz 8087 in a PC that calls for half that speed is wasteful, but won't result in any operational problems. Putting a five megahertz chip in a ten megahertz computer is, however, an invitation to miscalculation, a system crash, or the catastrophic failure of the chip.

The 287

The 80287, usually abbreviated to just 287, was introduced in 1985 by taking advantage of Intel's split-chip strategy. It retains the floating-point section of the 8087 but couples it with new interface logic to match the Intel's 80286 microprocessor chip.

As with the 8087, the bus control logic of the 287 is designed to link to an 826 and rely on the microprocessor host for system support. But unlike the 8087, the 287 coprocessor chip doesn't even have access to the address lines of the computer in which it is installed, so all memory-related operations are handled by the main microprocessor. This design allows the 287 to deal with both the real and protected modes of the 286 processor, enabling the 287 to address the full 16-megabyte range of that microprocessor. The 8087 operates only in real mode.

While both the 8087 and the 287 are packaged in a 40-pin DIP socket, the two chips are not pin-for-pin compatible and cannot be substituted for one another. This incompatibility should be obvious because the 8087 requires a full complement of address lines, while the 287 depends on its microprocessor host to handle all addressing functions.

Unlike the 8087, the 287 is designed to operate asynchronously. That is, the coprocessor does not necessarily operate at the same speed as its host microprocessor. The two chips, microprocessor and coprocessor, know how to adjust their operations, waiting as necessary to match their data transfer cycles.

Ordinarily, the 287 is connected with the same oscillator that runs the rest of a PC. However, an internal divider slows down the clock frequency entering the 80287 to one-third its original speed before it reaches the floating-point circuitry. Hence, an 287 operates at one-third the clock speed that is presented to it.

In most 286-based systems, the clock that runs the microprocessor is divided in half before being connected to the 286. Typically, the original double-speed clock is connected to the 287 so that the coprocessor effectively operates at two-thirds the microprocessor speed. For example, in an eight megahertz IBM AT the 287 coprocessor runs at 5.33 MHz.

Some systems give the 287 a dedicated clock of its own, allowing the engineer designing the system to operate the coprocessor at whatever speed he wants, thanks to the asynchronous possibilities of the chip. Using a dedicated clock can boost the data throughput of the 287 substantially.

While Intel at one time offered four different speeds of 287, the company's lineup was trimmed to two versions that operate at eight and ten megahertz, in 1990, eliminating versions that operated at five and six megahertz. A new design, discussed below, has made those two surviving 287 models obsolete also. Nevertheless, you may still encounter these now-discontinued versions of the 287 in older PCs and on the market for discount prices, so unambiguously identifying them is important.

A chip that's labeled only as a *80287* or bears the identification *80287-3* is rated to operate at up to five megahertz. The suffixes on the other discontinued 287s give the maximum speed rating of the chip in megahertz. Thus the *80287-6* runs at up to six megahertz;

the *80287-8* runs at up to eight megahertz; and the *80287-10* goes all the way to ten megahertz.

Because the 287 is based primarily on the 8087 floating-point circuitry, the chip is almost completely backwardly compatible with the 8087 and will execute most of the same software—though not all software because the floating-point unit is not a gate-for-gate copy of the 8087, but was improved somewhat in the upgrade. Differences in the two chips show up primarily in the way that they handle errors. Software can compensate for the differences in the chips, so a well-written program will run interchangeably on either coprocessor.

The Intel bus-control-logic design of the 287 that makes the coprocessor rely on its microprocessor host for addressing information earns the 287 an extra degree of flexibility. The chip is not inherently limited in any of its own addressing constraints, nor by the 16-megabyte memory-handling abilities of the 80286. As a result of this versatile design, the 287 is also able to operate with 386 microprocessors. For two years, in fact, it was the official Intel coprocessor for the 386.

But the 287 had been left behind by technology and the evolving IEEE floating-point standard. As it turned out, only after the 287 had been put into production was the IEEE floating-point standard finally written in its final form, now known as ANSI/IEEE 754-1985. In some subtle ways, the 287 and the finalized standard were at variance. Moreover, the 287 was designed with a 16-bit databus interface, which handicapped newer microprocessors that used 32-bit databuses. Consequently, the 287 is not the ideal math coprocessor, particularly for 386-based PCs. Nevertheless, a slow 287 is faster on floating-point operations than a 386 by itself, so even a lowly 287 can be a worthy addition to a PC that will accommodate one.

Eventually, Intel totally redesigned the floating-point unit of the 287 to create a new coprocessor more in line with the capabilities of the 386. The new floating-point unit design proved to be about five times faster than the original 287 on some operations and was first used in the 387 coprocessor, discussed below. But in January 1990, Intel adapted this new technology to the 80287 chip, in the process producing the two new, faster chips, the *287XL* and *287XLT*. The former is a direct, pin-compatible replacement for the 287 of days gone by. The 287XLT is designed for new PCs, primarily low-power laptop and notebook computers, and uses a *PLCC (Plastic Leadless Chip Carrier)* case that makes it incompatible with the sockets designed for other Intel coprocessor chips. Either of these advanced coprocessors will operate at speeds up to 12.5 MHz with either 80286 or 386 microprocessors designed to accommodate them. Because of the more efficient design of the new chips, they can calculate about 30 percent faster than the old 287s at the same clock speed.

The 287XL now entirely replaces Intel's old 287 line, giving you one chip to fit all existing applications—no more worries about matching chip speeds. In addition, the new floating-point unit in the 287XL and 287XLT will easily outperform that in older 287 chips, giving a bit of extra zip to math-intensive operations (though perhaps not enough to make it worthwhile replacing a plain 287 with a 287XL).

Beside the more efficient circuitry and compliance with the final IEEE floating-point standard, the new chips were also designed using a different silicon technology. They use *Complimentary Metal Oxide Semiconductor (CMOS)* technology rather than the *N*-channel *MOS (NMOS)* of the original. As a result, the new chips consume much less power than any of the old versions of the 287. While the old NMOS 287 chips were offered at the same time as their new revisions, the old and new versions were priced similarly. Obviously, Intel's intends to rid itself of its stock of the older chips and rely on the new one.

Your choices are not limited to Intel coprocessors for 286- and early 386-based computers, however. Advanced Micro Devices, which was licensed by Intel to manufacture the 286 microprocessor and (the AMD contends—there's a nasty lawsuit snarling this issue) to use the Intel's microcode in other products, offers its own version, the AMD80C287. Built using low-power CMOS technology, the AMD chip was initially offered in two speeds, ten and twelve megahertz. In that these chips use Intel's own microcode, compatibility is not an issue with them. You can use an AMD chip anywhere an Intel chip will fit, providing you observe the proper speed rating.

Integrated Information Technology (discussed below) also offers its own versions of 287-compatible coprocessors. These chips are based on IIT's own design, rather than the Intel microcode, which is both an advantage and disadvantage. They hold the potential of calculating faster but may miss achieving complete compatibility. Of course, any speed benefit is swamped by the I/O overhead of programs. And compatibility is likely a similar nonissue. The IIT chips are as compatible with the 287 as the 387 is, so you're unlikely to run into problems with any normal application.

The 387

When Intel began to design a coprocessor to match the 386, it chose to develop both a new bus interface unit and a new floating-point unit. The project fell behind schedule, and Intel hedged its bets by enlisting the 287 as the coprocessor for some early 386-based PCs and hiring Weitek Corporation to develop a version of its three-chip floating-point package, eventually named the 1167, for the 386.

All the while, it was carefully designing the 387 in Israel to implement the newly written IEEE floating-point standard. The design was totally fresh and blessed with the virtue of hindsight. Consequently, Intel was able to design the 387 floating-point unit to be faster than the one in the 8087/287 by a factor of about five once you combine the effects of higher potential clockspeeds and more efficient operation.

After introduction of the new floating-point unit in 1987 as part of the 387 math coprocessor, it became the foundation of all later Intel math coprocessors, including the 287XL, 287XTL, 387SX, and the 487SX. (The 387SX is essentially the same chip as the 387, but is designed to work with the 16-bit bus of the 386SX instead of a full 32-bit data bus.) Much of its design is also carried over into the 486 microprocessor's floating-point section.

The 387 promises a similar degree of backward compatibility with the 287 as the 287 does with the 8087. The primary differences appear in error handling, mostly because of changes in the IEEE standard. These differences are easily managed by properly written software. On some problems the 387 or 387SX may, in fact, deliver slightly different answers than would a 287—not to the extent of adding two and two and getting 22 but deriving transcendental functions that may differ in the far-right decimal place. Not that either microprocessor is wrong; the '387 and 387SX just conform better to current IEEE standard.

Another change Intel made in updating the floating-point units of the 387 was endowing the chip with a greater range of transcendental functions, including sine, cosine, tangent, arctangent, and logarithmic functions. As a result, while the 387 and 387SX should be able to run all programs written for the 287, the reverse in not necessarily true. Programs that take advantage of all the power of the 387 or 387SX may not run on the lesser chip. In general, however, code meant for the 8087 and 287 will run on either the 387 or 387SX.

Although it can operate asynchronously, a 387 generally operates at the same speed as the 386 it is installed with. Available versions have tracked the speed of the 386 as that microprocessor has become available in faster versions, all the way up to 33 megahertz. (USLI offers a clone of the 387 rated at 40MHz.) The speed ratings of different 387 chips can be identified by the part number on the chip itself. The 387 legend will be followed by a hypen and a two-digit number indicating the rating in megahertz. Consequently, a 387-25 will operate at speeds up to 25 MHz.

The 387 even looks like an 386, only smaller. Its square 68-pin PGA (Pin Grid Array) case has the same slate-like appearance as the microprocessor.

The 387 design has not been static. When it became necessary to boost the 387 to 33 MHz, further design improvements proved necessary. Intel switched from N-channel Metal Oxide Semiconductor (NMOS) technology to Complementary Metal Oxide Semiconductor (CMOS) and used new manufacturing processes that allowed details as fine as one micron to be etched in the chip's silicon. (Older 387s were limited to 1.5 micron details.) These improvements, along with some tinkering in the floating-point unit itself, yielded a performance improvement of about 20 percent.

The 33 MHz 387, introduced in April 1989, incorporates all of these advanced features. On October 1, 1990, the 16, 20, and 25 MHz versions of the 387 were also upgraded to the new technology. You can distinguish old-technology 387s from new-technology chips by the numeric code under the part number. Old 387s always begin this line of ten numbers with the letter "S." New technology chips lack the "S." You'll want chips without the "S."

The 387SX, a math coprocessor complement for the 386SX microprocessor, was introduced in January 1990, and all versions of it use the new technology. Two versions of this chip are currently available, 16 and 20 MHz to match the speeds of 386SX chips. You can tell the difference between the two by the speed rating silkscreened on the chip's case. As with the 387, the rating follows the chip designation and is given as two digits representing the megahertz rating.

387-compatible Chips

Unlike the 286 and 287, Intel chose not to license its 386 and 387 chips. Consequently, no company except Intel could legally produce its 387 design (AMD, in its lawsuit against Intel, claims to be licensed to use Intel's designs; whether it does is for the court to decide), forcing companies to reverse-engineer chips. Companies start with a list of all the functions the chip is to carry out and then create entirely new circuitry to handle those functions. Several companies have followed this approach—Cyrix Corporation, Integrated Information Technologies, and ULSI (the products of which are marketed by Specialty Development Corporation). Advanced Micro Devices is likely also working on such chips.

According to the various manufacturers, their designs are both hardware- and software-compatible with the Intel products. Because the 387-compatible chips are not slavish copies of the 387 itself, the various manufacturers have taken advantage of the design freedom to innovate. Most claim that they have added improvements to make their products more desirable than those made by Intel.

Cyrix Corporation

Although not originally conceived as a coprocessor company when founded in 1988, Cyrix Corporation quickly decided to make coprocessors its first product because they saw a ready market for the chips that lacked significant competition. The first of Cyrix's FasMath series of coprocessors were introduced in October 1989, as the 83D87, a pin-compatible replacement for the Intel 387. A lower-cost version for 386SX computers, the 83S87 was introduced in March 1990.

The Cyrix products are designed to be completely compatible with the Intel 387 family, although they are not copied from the chip through traditional reverse-engineering methods (x-ray a chip and determine its internal layout). Instead, Cyrix engineered its coprocessors with an entirely different logic design based on the documented and undocumented functions of the Intel products.

Perhaps the most important difference is that the Cyrix chips rely more on hard-wired logic than microcode. From this alternate design direction, they can achieve substantially greater speed than Intel's chips on floating-point operations.

Hard-wired logic is exactly what it sounds like. The bit-patterns that make up commands directly trigger state-changes in the solid-state circuitry of the chip. Each pattern—each logical instruction—must be specifically designed into the hardware of the coprocessor.

In microcode designs, instructions sent to the microprocessor cause the chip to run through several steps that make up the miniature internal program. The internal program tells the more general purpose logic of the chip to carry out the function required of it. The microcode design is the more structured approach. It gives the designer greater flexibility and can help get products to the market faster. It also allows complex instruction sets to be handled by general purpose circuits. But microcode can slow down the thinking process of the chip. Executing the microcode imposes another layer of overhead on every calculation.

On tasks that involve nothing but floating-point calculations, the hard-wired Cyrix chips can obtain answers in roughly half the time as the microcode-based Intel chips. Of course, only benchmarks (and not all of them) do nothing but floating-point operations. In real-world applications, input/output demands trim the Cyrix speed advantage dramatically. Even on the most math-intensive tasks, you should expect only about a 10 percent difference in the performance of the Cyrix 83D87, as compared to the Intel 387 on commercial applications.

Cyrix offers its 83S87 for 386SX computers in both 16 and 20 MHz versions. Four models of the 83D87 are available, rated at 16, 20, 25, and 33 MHz.

Beyond these pin-compatible I/O-mapped chips, Cyrix hopes to set a new high-performance coprocessor standard with its own line of memory-mapped coprocessors. The first of these products was the EMC87, which combined I/O-mapped instructions for compatibility with Intel's 387 with its own proprietary memory-mapped design for improved performance. Internally, the EMC387 is based on the same processor architecture as the 387, with eight 80-bit registers, and it has essentially the same command set.

The bus control logic of the EMC87 has been completely revamped, however, to the extent that Cyrix claims a fivefold improvement over the Intel part. The penalty is that the EMC87 is not pin-compatible with the Intel 387. Because the EMC87 is memory-mapped, it requires access to all the address lines used in 386 computers. Hence, it has a full complement of 112 pins and fits into the EMC socket normally reserved for a Weitek coprocessor.

Getting any of the speed improvement promised by the EMC87's memory-mapped architecture requires software particularly written for the EMC87. Applications that support the Intel 387 use only I/O-mapped instructions. The EMC87 will execute those instructions and deliver full 387 compatibility, but it won't work any faster than Cyrix's own I/O-mapped-only 83D87. Moreover, because the EMC87 uses its own proprietary command set, it is incompatible with the other leading memory-mapped coprocessor family, the chips made by Weitek. This incompatibility bodes ill for the memory-mapped coprocessor industry because it gives no common standard to which program could be written.

Understanding the need for availability of software to create a demand for the chip, Cyrix offers a code converter that adapts assembly language code from I/O-mapped to memory-mapped instructions for the EMC87. This code-converter will work with any assembly language file, including those produced by higher-level language compilers, such as Pascal or C. While these free code-converters may be interesting for software developers, they are of no value to you as an end user. They cannot convert commercial applications to make them compatible with the EMC87.

Until—and if—software publishers opt to take advantage of the EMC87 and write programs to match, the chip will remain more a curiosity than an added enhancement. However, because it is code-compatible with the Intel 387 and was originally priced at the same level as both the Cyrix 83D87 and Intel 387 (at the same speed ratings), the EMC87 could be a no-penalty hedge for optimists who believe in memory-mapped technology.

Integrated Information Technology

At its heart, Integrated Information Technology is a coprocessor company. Founded in 1988 by two engineers who left Intel to work for competing coprocessor-maker Weitek Corporation (one of these engineers was actually a cofounder of Weitek), the company now offers chips compatible with Intel's 80287 and 387. As with the Cyrix products, those from IIT were developed from the ground up, rather than reverse-engineered. Both are CMOS designs based on 1.2-micron technology.

The IIT coprocessor design differs from the Intel original in that the IIT 3C87 has 32 80-bit registers instead of a mere eight. These registers are divided into four banks and are designed to facilitate 4 × 4 matrix math, which can accelerate drawing performance in graphics applications. Using just one of those four banks simulates an Intel-architecture coprocessor. Using all four requires specially programs written that use the IIT 4 × 4 matrix instruction. So far only a handful of programs take advantage of this 4 × 4 matrix instruction. As with the Cyrix memory-mapped chip, the matrix ability should be viewed as an optimist's hedge. If it doesn't cost you anything, it doesn't hurt and it may bring future benefits should programmers ever decide to take advantage of the feature. Because of a better internal design to its floating-point unit, IIT claims that the 3C87 can calculate 50 percent faster than an Intel 387 in its math functions. Independent tests confirmed a speed advantage on benchmarks and commercial software from 3 to 36 percent.

Unlike the Cyrix chips, the IIT coprocessors don't exactly duplicate the operation of the Intel 387. The exception-(errors) handling of the Intel and IIT chips differs, much as it does between the 287 and 387. Some chip-makers have exploited that difference by writing special programs that show anomalous results when run on the IIT chips. With a bit of P. T. Barnum in their salesmanship, they claim that such results prove the 3C87 is inaccurate. According to IIT, however, such odd answers only crop up when you purposely try to exacerbate the exception handling differences by dividing by a near-zero number, such as $10-27$ (ten to the negative 27th power). On normal application software, no anomalous results should appear.

IIT did acknowledge that an early iteration of its 3C87 chip had an internal bug that resulted in errors in using its arctangent operation when running AutoCAD under *Unix* (and only with that application and operating system). This bug was corrected in June 1990, and the company reports that no other problems have been reported in the 100,000 chips it has shipped. In the unlikely event you run into that problem with the IIT chip, contact the company for a replacement.

ULSI

The initials stand for Ultra Larges Scale Integration, and that's the company's specialty, developing tiny products full of lots of circuitry. One of its products is a clone of the Intel 387, which ULSI calls the MathCo 83C87. The ULSI products are entirely socket-compatible with the various Intel chips that they mimic.

Reverse-engineered, the ULSI chips differ both in construction and performance. The ULSI products use CMOS technology and claim to be more efficient in their processing than the Intel products, requiring fewer clock cycles for each calculation. For example, while it takes an Intel chip 18 clock cycles to carry out a simple "add" instruction, the ULSI chip needs only three. Division, which takes an Intel chip 80 cycles, is handled by the ULSI chips in 40.

The best part of the ULSI line is that it extends the frontiers of speed to match faster microprocessors such as AMD's 40MHz 386. Five versions of the 83C87 are available, rated at 16, 20, 25, 33, and 40 megahertz. In addition, the company offers 387SX clones as well, the 83C87SX line. These chips are available at rated speeds of 16, 20, and 25 megahertz.

The ULSI line of coprocessor chips is marketed by Specialty Development Corporation of Austin, Texas.

Weitek Corporation

Formed in 1981 by former Intel engineers, Weitek Corporation has concentrated on making math coprocessor chips for a variety of computer platforms. It does not offer chips directly compatible with Intel's I/O-mapped designs. Instead, it has developed its own line of memory-mapped coprocessors.

By 1985, Weitek was producing floating-point coprocessors for a variety of workstations including those based on Motorola 68020 and Sun SPARC microprocessors. Around that time, Intel contracted with Weitek to develop a coprocessor for the 386 microprocessor. According to Weitek, the in-house Intel 387 program was behind schedule and Weitek developed its product in parallel with the 387 team.

Those efforts led to the Weitek 1167, the first of the Abacus line. The 1167 was not a single coprocessor chip but a small circuit board that combined two of the company's coprocessor elements used in 68020 computers along with interface logic to match the 386. The 1167 board actually included a socket into which you could plug a 387 to endow your PC with both coprocessors. The 387 could then run I/O-mapped instructions while the Weitek chips would handle memory-mapped instructions.

Although effective, the board-based design was hardly elegant, and in April 1988, Weitek introduced a single-chip equivalent to the 1167, the 3167. As with the 1167 board, the 3167 was designed to enhance Intel 386 microprocessors. In November 1989, Weitek introduced its 4167, a math coprocessor designed to enhance the Intel 486 microprocessor. The 4167 maintains compatibility with the Abacus 3167 and gives 486-based PCs the ability to run programs written with Weitek memory-mapped coprocessor instructions. Both the 3167 and 4167 are offered with ratings to match the speeds of the Intel coprocessors with which they work.

All Weitek chips plug into the 112-pin EMC sockets in computers that have them. They are not hardware compatible with Intel coprocessor designs. Nor will they run Intel I/O-mapped instructions. In fact, even according to Weitek, only a handful of commercial programs have built-in support for the company's Abacus series of coprocessors, about 38 applications at the time this is written. Most of those are specialized scientific packages, high-end CAD programs, or developmental software not exactly in the same product mainstream as Excel, Quattro, and 1-2-3. Unless you have software that explicitly supports one of the Weitek Abacus coprocessors, you won't see any speed improvement using one. The expensive chips just won't do anything.

The speed improvement you will see in comparison to Intel's 387 likely won't be great. When tested on one of the few applications that supports both I/O-mapped and memory-mapped coprocessors, the Weitek did little better than the 387 and its clones. In fact, on three common coprocessor-intensive tasks—loading and screen generation, mass entity deletion, and hidden-line removal—the

Weitek chip gave no significant improvement in performance over the results with the Intel-architecture chips. According to Weitek, the reason there's so little distinction between the various coprocessors on these tasks is that whenever substantial I/O overhead is present in the software, the effect of using the Abacus chip will be reduced down to the level of the 387. Of course, such overhead is present in nearly all commercial applications. The Weitek chips can deliver better performance (at least according to Weitek) if you optimize the I/O usage. For example, using a large RAM disk will minimize disk overhead and a high-end graphics coprocessor can speed up video displays, moving the software bottleneck to the coprocessor.

The 487

One of the major advances made by the Intel 486 microprocessor was its inclusion of coprocessor circuitry on the same silicon chip as the microprocessor. Far more than just a convenient package, the intimate relations between the two functions means intimate communications. The processor and coprocessor can toss instructions back and forth much more quickly than separate processor/coprocessor designs. In fact, on real-world tasks, you might see a two-fold improvement between the performance of a 486DX and a 386/387 combination operating at the same speed. Obviously, if you want the ultimate in math performance, forego a 386 and any coprocessor and opt for a 486DX instead.

The introduction of the 486SX in 1991 complicated matters. The chip, lacking a coprocessor of its own, was designed to be complemented with Intel's 487 math coprocessor. Of course, using two chips for the same purpose of the one-chip 486 undermines the 486's benefit of using internal communication between the processor and coprocessor. The Intel solution is surprising. The 487 is basically a complete 486DX dressed in different garb. Once installed in your PC, it takes over the function of the 486SX and math calculations, leaving the 486SX essentially idle. But the 487 is packaged differently from the 486—it has an extra pin—and is thus not socket-compatible with it. You cannot substitute one chip for the other. Moreover, the 487 will not work without a 486SX, so don't even think about trading in your microprocessor when upgrading to a 487.

Intel offers 487 chips in two speeds, 16 and 20 MHz., to complement its two models of 486SX chips. Again, they can be identified by the speed rating, which is silkscreened on the chip itself after its model designation. Although you can use a 20 MHz 487 with a 486SX microprocessor, there's no performance advantage in doing so. You'll want to match the speed of your 487 to your system's existing 486SX.

Making the Upgrade

Adding a coprocessor to your PC can be the easiest hardware upgrade you can make. All you need to do is slide a new chip into a socket. Before you can do that, however, you must find the right chip, perhaps prepare it to be inserted, orient it properly, then finally plug it in. Afterwards, you may also have to set up your system to recognize the new chip.

Finding the Right Chip

The correct coprocessor for your PC must match your system in several ways. The chip must be of the right variety to match your microprocessor. It must also have packaging and pin-out that are accommodated by your system. And it must be rated at the proper speed.

Your microprocessor is the first guide to your chip choice. If your PC is based on the 8088, 8086, 80186, 80188, V20, or V30 microprocessors, you must use an 8087 coprocessor. PCs based on 80286 microprocessors must use chips in the 287 family, such as Intel's 287 and 287XL. PCs based on the 386 microprocessor are best enhanced by the 387 coprocessor or one of its clones. However, some 386s may also be able to use the 287 family of coprocessors or a memory-mapped coprocessor. Computers based on the 486SX must be enhanced with the 487 coprocessor. The owners' manual of your PC should outline your microprocessor options. If you can't find your manual, the available sockets are a sufficient guide. While 486-based PCs don't ordinarily need coprocessors because of the built-

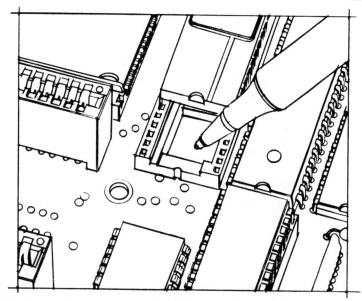

Figure 5.1 The proper orientation of 8087 and 80287 coprocessors is indicated by a notch at the end of the chip that matches a notch at the end of its socket. Be careful! Some ATs violate this rule.

in circuitry of the 486 chip itself, in most cases you can add a memory-mapped coprocessor to them.

The coprocessor socket or sockets inside your PC will determine which coprocessors you can physically add. All computers that use 8087 coprocessors will have 40-pin DIP sockets for that chip. Nearly all 286-based PCs will have the same socket, although some newer machines may have a square PLCC socket for the 286XLT coprocessor.

PCs based on the 386 microprocessor are likely to have the most socket options. Early machines will have both a 40-pin DIP socket to accommodate 287-family microprocessors and square 68-pin PGA sockets to accommodate 387-style coprocessors. Later machines may have either a 68-pin PGA for the 387 family or 112-pin PGA sockets for memory-mapped coprocessors. An examination of your PC's system board will reveal which options are available to you.

PCs equipped with 386SX chips will have PLCC sockets to accommodate the coprocessor. Machines accepting a 487 will have a waiting PGA socket.

Matching coprocessor speeds in 8088, 386, 386SX, and 486SX systems is easiest. In most cases, you will need a coprocessor that runs at the same speed as the microprocessor. An original IBM PC needs a five megahertz 8087 to match its 4.77 MHz clock speed. A 386-based PC that runs at 25 MHz will require a 25 MHz 387. And so on.

Speed issues arise with 80287 chips. In both 80286-based and 386-based PCs are likely to run at speeds at variance from the microprocessor speed. In all cases, the 287 chips will run slower than the microprocessor. How much slower is too important to guess at. The only way to be sure of the speed required from a 80287 coprocessor is to check the instruction manual of your PC or system board. Use a chip rated at the speed designated by your manual.

Intel publishes a very complete list of which of its chips it recommends for upgrading various PCs. In general, you can substitue the equivalent chips from other manufacturers providing you abide by the basic speed rules: Install a chip rated at the speed required by your PC or faster.

System Preparation

All coprocessors are installed internally inside PCs, so the first installation step you'll want to make is opening up the case of your PC. First, switch off the power to your computer, then pull out the power cord just to be certain you won't accidentally switch it on while you're doing the delicate work. Then slide off the top of the case.

Once you can see inside, locate the coprocessor socket. In most computers, it will be the only vacant socket on the system or microprocessor board. In some systems, you'll find two vacant sockets for expansion ROMs. The easy way to tell the difference between ROM and coprocessor sockets is that most ROM sockets—full or empty—come in pairs. Coprocessor sockets are loners. ROM sockets almost always use the DIP pin arrangement. Only 8087 and 287 coprocessor use this kind of socket. In general, coprocessors have more pins, 40 versus the 28 or so typical of ROMs. In systems that accommodate both a 287 and 387, the 287 socket will be DIP while the 387 socket will be PGA.

At this point, you should do whatever is necessary to gain easy access to the coprocessor socket. In most cases, that will mean re-

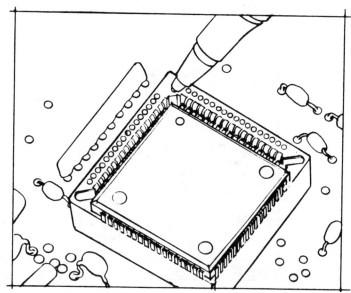

Figure 5.2 The proper orientation of 387SX chips is indicated by a flattened corner of the chip that matches a flattened corner of its socket. Just line everything up and press the chip in place.

moving one or more expansion boards. You'll want to be liberal in the number that you remove to give yourself as much room as possible. If you have to scrunch your hand to fit in, you're likely to misalign the coprocessor and skin your knuckles. Be sure to write down which board went where so you can put everything back where it came from when you reassemble your system.

You're now ready to prepare and install your coprocessor.

Preparing a Coprocessor

Before coprocessor chips packaged in DIP cases can be installed, the chips need to be prepared. Chips that need preparation include the 8087, 287, 286XL, and 80C287. Preparation is required because DIP chips are usually sold with their legs splayed. That is, the two rows of pins spread slightly apart. The spacing where the pins make the bend where they leave the chip's case matches the spacing of the holes in the chip socket. The spreading of the pins makes them difficult to properly insert.

Figure 5.3 The proper orientation of 387DX and 487SX chips is indicated by a flattened corner of the chip and a flattened corner *inside* the socket. 487SX sockets are larger and feature an extra pin that prevents improper insertion.

You need to ensure that each pin is bent at exactly a 90-degree angle. To do this, grasp the two ends of the chip between your index finger and thumb. Hold the chip with one of its rows of pins against a hard surface, such as a desktop, with the main body of the chip perpendicular to the surface. Apply pressure to the pins while holding the main body perpendicular so that the pins and the body of the chip form a right angle. Turn the chip over and do exactly the same thing with the other row of pins. When you're done, the pins should no longer spread apart. The chip is then ready to be plugged in.

PGA chips like the 387 and 487 as well as PLCC chips like the 287XLT and 387SX need no preparation. They can be pushed directly into their sockets.

Chip Orientation

In many PCs, the hardest part of installing a coprocessor is finding the socket into which the chip goes. Better PCs put the coprocessor

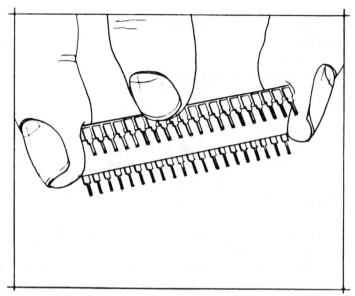

Figure 5.4 Before inserting a 8087 or 80287, straighten the pins on the chip by pressing each row flat against a hard, smooth surface such as a tabletop.

socket in an easy-to-access area. A few manufacturers lack the foresight to understand that you'd want to install a coprocessor and hide the socket in some unreachable place, perhaps under the power supply or drive bays. If you cannot reach the socket for your coprocessor, you can either take the wimp's way out and have your dealer do the dirty work or you can remove the drive bays or system board to gain access to the socket.

Before you slide the chip into its socket, you must be certain that the coprocessor is oriented properly—that the right end points in the right direction, that pin one on the chip goes into the socket hole meant for pin one.

Normally, you shouldn't have a problem. A notch at the end or corner of DIP-packaged coprocessor chips indicate the pin-one end, and a corresponding notch at the end of the socket indicates its pin-one end. Other chip styles have similar notches or other indications to help you identify pin one. In addition, most chips also indicate pin one with a recessed dot directly above or adjacent to the pin. All you have to do is match pin one on the chip with pin one on the socket.

Typically, DIP sockets have a notch at one end to correspond with the notch on the chip. Align the notches, and your chip is oriented properly.

Always double-check the alignment of a chip before pressing it in place. Improper alignment can result in bent pins and, if not discovered before you switch the power on, the demise of an expensive coprocessor chip.

Matters are not quite so simple with some of IBM's early ATs, which were manufactured with their DIP-style coprocessor socket oriented backwards. The sockets were put on their system boards by machines that had neither the eyes to detect a difference nor the motivation to care whether there was one. Consequently, if by chance you have such an AT and follow the standard notch code, your expensive coprocessor could still go up in smoke.

Here's how to know you're inserting your coprocessor correctly in an AT. The silkscreening on the system board (when it is visible) shows the correct orientation with the notch in the correct position. The blind insertion machine could not alter the silkscreened image. In most ATs, that means that the socket *should* have its notch at its end toward the front of the system unit. Make sure that the notch on the top of your 287 also points toward the front of the computer case if you have that kind of machine.

Note that most IBM PCs and XTs are just the opposite—the notch of the 8087 coprocessor that fits into those machines should face toward the rear of the case, matching the notch of the DIP socket it plugs into.

The 387 coprocessors and their clones also require proper orientation. The square PGA chip has one corner truncated more than the other three, corresponding to the location of pin one. You may also find a printed or embossed dot above this corner of the chip. The PGA socket for these chips should show a similar marking on their pin-one corner—either the outside edge of the socket will be similarly truncated or the socket may be doughnut shaped and its inner edge will show a slight bridging over corresponding to the pin-one corner. That is, you'll find three of the four inside corners of the socket will be square and the fourth angled at 45 degrees. The angle marks the orientation of the beveled corner of the coprocessor chip.

When fitting a 387 coprocessor into a 112-pin EMC socket, you'll notice that there's an extra hole in the socket in the bridged-over pin-one area. You can ignore this hole. On the EMC socket, the 387

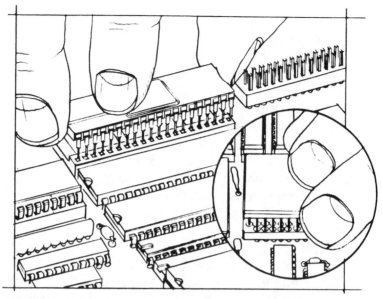

Figure 5.5 Be sure to line up the pins of 8087 and 80287 coprocessors with their sockets before pressing the chips down. Insure that all the leads are started in the proper holes before pressing down.

fits into the two rows of holes closest to the center of each side of the socket. It's normal for the outer row to remain vacant all the way around the chip. Make sure it looks the same on all four edges of the chip. If one edge is wider and shows two rows of pins and the opposite side shows none, you've installed the chip too far over by one row.

Memory-mapped chips cannot be inserted improperly into 112-pin EMC sockets because they have an extra pin corresponding to the extra hole in the EMC socket. Of course, you can try to force a chip into its socket improperly and damage it, so it's best to be sure you have the chip oriented properly before you squash it down. Again, the truncated corner of the chip corresponds to the pin-one placement. Match it with the truncated or bridged-over corner on the socket.

PLCC chips like the 387SX also have a beveled corner. Inside the PLCC socket, you should notice that one corner is correspondingly beveled. As with PGA sockets, you'll see three square corners and one angled at 45 degrees. The angled corner shows the proper orientation of the beveled corner of the PLCC chip.

Once your coprocessor is properly lined-up with its socket, you can press it in place. But your job is not yet done. Carefully inspect your work. Chips in DIP cases are particularly irksome in their ability to make an easy installation go bad. Their leads are apt to bump into the side of the hole for which they were meant, then curl under the chip or slide outside the socket entirely. With DIP chips, you should always verify that all leads are properly inserted into the matching holes. Be particularly on the lookout for leads that fold invisibly under the chip. Should you locate one or more leads that are not making good contact with the socket, you'll have to pull the coprocessor out of your PC and straighten the leads. The easiest way is to squeeze the leads flat between the jaws of long-nosed pliers.

Coprocessor chips in PGA packages pose few problems. Their pins are much more substantial and rigid than those of DIP chips. They bend only under forces so severe that you're unlikely to exert them except in anger or frustration. So if you're angry or frustrated (particularly with your coprocessor installation), put it aside for another day.

PLCC chips just require steady pressure to pop them down into their sockets. They are designed so that neither you nor an automatic insertion machine will do damage to the pins (actually, contact along the side of the chip) when you slide the chip into place. Just be sure to orient the chip properly before you press down—and be sure that you put the coprocessor in the right socket. PLCC chips are difficult to remove once you've pushed them into place.

Coprocessor System Set-Up

Even after you install a numeric coprocessor in your PC, it may not do you any good until you tell your computer that the chip is there. Although a coprocessor can be found using only software, IBM had tried to make coprocessor detection easier. Programs can avoid testing for a coprocessor by checking an *equipment flag*, a special memory location where system information is stored, to determine whether a coprocessor is present. The equipment flag is not set to indicate the presence of a coprocessor unless you tell your system that the chip is there.

Depending on the model of your computer, you tell it about a coprocessor either with a hardware setting or through software.

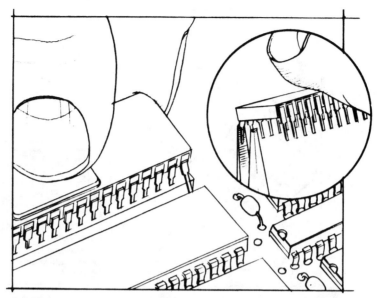

Figure 5.6 The most common failure of coprocessor installations is bending a pin outside the socket. If you discover this condition, remove the chip and straighten the pin with long-nosed pliers.

The PC and XT require that you throw a switch, one of many in a bank of DIP switches. The AT and all models of PS/2s learn about coprocessors through the software setup routine. In general, compatible computers follow the scheme used by the IBM model they emulate.

Software set-up means running the set-up program on the "Set-up" or "Reference" disk accompanying your computer or entering the set-up routines built into the BIOS of your PC. You'll want to reinstall all the expansion board that you removed for access to the coprocessor socket before you attempt the software set-up. Once the boards are back in, slide the power cord back into its socket, then boot up your PC. If your system uses hardware set-up, make the appropriate DIP switch adjustment, reseat all the expansion board you removed, and plug your system back in.

To set up the coprocessor through software you follow the same set-up procedure as you did when you originally bought and configured your computer. Just change the coprocessor option from No to Yes after you've installed your new chip.

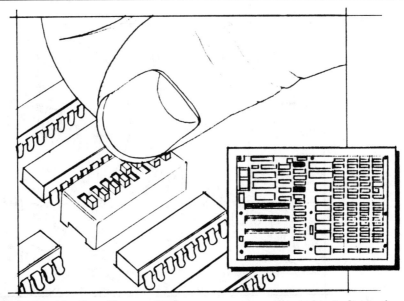

Figure 5.7 After installing an 8087 coprocessor, you'll need to indicate the chip is available to your system by throwing a system board DIP switch. Newer coprocessors require that you indicate their presence using the system's setup program.

Machines designed to use Weitek memory-mapped coprocessors make a special provision for it, either a DIP switch setting or a special entry during software-controlled set-up. Simply follow the instructions in your PC's owners' manual to make the correct adjustment to reflect installation of a Weitek chip. If you install a 387 on the WTL 1167 board, you'll have to indicate its presence to your computer, the same way as you would indicate that the 387 was your principal coprocessor.

Once you made the adjustments to your computer to show that you've installed a coprocessor, you need not do it again (unless the set-up memory of your AT or PS/2 loses power—in which case you'll have to go through the entire set-up process).

You'll want to check out your coprocessor before you completely reassemble your PC. Run a program that you know uses the coprocessor and assure yourself that everything is working properly. Once you're happy with the results, switch off your PC, put the top of the case back on, and screw everything back together. Your PC will now be able to race through numbers as if it had been born a prodigy.

6.

MEMORY

Memory upgrades are the most useful and frequent changes you're likely to make in your PC, but they are hardly the easiest or most trouble-free. However, with a bit of forethought you can easily master the idiosyncrasies of memory technology and make a quick and successful upgrade.

Of all the upgrades you're likely to make to your PC, the most inevitable is memory. Adding more memory will help you get your computer to do more of what you bought it for. If you want to add the versatility of a multitasking system, the glamor of a graphical user interface, or the utmost in speed, you'll want to stuff your system full with every megabyte it can hold.

Today's software is the best reason to add more memory to your PC. Step beyond older versions of DOS as your operating system, and your memory needs will start where the native endowment of most systems leaves off. You'll want four or more megabytes to get the most from UNIX, OS/2, or even the latest DOS incarnations such as Versions 5.0 and later. If you just want to try a multitasking extension to an older version of DOS—the pre-eminent example being Windows—your memory needs will similarly multiply. Switching between applications is quicker when you can keep the entire program and its data in memory, so the more memory you have, the more and the faster you can multitask applications. A growing number of programs, such as AutoCAD 386 and Paradox 386, incorporate their own DOS extenders and thus require more than the standard DOS 640K just to work. System speed-up utilities such as software-based disk caches and screen accelerators all rely on moving slower system operations to fast memory, and each one boosts the number of bytes you'll need installed in your PC. Maximum cache performance requires a megabyte or more of RAM, so if you want speed you'll need more memory. Scrimp on RAM and you'll shortchange your system's performance.

Adding memory means more than picking up the telephone and indiscriminately ordering a megabyte or two. All memory is not the same, and all is not equally useful to your system and the programs you run. Systems vary in the amount of RAM they can use and how you can install it. In fact, memory comes in more flavors than ice cream, and choosing the wrong one will give you something worse than a tummyache—you're likely to be stuck with unworkable, even unworking, memory chips.

There's really no big problem in adding memory to your PC, however. The main challenge is just matching your system's requirements to what's available on the market, what your programs need, and what will deliver the most speed. Each of these issues has many facets, but if you break it down and consider each one separately you'll find that most of your memory expansion decisions make themselves. Although you face such perplexing questions as whether you need expanded or extended memory, a memory board or loose memory chips, SIPs or DIPs, making the right buying decision is as simple as fitting together a two-piece jigsaw puzzle. As long as you know the kind of microprocessor in your computer and the provisions made in your machine for adding RAM, both pieces should fall right into place.

Memory Addressing

One of the biggest considerations when you add memory to your PC is how much to add. In the abstract you probably want as much as you can get, an amount limited not so much by common sense but by the uncommon dollars in your computer budget. But an unlimited amount of memory is not necessarily better than a few megabytes.

To be at all useful, whatever memory you add to your PC must be both usable and used. And that can be a problem because not all programs take advantage of every byte that you add to your PC. Moreover, computers cannot handle unlimited amounts of memory. Practical design factors limit capacities not just to finite amounts but in some cases to meager memory capacities.

Both limits arise from a common cause—addressability. For memory to be used by programs, it must be addressed. And logical and mechanical design factors limit how much memory a given PC can address.

Four factors limit the addressability of the memory in a PC—your programs, your operating system, your microprocessor, and your system's architecture. The maximum amount of memory that you can put to work is set by the smallest of these constraints.

Program Limits

Nearly every program that anyone has ever written includes some internal reference to memory. That is, the program assumes that some kind of memory will be at its disposal and that memory will be at a specific location and is accessed in a particular way. For example, every DOS program assumes the DOS environment that operates in your microprocessor's real mode and is thus limited to one megabyte of memory. A program that's written to run strictly under DOS doesn't even know that other memory types exist and certainly cannot figure out how to reach anything beyond DOS memory. Consequently, programs written with DOS in mind cannot use anything besides DOS memory. Moreover, they can't by themselves abide by any changes in DOS that might blast through the familiar 640K barrier. What they expect to address and what the range of memory actually is would then vary and the program would likely run erratically. Of course, the first tiny error in that erratic operation will crash your system.

In recent years some programs have been written with an eye beyond DOS. These applications can stretch beyond the constraints of DOS when other memory is available and take advantage of it. But these programs, too, are limited in the kinds of memory that they understand. They can't make use of just any memory. It must be the kind that they are specifically written to use. To a program, memory is kept behind locked doors—and the key to each door must be within the program's grasp for it to get at that memory.

In some cases you can add operating environments that will let programs written only to work with DOS memory take advantage of other memory types. But these operating environments don't change the capabilities of your applications. As a substitute, they offer a subtle subterfuge—they make your programs think that another kind of memory is ordinary DOS RAM. Your program then uses this converted memory as if it were standard DOS memory. When run under such an operating environment, the power of your program is not enhanced even though the power of your PC may be. The program can take advantage of no more memory than it could without the operating environment. You and your PC, on the other hand, can use more of the memory inside your PC when using an operating environment even though the capabilities of individual programs are not changed.

Operating System Limits

The amount of memory that you can effectively use is also constrained by your operating system, especially if you use DOS. After all, an operating system is nothing more than a set of computer programs that take care of some of the housekeeping involved in running your computer.

DOS is a particular culprit because it is written just like old-fashioned programs and assumes that your PC can address no more than one megabyte of memory, of which 640K at most is available to it. DOS simply has no conception that larger amounts of memory are possible, so it makes no attempt to address them. DOS is bound by the rules of the real mode of Intel microprocessors so it cannot even operate in the protected mode that would open up more megabytes to it.

Even DOS after Version 5.0, which was written with the awareness of other types of memory and megabytes of it, cannot unlock substantially greater reserves for your programs than earlier versions. It has to duplicate the functions of old DOS versions to keep compatible with them—and the programs written to use them. Certainly DOS Version 5.0 knows new memory-handling tricks, but your DOS applications are all old dogs. They refuse to learn anything new—and they may just bite you if you try to outsmart them.

Programs with DOS extenders that address more than one megabyte of RAM can run under DOS because they forego most of what DOS offers. The applications use DOS only to start loading themselves into memory. After a special *loader* routine has been moved into memory and starts executing, it takes over from DOS and finishes moving the rest of the program into memory. Because DOS is no longer involved in loading the program, code can be moved into areas that would not normally be addressable by DOS. Once all the code is loaded, the program runs by itself, ignoring DOS and its memory constraints. Programs without DOS extenders typically rely on DOS for support for read and writing files and the like. Programs with DOS extenders handle these operations themselves. They avoid the DOS addressing problems by avoiding DOS and acting as their own operating systems while they are in control of your PC.

Microprocessor Limits

Every Intel microprocessor has explicit memory-handling limits dictated by its design. Specifically, the amount of memory that a particular microprocessor can address is constrained by the number of address lines assigned to that microprocessor and internal design features. Ordinarily, a microprocessor can directly address no more memory than its address lines will permit.

A microprocessor needs some way of uniquely identifying each memory location it can access. The address lines permit this by assigning a memory location to each different pattern that can be coded by the chip's address lines. The number of available patterns then determines how much memory can be addressed. These patterns are, of course, simply a digital code.

The on/off patterns of the 20 address lines of the 8088 and 8086 microprocessors can uniquely define 2^{20} addresses, the one megabyte addressing limit of DOS, a total of 1,048,576 bytes. Because 286 microprocessors have 24 addressing lines, they can directly access up to 2^{24} bytes of RAM—that's 16 megabytes or 16,777,216 bytes. With a full 32 address lines, 386 and 486 microprocessors can directly access four gigabytes of memory—that's 4,294,967,296 bytes. You're unlikely to need more than that amount of addressibility soon, particularly considering most programs are still written with the DOS constraints in mind.

Architectural Limits

Not all computers can take advantage of all the memory that their microprocessors could address. For example, 386-based PCs that use the class AT bus for expansion generally permit the direct addressing of only 16 megabytes. The reason for this memory-addressing shortfall is that the AT bus was designed with only 24 addressing lines, rather than the full 32 of the microprocessor. A few classic-bus computers break through this limit by the expedient of forcing you to keep all memory in proprietary expansion, forcing it off the bus. To gain greater capacity, these systems force you to limit your expansion options.

Both the advanced PC expansion buses, EISA and Micro Channel, extend their address buses to a full 32 bits. But other aspects of computer design may still limit internal addressing to levels below those allowed by the system's microprocessor. For example, most of the initial 386-based EISA computers allowed up to 32 megabytes of RAM to be installed—more than AT-bus machines but far within the four gigabyte constraint imposed by their microprocessors.

Some special architectures allow microprocessors to address more memory than the amount for which they were designed. The most popular of the techniques used is *bank-switching*, in which additional memory banks can be switched in and out of the standard addressing range of the chip. The maximum limit of a bank-switched system is, at most, the product of the amount of memory a microprocessor can directly address and the number of banks that can be switched. Potentially prodigious amounts of memory can be handled by bank-switching. In practice, however, the 386 and later microprocessors have made the technique virtually obsolete because they can directly address so much more memory than can be practically used today. Even at a reasonable $50 a megabyte, four gigabytes of memory would cost $200,000—and you'd still have the challenge of fitting 4,000 memory modules inside your system. Even with memory boards able to pack 32 megabytes each, you'd still need 125 boards and expansion slots to match. (And, incidentally, if you assume a soft error rate of once a year per megabyte of memory—not an unreasonable figure—your computer equipped with four gigabytes of RAM would crash more than ten times per day from memory parity errors.) Even if such bodacious byte totals were not impractical today, you would not need to worry about their ramifications simply because of all the other constraints on memory addressing.

Types of Memory

All the megabytes inside a PC are not the same. In fact, the memory that can be used by your programs can be divided into four types: *conventional, extended, expanded,* and *cache*. Thee four types differ primarily in how they are accessed, which determines how they are used and the benefits each brings to your PC.

Conventional Memory

Sometimes called DOS memory, conventional memory refers to the 640K (or so) that can be used directly by DOS. It's conventional because it's the only kind of memory accessible by the conventional computers that came before the "advanced" IBM AT was marketed. It's also termed "DOS memory" because it is the only kind of memory that DOS was written to use.

Conventional memory is often termed *real-mode memory* because it is directly addressable in the real operating mode of Intel microprocessors. Sometimes it's called *base memory* because every PC has at least a small amount (most now have a full complement) of this memory, which serves as a foundation of the system. This base memory must be present because all Intel microprocessors boot up in real mode and need at least some memory available in real mode to carry out any operations.

Although conventional memory is probably the most useful in your PC, it's also limited. The original PC design pegged the maximum at 640 kilobytes, forcing all machine wishing to remain compatible to do likewise. This limit was only partly imposed by the 8088 microprocessor of the original IBM PC. Although the chip could handle one full megabyte of memory (that's 1024K bytes), IBM reserved 384K of the total addressing range for use by internal system functions such as the Basic Input/Output System (BIOS) and video display systems.

The reserved 384K memory area above the DOS addressing range is often termed *high memory* (microsoft calls it high DOS memory) because it is at the upper end of the addressing range of the 8088 microprocessor. In most PCs, the entire addressing range reserved for this high memory is not used. The upper 64K of it is generally given over to your PC's BIOS (and, in IBM computers, the built-in cassette BASIC interpreter language); another 64K block is relegated to use by display systems; and another 8K or so is devoted to the extra BIOS code needed by hard disk systems. Networks and other peripherals may also use limited high memory areas.

The leftover high memory addressing range cannot be used for DOS applications for two reasons. First, this memory area is reserved, meaning that no program writer can assume that any particular range of it is free for use by his or her applications. While a program might be able to snare a few bytes of this range in one PC, in another system it may bump into another function that's also trying to use the same memory. Such memory conflicts generally translate into system crashes. Moreover, DOS requires contiguous memory. That is, DOS can only operate with a continuous range of addresses under its control. It cannot jump over blocks of reserved memory to expand its territory.

For software designers, such constraints are more often inspirations rather than hard and fast limits. Working around some of the limits of DOS memory *is* in fact possible in some particular situations.

The first requirement, sidestepping the rules of reserved memory, is possible by customizing control software to suit each particular machine in which it runs. The program goes out and checks which addressing ranges are used and which lack associated ROM or RAM. If no physical memory is assigned to a particular addressing range, then that range could be used for extending conventional memory.

Conquering the second constraint depends on the kind of microprocessor in your computer. If you have 8088-based PCs or a 80286-based ATs, you can take advantage of a number of memory expansion boards that allow part of their RAM endowment to be addressed within the one megabyte abilities of the 8088 microprocessor but above the nominal 640K limit of DOS. These boards allow you to push the limits of conventional memory upward by appropriating the addressing range reserved for display adapters but not used in some systems. The memory range used by a monochrome display adapter (MDA) starts 64K above the 640K conventional memory limit. If you use only a MDA video board, you may be able to reassign the intervening 64K of addresses to conventional memory—providing you buy a memory expansion board that's capable of putting some of its chips in this range. The addressing range used by a Color Graphics Adapter (CGA) starts 32K above the MDA range, so systems with only a CGA adapter hold the potential for hosting 96K of additional conventional memory—again, with the proper memory board.

Note that when using special memory board hardware to take advantage of extra addressing ranges for conventional memory, you must be sure that the normal 640K conventional range is completely filled before you try to add on above the 640K limit. The base 640K must be complete to assure that whatever extra conventional memory you add is contiguous with all the bytes in the normal range. No gaps are permitted if you expect DOS to work.

In systems that support it, *memory remapping* can also extend the usable range of conventional memory. Systems capable of such support include nearly all PCs equipped with 386 and more recent microprocessors, Micro Channel PS/2s, and other PCs with special memory management hardware (such as a 286 equipped with an ALL ChargeCard).

Memory remapping can be likened to a renaming system—memory that's located in one address range is simply reassigned addresses in another range. In these systems, RAM nominally addressed above the conventional memory area (even memory above the one-megabyte maximum addressing range of 8088 microprocessors) can be logically relocated at the top of the base 640K to extend the range of DOS. In most cases, this remapping is handled by special memory management software that typically also allows you to take advantage of noncontinuous ranges of addresses in the high memory area for relocating driver software and terminate-and-stay resident programs. This memory is remapped into blocks called upper memory blocks (called VMB by microsoft.).

Unless you're willing to put up with old-fashioned text-only displays or clunky, chunky CGA graphics, however, this added DOS memory won't be available to you. Newer display systems like the Extended Graphics Adapter (EGA) and Video Graphics Array (VGA) occupy the addressing range that begins exactly at the top of the conventional memory 640K limit. You can't slip any more conventional memory in because it could not be contiguous with the base 640K range.

However, with the memory management software used for remapping 386 machines you can get the effect of more DOS memory by moving drivers and such out of the base 640K, but you can't actually increase the range available to DOS programs.

The term "high memory" (High Memory Area in microsoft terminology) is sometimes used to refer to another memory area besides the upper 384K addressing range of real mode. In this second definition, high memory refers to the 64K segment of RAM that's addressed just above the base-one megabyte. With 80286 and more recent microprocessors, software can treat this memory as a special case for remapping purposes, using it as if it were real-mode memory even though it is addressed outside the real-mode range. For example, DOS Version 5.0 uses this high-memory area (when it is available) for loading most of it, kernel, giving you more of the lower 640K for your programs.

The reason this high-memory area exists is linked to the way Intel designed its microprocessors. Normal memory addressing in 8088 computers wraps around. That is, if your program tries to address a memory area located above the one-megabyte limit, the microprocessor ignores the part of the address above one megabyte and starts counting at the beginning of conventional memory again. The 80286 (and later) microprocessors don't wrap around because they have the capacity to address memory above the conventional memory area. When a program meant for the 8088 attempts to wrap around, it ends up trying to access memory above the conventional limit which, strictly speaking, is extended memory (see below). A quirk in the 80286 design allows some memory management programs to use this extended memory as if it were conventional memory. It gives the memory management software an extra 64K address range in which driver software and TSR programs can be relocated. DOS versions before 5.0 and application software (even when running under DOS 5.0) cannot in themselves do anything useful with this memory because it is not contiguous with the lower 640K of conventional memory.

Expanded Memory

In 1983, just two years after the IBM PC made older computers with mere 64K maximum memory effectively obsolete, the PC's own 640K limit was showing itself as a roadblock to the use of more complex programs and large amounts of data. Consequently, a consortium of companies led by Lotus Development Corporation, Intel Corporation, and Microsoft Corporation developed what they termed the Expanded Memory Specification as a means for breaking through the 640K barrier. Interchangeably termed expanded memory, *LIM memory* (for the names of its developers), or *EMS*, this technique takes advantage of bank-switching to allow microprocessors to address memory that would otherwise be beyond their reach.

Bank-switching works by dividing the additional system memory into a number of discrete blocks or memory banks that are not directly linked to the microprocessor. Instead, each bank is connected to a software-controlled hardware switch. Through software commands, each block can be individually switched into the addressing range and control of the microprocessor. The total memory held in all the memory banks can thus be accessed through a small range of addresses called a *page frame* that's carved out of the conventional memory area. Consequently, even a primitive microprocessor like an 8088 can access multiple megabytes of memory.

Using the latest incarnation of EMS, Version 4.0, up to 32 megabytes can be shifted into the conventional addressing range in 16K banks. While the original EMS design used a 64K page frame located in high memory, EMS 4.0 also allows bank-switching to take place within the DOS 640K addressing range. The difference is important because it puts EMS 4.0 within the contiguous addressing range of DOS and allows program code to be bank-switched. This permits specially written programs larger than 640K to run on 8088 systems. The earlier EMS 3.2 specification would only allow the storage of data in bank-switched memory.

Expanded memory doesn't come for free. It requires both hardware and software additions to your system. Nearly all 8088- and 8086-based computers, as well as most 80286 machines, ordinarily require a special EMS memory board to take advantage of LIM 4.0 expanded memory. That's because most earlier PCs don't know how to bank-switch by themselves. They lack the hardware facilities for disconnecting and reconnecting banks of memory. The EMS board adds the necessary control circuitry along with bank-oriented memory. In addition, a software driver is required to match your applications to the EMS facilities of your system. Among other things, the driver tells programs which EMS features are available and how to use them, the location of the page frame (which can vary to allow for systems that have different configurations), and the amount of memory that's available. The page frame used by the EMS board takes over a 64K range of high memory that cannot be used for any other purpose.

Some 286 computers and all 386 and later machines can simulate bank-switching with their built-in memory mapping abilities. Most memory management software packages include the driver software necessary to convert extended memory into bank-switched EMS.

Expanded memory emulation programs sometimes called *LIMulators* can almost completely mimic EMS, even on 8088 machines.

On 286 computers, this software simulates EMS using extended memory. On 8088 machines, the software uses disk memory to simulate EMS. In either case, the LIMulation software copies code from the page frame to the available disk or extended memory as needed. The copying operation can severely slow performance, but it offers you the advantage of using larger data sets when you really need to.

Note that neither 8088 nor ordinary 286-based computers can exactly duplicate EMS 4.0 using software alone. Some EMS 4.0 functions require explicit hardware features that cannot be duplicated even through software simulation with a LIMulator. As a result, some programs may not operate properly with simulated EMS. However, most virtual memory managers come close enough to the EMS 4.0 standard that you can expect the majority of your expanded memory applications to use virtual EMS as if it were the real thing.

Some EMS 4.0 hardware also has its limitations. Many of these are traceable to the design of the specification, a cooperative effort among a number of manufacturers, each looking out for its own best interest. In fact, if you think a camel is a horse designed by a committee, EMS 4.0 would appear more like it was crafted by an entire congress.

While EMS 4.0 was meant to eliminate the shortcomings of the previous versions of the standard—in particular, to allow programs to run in expanded memory and give multitasking capabilities. But some memory boards that conform to the EMS 4.0 standard are not capable of multitasking. This incongruity results from the way that the EMS 4.0 standard specifies page-mapping registers.

Page-mapping registers are a part of the special EMS board hardware that records which bank of physical memory is assigned to which logical memory pages. That is, the register indicates which bank of RAM chips stores the bits used by a program or task. When a certain piece of code or data is required, the register points to its physical location in the memory hardware.

While one set of page-mapping registers is necessary if an EMS 4.0 board is to work at all, multiple sets allow the control software of multitasking systems to instantly shift between applications. When the supervisory software transfers control from one task to another—typically on the order of 18 times per second—it only needs to peek at the second set of registers to see where it can reach the needed program code in memory.

The weakness of the EMS 4.0 standard is that it allows a conforming product to have one *or* more sets of page-mapping registers. Boards with only one set have hardware enough to track only one task.

The EMS 4.0 standard skirts around this issue by providing a means of simulating multiple registers. The EMS 4.0 driver included with any expanded memory board includes code to support function calls made by programs using EMS 4.0 memory. These function calls comprise a BIOS-in-miniature. As with a computer's BIOS, these EMS function calls match generic software to the specific hardware product.

One such function call handles shifting between registers. With expanded memory boards that have only one set of page-mapping registers, this function call executes a complicated pirouette each time a multitasking system shifts between tasks. It must copy the values from its registers to reserved RAM, find the next set of register values elsewhere in RAM, and transcribe the alternate values into the registers. This process can take so long that it makes true concurrency untenable.

The reason stunted EMS boards with but a single set of page-mapping registers are allowed to fit the EMS 4.0 standard is likely rooted in the committee nature of the specification. The companies that promulgated the EMS 4.0 standard all had existing products, some of which were designed for an intermediate kind of memory called *Enhanced Expanded Memory Specification* or *EEMS* standard (which requires two sets of page-mapping registers) and others that conformed to the earlier EMS 3.2 (which only requires one). By not specifying the number of registers to be used and using driver software as a Band-Aid, makers of both kinds of boards almost instantly had products that could be sold under the new EMS 4.0 banner. Software designs are usually easier to change than hardware.

The bottom line is that you should be careful when buying an EMS 4.0 board to upgrade your PC. Although most new boards now support multiple page-mapping registers, some older products do not. You may inadvertently buy a board legitimately labeled as following the EMS 4.0 standard that won't support multitasking in your system. If you plan on running a multitasking system, you'll want to be sure that any EMS 4.0 boards you buy support multiple page-mapping registers.

Extended Memory

When new microprocessors were added to PCs to improve performance—first the 80286 in 1984, then the 80386 in 1987, and the 80486 in 1989—they brought along a side benefit; greatly broadened addressing ranges. The 80286 is endowed with an addressing potential of 16 megabytes. The 80386 (SX and DX) and 80486 all are equipped to handle 4096 megabytes.

These larger memory areas are directly accessible to the respective microprocessors, so bank-switching is not required. Nothing about the microprocessors prohibits the use of bank-switched memory, however, so you can still use EMS in your AT or 386.

Because the increased memory capacity linearly extends the addressing range of the microprocessor, this kind of RAM is termed *extended memory*. Adding memory on the system board of an AT-class or more powerful computer will usually endow it with extended memory. Computers based on the 8088 and 8086 microprocessor are incompatible with extended memory—they simply cannot reach it because they don't have the necessary address lines. If you don't use an EMS board, any memory you add to an 80286, 386, or 486 computer beyond its conventional memory base will be extended memory. Most memory upgrades will be extended memory. When extended memory is controlled by a memory manager such as HIMEM.SYS included with DOS 5.0, the memory in this area is called extended memory specification (XMS) by Microsoft.

DOS and ordinary DOS applications do not normally use extended memory, but advanced operating systems such as UNIX and OS/2 can. Memory management software can turn extended memory into EMS and make it useful to a wider range of software. The special 386 versions of DOS programs typically require extended memory.

Cache Memory

While cache memory is used by programs and directly accessed by microprocessors, it differs from ordinary RAM in that your programs don't really know that it's there. It is functionally invisible.

The purpose of the cache is to match a high-speed microprocessor to slower RAM memory chips.

Since the introduction of 16 MHz microprocessors, computers have outrun the capabilities of most memory chips. Only the fastest, most expensive RAM chips can keep up with the high clock rates of today's microprocessors. A cache is a buffer that fits between a fast microprocessor and slow memory to help the two get along. By using a modest block (typically 8K to 64K) of fast but expensive static memory as a cache, designers can construct computers using much more affordable, though more laggardly, dynamic memory chips. Some microprocessors even have their own, built-in caches. The 486DX and 486SX each have an 8K memory cache built into their silicon circuitry.

Some means of matching memory to microprocessor speed is mandatory because when a 33 MHz computer operates with zero wait states, it needs to be able to access memory every 33 nanoseconds. Only fast static RAM chips work at such speeds. Affordable dynamic memory chips require 60 to 80 nanoseconds between accesses.

The cache bridges that difference. The microprocessor is connected only to the fast memory of the cache. A special device, *the cache controller*, attempts to anticipate the bytes that the microprocessor will need for its next thought and loads them from main memory into the cache.

The cache controller is not clairvoyant. Instead, it essentially guesses at which bytes to load into the cache according to an algorithm. For example, the simplest algorithm merely assumes that the next bytes needed will be in the same address range as previously required bytes. The algorithm simply stuffs the cache with a block of memory from a particular address range. Caching algorithms must also take into account the needs of OS/2, multitasking, and multiuser operating systems. Such caches need to hold bytes from each task so that they are available when execution shifts between tasks, on the order of 10 to 50 times a second.

When the cache controller does not properly anticipate what the microprocessor requires, the necessary bytes must be retrieved directly from main memory. This slows the system to main memory speed by piling wait states onto the microprocessor.

Real computers further complicate cache designs. Besides the microprocessor, other devices such as a DMA (Direct Memory Access) controller may change main memory, and those changes must be constantly reconciled with the cache. Moreover, when bytes are written to the cache, main memory must immediately made to conform.

On the other hand, a properly designed cache can increase the throughput of a computer even beyond what its microprocessor speed might seem to allow. Both EISA and Micro Channel computer designs allow for the system microprocessor to work on data in cache memory while other system components deal with main memory, thereby achieving a limited degree of parallel processing.

The principal measure of the quality of a cache is its "hit ratio"—the number of bytes properly anticipated over the number of bytes actually used by the microprocessor. The hit ratio is equal to the percentage of the time the microprocessor operates without wait states. In actual caches, the hit ratio varies with the algorithms used by the cache controller and the size of the cache. A larger cache naturally has a higher hit ratio because it's more likely a given byte will be in the cache. As cache size increases, so does the probability that the next byte needed by the microprocessor will be found inside the cache where its retrieval requires no wait states. (If the needed byte is outside the cache, wait states may need to be imposed to match memory access with microprocessor speed.) Typically, a 32K cache can yield a hit ratio of better than 90 percent.

The relationship between performance and cache size is not linear, however. As cache size increases, it quickly approaches a point of diminishing returns. Expanding a cache beyond 32K with its 90 percent hit ratio would, for example, raise overall system performance by only a few percent. Nevertheless, if you want the best performance from your system, you want the largest possible cache. That's why many 486 systems have external caches to supplement the chip's internal 8K cache.

Some PCs have expandable or scalable caches, meant for upgrading. These typically require special static RAM chips or special add-in cache assemblies that are available solely from the computer manufacturer. Because these designs are proprietary, no general instructions can describe all cache expansion approaches. However, most are simple plug-and-play installations that require only that you take precautions against static discharges.

Unlike other memory upgrades, adding cache memory won't change the size or number of programs that you can run on your PC. Cache upgrades are strictly for improving performance.

Choosing a Memory Type

When you think about a memory upgrade, you will, for the most part, be concerned with expanded and extended memory because nearly all PCs sold today are filled to their conventional memory capacity. Which of the two to choose—expanded or extended—depends first on your software. If your software allows you a choice, then performance should be your next concern. If your software does not allow a choice—if your favorite program or operating environment requires a particular kind of memory—then you'll need to buy memory to match the application.

Application Considerations

Because DOS-based programs only know how to deal with conventional memory, both expanded and extended memory are off-limits to them. To take advantage of either form of memory you need special software—applications written particularly to use a given memory type, operating environments designed to push DOS programs into extended or expanded memory, or another operating system.

Most applications will *not* recognize EMS or extended memory. The only programs that can take advantage of memory beyond the conventional addressing range are those that are specifically written to do so. In other words, EMS is valuable only when you have software that requires it. Do not consider enhancing your PC with EMS memory if you do not have an application that needs it. Don't add extended memory if you don't have a program or operating system (such as DOS 5.0 or OS/2 2.0) that can use it.

A number of applications have been written to take advantage of expanded memory. Versions of Lotus 1-2-3 numbered lower than 3.0 are a cases in point, although most programs that deal with truly large amounts of data now have expanded memory abilities. Programs that use expanded memory will specifically state their needs and abilities in their specifications. If a program does not explicitly assert expanded memory capabilities, it probably won't gain from any expanded memory upgrade you make to your PC.

Recently, a number of programs have been rewritten to take advantage of the enhanced memory-handling abilities of the 80386 and 80486 microprocessors. AutoCAD 386 and Paradox 386 are examples. These programs use extended memory, megabytes of it. Nearly all non-DOS operating systems use extended memory. Version 5.0 and later of DOS can also take advantage of extended memory and use it for its own code, for relocating memory-resident utility programs, for disk caching, and for use by EMS-ready applications.

Obviously, if the application that you use most needs expanded or extended memory, you should dose your computer with the kind of memory that your favorite program can exploit. Your choice is often not that easy, however. Some advanced operating environments like Windows 3.0 can use either expanded or extended memory. In fact, Windows 3.0 can even convert extended memory into expanded for programs that need it. You can also turn extended memory into expanded memory using a LIMulator.

Performance Considerations

Whether this software-generated EMS is better than a hardware EMS board depends on your computer system. In some systems, software-based EMS can be two to four times faster than a dedicated EMS board. In others, the board beats emulated EMS. The determining factor is the relationship between the speed at which your PC's microprocessor operates and the speed of its expansion bus.

If your computer is based on a 80386DX or 80486 microprocessor, you should always add extended memory to the system board or use proprietary memory expansion boards. Plugging any memory board, extended or expanded, into an expansion slot will seriously degrade performance because the expansion buses of these computers operate much more slowly than do their proprietary memory sockets and slots. If you need expanded memory in such a computer, use a LIMulator to convert extended RAM into expanded. You'll get much better performance than using an EMS memory board.

Should your PC be based on an 8088 or 8086 microprocessor, your decision is even easier. Once your machine has its full 640K conventional memory quota, you can add only expanded memory.

And that memory must be in the form of an EMS board installed in an expansion slot. Nothing else works—or will fit.

The 286 and 386SX microprocessors are special, more complex matters. System board and expansion board memory are equally quick in slower models in which the expansion bus operates at the same clock speed as the microprocessor. Examples of such machines include all genuine IBM ATs, all non-Micro Channel PS/2s, PS/1s, and compatible computers operating with microprocessor speeds of 10 MHz or less. In these machines true EMS boards will generally be faster than using a software-based LIMulator.

In similar machines with quicker clocks, however, memory that's added directly to the system board or through proprietary memory expansion boards will be faster than any expansion slot memory. Should you have one of these computers and software that will work with either extended or expanded memory, give it extended. Ordinary extended memory will, in every case, be faster than expanded memory emulated with software, and you'll have one less driver stealing memory from your system. If, however, your favorite program demands expanded memory, use a LIMulator. It will still outperform memory that's handicapped by expansion bus speed.

Hardware Considerations

Of course, any memory upgrade you add to your PC must meet one further compatibility—it must be physically compatible with your computer. It must fit.

Matching a memory board is more than a matter of finding a board that will slide into a slot. After all, even a ten-year-old eight-bit memory card will fit nearly every available PC (except, of course, Micro Channel machines). But an eight-bit board would hardly be a good match for a fast EISA-based super-server. Not only would the eight-bit board not exploit the full 32-bit potential and performance of the EISA machine, it would likely not work at all. The addresses at which an eight-bit memory card could locate memory would undoubtedly be within the same range as the base memory already installed inside the EISA computer. The addresses of the board's RAM cannot be changed to a range that would not conflict.

The first hardware issue is where to put additional memory. The chief choices are threefold: on the system board, on proprietary memory expansion boards, and on conventional expansion card in system expansion slots (slotted memory). This short list is arranged in order of desirability—and what is often necessity. System board memory is best, slotted memory the best to avoid.

System Board Memory is generally the fastest in any PC. It's connected directly to the microprocessor, if just through the necessary detour of some control logic. In most PCs, system board memory matches the width of the microprocessor input/output channel and it's generally the best match for microprocessor speed. It has the potential to be fastest because its signals need to travel the least. Because the system designer has complete control over the connection design, it can be crafted to minimize reactive effects that slow circuitry down and increase unwanted radiation.

Most PCs are designed to give a preference to system board memory. Most, in fact, require that you fill the system board memory sockets to capacity before you venture into the territory of other memory upgrades. Hardly a handicap, that's usually the best strategy. In other words, if the manufacturer of your PC provides you with empty sockets on the system board for memory expansion, fill them first.

Proprietary Memory Expansion uses special memory boards that are unique to each manufacturer, perhaps even to each PC, to add more RAM. These boards are proprietary for a good reason. They use exactly the same memory architecture as system board memory, matching the microprocessor in bus width, interconnection method, and as closely as possible in speed. Because there's no industry-wide agreed-on standard for memory architecture, computer makers are forced to go in their own directions.

The good news is that these boards match system board memory in performance. That means they are *fast*. The bad news is that, except for a few rare cases, the proprietary nature of these boards makes them obtainable only from the manufacturer (or vendor) of your PC. The exceptions are the products of the largest computer makers such as Compaq and IBM. These machines have achieved sufficient volume that some aftermarket companies have found it profitable to make and sell accessories for them.

The rule is simple in buying a proprietary memory board—get what fits from whoever sold you your PC. If boards are offered with different capacities for memory chips or modules (not installed chips, but the number of sockets into which memory can be installed), it's best to opt for those with the higher capacity. Eventually you'll probably want as much memory as you can squeeze into your PC. You might have to toss out a low-capacity board when you want to further increase your PC's memory endowment in the future.

In general, proprietary memory boards use standard memory chips and modules. When the boards are available both with and without their full memory quotas, be sure to evaluate the price charged for the chips installed on the board. If the premium for buying memory from the computer manufacturer is negligible (some vendors actually charge little or no markup as a sign of goodwill), then you're probably best off buying the boards stuffed—complete with memory. However, some computer makers see memory boards as a profit center—even an exploitation center—and levy heavy premiums on preinstalled chips. In these cases, you'll get a better deal by buying the board without any chips installed—so called *0K RAM* boards—and installing your own memory on them.

Slotted Memory fits into your PC's standard expansion slots, the same slots that accommodate everything from hard disk adapters to game ports. Today, slotted memory boards are nearly commodity products. Boards will fit a wide variety of PCs without regard to concerns such as memory architecture.

In the original IBM design of the PC and XT, slotted memory was the prime—and only—expansion choice. The expansion buses of these machines were designed to match the performance of the system microprocessor. Adding memory to the expansion slot thus was no performance hardship. As microprocessor clock speeds increased, but the bus speed stayed nearly constant to accommodate old expansion boards, slotted memory became penalty memory. Every access to the bus meant a waiting period for the system microprocessor. The faster the microprocessor, the worse the idea of putting memory in expansion slots.

The slot penalty is minimal for PCs, XTs, and other machines of their class. In fact, putting memory in an expansion slot is the only option for many of these machines. For AT-class computers that operate at eight megahertz or less and many ten megahertz machines (including IBM's low-end PS/2s), slotted memory is equally as effective. At microprocessor speeds in excess of ten megahertz, however, the slots run more slowly than the microprocessor, and the wait states begin to add up. The higher the microprocessor clock speed, the longer the wait for slotted memory.

Sometimes, however, slotted memory cannot be avoided; for example, to expand an XT, to add EMS to a fast AT, or to go beyond the expansion limit of some system boards. In such situations, you'll have to follow a few rules to be sure that your memory board will be compatible with your PC.

First, ensure that the bus of the memory board matches the widest expansion bus available in your system. This bus-matching is important for two reasons. The widest possible bus ensures that memory transfers can be made as quickly as the expansion bus permits. With a wide-bus board although you may have to endure some wait states, you won't have to delay for unnecessary wait states. In addition, a wider bus gives the expansion board a wider potential address range. Boards designed for the eight-bit XT bus cannot be addressed outside the one-megabyte range of conventional memory because only 20 address lines are available on the narrow bus. Similarly, 16-bit memory boards designed for AT-style computers cannot range beyond the 16-megabyte addressing limit of the 24 address lines of the AT bus. Boards that use the 32-bit EISA bus have the full four-gigabyte 386 address range available to them, as do modern 32-bit Micro Channel boards. Some early 32-bit Micro Channel memory boards were, however, limited in their addressability to the 16-megabyte AT range.

Even though a board uses a wide bus, you have no guarantee that it takes advantage of the full range and flexibility of the bus's addressability limits. A memory board needs to be versatile enough to locate its memory anywhere in the available address range so that it can extend the contiguous memory of your PC. Most memory boards provide some method of indicating the starting address for the memory they hold, either through dip switch settings or nonvolatile latches set with a software configuration routine. Boards with adjustable capacity typically allow you to set the starting and ending addresses of the board. Be sure whatever slotted memory board you buy can locate its memory in the range you require.

Early PC, XT, and AT expansion boards usually included additional functions beyond mere memory so that you could add ports and possibly a clock (for PCs and XTs) while consuming a single expansion slot. As long as these extra features can be switched off or relocated—so you can avoid conflict with the ports already installed in your PC—there is no reason not to take advantage of such multifunction boards. In fact, they can be a good value. But don't pay extra for ports when you don't need them.

The trend today is to boards that offer memory alone— and lots of it. As with proprietary memory boards, the ultimate chip capacity is your primary concern. Be sure to get a board that will allow for as much expansion memory as you need today and for whatever more you'll need in the foreseeable future. Check the price per megabyte of already-installed memory and ensure that you can't do better by buying and installing the RAM chips yourself.

Slotted memory boards often give you the option of configuring the bytes they offer as extended or expanded RAM. The best boards are those that handle this selection through board hardware by assigning memory banks to one or another function. Other boards may offer a viable alternative in RAM that's configured only as extended memory but includes an expanded memory emulator as standard equipment. A few boards come with their entire capacity predesignated as expanded memory and use an extended memory emulator for setting up your PC with a greater endowment of extended memory. Simulating extended memory with expanded should be viewed as a convenience feature only because extended memory emulation causes performance to suffer dramatically. Avoid boards that only emulate extended memory unless you're sure you'll only need expanded memory to satisfy the needs of your present and future applications.

Selecting Memory Chips and Modules

Once you know where you want to add expansion memory, you need to consider how to fit the memory in. If you've opted for a proprietary or slotted memory board that's already stuffed, your decision is already made. But if you've opted for a bare board with

0K of RAM or to add chips directly to your system board, the tough work begins—finding the right chips. Four factors separate the available types of memory chips: capacity, packaging, technology, and speed. You've got to make the right match for each of the four, otherwise your chip investment will be wasted.

Packaging

How a memory chip physically installs inside your PC or on its board and how it interconnects with your system's electrical circuitry is determined by its packaging. Two basic package styles are widely used in today's PCs: loose chips and memory modules.

Loose chips are simply integrated circuits, the small wafers of silicon that actually remember the data you want to store. Each loose chip has a separate package, usually a shell of black epoxy plastic with a number of silver-colored leg-like leads extending away from it.

The arrangement of these leads gives each of the individual chip package types its name. The most common chips have two parallel rows of leads arranged so that the wide flat surface of the chip lies parallel to the circuit board they plug into. These are called *DIPs*, for *Dual In-line Package*. Some chips have a single row of pins or leads, earning them the name *Single In-line Package* or *SIP*, and install perpendicular to their host circuit board. A third variant has two rows of leads, like a DIP, but put them on an edge like SIP, and arranges the leads so that the two rows are offset from one another. This zig-zag pattern of pins gives its name to the package, the *Zig-zag In-line Package* or *ZIP*. (See Figure 6.1)

Although the chips with the same package style may look similar, there can be some not-so-subtle differences between them. For example, the number of leads (pins or legs) that sprout out of the chip. DIP circuits, for example, have anywhere from 6 to 80 leads. Memory chips typically have from 14 to 20 leads.

The most important consideration with chip packaging is that the chips you buy physically fit inside the sockets in your computer. A chip with too many leads just won't work in a smaller socket. Some systems, however, give you the option of chips for their sockets—allowing you to put smaller 16-pin chips in 20-pin sockets. In such situations, it's important to be sure you put the chips in the correct end of the socket.

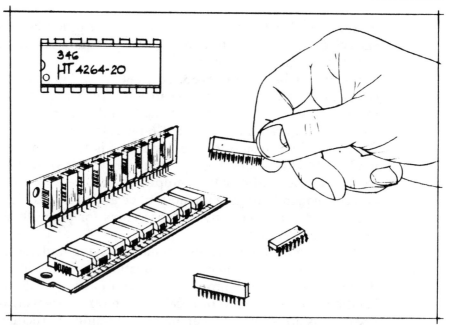

Figure 6.1 Memory comes in a variety of packages. Clockwise from the upper left: a DIP chip; a ZIP chip (between fingers); another DIP, a SIP; a SIMM; and a SIPP.

Before you order chips, check what package you need and how many leads there are per chip. The manual accompanying your PC or system board should describe the type of memory used. If not, you'll have to take a look inside your PC.

Chips are traditionally rated by the number of bits of data they can store. For instance, a 256-kilobit memory chip stores about 256 thousand bits of data or about 32 thousand bytes. In most computer designs, each byte of memory is stored in several memory chips that are connected in parallel. That is, the byte is divided into its constituent eight bits, and each bit is stored at the same address in a separate memory chip. Consequently, the smallest practical increment of memory expansion involves eight chips, oftentimes called an eight-bit bank of memory.

Most personal computers add a ninth chip to each bank for parity-checking. That is, the ninth chip provides a means for verifying that the data coded by the other eight is correct and has not changed since it was originally stored. Hence, chips are generally added to PCs in one or more groups of nine. (Some laptops, very inexpensive desktop computers, and many Apple Macintosh models lack this parity-checking facility. They require you to add memory chips in groups of eight.)

Today's high-powered 8086, 286, 386, and 486 require an even larger increment of memory expansion. The 8086, 286, and 386SX microprocessors normally move data to and from memory 16 bits at a time. (They are said to have a "16-bit data path.") Consequently, the minimal expansion for these systems is two eight-bit banks (a total of 18 chips—don't forget the parity chips) at a time. The 386DX, 486SX, and 486DX microprocessors use a 32-bit data path and consequently require memory to be added in 36-chip banks. In other words, if you're buying loose chips for your 386 PC, you'll need to get 36 at a time.

Dealing with all those chips can make playing roulette seem like a sure thing—potential memory installation problems increase each time you push a chip into a socket—you have a greater chance of bending a lead of a chip or breaking one off. Moreover, the memory-expansion effort can get time-consuming, particularly when you have more chips to install than patience. And the space required for chips can become outrageous. Putting a few megabytes of loose chips on a system board can take a quarter or more of the available board surface.

One result of these problems is that most manufacturers of higher-powered computers use memory modules instead of individual chips. In general, a memory module is simply a small circuit board that holds nine (sometimes, though rarely, eight) discrete chips or their equivalent as one easy-to-plug-in assembly. To make contact with their sockets, modules use either edge-connectors similar to those on expansion boards or projecting pins like the leads of integrated circuits. By convention, a module of the former type is called a *SIMM* (for *Single In-line Memory Module*) and of the latter type a *SIPP* (for *Single In-line Pin Package*). While arguments can be made as to which is best (SIPPs can be soldered directly to circuit boards, SIMMs work better in sockets) the only important issue is that you get the correct package to match your computer.

Capacity

The amount of information a chip or memory module can store is its *capacity*. The capacity you need is easy to determine: Just get chips that store the number of bits (or bytes, in the case of memory modules) that your system uses. The basic choices are 64K, 256K, 1M, 4M, and, eventually, 16M chips. Your computer or memory board manual should tell you what size chips to use.

Note that today's 256K and one-megabit chips come in two different styles. In the most familiar arrangement, the entire capacity of the chip is addressed as a single bit-wide unit. Other chips internally divide the capacity of the chip into four independent banks. The former, single-bank chips can be more specifically described as 1×256 kilobit and 1×1 megabit chips, while the four-bank chips are describe as 4×64 kilobit and 4×256 kilobit. The four-bank chips are useful in some system designs that will be discussed below.

Some systems, particular those manufactured by IBM, use oddball chip sizes. For example, in some PS/2s you'll find 768K chips in hermetically sealed metal cases. These were actually designed to be one-megabyte chips, but didn't pass the necessary quality assurance tests—in each chip one 256K bank proved bad while the other three banks inside met or exceeded their design specifications. IBM made the best of an otherwise bad chip and packaged each slice of silicon with three good banks as a 768K RAM chip. (There's nothing wrong with the three remaining internal banks, so don't think you're getting a second-rate chip.) These chips are not available on the open market. They are used for standard system memory only—never for expansion memory.

Early ATs used another oddball memory size, 128K modules. These actually were double-decked 64K chips, soldered together to put 128K in a single DIP socket. In that ATs were sold without their full 640K system board quota, you may encounter a need for these two-story integrated circuits should you want to expand your AT's memory. Unfortunately, these are difficult to find, particularly at a favorable price. But many AT memory boards allow you to backfill your system's conventional memory area from the RAM chips on the board. Look for such a memory board if your AT uses 128K modules and you want to upgrade it.

In many clone computers you'll find a jumper or switch that will let you select between two or more chip types. Just make sure you match chip type to the settings. Note that chips of different capacities don't mix well within a memory bank—all chips in a memory bank must be the same size.

Of course, there is an exception to this rule. Some systems build a bank of memory from two 4 × 256K chips (for eight bits of data) and one 1 × 256K chip (one bit for parity). As with the IBM oddball memory choices, this arrangement is most often used solely for soldered-down standard-equipment memory while expansion memory banks take more normal, all-chips-the-same form.

Memory modules, too, are available in various sizes. Currently popular sizes include 256K, 1MB, 2MB, 4MB, and 8MB, with 16MB modules promised. Memory modules—SIMMs or SIPPs—are designed to store bytes rather than bits of data, and are rated in their byte capacity. Only one SIMM is needed for an eight-bit memory bank.

Advanced microprocessors may require 16- or 32-bit banks to optimally match their data connections. Rather than using wider memory modules, most such computers use multiple SIMMs to make wider banks. A 16-bit wide memory bus uses two modules; a 32-bit bus, four. As with loose chips, all memory modules within a given bank must be the same capacity. Many computers allow you to mix capacities of memory modules on a single memory board or on the system board, but even in these PCs each bank is made from modules that have the same capacity rating, while the different banks may vary in the module capacity they use.

SIMMs can offer wider data paths, however, and in some machines a single SIMM may make an entire memory bank. In these computers, you're often free to use whatever size module you want in whatever socket is available.

Some PCs will accommodate different memory module capacities. These may require you to set a jumper to indicate the correct capacity for the modules you use. Many newer machines can detect the size of memory modules that you've installed and automatically adjust themselves to match.

When upgrading the memory of any PC, the cardinal rule is to make sure that you match the capacity of chips you buy to the needs of your system. You should check the manual accompanying your PC or its system board to determine the variety of chips or memory modules that it uses, as well as whatever configuration steps may be required to match different capacities of chip and modules.

Technology

The manner in which a chip functions electrically is called its technology. Most memory chips are *dynamic random access memory* or *DRAM* chips. They are "dynamic" because they store data as electrical charges that slowly bleed off and must be periodically replenished or refreshed to maintain the accuracy of their contents.

With ordinary or "standard" DRAM chip designs, each chip requires a recovery period between successive read or write operations, possibly imposing a delay between repeated accesses of the chip. The time required for this recovery is called the access time of the chip, and it is the principal limit on memory speed.

To minimize the delays imposed in repeatedly accessing a memory chip, alternative memory chip designs have been created. *Page-mode memory* chips allow repeated accesses within a single block of memory on the chip—the block being called a *page*—to be made without imposing a recovery period. A similar chip, called *static-column RAM* chips allows repeated access within a column (another memory block arrangement) to be made without the recovery delays. Either kind of special DRAM chip can speed up the operation of the host computer by minimizing microprocessor wait states.

From an upgrade standpoint, the most important consideration with these DRAM chip designs is that they are not interchangeable with ordinary DRAM chips. If your computer calls for one of these technologies, be sure you get matching chips.

Other memory technologies that you might encounter in upgrading your PC include *Static RAM* or *SRAM* and *Video RAM* (also called *VRAM* or *dual-ported RAM*). You may also encounter the terms *PROM, EPROM* (or *EEPROM*), *Flash memory*, and *interleaved memory* when scouring ads. In general, you do not have to worry about these terms when upgrading your PC's main memory.

Static RAM represents an entirely different memory technology that stores data in the positions of electronic switches called flip-flops. SRAM chips do not require refreshing and can usually operate at higher speeds than DRAM. This kind of memory is rarely used in the main memory banks of PCs because it is more expensive. Then again, because of its speed, SRAM is the top choice for cache memory. SRAM and DRAM chips are not interchangeable.

Video RAM chips are a special case of DRAM chips that are designed with two ports or means of access. While data are being written to the chip from one port, they can be read from the other. This design has an important advantage in making display systems because it allow the screen image to be updated (writing to the chips) while the data in the chips are sent to the monitor screen (reading the chips). Again, VRAM chips are not interchangeable with standard DRAM chips.

ROM, PROM, and EPROM are all forms of Read-Only Memory, hence the suffix -ROM of each. By their very nature, they are not compatible with the working memory of your PC because they cannot be written to by your computer's normal memory-support electronics. ROM chips have their contents fixed inside them when they are made. PROM chips can be programmed at a later date (the "P" in the name stands for "Programmable"). EPROM chips can be reused, erased, and reprogrammed as needs arise. The "E" in the name stands for "Erasable." Erasing generally means shining bright ultraviolet light through a window in the top of the chip. EEPROM ("Electrically Erasable PROM") can be erased with electrical signals, although not the same ones used in writing to standard DRAM chips. ROM chips and RAM chips cannot be substituted for one another in an upgrade.

Flash ROM is a special kind of EEPROM that is designed for repeated erasing and reprogramming. While it can work much like random access memory, rather than pure read-only memory, Flash ROM chips require different kinds of signals for updating their contents than do RAM chips. As a result, you cannot substitute one for another.

Interleaved memory is not a kind of chip, but an arrangement of memory banks. By dividing the entire memory of a computer so that half of it is being refreshed while the other half is being used, a designer can trim the number of wait states imposed by the memory system. On the average, half of the memory in the computer will be ready for use at any time without waiting, having been refreshed during the previous memory access. As long as memory accesses alternate between the two divisions of memory, no waiting will be imposed. Statistically, this will happen half of the time, so waiting is cut in half. Some systems use a four-way interleave, splitting memory into four parts, which can statistically trim wait-states to one-quarter what would normally be required by a given speed of DRAM chip.

Memory interleaving can be important when you upgrade your PC. Although it won't influence the technology of the chips or modules that you need, it may determine their number. For a two-way interleave, you need twice as many banks as with noninterleaved memory—and the banks must be the same size. This need can put important restrictions on what upgrades are allowed in your PC. You may not be able to get away with adding just a megabyte each time you want to expand the memory of your system. For example, 386 computers that use two-way interleaving may require memory upgrades in increments of two megabytes using 256KB SIMMs and eight megabytes using 1MB SIMMs.

Many systems make memory interleaving optional. With an odd number of memory banks, they operate without interleaving. With an even number, they use interleaving. Consequently such machines deliver better performance when upgraded to an even number of banks. If you have such a PC, you'll want to be sure that when you're finished with your memory upgrade your system is equipped with a number of memory banks that puts memory interleaving to work.

Speed

All memory chips and memory modules are rated to operate at a given speed. The speed rating of a dynamic RAM chip or module indicates how long it needs to recover between successive operations. The speed rating describes the maximum rate at which the memory can reliably operate. Unlike microprocessor speeds, which are given in megahertz, however, memory ratings are in the reciprocal value, nanoseconds. The higher the megahertz of a chip, the lower the nanosecond rating of the memory it requires.

Typical ratings for dynamic memory are 60, 70, 80, 100, 120, 150, and 200 nanoseconds. Static RAM chips may be rated at 35 or 25 nanoseconds. Lower numbers indicate faster memory. In most cases, faster memory is more expensive. Sometimes, however, you may find an insignificant price difference between memory of different speed ratings. Choose the faster memory when you have the option.

The basic speed rules are simple. Memory chips must be able to operate at least as fast as your system requires them to. Faster chips will work in place of slower chips, but not the other way around.

Faster chips will not, however, make your computer run quicker—the speed at which memory operates is set by the host PC's internal clock and the number of wait states set by your system's circuitry. Faster chips have a higher speed potential, which will allow you to install them later in a quicker computer should you ever upgrade your system or system board. Moreover, with faster memory you may be able to cut the number of memory wait states imposed if your PC makes that option programmable.

If you are in doubt about what memory chip speed you require, simply look at the chips already installed in your PC. Memory chips are easy to locate because they are typically the only integrated circuits that occur in blocks of identical chips. Memory modules appear like small circuit boards projecting up from your system board. Both chips and memory modules will be marked with a speed rating as the last digit of the identifying number silkscreened on top. Note that for speeds of 100 nanoseconds or slower, the right-hand zero is usually not printed, so a chip ending with the suffix -12 is rated at 120 nanoseconds, while -80 indicates 80 nanoseconds.

Memory modules often have ratings stenciled on their circuit boards. If not, the speed ratings of the individual chips on the modules should be plainly readable. Most modules are rated at the same speed as their individual chip ratings.

Because computers vary in the number of memory wait states they impose, your PC's microprocessor clock speed is not a reliable indication of its memory speed. Two computers with identical microprocessors operating at identical speeds may require two different memory speeds. While a memory cache tends to isolate main memory from the speed needs of the host microprocessor, it does not eliminate speed concerns. Even cache-isolated memory must operate at a minimum speed, albeit one lower than if no cache were present.

In general, however, 4.77 MHz PCs and XTs will operate with 200 nanosecond memory. AT-class machines based on six-or eight-megahertz 286 microprocessors typically require 150 or 120 nanosecond memory. Quicker computers require quicker memory. Very generally, for example, 386 and 486 computers require 80 to 60 nanosecond memory—the fastest DRAM that's widely available.

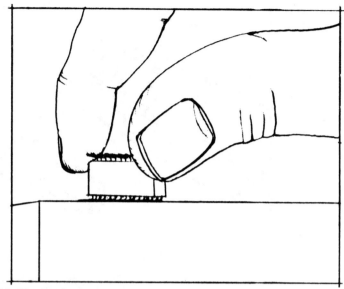

Figure 6.2 The leads on most DIP chips are spread too far apart when the chips are sold. Before you install the chips, bend the leads perpendicular to the body of the chip. Hold the chip by the ends between your fingers and press one side, then the other, against a flat, smooth surface to straighten the leads.

Chip and Memory Module Installation

The first steps in upgrading the memory of your PC is to determine what kind of memory you need, locate a supplier, and order it. If you outline exactly what kind of memory you need—package, speed, technology, and capacity—most suppliers can identify what chips to send you. Alternately, you can work from the chip designation, the numbers printed on the chip.

While you'd expect matching numbers to be the easiest way to locate memory chips, this simple process is complicated by every manufacturer using its own designations for its products. Memory chips with exactly the same characteristics and vital statistics will wear entirely different designations when offered by different companies.

The best you can do with chip designations is to use a list of chip equivalencies, or ask your vendor to check for you. Match the

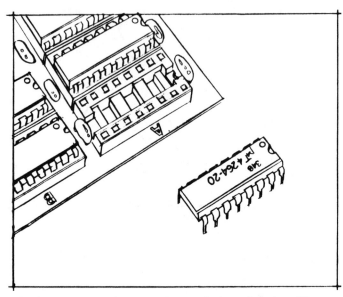

Figure 6.3 Assuring proper alignment is mandatory when installing memory chips. Insure that the pine-one end of each chip is aligned with the pin-one end of each socket. On chips, pin one is indicated by a circular depression adjacent to the pin and/or a motch in the end of the chip package. A notch indicates the corresponding end of the socket.

designation of the chips in your PC with one of those listed, and the chips in the same class should serve equivalently. You'll then have to make another match—with the brand or brands that each chip vendor you contact carries. No wonder most people order by package, capacity, speed, and technology, rather than designation.

After the new memory-enhancement accessories that you order are delivered, you have to install them. With boards that you buy with memory already in their sockets, that's easy—just plug them in. With loose chips you have to install yourself, either on your system board or on a memory board shipped with 0K installed, you have to do the chip-work yourself. And you have to be careful. Each chip must be properly prepared and aligned before you press it into place.

Preparing Chips

Most loose chips used for memory upgrades are packaged as DIPs. As with other DIP components, you may have to prepare the pins of each chip before you press it into its socket. DIPs are usually delivered with their leads spread slightly apart. Chip sockets are designed for leads that are aligned at perfect right angles with the chip case. You can cope with this spread in two ways.

The more difficult method of making chips fit is by pressuring each chip into its socket. Insert the leads on one side of the chip part way into one side of the socket. Then press the chip firmly toward that side until the lead on the other side of the chip can be pressed into the socket. If you've not inserted chips before, this method can be frustrating and dangerous, potentially resulting in broken leads. If you don't get the first side far enough into the socket, some of the leads will pop out. If you press the chip down, the errant lead will project out of the socket, and the chip won't work. If you press the chip too far down into the socket to begin with, you won't be able to fit the leads on the other side into the socket. Each bad bend of a lead increases the likelihood that it breaks off.

The alternate method of chip installation is to prepare each chip beforehand by properly bending its leads. You can do it the same way as with larger chips or use a tool to help in the bending. An ordinary pencil works well. Hold the two short ends of one chip between your finger and thumb with the leads on one side resting against a tabletop and the body of the chip perpendicular to the surface. Let the tips of the leads touch the surface while the body of the chip remains slightly above. Then press with the pencil on the leads on the other side until both sets of leads are parallel to the tabletop, and perpendicular to the body of the chip.

The best alternative in chip installation requires a chip insertion tool. The tool holds each chip securely without your needing to touch the chip leads (and risk static damage), bends the legs into the proper position, and gives you a longer reach to more easily press each chip home. If you have a tool, use it. If you plan to do a lot of upgrading with discrete memory chips, buy one.

Generally, SIP and ZIP chips need no preparation. Sometimes, however, the leads of these chips may be slightly bent when the chips are delivered. Rather than trying to work a chip with bent leads into a socket, it's a better idea to first ensure all the leads are properly aligned. You can do this by simply bending them back into alignment. Use long-nosed pliers to grip the flat width of the entire length of the lead. Squeezing the jaws of the pliers will flat-

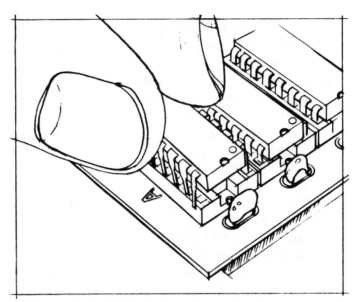

Figure 6.4 Place each chip lightly in its socket. Insure the notches in the ends of the chip and socket line up. Also make sure all of the leads of the chip fit properly in their matching socket holes. In particular, insure no leads bend over the edge of the socket (as shown here) or bend under the chip.

ten most leads straight. You can make more major adjustment by gently bending the lead into the proper position. Be careful, lest you break off a lead in trying to straighten it.

Which Sockets?

Just as all memory chips and modules are not created equal, neither are their sockets. Most computers assign addresses to memory chips and modules based upon the physical sockets in which they are placed. For memory to be contiguous, the memory modules and chips have to be installed in the sockets that are assigned the next highest addresses in the computer. In other words, which sockets you use can be important.

In most—but not all—cases a bank of memory chips on a system board or memory expansion board comprises a single row. The rows are numbered zero through whatever, and the instructions for your PC or board list in what order to fill the banks. As long as you fill all the banks needed for a certain memory level, it doesn't matter what order you put the chips into their sockets. Just make sure you have filled all of the banks required, be it zero through three or zero through eight. Note that some systems divide the banks into odd and even numbers to complicate things—the first bank may include what's numbered as Bank 0 and Bank 1 in the stenciling on the system board. The only sure-fire rule is to follow the instructions.

While memory modules eliminate the worries about rows of discrete chips, they still may require that you fill their sockets in a particular order, one that may not correspond to their numbering. Again, the only way to be certain is to check your instruction manual.

In only two cases do you not have to worry about which sockets you fill when you upgrade your system's memory—when you fill all the sockets and when you have a system smart enough to detect what kind of chips you've installed where. For example, IBM's PS/2 Models 90 and 95 allow you to plug any size or speed rating of memory module in any module socket, and the computer will configure itself to accept what you do. Of course, when you fill all the sockets, there are no holes left to interrupt the continuity of memory address assignments.

Chip Orientation

Chip manufacturers have added one more consideration to improve the odds that your upgrade will fail. The alignment of chips in their sockets is critical. Chips will fit in equally easily in either of two orientations. Pointed in one direction, the chips will work properly. Pointed in the other direction, they are likely to self-destruct the moment you switch on the power to your PC. Clearly, you'll want to be certain to ensure your chips are all oriented properly.

Fortunately, determining the proper orientation is easy. All you need to do is be careful, observant, and double-check your work. There's only one rule—pin one of each chip must go into the matching pin-one hole in each socket.

Two indications of pin one are used, either separately or together. Most of the time, pin one on the chip is marked by a small depression or dimple in the plastic on the top of the chip's package

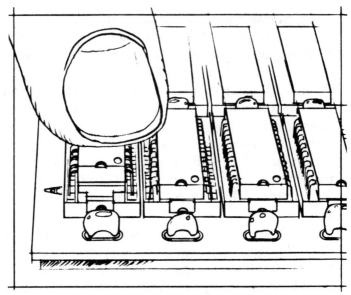

Figure 6.5 Once you're certain the chip is aligned properly and all leads are correctly started in their holes, press each chip into its socket with firm, even finger pressure.

adjacent to pin one. The pin-one end of the chip may also be indicated by a notch at the end of the chip package.

Chip sockets are usually marked for pin one by a notch at their ends. Sometimes, however, other indications are given. For example, a socket that's more of a skeleton with notch-like cutouts at each end may have pin one marked by a tiny notch near the pin-one hole. Other indications to look for are silkscreened numbers on the circuit board itself. On the bottom of the circuit board, pin one may be indicated by a different shape to the tab to which the socket pin in soldered. For example, 17 of the tabs on the opposite side of the circuit board beneath the chip socket may be roughly rectangular while pin one (which must be at one of the corners) will be elliptical. Or the bulk of the pin pads may be rounded while the pin-one tab may be square. The basic rule is that if a single solder tab is different from the rest, and is located on a corner it marks pin one.

The rule for proper chip installation is that you put the dimpled or notched end of the chip in the notched end of the socket. This assures that pin one will be in hole one.

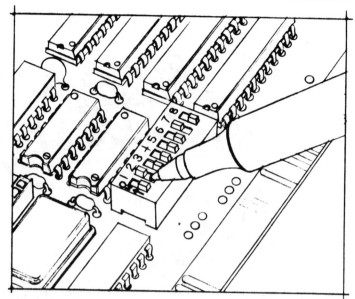

Figure 6.6 In first generation PCs, you'll need to indicate that you've added memory to the system by adjusting a DIP switch or jumper. More modern computers automatically adjust for any memory you've installed when you run the system setup program.

In general, all the chips in a bank of memory will be oriented in the same direction. If, when you double-check your work, you detect a chip or two that look different from the rest, check to be sure that they are oriented to match their sockets.

Plugging in Modules

Another of the advantages of memory modules is that you're prevented from installing them improperly and thereby destroying them, at least when you're dealing with SIMMs. A tab on each SIMM prevents it from being snapped into its socket backwards. SIPPs, alas, are like chips and can be improperly installed. You have to observe the markings on SIPPs and their sockets to be sure of installation success. Fortunately, few systems use SIPPs for memory expansion.

Installing a SIMM is easy once you know how—and pretty confusing until you learn how. Instead of being inserted into the socket at the angle at which it will finally rest, you slide a SIMM into its

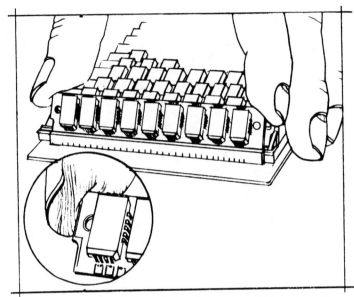

Figure 6.7 Hold SIMMs and SIPPs only by their edges. When installing a SIMM in a socket, first press the SIMM down nearly vertically into the socket. Note that a notch at one end of the SIMM (inset) will insure that the SIMM is correctly aligned.

socket at a different angle, often straight up and press down until it firmly engages the contacts at the bottom of the socket. Once you have the SIMM as far down in the socket as it will go—with both ends equally far down—you lean it back into place. A snap at either edge will then grab hold of the edges of the SIMM and lock the module into place.

At the two ends of each SIMM socket are posts that prevent it from being pressed further backwards. These posts indicate to you which way a SIMM is to face when you insert it. When a SIMM has memory chips solely on one side, the side with the chips faces forward, away from the posts. Sockets that hold SIMMs at an angle to the vertical always put the component side of single-sided SIMMs upward.

SIMMs with chips on two sides are trickier. Examine the SIMM and you'll see that one side has an extra bit of circuit board that acts as a keying tab. Examine the SIMM socket and you'll see a matching part of the socket into which the key fits.

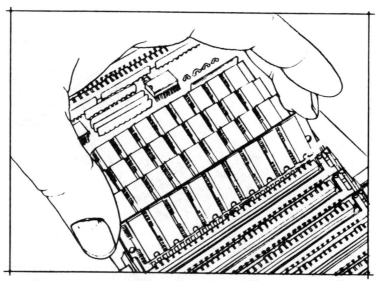

Figure 6.8 Once you've pressed the SIMM down against the contacts in its socket as far as it will go, press backward on the SIMM until it latches on the ends of the socket. Each end will definitely snap into place.

At either end of a SIMM socket you'll note the fail-safe scheme that ensures that you've got each SIMM properly in its socket. A plastic finger at either end of the socket is designed to snap into a hole in the SIMM. If the finger doesn't engage the hole, the SIMM isn't deep enough into its socket.

Also at each end of the socket is another finger that snaps over each of the two short edges of the SIMM to latch it in place. If you have to remove a SIMM or simply loosen it up to push it more firmly into place, you'll have to unlatch these fingers. Just push them outward one at a time until you can press the edge of the SIMM forward. Once you do one side, freeing the other side will loosen the whole SIMM for pressing deeper down or removing from its socket.

Determining the alignment of SIPPs is more problematic. The best guide is the numbering of pins. Both the pins of the SIPPs and the holes in its socket should be numbered, usually with nearby silkscreen identifications on the circuit board. In most PCs, all the SIPPs face the same direction, so you can use existing rows of SIPPs as your guides. In any case, you should double-check your work

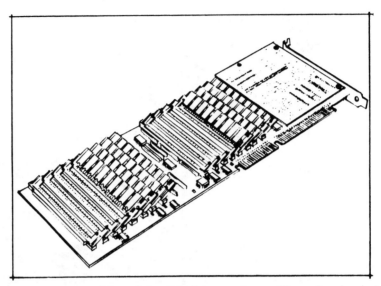

Figure 6.9 Be sure you fill each bank before starting to fill another bank. In 286 and 386SX machines, a bank requires two SIMMs; in 386DX and 486 machines, a bank requires four SIMMs. Check you manual to find out which banks need to be filled first.

even more carefully than when installing loose chips. After all, a mistake with a SIPP can potentially ruin nine or more chips in the same instant.

Inspect Your Work

A memory upgrade isn't finished when you'll slide all the necessary chips and SIMMs into place. Take a second look and assure yourself that simple mechanical errors won't mar your upgrade and prevent its operation.

The most important double-take to make is the check of chip (and SIPP) alignment. Remember, a mistake here can mean your hundreds-of-dollars investment in memory will soon be worthless silicon sand.

Another thing to check after you insert chips is to make sure that each of the pins of each chip fits exactly into its socket. After you push each chip in, make sure that none of its leads fold under the chip or slip outside of the socket. If a lead does, remove the chip from the socket, straighten the lead (squeezing it flat with long-

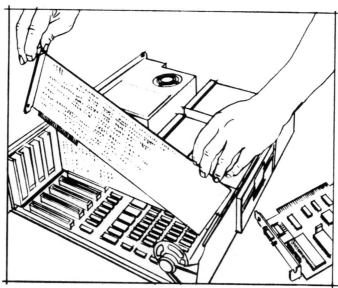

Figure 6.10 After you've added all the chips or SIMMs to an add-in memory board, adjust any DIP switches or jumpers on the board as required. Then install the board in a matching expension slot. Proprietary boards must, of course, be installed in the specially memory slots in your system.

nosed pliers is perhaps the best way), and carefully slide the chip back into the socket. Remember, an ounce of prevention is the best buy in the memory market today.

System Set-up

Once you've installed all the chips and boards, you have to tell your computer what you've done so that it can recognize its new memory. With early computers—PCs, XTs, and their clones—you'll have to set dip switches or jumpers. Because each model of computer has its own settings, you'll need to check in your PC's instruction manual. ATs and later computers will require that you run the set-up program that came with the machine, either on disk or stored in its memory.

As you relax, knowing that you've done a good job and successfully upgraded the RAM of your PC, you'll find that your work is hardly over. Soon you'll find that you need some new application that will require even more memory. And you'll be in for another round of memory upgrading.

7.

HARD DISK UPGRADES

With so many applications your hard disk determines overall system performance. In all systems, the disk determines your maximum on-line storage capacity. Upgrading your hard disk can give you more speed, the ability to handle more and larger files, and the satisfaction of building your PC into something better.

If the Duchess of Windsor had a PC, she'd probably have said that you can never have a hard disk that is too big or too fast, rather than quipping some nonsense about weight and wealth. The simple truth is this: No matter how large the hard disk that you bought with your PC, no matter how close to the top of the performance spectrum it rated when you bought it, if it's more than a few years old, it ranks near the top no more.

If your hard disk drive is no longer big or fast enough for you, you're in line for a hard disk upgrade. If your PC entirely lacks a hard disk, a hard disk of any sort is a mandatory upgrade. A personal computer without a hard disk is like a day spent without opening your eyes—the sunshine is there, but you're just not taking the rudimentary steps required to truly appreciate it. A hard disk will makes your PC faster, more powerful, and, above all, easier to use.

As with any PC upgrade, the hardest part about replacing a hard disk is matching the one perfect product to your PC and your own needs. The task can seem formidable because hard disks seem to have their own language that's a mixture of gibberish and alphabet soup. But once you sort through the verbiage, finding the best buy just means a little fingertip shopping. Order the drive and the easiest work is ahead of you—installing the disk in your computer.

The complicating factors are many—you need to determine the capacity of the disk you want to add to your PC. You have to determine what performance level you require—from the slowest, minimal disk to multiple drive systems that race along faster than a mere single disk can. You also need to consider issues that seem tangential, but actually govern many of your other choices: Which interface and interconnection architecture do you need? Do you need a hardware cache or similar technological speed-up? And how much of what you could possibly add to your PC can you actually afford? The decisions are not easy. Veering off in the wrong direction is easier than finding the right path—and almost inevitable if you don't know what you're doing or the basics about disk designs or options.

The Hard Disk as a System

Although most people discuss hard disks as if they were a single, well-defined thing, they are not. Hard disks must be considered as a system made from a number of inter related and interworking parts. Those constituents are spread throughout your PC. Part of the hard disk system is locked in your system's *BIOS*, either hard-coded as part of the ROM chips on your system board or as an add-in extension ROM carried on your system's hard disk controller (should the disk controller be an expansion board rather than being built into the system board circuitry). The drive mechanism is linked to your system through a connection called an *interface* where the signals of your PC and hard disk take a common, mutually understandable form. This interface may be related to a separate *disk controller*, which translates the demands of your PC for data into instructions that tell the hard disk how to operate, or those functions may be built into the disk itself as *integrated drive electronics*.

The hard disk itself is a multifaceted entity. The disk itself that gives the product its name is more properly called a *platter*, and it is simply a solid circle of aluminum or some other foundation material (to engineers, a *substrate*) that offers a rigid support that can serve as a carrier for a magnetic medium upon which a digital code can be stored. The substrate is inflexible, hence the name *hard* disk. It's designed to remain as flat as possible and never change its shape, unlike flexible or floppy disks that bend as the need arises.

Tiny areas of the medium on the surface of the platter called *magnetic domains*, are magnetized to store bits of digital code. The disk platter itself has no means of putting those bits in place nor can it do anything with those that are already present. For those operations to be usefully accomplished, the platter also requires the efforts of a reading and writing mechanism and a locating mechanism. Together with the electronics required to operate those additional parts, the complete unit makes up a hard disk drive.

Three separate electronic and mechanical functions are required in the operation of the hard disk drive. Signals must be amplified;

that is, the weak logic pulses in the computer must be strengthened up to a level that will change the magnetic medium during a write operation (putting information on the disk) and the tiny signals created in reading the stored magnetism must also be beefed up to the level necessary for the operation of digital circuitry. Second, a mechanism called a *head actuator* must be able to move the head at any point along the radius of the disk to pick out a particular magnetic domain for reading or writing. The third element is another mechanism that spins the disk, usually at a constantly and carefully controlled rate, so that the second dimension of the location of a magnetic domain—along the circumferance of a circle traced by the head actuator—can be pinpointed. This prime motivator is termed a *spindle motor*.

Differences in each of the constituent parts of a hard disk system affect the performance it can give to your system, as well as how and whether it can be connected to your PC at all.

In many cases you're in luck. You don't have to worry about all the details because you won't have any choice. Moreover, the manufacturer may simply not reveal some of the innermost secrets of its drive construction to you. And, for the most part, these details won't matter. For example, all hard disks spin at approximately the same rate, 3600 revolutions per minute, and most platters have aluminum substrates. Even if a disk manufacturer were to slow the spin of its drives to 3590 RPM and substitute a substrate of glass for the aluminum, the changes wouldn't affect how your PC uses the drive or how you connect the drive to your system.

Other changes are more meaningful for your upgrade. In particular, with older drives you'll need to know some of the intimate details of the internal geometry of the hard disk in order to match it to your PC. If you want to be at all successful in making your upgrade, you'll also be concerned with the specifics of the connection between your PC and the disk. After all, if you can't plug a hard disk into your PC, your upgrade won't stand much of a chance of success.

The most important connection consideration you need to investigate is the disk interface. As with crossing the street, you have to look both ways—at what your PC wants and what any prospective hard disk uses.

Interface Designs

By itself, a disk drive is a clever curiosity about as useful as a snowball paperweight—while a blizzard of activity inside may dazzle you, nothing can get out. Rather than a mass storage device, a disconnected hard disk would be nothing more than a curiosity, an unopenable time capsule holding a record of the long-forgotten past.

To be at all useful, a hard disk drive must somehow connect with your PC, to transfer information from its vast repository to the microprocessor. And to get the most value from that storage, the transfers should be as quick as possible so there's no waiting time.

But more than just a pathway for data, the hard disk requires other links to your computer. Without some means for telling the drive which bytes were wanted—how to move the head actuator, where to look on the disk during its round-and-round spin—the digital output of the hard disk drive would be a stream-of-unconsciousness flurry of random pulses. The disk drive thus requires control signals to tell it which bytes to discharge and where to store those sent to it.

Where these two groups of signals—the data and the control—link between the hard disk drive and its computer host is the *disk interface*. Its physical embodiment is a connector of some sort. That stands to reason since, if the drive and computer could not be detached, they would be one unit that wouldn't require an interface at all. The drive and computer could be one assembly, crafted together as a single piece.

Of course, were drives a permanent part of your PC, you wouldn't have any upgrade problems. Nor would you be able to upgrade your PC when you need to. Your system would be a unalterable, sealed box (which could be called a "laptop computer").

The existence of the disk interfaces is important because the connection scheme gives you a choice. But it also makes matching the drive to your PC critical. If the interface used by your PC and a hard disk don't match, no useful information can be passed between them. The mismatched situation would be like connecting your electric line to the tap on your sink—if you expect it to work, you may be shocked at the outcome.

Although there's always a connector somewhere between the hard disk and its PC host—if just for the computer manufacturer's convenience in putting everything together—electrically and logically the location of the disk interface varies. In some designs, the connection is made as close to the storage medium as possible. The data pulses read from the disk are passed directly to the computer host without any processing (except conditioning and buffering to bring them in line with accepted digital standards). The host is charged with creating the data format that will be written to the hard disk. Other interfaces put this processing power on the disk drive itself. The drive processes the data stream from its read/write head and presents the result to the system host in a more organized standard digital format.

In the former case, the signals appearing at the interface are a function of the device that generates and uses them; the signal arrangement is peculiar to that device. Consequently, this connection scheme is called a *device-level interface*. With the latter variety of connection, the signals are those normally used by the host system, so it is termed a *system-level interface*. The first of the two systems might also be distinguished as a low-level interface because of their intimate connection and the lower levels of sophistication of its signals, much as a hardware-specific language like an assembler is a lower-level language. Correspondingly, a system-level interface can also be termed a high-level interface.

To understand the differences between device-level and system-level connection schemes, you need to know a bit about how your PC processes data, how information is stored on disk, and how the two differ. PCs are essentially *parallel* devices. They process data in multiple-bit chunks called *bytes*, *words*, and *double-words*. Just as a byte is eight bits, a word is two bytes, and a double-word two words. Depending on its bus and register design, a microprocessor manipulates each one of these data formats in a single gulp and transfers it to and from memory; its expansion bus is a single unit using 8, 16, or 32 parallel connections.

Disk drives store information serially. They write a single, long stream of information as a pattern of flux changes in the magnetic medium of the disk. In addition to the actual data, formatting characters are embedded in this data stream so that the information can be properly located. Typically, lengthy strings of bits are grouped together into sectors (typically 512 bytes or 4096 bits long) that are preceded by another string of bits identifying the sector.

The read/write head of the disk drive scans the disk surface as the disk spins under it, reading a continuous string of bits. A special electronic circuit called a *data separator* sorts out the information inside the sectors from the sector identification information. Then another circuit translates the serial string of data into the parallel format that can be accepted by your PC.

In device-level disk interface design, the input and output of a disk drive is the raw stream of data to be written to or read from the disk. The data separation and format-changing functions are carried out in the *hard disk controller*, which is an expansion board separate from the hard disk drive itself. The rate at which information is moved between hard disk and hard disk controller is determined by the density of the flux changes on the disk and how quickly the disk spins. The combination of these two values yields the number that is usually quoted as the *data transfer rate* of a conventional hard disk. Note that this value overstates the amount of information that's actually transferred. The data stream includes both active data as well as the formatting information (about which your PC and programs could care less), and even some nonsense bits used for padding out the length of a disk track to allow for speed variations.

Besides the need for format conversion, the serial data connection between disk and controller also imposes a technological speed limit. The faster the data rate and higher the frequency of a connection, the more troublesome it is for the designer. Higher frequencies are more subject to noise and create more interference-causing radiation. To minimize these detrimental effects, high frequency connections must be kept short and be carefully designed. Limiting the frequency at the disk interface minimizes such problems, but also constrains the flow of information between a drive and its computer host.

The system-level interfaces move the data separator onto the disk drive itself. The drive can then deliver information to your computer system in the format it prefers—parallel—8, 16, even 32 bits at a time. Because the information is being moved out of the drive through a parallel connection, the actual operating frequency of the link can be lower for a given throughput. (With eight data paths, for example, information need only travel at one-eighth the speed to achieve the same throughput as a single serial connection.) Moreover, because the formatting information is sorted out in the data separator, this digital chaff need not waste the valuable bandwidth of the disk-to-PC connection.

Note that because the disk controller functions are part of a hard disk with a system-level interface, these drives do not have separate hard disk controllers. If they require a special expansion board to connect with your PC, this board is termed a *host adapter* because it merely translates signals rather than controlling the drive. Figure 7.1 illustrates the fundamental differences between the two interface types and their associated parts.

Device-level Interfaces

The first and still most common interfaces used by PCs are device-level. The primary reason for this choice relates back to the first hard disk drives in PCs. At the time IBM thought of endowing the XT with a hard disk, the only drive standard available was a device-level interface called *ST506*. Pragmatic considerations made this device-level connection necessary. The electronics required for signal processing would not have fit on the drive mechanism using the technology available at the time. Moreover, because a device-level interface is essentially system independent, this connection choice allowed drive makers to maximize their market. Because the drives didn't match any particular computer, they were equally adept (or not adept) at working with any computer. Since there was no truly dominant personal computer standard before the first PC, the use of a device-level interface broadened the market for a disk maker's products.

In fact, the design effort in connecting a hard disk to the small computers was originally backward from today's perspective. PCs—and their software in particular—were engineered to match hard disks. Consequently, PCs were tied tightly to device-level interfaces. Part of this heritage resulted in a system design in which some PC software takes direct control of the most intimate aspects of hard disk hardware. This software expects any hard disk drive (and its interface) to react in specific ways upon the software's command. For example, some software might itself examine the sector-formatting bits on the disk by prying into the circuits of the disk controller. (Old copy-protection schemes, for example, worked in

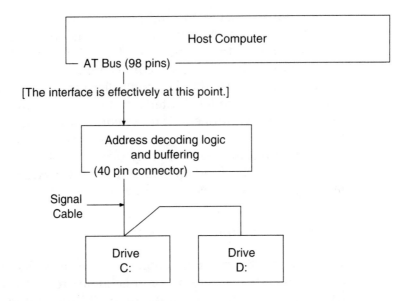

Device Interface (ST506 or ESDI in example):

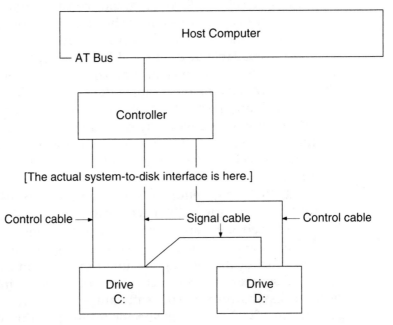

Figure 7.1 Design difference between device and system interfaces System interface (ATA Interface in this example):

this way.) DOS itself was designed to best process disk information when it is delivered in the form that a device-level interface packages it.

While the original ST506 disk interface was more than a match for the speed abilities of the IBM XT and about equal to the performance of the original AT, faster computers raced far ahead of its abilities to handle data. To cope with the demands for increased performance, the hard disk industry got together and created a better ST506 standard, which was called the *Enhanced Standard Device Interface* or *ESDI*.

As its name implies, ESDI was still a device-level interface, but was given greater performance reach and a host of standardized design improvements. These include new commands and special reserved areas on the disk itself for storing set-up parameters and bad track data. Whereas an ST506 connection was limited to a data transfer rate of five million bits per second, today's best ESDI hard disks can quadruple that.

ESDI's ancestry is easy to see. ESDI drives use the same wiring system as do ST506 drives—the same connectors, the same pair of cables, the same twist in the middle to distinguish the first from the second drive in the IBM system that you'll encounter if you choose to connect one of these drives to your system (see Figure 7.2.). But this ancestry does not follow through with compatibility. ESDI drives cannot be interchanged with ST506 hard disks. Although the cables match, the signals do not. Consequently, what may look like a simple upgrade—slide your slow old ST506 drive out and a quick new ESDI in—won't work. You'll need a new ESDI disk controller to match the new drive.

System-level Interfaces. Nearly simultaneous with the development of ESDI, disk companies began working on a new system-level interface, now known as the *Small Computer System Interface* or *SCSI*. This interface represented a complete rethinking of how peripherals should be attached to PCs. SCSI was designed to be more intelligent and more independent. For example, transfers can be made across a SCSI connection without the need for the host computer to control them. Because it is a higher-level interface, it permits the connection of not just hard disks, but almost any other device to a PC.

Figure 7.2 ST506 and ESDI hard disks use two cables in addition to a power connector. Each drive gets its own signal cable (narrow cable in illustration) and two drives daisy-chain to a control cable (the wide cable above). In the IBM scheme drive C: connects to the end of the control cable adjacent to the twist; drive D: attaches to the middle connector.

So far, the most intriguing aspect of SCSI from a hard disk user's perspective is its performance. It has the potential to outrun both ST506 and ESDI, and a new revised version of SCSI—*SCSI 2*—far exceeds the performance of existing drive mechanisms. For the most part, the higher speed of SCSI remains but a promise, however. Current SCSI systems are limited by the mechanical designs of their hard disks and the throughput available on expansion buses, rather than the interface standard.

But SCSI falls short of being the dream interface for PCs. Its undoing is its very advantage. PCs weren't designed for hard disks with system-level interfaces. The first symptom of this problem was the performance hit taken by early SCSI implementations. Because data formats had to be translated in going from PC to SCSI, the data transfer rate was substantially slowed, so that a few years ago SCSI ran a poor second to ESDI when it came to throughput. Since then, SCSI has been better matched to PCs.

But SCSI systems are still plagued by another problem: *compatibility*. Some SCSI systems won't work with some PCs. Worse yet, some SCSI products won't work with other SCSI products.

The problem is that much of the original SCSI design was optional. Manufacturers could choose to implement just a few, many, or all of its features. Consequently, one SCSI product might have expected something that a second device is incapable of delivering because its manufacturer decided that particular feature wasn't necessary. This problem arises when you want to connect SCSI hard disks to a single-host adapter or even if you want to play the mix-and-match game yourself and connect a drive from one manufacturer with a host adapter from another. In theory, you can connect up to seven SCSI devices to a single SCSI host adapter. In practice, this probably won't work because of the SCSI options policy.

In other words, if you plan to mix and match devices, SCSI can be a big headache. On the other hand, a matched SCSI system can rival the performance of any PC disk interface and will usually present few installation problems. The bottom line is that you need not fear SCSI drives—just plan to buy a SCSI hard disk and its host adapter either as a matched pair or with an explicit assurance that the drive will work with the host adapter you plan to use.

A fourth interface standard that's commonly called *Integrated Drive Electronics* or *IDE* promises to take over the link between new hard disks and PC designs. IDE combines higher speed with a design that's optimized to match with PCs that follow the IBM standard, building in the compatibility that's necessary for software that wants to take direct hardware control. Because it uses a parallel data connection, IDE holds the potential of moving data as fast as the expansion bus in your PC can accept them, although (as with SCSI) current drives don't reach those rates.

IDE is actually a generalized term that refers to several different interfaces. Most often it refers to an interface that's more correctly termed the *AT Attachment* because it uses a modification of the classic AT expansion bus as its connection point. Another IDE design is based on Micro Channel Architecture. Strictly speaking, SCSI hard disks are also IDE.

IDE drives that use the AT Attachment design are able to transfer data 8 or 16 bits at a time, depending on how they are engineered and what your PC will accept. Even some 32-bit computers provide only 8-bit connections for AT Attachment drives.

Hard disks that use the AT Attachment interface are designed to operate at the normal speed of your PC's expansion bus—nominally eight megahertz—using normal data transfer methods (which take two bus cycles to move a word of data). As a result, the speed limit imposed by the interface is about eight megabytes per second (16-bits divided by 8-bits-per-byte times 8 megahertz divided by the 2 cycles per transfer). The mathematical limit of the standard ST506 interface is five megahertz or 0.625 megabytes per second, although the actual throughput is actually lower once the time wasted on sector identification information is taken into account. ESDI, the improved ST506 interface, currently is limited to 20 megahertz—that's only 2.5 megabytes per second—of raw data transfers, as is SCSI. Clearly, the AT Attachment hold the most promise for future performance.

It currently doesn't deliver anywhere near that performance level because most AT Attachment drives use the same mechanical parts as their ESDI siblings. That is, they rotate at the same speed and pack data with the same density, with the result that they can achieve only the same data transfer rate. As AT Attachment technology matures, however, drives are being designed from the ground up to match the interface. With luck—and adequate development time—these drives will deliver on the performance promise of the interface.

As it stands now, performance is not a compelling reason to choose one hard disk interface over another, with the exception of primeval ST506, which you can safely ignore except when you need to match a vintage controller. Choose a drive that delivers the speed that you need, while making sure its interface matches your system (or that you can match it to your system).

Hard Disk Controllers and Host Adapters Issues

When you want to add a hard disk to your PC, one of the most important considerations is that you have something into which to plug the disk. With ST506 and ESDI drives, the place to plug in is the disk controller. With SCSI and AT Attachment (and other IDE) drives, you'll plug into a host adapter. In any case, you're dealing with more than a mere connector. Each of these links to your system has its own particular design features that you need to consider.

If you don't plan on upgrading to a drive that uses a different interface than the hard disk currently in your PC (for example, simply to increase the storage capacity of your system), your only controller concern is making the match. That is, the new drive must use the same interface as your existing controller. Once you've made the match, you should be able to plug the new drive in without altering the rest of your system.

If you plan to upgrade your controller along with your hard disk, however, you have more issues to think about, such as your system's floppy disk drives. For a brief period (from the introduction of the AT in 1984 to the introduction of the PS/2 series in 1987), IBM combined floppy and hard disk control functions on a single expansion board. Many compatible computer makers continue to do so today. If you plan on replacing the hard disk controller in such a PC, you'll need to get a controller or host adapter that also includes floppy disk circuitry or a separate floppy disk controller. Not all hard disk controllers have such circuitry built in, so you'll have to be careful when you shop.

You'll also want to match the expansion bus connection of the controller to your PC. If you have an old, 8-bit system, you'll want an 8-bit controller. Classic AT-bus computers should get 16-bit controllers. And EISA and Micro Channel computers need controllers and host adapters that match their advanced circuitry *if* you want to be assured of the best possible performance.

Caching controllers At the top of the line for most hard disk controller and host adapter manufacturers are the *caching controllers*. These are specialized devices that do more than just match a drive to your PC. In addition, they incorporate a large block of RAM, often megabytes, to make the connected hard disk drive appear faster.

A disk cache works like a memory cache. Information once read from your disk is stored in the cache so that if it is ever needed again, it can be retrieved at the fastest possible speed. Some caching systems actually make your hard disk read more data from your disk than your computer wants, anticipating that your PC and its programs will want what comes next on the disk.

In many systems, a software cache can be as effective—often even faster—than a hardware caching controller. Hardware and software caches rate are about equal, when equipped with the same amount of memory, in reducing the average access time of a hard disk system. More memory—megabytes of it—will make either form of cache quicker. The bigger the cache, the more likely disk-based data can be duplicated in the cache. (If a cache were as large as your hard disk, all of the disk's data would be in RAM and there would never be a miss!) Typical hardware-based disk controller caches range from one hard disk track, about 8K for ST506 disks, 17K for most ESDI disks, to multiple megabytes. More is better but, of course, more costly, too.

Software caches earn an edge because once you buy the caching program (at about $100 retail), memory is the only additional expense. At today's $50 per megabyte prices, you can build a huge software cache for the price of an entry-level hardware-based cache.

Buying a caching controller is much the same as with any other disk controller. You need to match the interface used by the controller with that of the hard disk you want to use—ST506, ESDI, IDE (AT Attachment), or SCSI. Be careful, however. You need to check what utility software you use in conjunction with a caching controller. Some hard disk utilities are not compatible with some caching controllers. The utility tries to take direct control of the hard disk drive itself, but the elaborate circuitry of the controller stands in its way, frustrating and confusing its efforts.

A caching controller delivers the biggest benefits to computers that use advanced 32-bit expansion buses—EISA and Micro Channel machines—although it can make a noticeable improvement in response to almost any computer. They work best in applications that require the repeated use of the same disk-based information, for example, compiling programs.

Caching controllers are for people who want the ultimate in disk performance—and are prepared to pay a premium price for it. Both software and hardware caches hold the potential of quickening not just how fast data can be found on your hard disk, but also how fast a block of data can be read into your PC. Data that are stored in a disk cache can be transferred at RAM speed instead of depending on the read/write head to skitter across the disk to find each byte then slowly read blocks of data from the disk. The performance improvement on a cache hit could range from a factor of five to twenty.

In transferring information, the software cache gets a speed edge in most PCs because it buffers your system's expansion bus as well as the hard disk. In 32-bit systems that use 16-bit expansion buses (as do all ISA computers, ATs, and 386-based PCs with AT-style expansion buses), the software cache helps avoid the narrow-bus bottleneck. On the other hand, disk controllers with built-in hardware caches take the lead in PCs with full 32-bit buses (such as machines based on the EISA and Micro Channel expansion buses) if the controllers use bus-mastering. Bus-mastering relieves the system microprocessor from much of the disk overhead, potentially accelerating data transfers.

Beyond these common concerns for all disk interfaces, controllers and host adapters for each of the various disk interfaces add their own particular match-up and buying concerns. Each one of the popular hard disk interfaces raises its own particular issues that you must consider when searching out the best product with which to build your upgrade. The following is a look at the most important of these considerations for the different varieties of controller and host adapter:

ST506 Controllers For most people, the old ST506 interface is something to upgrade from and not to. But there are still some compelling reasons to consider ST506 systems and their controllers. First is the goodbye syndrome. Because ST506 technology is waving farewell, there are some intriguingly good buys available in the marketplace. Pore through the advertising ghetto in the backs of magazines, and you'll find a wonderland of aging, near and past obsolete products at prices that make yesterday's technologies finally make sense. If you're not mesmerized by performance numbers and are looking for nothing more than good, safe storage— yeoman class—ST506 certainly deserves consideration.

There's another reason to consider the mother of all interfaces—it may be exactly what your PC wants. If you have an older AT-class computer that already has a hard disk controller (for example, you want to upgrade to a bigger drive or add a second drive to your system for more capacity), you will likely need to buy an ST506 drive to match the controller. Certainly you can upgrade the controller at the same time to advance to a newer interface, but then you'll have to put your old disk to pasture or struggle to try to make two unmatched controllers work in the same PC. It can be done, but you can pound nails into your head, too. Whether either is a good idea depends only on how much suffering you're willing to endure. Trying to get disk controllers to cohabitate is enough to make grown programmers weep. Besides, in an AT-class PC you don't stand much to gain from the higher transfer rates of newer interfaces. Buying into new technology will be paying for performance you cannot see.

Most ST506 hard disk controllers can handle two drives, and in most cases those drives can have different capacities. Some old ST506 controllers are an exception. For example, those in the original IBM XT will work only with ten megabyte hard disks. Others were designed for particular disk drive units and match only those. In such circumstances, a new drive may require a new controller.

Another worry is when you acquire a large ST506 drive that you want to add to your old, generally agreeable controller. Many vintage ST506 controllers don't understand hard disks that have more than 1024 cylinders or tracks. While that omission is understandable (the PC BIOS does not allow for more cylinders), it can mean wasted space on your hard disk. Cylinders capable of storing extra megabytes may be available on your hard disk, yet inaccessible to your controller. To get the full value from your purchase of a larger hard disk, you may need to buy a more up-to-date controller. That's not necessarily bad—you may gain some other benefits, such as caching at the same time—but you'll have to add the price of the controller to that of the hard disk to calculate the true cost of your upgrade.

RLL Controllers All ST506 controllers are not created equal. Hard disk drives that use device-level interfaces never look at the actual pattern of digital code that's being scribbled on their surfaces. The information-coding process is carried out by the controller. That means that the controller could use any pattern it wants to represent data. It could, for example, use 10110101 to signify a single bit of data. Certainly that code is inefficient, but the example does show the extent of freedom that a disk controller designer has.

The ST506 standard does not specify what code is to be used for storing data. In fact, a new generation of hard disk controllers have been designed to use a code that's more efficient, allowing more data to be packed on a given disk.

The standard form of data coding used by most ST506 disks is called *Modified Frequency Modulation*, or *MFM*, which specifies that data be transferred between the disk drive and its controller at a rate of five million bits per second—five megahertz. Each bit of data is coded as the presence or absence of a flux transition on the disk.

You don't need to know what MFM means. All that's important is that MFM is actually the *least* dense way that information is coded and stored on hard disks today. As a result, hard disk drives that use the ST506 interface and MFM data coding store less information in a given area and transfer data more slowly than any other current drive technology.

Many (but hardly all) ST506 drives can also use a more advanced form of data coding called 2,7 *Run Length Limited* coding, or *RLL* for short. This is a special modulation method that allows information to be packed 50 percent denser on the hard disk surface. Because 50 percent more data pass under the read/write head with every spin, RLL increases the peak data transfer rate of ST506 hard disk by 50 percent to 7.5 megahertz. It also increases the capacity of a given disk drive by 50 percent. An advanced form of RLL, cleverly termed *Advanced RLL (ARLL)* coding, puts 100 percent more data on a given disk.

To use RLL in your PC, you need an *RLL controller*, a hard disk controller specifically designed to use RLL. You can't just reprogram your ordinary controller to use RLL because the data coding is set by the actual controller hardware. Most disk controller makers now offer RLL controllers to match their MFM models. Note that an RLL controller that has both floppy and hard disk functions uses RLL only for the hard disk. If you used RLL for floppies (which you can't), you couldn't read distribution disks or exchange floppies you make with other people.

Although the data coding used by a system is determined by the disk controller (which actually does the translation), you must also be certain to get an RLL-certified disk to match the controller. RLL demands disks with wider-bandwidth electronics and better-quality magnetic media. Disks that are not RLL-certified may work initially with RLL controllers, but may gradually or catastrophically lose data. On the other hand, RLL-certified disks will work with ordinary MFM coding without a problem.

The issue of RLL also raises one caveat when shopping for hard disks. Some vendors list only the RLL capacity of RLL-certified drives. This is a misleading practice because it can distort the available storage you might expect to get if you don't hook the drive to an RLL controller. When ordering an ST506 hard disk, be sure to ask whether the drive is RLL-certified and whether the listed capacity is with MFM or RLL data coding.

Data coding is not a concern with other hard disk interfaces. The ESDI standard specifies the data coding to be used, so with an ESDI drive you don't have to worry about such mismatches. With system-level interfaces (IDE and SCSI) data coding is irrelevant because neither you nor your PC ever see the raw signals on the disk.

ESDI controllers The issues in selecting an ESDI controller are much the same as selecting one that uses the ST506 standard. Most ESDI controllers handle two drives. For the most part, ESDI controllers are insensitive to drive capacity. However, as with ST506, some early ESDI controllers were incapable of handling drives with more than 1024 cylinders. If you plan on upgrading to a larger drive, you'll want to be sure that the controller you choose can handle it.

While you don't have to worry about data coding with an ESDI hard disk, you do face another issue: matching the transfer rates of disk and the controller. Not all ESDI hard disks transfer information at the same speed. The first ESDI drives moved data at ten million bits per second. Later generations of equipment upped that speed to 15, then 20 megahertz. Your ESDI controller must be capable of operating at least as fast as your drive does if you want to get all the performance that you pay for. If you opt for a 15 MHz ESDI hard disk, you'll need a controller rated to transfer data at a speed of 15 MHz. or higher. A higher-speed controller—for example 20 MHz—will work, too, but it won't increase the transfer rate of the slower drive. If you do use a higher-speed controller with a slower EDSI drive, you certainly pay for performance that you don't need, but you'll also be hedging against the future should you later want to upgrade to a still faster hard disk.

The general rule is to match speed ratings of ESDI drives and controllers. Otherwise, the slower component will limit the maximum transfer rate of the entire system.

IDE Host Adapters Because the control electronics of IDE and SCSI hard disks are built into the drive mechanism itself, these devices do not need separate disk controller that you would have to plug into an expansion slot of your PC. But you can't plug one of these drives into a slot even if you could find a way to physically squeeze it in. Both IDE and SCSI drives still require you to use some kind of host adapter—either an expansion board or circuitry built into your PC's motherboard—to match them to your PC's expansion bus. Such a host adapter is often substantially less expensive than a true disk controller, although high-performance host adapters can demand a price premium.

One of the attractions of IDE is supposed to be that its most popular form (ATA) uses the AT expansion bus as its connection. That's not exactly true. IDE drives require signals somewhat different from those in your PC's slots. To make individual drives independent from the particular design of the computer that they are installed inside, IDE drives require that your PC send them commands through special registers.

The host adapter circuitry for IDE also requires address-decoding logic to match bus signals to the drive. Although this design adds to the complexity of the host adapter, it also allows the IDE drives to be more host independent. That is, the designer of a computer system can choose to locate the IDE system at any port or memory address without the drive needing to have an abundance of switches and jumpers to select alternate locations for compatibility reasons.

The actual data traveling to and from an IDE drive are, however, loaded directly onto the expansion bus of its host computer. This aspect of the IDE design makes the system an excellent match for most PCs. It does not work for Micro Channel machines because of the different bus design used by the IBM design, although an alternate form of IDE for such computers is being developed.

IDE also isolates your system from the data coding on the drive because no part of your PC ever sees the actual data stream going to the read/write head. IDE manufacturers are free to exploit novel technologies like run-length-limited recording and zone-bit recording to squeeze more information on each disk. But these special technologies are hidden from you, embedded in the drive itself. Exactly what technology the manufacturer uses in a particular drive is not an issue when you buy or connect the IDE drive. You only need to worry about the IDE interface itself. You don't have to mix and match drives and controllers as you would with ST506 drives that use RLL.

Under the AT Attachment IDE standard, up to two hard disks can be connected to a single host adapter. One drive is described as the master; the other, the slave. The names are merely terms of convenience. Ordinarily the master doesn't control the slave.

Today, all new drives that follow the AT Attachment standard can be interconnected in this master-slave relationship. But this co-operation does not hold true for all IDE hard disks. Early units were particular about any other drives that might be connected to them. Typically an IDE drive from one manufacturer would refuse to share a host adapter with a drive from a different manufacturer. Note that this is a characteristic of the drives and not the host adapter. All host adapters deliver essentially the same signals to one- or two-drive systems. Incompatibilities limiting expansion on the host adapter arise between the drives—the drive-to-drive connection—not in the host adapter-to-drive link.

If you are buying a second IDE drive for your PC, this lack of compatibility between older hard disks can be an important issue. About the only way to assure yourself a second drive will work with your existing drive is to duplicate what you already have. The next best choice is to get a second drive from the same manufacturer as your first. Not matching manufacturers when making an upgrade is extremely risky.

SCSI Host Adapters The job of a SCSI host adapter is much more complex because SCSI effectively functions as an expansion bus in its own right. Moreover, SCSI was not particularly tailored for PCs, but rather was designed as a universal interface, one that serves not only different computer architectures but also a variety of peripherals, from hard disks to scanners and operating systems. The SCSI host adapter must match the signals designed for its universal bus to the particular requirements of the PC bus and DOS. The required translation is more challenging than the work required of other controllers and host adapters because SCSI structures information in the form of blocks and DOS thinks in terms of clusters. Other interfaces work directly with DOS and clusters.

The translation abilities of the host adapter imposes a limit on transfer speed of SCSI systems. This limit can be either above or below the inherent speed limit imposed by the design of a SCSI hard disk. Consequently, the performance of a SCSI host adapter is as important as, or more than, the speed of the hard disk it is connected to. Early SCSI host adapters choked on the conversion process, and system throughput suffered. In the last few years, however, the efficiency of SCSI systems has improved immeasurably. When you shop for a SCSI host adapter, you want to look for newer products. Although old, laggardly host adapters may turn up occasionally, they can impose a drastic performance penalty on your SCSI hard disk and your PC.

Besides performance issues, your choice of SCSI host adapter will determine whether and how any hard disk you connect to it can boot your PC. Some host adapters have on-board BIOSs with boot capabilities (though this potential may be limited on one of the many devices attached to the SCSI adapter). Older SCSI host adapters often have no booting potentials. If you need to boot from a SCSI disk, you'll want to be sure the host adapter you buy has this capability.

The SCSI host adapter choice will also determine your flexibility in assigning device identifications and priorities to the peripherals you attach to it. Some host adapters require that your boot drive have a particular SCSI identification. Others will boot from any device connected to the SCSI host adapter. Although it's normally no trouble to assign a SCSI hard disk to the identification number that's predesigned to boot the host PC, the ability to easily change boot assignments can make your life easier (particularly if you have multiple hard disks set up with different operating systems).

The use of blocks, rather than clusters, as storage units in SCSI devices also has its benefits. It isolates your system from the details of disk data. Your PC simply doesn't care about the physical configuration of the disk or its data storage format. As with new IDE drives, drive manufacturers are free to use any exotic drive geometry and data coding they want. You simply don't have to worry about what's going on inside the drive.

One of the greatest promises of SCSI is its ability to serve as a high-speed, universal interface. Its design allows up to seven disparate devices to be connected to a single host adapter. Already SCSI-based CD ROM, magneto-optical rewriteable optical disks, tape drives, and scanners are available in addition to hard disks. Using

SCSI, even a computer with a limited number of expansion slots could accommodate more peripherals that would be prudent.

However, SCSI has not been refined to the point that any mixture of peripherals attached to a single host adapter will plug and play. Some SCSI devices get along about as well as a squad of five-year-olds equipped with a single candy bar. The SCSI standard is partly to blame, because in the past it has allowed manufacturers to select the features to implement. All SCSI devices did not support all SCSI features, and those that did might take their own direction in how to do it.

When you want to mix standard SCSI and SCSI-2 devices you can do it about as easily as mixing standard SCSI devices alone. That means you'll still have to rely on manufacturers and system integrators to assure that devices and host adapters will be compatible. In general, a SCSI-2 host adapter should have no problem handling standard SCSI devices.

SCSI-2 promises to unify the standard and make it more universal because it makes more SCSI design features a mandatory part of every host adapter and device. The reverse is not so assured. In the long run, that gives SCSI-2 great promise, particularly for your next host adapter choice. In the short term, however, don't expect the installation of a SCSI drive to be as easy as an IDE or ESDI hard disk, and don't get your hopes up that one SCSI host adapter will serve all the peripherals you want to connect.

Capacity Issues

Capacity and host adapter choice are often related issues in choosing a hard disk for an upgrade. Most of the time, you'll want to decide on host adapter first—or the decision is already made for you by the equipment that's inside your PC. You'll want to get a disk that matches the interface available. But if your goal is solely to add storage capacity to your system, it often pays to keep an open mind about the disk interface. You should be willing to change interfaces should you find a large drive with a particularly attractive cost per megabyte.

When capacity is your motivation for upgrading your hard disk, the proper place to begin is by considering how much hard disk you need. After all, if the primary reason you're making an upgrade is that your present drive is too small, you should have some idea of what size is adequate.

Odds are that if you had your druthers, you'd rather have the largest possible hard disk. Bigger certainly is better. Even when you plan for the future, supposedly spare disk space can disappear at a surprising rate. What once was a generous amount of disk space now can be niggardly indeed. Imagine trying to make do with the ten megabytes that were standard in an XT or the 20 IBM originally packed in an AT. Those capacities are becoming impossible to find today except as special-purpose products— removables, hard disk cards, and laptop drives. Today's top-selling hard disks average around 60 megabytes, and the most sought-after size soon will reach the the 100- to 150-megabyte range. And if you have a real need for hard disk storage space, you can find drives with 180, 330, even 1200 megabytes.

With capacity the primary trade-off is, as always, price. Larger drives cost more. But as capacities increase, the cost per megabyte of storage falls. If you're just counting bytes and not trying to match a budget, a drive with greater capacity is a better buy. It's also likely to be faster because the largest drives are top-of-the-line products on which manufacturers concentrate their development efforts.

Even if you disregard the huge prices demanded for the most capacious hard disks, there are two good reasons for not buying a huge hard disk. You might want the virtue of redundancy, the "don't put all your eggs in one hard disk" philosophy, and opt for a pair of smaller drives instead of one overwhelming disk. Or you might not have space in your PC for a gigabyte-size drive that requires a full-size disk bay.

Putting half a gigabyte of your most important data on a single hard disk is an invitation to disaster. If you keep regular backups, you might not lose everything with a head crash, but you'll still be out of action until you can get the disk repaired. Spread what you have across two disks and make your most important files redundant, and you'll be better able to weather such emergencies. In addition, the one drive that fails will cost less to repair or replace. (Many disk repair companies set their charges according to capacity rather than by time and materials.)

Going a step further, in a two-drive system you could use one drive to back up the other. This is now an accepted strategy in networking and deserves consideration even in single-user applications when your time is more valuable than the often-minimal expense of a second hard disk.

As the capacities of hard disks have increased, the drives themselves also have become physically smaller. Just a few years ago, the physical size of a disk drive determined how much it held and how much storage capacity you could stuff into your system. Today, however, the disk drive manufacturers have increased the density of data that can be written to a disk to the extent that $3\frac{1}{2}$-inch drives hold more than $5\frac{1}{4}$-inch units used to. Readily available $3\frac{1}{2}$-inch drives, which will fit in all but the smallest of laptop computers, can hold 600 megabytes—more than you'll want for anything but a high-powered workstation (at least today).

Drive Size and Form Factor

Matching the size of a drive to your PC can be more important than matching its capacity. After all, you can still work with a hard disk that's somewhat over (or under) the storage capacity you need. But if a drive is too large to fit inside your PC, connecting it may be more than troublesome.

Today, a large capacity hard disk can be small indeed. For example, IBM is planning a 1.2 gigabyte drive that neatly fits into a $3\frac{1}{2}$-inch form factor. Cost is another matter. Pint-size drives use newer technology and generally cost more per megabyte of storage than giant-size drives of the same capacity. Even when comparing $5\frac{1}{4}$-inch drives, you'll likely find that full-height units are less costly than half-height drives. Some of the 8-inch drives you'll find scattered in ads can offer you the lowest cost-per-megabyte of all.

If you've got the space for them, there's no performance or capacity reason to look askance at a king-size drives. Most were flagship products at the time when they were first introduced. Since then, the wind has blown out of their sails and buyers have turned their attention to the sleek modern products. They are priced as leftovers and close-outs. If you're willing to make allowances for square-rigged technology, however, you can still put them to work.

Moreover, some people believe that size correlates with reliability. Eight-inch and full-height $5\frac{1}{4}$-inch hard disks are held in high regard by these folks as being the battleships of mass storage, able to withstand anything short of a Congressional budget cut.

Don't be misled. Size does have a bearing on the reliability of hard disks—but in the opposite direction. The latest, tiny hard disks are built using the newest semiconductor technologies—surface mount components, application-specific integrated circuits (ASICs), and very large scale integration (VLSI)—which reduces the number of parts in the electronics of a hard disk to a handful instead of a bag full. The fewer components, the less there is to go wrong and the more reliable the drive can be.

In addition, a small drive has Newton on its side. Because all the parts of a tiny hard disk are tinier, they have less inertia when they move. They are less likely to rattle themselves to death as the drive operates. And the smaller, lighter-weight head is less apt to destroy the disk should it crash. Although the price per pound of a small disk is higher, it can be worth it.

Larger drives also consume more power. If the power supply in your PC is already stretched to the limit—and if you have an original IBM PC, it certainly is—an old-technology drive may demand more watts than your system can supply. The latest $\frac{1}{2}$-inch drives require so little power that you probably won't have to enhance even the 63.5-watt power supply of the original PC to add one in.

But there's another side to the power supply story. Paying more for a low-power hard disk can be false economy. A power supply upgrade costs far less than the price differential between an old-technology, power-hungry hard disk and the latest miserly model. You can upgrade your power supply, select an old-fashioned hard disk, and save a bundle.

If a big hard disk doesn't fit inside the chassis of your PC, matters are not quite so simple. While you can find external chassis in which to mount an expansion hard disk, making your own external drive system isn't easy. Most of today's hard disk controllers make no provision for external cables, so you'll have to rig your own way of getting control signals out of your PC. Worse, the cables themselves can be hard to get. While there are many ready sources of supply for internal hard disk cables, vendors of those for external hard disk drives are rare.

Laptop and notebook PCs make size constraints an insurmountable issue, but one that you don't have to worry about. Most laptop and notebook PCs are designed with proprietary hard disks (if they have hard disks at all). The only products that will match a particular make and model of laptop PC are those offered by the computer's maker. Most notebook PCs aren't even field-upgradable, so there's no reason to look in the aftermarket for new hard disks.

Hard Disk Cards As you balance your new hard disk in its drive bay with one hand, hold a mounting screw in place with another hand, and twist the screwdriver with your other hand, you might wish or hope for an easier way to upgrade the disk storage of your PC. The hard disk card is exactly what you should be looking for.

A hard disk card is a clever idea. It mates a miniature disk drive with the expansion board that's needed to control its operation and to adapt it to a PC slot. The entire assembly slides into an ordinary expansion slot like any other expansion board.

This system has several virtues. The hard disk card is easier to install—it plugs in as easily as any expansion board and doesn't require three hands and bloody knuckles to wrestle the drive and its cables into place. The hard disk card also saves a drive bay. If your computer doesn't have an extra bay for adding a new disk drive, the disk card still allows you to add up to 120 megabytes to your system's storage. Moreover, because the controller and disk drive is sold together as a single assembly, you don't have to worry about matching them. An engineer has already done that for you.

The thinnest, fastest, and best-integrated hard disk cards are made by Plus Development Corporation, and this situation is certain to continue because Plus has a patent on putting hard disks in a single expansion slot. The product embodying this technology is called the HardCard.

The original model of this product line was the first trendsetting disk that fit into an expansion slot. With each generation (Hard-Cards are currently on their third) the Plus drives have gained more capacity and speed. In regard to performance particularly, they are (within their capacity ranges) the equals of any drive that you can fit into a bay today.

The tradeoff for the convenience and bay-saving capacity of the HardCard line is the price. You'll generally pay more for such a slottable hard disk card than for a unit you install in a disk bay.

A number of companies have developed their own versions of hard disk card by matching $3\frac{1}{2}$-inch disk drives to short controller cards so that they, too, will fit into your system's expansion slots.

Although they lack the crafted-as-a-single-piece feel of a true Hard-Card, they can be effective, bay-saving storage add-ons for your system. However, these packages are two slots thick, robbing your PC of its valuable expansion room. On the other hand, these more generic hard disk cards are readily available and relatively inexpensive, typically costing little more than a drive and its associated controller or host adapter.

The same considerations apply to buying a hard disk card as apply to the purchase of any hard disk. You need to match the capacity and speed of the drive to your needs and budget. More importantly, you must have the right kind of space available inside your system to accommodate the drive. Some hard disk cards require 16-bit slots, some work in 8-bit slots. Some have particular requirements about which expansion slots they will fit in particular computer models.

Should you want to buy a hard disk card from a mail-order supplier, you'll want to describe exactly the slots in your system that you have available to accommodate it. Some hard disk cards are made to overflow slots behind the power supply in your system, others steal a bit of extra space from the left-hand side of the expansion area. Make sure it will fit before you waste your time and postage on a round-trip ticket for a peripheral not suited to your PC.

Hard Disk Arrays

When you shop for a new computer, a term you're sure to run into today is *drive array*. While hard disk manufacturers continue to improve the capacity and throughput of their products, the gains are modest, matters of refinement rather than breakthrough. Drive arrays, on the other hand, can deliver quantum improvement and do it immediately. However, drive arrays are currently so costly and pack so much capacity that you're unlikely to need one with a single-user system. But the technology is working its way into the mainstream, so you should make yourself familiar with it.

The premise of the drive array is elementary—combine a number of individual hard disks to create a massive virtual system. But a drive array is more than several hard disks connected to a single controller. In an array, the drives are coordinated, and the specially designed controller allocates information among them. The spin of each drive in the array is synchronized, and any single data byte may be spread among several physical hard disks.

The obvious benefit is capacity. Two disks can hold more than one, and four more than two. But drive array technology can also accelerate mass store performance and increase reliability. The secret to both of these innovations is the way the various hard disks in the drive array are combined. They are not arranged in a serial list where the second drive takes over once the capacity of the first is completely used up. Instead, every byte of data is split between drives. For example, in a four drive system, two bits of every byte might come from the first hard disk, the next two bits from the second drive, and so on. The four drives could then pour a single byte into the data stream four times faster—moving all the information in the byte would only take as long as it would for a single drive to move two bits.

Sacrificing part of the potential speed and capacity of the drive array can yield great reliability, even fault-tolerant systems. The key is redundancy. Instead of a straight division of the bits of each byte the array stores, the information split between the drives can overlap. For example, in the four drive system, instead of each drive getting two bits of each byte, each drive might store four. The first drive would take the first four bits of a given byte, the second drive the third, fourth, fifth, and sixth bits; the third, the fifth, sixth, seventh, and eighth; the fourth, the seventh, eighth, first, and second. The overlap allows the correct information to be pulled from another drive when one encounters an error. Better yet, if any single hard disk should fail, all of the data it stored could be reconstituted from the other drives.

This kind of system is said to be *fault-tolerant*. A single error or failure won't shut down the entire system. Fault-tolerant drive arrays are extremely valuable in network applications because the crash of a single hard disk will not bring down the network. A massive equipment failure thus becomes a bother, rather than a disaster.

The example array represents the most primitive of drive array implementations. Advanced information coding methods allow higher efficiencies in storage, so a strict duplication of every bit is not required. Moreover, advanced drive arrays even allow a failed drive to be replaced and the data that was stored upon it reconstructed without interrupting the normal operation of the array. A network server with such a drive array wouldn't have to be shut down even for disk repairs.

Just connecting four drives to an SCSI controller won't create a drive array. An array requires special electronics to handle the digital coding and control of the individual drives. The electronics of these systems are proprietary to their manufacturers. The array controller then connects to your PC through a proprietary or standard interface. SCSI is becoming the top choice for use with drive arrays.

Performance Issues

Getting more performance from your system is another reason to upgrade your hard disk. In some cases, a faster drive can make more of an improvement than adding a turbo board or other accelerator to your system. Better yet, the difference is one you can see and feel. A faster hard disk can make your PC more responsive. That is, when you press a key, your computer will react more quickly to your wishes—loading programs, listing directories, carrying out simple DOS commands with noticeably less hesitation.

For many people, speed is more than an issue of hard disk performance. It's also measures technical savvy, both on the part of the designer and manufacturer of equipment and on the part of the buyer. In these days in which technical breakthroughs strike like lightning, the newer, better whatevers—be they hard disks, display adapters, or entire PCs—are always faster. Moreover, the power elite of PC-dom sees buying anything other than the fastest products in its class as an admission of inferiority. By accepting a slower drive, you acknowledge that your time is not so valuable that you need the best performance. Or that you didn't know any better. Or that you just own second-rate equipment.

Actually, there's some truth to those contentions—but that doesn't mean that you absolutely require the fastest hard disk in all situations and inside every PC. Rather, the better strategy is to find one with performance that matches your needs—that is, you should not pay more for a hard disk drive that's faster but cannot benefit your system and the way you work with it. Don't buy performance that you won't see or can't use.

Access Time

The speed factor that determines the response of a hard disk is called its *average access time*, a self-explanatory name. This term refers to how long it takes the drive to find or access any given byte stored on the disk, on the average, usually expressed in milliseconds (ms), or thousandths of a second. For example, a disk with an average access time of 20 ms will be able to locate a given block of data in about 20 ms, with the actual time stretching from instantly to about 40 ms. The average access time is the speed you'll find listed in nearly every ad you can find in just about every computer magazine. A lower figure means a faster drive.

The average access time is more important than merely a measure of how snappy your disk will respond. It also determines how quickly the drive can perform when confronted with the need to gather together a lot of data that are dispersed across the disk, for example, sorting through a database.

In days gone by, computer power users worried over what kind of head actuator their disk drive used. The head actuator is the mechanism that moves the read/write head, and the speed of the read/write head determines the average access time. In today's hard disk market, you don't have to worry about such details. The speed of all head actuators has improved and, besides, when you're interested in performance it doesn't matter how the head gets where it's going as long as it gets there—and gets there fast. If a disk delivers a faster average access time, it will be more responsive no matter what technology it uses.

One good reason not to worry about head actuator technology is that there's not a lot of difference between better drive mechanisms any more. To get speed ratings down to the sub-28-millisecond levels expected in today's marketplace (as well as squeeze more data into a smaller drive), manufacturers have had to refine their mechanisms and choose the better technology—servo-controlled head actuators. Certainly there are differences of quality between mechanisms, but the average access speed that they deliver is one of the best indications you have of that quality.

Any hard disk with an average access time greater than 40 ms cannot be considered state of the art, and the dividing line is quickly slipping down to 28 ms. In fast 386- and 486-based PCs, you'll probably want one of the 15–16 millisecond wonder drives.

Knowing the average access speed of a hard disk alone isn't enough. You also need to be able to put that speed into perspective. You need to know how much speed you need, whether the extra $100 that buys you a 28 ms drive instead of a 40 ms drive is really worth it. The answer is that it depends—on what kind of PC you have, on what kind of controller you have, on what software strategies you are willing to adopt, and on what you expect.

Some guidelines can be drawn from the drives that IBM has offered with its products. For example, the hard disk of the original XT was rated at an average access time of 80 ms (and often delivered performance closer to 100 ms). The AT got a hard disk rated at 40 ms to match its 8 MHz. 286 microprocessor. The 386-based PS/2 Model 70 got a 28 ms drive, and the 486-based Model 90 got a 16 ms hard disk. If you match the microprocessor in your PC with a hard disk at the speed chosen by IBM you'll get performance that's somewhere between satisfactory and the minimum that's acceptable, depending on your personal impatience. On the other hand, a faster drive won't hurt anything if you don't mind paying for it.

That's not to say that you should never attach a slower drive to your 386. Because they are older and in less demand, slower drives are less expensive. That price advantage makes slow drives useful in many circumstances. For example, if you want to use a second hard drive as a backup system, a slower drive may be an excellent choice. And if you go through dollars faster than bytes, a slower drive may be the best you can afford—any hard disk drive is usually better than none.

Caching Concerns

If the disk controller in your PC or the one you intend to buy to match your new disk has a built-in cache, you should be better able to tolerate a slower drive. An effective hardware caching controller can accelerate disk access times to below one millisecond when the data your system needs are stored in the cache (that is, when the cache makes a hit), completely isolating you from the performance delays of the slower hard disk drive.

However, anyone opting to pay the price of a cached controller is probably looking for the best performance possible and probably has a flexible view of pricing. If you pay extra for a caching controller—prices range from $500 to $2,000—you might as well pay a little more for a quicker drive to match. It won't be wasted. Adding a faster drive to a cached controller can further improve system performance because the quicker drive will trim access times when the cache misses.

Data Transfer Rate

If you need to process information, finding a byte isn't enough. You also must be able to move it from disk storage into your computer's memory where it can be worked upon. Consequently, average access time in itself is only half of the speed story. Another measurement, the *data transfer rate*, tells the rest—how quickly a hard disk drive can move information into memory. Customarily, the data transfer rate of a hard disk drive is reported in megahertz: how many millions of bits can dash from disk to RAM in a second.

The data transfer rate that's most often quoted for a hard disk drive may be the most misleading figure in all of computerdom. The number that's universally published is the peak transfer rate, the fastest that information can possibly move if nothing stands in its way. The path is never so clear, however, and the actual transfer rate that a hard disk can achieve when moving real data rarely approaches even half the peak rate. Nevertheless, the peak data transfer rate is useful as a relative figure. A drive with a higher peak rate will likely operate faster than one with a low rate and will consequently be more desirable.

For most hard disk systems, the peak transfer rate is governed by two factors: how fast the disk spins and how tightly information is packed on the disk. The former is almost universal, about 3,600 revolutions per minute. Although the latter is somewhat flexible, standards have emerged, based on the interfaces—the connections—that link the drive to your computer.

Not all personal computers need the high transfer rate performance of one of the newer high-performance disk interfaces. Older, slower computers can't deal with the data supplied by a hard disk with a fast interface, so added performance would be wasted on them. In general, the ST506 interface is more than fast enough for computers based on the 8088 and 8086 microprocessors. These systems will benefit from the increased capacity won by using an RLL system, but won't gain appreciable speed from it. While PCs based on the 286 microprocessor will gain some speed from a faster interface, unless the microprocessor operates at high speed (from 12 to 16 megahertz) it probably won't gain enough performance to outweigh the higher cost of a fast ESDI or SCSI interface. Because the most common IDE interface is basically designed around the AT interface, IDE drives are a particularly good match for AT-like systems based on the 286, though some IDE drives handily outclass ATs. Both the 386 and 486 microprocessors are so fast that their capabilities are constrained by slower disk interfaces. An ESDI or SCSI disk drive will be the best match for a computer based on one of these microprocessors.

Hard Disk Reliability

Reliability means many things when referring to a hard disk drive. Most important, a reliable drive is one from which you can read your data whenever you want to. One that doesn't deliver data on demand doesn't belong in your PC—or any computer.

The gremlins, goblins, and glitches that can interfere with the smooth transfer of your data are many and arise from diverse causes. Some problems are purely electrical in nature. Something could go awry with the electronics of your drive, preventing it from processing data, garbling what is found, or fouling the operation of the mechanism by failing to issue the proper commands or making illogical demands. The mechanical parts of the drive can also break. The motor may stop spinning, a head can come loose, connectors can separate. And the media itself can suffer the ravages of time, simply by self-erasing or by becoming physically flaky. Worst of all, the various ills can combine to make a fatal malaise—an errant electrical command might cause a mechanical malfunction that crashes the hard disk drive's head into the media, furrowing it forever with read errors straight across the corporate database.

Looking at a drive might seem to tell little about its long-term prospects. But you can get a good idea from hefting a product in your hand and carefully examining it. Moreover, knowing a bit about the technology can lead you to products that are inherently more reliable.

The most general guideline to the reliability of a hard disk drive is the *MTBF* figure given in its specification sheet. This figure expresses the *mean time between failures* of the product. As formal and precise as the definition sounds, it is less than it seems. No drive is guaranteed to run trouble-free for the entire period given for its MTBF rating. After all, some of the MTBF figures are awe-inspiring—some rated up to 50,000 hours. That's nearly six years of continuous spinning, two decades of normal eight-hour weekday work.

Your first indication that something is amiss with the MTBF is the disk warranty. Although a given drive may last more than five years in worst-case continuous operation according to its MTBF, it's likely to be backed only by a one-year warranty. Such a manufacturer obviously doesn't put a lot of faith in MTBF, and neither should you.

As should be obvious, a MTBF is only a calculated value. After all, how can a manufacturer hang a five-year rating on a product that's been on the market only for a few weeks? To determine MTBF, the drive maker looks at each individual component that goes into making the drive, takes the published life expectancies of each one, and mathematically combines these values to achieve a number, the MTBF. In theory, this figure should be a reasonable representation of what you should expect from your hard disk drive. But there are so many variables that the MTBF figure does not take into account that it is no assurance that your drive will actually run into the next century without difficulty.

And yet the MTBF has some relevance because the factors going into it do influence drive life. For example, the fewer, more reliable parts a drive has, the higher the MTBF. It's almost tautological. The less there is to go wrong, the less likely something will go wrong.

Even if you're not privy to the manufacturer's specification sheet—it's rare for most end users to get their hands on the product literature of hard disk drive manufacturers—you can still see potential differences in reliability that parallel MTBF. A drive that is covered with printed circuit boards is likely to be less reliable than one that has a few square inches of circuitry. Compare a vintage drive, some of which have three boards arrayed around them, to a recent $3\frac{1}{2}$-inch product. You could count the chips on the new drive but could do little better than guess at the component count on the veteran unit.

Common sense can sometimes be misleading, however. For example, a big, hefty, sturdy drive would seem to be built for longer life than a flyweight laptop unit. But that's not necessarily the case.

Old drives had to be big because of the state of technology when they were designed. Storage densities limited miniaturization. Physically large drives required robust mechanisms to get anywhere near acceptable speed. Jerking a heavy head mechanism around requires powerful components. Feel an old full-height hard disk in operation. Some can make a whole PC hop around like Mexican jumping beans on a sizzling afternoon when they sort a database. You might expect something to rattle loose, and inevitably it will. Consequently, there's no particular reliability reason to favor a full-height drive over a half-height or a $5\frac{1}{4}$-inch drive over a $3\frac{1}{2}$-inch or smaller unit.

In the developing days of hard disks, there were several features that improved a product's long-term prospects that were worth looking for. Among these were hard, plated disk media instead of softer oxide-coated platters and an automatic park-and-lock mechanism that assured a drive wouldn't crash when you turned it off or moved it. If you're buying a drive with an older design through the mail-order channel, you'll want to check for these features. Newer drives almost universally make these features—or even better protections—standard equipment.

Although the potential for disk head crashes hasn't been eliminated, newer drives are much less likely to suffer from them. Miniaturization is a primary reason. To achieve the high data-densities needed for packing hundreds of megabytes into a laptop-size package, drive makers have been forced to use more exotic (at least from the past perspective) recording media. Instead of being coated with a compound consisting of magnetic particles and glue, they are vapor plated (a process sometimes called "sputtering") with a solid magnetic surface. These sputtered and plated magnetic surfaces are inevitably harder than more conventional, lower-density recording compounds. In addition, as the drive mechanism is reduced in size, its mass goes down, cutting the momentum of a crashing head and reducing its destructive force. And finally, enough people screamed and complained about disk disasters that drive makers had to listen. Park-and-lock style mechanisms in which the read/write heads automatically retract when the drive shuts down have become a standard feature of most hard disks. Unlike days gone by, no single disk model is particularly prone to head crashes any more.

There's one value that's more misleading than the MTBF number—*MTTR*, the *mean time to repair*. Typically, this figure is 15 to 30 minutes. Even at the $75 to $100 per hour computer service people charge, that would seem to make hard disk repairs amazingly affordable. Actually, however, the MTTR number is better read as *mean time to replace*—simply how long it takes to pull your old drive out and shove in a new one. To estimate the cost of fixing your PC after a disk failure, add the price of a new disk to the labor charge for pulling out your old drive and sliding in a new one.

Just to tie down the loose ends of this repair policy, consider what happens to disks after their demise and they've been replaced. A growing number of dead drives are eventually recycled, resulting in the proliferation of refurbished hard disks on the market. As with any product, there's little reason to look askance at a refurbished product when the refurbishing is done right. (Ever try to buy a new water pump or alternator for your car?) But if you don't know who's done the hard disk refurbishing or where the work was done, you *don't* want to buy the disk. It's easy to open up a hard disk, rattle and readjust the parts, blow out the debris, and screw it back together again. The drive will work like new, often for an amazingly short time.

Unless disk refurbishment is done in a clean room—a environmentally controlled chamber from which all dust and contamination has been eliminated—enough junk can settle out of the air to make a disk platter into a rotary sander. A clean room costs in the vicinity of a million dollars to set up. Little wonder few garage-based shops have them. In other words, buying a refurbished drive from a disreputable company is a lot like gaming in Las Vegas. In the long run, the odds assure that you will lose. If you're lucky, you'll only lose your initial investment.

Choosing a Vendor

When it comes to issues of reliability, you'll find it more profitable to consider *when* your hard disk fails, rather pondering the probabilities of *if*. Given enough time—and you'll want to use your hard disk drive as long as possible—something is going to go awry. So you need to concern yourself with what you can do when the inevitable sneaks up on you. You need to know who you can call for help, what kind of help you'll get under the warranty terms of your drive, and what to do when you discover that your warranty ran out long before your luck did.

Most hard disk makers require you to travel the dealer route, so when reliability is your concern, where you buy your disk is more an issue than how it is made. You should shop for a vendor as critically as you shop for the drive. Check the vendor's policies in regard to the big initial headaches—incompatibility with your system and dead-on-arrival drives. The vendor should allow you to return the failed product without delay or charge. After all, the freight company will pay the vendor for the damage it wreaks.

If you tell the dealer what kind of computer you intend to install the drive in (and what host adapter or controller you're going to use, if you don't buy one with the drive), the dealer is obligated to stand behind your success in getting it to work by law. The dealer telling you that a drive will work in a particular situation creates a *warranty of fitness* for particular purpose, which gives you certain rights under the terms of the Uniform Commercial Code. However, with an uncooperative company, enforcing those rights may be more trouble than a hard disk is worth, so it pays to find a company that will stand behind what it sells.

Although the hard disk manufacturer is not your first line of defense against failure, it may be your fallback position. Lowball hard disk vendors often have painfully brief lives, which means you can be left with no one to turn to when your hard disk crashes to a halt. If you worry about such possibilities, you'll want to choose a drive manufacturer who will offer some help. The quality and availability of manufacturer-based assistance varies widely, from complete toll-free telephone support to free-but-you-pay-for-the-call help to a feel-free-to-call-someone-else philosophy. Check what's offered before you commit to a particular manufacturer's product and you may save yourself a headache later.

Evaluating Costs

When it comes to twentieth century fiction, hard disk prices may win the Nobel prize. The hard disk prices you see in some advertisements may be only part of what you'll end up paying for a new drive for your PC. Remember, a working hard disk is a complete system, but disk vendors are prone to listing the price of only a single part of that system, the drive itself. To calculate the actual cost of upgrading your hard disk, you'll have to factor in the expense of the rest of the disk drive system.

Typically, a hard disk drive is sold simply as a mechanism, exactly as it is ushered down the production line and out of the factory. You get a box, unopened and uninspected throughout its journey from factory to your doorstep. Your get exactly what the factory packed inside—a hard disk drive. You won't see any of the amenities necessary for connecting the drive to your PC and making it work.

The first thing a raw drive needs is a method of connection. Put simply, you need cables. While some PCs come with the cables they need for connecting a hard disk, don't count on it. Before you order a disk, check to see what your PC offers.

If you are advancing to a new disk interface, the odds are you'll need new cables. The lack of extra cables built into your PC is a forgivable sin on the part of the maker of your computer. After all, the manufacturer has no way of knowing what obscure things you might plug in. But don't forgive a disk vendor who slights you on cables. He should know that you'll need cables, so he should include them in what he sells. If he doesn't, don't forget to figure cabling costs into the price of the raw drives that are advertised. While you can buy some cables for three or four dollars from some vendors, you might find them to be a ten dollar (or more) premium when you buy your disk. You'll want to take that into account when comparison shopping.

The cables have to connect to something. In general, that means a disk controller or host adapter. If you're simply adding a second drive of the same type to your PC, you might not need a new controller or host adapter. Move to a new interface or add a much larger drive, however, and you're likely to face another additional charge.

Many of today's latest PCs have built-in support for IDE hard disks. Older machines will require a host adapter board that may add $20–50 to the total cost of the system. Adding a second IDE hard disk is more problematic. The ability to connect a second drive depends on the hard disk drives themselves, not the host adapter. With first-generation IDE drives, you have no guarantee that two drives will work with one another, particularly if they are made by different manufacturers. Check IDE drive compatibility before you buy.

With SCSI, too, you'll also need a host adapter that should be factored into the purchase price. However, you'll probably want to acquire a matched adapter from the same source as the hard disk to assure yourself of compatibility. If your system already has an SCSI adapter, you might think you can get away without adding another (after all, a SCSI host adapter can handle seven devices). But each SCSI device you chain onto a host adapter increases the potential for incompatibilities to arise. Unless you choose a SCSI drive that matches one already attached to your SCSI host adapter, you may run into compatibility headaches. So you are likely to end up in the market for another host adapter (and one that will happily co-reside with the adapter you already have).

Software is also an issue when it comes to pricing hard disk drives. Depending on your PC and DOS version, you may absolutely need a hard disk preparation program for larger hard disks.

Many PCs do not have drive tables that support all available hard disks. That is, the drive parameters listed in the set-up programs for most PCs don't list all possible or available arrangements of heads and cylinders. If you acquire a drive that doesn't match parameters available in your system, you face two choices—either give up some capacity and opt for a listed value that's close but smaller, or use a proprietary program to match the drive to your PC.

The latter strategy offers two important benefits. It allows you to put more of the disk capacity for which you paid to work and it can allow greater flexibility in configuring your drive—you can partition the disk in a greater number of ways, even with multiple operating systems.

But straying from the officially sanctioned set-up procedure can lead to problems later on. In particular, proprietary set-up programs may be incompatible with some software, such as operating environments that try to take lower-level or direct control of your system's hardware. In addition, you may have to pay extra for the proprietary set-up software, another cost to factor in to the price of the new hard disk.

Of course, that price often buys you more than a way to exploit the full capacity of your hard disk. The proprietary set-up programs often include disk formatting, optimization, and diagnostic utilities as well. These side benefits by themselves may be worth the price of the set-up program.

Upgrade Method

Before you start to install a hard disk upgrade, you'll want to take three preparatory steps—backing up your old hard disk, reconfiguring your system's set-up memory, then finally removing your old hard disk from your computer.

Backing up is the most time-consuming part and, unless you have or can borrow a tape drive, will require a big stack of floppy disks. If you don't have any special backup software, use the DOS BACKUP program or, to play things safe, use XCOPY instead. If you want to really be safe, make two backup copies.

If you have an AT or more recent computer that is configured using a set-up program, you'll want to configure your system for your new hard disk *before* you remove your old hard disk. This will eliminate the lengthy wait and error message that inevitably pops up when you switch drives without telling your PC.

To configure your system, run its set-up program either from disk or by pressing the appropriate keys, whichever way your computer accesses its set-up utility.

If you are planning on using an automatic set-up program, such as On Track Computer System's Disk Manager or Storage Dimension's SpeedStor, check the program's instructions for the proper hard disk type for which to set your system. If you don't plan on using proprietary software, change the hard disk listed in the set-up to match the parameters of your new drive (or the one that most closely matches it without exceeding its capacity, head, or cylinder count) unless you are changing controllers. In the latter case, check to see what parameters the new controller requires. Some disk controllers—particularly SCSI systems—require you to set your system to think that it has *no* hard disks.

Once you save your new configuration, turn off your PC and disconnect all cables from it. This is a safety step that ensures that no stray electrical currents can get into your computer and harm its circuits (or you) during your installation. It will also give you greater freedom in installing your drive should you need to cant your system unit to get at a hidden screw—or should you need to turn your PC upside down and shake it to retrieve a screw that accidentally falls inside. (You'll only want to shake your computer after you've removed your old disk and before you've installed a new one. *Never* violently shake your computer when it has a hard disk inside it.)

Remove your hard disk by first unscrewing all the hardware that holds it in place. Even after the screws are out, the drive's cables will loosely hold the drive in place. You'll be able to shift the drive a bit, which will make disconnecting its cables easier.

If you're going to upgrade to a new hard disk that uses the same interface and controller as the old, only disconnect the cables from the drive itself. Leave them attached to the controller. If you're replacing both drive and controller, you can safely remove both ends of the cables.

Finally, remove the hard disk from your PC. You must also remove the old controller if you are going to replace it.

Mechanical Installation

The easiest part of upgrading your hard disk is physically installing the drive in your computer. All the work is mechanical, and what you have to do is obvious. You can put a screwdriver to work and almost put your mind on hold.

The most complex issue is determining the means by which your drive should be secured to your computer's chassis. This should become obvious when you remove your old hard disk.

A number of mounting schemes are used by various computer makers. The most straightforward is the direct mounting scheme used by the IBM XT and a wide number of compatible manufacturers. The drive is directly screwed into the disk bay using either of the sets of screw holes on the sides or bottom of $5\frac{1}{4}$-inch and $3\frac{1}{2}$-inch drives. Although some PCs use only two screws on one side of a drive to hold it in place, one-side mounting usually isn't very secure. The original 10-megabyte IBM XT, for example, hides a third screw that fits into the bottom of its hard disk. Don't overlook this screw when removing your old hard disk from your XT or when you install an upgrade.

IBM introduced a new, more secure mounting scheme in the AT, and many compatible manufacturers use the same scheme or a vari-

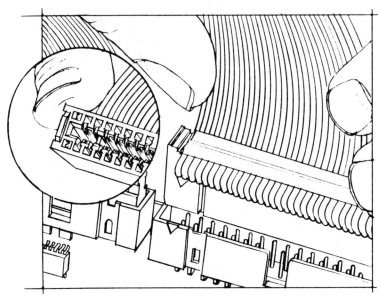

Figure 7.3 You can distinquish the drive end from controlled end of ST506 and ESDI cables by the connectors used. The drive end uses an edge connector (inset) that has a slot that runs its full length. The controller end will typically use a pin connector (main drawing) that has two rows of square holes that match the rows of square pins on the controller.

ation on it. In the AT, mounting rails are attached to the sides of the drive that allow you to slide it into place. The rails fit into guide slots that hold the drive assembly securely on both sides. Many hard disks come with AT mounting kits or with the rails already installed on the sides of the drive.

Some AT compatibles—notably Compaq Deskpros—use a similar mounting scheme with slightly wider rails that are incompatible with standard AT rails and the AT chassis. If you have one of these machines or a similar computer, you'll either have to recycle your old rails (remove them from your old drive and switch them to the new drive) or attempt to get new rails to match your computer, which can sometimes be a challenge.

Another variety of AT compatibles use drive-mounting rails that are narrower and, consequently, also incompatible with IBM rails. Most machines that use these narrow rails preinstall a set in each drive bay of the computer, even those without drives. In this case, you only need detach the rails from the chassis, screw them to your disk, and slide the disk into place.

Rails are held in the computer chassis in one of two ways. IBM-style systems use small brackets that push the rails to the end of their travel in the bay. Some compatibles make the brackets part of the drive rails. In either case, one screw holds each bracket in place. Just unscrew to slide the old drive out and screw the bracket back in to hold your drive upgrade in place.

Tower-style IBM PS/2's are the same width as those used in the AT, so AT rails will work in their internal $5\frac{1}{4}$-inch drive cages. To loosen a drive in one of these computers so that you can slide it out of the chassis, press down on each of the large blue daisy-like knobs above the drive and turn it counterclockwise with the palm of your hand until the drive can slide out.

Desktop PS/2s use plastic sleds to hold their $3\frac{1}{2}$-inch drives. The drive screws into the sled using the screw holes in its bottom, then the sled slides into place. A plastic tab at the end of the sled locks the whole assembly in place. To remove one of these drives, press down on the wide tab under and at the front of the drive, then slide the sled forward.

In most systems, you'll find it's easier to plug the cables into your new hard disk upgrade after you've put the drive near its final position, but not secured into place. For example, in ATs, slide the drive part way back into its bay, connect the cables, then slide the drive all the way back and screw the rail brackets into place.

If you need to install a new disk controller or host adapter, you can put it into an expansion slot before or after you installed your hard disk. The best slot to use is the one closest to the hard disk bay that has a connector that matches the one on the bottom of the controller.

For example, make sure that a 16-bit controller is installed in a 16-bit expansion slot. Similarly, 32-bit Micro Channel controllers should only be installed in 32-bit expansion slots. EISA controllers should only be installed in EISA expansion slots.

Cable Connections

The interface your hard disk upgrade uses will determine the number and kind of cables you'll have to connect. In most cases, you'll need to connect two or three cables to your upgraded hard disk.

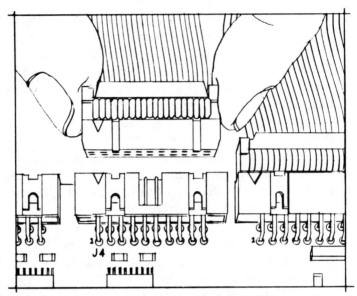

Figure 7.4 You'll have an easier time if you install all cables on the controller or host adapter for your disk drive *before* you slide the board into an expansion slot. In most cases, you'll find J4 on ST506 and ESDI controllers provides signals for the c: drive.

All drives will require a power connection, the white nylon modular connector at the end of the set of four wires (sometimes three) that emerge from your computer's power supply. You can't make a mistake plugging in this connector. Two of its corners are beveled so you cannot insert it improperly.

The only difficulty you may encounter with a drive power connector is the high effort that's sometimes required to push the connector into its jack. Try to put a finger or thumb under the jack when you push the connector in so you don't unduly stress the circuit board on the disk drive.

ST506 and ESDI hard disks require two additional cables—a wide, flat control cable and a narrow, flat data cable. In theory, the connectors on these cables are keyed to prevent you from attaching them improperly. A thin plastic tab inside the cable connector fits into a slot cut in the edge connector on the disk drive. On the controller end, one of the holes in the cable connector is usually plugged and the corresponding pin on the controller connector is missing.

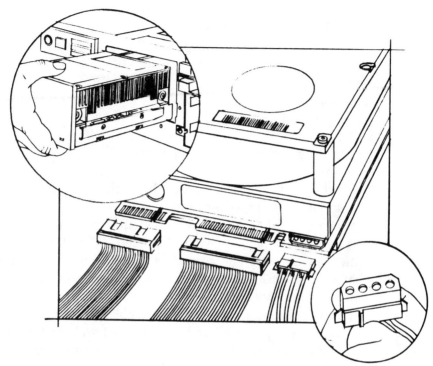

Figure 7.5 Slide your drive part-ways but not all the way into its bay. With the drive still loose plug in its cables. Be sure the red or blue stripe on ST506 and ESDI cables goes to the side of the drive edge connector closest to the notch in the connector. Power connectors (inset) have two beveled edges so you cannot insert them properly.

Sometimes the plastic key or the plug is absent from a connector. Although putting a connector in backwards shouldn't harm your new drive or its controller, it will prevent the drive from working—and give someone in technical support a migraine. You can avoid such mistakes by ensuring that the (usually red) stripe on the edge of each cable is on the same side as the slot in the edge connector on the drive. The stripe also corresponds to the side of the connector that mates with pin one on the connector on the controller. Pin one is usually marked with a silk-screened number.

Each ST506 or ESDI drive in a computer requires an independent data cable, run to a separate connector on the disk controller. When upgrading a drive, be sure you connect the data cable to the same connector as the old drive. In most cases, connect or J4 on the controller goes to the first disk drive in your computer (drive C:); connect J3 to the second drive (D:).

Control cables are daisy-chained. That is, a single cable attaches to the disk controller and has two additional connectors to accommodate two disk drives. In the IBM system, the first hard disk (C:) gets attached to the connector at the end of the cable (the one nearest the twisted section of the cable); the second drive (D:) attaches to the connector in the middle of the cable. If there are two twists in the cable on either side of a connector, that connector goes to the first drive.

For this system to work properly, each hard disk in your system should have its drive select jumpers or switches set to indicate that it is the *second* hard disk in your system. On most hard disks, you'll find a set of jumpers or switches labeled DS0 to DS3, DS1 to DS4, or something similar. The correct setting is the second in the series. That is, use DS1 when the labels start with DS0; DS2 when the counting starts with DS1.

IDE drives require only a single cable in addition to the power connector. Just plug one end into the system board or host adapter board and the other into the drive. If the connectors on the cable are not keyed, ensure that the (usually) red stripe on the cable is nearest pin one on the adapter and hard disk connectors.

In systems that accommodate two IDE drives, the two are daisy-chained together. Either drive can be connected to either cable connector—a switch on the drive determines whether it will operate as either the first or second hard disk. You'll have to refer to the drive's instruction manual to find the proper settings.

SCSI drives use a simple daisy-chain cable but add several complexities. Again, you must ensure the strip at the edge of the cable aligns with pin one on the drive or other device connector.

The first and last device in a SCSI chain must also be terminated. (The host adapter is usually considered the first device.) On most SCSI disk drives, you'll find a row of three terminating resistors packs. If the SCSI hard disk is not the last in the daisy-chain, remove all three of these resistor packs.

Each device in the SCSI chain must be assigned its own, unique SCSI identification number, zero through seven. The host adapter is usually seven. Some controllers require you to set the boot disk in your system to a particular value (usually zero). IBM, on the

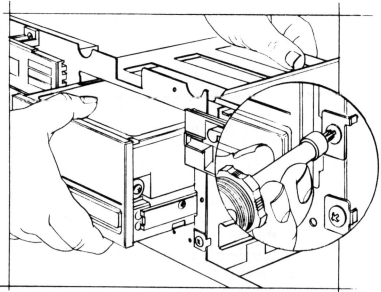

Figure 7.6 Once you have all the connectors plugged in slide the drive all the way back into its bay. You can then screw it into place. With AT-style systems, small metal brackets (insert) hold the drive rails in the bay.

other hand, sets its drive as device six. Check your disk drive manual to find out how to set its SCSI identification.

Software Set-up

Once your hard disk upgrade is physically installed, you face the challenge of software set-up. This process involves several steps—matching the new drive to your computer, low-level formatting the drive, partitioning the drive for DOS, DOS-formatting the drive, and, finally, restoring your file backups to it.

The easiest way to get through these steps is to use proprietary disk installation software mentioned earlier. One of these programs, which is often supplied with hard disks sold for upgrades, will automatically handle all the necessary installation steps except restoring your files to your new disk. Their step-by-step prompted menu systems need little explanation.

System Configuration

If you don't have automatic installation software, you should have configured your system to accept your new hard disk before you removed the old drive. If you did not, run your system's set-up procedure and make sure the hard disk parameters listed there match those the drive manufacturer lists for the model of hard disk you've installed or that your disk controller requires.

Many newer IDE drives now offer a feature called translation mode. Thanks to a microprocessor in the disk drive electronics, the drive can determine what configuration of hard disk your system expects and adjust itself to mimic that drive layout (within the limitations of the drive's capacity, of course). Your system is isolated from the actual layout of heads and cylinders on the drive and only sees the logical configuration the drive wants your PC to know about.

The isolation of the physical format of the drive from what your PC sees has another important implication. It allows the drive maker to use any geometry he pleases, free from the BIOS and DOS restrictions on disk architecture. For example, DOS doesn't understand disks with greater than 1024 cylinders. An IDE drive with excess cylinders could configure itself to logically look as if it had more heads and fewer cylinders.

Low-level Formatting

The next step is low-level formatting. This requires a special program, not the FORMAT utility that is part of DOS. Drive vendors usually will supply such a program if it is necessary—and if you ask for it. You don't need one if you have a PS/2, a compatible that includes a low-level formatting utility with DOS, or a controller with the procedure built in.

IBM's formatting program is hidden on the Reference Disk that's included with all PS/2 models. To access it, simply press the Ctrl-A two-key combination at the main set-up menu you see after you boot up from the Reference Disk.

The low-level formatting program included with DOS by IBM-compatible computer manufacturers is typically called LLFORMAT,

HDINIT, HDPREP, or some other obscure name. You'll have to consult your MS-DOS manual to find out the magic word.

Most new disk controllers include a low-level formatting utility as part of their ROM BIOS. Running these utilities is easy once you know the trick. First you must run the DOS DEBUG utility. Once DEBUG loads, you'll see a new prompt on the screen, a simple flashing hyphen. Typing G=C800:5 or G=C800:6 then pressing Enter will start the program with most popular disk controllers. (These numbers may be different if you have more than one disk controller in your PC. Check the controller instructions.)

Which of these two commands to use depends on the perversities of the controller manufacturer. You can be sure only by checking with the (often indecipherable) instructions accompanying the controller. Or you can try both commands. If you make the wrong choice the first time your system will likely crash, but you can reboot with no adverse effect and try the other choice.

If none of these low-level formatting options are available to you, you'll need to get a special program to accomplish the chore. Most disk diagnostics packages include the necessary utility along with their other performance-enhancing options. Gibson Research Spin-Rite and Golden Bow Systems Vopt and Vfeature are some of your choices.

Disk Partitioning

Partitioning is ordinarily handled by the DOS FDISK program. Different partitioning options are available under the various versions of DOS. You'll find it's a good idea to upgrade to a more recent version of DOS when you upgrade your hard disk so you can take advantage of the latest partitioning options.

In most cases, you'll want at least DOS Version 3.3, which will allow you to install multiple DOS partitions on your hard disk. With DOS 3.3 you'll have to divide any disk larger than 33 megabytes into at least two partitions. You'll also be limited to virtual drives no larger than 33 megabytes. DOS 4.01 will allow you to partition most drives as a single, large disk or to subdivide it into virtual drives of whatever size you like.

DOS Formatting

The final step in disk preparation is DOS formatting, which requires only running the DOS FORMAT program for each of the
virtual drives created by your upgrade hard disk. You'll want to
choose the /S option for the drive C: disk.

Restoring Files

Once your new hard disk is fully configured and formatted, you
can restore all the files from your old hard disk back to it. If you've
had some hardware experience, you can speed up this step by first
installing your new hard disk as a second drive without first removing the drive you want to replace. Use XCOPY with the /S option to
copy all the files from your old disk to the new. Then remove your
old disk from the system and reconfigure your new disk as the first
drive.

Not counting the waiting time—the ordeal of backing up, formatting, and restoring—you can probably install a hard disk upgrade
in less time than it took to read this chapter. That's certainly quicker
than it takes to achieve unlimited wealth and weight loss. And
you'll reward yourself with something nearly as valuable—more
storage capacity and speed for your PC.

8.

FLOPPY DISK UPGRADES

Even after ten years of intense development, high-tech networks remain only the number two choice for exchanging data. Number one is, of course, the lowly floppy disk. Floppy disk drives are slow, they hold meager amounts of data, and they come in a confusion of styles. Yet they remain the first choice for exchanging—as well as distributing and backing up—information available for personal computers.

Floppies are cheap and—though not indestructable—are reasonably reliable repositories of data. They are as familiar as the front panel of any PC. And when you have a 370K file to store and a 360K disk or, worse, a $3\frac{1}{2}$-inch disk from a friend and only a $5\frac{1}{4}$-inch drive, floppies can be as frustrating as the most twisted government bureaucracy. If you have data on a floppy disk that doesn't fit the drive in your PC, you're hardly better off than not having the data at all. And that's the problem. Floppy disks seem to come in more flavors than ice cream, and the one that you want most is generally the kind your disk drive can't handle.

Fortunately, even though floppy disks aren't always compatible with different drives, most floppy disk drive types are compatible with most PCs—or can be made that way. You can add the size of floppy disk drive you most commonly need to a vacant slot inside your PC. Or you can oust an old floppy for one with greater storage or that will allow you to exchange files with your friends, business associates, or your laptop computer. After a few minutes work, new floppy disk storage opportunities will await you.

Floppy Standards

In making a floppy disk drive upgrade, the primary problem is the same one haunting all those disks that won't fit your current drive—variety. There are so many different kinds of drives—each with its own compatibilities and incompatibilities—that deciding on *which* kind of floppy upgrade you need can be its own challenge.

Floppy disk drives are the classic victims of their own success. Once IBM saw how successful its floppy disk standard was, the company came up with several more. Instead of the world being plagued with innumerable data formats on $5\frac{1}{4}$-inch floppy disks— most of which could be read and written in garden variety disk drives but with their own, special software—IBM even made the drives physically different. Of course, the changes were all made in the name of progress, a steady progression of capacities. In ten years, the changes and incompatibilities have squeezed 18 times more information into less than half the original disk surface area.

Before the IBM PC was introduced in August 1981, every small computer that used $5\frac{1}{4}$-inch floppy disks had its own generally incompatible floppy disk storage format. Floppy disks back then were like hard disks today—each computer formatted its floppy disks with a seemingly different number of tracks and sectors. The floppy disks themselves were varied. Some were designed for hard sectors with multiple index holes, while others had a single index hold for soft sectoring.

After the IBM PC became the wild and unexpected success that it did, the IBM arrangement of data on floppy disks became the standard—40 tracks of eight sectors each, with each sector holding 512 bytes of data. But in the race to keep up with the latest technology, over the years IBM has squeezed in more sectors and tracks while trimming disk diameter from $5\frac{1}{4}$ to $3\frac{1}{2}$ inches (a reduction in recordable surface of about 56 percent). In the process, IBM has used no less than six types of floppy disks in the six years between the inception of the first PC and the introduction of the PS/2—that averages nearly a new disk format every year! In order of appearance, these were: single-sided, double-density $5\frac{1}{4}$-inch; double-sided, double-density $5\frac{1}{4}$-inch; double-sided, high-density $5\frac{1}{4}$-inch; doubled-sided $3\frac{1}{2}$-inch; double-sided, high-density $3\frac{1}{2}$-inch; and double-sided, extra-density (or quad-density) $3\frac{1}{2}$-inch.

Capacity is perhaps the most distinguishing characteristic of these floppy disk drives. The original single-sided drives of the first PCs held 160 kilobytes of data under the first versions of DOS 1.0 and 1.1. This capacity was extended to 180 kilobytes by the slightly different format used by DOS Versions 2.0 and later. The newer DOS versions packed nine 512-byte sectors on each of the disk's 40 tracks. The old DOS versions could only fit eight.

Double-sided $5\frac{1}{4}$-inch disks simply doubled the capacity of the single-sized variety. With eight sectors per track, they hold 320K bytes; with nine sectors per track, 360K. In that the same disk media will hold either 320K and 360K, dependent only on how you format them, you can guess which is the most popular—and the default capacity when you format.

While high-density $5\frac{1}{4}$-inch disk drives can read both single- and double-sided, double-density disks, at high-density they operate only at high-density, in which case they can pack 1.2 megabytes on a single disk (with no bad sectors). All double-density $3\frac{1}{2}$-inch disks are double-sided in the IBM scheme and hold 720 kilobytes. High-density $3\frac{1}{2}$-inch floppies, also all double-sided, hold 1.44 megabytes; and quad-density disks hold 2.88 megabytes, always on both sides.

Floppy Drive Compatibility

In general, the newer drives of a particular media size are backwardly compatible with disks made with older technologies. That is, whatever you create with a primeval drive will be readable on a newer system as long as the disk will fit properly in the floppy disk drive.

Going the other direction is chancy—while DOS can help more advanced floppy disk drives work sort of like older drives, problems arise. You can force DOS to make single-sided disks that will work with the single-sided, 160K capacity drives of the first PCs by adding the /1 option when you format new floppies.

Note that while single-sided disks can be read and written in double-sided drives, double-sided disks can neither be read nor written in single-sided drives. You can't read just one side at a time when you put a double-sided disk in a single-sided drive because DOS alternates sides when it reads the disk—half the sectors in a file will be on one side of the disk, the other half on the other. This odd arrangement is actually the more efficient arrangement because it requires less disk drive head movement—but it frustrates any hope of using a single-sided drive for anything useful any more. Virtually no commercial program distribution disks are single-sided, and none of your friends are likely to have single-sided disks, either. The odds are better than 600:1 against it— in a universe of tens of millions of PCs, the number of installed single-sided disks can be measured in the tens of thousands. Consequently, this command isn't really useful. Nearly every software publisher assumes that you have double-sided drives. If you don't, you should get them—the increase in capacity and convenience is well worth the $50 price and minimal trouble of upgrading.

A bigger problem arises with high-density disk drives. While double-density disks can be read in a high-density (or quad-density) drive, a double-density drive cannot read high-density disks. The /4 option is *supposed* to let you use a high-density drive to format disks to be readable in double-density drives. But high-density $5\frac{1}{4}$-inch drives use narrower heads than double-density units so they can squeeze in more tracks, 80 per high-density disk versus 40 for double-density. In writing double-density disks, the narrow high-density head leaves a band of unaltered disk around the information it does write, and a double-density head will read the extraneous noise extending from either side of the narrower track along with the desired information. As a result, the double-density drive may find a jumble of bits and mistake the data that it reads, producing errors.

The problem should not arise with $3\frac{1}{2}$-inch disks because the width of the heads used for double- and high-density drives are the same. Instead of more tracks, high-density $3\frac{1}{2}$-inch drives squeeze more information on each track. In theory, a high-density $3\frac{1}{2}$-inch drive should be equally adept at making double- and high-density disks.

If there is any sense to be made from this situation it's that for true compatibility with all IBM disk formats, you need at least three different floppy disk drives: a double- and a high-density $5\frac{1}{4}$-inch and a high-density $3\frac{1}{2}$-inch drive. Most PC floppy disk controllers will operate only two drives. So you are forced to choose your favorites for your system.

The double-density $5\frac{1}{4}$-inch drive is the universal exchange standard. If you want reliably to move information to the widest reach of PCs, you'll want a double-density $5\frac{1}{4}$-inch drive. If you care more about capacity—particularly for making backups—you'll want to consider a high-density drive. Which size depends on what other computers you have (or plan to have) and what you think about the future. If you have a laptop computer or are planning to purchase one some day, you'll want consider a high-density $3\frac{1}{2}$-inch drive. You can safely consider single-sided $5\frac{1}{4}$-inch and double-density $3\frac{1}{2}$-inch disk drives obsolete.

Floppy Disk Compatibility

Outwardly, all floppy disks appear to come in two sizes, period. Any $5\frac{1}{4}$-inch floppy disk fits into any $5\frac{1}{4}$-inch floppy disk drive. Any $3\frac{1}{2}$-inch disk fits into any $3\frac{1}{2}$-inch drive. Yet, despite the visual similarity in floppy disks, the prices for disks *for disk formats* vary by factors as large as 20 to 1. To some people, this is a major scam. Others know better.

The differences between floppy disks is more than a matter of marketing, name brands, and quality control. High-density disks are physically different from low- or double-density disks. If you upgrade your floppy disk drive, you'll also have to upgrade the kind of disks that you buy.

The magnetic media that are used for storing information on floppy disks are scientifically described by several properties. Among the most important of these is *coercivity*, a property that describes the strength of a magnetic field that is required to write data onto the medium. Coercivitity is measured in *Oersteds*. As applied to floppy disks, the coercivity of a disk indicates how strong a magnetic field a disk read/write head must generate to write data on the disk.

Higher-density floppy disks have higher coercivity media, and high-density floppy disk drives are designed to generate stronger signals to write to the disks. Higher coercivities help with high-density disks because they increase the strength of the recorded signal (which compensates for the smaller area on the disk to which each bit is written on a high-density drive) and they make storage more secure because it's less likely to be erased accidentally.

In general, you can't tell high-density and double-density disks apart without reading their labels. To the naked eye, the particles of magnetic medium look identical. Nor can your disk drive see the difference. Should you tell your drive to format a $5\frac{1}{4}$-inch double-density disk as high-density, it will try to follow your command. Try this and you're apt to get a lot of bad sectors or the disk may be rejected entirely because the first track tests bad. Worse, because of the coercivity difference between double-density media and the high-density disks the drive expects and writes with, the data you store on the sectors that are supposedly good may deteriorate over time.

The same concepts apply to $3\frac{1}{2}$-inch disks but with two differences. One, the difference in coercivity is not as great between double- and high-density $3\frac{1}{2}$-inch floppy disks as it is with $5\frac{1}{4}$-inch disks. Two, many $3\frac{1}{2}$-inch disk drives can actually tell the difference between double- and high-density disks because high-density disks are coded with a special hole in the plastic disk shell. It's located opposite the hole used for write-protection. The presence of this hole indicates a high-density disk, and the disk drive can detect the hole. Some machines, notably IBM's PS/2s, ignore the signal from the hole sensor, so they will let you try to format double-density $3\frac{1}{2}$-inch disks as high-density—with dismal results.

Entrepreneurs have taken advantage of the disparity between prices and coercivities in $3\frac{1}{2}$-inch floppy disks—the small coercivity difference but large price difference—by developing special punches that allow you to slice the high-density sensing hole in double-density $3\frac{1}{2}$-inch disk shells. Punch the hole, and you can convince a high-density $3\frac{1}{2}$-inch disk drive to use a double-density disk as if it were a high-density disk. Owners of some IBM PS/2s have it even easier—their machines will assume that every disk you feed into the machine is high-density unless the machine is told otherwise by adding a complex option to the format command.

In theory, this subterfuge could save you between $1 and $5 per disk, just by punching the hole and doubling the formatted capacity of a double-density disk. But consider such a cost-saving strategy the technological equivalent of jumping off a cliff. Just because you can do it doesn't mean you should do it. The price you pay for punching the hole is in reliability. Although a double-density disk may format fine as a high-density disk, it will be more apt to go bad over time. In six months or so, you may begin to encounter read errors in the data you store on such disks. Eventually, you will lose an important file to this problem, and the time you spend recovering the file—if you can at all—will more than offset whatever savings you made punching the hole. In other words, you won't want to use such altered disks for serious data storage.

There's even a worse strategy than buying the expensive hole punch to try to increase disk capacity—doing it yourself. You could take an electric drill and bore the needed sensing hole in the disk shell. You would ruin the disk and the disk drive with the detritus of the drilling. The tiny shards of plastic that inevitably get shorn off during drilling can lodge in the disk shell, under the read/write head of the drive, or in the drive mechanism itself, fouling both disk and drive. Don't risk it to save a few cents.

A related cost-saving trick is to buy cheaper, single-sided disks and format them double-sided. This strategy is often successful because there is no physical difference between single- and double-sided disks. All floppy disks have magnetic media on two sides. Single-sided disks are only certified for use on one side. Certification as single-sided can mean that the disks are tested only on one side—or that they are tested on both sides and only one side was found to be good. In the former case, you may be able to cash in by doing your own testing simply by formatting the disks double-sided and seeing if you encounter any errors. Be forewarned, however, that disk makers vow that their testing is more rigorous than anything you can do and that your PC may think a marginal disk sector is good enough, even though it might go bad at a later date.

DOS Considerations

When upgrading to a new floppy disk format, don't forget to make sure the version of DOS that you plan to use will support your new drive. The history of DOS is mostly a story of updates to accommodate new kinds of disk drives (as well as incorporate other advanced features). Part of nearly every revision of DOS has included changes to accommodate new floppy disk formats.

The whole PC and floppy disk story began with DOS Version 1.0, which was introduced along with the original IBM PC in 1981. Its principal claim to fame was that it booted up the PC and let the world see what personal computers could do. As far as floppy disks were concerned, that wasn't much. It could handle only single-sided, double-density $5\frac{1}{4}$-inch disk drives and store a measley 160K per disk. Each disk side was formatted with 40 tracks of eight sectors with 512 bytes in each.

DOS 1.1, introduced later in 1981, opened a new world to the floppy disk—the second side. It allowed the use or either single- or double-sided disk drives with double-density disks. The maximum capacity per disk it allowed was 320K with the same storage format as DOS 1.0 used, on each side of each disk.

In 1982, when IBM introduced the XT with its ten-megabyte hard disk, DOS was upgraded to Version 2.0. More than an upgrade,

DOS 2.0 was reworked from the ground up to include tree-structured directories and other features useful in running a hard disk. DOS also grew substantially, rudely cutting into the capacity of DOS system disks. To counteract the larger disk space requirements, the capacity of floppies was increased by altering the disk format. While floppy disks still packed 40 tracks per disk side, a simple timing change allowed DOS 2.0 to squeeze nine 512-byte sectors into each track. The capacity of a single-sided disk was thus increased 12.5 percent to 180K; a double-sided disk to 360K.

Unlike previous upgrades, the move to DOS 2.1 in 1983 brought no additional floppy disk capacity. However, changes were made in the operating system to allow the use of half-height floppy disk drives. (Timing requirements were relaxed because early half-height floppy disk drives were not as precise as their larger forebears.) The motivating factor in this change was the introduction of the PCjr, which was equipped with a half-height drive.

In 1984, DOS again went through a major alteration, to Version 3.0. Introduced to support the new 286-based IBM Personal Computer AT, DOS 3.0 was designed to support high-density, $5\frac{1}{4}$-inch disk drives. The track count of each disk was increased to 80 per side. This closer spacing of tracks required a narrower read/write head, leading to the backward compatibility problems in writing double-density disks. Each of these tracks was split among 15 sectors to achieve a total disk capacity of 1.2 megabytes.

DOS 3.1 was promised at the same time as DOS 3.0 was introduced. When introduced, it made no change in floppy storage. Instead, it added file control facilities such as record locking that were required for reliable network operation.

DOS 3.2, on the other hand, broke new ground. It was the first DOS to support $3\frac{1}{2}$-inch diskettes. It was introduced in 1986 to accommodate the IBM Convertible, an unlamented laptop computer. DOS 3.2 supported double-sided, double-density, $3\frac{1}{2}$-inch disk drives with a total capacity of 720K. (IBM fortunately passed over on single-sided $3\frac{1}{2}$-inch disks.) Each disk side was formatted with 80 tracks with 9 sectors each.

To accompany IBM's new range of Personal Systems/2 first introduced in 1987, DOS 3.3 made its debut. The principal change as far as floppy disks were concerned was the support of a new format, high-density $3\frac{1}{2}$-inch disks. The capacity of the little disks was doubled (to 1.44 megabytes) by increasing the number of sectors per track. The track count was kept at 80 per disk side. As a result, there were no backwards compatibility problems as there were with double- and high-density $5\frac{1}{4}$-inch floppies.

DOS 4.0 added a user-friendly shell (interface) and extended support for larger hard disk partitions. However, the floppy capabilities of DOS 4.0 were unchanged from DOS 3.3.

DOS 5.0, introduced in 1991, brought the new extra-density $3\frac{1}{2}$-inch floppy disks into the DOS fold along with its added memory management abilities.

Digital Research published several of its own versions of DOS (called DR DOS) to compete with the Microsoft/IBM operating system. The DR DOS versions mirrored the floppy disk capabilities of the Microsoft/IBM DOS available at the time. In that all versions of DR DOS were introduced subsequent to 1987, all have support for all IBM standard floppy formats through $3\frac{1}{2}$-inch high-density disks.

The one fact you should remember from this history lesson is that if you want to move up to high-density, $3\frac{1}{2}$-inch floppy disks (the most common floppy disk upgrade), you'll want to upgrade any older version of DOS you might be using to Version 3.3 or later. Any version of DR DOS will also work. For extra-density $3\frac{1}{2}$-inch floppies, you'll want MS DOS 5.0 or DR DOS 6.0. All of the DOS considerations in floppy disk compatibility are summed up in Figure 8.1.

PC Compatibility Issues

If having to sort through such a diverse array of drive types and DOS versions seems an irritation, making them work together is a plague. Many, if not most, PCs will not operate all floppy formats in their factory configurations. The reasons are various and range from the understandable—the IBM PC was designed before $3\frac{1}{2}$-inch floppies even existed and consequently make no allowance for them—to the outrageous—except for the very latest models, IBM PS/2 won't recognize high-density $5\frac{1}{4}$-inch floppy drives. In between is a vast middle ground of system compatibilities. Some PCs will accept any floppy drive type, others will seem to work but will grant you a generous share of disk errors.

Figure 8.1 DRIVPARM.SYS command options:

OPTIONS UNDER DOS 3.3:

/d: Physical drive on which to act, numbered starting with 0 as the first floppy disk drive (A:) This is the only mandatory parameter. You must specify on which drive the dirver is to work.

/f: Form factor option, which specifies drive type as follows:
    0 Double-density 5.25-inch floppy drive
    1 High-density 5.25-inch floppy
    2 Double-density 3.5-inch floppy drive
    7 High-density 3.5-inch floppy drive
    If not specified, DOS assumes a value of 2 for /f;

/h: The number of drive heads, which corresponds to sides of a floppy disk drive. While DOS accepts any value from 1 to 99, the default is 2.

 i/ Indicates that the drive is an electrically compatible 3.5-inch floppy. You must use this option if your system does not have internal support for 3.5-inch drives.

/n Indicates that the drive does not use removable media. Do not use this option with floppy disk drives.

/s: The number of sectors per track on the disk. DOS will accept any value between 1 and 99 with the default being 9.

/t: The number of tracks on each side of the disk. DOS will accept any value between 1 and 999 with a default of 80.

OPTIONS UNDER DOS 5.0:

/c Indicates that the drive can detect when the drive door is closed. This can speed up some operations with floppy disk drives that support the feature. Check your floppy disk drive's manual to see if it supports this feature.

/d: Physical drive on which to act, numbered starting with 0 as the first floppy disk drive (A:) and going upward to number 255. This is the only mandatory parameter. You must specify on which drive the driver is to work.

/f: Form factor option, which specifies drive type as follows:
    0 Double-density 5.25-inch floppy drive
    1 High-density 5.25-inch floppy
    2 Double-density 3.5-inch floppy drive

> 5 Hard disk drive
> 6 Tape drive
> 7 High-density 3.5-inch floppy drive
> 8 Read/write optical disk drive
> 9 Extra-density 3.5-inch drive (2.88MB)
>
> If not specified, DOS assumes a value of 2 for /F:

/h: The number of drive heads, which corresponds to sides of a floppy disk drive. While DOS accepts any value from 1 to 99, the default varies with the form factor (/f: option) you select.

/i Indicates that the drive is an electrically-compatible 3.5-inch floppy. You must use this option if your system does not have internal support for 3.5-inch drives.

/n Indicates that the drive does not use removable media. Do not use this option with floppy disk drives.

/s: The number of sectors per track on the disk. DOS will accept any value between 1 and 99 with the default varying with the form factor (/f:) option that you select.

/t: The number of tracks on each side of the disk. DOS will accept any value between 1 and 999 with a default that depends on the form factor (/f:) option that you choose to use.

OPTIONS UNDER DOS 3.3

/d: Physical drive on which to act, numbered starting with 0 as the first floppy disk drive (A:) This is the only mandatory parameter. You must specify on which drive the driver is to work.

/f: Form factor option, which specifies drive type as follows:
>   0 Double-density 5.25-inch floppy drive
>   1 High-density 5.25-inch floppy
>   2 Double-density 3.5-inch floppy drive
>
> If not specified, DOS assumes a value of 2 for /f:

/h: The number of drive heads, which corresponds to sides of a floppy disk drive. While DOS accepts any value from 1 to 99, the default is 2.

/i Indicates that the drive is an electrically-compatible 3.5-inch floppy. You must use this option if your system does not have internal support for 3.5-inch drives.

/s: The number of sectors per track on the disk. DOS will accept any value between 1 and 99 with the default being 9.

/t: The number of tracks on each side of the disk. DOS will accept any value between 1 and 999 with a default of 80.

OPTIONS UNDER DOS 5.0:

/c Indicates that the drive can detect when the drive door is closed. This can speed up some operations with floppy disk drives that support the feature. Check your floppy disk drive's manual to see if it supports this feature.

/d: Physical drive on which to act, numbered starting with 0 as the first floppy disk drive (A:) and going upward to number 255. This is the only mandatory parameter. You must specify on which drive the driver is to work.

/f: Form factor option, which specifies drive type as follows:
    0 Double-density 5.25-inch floppy drive
    1 High-density 5.25-inch floppy drive
    2 Double-density 3.5-inch floppy drive
    7 High-density 3.5-inch floppy drive
    9 Extra-density 3.5-inch drive (2.88MB)
If not specified, DOS assumes a value of 2 for /f:

/h: The number of drive heads, which corresponds to sides of a floppy disk drive. While DOS accepts any value from 1 to 99, the default varies with the form factor (/f: option) you select.

/i Indicates that the drive is an electrically-compatible 3.5-inch floppy. You must use this option if your system does not have internal support for 3.5-inch drives.

/s: The number of sectors per track on the disk. DOS will accept any value between 1 and 99. The default varies with the form factor (/f:) option you use. These values are as follows:

Form Factor Option	Default Sectors
0	9
1	15
2	9
7	18
9	36

/t: The number of tracks on each side of the disk. DOS will accept any value between 1 and 999 with a default of 80 except when the form factor (/f:) options is zero, in which case the default is 40.

In truth, most computer systems have exactly the right electronic hardware needed to operate any standard floppy disk drive, specifically a type 765 disk controller chip. (The latest PCs that are built using Application Specific Integrated Circuits [ASICs] typically emulate a 765 disk controller in one of their VLSI chips.) Systems with compatibility problems simply don't take advantage of all the features and abilities of this chip.

Rather than a hardware omission, the floppy problem arises from a firmware shortcoming. The primary culprit is generally your system BIOS. The BIOS stores all the instructions your computer knows on its own for matching the 765 to different floppy disk types. If your system BIOS lacks the instructions needed to make a $3\frac{1}{2}$-inch drive work, for example, you can't plug such a drive into your PC and expect it to play.

The code in your PC's BIOS contains the values needed by the 765 floppy disk controller chip to understand the storage format on different styles of floppy disks. If your BIOS contains the correct values for the type of floppy disk drive that you want to install, your system will be able to operate the drive. If not, you'll have to compensate for this omission in some way.

Note that this omission probably was not intentional on the part of the manufacturer of your PC. The necessary values for the various kinds of floppy disk drive have been introduced one by one throughout the history of the personal computer. If your PC (or, more to the point, its BIOS) was engineered before a specific kind of floppy drive was accepted as a standard for IBM-style computers, then your system's BIOS is unlikely to accommodate that type of drive. Most modern PCs have nascent in their BIOSs the values they need for all earlier drive types.

Determining whether your PC is compatible with a given type of floppy disk drive can be as easy a checking your systems owner's manual or as difficult as trial-and-error experimentation. The simplest case is when you just want to duplicate the floppy you already have installed in your system. In almost every case, PCs will accept a second drive of the same format as the first, factory-installed drive. After all, having one drive that works assures you that you have the BIOS support for that drive type.

The only likely problems are a lack of space—for example, a small footprint PC may have given over its second drive bay to a hard disk—or lack of a floppy disk controller channel because the second channel of the system's floppy disk controller has been given over to a tape backup system.

If your system already has a high-density drive of a given floppy disk size, the odds are again favorable that your system will also be able to control a double-density drive of the same size. With $5\frac{1}{4}$-inch drives, this was the most popular upgrade until the introduction of $3\frac{1}{2}$-inch drives. The double-density drive provided complete compatibility with double-density floppies from other machines, something the high-density drive could not do. With $3\frac{1}{2}$-inch drives, however, this strategy is pointless. The high-density drive can read and write double-density disks as well as a double-density drive can. With the price difference between double- and high-density $3\frac{1}{2}$-inch floppy disk drives averaging about $10, opting for lower density and half the capacity doesn't make sense.

Adding a drive that uses a different disk size than your PC's existing floppy is the chancy upgrade. You must first determine the inherent compatibility of your system. One place to start your investigation is with a look at the date your system was made. Computers designed before the IBM AT was announced in August 1984 are likely to recognize only double-density (360K) $5\frac{1}{4}$-inch floppy disk drives, not high-density $5\frac{1}{4}$-inch drives introduced with the first AT. Systems designed before IBM introduced its ill-starred PC Convertible laptop computer are unlikely to use double-density $3\frac{1}{2}$-inch drives because—guess what—IBM introduced the 720K format with that machine. IBM began using high-density $3\frac{1}{2}$-inch drives with the introduction of its PS/2 series in 1987, although a few manufacturers anticipated this format.

If you don't know when your system was designed or introduced (and most people don't), you're not out of luck. You can take a quick look at your PC's set-up procedure (either the set-up procedure you can select from the keyboard when your computer boots or the disk-based set-up program that accompanied your computer when you bought it). Check the options that set-up gives you for floppy disk drives.

The set-up program used by most computers since the introduction of the AT includes a set of choices from which you select which style of floppy disk drive you have installed as drive A: and B:. Check what your choices are. If the style of floppy disk drive that you want to install is listed in set-up (you might have to step through all the options to see it), then you're home free—your floppy disk upgrade will work with your PC after a simple mechanical installation job.

What? Your system doesn't use a set-up procedure? In that case you have a computer designed by the old school—that is, in the days before the AT. Consequently, your system most likely knows only about double-density $5\frac{1}{4}$-inch floppy disk drives.

Laptop Compatibility Issues

Laptop computers present their own compatibility issues. Most laptop manufacturers recognize the problem of media incompatibility and allow for some means of connecting an external $5\frac{1}{4}$-inch floppy disk drive to their products—internal drive just don't fit in the tight confines of the typical laptop. Most of these add-on drives attach to dedicated proprietary floppy disk ports, typically a large connector on the rear of the laptop PC. The manufacturers of these machines offer their own products (typically expensive) for this upgrade.

For these systems, the upgrade chore itself is trivial—plug in the drive. The rest of the process has been integrated into a simple procedure by the manufacturer so you can't go wrong.

Third-party products for laptop floppy disk upgrades are rare because of the proprietary nature of the interface. An aftermarket manufacturer would be forced into engineering a different connection scheme for each laptop computer for which it wanted to offer upgrade products. With the individual sales of every laptop computer model being tiny compared to the huge volume of almost-generic desktop machines, third-party support of add-in laptop floppy disk drives doesn't make economic sense—particularly considering the market is temporary. Eventually, the world will convert to $3\frac{1}{2}$-inch disks, and the value of clunky, add-on $5\frac{1}{4}$-inch drives for laptops will plummet.

If you need to share disks between your desktop and laptop computers, it will be much more economical and convenient to add a $3\frac{1}{2}$-inch drive to the desktop machine instead of adding a $5\frac{1}{4}$-inch drive to the laptop. The drive itself will be cheaper because of the existence of common interface standards and the competition among suppliers. Moreover, instead of buying an engineered add-on system, you can often get away with adding a raw drive to your desktop machine. While a proprietary plug-in laptop floppy disk drive might list for $300 or more, you can add a floppy drive to your desktop PC for about one-sixth that.

Moreover, your desktop PC is a more convenient place to add a drive. You'll more likely to have room in your desktop PC—room both to fit the drive in place and working room when you make the upgrade. And your installation will be permanent, with no need to plug and unplug an external drive when you head for the road. Even if tight space in your desktop machine means you have to make any floppy upgrade to it externally, you still won't be bothered by playing musical cables every time you want to pack your laptop PC into your attache case.

Improving Compatibility

The lack of direct support for a given floppy disk drive type by your PC does not mean that you're forever precluded from adding that kind of floppy as an upgrade. The omission merely means an extra step to the process—you have to teach your computer how to handle the renegade drive. Fortunately, educating your PC is a less traumatic process than sending a five-year-old to kindergarten or even a teen to reform school. In fact, not one but three different strategies can give your PC the remedial education it needs: adding driver software to compensate for BIOS shortcomings, upgrading your floppy disk controller along with the floppy disk drive, and upgrading the BIOS of your computer.

The first is the universal approach, the least expensive, and the one that requires the least tinkering with the solid-state secrets of your PC. It's also the most limited and, occasionally, irritating. Adding new BIOS chips to your PC will make up for the deficiencies built in due to the lack of prescience on part of its designers. But a new BIOS can adversely affect the other compatibilities of your system. For many people, the optimum trade-off is the insertion of a new floppy controller. The add-in controller comes close to being the best of all possible worlds—it can add its own bit of BIOS without the need to tinker with chips or disturb the inherent compatibilities of your system. In most cases, you won't need to bother with software drivers. And, hardly incidentally, a new controller may also be the most costly way of upgrading your PC for compatibility with a new floppy drive type.

Software Drivers

Driver software supplements the code that's contained in your system BIOS with special instructions for handling the new type of floppy disk drive. DOS loads the driver software through your system's CONFIG.SYS file just as it would any other device driver. That's the first limitation of using driver software—your system has to boot up with DOS before the driver can be read. Consequently, driver software is not an adequate solution for your boot floppy (drive A:) because your system wouldn't know how to operate the new drive type until it used the drive for booting up. If booting up is pulling your system up by its own bootstraps (which is the phrase from which the "boot" term is alleged to have arisen), trying to boot up from a floppy drive not supported by your system is like trying to pull up your system by the straps of a strapless evening gown. There's nothing for it to get hold of.

Worse, because the driver loads after DOS takes control of your PC, driver software is operating-system specific. If you don't use DOS, you may be out of luck. You'll need a different driver for DOS than you will for OS/2 or UNIX. You may not be able to find driver software for operating systems other than DOS, so if you're planning on moving up to a new operating system you probably won't want your new floppy disk drive to take the driver route. If your dealer admits that no driver for advanced operating systems is available today but one will be released shortly, wait until shortly before you buy the drive. Never rely on anyone's promise that a driver for a given operating system may be available in the future—you want to use your floppy disk drive *now*—or at least sometime within your lifetime.

Driver software also raises software compatibility concerns. Some software, such as some disk utilities and backup programs, takes direct hardware control of floppy disk drives and ignores software drivers. These applications may not work on floppy disk drives that use software drivers—and that's not a very reassuring situation if you've ever had to unerase a file before. Imagine if you couldn't recover a file that you accidentally erased. Worse than not working at all, the file recovery software may try to work and spin the floppy disk drive into chaotic operation that may destroy the rest of the data on the floppy in the drive.

Software drivers also add petty irritations. For example, because DOS brings them to life after all other disk drives in your system have been initialized through your system's BIOS, they take on drive letter identifications further down the line than the last BIOS-based drive. So your new driver-based floppy will likely be recognized as drive D: rather than drive B:. You can use the facilities of DOS to rename the drives to a more conventional alphabetical order, but you'll then be surprised how often error messages will pop up to tell you a given DOS utility won't work on a renamed drive. You'll likely end up grumbling that the savings of using software alone for the upgrade was false economy.

All told, software drivers are technically the least desirable way of matching a foreign floppy disk drive to a PC. Unfortunately, they are also the only universal method of doing so, sometimes the only method permitted by a given PC. Apart from the perfect hardware match, driver software is also the least expensive means of matching a floppy to your PC.

Many floppy disk upgrade kits include a software driver to help you upgrade systems that need one. Note that this driver is used in addition to the DRIVER.SYS program that comes with recent versions of DOS. The driver that comes with the floppy disk drive tells your PC how to operate the floppy disk drive; DRIVER.SYS tells your system how to recognize that new floppy disk drive. You must make two entries in your CONFIG.SYS file. The driver supplied with your disk drive should be listed first because it must tell DOS that the drive is there before DOS can deduce what the deuce to do with it.

In some cases, a few later generation PCs (generally AT-class machines and better) that originally were not designed for $3\frac{1}{2}$-inch floppy disk drives can be coaxed into operating them using DRIVE.SYS alone. You boot your system normally—potentially with error messages and odd sounds from the floppy disk drive. DOS then reads the DRIVER.SYS entry in your CONFIG.SYS file and, from the options given there, reconfigures the floppy to work properly. The only catch is that you then have two drive letters assigned to the new floppy—the drive's hardware assignment that doesn't work right and a software assignment that does.

Some (but not all) versions of MS-DOS and DR-DOS—but importantly *not* IBM's PC-DOS—include an additional driver program called DRIVPARM.SYS that sidesteps this drive-letter duplication. DRIVPARM.SYS resets the drive-type information provided by your system BIOS to reflect the new parameters. The drive on which DRIVPARM.SYS works keeps its original drive-letter assignment but assumes a new personality—one that works. Then again, DRIVER.SYS can be used to give you greater system flexibility. You can give the same drive several names to make your normal system usage easier. Note that some manufacturers include DRIVPARM.SYS with the DOS that accompanies their systems when sold; other manufacturers using the same DOS version number may not include DRIVPARM.SYS. The inclusion of this utility is the manufacturer's choice and not specifically linked to a particular DOS version number.

When you give multiple DRIVPARM.SYS commands for the same floppy disk drive, the last command listed in your CONFIG.SYS file prevails. If you give multiple DRIVER.SYS commands for the same floppy disk drive, you end up with mulitple drive letters, one for each time you include DRIVER.SYS in your system's CONFIG.SYS file. These drives take their drive letter assignments in alphabetical order according to their order listed in CONFIG.SYS. The first DRIVER.SYS entry gets the first available drive letter.

The options for DRIVER.SYS and DRIVPARM.SYS are the same. You should specify three options: drive number, as /d:; form factor, as /f:; and the $3\frac{1}{2}$-inch indicator, /i:. In most cases, that will be enough for DOS to understand what kind of floppy disk drive you have installed.

The drive number indicates which channel of the floppy disk controller is connected to the drive that DOS is to act on. As with most computer things, counting starts with zero. Hence, use /d:1 to indicate the B: (second) floppy drive.

Four principal form factor options describe the most common floppy drives: /f:0 for double-density $5\frac{1}{4}$-inch drives; /f:1 for high-density $5\frac{1}{4}$-inch drives; /f:2 for double-density $3\frac{1}{2}$-inch disk drives, and /f:7 for high-density $3\frac{1}{2}$-inch floppy disk drives. The default settings for these form factor options take care of the necessary head and sector settings.

The /i: option indicates that you are using a $3\frac{1}{2}$-inch floppy disk drive that is connected to your existing floppy disk controller as either Drive A or Drive B, but for which your system lacks BIOS support. This option may not be available (or work) with all PCs. In systems in which it does work, using DRIVPARM is the easiest way to get a new floppy disk drive running. If this option is not available, you'll need to try other upgade methods.

Floppy Controller Upgrade

In many PCs you can match an odd floppy disk drive by upgrading your floppy disk controller. Many—but far from all—modern floppy disk controllers come equipped with an add-on BIOS that adds the necessary instructions to your system's existing BIOS to allow it to control any standard floppy disk drive type. In most PCs, this add-on BIOS is automatically detected when the system boots up. Its extra code is added to the rest of the BIOS to endow your system with support for newer floppy disk drive types.

When you shop for a new floppy disk controller that can add BIOS support to your PC, you have to be careful, however. Older floppy disk controllers, many combined floppy and hard disk controllers, and the least expensive controllers do not have the necessary BIOS code built in. You will have to ask when you order a particular controller whether it has its own BIOS. Better yet, check when you order a floppy controller upgrade to be sure that it will allow you to use a specific floppy disk drive type with your PC. Be sure that the vendor you choose will allow you to return the controller (without a restocking charge) if it does not work the way the salesman assures you it will in upgrading to a new floppy drive type.

Not all PCs will accept the BIOS of a new floppy disk controller, so this upgrade option may not be available to you. In particular, IBM's very first batch of PCs—those that could accommodate only 64K of RAM on their system boards—have primitive BIOSs that cannot be extended by the add-in BIOS on a floppy controller. (Although you used to be able to upgrade the BIOS of these PCs to an extendable BIOS, IBM no longer offers this BIOS upgrade.)

Computers that have their floppy disk control circuitry built into their system boards will require that you disable the system board floppy circuitry before you add a new controller card. If you cannot disable the system board floppy disk control circuitry of your PC, then you may not be able to add a new controller. Even if you can, the existing controller circuitry wil take precedence, putting drive letters A and B off-limits to your new floppy disks.

Micro Channel PS/2s also forecloses on the possibility of controller-based BIOS upgrades because Micro Channel-based floppy controller cards are virtually impossible to find. That's not a great loss because all Micro Channel computers have innate abilities to handle both double-density and high-density $3\frac{1}{2}$-inch floppy disk drives. However, most IBM Micro Channel computers lack the capability to control high-density $5\frac{1}{4}$-inch floppies. The first IBM Micro Channel computers to support this drive format were the PS/2 Models 90 and 95. Consider high-density $5\frac{1}{4}$-inch drives off-limits to older PS/2s.

New floppy disk drive controllers are available in an amazing array of designs. Most have two channels—meaning you can connect only two floppy drives to them. Some have more, typically up to four. If you are planning to add a tape backup system someday (or already have one), the four-channel controllers offer the advantage of a place to directly plug in QIC-40 and QIC-80 tape drives.

In purchasing a new floppy controller, your first concern should be the BIOS. After all, that's why you're buying the controller in the first place. You want to be sure that the controller will support the floppy drive formats that you want to use. Next, consider how many channels the controller offers and whether the controller will cohabitate with your existing controller. That is, verify that you can get up to four channels in your PC, either on one new card or by a combination of your new and old controller cards.

Size and interface design are not major issues in selecting floppy controllers. Nearly every board you can find will be a short card that will fit into any expansion slot. That's because today not much circuitry is necessary for controlling a floppy disk drive—and there's no point in wasting board space you don't need. Bus interface is not an issue because floppy disk drives operate so slowly that even the vintage eight-bit PC expansion bus is not challenged to pass through the data as fast as the drive reads them. At the other end of the connection, there are not any interface compatibility worries, either. Floppy disk connections are standard throughout the world of PCs.

Adding a New BIOS

The most satisfying solution to the floppy incompatibility problem is adding a new BIOS to your PC so that all the needed floppy disk instructions will be built into your computer. This change requires that you remove one, two, or four large integrated circuit chips from the system board of your PC and replace them with new ones. That part of the job takes only a few minutes (after you open and disassemble your PC). The more difficult part is finding a BIOS upgrade that will work with your computer.

Although several companies manufacture BIOSs, these companies aim their sales efforts at providing chips directly to computer makers. They don't ordinarily deal in single-piece quantities with individual end-users like you. Moreover, unless a BIOS upgrade is available from the original maker of your PC, you have no guarantee that the new BIOS will actually operate with your computer. In other words, you generally cannot buy a BIOS off the shelf. What you can do is contact the dealer who originally sold you your computer and ask if its manufacturer offers a BIOS upgrade. If such an upgrade is available, your dealer will be the best (and likely only) source of supply.

A number of aftermarket suppliers offer what purport to be generic BIOS upgrades for PCs. The problem with these is that they may or may not work, depending on your PC and the BIOS. The only way to be sure is to try one out—but vendors are unlikely to extend this priviledge to you because the chances are good you'll destroy the replacement BIOS installing it, removing it, or just shipping it. The next best strategy is to get the vendor's absolute assurance that a given BIOS will both work with your PC and upgrade its floppy-handling abilities—and to be sure the vendor stands behind that assurance with a money-back guarantee.

BIOS chips come in varying numbers and even different chip types. The number of chips your PC uses does not have to be absolutely matched. For example, many machines in the IBM AT line have four BIOS sockets, but in most cases only two are filled with chips.

A more important consideration is the width of the BIOS memory. Eight-bit PCs use eight-bit BIOSs. Sixteen-bit PCs usually use 16-bit BIOSs. But most 32-bit PCs use only 16-bit BIOSs. And some machines use just eight-bit BIOSs, which they remap into 32-bit memory using ROM shadowing.

Fortunately, you don't have to worry about most of the 32-bit machines, such as those based on 386 or 486 microprocessors because they have code for $3\frac{1}{2}$-inch floppies built in. But you will have to ensure that you get the right width of BIOS to match your earlier computer. In most cases, you're best off asking for a BIOS to match the make and model of your PC. Failing that, figure you need an eight-bit BIOS for a computer based on the 8088 microprocessor and a 16-bit BIOS for a PC based on the 80286 chip.

Finding the BIOS chips inside your PC is merely a matter of looking for the labels. Most BIOSs are packaged in EPROM chips. Unlike normal integrated circuits, which have solid black cases, EPROM chips have a small round window in the center. (This window allows you to erase the chip by shining ultraviolet light into it.) In most cases, this window is covered up by a stick-on paper or plastic label which both identifies the chip and shields the chip from inadvertent erasure. Among the other nomenclature on the label will be the copyright notice of the company that actually wrote the BIOS inside the chip.

In most IBM-compatible PCs you'll find three chips with such labels. One chip will be by itself somewhere near the back panel of the machine, usually very close to the keyboard connector. This chip holds the keyboard BIOS and is of no concern to you when you need to upgrade your BIOS to handle new floppy drive types. The other labeled chips are usually found in pairs somewhere in proximity of the system microprocessor. These are the actual BIOS chips that you should be concerned with upgrading.

In 16-bit PCs, you should note that one of the two chips is labeled "odd" in some way, the other "even." That's because the 16-bit addressing range is split among two chips, one of which handles the odd addresses, the other the even addresses. When you substitute new chips for old, it is important that you place the new "odd" chip in the same socket from which you removed the old "odd" chip. You must also match the even chips.

In other machines you are challenged to match "U" numbers. Most integrated circuits are identified in the silkscreened legends on the system board with names in the form of the letter "U" followed by a unique number, for example U47. Replacement BIOS packs should tell you which chip numbers to switch with what upgrades. If not, call and verify which chip to replace with which other one. Trial and error has no place in BIOS upgrading.

It's also important to ensure that the alignment of any new BIOS chips matches the old—that is, the chips themselves must "point" in the right direction. Figuring out which is the proper direction (and telling one end of a chip from the other) is easy. All EPROM chips are notched at one end. Make sure that the new chips you put into your PC have their notches pointing in the same direction as did the notches on the old chips.

Normally you can depend on the chip socket to tell you which direction the notch goes. The socket will have a notch or some other way of distinguishing one end of itself from the other. However, this method is sometimes unreliable. For example, some early IBM AT computers had their sockets installed backwards by automatic insertion machinery. Put a chip in aligned in what looks like the proper direction, and these machines will summarily blow it up with a brief but bright flash sparkling out of the erasing window. In other words, the orientation of old chips is a more dependable guide than the chip socket for proper IC alignment.

Physical Considerations

Once you've established what you need to get your floppy disk upgrade running, you need to decide where to put it. Somehow the drive must attach to your PC; preferably, it should fit inside the chassis of your computer as if it were installed there by the factory. Your choice of how to physically install the drive depends on the layout of your PC and how many and what kind of its drive bays remain unfilled.

Internal Versus External Installation

All else being equal, the most convenient place to put a floppy disk drive is inside your computer's chassis. If your system has an open drive bay large enough to fit a new floppy disk drive or one that's larger, you're all set. Today, the magic drive bay size is a half-height, $5\frac{1}{4}$-inch bay. Most of today's floppy disk drives are designed to fit one of these or can readily be adapted to fit one. Of course, $3\frac{1}{2}$-inch drives also will perfectly fit a $3\frac{1}{2}$-inch bay if you have one of those available instead. Just don't plan on sliding a $5\frac{1}{4}$-inch drive into a $3\frac{1}{2}$ inch bay—you'd have an easier time fitting a peck of peaches in a two-quart basket.

External floppy disks are available if your system doesn't have room to accommodate the drive that you want. For example, all PS/2 except the new Models 90 and 95 are designed for external mounting of $5\frac{1}{4}$-inch floppy disk drives. Opt for an external chassis and you can connect just about any floppy disk to any PC. (There will be other complications for such an installation, which we'll discuss later.)

In most cases, you'll want to buy an external floppy disk system as a complete kit—drive already mounted in an external chassis, cables, and software. Although several vendors offer cases you can use for your own external floppy disk system, you're likely to encounter more problems trying to roll your own system than the cost savings will justify. For example, few floppy controllers provide jacks to plug in external cables. In addition, to connect the chassis to your PC, you'll have to get a shielded floppy disk cable to minimize interference both to the floppy signals and emitted by them. And you'll need specialized wiring for inside the external drive unit along with a power supply. Opting for a ready-made external drive system will eliminate all these worries—for a price—and give you a streamlined installation job.

Mounting Hardware

If you choose to use a ready-made external floppy disk system, be sure when you order that you'll get everything that you'll need to install the drive and secure it. The necessities include a drive of the correct format and proper capacity; a case for it (preferrably with a built-in power supply); hardware to mount the drive in the case; the required connecting cable sufficiently long for you to install the completed drive unit in a convenient place; a floppy disk controller or some means of adapting the signals from your existing controller for external transmission (including a reasonable mounting system for the required cable jack, for example a card-retaining bracket to hold the jack); and the software required to ensure the BIOS compatibility of the new drive with your old PC.

Internal floppy disk upgrades bring their own concerns. Although a little drive has more than enough room to comfortably fit in a larger bay, properly mounting the drive requires more than just space. You'll also need mounting hardware. In addition, putting a $3\frac{1}{2}$-inch drive in a $5\frac{1}{4}$-inch slot requires an adapter. Sometimes you're lucky. Many $3\frac{1}{2}$-inch floppy disk drives either come packaged with adapters or have adapters available for them at a small charge (typically less than $10). Some drives are even sold as complete kits that include front panels of black and beige (to match the XT and AT color schemes) in both $3\frac{1}{2}$-inch and $5\frac{1}{4}$-inch sizes. Other times you don't fare so well, however. The lowest-priced drives are often sold bare, without even the screws you'll need to attach them to your PC's drive bays. Most advertisements won't tell you what's included, so you'll have to ask when you order. Be certain that the vendor you choose will supply the hardware or adapter you'll need, even if at an extra charge.

The mounting hardware you'll need varies with the computer you plan to install the floppy drive inside. In general, you'll want to use four $\frac{6}{32} \times \frac{1}{4}$-inch screws to mount most floppy disk drives in the typical drive bay. Binder head screws are best for drives that screw directly into the sides of the bay. These flattened screwheads will give you maximum clearance. If you're going to mount rails to the drive, use flathead screws instead. These will fit flush into the recesses in most drive-mounting rails.

If you have an AT-style computer that uses rails for mounting disk drives, you'll need rails for your new floppy disk if spares didn't come with your PC. Many disk vendors can supply rails at a modest charge (if any). Sometimes AT rails are even included in drive-mounting kits. Mounting hardware for compatible computers is another story. Because different computer manufacturers use rails of different—often uncommon—sizes, you may not be able to get rails from your drive vendor. You'll have to let your salesperson know the kind of computer you have to see if he can supply you with the right rails. If the disk vendor can't supply the right rails (and with obscure brands of PC, that can be likely) you'll have to contact the dealer who sold you your computer to get the rails. Before you go to all of that trouble, however, check to see if the maker of your computer has anticipated your problem and included extra rails with the system. Extra rails sometimes are packed with computers loose—typically rattling around in a plastic bag with a variety of other extra pieces inside the box the computer was shipped in—or already installed in drive bays. Save yourself, the drive vendor, and your wallet a little trouble by ensuring you need rails before you ask for them.

Floppy Drive Cables

If you're simply replacing an existing floppy disk drive with one of a different format or greater capacity, or if you're adding a second drive inside your PC, you shouldn't need a cable. Most PCs come with a cable designed to handle two floppy disk drives already attached to their floppy disk control circuitry. Most systems also have a spare power connector to accommodate a second floppy.

Every rule has its exceptions, and your PC might just be one of them. To avoid unpleasant surprises when you start your floppy installation, check the resources inside your PC. Remove the lid from the case and examine the floppy drive cable for a connector for the second drive.

The floppy cable is easy to find—simply look at the back of the floppy drive already in your system. There you'll find a wide, flat ribbon cable leading to an expansion board or to the system board itself (depending on the location of your PC's floppy disk control circuitry). In systems equipped for two floppies, you'll generally find a connector in the middle of this cable, ready and waiting for the additional floppy disk drive.

To check for a power supply cable for an additional floppy disk drive, look for the power supply in your PC. In most cases, the power supply is a shiny, chrome-plated box most often in the right rear corner of the chassis.

Several bundles of wires emerge somewhere from inside most power supplies, typically the left side. Some of these bundles are made from groups of four wires—typically a red, a yellow, and two black wires—leading to a white nylon connector. One of these groups of four wires will lead to your existing floppy disk drive, where the connector will be plugged in. Check the wires emerging from the power supply to see if there is a set of four wires and nylon connector not attached to anything. If so, you've found the power cable your floppy disk upgrade will need.

If your floppy disk control cable doesn't have a second connector, you'll need a new floppy cable that does have two. If you don't have a spare power cable, you'll need a Y-cable (sometimes spelled wye-cable) or splitter—a wire that plugs into the nylon power connector and yields two duplicates of that connector. And if you're adding a third or fourth floppy to your system, you'll absolutely need a control cable for your floppy or floppies. Be sure to order them when you order your disk drive.

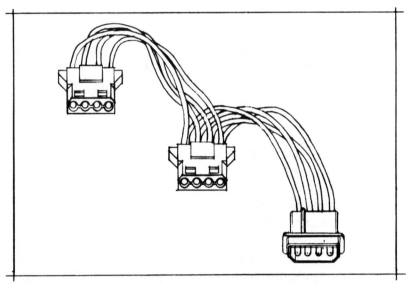

Figure 8.2 If your PC lacks sufficient power connectors for your new drive, you'll need a wye cable (shown). Plug the female end (lowest in drawing) of the wye cable into one of your system's power connector. The wye cable then provides two male power connectors for drives and other devices.

Connecting Cables

Floppy disk drives ordinarily require two connections with your computer. A single wide, flat ribbon cable carries both control and data signals to and from the drive. A four-wire power cable supplies the drive with the current it needs to run its electronics and spin its motors.

To avoid surprises, check and be certain that your PC has a spare power connector before you order your floppy disk drive. If you don't have a spare connector, you'll need to order one of those Y-cables to add another power connector to your system. It's called a Y-cable because it's shaped like the letter "Y" having a jack that plugs into one of the power connectors from your PC's power supply at its base and two plug suitable for disk drives, one at the end of each branch of the "Y."

Beveled corners on drive power connectors prevent you from inserting them improperly. If you cannot fit a power plug into a

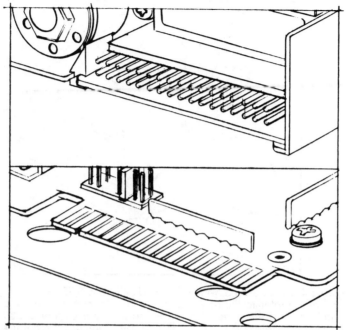

Figure 8.3 Most $5\frac{1}{4}$-inch floppy disk drives use edge connectors (bottom) for their signal cables. Most $3\frac{1}{2}$-inch floppy disk drives use pin connectors (top).

power jack on a floppy drive, try turning the plug over and trying again.

Most computers are prewired with a signal cable for two floppy disk drives, so if you're just going to add a second drive to your PC you won't need any other cabling. If you're adding a new floppy disk controller, however, you may require a new cable.

Two styles of connectors are used for linking floppy disk to their controllers. The original IBM design used by the controllers in PC and XT computers, as well as nearly all $5\frac{1}{4}$-inch disk drives, was an edge connector, a short extension to a printed circuit board that has contacts etched into it and is plated with gold. AT and newer controllers and many $3\frac{1}{2}$-inch floppy disk drives use pin connectors (sometimes called headers), short sharp gold-plated pins in two rows that project up from the circuit board. Edge connectors and pin connectors are not interchangeable, so the cable you get must match the connector style used by your drive and controller.

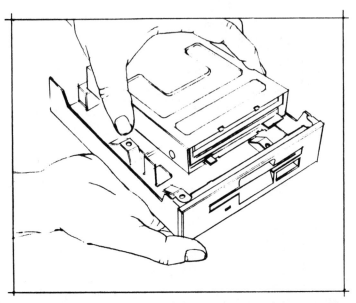

Figure 8.4 To install a 3.5-inch floppy disk into a 5.25-inch bay, you'll need to install an adapter to the drive. Adapters may consist of one piece that attached to the bottom of the drive (shown) or separate pieces that attach to either side. Be sure the bezel on the front of the adapter matches the color scheme of your PC-black or beige.

As with hard disk cables, floppy drive signal cables typically have three connectors—one plugs into the controller and the other two fit disk drives. One drive connector is in the middle of the cable, the other is at one end. The controller connector resides at the other end. You can distinguish the drive end from the controller end of the cable because a section of the cable is twisted near the end holding the drive connector (see Figure 8.3). Note that this twist looks similar to the one in a hard disk cable but it occurs on different wires of the cable. You cannot substitute a floppy drive signal cable for a hard disk cable or vice versa.

The connector with the twist always goes to the first floppy disk drive in a computer system, drive A:. The connector in the center goes to drive B:.

Signal cables are supposed to be keyed so you can't plug them in improperly. The key is a thin tab of plastic wedged into the plug positioned so that the key mates with a slot cut in the edge connector on the disk drive. Sometimes, however, the plastic tab falls out of the connector. Sometimes cable manufacturers simply neglect to put the key in place. Without the key, of course, you can inadvertently slide the connector in backwards. This is not a fatal condition, but it will prevent the drive from working. Inversion of this connector is the first thing to look for if a floppy disk upgrade does not work. If you want to avoid problems, make sure you've plugged the signal cable in properly by keeping the side of the connector nearest the red (or, sometimes, blue) stripe on the cable on the side of the edge connector that has the keying slot nearest it.

Upgrade Mechanics

The actual mechanics of upgrading your PC with a floppy disk drive are easy, simply a matter of getting your system ready, setting the drive inside, and going to work.

Readying your system means making sure you have space and connectors available for your new floppy disk drive. This means doing your homework before you order your new floppy disk drive so that you get all the supplies that you need. Turn off your PC, disconnect its power cable, then open it up and take a look around. Count the power connectors and check the drive signal cable. Examine the bay where you plan to put the drive. Check to see whether it requires only mounting screws or if it demands new drive rails. Make a list of what you'll need and order the mounting hardware and cables, if required, at the same time you order your new drive. Once your inspection is over, put your PC back together so that you can keep it at work until your new floppy disk arrives.

When you finally get the drive slated for your upgrade along with its mounting hardware, it's time to dig into your PC again. Follow the same procedure as before—switch off the computer, unplug its power cord, and remove the cover from the case. Once you're inside your system, the first step is to prepare a drive bay for the new floppy disk drive. If you plan on replacing an existing drive with your upgrade, you'll first need to remove the old drive. Remove the screws holding the drive or its rails in place inside its bay. Slide the drive slightly forward, then remove the two cables from its rear. Finally you can slide the drive out of your PC. If the drive was mounted on rails that you plan to reuse, remove the rails from the drive.

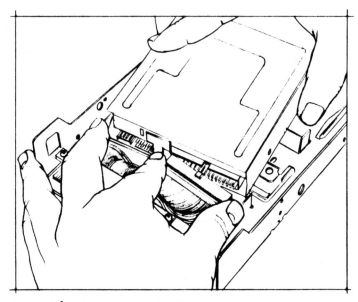

Figure 8.5 Most $3\frac{1}{2}$-inch drive bay adapters include cable adapters to convert the pin connectors on the drive to the edge connectors used in the rest of the system. You'll want to attach the cable adapter to the drive before you screw the drive into its bay adapter.

If you're planning to slide your new floppy disk drive into a vacant drive bay, you'll want to prepare that bay, too. If the bay has rails in it waiting for a drive upgrade, remove the rails so you can later mount them on the new drive. If the bay requires you to screw the new drive directly to the side of the bay, ensure that no cables protrude into the bay to impede your upgrade efforts.

Next, prepare your new floppy disk drive. In most cases, you shouldn't have to make any adjustments to the drive itself—the jumpers and switches (if any) on most drives today are set to operate with PCs. However, you may need to deal with the drive *terminator*. A terminator is a package of resistors that ensures signals going to and from the drive are at the proper level. No matter whether you have one or two floppy disk drives connected to a cable, you should have only one terminator, located on the drive attached at the end of the cable. If the drive you're installing is to be the second drive connected to a controller, you should remove the terminator resistor pack from the drive to keep the terminator count down to one. The terminator looks like either a socketed integrated

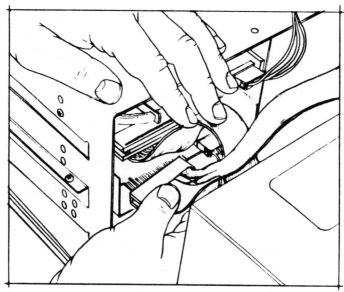

Figure 8.6 After you slide your floppy disk upgrade into its bay but before you screw it into place, connect the signal and power cables to it. The floppy with the connector nearest the twist in the signal cable is drive A:, here shown as the *lower* of the two drives.

circuit (typically the only one on the drive) or a small plastic strip with nine pins jutting down into the circuit board. One peripheral manufacturer claims that with recent PCs and controllers you no longer have to worry about terminators—just leave them in place. That's the easy way out, and if your drive works okay there's nothing to worry about. But you may want to remove the terminator now anyhow because if you do get many drive errors from your new floppy, the first thing to check will be the terminator—which will mean pulling the drive back out of your computer again.

If you're installing a $3\frac{1}{2}$-inch drive in a $5\frac{1}{4}$-inch slot, the next step is to get the drive ready by mounting it in its drive-bay adapter. First, physically install the drive in its adapter. Two kinds of adapters are popular. One comprises two angles of sheet metal that mount on either side of the drive to extend its sides. Others are U-shaped pieces that may attach to the side or bottom of the drive. In either case, install the adapter now.

You may also have to adapt the signal connector of a $3\frac{1}{2}$-inch drive to match the connector cable used by $5\frac{1}{4}$-inch drives. Some $3\frac{1}{2}$-

Figure 8.7 Once the cables are connected, push your new floppy all the way into its bay and screw it into place. You'll have to run your system's setup program to let your PC know what kind of drive you've installed.

inch drives use pin connectors and a miniature power connector. Their drive-bay adapter kits usually include a small circuit board that converts its connectors to those more common among floppy disk drives. If this converter is just a board that plugs into the back of the drive, install it after you've mounted the drive in its bay adapter. If, however, the converter is a board mounted on the bay adapter, connect its short cables to the drive before you screw the drive into the adapter.

After you've made the necessary connections, put the little drive in place inside its adapter, line up the screw holes, and start each of the four (or so) screws that will hold it in place. After you've started all four screws, tighten them one by one. When you're done, make sure that you've not distorted the shape of the drive by screwing it in too tightly and out of alignment. Slide a disk into the drive and make sure that pressing the release button on the front of the drive pops the disk out. If not, loosen the screws and adjust the drive so that the release button operates smoothly when you've got a disk in the drive. When you're satisfied that the drive ejects disks properly, retighten the screws and check again.

At this point, you can treat an adapted $3\frac{1}{2}$-inch drive and a true $5\frac{1}{4}$-inch drive interchangeably. If your PC uses drive-mounting rails, install them on the drive or its adapter. Then slide the adapter-and-drive into place inside your PC. Connect the power cable and signal cable before you permanently screw the drive in, so that you can more easily access the connectors. Then slide the drive into its final position in your PC. When using drive-mounting rails, you'll generally want to push the drive back as far as it will go in the bay. In direct-mounting systems, you'll need to line up the hole on the side of the drive with the holes in the side of the drive bay.

With rail-mounted drives, you can immediately screw the rails into place. With a direct-mount drive, you'll want to start each of the four (or so) screws that hold the drive into place without tightening them completely. After all four are started, then tighten the screws one by one. By leaving the drive a bit loose before you tighten the screws, you can more easily adjust its position to get all four screws properly started in their holes.

Once you've tightened all the screws, test the drive, then—when you're sure the new floppy disk drive is working properly—reassemble your PC.

PS/2 Considerations

Because of their case design, most PS/2s require you to add $5\frac{1}{4}$-inch floppy disk drives externally. To do so, you first must install a connector somewhere on or in the system into which you can plug the external drive. Companies that offer external drives for PS/2s sell complete kits that make the job easier. The installation process described here is based on a particular manufacturer's kits, although those of other manufacturers are similar.

The various PS/2 models use different drive connection systems that will complicate your installation job. For example, the PS/2 Model 30 286 uses a cable from the system board to the drive; the Model 50 uses an *interposer* board, a T-shaped circuit board that floppy disk drives plug into. Signals from these interconnection schemes must be routed to a rear panel connector into which you can plug the external drive unit.

In systems that use cables, you'll need to plug an adapter into the existing drive B: cable (the one that is unused) and run an extension cable to the rear panel of the system's expansion slots. Then just

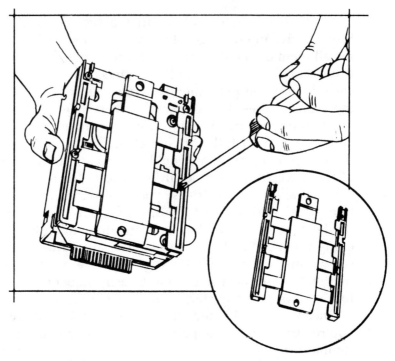

Figure 8.8 To install a floppy disk drive (or other $3\frac{1}{2}$-inch device) in a PS/2, you'll first need to mount a sled (insert) on the bottom of the drive. The sled secures with four screws. Once the sled is attached, you can simply side the drive into your PS/2.

screw into place the retaining bracket holding the external drive connector. In systems with interposer boards, you'll need to plug an adapter into the interposer board, then plug the extension cable into the adapter. Finally, install the external connector in an expansion slot. All the adapters, cables, and connectors should be supplied in a PS/2 floppy disk upgrade kit.

Note that some PS/2 upgrade manufacturers put a single integrated circuit on their cable adapters for floppy disks. This is a buffer chip that ensures sufficient signal strength to traverse the internal and external extension cables without errors. It is powered by the electricity that's supplied to the floppy disk drive through its connector cable.

IBM has complicated matters in ordering adapter kits for external drives by using different connectors in various PS/2 production runs. Early PS/2s used floppies with edge connectors. More recent designs use drives with pin connectors. The division is by time and

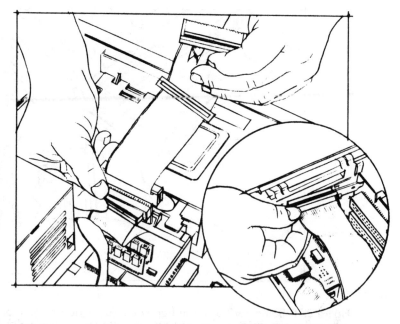

Figure 8.9 Some external upgrade PS/2 floppies require you to plug in an extender cable, then route it the back of the machine when you add the external connector at the rear of the expension slot. After you reassemble your PS/2, simply plug the external floppy into the new connector.

not along model lines, so you have to check your PS/2 to see what kind of connectors it uses. Upgrade kit manufacturers often sidestep the problem by including pin-to-edge connector converters with their kits. You may want to check the kind of connector your system uses before you order your upgrade kit.

After the external connector is installed on the back of your PS/2, the only mechanical step left is plugging in the external drive. You want to screw the connector in to ensure that it's always plugged into your PC. Otherwise the connection may become loose and you will get error messages when you boot up your system or try to access the drive. An ounce of prevention is worth several pounds of frustration.

Final Steps

After you've performed the mechanical installation, you'll need to complete the software part of the floppy disk installation proce-

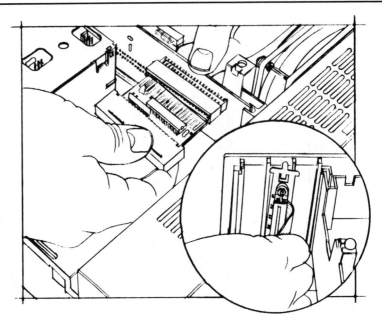

Figure 8.10 Some PS/2 external floppy upgrades add a small adapter board with buffer circuits on it. Plug the adapter into the connector for the second internal floppy, route the cable to the rear of the machine and add the external connector to the rear of an expension slot (inset).

dure, no matter whether you're upgrading a PS/2 or PC. If you have a modern PC that uses a set-up program either encoded into its BIOS or loaded from a floppy disk, simply run the set-up procedure. If your older PC requires that you use software drivers to match the floppy disk to your system, follow the instructions that came with the driver and add the drivers to the entries of your system's CONFIG.SYS file. PS/2s will, of course, require you run the set-up procedure on your system's Reference Diskette and add a driver to use a high-density $5\frac{1}{4}$-inch floppy.

Once that's done, you're ready to use your floppy for exchanging data, backing up your hard disk or just ensuring you have access to the greatest range of software available for any kind of computer in the world.

9.
OPTICAL DISK DRIVES

Optical storage technologies promise a unique mixture of permanence, removable cartridges, and high capacities. Although they can't yet substitute for hard disks, you can take advantage of CD ROM, WORM, and rewritable optical drives for a growing variety of purposes for which they are actually better suited than are traditional magnetic storage media.

The decade-long dominance of the Winchester disk in desktop computers is drawing to an end, at least if you believe the manufacturers of disk drives based on the various optical technologies. Digital storage systems based on light beams can pack more information into thin, square cartridges and silvery disks than conventional magnetic systems can squeeze into a multiplatter stack. With optical storage technology, you can put a complete encyclopedia on line, permanently store bookkeeping records for longer than Rip van Winkle might need them, or hold the working drawings for the entire Brooklyn Bridge replacement you're working on. Optical storage can make permanent, unalterable records for quick and easy distribution of huge amounts of reading material (including the illustrations, of course).

Not only can publishers put their latest oeuvres onto optical media, but with the right drive, you can, too. Because all optical disk systems use compact cartridges or other removable media of some sort, a single drive can hold an unlimited amount of information—hundreds of megabytes on line for instant recall and gigabytes (or whatever you want) off line, waiting for you to slide them into play.

The scourge of magnetic disks is also absent from optical storage. Optical recording is a noncontact sport. The only thing that ever touches the data on a disk is a light beam. Consequently, disks do not wear out (as flexible magnetic media do), nor do they suffer head crashes. The optical assembly that reads or writes to the disk can be located a safe distance from the disk surface instead of flying the precarious microinches above, as magnetic systems require. Moreover, while magnetic disks put the actual recording medium in harm's way directly under the head (and in many cases the medium is devastatingly soft), optical disks protect your data behind a transparent plastic shield through which a laser beam can be precisely focused.

All that said, optical storage systems have two definite downsides. They are expensive, at least from the standpoint of initial investment. Drive units that permit you to both read and write on optical disks (unlike magnetic media, you can't take for granted the ability to write data to disk) cost three to five times more than conventional hard disks of about equal capacity per disk. Drives that only read data from optical disks cost two to three times more than their nearly identical cousins, audio-only Compact Disc players.

From an upgrade standpoint, optical systems are also somewhat more difficult to meld with your existing PC. Today's computers were simply not designed with optical storage in mind. Consequently, you'll end up navigating an installation process that uses either a proprietary connection scheme or an SCSI link. Even the size of the drives can be an upgrade challenge because most optical drives use $5\frac{1}{4}$-inch media. The disks themselves, let alone the drives that spin them, won't fit in smaller PCs.

Once you've made the upgrade, however, you won't have to worry about these installation problems again. You'll find that optical systems are, at worst, only a bit more complicated to deal with than conventional media.

If you can afford to put up with the disadvantages and you have the right applications, an optical storage system can be one of the best storage upgrades you can add to your PC. Optical storage can provide a writer (or college student) with instant access to information that, when the system is heavily used, is much less expensive than on line database services. The combination of large capacity and removability makes optical storage an excellent backup system, one that can (in a pinch) directly substitute for a failed magnetic hard disk. Some drives make your storage records permanent, providing the perfect, unalterable audit trail.

It's nearly certain you'll have to face optical data storage sooner or later. Even if you don't have an immediate need for an optical upgrade, or if buying an optical system would prohibit you from indulging in regular meals, the newly emerging technologies simply have too many advantages over conventional magnetic disk storage systems to ignore. Costs are falling precipitously. And new generations of equipment are emerging quickly enough to put the reproduction ability of bunnies to shame. Optical recording is no fad, but a real and valuable technology—and likely a worthwhile upgrade for your PC.

Three Optical Technologies

Today, optical storage is not a single technology but three, each distinguished by the means by which data can be stored on the disk—and who puts the data there. Either the information comes prerecorded, or it can be written once but never changed, or it can be written and altered almost as easily and conveniently as using a conventional hard disk drive. The first is the *CD ROM* drive, appropriately named because it uses optical discs patterned after the CDs used in stereo systems, and functions as Read-Only Memory (hence, ROM). The second is the *WORM* drive—Write Once, Read Many (or Multiple) times. The last, and the most versatile, goes by many names—*rewritable optical, erasable optical*, and *magneto-optical*. The first two describe what the technology does. The last is a name derived from the combination of technologies used in reading and writing the disk.

As its name implies, CD ROM is fundamentally an adaptation of the Compact Disc digital audio recording system. As with audio CDs, digital data are written to master discs using special recording equipment that makes microscopic pits on the surface of a disk. The information encoded in the pits can be read simply by detecting changes in reflectivity (the pits are darker than background of the shiny silver disk). Because these data pits are a mechanical feature, merely dimples in the disk, they can be duplicated millions of times with pressing equipment similar to that used to squeeze out old-fashioned LP albums. Once a CD ROM disc is pressed, however, the data it holds cannot be altered. The pits are present for eternity.

Sometimes the terms rewritable CD ROM and erasable CD ROM pop up in the media. Note that these words are self-contradictions—something that's rewritable can't be read-only (as in the acronym ROM). While some systems have been proposed that allow you to write your own CDs—notably Tandy Corporation's long-promised THOR and Sony's miniaturized recordable CDs promised for 1992 release—these are not a ROM at all, but rewritable systems enhanced with the capability of reading CDs.

Although WORM drives have similarities to CD ROMs, they upset the basic definition by putting writing abilities inside the disk drive. As with CD ROMs, WORM drives store data as physical changes in the disk surface, but they don't change the disk in the same way as WORMs. Digging pits would be difficult in the WORM medium because it is safely encapsulated in transparent plastic. Instead of digging, WORMs work by darkening. That is, WORM drives usually just darken the disk surface or evaporate part of it rather than blasting away at it.

Unlike CD ROMs, duplicate WORM disks cannot be stamped. The darkened or evaporated surface does not lend itself to stamping. Moreover, the optical surface of a WORM disk is already sealed out of harm's way by a plastic coating that's laid on the disk during the manufacture of blanks. Consequently, every WORM disk must be written individually. Each disk is either an original—or that wonderful oxymoron, an original copy. If there ever were a million-selling prerecorded WORM disk, you wouldn't want to be responsible for duplicating it.

In contrast to these two unchangeable optical media types, rewritable optical drives accomplish exactly what their name implies. Data can be written on their disks in a form that can be read optically. The written data need not be permanent, however, but can later be changed and rewritten essentially whenever you want. The idea of rewritable optical storage is so compelling that various manufacturers have developed (or are developing) at least three technologies—dye-polymer, phase-change, and magneto-optical— that yield both the high storage densities that only optical media can provide along with the potential for upgrading their storage contents as your data change.

Which of the three optical storage systems you want for your PC upgrade depends on your purpose. Each system has its own strengths that make it most suitable for a particular application.

The easiest to dispense with is WORM. The unalterable nature of WORM puts it out of the data storage mainstream, but it can be eminently useful—even necessary—in some applications in which permanence is a virtue. Unalterability and archival storage go hand in hand. If you regularly create records of some sort that you need to preserve for posterity or the prying eyes of the auditor, WORM makes an excellent choice. You can dump hundreds of megabytes on a disk and know that no one will sneak into the office in the evening and make changes. Moreover, the optical nature of the storage assures that your archives will be as close to eternal as today's technologies allow. Estimates of the life of WORM media *start* at ten years, a point at which magnetic storage can become chancy. From there, the life expectancy of WORM soars into the centuries. The large capacity of WORM cartridges means that you can put a year of business files on one disk or keep all the engineering drawings—originals and revisions—in the same convenient package.

Because of its removable cartridge nature, recordability, high capacity, and permanence, WORM media can also make an excellent data exchange medium. You can send hundreds of megabytes across the country as easily as dropping a cartridge into a Federal Express envelope. You will be sure that the data that are distributed will always remain the same, unalterable in the field office no matter how creative the workers there may be. On the downside, however, each WORM disk must be individually written and the disks themselves can be costly. While neither is an obstacle when you're sending one copy across the continent, distributing information to a thousand dealers is another matter.

When megabytes must be sown to the four winds, Compact Disc storage is typically the more affordable alternative. Duplicate CDs can be stamped for under $10 each in modest quantities, while each WORM cartridge will add an extra a $100-plus price penalty in addition to the time needed for individual duplication. Make a million of a CD ROM and you can figure the cost as a dollar or two a copy.

This easy duplication and low cost make CD ROM the premiere digital publishing medium. Already, hundreds of CD ROM titles are available, each one holding an encyclopedia of data. You only need to upgrade to a CD ROM player to give yourself nearly instant access to any word in any of these encyclopedia sets. Moreover, you can search for that information with computer speed.

The only problem with CD ROM is cost. Neither the drives nor the Compact Discs themselves are inordinately expensive—in mass-market quantities CDs cost no more than a hardcover book to make—but the data they contain are valued (by the publishers) in the thousands of dollars. If you're used to paying $15 for an audio Compact Disc, the $300 toll for a popular CD ROM seems outrageous—notwithstanding that the same information in paper form would cost many times as much.

Rewritable optical storage appears to be the strongest contender to wrest the storage laurels from the Winchester family. Rewritable optical promises the same massive storage capabilities along with removable cartridges and greater reliability of other optical media. Alas, rewritable has its own drawbacks. Currently, the drives are substantially more expensive than Winchester hard disks. And current products are notoriously slow, fitting almost midways in the continuum running between floppy disks and the best hard disks.

Currently, then, the best applications of rewritable optical are those that exploit its strengths while not suffering from its weaknesses. It can be an archival medium like WORM when unalterability is not an issue. It also allows hundreds of megabytes to be transferred between systems as convenient cartridges, which can be reused for the next job. And rewritable operates as a superb backup system, with the ability to perform disk mirroring and even to substitute for a failed hard disk (at least for patient people).

New developments promise to minimize the disadvantages of rewritable optical. The drives are getting faster and prices are coming down. But magnetic drives are a moving target, getting cheaper and faster themselves. Still, where rewritable optical qualifies as the best choice, it's getting even better.

CD ROM Background

The very name CD ROM brings together the two concepts that give the medium its power. Like the ROM chips inside your PC, CD ROM is a source of digital code designed for delivery and not alteration. Rather than stamp-sized slices of silicon, with CD ROM the delivery vehicle is the small, silvery platter of a Compact Disc, about five inches in diameter, with a more than superficial resemblance to the CDs that spin in your stereo system. The resemblance is hardly a coincidence. The essence of your stereo's CD system is that music is stored digitally. CD ROMs merely substitute other data for the melodic digits on the disks.

The audio CDs and CD ROM discs are so similar that most CD ROM systems that work with your PC will, in fact, play the music CDs in your collection—providing you have the right software. Music abilities are built into most computer CD ROM players. They even have headphone jacks on the front or audio outputs on the back to provide for your listening as well as data processing enjoyment. The software you need to make one of these CD ROM players do double-duty playing audio should be included with any audio-capable CD ROM drive that you buy.

The similarity between stereo and computer CDs extends further. As with music CDs, the digital CDs for your computer are a publishing medium. Like newspapers, books, videos, and records, CD ROMs provide a means through which you can carry home entertainment and information in a convenient form. You cannot write to a CD ROM disk; you buy each one already filled with the information that you want.

The CD ROM medium is perfectly suited to this application. The disks themselves are easy to manufacturer—they can be made on the same presses as music discs—and inexpensive compared to more traditional publishing processes. The capacity of the typical CD ROM disk—300,000 pages of text—is about the equivalent of 150 full-length books. At today's bookstore prices of $20-30 per volume, publishing the information on one CD ROM on paper might cost $3,000–4,500. The retail price of a commercial CD ROM disk that holds the same words would costs between one-third and one-thirtieth of that.

The downside of CD ROM is that using the disks requires that you add a special piece of equipment to your PC: that CD ROM player with an earphone jack. More expensive than its stereo-only equivalent, a CD ROM player can cost from $300 to over $1,300, depending on how it is meant to be installed (internal or external), the accessories that come with it, and even how many disks it accommodates.

Fortunately, you need only one CD ROM player for as many disks as you want to use. Much like the one in your stereo system, the computer CD ROM player allows you to interchange disks, so one player allows access to an entire library of CD ROM media.

Computer CD ROM players are more expensive than stereo models because the computer-connected equipment must be more accurate. A tiny musical flaw that might pass unnoticed even by trained ears could have disastrous consequences in a data stream. For example, a single bit error can change the "not" in the Seventh Commandment to "now" and provide an entirely new meaning to an electronic Bible (not to mention your life). To minimize, if not eliminate, such problems computer CD ROM players have error-correction circuitry that's much more powerful than that built into stereo equipment.

Another difference between stereo and computer CD ROM players is that the latter must be connected to and controlled by your PC. By itself, the computer CD ROM player does nothing but spin its disk. Your computer must tell the player what information to look for and read out. And your computer is needed to display—visually and aurally—the information the CD ROM player finds, be it text, a graphic image, or a musical selection.

The bottom line is, of course, that you have to buy a CD ROM player and attach it to your PC if you want to take advantage of the hundreds of disks that are already available—and the thousands that will undoubtedly be published in the coming years. But you're in luck. A CD ROM player is one of the easiest additions you can make to your computer. If you've ever plugged in an expansion board, you can probably accomplish the mechanical part of the installation in ten minutes.

CD ROM Media

The best part about CD ROM disks is not their huge storage capacity but that they combine that capacity with familiarity. You don't have to be a genius to deal with the mechanism as you do when loading a computer tape on a mainframe. If you can manage to play music on your stereo you can use CD ROMs.

The disks themselves store information exactly the same way it's stored on the CDs in your stereo system, only instead of getting up to 80 minutes of music, a CD ROM disk hold about 600 megabytes of data. Those data can be anything from simple text to SuperVGA images, to programs, and the full circle back to music.

The silver disk puts digital data into optical form. The digital data on CD ROM are coded as pattern of bits represented by the presence or absence of those pits blasted into the surface of the CD. The overall CD is shiny and reflects light well; the pits don't. A laser beam is focused on the disk and reflects back into a photodetector, which can tell the difference in the brightness of the reflection of a pit or unharmed disk. The pattern of bits codes digital data.

Because CDs are noncontact media—the data pits are sealed within layers of the disk itself and are never touched by anything other than a light beam—they never wear out and acquire errors only when you abuse the disks themselves purposely or carelessly (for example, by scratching them against one another when not storing them in their plastic jewel boxes). Although error correction prevents errors from showing up in the data, a bad scratch can prevent a disk from being read at all.

Music and data CD disks are manufactured in the same way. First a master is recorded on a special machine with a high-powered laser that blasts the pits in a blank recording master. The master is made into a mold that is then used to stamp out copies of the original CD, much like dies are used to stamp out coins. The principal differences are that a CD has only one finished side and much finer detailing than does a quarter or half dollar—and they cost more.

Actually, the precision of the CD manufacturing process isn't a significant part of the cost of the disk. Most of the price is attributable to the cost of the data on the disk, the royalty that's paid to the people who create, compile, or confuse the information that's to be distributed. You pay a similar price for the data that are stored in books, only for your book purchase you get something bigger and more tangible—it feels like it should be worth more.

While the cost of manufacturing a single book or CD ROM disk are on the same order of magnitude, CD ROMs appear to give you less for more because they hold so much information. Data weigh more in book form, so those who buy by the pound think books are the better value. On a fact-for-fact and pennies-per-fact basis, however, CD ROMs are substantially less expensive than books. The data are just as valuable, but they are less tangible.

CD ROM Players

Perhaps the most welcome feature of a new CD ROM player is that you don't need to learn anything new to use it. You probably already know all the ins and outs of CDs from playing them on your stereo. Many CD ROM players accept disks exactly like stereos do—with drawers that slide out at the press of a button. Just lay your disk in the drawer, press the button again, and it's loaded.

Some CD ROM players make the job even easier. You load your disks into a special carrier that resembles the plastic jewel box case that most commercial music CDs come in. When you want to load a disk into the CD ROM player, you slide the whole carrier into a

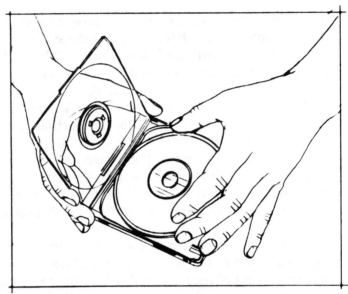

Figure 9.1 Many CD ROM drives are now designed to use disk carriers that prevent smudges and scratches to the disks. Loan a carrier as you would a music CD jewel box, but be sure to first slide the disk under the overhand near the carrier's hinge.

waiting slot. Most people buy a carrier for each CD ROM disk they have because of this convenience and the extra protection the carrier affords the disk—no scratches and no fingerprints, guaranteed! CD ROM changers use multiple-disk cartridges exactly like those used by audio CD changers.

Once a CD ROM player is properly installed in your computer system, you can access the disk you slide in as if it were just another DOS drive. The CD ROM player will have its own drive letter, and you can check what's on the disk as simply as executing a DIR command.

You might not have access to the data that are stored on the disk so easily, however. Most CD ROMs contain their own searching software that you must run to read the data stored there. But don't worry about having to learn to use another software package. Most of these programs will give you a menu-driven interface that's easy to use and completely intuitive. Sponges and several varieties of lichens are reputed to have mastered the ins and outs of these programs.

While easy on you, these programs are not easy on your system. They may require a huge amount of memory to run. Most will demand your system be filled to its full DOS 640K limit. In fact, these memory-hogging programs may even require you to eject your favorite TSR programs before you can start to use your CD ROM.

The CD ROM programs may carve their own storage space from your hard disk, hundreds of kilobytes of it for their files. To compound the misery, each CD ROM disc you have will likely require its own data access software. If you get several CD ROM discs, you'll need quite a lot of storage just for the programs that accompany each one.

In other words, if you want to install and use a CD ROM player, you'll have to start with a PC with a full dose of DOS memory—640K—one that includes a hard disk drive. CD ROM driver and retrieval software will also require that you use DOS Version 3.10 or later on your system.

Although CD ROM players are built around laser beams and optical technology, don't expect to get data at the speed of light. Compared to hard disks, most CD ROM players are glacial in their access times—that is, how long it takes the drive to find the information you want after it receives a command. For example, with today's better hard disk drives, the average access time is about 15-25 milliseconds. The best of today's CD ROM players have access times on the order of 350 milliseconds, many scoring as high as 500 milliseconds. Those numbers mean that after you press the Enter key to tell your CD ROM player what to do, it will delay about half a second (on the average) before it locates the first bit of information you need.

Once the information is found, it must be transferred to your PC. This additional step can take even longer. While text might pop up on your screen, graphics can take painfully long to display. While a screen of text comprises only about 2,000 bytes of data, a screen image may take a million. Each one has to be transferred individually from the CD ROM player into your PC. After the transfer, the images have to be processed before they can be displayed, eating up more time. As a consequence, painting a full-screen high-resolution image on a 286-based computer can take ten seconds or more.

Compared to the alternative, finding the right book and paging through to the entry you want, CD ROM is lightning-like indeed.

For example, searching through the 150 books on the disk *U.S. History on CD ROM* for a keyword takes but a few seconds. You can zoom in on what you need to know in less time than it takes to get to the bookshelf. For those who need answers quickly, CD ROM still rates among the fastest ways of getting them.

The bottom line is that speed is relative. Fast depends on what you make a comparison to. Put a Winchester hard disk and a CD ROM on the balance, and the magnetic hard disk will weigh down its side with milliseconds and megahertz. But compare CD ROM to using printing media and the computer will prove its advantage. Hours of searching can be reduced to minutes—an advantage not readily translated into numbers, but a godsend when you need to do research.

CD ROM Standards

Unlike other peripherals that you might want to add to your PC, the CD ROM player and its media have been completely standardized. The same CD ROM discs will fit the currently available mechanisms so that you're assured your new digital library will be readable and should remain so far into the future. You don't have to worry about how a given brand may affect the compatibility of your CD ROM system.

You do have to ensure that the CD ROM discs that you buy are compatible with your computer's software architecture. Many disks are sold in special versions for PCs or Macintosh computers, with different access software to match the target computer. Hence, when you order a disk, it is important to specify what kind of computer you plan using it on.

The data on CD ROM discs are stored in a particular format—an arrangement of tracks and sectors similar to that of hard disks—and, thankfully, one format has become a standard across the industry. Nearly all CD ROM discs and CD ROM players available today conform to the *High Sierra format* or its more recent upgrade, the ISO 9660 specification.

The only practical difference between these two standards is that the driver software supplied with some CD ROM players, particularly older ones, meant for use with High Sierra formatted disks may not recognize ISO 9660 disks. You're likely to get an error message that says something like "Disc not High Sierra." The problem is that the old version of the Microsoft CD ROM extensions—the driver that adapts your CD ROM player to work with DOS—cannot recognize ISO 9660 disks.

To meld CD ROM technology with DOS, Microsoft Corporation created a standard bit of operating code to add onto DOS to make the players work. These are called the DOS *CD ROM extensions*, and several versions have been written. The CD ROM extensions before Version 2.0 exhibit the incompatibility problem between High Sierra and ISO 9660 noted above. The solution is to buy a software upgrade to the CD ROM extensions that came with your CD ROM player from the vendor who sold you the equipment. A better solution is to avoid the problem and ensure any CD ROM player you purchase comes with Version 2.0 or later of the Microsoft CD ROM extensions.

The connection between CD ROM players and your PC also has been, for the most part, standardized. Nearly all CD ROM players that you can buy today use the *Small Computer Systems Interface* or *SCSI* to link with your computer. A few CD ROM players connect through a serial port, but when you're talking about moving 600 megabytes of data around, a 9,600-bit-per-second connection amounts to trying to drain a lake using a sponge. You won't want to mess with serial-linked CD ROM players unless you have from now till the glaciers come home to wait for your data.

But life isn't easy with SCSI, either. While the SCSI connection is quicker than serial—by a factor approaching one thousand—it can be ornery. In fact, SCSI is one of the most complicated interfaces to get operating properly, particularly with a PC. However, if you take the installation step by step, you should run into few difficulties.

WORM Drives

WORM drives might be called an orphan technology. Unlike other products that disappear in the dust riled up by onrushing technology, WORM drives have hung on, always on the periphery of the consciousness of the computer industry, just as orphans and other social problems always lurk in the background. Like orphans, WORM drives hold great promise, at least if you take the time to investigate their potentials.

WORM drives are orphans, too, because they have no close kin—cousins, maybe, but no real brothers and sisters, no parents (of course), and likely no offspring. They are related to other optical technologies as people are related to jellyfish and birds of paradise.

Despite their common design elements—lasers and small plastic-encapsulated metalized disks—WORM drives and the CD ROMs are very much different. As the name implies, the CD ROM is a Read-Only Memory device loosely based on the Compact Disc system that's been the hottest thing in the hi-fi world for the last few years. In contrast with CD ROM disks, which can be written only at the factory, WORM is designed to be written on by the end user.

The one-way data flow means that WORM drives are necessarily more expensive than CD ROM players simply because CD ROM players don't need recording circuitry. While you can find CD ROM players as cheaply as $300, WORMs list for up to about $4,000. The huge cost difference—much more than could be justified by a couple bucks of recording circuitry—results from the cost savings accrued through quantities of scale. CD ROM players benefit from their similarity to audio machines, which are made by the million while a few thousand WORM drives might be sold every year. Additionally, WORM drives need higher-powered lasers to do their work writing data.

You'd think both WORM drives and rewritable optical units would be very similar. After all, both use light beams to read and write by changing the reflectivity of disks held in cartridges. But dig deeper and you'll see they're not. Although the functional difference between WORM drives and rewritable optical storage is the number of times a given part of the storage medium can be written to, the two systems use fundamentally different technologies. Although both systems are based on laser technology, their operating principles are quite unalike. Most erasable disks rely on a special optically bistable medium that can be shifted between two states of reflectivity (which may differ only by a few percent) under the joint influence of the laser and a magnetic field. Hence, they are magneto-optical systems. The WORM drive uses a laser to alter the reflectivity of the disk or to ablate a hole in a thin metal film (actually, the laser only pokes a tiny hole in the medium; surface tension enlarges it to its final form).

Most importantly, the WORM drive is not an unsuccessful or incomplete erasable optical disk system. In its present form, the

WORM is a completely functional product with its own unique purposes. When used in the right applications, the unalterable nature of WORM data is a virtue, not a weakness.

The WORM disk provides a permanent archive of the information it records. The WORM works when you want to grow huge, enduring databases yourself; need to maintain a full audit trail through months and megabytes of bookkeeping records; or demand step-by-step backups covering the full evolution of a project. Because they are unalterable, these WORM records cannot be accidentally or purposely changed or manipulated. In these applications, immutability becomes a virtue.

Nor do WORM disks suffer from the ravages of time. While common phenomena like the magnetic fields of telephone bells and the aurora borealis conspire against all forms of magnetic storage, today's optical WORM disks are safe from just about everything except acetone rains. The *claimed* life for WORM optical cartridges is ten years, versus three years for magnetic media. Barring cataclysm, the data on a WORM cartridges will endure longer than the expected life of the host computer into further decades.

WORM Systems

Because WORM is a specialized, niche technology, the range of available products is small. While about a dozen manufacturers are active in the area, the majority of drives currently sold are made by a couple of manufacturers, Literal (formerly Information Storage Inc.) and Panasonic. Normally, you wouldn't have to worry about who made a disk drive because the various products would be interchangeable to some extent, the way that CD ROMs, rewriteable optical cartridges, and floppy disks have been standardized. But the WORM industry is not guided by a single standard. Instead, you have your choice of a number of incompatible standards, each advocated by its particular manufacturer or a small group of manufacturers. Hence, the manufacturer you choose will determine the standard you get, which will determine the capabilities of the drive.

The confusion is abetted rather than absolved by standards organizations. While two standard-setting organizations have embraced the optical field—the International Standards Organization (ISO) and the American National Standards Institute (ANSI)—the leading WORM manufacturer also follows its own, proprietary standard.

And the differences aren't little, easily resolvable things like sector size or color of the cartridges. The standards vary about such indisputable differences as the size of the cartridge, the capacity of the cartridge, and the data storage format on the cartridge. For example, today most WORM cartridges use discs measuring about $5\frac{1}{4}$-inches in diameter, but the protective shell wrapped around these discs varies in thickness and mechanical accouterments—rendering different manufacturer's products non-interchangeable. You can't slide a cartridge meant for one drive into a drive made under another WORM standard.

The digital contents of the cartridges also varies. The ISO standard allows for a total cartridge capacity of about 650 megabytes. Among others, Pioneer, Laser Magnetic Storage, and Hitachi make drives that conform to ISO specifications. Literal makes drives that conform to the ANSI standard and hold about 1.2 gigabytes per disk. Another Literal product uses a somewhat thicker cartridge (but the same disk inside) that meets the ISO standard but packs an incompatible capacity of 1.2 gigabytes. Panasonic follows the beat of its own drummer and is able to fit about 940 megabytes into its proprietary cartridge. While you might be tempted to follow the standards organization of your choice rather than a proprietary system, take note that the Panasonic proprietary standard yields the lowest cost per megabyte of WORM systems.

Besides the $5\frac{1}{4}$-inch WORM drives most often used by personal computers, larger systems are also available for applications that are even more specialized. Among the most popular of these are 12-inch disks that provide the basis for immense digital libraries and information retrieval systems. A single 12-inch cartridge can hold six megabytes—3.2 per side. Those prodigious amounts can be multiplied by juke boxes, WORM cartridge changers that automatically select and load cartridges when the data stored on them are required. The leading manufacturer of 12-inch WORM systems is Sony.

In general, the cartridges used by personal computer WORM systems consist of a thin metalized film medium encapsulated in a clear polycarbonate plastic disk. The actual disk is further protected by a high-impact plastic shell with a sliding metal door that allows access for the optical read/write head of the drive.

WORM disks are sold with the optical equivalent of a low-level format already in place. Some of the first WORM drives formatted their cartridges with grooves that the laser beam tracked to write and read information. This style of formatting has been superseded in nearly all existing drives by flat disks on which servo information is blasted onto (and through) the disk with a laser. As with floppy disks, WORM disks can be either single-sided or double-sided. But unlike magnetic media, however, WORM cartridges must be physically flipped over to access the second side, exactly as you would with an old-fashioned vinyl phonograph record.

WORM drives themselves conform to the $5\frac{1}{4}$-inch form factor used by older hard disks. (Except, of course, those that use 12-inch and other size cartridges!) Nearly all available WORM drives require a full-height drive bay, although a half-height model is available from Ricoh. While at one time all WORM drives used proprietary interfaces, the SCSI connection is now dominant in the field. Nearly any WORM drive that you buy today will have an SCSI interface.

WORM Applications

Today's WORM technology lends itself best to three applications: data acquisition, archival backup storage, and data retrieval systems. In that all WORM drives deliver very much the same physical virtues (cartridges, archival integrity, and so on), software best distinguishes different products and how they are better suited to one application than another.

If you are typical among those who need a backup system, you probably hope to need a WORN—Write Once Read Never—system more than a WORM. Backups are something that you hope to *never, never, never* need.

In that you hope you won't ever have to pry your data back off your WORM, the most important aspect of the WORM when backing up is how fast and conveniently you can transfer information to it. The critical elements in forming your purchase decision should be the ease of use of the backup software (if any) accompanying each system and its speed in transferring information to disk. Although you need the assurance that the restoration process will work (and be able to recover as much or as little as you lose), restoration time won't be too important to you unless your disasters come with painful regularity—in which case you may need other forms of therapy than what the WORM provides.

When you need to work with your archives—searching through them for a particular phrase or drawing—speed in the other direction becomes more important. You need a system that reads from the disk quickly. For instance, if you plan to file your boilerplate forms and contracts on optical disk or build a database of magazine articles, you'll want to be able to recall files fast.

You'll also want to explore the ease-of-use of the systems, whether all functions require you to type commands or just select from a menu. Installation can be bothersome, but you only do it once. Besides, this book should help you find your way through the worst of its trials.

Because a WORM drive is such a specialized and expensive proposition, you'll probably want to explore the products more thoroughly than you would other computer purchases before you buy. Try them out if you can. In particular, get a demonstration of the software accompanying the drive.

Rewritable Optical Disks

The ultimate goal of most developers of optical drives is to create a product that combines all the advantages of optical storage (long life, reliability, storage density) with the flexibility, speed, and ease of use of conventional magnetic drives. Above all, the medium must be erasable and reusable so that files can be updated over and over again. The promise of this grand unification of benefits has provided incentive for research and development of several rewritable optical storage technologies—dye-polymer, phase-change, and magneto-optical media.

Dye-polymer storage

The premiere example of the first of these technologies, and the one that has received the most publicity, is the aforementioned CD-compatible THOR system, promoted as a Compact Disc on which you can record. THOR itself is an acronym for Tandy High-performance Optical Recording system. As with any of the dye-polymer systems, THOR relies on translucent disks with a dye-tinted inner layer that swells into a bump when heated by a laser. The bump changes the reflectivity of the disk and can be detected by the same optical system as is used in a Compact Disc player. A second laser can make the bump relax, effectively erasing the data that have been previously written. As of this writing, THOR remains in development and is not available commercially.

Phase-change storage

In phase-change rewritable optical systems, the recording medium is cycled between crystalline and amorphous states to store the ones and zeros of digital code. That is, the recordable material can arrange itself into the regularly ordered lattice of a crystal or into a form in which its constituent molecules are randomly organized like a compressed powder. While the chemical make-up of the medium remains the same as it changes between states, its reflectivity is altered. The result is that the medium can be made into tiny light and dark patches that can be used to encode digital information.

In effect, these state changes are effectively the same media alteration that's used in some WORM drives. Some commercial products actually use this technology to function as dual-purpose units—a single drive can handle both rewritable and WORM cartridges. Just slide in the kind of disk you want to use—almost. Differing WORM and rewritable cartridge standards complicate matters.

Magneto-optical Storage

The third technological choice, magneto-optical, is currently the most widely used rewritable optical method. Consequently, most rewritable optical drives are today called *MO drives*.

The magneto-optical name describes the principal used in these products. The recording medium in each disk is basically a magnetic material, and it relies on magnetic fields to store information. The difference between MO drives and conventional magnetic disk drives is that the MO product uses a tightly focused laser beam to supplement a magnetic field to write data onto the disk. The laser itself is used without the magnetic assist to read the disk.

The combination of optical and magnetic technologies results from necessity. Because the MO medium must be used over and over again, it poses problems in writing data. Unlike CD ROM mastering machines, for example, the MO laser cannot be used destructively to blast pits or holes in the MO medium. The physically damaged disk would be difficult to reuse. But other than blasting away the medium and its magnetic field, a laser by itself cannot alter the magnetic alignment of the material. Nor would writing magnetically offer hope of delivering the unique advantages of optical storage. If a magnetic head were used to write data, it could pack information no more densely than the information would be packed on a conventional Winchester disk. There would be no incentive to use the fine probe of a laser beam to read the disk—no reason for optical technology to be used at all.

A technological twist allows the light beam to read magnetic fields. The laser, which is bounced off the disk to read its data, is polarized. That is, the plane of orientation of its photons in the laser beam are all aligned in one direction. When the polarized beam strikes the magnetically aligned particles of the disk, the magnetic field of the media particles causes the plane of polarization of the light beam to rotate slightly, a phenomenon called the *Kerr effect*. While small (as little as a 1 percent shift in early MO media but now reportedly up to 7 percent), this change in polarization can be detected as reliably as the direct magnetic reading of a Winchester disk.

One important difference separates MO from both phase-change and dye-polymer technologies. The latter two rely on a physical change in the properties of the optical medium that results in a change in reflectivity, while the magnetic field reversal used by MO drives is not a physical change of state. The magnetic particles never change or even move.

Materials that undergo physical changes of state suffer stress that can reduce the effective life of the material because of fatigue. It's like the metal shell of an airliner that must expand and contract each time the cabin is pressurized. After too many cycles, the material may fatigue and fail, potentially giving everyone onboard a clear view of the heroic measures of the captain in preventing disaster. The media used for both dye-polymer and phase-change rewritable optical disks have limited lives because of such fatigue. Magneto-optical media do not.

Whether these fatigue-prone technologies can be used successfully as computer storage depends on their use and the number of state changes they can safely endure. Typical phase-change media are rated for lives in excess of ten thousand cycles. While just a few thousand cycles may sound sufficient for use in computer disk storage, even a million cycles may be woefully inadequate in a conventional PC mass storage system. While you may not erase and rewrite the entire contents of your disk drive very often, DOS busily rewrites the file allocation table on the disk every time you create or add to a file. That may happen thousands of times a day. If used like an ordinary magnetic disk, state-change optical media may quickly fail with errors occurring first in the most important storage area on the disk, the FAT.

That's not to say phase-change and dye-polymer media are entirely unworkable. They're just not amenable to normal DOS operations. By clever engineering FAT changes can be minimized, for example by moving the FAT before it becomes overwrought. State-change disks can also be effective when buffered by traditional magnetic hard disk media—ongoing changes are made to the hard disk and only occasionally are those changes spooled off to the optical drive. State-change disks are also suitable for specialized applications that require a limited number of write cycles. A writable digital disk storage system for home audio is an example, the purpose for which the Tandy THOR system is primarily targeted. Because most people will record only a few times (even a few thousand) on a given part of a disk, the medium would not be unduly stressed.

Changes in magnetic polarity are well understood and generally believed to be completely reversible. After all, that's how traditional magnetic media—hard disks and floppies—work. Because MO drives are based on this well-understood principle, they are generally considered to be capable of an unlimited number of write-rewrite cycles. There's no worry about stress, fatigue, failure, and data loss.

How Magneto-optical Drives Work

Instead of using optical or magnetic principles alone, MO drives combine them. They use a conventional magnetic field, called the *bias field*, to write data onto the disk. Of course, this field is limited by the same factors in Winchester disks—the size of the magnetic domains that are written is limited by the distance between the read-write head and the medium and is, at any practical distance, much larger that the size of a spot created by a focused laser. To get the size of a magnetic domain down to truly minuscule size, MO drives use the laser beam to assist magnetic writing. In effect, the laser illuminates a tiny area within a larger magnetic field, and only this area is affected by the field.

This optical-assist in magnetic recording works because of the particular magnetic medium chosen for use in MO disks. This medium differs from that of ordinary Winchester drives in having a higher *coercivity*, a resistance to changing its magnetic orientation. In fact, the coercivity of a MO disk is about an order-of-magnitude higher than the 600 or so Oersteds of coercivity of the typical Winchester disk.

This high coercivity alone gives MO disks one of their biggest advantages over traditional Winchesters—they are virtually immune to self-erasure. All magnetic media tend to self-erase; that is, with passing time their magnetic fields lose intensity because of the combined effects of all external and internal magnetic fields upon them. The fields just get weaker. The higher the coercivity, the better a medium resists self-erasure. Consequently, MO disks with their high coercivities are able to maintain data more reliably over a longer period than Winchester disks. The quoted lifetime for MO disks is ten years. While that's difficult to prove because MO drives have not even existed for ten years, many people in the industry view that claimed lifetime as conservative. Traditional magnetic media require refreshing every few years to guarantee the integrity of their contents. Mainframe computer data tapes are typically refreshed every two years. MO media promise to substantially extend the time between refreshes, if not eliminating the need for refreshing entirely.

The high coercivity of MO media also makes the disks resistant to the effects of stray magnetic fields. While a refrigerator magnet means death to the data stored on a floppy disk, it would likely have no effect on an MO disk (but you still wouldn't want to clamp your MO disks to your system unit with refrigerator magnets). This resistance to stray fields means that you have to worry less about where and how you store MO cartridges.

Along with such benefits, the higher coercivity of MO media brings another challenge: Obtaining a high enough magnetic flux to change the magnetic orientation of the media while keeping the size of recorded domains small. Reducing this high coercivity is how the laser assists the bias magnet in an MO drive.

The coercivity of the magnetic medium used by MO disks, as with virtually all magnetic materials, decreases as its temperature increases and becomes zero at a media-dependent value called the *Curie temperature*. By warming the MO disk medium sufficiently close to the Curie temperature, the necessary field strength to initiate a change can be reduced to a practical level. The magnetic medium used by MO disks is specifically engineered for a low Curie temperature, about 150 degrees Celsius.

The same laser that's used for reading the MO disk can simply be increased in intensity to heat the recording medium past its Curie temperature. This laser beam can be tightly focused to achieve a tiny spot size. While the magnetic field acting on the medium may cover a wide area, only the tiny spot heated by the laser actually changes its magnetic orientation because only that tiny spot is heated high enough to have a sufficiently low coercivity.

The Magneto-optical Drawback

The design of today's MO drives has one intrinsic drawback. The bias magnetic field must remain oriented in a single direction during the writing process. It cannot change because the high inductance of the electromagnet that forms the field prevents the rapid switching of the magnet's polarities. Consequently, the bias magnet in today's MO drives can align magnetic fields in a given area of a disk track in only one direction each time that portion of a track passes beneath the read/write head. For example, when the bias field is polarized in the upward direction, it can change downward-oriented fields on the disk to upward polarity but it cannot alter upward-oriented field to the downward direction.

In order to work reliably, the MO recording process requires that all fields on an area to be written are oriented in a single direction before the data are written. In other words, a given disk area must be separately erased before it can be recorded. In conventional MO drive designs, this erasure process requires a separate pass under the bias magnet with the polarity of the magnet temporarily reversed. After one pass for erasing previously written material, the actual information is written on a second pass, changing only the areas to be changed with laser heating.

The penalty for this two-step process is an apparent increase in the average access time of MO drives when writing data, which is already slow for other reasons. Although speeds vary, many MO drives spin their disks at a leisurely 2,400 revolutions per minute, roughly a third slower than Winchester disks (which typically operate at about 3,600 RPM). Each turn of such an MO disk therefore requires 25 milliseconds. Even discounting head movement, the average access time for writing to an MO drive cannot possibly be faster than at least 37.5 milliseconds. (On the average, the data to be erased will be half a spin away from the read-write head—12.5 milliseconds—and a second spin to write the data will take an additional 25 milliseconds.) Understandably most manufacturers are working on "one-pass" MO drives and are speeding the spins of their disks.

The MO drive also suffers another performance handicap. While Winchester read-write heads are typically flyweight mechanisms weighing a fraction of a gram, the read-write heads of MO drives are massive assemblies of magnetic and optical parts. Typically, this MO head mounts on a sled that slides on parallel steel tubes. Moving that massive head requires a robust mechanism and, thanks to the principal of inertia, takes substantially longer to speed up, slow down, and settle as compared to a Winchester head. In fact, when it comes to average access time, there is almost no comparison between Winchesters, which can now write data as quickly as 15 milliseconds between random bytes, and MO drives which, at their current best, are no faster than 60 ms—not counting the twice-around write penalty.

The optical sled used by MO drives isn't without its redeeming qualities, however. Unlike the Winchester drive head, which must fly microinches above the media surface to pack data tightly on the disk, optical heads can work at a distance. The guide rods absolutely fix the distance between head and disk that's truly huge compared to Winchesters—and with that distance comes safety. Head crashes are impossible on MO drives because the head is restrained from moving close to the media. In fact, only the laser beam ever touches the disk surface (or should—keep your fingers out of the protective door in the MO cartridge!). As with CDs, the optically active surface of an MO disk is sealed beneath a tough layer of transparent plastic, again minimizing damage. The laser beam focuses through the clear covering. Because the beam is out of focus at the surface of the disk and only converges to a spot underneath the clear surface layer, the effect of imperfections such as scratches or dust on the top of the disk have relatively little effect on the accuracy of disk reading or writing. Of course, MO drives also incorporate error-correction to minimize the appearance of errors in the stream of stored data.

Magneto-optical Media Considerations

Clearly, speed is not a compelling reason to upgrade to an MO drive. You'll get substantially better performance from a good Winchester magnetic hard disk. And Winchesters will always have a performance advantage over MO products, at least if you believe the predictions made by hard disk manufacturers. But MO drives have their own distinct advantages that can make them an excellent choice for some applications.

Capacity is often cited as one advantage of MO products. That's not necessarily true. Today $3\frac{1}{2}$-inch magneto-optical drives offer no dramatic capacity difference from run-of-the-mill magnetic hard disks. They allow only about 125 megabytes of on-line storage per cartridge side. Small optical cartridges make their case with other virtues.

Even $5\frac{1}{4}$-inch magneto-optical drives do not outshine the capacities of magnetic drives despite their greater storage densities. But direct comparisons between Winchester and MO capacities are misleading. The quoted capacities of both types of drives are in roughly the same ballpark, but the technologies are playing different games. Drives using $5\frac{1}{4}$-inch disks may quote roughly similar capacities for either technology, a maximum of about a gigabyte. But Winchester drives might use up to eight internal disks or platters (15 recordable surfaces) to achieve that capacity while the higher data-packing density of MO drives allow them to reach the same figure with a single platter locked inside a removable cartridge.

The capacities quoted for MO cartridges are misleading, however. Although MO drives are quoted with capacities in the range 600 to 1,000 megabytes, only half of the figure that manufacturers commonly quote is on-line storage. The discs in today's cartridges array their storage across two sides, and current MO drives have a single read/write head, so only one side of a cartridge can be read from or written to at a time. To access the other side, you have to physically remove the cartridge from the drive, flip it over, and slide it back in. Consequently, only half of the total capacity of the cartridge is actually on line at a time.

On the other hand, while MO drives are usually rated with capacities per cartridge, a single drive has an effectively unlimited capacity. Run out of space, and you only need slide in a new cartridge or flip over the one that's in the drive. You can stock up on as many cartridges as you can afford (the price per cartridge currently is about $250). Of course, only about 300 megabytes of that unlimited total can be accessed at a time.

Most makers of MO drives also offer jukebox systems, sometimes termed *autochangers*. These units can automatically shift among several disks to achieve astonishing near-line storage abilities, 50 to 100 gigabytes. It's called near-line storage because you have to put up with a slight wait as the autochanger finds the correct cartridge and spins it up to speed. The jukeboxes are not priced to put them in the budgets of most individual PC owners. They are products for information servers.

Magneto-optical Standards

Data exchange depends on standardization. The cartridges written on one machine must be readable by others. In the last year, MO drives have gone a long way to achieve the necessary standardization to the extent that the International Standards Organization (ISO) has propounded a set of specifications for $5\frac{1}{4}$-inch and $3\frac{1}{2}$-inch MO cartridges. The ISO standard guarantees that any ISO-standard cartridge can be used in any drive supporting the ISO standard. Although that sounds like a straightforward statement, it has its complexities.

For $5\frac{1}{4}$-inch MO disks, the ISO standard is actually a dual standard. It allows cartridges of two types, those that store data in 1024-byte sectors and those that store data in 512-byte sectors. Because larger sectors mean less overhead—among other things, fewer sector identification markers are required—1024-byte-per-sector cartridges can store more data, about 650 megabytes per cartridge (about 325 per side) versus 594 (often rounded to 600) megabytes for 512-byte per sector cartridges (about 297 megabytes per side). The actual capacity of each cartridge varies and is inevitably smaller than these figures because, as with hard disks, magneto-optical cartridges may have bad sectors that cannot be used for data storage.

Under the ISO standard, a drive must be able to read and write both types of cartridges. Drives produced before the standard was adopted (or by companies not recognizing the standard) may be limited to one or the other size. Some manufacturers offer drives that support not only ISO cartridge standards but their own, proprietary storage formats. For example, the Tahiti drive produced by Maxtor augments its ISO abilities with a special format and data storage method that packs up to one gigabyte per cartridge. Using constant linear velocity recording, it fills the longer, outer tracks of each disk with more sectors full of data. The ISO standards call for constant angular velocity recording (meaning the disk spins at a constant rate), which puts the same number of sectors—and the same amount of data—on every disk track.

As with all too many personal computer *standards*, the ISO standard is *not* a panacea that guarantees cartridges written in one MO drive will be readable by another. Although the ISO standard does specify the physical format in which data are stored on the disk, it does not indicate the logical format. Different system integrators may opt for their own disk partitioning schemes, and the software drivers used by one MO system vendor may not recognize the partitioning used by another maker. Note that few MO drive integrators opt to use standard DOS partitioning, although the introduction of Version 5.0 may change their perspective on DOS.

Compatibility is not the only issue that partitioning affects in MO drives. The way the capacity of an MO cartridge (as well as the disk's formatting and even the number of bytes per sector) has a perhaps unexpected effect on the data throughput performance of a drive. A cartridge partitioned for standard 32-megabyte DOS volumes may deliver half the effective throughput of a drive using a proprietary partitioning scheme that allows the entire capacity of one cartridge side to be addressed as a single volume. This performance effect arises because of larger volumes on MO cartridges result in larger DOS storage clusters, and larger clusters reduce the overhead involved in extended data transfers.

Performance of MO drives also varies more widely than conventional hard disks because the ISO standard specifies that MO drives use the Small Computer System Interface (SCSI) to connect to their hosts. While this interface choice has its advantage in flexibility (for example, up to seven SCSI devices can be connected to a single host adapter), SCSI also can be a handicap for DOS users. ISO magneto-optical drives, like all SCSI devices in DOS-based computers, can be severely constrained by the performance of the SCSI host adapter used. A good SCSI host adapter will allow an MO drive to transfer data at the speed data can be recovered from the spinning disk, a rate on par with today's best Winchester hard disks. A poor SCSI adapter may limit mass storage throughput to 10 percent of its possible peak rate and make the overall system look painfully slow. Worse, SCSI systems do not integrate seamlessly with today's PCs and DOS. With many of today's MO systems, installation can be a headache, particularly if you try to connect devices from more than one manufacturer to a single SCSI host adapter.

MO Cartridges

The strongest point of the ISO standard is that it strictly defines the MO cartridge and the media it contains. Not only does this aspect of the standard assure physical compatibility of cartridges, it also ensures that multiple sources of supply will be available, potentially making media less expensive.

Despite their common name, most $5\frac{1}{4}$-inch cartridges are filled with optical disk platters that actually measure 130 millimeters (5.12 inches) in diameter. The cartridges themselves measure .43 by 5.31 by 6.02 inches (HWD) and somewhat resemble $3\frac{1}{2}$-inch floppy disks in that the disk itself is protected by a sliding metal shutter.

The magnetic medium on an MO disk is constructed from several layers. First, the plastic substrate of the disk is isolated with a dielectric coating. The actual magneto-optical compound—an alloy of terbium (a rare-earth element), iron, and cobalt—comes next, protected by another dielectric coating. A layer of aluminum atop this provides a reflective surface for the tracking mechanism. This sandwich is then covered by 0.30 millimeters of transparent plastic. Disks are made single-sided, then two are glued together back-to-back to produce two-sided media.

Unlike conventional Winchester disks that store data on a number of concentric tracks or cylinders, under the ISO standard MO drives use a single, continuous spiral track much like the groove on an old vinyl phonograph record. The spiral optimizes the data transfer of the drive because the read/write head does not need to be moved between tracks during extended data transfers. It instead smoothly scans across the disk.

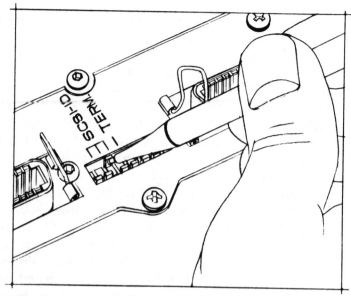

Figure 9.2 The first step in installing any SCSI-based optical drive is to set the SCSI ID on the drive itself. SCSI devices use DIP switches (shown), rotary switches, or jumpers to set their IDs. Each device must have an unambiguous ID.

Magneto-optical Applications

The spiral tracks of MO cartridges demonstrate that designers of the drives recognize that the technology is not at its best when randomly accessing data, but rather favors large sequential transfers. Consequently, current MO drive systems are not aimed at universally replacing Winchester hard disks as primary mass storage media. Their role today is seen as secondary mass storage—the uncharted territory that lies between hard disks and streaming tape.

In other words, MO drives are not for every application, but they have significant strengths that make a particularly good chioce when a safe, secure means of storing hundreds of megabytes is required. Graphics and audio/visual systems are particular candidates because MO cartridges provide the capacity needed for easy exchange of extremely large files. Engineers, for example, can put huge CAD files on disks to archive them.

MO drives can also make an excellent backup medium, particularly for network applications. A single cartridge can back up all but the largest hard disks. Moreover, the ability to rewrite cartridges allows them to fit traditional into backup arrangement in which backup media are routinely recycled. Compared to tape media, restoration of files from MO disks is fast and easy. However, MO cartridges are substantially more expensive than open-reel or cartridge tapes of the same capacity by a factor of at least two.

MO disks can also serve as an excellent archival medium. Cartridges are compact enough to carry several in a briefcase or lock securely in a safe. Data stored on them is safe for long-term storage because MO media are virtually free from self-erasure and resist external magnetic perils, thanks to their high coercivity.

In some systems, MO drives could replace hard disks as the primary mass storage system. With suitable caching software, the apparent performance of MO disks can be hoisted nearly to the level of a conventional hard disk. The lag in access time will still become apparent during cache misses, however.

Writing an obituary for hard disks is probably premature. Rewritable magneto-optical disks probably won't displace Winchester technology soon. Like most new technologies, MO will likely achieve its greatest success in a new role, one that it will likely define itself. As it stands now, MO technology is both useful and available. And it affords possibilities that may change the way you use your PC.

Optical Drive Installation

Because all of today's optical drives use an SCSI connection, you can follow the same procedure to install any current optical device, be it CD ROM, WORM, or magneto-optical. Once you understand the ins and outs of the SCSI connection, installing an optical drive is easy, an ordinary mechanical installation followed by SCSI set-up.

Note that your system will have to have a pretty hefty array of other equipment to take advantage of your optical drive. In most cases, you'll need a hard disk. Even when CD ROM or WORM software doesn't demand a hard disk, you'll need one to make such drives useful. A rewritable optical drive can substitute for a hard

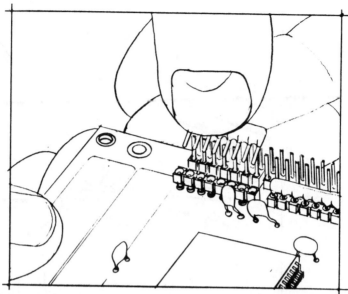

Figure 9.3 Next, make sure that your SCSI system is properly terminated. The first device (typically the SCSI host adapter) and last device should be terminated. Remove terminations of the other devices in the chain by throwing the appropriate switch or physically removing the termination resistors as shown here.

disk, but in nearly all practical applications you'll use the optical drive to supplement rather than replace a magnetic drive.

In addition to the hard disk, you'll want at least the DOS maximum of 640K of memory to accommodate the SCSI drivers and other software that accompanies your optical drive. Some systems—particularly CD ROMs—will benefit from extended or expanded memory. Some even demand it. You'll want to make sure that you have sufficient RAM to get your drive operating.

You'll also want an up-to-date version of DOS. Most optical systems require DOS 3.3 or later. If you have an earlier version, you'll need to update before you upgrade to optical.

Once you're sure your PC is properly equipped to use your optical drive, you can begin the upgrade.

The first step is to set up the details of your SCSI system. Check the documentation that accompanied your optical drive player to determine whether it requires you to set a particular SCSI ID number to be properly recognized by its software driver. If so, set the number on your optical drive to match what the software driver

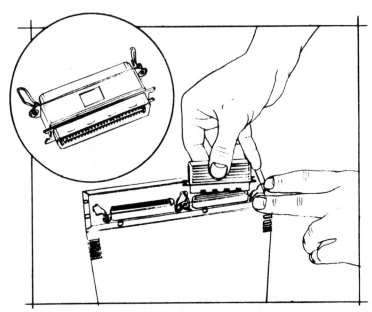

Figure 9.4 Some SCSi devices use external terminations (inset) that plug into the second SCSI connector on the last device in the SCSI chain. Clip the termination plug into place so that it doesn't become loose.

documentation specifies. If the driver does not require a specific number, you'll still want to check the SCSI ID number of your optical drive to ensure it does not conflict with any other SCSI device you plan to connect. Anyhow, you'll need to know this number later during the software installation process. *Write it down.* A good place to record it for quick access when you need to know it is the title page of the equipment manual.

Next, check the SCSI termination on your new optical drive. If you plan to make the optical drive the only SCSI device you will connect to the host adapter, or if you want the new optical drive to be the last device in your SCSI chain, you should set the drive to terminate. Otherwise, it should not terminate the SCSI line.

In most cases, you'll adjust the termination either by setting a switch or plugging a dummy termination plug into the drive. To use an external termination, just slide the dummy termination plug into one of the two SCSI jacks on the back of the optical drive, then snap the retaining wires toward the center of the connector to hold it securely in place. Otherwise remove the termination resistors from the drive or switch the termination off. Because the easiest way to install an optical drive is as the only SCSI device connected to a host adapter, you'll probably want to terminate the SCSI connection at your hard disk.

Optical drives delivered bare for internal installation nearly always have termination resistors already installed on the electronic circuit board on the drive itself. In single-drive internal installations, you shouldn't need to alter the drive or system terminations in any way.

Once you've set the drive terminations, check the instructions accompanying your optical drive to see if your SCSI host adapter requires any hardware set-up. Most SCSI host adapters come already set up to work in PCs that have a single hard disk controller. If you've added a lot of disks or expansion boards to your PC—or another SCSI controller—you'll want to check to see if you need to change jumper settings to accommodate the new SCSI host adapter. If such adjustments are, in fact, required, follow the drive's installation manual in making them. In general, you'll throw a DIP switch or two or alter some jumper settings.

After you set up the host adapter, you're ready for the mechanical part of the installation of your optical drive. Start by switching off your PC. You should never install an expansion board or drive (magnetic or optical) in your computer while the power it on. For safety's sake (for both you and the SCSI host adapter), disconnect your PC's power cable. Now open your PC's case so you have access to its expansion slots and, if you will install the drive internally, its disk drive bays.

For internal drive installations, position the drive in the bay you choose to use, but do not secure it in place. Connect the power cable—one of the cables made from four discrete wires coming from your PC's power supply—but not the SCSI cable—to the drive. Because the white nylon connector at the end of the power cable is keyed, you cannot install it improperly. If it doesn't fit into the jack on the back of the drive, invert the connector (twist it over 180 degrees) and try again.

Next install the SCSI host adapter in a vacant expansion slot in your PC. You can usually just plug the host adapter into any expansion slot into which it fits. Be certain to twist the board's retaining bracket screw firmly in place.

Figure 9.5 Once you set the terminations and SCSI ID numbers, install your SCSI host adapter. Be sure to match the bus width to the needs of the host adapter. Screw the host adapter in place, then plug your SCSI cable into it (inset).

Should you choose to install your optical drive internally, the best slot to use is the one immediately adjacent to your hard disk controller, the rightmost free slot, or simply the one closest to the drive. Your principal concern is to make the challenge of routing the SCSI cable from the host adapter to the drive as easy as possible.

Now attach one end of the SCSI cable supplied with your optical drive to the host adapter. If you are installing the optical drive externally, screw the cable in place to the jack on the back of the host adapter. Connect the other end of the SCSI cable to your optical drive.

If you're making an external installation and you plan to connect other SCSI devices, plug the SCSI from the host adapter into one of the jacks on the drive and plug the cable leading to the next SCSI device to the other jack on the drive. If your drive uses an external termination and is the only SCSI drive to be connected to your host adapter, the jack to use should be obvious—it's the only one free because the other SCSI jack is filled with the termination.

If you're making an internal installation, fold the SCSI ribbon cable so that it smoothly flows from host adapter to the drive. Plug the connector (the last connector on the cable if there is more than one) into the SCSI drive. Professional installers make hard right-angle and 45-degree bends in the ribbon cables, folding the cable tightly against itself so that it doesn't push out all over everything like honeysuckle in a too-fertile spring. Because you haven't secured the drive in place (at least if you've been following these instructions), you should be able to pull it out slightly to reach the jack on the drive. Once both ends of the SCSI cable are connected, secure your internal drive in place.

It's safe now to plug the power cable back into your PC. If you've made an external drive installation, also connect the power cable to your drive and plug the other end of the cable into utility power.

Some optical drives are shipped with "dummy" disks installed to protect the mechanism from shipping damage. Sometimes you must mechanically release this disk before you switch on the power to your drive. Others will eject the dummy disks—either automatically or upon your command—after you power up the drive. Check the instructions accompanying your drive for the proper method of removing any dummy shipping disks.

Once everything is plugged in, and shipping disks that require removal are removed, turn on your optical drive (if you've installed it externally) and boot up the computer. While you're waiting for your computer to come up, follow the drive-makers instructions for loading a disk or cartridge into the drive. (Most optical drives must be turned on to load and unload disks.)

Your PC may boot differently from the way you've become accustomed. The first time you boot up after you've installed an SCSI host adapter you'll probably see new messages on your monitor screen, possibly even an error message alerting you that your new drive isn't ready for use. Often—but not always—these messages can be ignored the first time because you have to run some set-up software to properly configure your new drive. If, however, you persist in getting an error message after you've performed the entire software installation for your new optical drive, you'd better check out what's causing the messages.

When your system boots the first time after you've installed your optical drive, follow the procedure in the drive's instruction manual to configure it and install any necessary software drivers. Typically,

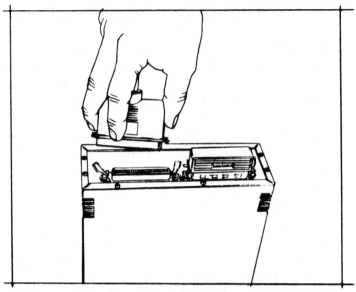

Figure 9.6 Connect all the other SCSI devices in turn. Each SCSI device except the last (shown here) will have two cables—one leading to the device, and one going to the next device in the chain.

you will receive a diskette with the optical drive that has an automatic installation program on it. Most of the time you can slide this disk into your A: floppy disk drive, log onto that drive, and run a program called SETUP or INSTALL. These programs are usually self-explanatory. Check the instructions that came with your drive to find out the proper name of the set-up program.

Once you've installed the software driver, reboot your computer to put the driver into memory. You should see a new boot-up message informing you that the drive has been installed properly. If the software of your optical system supports DOS directly, verify that the new drive operates properly by using the DIR command on it, ensuring that you have a disk in the drive. Otherwise, follow the drive-makers instructions for using the drive to verify that it works.

Once you've confirmed that you can see a directory of the contents of the cartridge in your optical drive or have otherwise verified that the drive is working properly, turn off your PC and reinstall the cover to its case. Your optical drive system is now ready to use. Follow the instructions for the software that accompanied the drive to use it.

10.

ADDING PORTS AND MODEMS

To connect your PC to an external peripheral, you'll need a port of some kind. The two most common are serial ports, which are used for everything from mice to speech synthesizers, and *parallel* ports, which are primarily used for printers, but are increasingly finding application for data transfer. To extend the reach of your PC from your office to the world, you'll also want a modem, a supercharged, special-purpose serial port.

Ports, ports, and more ports—that's what you need to tie your PC to all the peripherals you want and dream about. A mouse, a modem, a plotter, a speech synthesizer, a file transfer link with your laptop—each of those goodies probably demands a serial connection. And those that abstain from speaking serially want instead a parallel port. Because most PCs only come with one or two ports, eventually you'll need to add ports—perhaps in the form of an internal modem—to your PC.

Without enough ports, you have to twist into the contortions of a combination switchboard operator and sideshow India rubber man on amphetamines, plugging and unplugging cables every time you want to connect something to the single serial and parallel port that are standard on most PCs. Little wonder that ports are the most common, most needed, and—surprisingly—least expensive upgrades granted PCs. An extra port can cost as little as $10 to $20 and install in minutes. Just order a board from just about any ad in any computer magazine and slide the board into an expansion slot.

Only afterward will you discover the truth, in the two evenings you spend figuring out why your new ports won't work. While serial and parallel ports are among the easiest and cheapest upgrades you can make, they are not without their own idiosyncrasies. You can't just add ports willy-nilly, nor can you expect all port hardware to work in every PC.

Not all serial ports are the same, nor are all parallel ports. Some have different speed capabilities. Some have different computer compatibilities. And some may just not do what you want them to. Moreover, the ports you can add depend on what ports you have. What will work may depend on what software you plan to run.

Don't give up. With a little insight and planning, you can be sure your new ports will be the perfect upgrades for your PC. All you need to know is how to pick the right board and bring all its features to life.

Serial Ports

If ports were nothing more than connections to be made on the rear panel of your PC, you wouldn't have any worries about installing a second, third, or fourth serial port. But ports have to go deeper. They must link not only with the hardware of your PC but with your software, too. After all, a mouse connected to a serial port does you no good if Windows can't follow its pawprints, nor will your modem be a benefit when your terminal program doesn't know it's connected.

The necessary linkages between ports and your system are made at several levels. The port ties into your expansion slots so that your PC's electrical signals can cross over its circuits. It logically links to your system's BIOS so that your PC hardware knows at what addresses it can send instructions to the registers on the port expansion board. And DOS couples with it by assigning a name to the port. Only after all these linkages are made can programs that take advantage of DOS services know where to go when they want to communicate. More importantly, these linkages conspire together to limit both the speed and number of ports that you can attach to your PC. While you can beat some of the limits, others are more stalwart in their obstinancy.

The roots of the primary port problems are more than a decade old. When IBM initially crafted the PC, the company's engineers really had no conception of what the machine would be used for. They had no idea that you might want to connect all manner of external devices to your Personal Computer because no one had ever attached a PC to anything before. After all, virtually no one (in comparison to today, anyhow) had a PC to link up or anything to connect to one.

The good news is that when they designed the original PC BIOS—which for complete compatibility every clone computer must match—the IBM engineers allowed space for identifying four ports each of both the serial and parallel persuasions. But the bad news is that when they assigned the addresses from which these ports could operate, they allowed for only two serial ports and three parallel ports. This limit applied whether ports were available on the rear panel of your PC or were embedded in internal devices like modems. DOS allowed for an equal number of names to match the assignments. As a result, even though you could load up to four serial port addresses into your system's BIOS, until DOS Version 3.3 was released only two serial ports could be recognized by the operating system and most applications.

While some board hardware could add supernumerary serial ports, these could link only to proprietary programs because the logical addresses used by the additional ports were nonstandard. For example, a number of internal modems were located at logical addresses recognized by some communications programs but not by other software. Only the software knowing these proprietary addresses would work with these ports. DOS 3.3 and later—introduced with the first of IBM's PS/2s—finally expanded its understanding to four serial ports, and the new machines assigned standard addresses to them. Consequently, if you plan on adding serial ports to stretch your system's quota beyond two, you'll need DOS 3.3 or later.

On the other hand, the original bequest of three parallel ports has proved bountiful enough that designers have made no new provisions for adding more to PCs. No matter the version of DOS you have, you can handle three parallel ports.

There are other compatibility problems with ports. Speed is one. In the original IBM design, serial ports were designed to operate at rates of 50 to 9,600 bits per second. This speed was pushed up to 19,200 bits per second in the new PS/2 Models 90 and 95. Even that is not sufficient to run today's latest external high-speed modems at full speed. Consequently, some companies have developed special, high-speed serial ports that operate at 38,400 bits per second.

Surprisingly, many programs that use serial ports—in particular, data transfer utilities—operate at even higher speeds, say 115,200 bits per second or so, using conventional low-speed serial ports. The reason is that IBM's rating includes the overhead of using the BIOS to communicate with the serial port, which imposes software overhead. Moving a single character to a serial port requires your PC to execute hundreds of instructions. Data transfer programs that take direct control avoid the use of the BIOS and cut overhead per character to a few instructions. The actual operating speed of a serial port is determined by a divisor that's set in the register of a timing circuit. Using a big divisor, IBM put the brakes on serial circuitry to limit its speed to 9,600 bps or so. By reprogramming this time base—essentially eliminating the divisor—fast file transfer programs can accelerate nearly any serial port to its hardware-enforced limit of 115,200 bps. Commercial communications programs and modem applications require the protection and assurances provided by using the overhead-consuming routines and are thus limited to the nominal port ratings that IBM and other manufacturers put on their products.

Timing circuitry and overhead is not the only speed constraint on serial operation, however. The actual processing capacity of the chips used to generate the serial signals used by the serial port limits how quickly they can react to the commands sent by your PC. Some chips are not fast enough to keep up with today's PCs.

The chips in question are called UARTs (Universal Asynchronous Receiver/Transmitters). Three different UART chips are used in PC applications. They share a family resemblance, which allows them to all operate with the same software but differ in their speed capabilities.

The UART used by the original IBM PC was termed the *8450*, and it's the slow child of the family. It's not even capable of operating at the speeds demanded by an ordinary 80286-based PC. While the 8450 will work in the original PC, XT, and most eight-bit "turbo" computers, it can't cut it in ATs and more powerful machines based on the 386 and 486 microprocessors.

For these faster PCs, the minimal UART chip is the 8450's successor, the *16450*. This chip will work in nearly any computer. It can keep up with the fastest—at least at the nominal serial port speed rating—and doesn't mind holding back when dropped into a slow PC.

But the 16450 has been itself supplanted by a new, improved chip, the *16550*. Completely backward in its compatibility with the 16450, the 16550 adds a 16-byte first-in, first-out buffer, which allows the new chip to keep communicating even when a multitasking computer turns its attention to other projects. When properly programmed (and using the right software), the 16550 can carry out its 16 bytes of communications on its own. By the time the 16550 runs out of data, the multiprocessing system will probably have had a chance to restock its buffer. This ability to communicate on its own allows a fast, continuous flow of data even under multitasking systems.

Because the newer, faster UART chips are backwardly compatible with the older ones and because they do not suffer from being operated too slowly, your biggest concern in buying a port upgrade is to be sure you get a product that uses UART chips fast enough for your PC. Or even the fastest possible UART chips. If you ever plan on using a serial port board in an AT, for example, you need a 16450 or better UART chip on it. The 16450 and 16550 are pin-for-pin compatible with one another, so you can always upgrade the older chip for the newer one simply by pulling out the old and inserting the new. If you have even vague plans of trying this upgrade, be sure that any serial port board you buy puts a socket underneath its UART chips.

Some system units and a few aftermarket boards don't use UARTs at all. Instead they substitute VLSI (Very Large Scale Integration) chips that have several functions built in. For example, the Western Digital 16C552 combines the the electrical equivalent of two 16550 UARTs and a parallel port into one chip. Port boards that use VLSI chips are capable of matching the speed needs of any PC.

Many port boards come standard with a single serial port but provide provisions for you to later add a second one. Usually all you need to add is a UART chip and a cable. While any of the above three UARTs may fit in the waiting socket, you're best off getting the best. The latest design assures the highest speeds and most reliable operation.

Parallel Ports

Parallel ports are simpler than serial in that no special circuitry is needed to change data from one format to another. Computers think in parallel fashion, and deliver data that way to their port circuits. Data bound for a serial port must be translated by a UART chip before they go out.

Although they are simpler than serial ports, not all parallel ports are the same, however. The printer ports of the original IBM PC were exactly that—output-only ports designed to connect to printers. In later machines, these ports developed bidirectional abilities so that they could both transmit and receive data. (IBM first announced this ability with the introduction of its PS/2 line, but the feature was actually available on earlier machines.)

Nearly all parallel products that come as factory equipment in today's PCs are bidirectional, and some system accessories take advantage of this feature for higher-speed data transfers. For example, laptop file exchange programs (like the more recent versions of Traveling Software's LapLink) can use parallel connections to double or triple their transfer speed.

Not all parallel ports on upgrade boards are bidirectional, however. Because two-way parallel ports require bidirectional logic buffers—which are more expensive than the one-way kind—the least expensive port upgrade boards are likely unidirectional. Be wary of these boards. If you want to use your new port for more than just printing, you'll want it to go both ways. Ask when you order to be sure that any parallel port you buy is truly bidirectional.

In coming years, you may face a new port design choice—*bus mastering ports*. The ports take advantage of a new technology that is only useful in EISA and Micro Channel computers. Thanks to the advanced expansion buses in these systems, the specially designed bus-mastering ports can take control of data transfers from your system's microprocessor. With this control shift, your system will be able to speed up data transfers by eliminating most of the work its microprocessor would ordinary have to do, moving the tough part of the transfer to the circuitry of the bus mastering board. IBM's latest high-performance systems, its Models 90 and 95, use bus-mastering serial and parallel ports. Few bus-mastering port upgrades are currently available, although that may change as designers try to eke out more speed for their products.

Port Addresses

When you install ports in your PC, they must be assigned input/output addresses through which your system, using its BIOS, can communicate with the registers on the port adapter board. These addresses must be unique for each port so each one can be unambiguously identified. Typically, you assign the addresses used by most port upgrade boards by changing jumpers on the board or running set-up software.

When your PC boots up, it checks for these port addresses by querying the board and loads the address values into the PC's memory at a special location. DOS then checks that location to find which ports are available and assigns a name to each port based on its position in memory.

The BIOS rules of loading port addresses are the most important. Your system goes in quest of ports in a particular order. It searches for serial ports in this sequence: 3F8(Hex), 2F8(Hex), 3E8(Hex), and, finally, 2E8(Hex). It looks for parallel ports in this order: 3BC(Hex), 378(Hex), and 278(Hex). As it finds each port of a particular type, it plugs the corresponding address value into the locations reserved for that purpose in the *BIOS data area*, the lowest reaches of your PC's RAM, which start at absolute memory address 0400(Hex). The first eight bytes here hold the four serial port addresses; the next eight bytes are reserved for parallel port addresses. When DOS loads, it reads the addresses from the BIOS data area and assigns each one a name in exactly the order in which they are listed in the BIOS data—COM1 through COM4 for serial ports, LPT1 through LPT3 for parallel ports, with the name PRN also assigned to LPT1 as a default.

The scheme can result in some perplexing effects when you make an upgrade. For example, when you plug in a second parallel port, its address may occur earlier in the sequence than the port you already have installed. The new port will then preempt LPT1 and take that designation itself. As a result, the printer or other device you had connected to the first port won't respond like it used to after you add the upgrade. Your software will still send data out LPT1 but it will go to the new port and ignore the old one (which has become LPT2).

The practical outcome of this switch-hitting of ports is that you may think you've ruined your PC by upgrading it when, in fact, all is well. You just have to let your software know the changes that you've made to your system. Either reinstall your software and advise it of your revised port assignments, or rearrange the cables on the back of your PC to match the new port nomenclature.

Worse than this name-changing confusion is when you err in configuring your new ports by inadvertently assigning two ports the same addresses. As a result, one, the other, or neither port may work. In this case, you'll have to change the hardware settings on one of the ports so that each port has its own unique address.

OS/2 uses different addresses for its serial ports beyond the first two. In addition, it will accommodate up to eight serial ports. If you plan on using a port upgrade with OS/2, make sure that it will respond to the addresses used by that operating system. Table 10.1 summarizes the addresses used by OS/2 ports.

Table 10.1 Input/output port assignments for OS/2 serial ports.

OS/2 Port Name	I/O Port Address (Hexadecimal)
SERIAL 1	03F8
SERIAL 2	02F8
SERIAL 3	3220
SERIAL 4	3228
SERIAL 5	4220
SERIAL 6	5228
SERIAL 7	5220
SERIAL 8	5228

Most serial ports require that you assign them an interrupt for them to work properly. While some port upgrade boards automatically select the interrupt to use based on the port address you designate, others make interrupt assignment an additional step, seemingly just to confuse you. The serial port assigned to COM1 normally should be given hardware Interrupt Request (IRQ) 4. Serial port COM2 normally uses IRQ3. COM3 shares IRQ3 with COM2, and COM4 shares IRQ4 with COM1. Parallel port interrupts are usually not assignable.

One of the biggest problems you'll face when you want to add another port or two is that not all port upgrade boards know all the I/O address assignments. Many ports allow you to assign their serial ports as COM1 or COM2 only. With such a board you won't be able to get more than two ports to work in your system, no matter how many boards you add or how many serial ports are already installed in your PC. In other words, be sure that the serial ports on any upgrade board you buy can be assigned as COM3 or COM4 as well as COM1 and COM2. If you plan on using OS/2, you'll need even greater flexibility.

When assigning names to serial ports, don't forget that internal modems have their own, embedded serial ports that take an address like any other serial port. If you have an internal modem, one fewer port address will be available for your upgrade. The modem's serial port address may also conflict with the address of other ports, so you'll need to know the value that's assigned to it.

You'll also want to study up on your system unit because many PCs now have at least one serial and one parallel port installed on their motherboards. Be sure you know which ports are already installed, what addresses they use, and how to reassign their port addresses (or how to switch off the ports).

Port Connectors

A seemingly trivial concern with important implications is the connector used by your port upgrades. If you already have something to plug into the port, you'll want to be sure the connectors match. If they don't, you'll need to get the appropriate adapters.

With serial ports two styles of connector are popular, 9-pin and 25-pin male D-shells. The original PC used the 25-pin scheme. Because the AT put both a parallel and serial port on the same expansion board, which was limited in size by the original design of PC-option retaining brackets (the metal strip on the back of each expansion board), there was not enough room for a full 25-pin jack for each. The parallel port needed all 25 connections and couldn't be shrunk, so the serial port was trimmed to its essentials, nine pins. Port boards that offer a parallel and a serial port attached to the same retaining bracket use the AT scheme. PS/2s reverted back to the 25-pin serial-port scheme because their connectors were mounted on the rear panel of the machine rather than on the retaining bracket of an expansion board. Most port upgrade boards that offer a second serial port usually move the second serial port to a separate retaining bracket and give it a 25-pin jack.

The only difference between 9-pin and 25-pin jacks is that you might need an adapter to match certain peripherals to one or the other. Most mice, for example, use 9-pin connectors but come with adapters to mate them with 25-pin jacks. As long as you have matching cables or adapters, the style of jack used for a serial port does not matter. The two styles use the same signals and work the same with standard serial devices.

Parallel ports are standardized with 25-pin female D-shell connectors. Game ports, when offered by upgrade products, also follow a standard, using female 15-pin D-shell connectors. To distinguish game ports from VGA outputs, which also use 15-pin D-shell connectors, look at the arrangement of pins. The pins on game ports are arranged in two rows, while the 15-pin connectors used by VGA adapters use three rows of pins.

Shopping for Port Adapters

Unlike other products, such as hard disks and display adapters, that you might buy as upgrades, you'll find a glaring lack of brand names among port expansion products. The fierce competition has resulted in low prices—so low in fact that most brand name suppliers can't or won't compete. Most of the port products that you find will consequently be inexpensive, anonymous, and likely oriental.

That's not to say that they are not very good. Port technology is rudimentary in comparison with today's latest 33 MHz 486 computers, so it doesn't take a bevy of rocket scientists with silicon slide rules to design the circuits or the latest surface-mount equipment to make the boards. Most port expansion products will work unerringly in most PCs.

Of course, you can still get a bad board, so you need to rely more on vendor support than for brand name products. Because you have no one else to turn to when something goes wrong, pick a vendor whom you trust and upon whom you can depend.

You also need to be sure that the port upgrade that you choose includes the features that you need, for example, port addressability and bidirectional parallel ports. You'll want to select a vendor who can answer your questions about his product, deliver what you want, and accept it back if it does not meet your expectations and needs.

The one exception to the no-name port board philosophy is the high-speed super serial port that can operate at 38,400 bits per second even when allowing for full DOS overhead. The boards, necessary for the highest speed of today's modems, are available only from a few manufacturers with well-known brand names. They also cost substantially more than the generic offshore competition. That's the price you have to pay to get the best performance for your PC.

The typical port expansion board will be half the length of a standard expansion slot (there's so little circuitry that a lot of board space is not required), the height of an XT expansion slot, and use an 8-bit bus interface connector. There's little need for a 16-bit interface because the ports themselves limit the transfer rate well below that which the eight-bit ISA bus can handle.

Most of these boards will be equipped as standard equipment with one parallel and one serial port. Some make a second serial port an inexpensive (say, $10) option. The second-serial option kit buys you another UART, a short length of cable, and a mounting bracket. You will inevitably need a second serial port, so the option is well worth the price.

Some port boards also include a game port for connecting a joystick. Although you might not regard having a game port as a big advantage, it's certainly no disadvantage. Consider it a free bonus.

Multifunction boards that combine memory and ports are still available for some kinds of PCs. Some of these are even backed with name brands. A multifunction board that uses an 8-bit bus connection can be a worthwhile addition to a PC or XT if you can also use the memory expansion. Similarly, a 16-bit card will benefit a six- or eight-megahertz AT. However, avoid adding such memory boards to faster, most powerful computers (any machine rated at 12 megahertz or faster) because such a board can slow overall system performance on memory operations.

Port Preparation

The first thing to do when you're considering port expansion—even before you buy a board—is to make a list of the port locations used by your existing ports to determine available port address assignments and whether adding another port is even feasible. You have several options in determining the ports already installed in your computer. First, check your system's documentation and that included with all the expansion boards installed inside your PC. These should list the ports already provided (and thus the addresses used) by your PC. You can also use commercial system-reporting software such as *Check It*, *InfoSpotter*, or *System Sleuth* to determine what port addresses your system already uses and which are available. Be wary, however. These products are not infallible. Sometimes they make mistakes and miss ports or incorrectly identify them. Another tool that has the advantage of being free is the DEBUG program that's typically included with DOS.

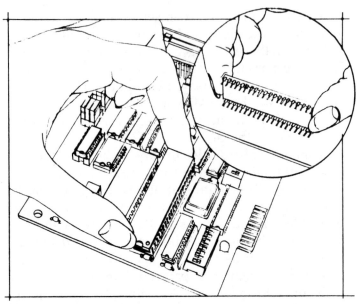

Figure 10.1 Most port upgrade boards require that you install a second UART chip to add a second serial port. Prepare the board before you plug it into your PC by sliding the chip into the vacant slot on the board. First, staighten the pins of the chip (inset), insure that the notch on the chip and socket line up, then push in the chip.

DEBUG allows you to check what's stored in your system's memory, including the BIOS data area.

To determine what ports are used using DEBUG, first run the DEBUG program itself. After it loads, it will present you with a hyphen as a prompt. It may not look like much, but that hyphen is the key to a powerful tool. To use it, type the following command at that DEBUG hypen prompt:

D 40:0

This tells DEBUG to display the contents of the 40th paragraph of memory (if you count hexadecimally like your PC does). In other words, you are asking to see the contents of your system's memory at absolute address 400(Hex), the part of the BIOS data area where the various port assignments are stored. After you type the command, you should see a block of numbers displayed on your screen, similar to this:

```
-d  40:0
0040:0000  F8  03  F8  02  00  00  00  00-78  03  00  00  00  00  00  00   ........x.......
0040:0010  2D  44  04  80  02  00  00  80-00  00  28  00  28  00  34  05   -D........(.(.4.
0040:0020  30  0B  3A  27  30  0B  0D  1C-06  21  64  20  65  12  67  22   0.:'0....!d e.g'
0040:0030  08  0E  62  30  75  16  67  22-0D  1C  64  20  20  39  00  80   ..b0u.g'..d 9..
0040:0040  AB  00  C0  00  00  00  01  03-02  03  50  00  00  10  00  00   ..........P.....
0040:0050  00  18  00  00  00  00  00  00-00  00  00  00  00  00  00  00   ................
0040:0060  07  06  00  D4  03  29  30  00-00  00  00  00  50  00  0F  00   .....)0.....P...
0040:0070  00  00  00  00  00  00  00  00-14  14  14  14  01  01  01  01   ................
```

Your concern is the top line, which shows the first paragraph—16 bytes or 10(Hex) bytes—of memory at location 400(Hex). The numbers on the far left are sign posts to tell you where you are in memory. The block of two-digit numbers left of the central hyphen on the first line are eight bytes used for storing the addresses used by serial port assignments, the eight bytes on the right hold the parallel port assignments.

Each port assignment is split among two numbers (actually byte values), the two bytes given in reverse order according to the byte arrangement convention of Intel Corporation. The first pair of numbers is COM1, the second pair COM2, and so on. An assignment of 0000 indicates that no port of that number is present. In the example above, two serial ports are assigned, COM1 at 03F8 and COM2 at 02F8, and one parallel port, LPT1 at 0378. The last two byte entries in the parallel port section are irrelevant because only three such ports are allowed. Ignore any numbers you find there.

Rather than relying exclusively on any one of the three methods of port determination—documentation, commercial software, and DOS DEBUG—the best strategy is to use all three to cross-check one another. In general, the most reliable is DEBUG because it does no interpretation of the facts that might result in an erroneous display.

Once you know how many ports you actually have assigned, you can calculate how many you can add. Choose a port expansion product that matches or exceeds your needs. In most cases, you can switch off the ports that conflict with existing ports, either on your

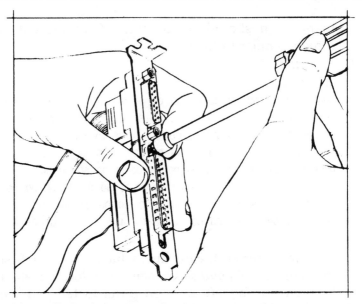

Figure 10.2 You'll also have to install extra port connectors in a retaining bracket. Slide the connectors through the rear of the bracket, then screw the connectors in from the front. A nutdriver is the best tool.

system board (for ports originating there) or on your port expansion board (for the ports it provides).

Next is the tough part: Finding the one right port board for your needs. You'll end up checking magazine ads, perhaps even visiting your dealer. When you order, be sure you let the vendor know how many ports you want to add and what locations you have available for those ports. If you need a port at COM3, let the vendor know. And make sure that the parallel ports you get are truly bidirectional and that each serial port is equipped with at least a 16450 UART chip.

Port Installation

When you get your new port board, your first job is to configure it to match your system, to fold the ports it provides around the ones your PC has installed. Once you know the addresses that your PC already uses for its ports, you can assign nonconflicting addresses to your new port adapter board. In most cases, you will have to set

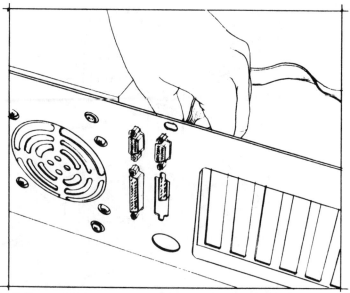

Figure 10.3 If your PC has cut-outs on its rear panel, use them instead of wasting a slot for the extra port connectors. Slide the connectors through the chassis from the inside, then screw in the hardware from outside.

DIP switches or jumpers on the board to assign its addresses. Because every port adapter board uses a different array of switches and jumpers to make its settings, no general directions apply to selecting the right switch and jumper positions. Check the documentation accompanying the board for the proper switch and jumper settings.

If you're adding more than the one parallel and one serial port that are available on most port upgrade boards, you'll need to do a bit more preparation. A second serial port may require that you install an additional UART (which you should order with the board). Fortunately, the chip installation process is easy. A UART is installed like any other integrated circuit. First, prepare the leads (legs) of the chip so that they are at right angles to the body of the chip so they fit properly into the chips socket. Hold the chip longways between your fingers and press the whole row of pins on one side of the chip down against a smooth, flat surface (such as a desktop) until the leads form a 90-degree angle with the body of the chip. Once the pins are straight, align the chip over the socket that's waiting for it. You must be sure to properly orient the chip,

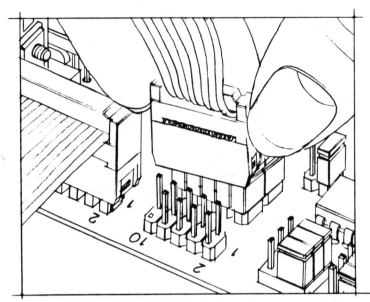

Figure 10.4 Before you slide the port adapter board into an expansion slot, plug the cables from the external connectors into it. Be sure to observe polarity. The side of the connector nearest the red or blue stripe on the cable goes to pin one on the port adapter board.

lining up the notch that appears on one edge of the chip with corresponding notch in its socket. Finally, press the chip into its socket. Double-check your work and double-check to ensure that it is oriented properly and that none of the chip's pins have folded underneath the chip or have splayed outward from the socket.

Most port boards only have room for two connectors on their retaining brackets. When you add more than one serial port from a single board, or if you have a game port on the board, you'll have to attach the supernumerary jacks to the upgrade board using short cables, which should be supplied with the board. The second serial port will likely use a 25-pin jack and the game port a 15-pin jack, each tethered to a short ribbon cable.

To hold these jacks in most PCs, you'll need to mount them on an additional retaining bracket. Sometimes they are supplied already installed in a bracket. Otherwise you may have to install them in a bracket yourself. If the jacks and bracket are delivered as separate pieces, put them together by first removing the two screws and nuts at the outer ends of each jack, then push the jack through

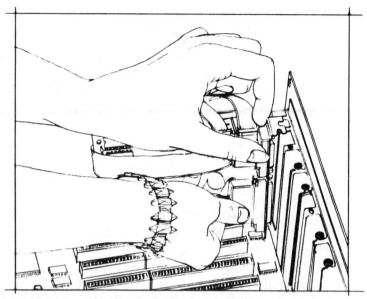

Figure 10.5 Slide the port adapter board into a vacant slot. Then slide the retaining bracket with the external connectors into the adjacent slot. Screw both the port adapter and extra retaining bracket into place.

the matching hole in the retaining bracket, and finally reinsert the hardware you removed to hold the jack securely in place. Some PCs have cutouts on their rear panels to accept these extra jacks directly. You can save an expansion slot if you use these cutouts instead of an additional retaining bracket. If you plan to make use of these cutouts, first remove the hardware from the extra port connectors and any small blank panels blocking the cutouts now—but don't yet install the jacks in the cutouts.

Before you install the port upgrade board in your PC, attach the extra serial and game port connector cables to it. As with the UART chip, proper orientation is important. The side of the cable with a red (or blue) stripe should be aligned with pin one of the header that the connector plugs into on the upgrade board. Pin one is usually identified by a small silkscreened number on the board.

Once the cables are attached, slide the board into any vacant expansion slot in your PC and screw it in place. Any slot will do in most cases. Because port adapters use 8-bit interfaces, you can use 8- or 16-bit expansion slots. And because most port adapters are short cards, you can take advantage of the abbreviated slots behind your disk drives. Once you've slid the board into the slot of your choice, locate a nearby slot to use for the optional second retaining bracket for the extra port jacks. Remove the retaining bracket from this slot. Finally, install the second port adapter retaining bracket in this slot. If you've opted to install the extra jacks in rear-panel cutouts, now is the time to do so. Use the hardware you removed from the jacks earlier.

Once you've screwed everything in and organized the cables, you're finished the hardware part of your upgrade. Check your work by running DEBUG again to see your new address assignments.

Before you use your new ports, you'll want to verify that you haven't changed the names of any of your old ones. Try using your already-installed peripherals, and verify that they work like they used to. If not, reinstall your software—each and every program you normally use that sends something out either a parallel or serial port—to reflect the new port designations or rearrange the peripheral cables you've plugged into the various ports on your PC.

Modems

If you want to extend the reach of your PC from its serial ports to link to any other computer in the world through the dial-up telephone network, you absolutely need a modem. More than a matter of manifesto or electrical necessity, it's the law. You cannot let your PC and telephone line directly conspire together without a modem to bridge them. So sayeth the FCC, the steward of the wires and airwaves of United States.

Although the need for a modem is foregone once you decide on a dial-up telephone link, your choice of modem is hardly so simple a decision. Besides manufacturers and models, you have to pick a standard to follow. Where once all was orderly and the decision was easy—you had but two choices, and both of those were dictated by the iron hand of Mother Bell—today the selection of modem standards is wider than that of telephone companies.

Distinguishing this surfeit of standards is an alphabet soup of acronyms, an assortment of speeds, and more features than Detroit can list as options on the sticker of the latest highway hog. Today you can find standard modems that push data through at rates as high as 38,400 bits per second, that can send a fax to the local delicatessen to bring lox and a bagel to your doorstep, or can field dozens of phone calls while you waste away in your hot tub sipping imported mineral water.

Finding the right one can be as daunting as prospecting in the wilderness. You have a general idea of what you're looking for—wealth, fame, fortune, and saving telephone line charges—but only a faint inkling of an idea what form the object of your quest will take. When prospecting, you can turn over rocks and poke around with a stick or you can hire a survey company with a geophysical network of linked seismographs to scientifically narrow the search. Fortunately, finding a modem can be a simpler sortie (if less exciting), with this chapter substituting for the geologist's survey.

Modem Function and Purpose

Along with the meaning of life, one question has perplexed more computer owners than perhaps any other: Why do I need a modem? After all, the modem seems to be the most contrived computer accessory ever foisted on an otherwise astute segment of the buying public. Both your PC and your telephone deal in the same stuff—electrical signals—so connecting them should be a job of nothing more than clipping in a patch cord. The requirement for using a modem is enough to make you suspect that the modem industry has a Congressional lobby second only to that of the National Rifle Association.

Far from a conspiracy of the communications-industrial complex, modems exist for the very good reason that computers and telephone lines get along about as well as crude oil and cormorants. While both computers and telephones use electricity for their communications signals, that's about like saying people and parrots use the same medium, sound waves in air. While computers use digital electric signals, telephones are based on analog technology. Although superficially similar, neither can make sense out of the other.

Much of that signal difference has to do with history. The first pained words out of Alexander Graham Bell's speaking telegraph were analog electrical signals. Little has changed since then. If Dr. Bell could sneak into the late 20th century and steal back to the 19th with a $5 telephone, he'd have almost no problem getting it to work with his own fledgling equipment. On the other hand, the technology of today is digital. Noise-free and error-free, digital signals can be transmitted over vast distances (say, from Neptune) without degradation. Digital signals are the same electricity that courses through your PC as its brain waves. Yet these same signals are completely incompatible with the century-old telephone system.

(Strictly speaking, digital communications are older the analog kind. The conventional telegraph predates the telephone by nearly three decades—Samuel F. B. Morse wondered what God had wrought in 1844—but most folks never installed telegraphs in their homes and otherwise failed to take advantage of the certainty of digital technology until the advent of the PC.)

The job of the modem is to accommodate today's digital pulses to a telephone network still firmly rooted in the 19th century. The modem converts digital data into audio-like signals that can be carried over telephone lines as if they were voice communications. Like electrical goodwill ambassadors, they help hostile signals get along together by making them converse.

Modems translate digital signals into analog through a process called *modulation*. In fact, the word *modem* is just a contraction for *modulator/demodulator*, a functional description of a modem's work. Modulation is the secret. The best of today's modems take advantage of modern modulation methods to squeeze in more than a dozen data bits where only one should fit. Modulation also is the great performance separator between modems. Faster modems—the one's that can operate up to 38,400 bits per second—use newer, more exotic modulation methods.

But modulation is not enough to reach the highest data rates. The latest modems can squeeze information through the telephone line faster by condensing it down to its essence, reducing or eliminating redundant information. By compressing your data, the modem can cut the time your telephone must be connected—and costing you money—to transfer a file of a given size. Because today's high data transmissions rates press against (and often beyond) the ability of an ordinary telephone connection to carry them, modems also need some way to detect—and, if possible, correct—any errors that might sneak in.

In addition, modems must carry out a number of seemingly trivial but important tasks in making and continuing the connection.

For example, a modem must be able to tell the difference between different transmission speeds so that it can automatically connect with another modem. Such speed-seeking is not a mere convenience. You couldn't tell one speed from another by yourself, even if you had perfect pitch and the hearing of a Pekinese pooch.

Most modems are boxes chock full of convenience features that can make using them fast, simple, and automatic. The best of today's modems not only make and monitor the connection, but even improve it. They dial the phone for you, even remembering the number you want and trying again and again. They listen in until they're sure of good contact, and only then let you transmit across the telephone line.

Understandably, modems are available in a great variety and choosing the right one is more difficult than plugging one in and connecting up. If you know what to look for—and what all the confusing terms mean—you'll be able to make the right choice as easily as selecting the right candy from the store.

Modem Standards

Neither men nor modems are islands. Above all, they must communicate and share their ideas with others. One modem would do the world no good—it would just send data out into the vast analog unknown, never to be seen (or heard) again—sort of like writing a letter to the editor of your local newspaper.

But having two modems isn't automatically enough. Like people, modems must speak the same language for the utterances of one to be understood by the other. Modulation is part of the modem language. In addition, modems must be able to understand the error-correction features and data compression routines used by one another. Unlike most human beings who speak any of a zillion languages and dialects, each somewhat ill-defined, modems are much more precise in the languages they use. The have their own equivalent of the French Academy—standards organizations.

In the United States, the first standards were set long ago by the most powerful force in the telecommunications industry—the telephone company. More specifically, the American Telephone and Telegraph Company, the Bell System, which promoted various Bell standards, the most famous being Bell 103 and Bell 212A. After the

Bell System was split into AT&T and the seven regional operating companies (Baby Bells, a situation also known as AT&T and the seven dwarfs), other long distance carriers broke into the telephone monopoly. Moreover, other nations have (not surprisingly) become interested in telecommunications.

As a result of these developments, the onus and ability to set standards moved from AT&T to an international standards organization, the *Comite Consultatif International Telegraphique et Telephonique* or CCITT (in English, that's International Telegraph and Telephone Consultative Committee). All of the high-speed standards used by modems today and the immediate future are sanctioned by the CCITT. These standards include v.22bis, v.32, v.32bis, v.42, and v.42bis.

Along the way, a modem and software maker, Microcom, developed a series of standards prefixed with the letters MNP, such as MNP4 and MNP5. The letters stand for Microcom Networking Protocol.

Standards are important when buying a modem because they are your best assurance that a given modem can successfully connect with any other modem in the world. In addition, the standards you choose will determine how fast your modem can transfer data and how reliably it will work. The kind of communications you want to carry out will determine what kind of modem you need. If you're just going to send files electronically between offices, you can buy two nonstandard modems and get more speed for your investment. But if you want to communicate with the rest of the world, you'll want to get a modem that meets the international standards. The following are the most popular standards for modems that are connected to PCs.

Bell 103 comes first in any list of modem standards not just alphabetically but because it was the first widely adopted standard, and it remains the standard of last resort, the one that will work when all else fails. It allows data transmissions at a very low speed.

Bell 103 uses a kind of modulation called *Frequency Shift Keying*, or *FSK*, in which different tone frequencies signify digital one and digital zero. Each change in the modem's signal thus carries one bit of digital information. Consequently, the Bell 103 standard is the only one in which the baud rate (the rate at which signal changes) is equal to the data rate. Bell 103 modems operate at a maximum data rate of 300 bps.

FSK signals are so resistant to noise and other line problems because frequency varies little, even with disastrous changes in a telephone connection or its routing. In fact, FSK is so reliable and straightforward that sound waves can carry it effectively. Thus a Bell 103 signal can be sent down a telephone line without direct electrical connection by putting a loudspeaker against (or near) a telephone microphone, a technique called *acoustic coupling*.

Bell 103 is the one popular modem standard that works most reliably with acoustic couplers, although some 1,200 and 2,400 bps acoustic couplers are available. In dire situations where a direct connection cannot be made to a telephone circuit, the Bell 103 standard attached with an acoustical coupler can be a safe haven.

Bell 212A is the next logical step in a standards discussion because it was the next modem standard to find wide application in the United States. It achieves a data transfer rate of 1,200 bits per second by switching to phase modulation from FSK.

In phase modulation, a fixed tone called a *carrier wave* is altered so that the phased of its wave cycles are altered to specific phase angles in relation to the unchanged carrier. For instance, in quadrature modulation (which is used by Bell 212A modems), each state differs from the unmodulated carrier wave by a phase angle of 0, 90, 180, or 270 degrees.

Under Bell 212A, the carrier wave can change up to 600 times per second or 600 baud. The four different phase states are sufficient to encode the four different patterns of two digital bits. Consequently, each baud (signal change) with its four states can carry two bits of information, doubling the actual throughput to twice the baud rate. Consequently a Bell 212A modem operates at 600 baud and transfers information at 1,200 bits per second.

While perhaps today's most widely used communication standard in America, many foreign countries prohibit the use of Bell 212A, preferring instead the similar international standard, v.22, discussed below.

LAPB stands for Link Access Procedure, Balanced, an error correction protocol designed for X.25 packet-switched services like Telebit and Tymnet. Some high-speed modem makers adapted this standard to their dial-up modem products before the v.42 standard (see below) was agreed upon. For example, the Hayes Smartmodem 9600 from Hayes Microcomputer Products includes LAPB error-control capabilities.

LAPM is an acronym for Link Access Procedure for Modems and is the error-correction protocol used by the CCITT v.42 standard noted below.

Microcom Networking Protocol is an entire hierarchy of standards, starting with MNP Class 1, a no-longer-used error-correction protocol to MNP Class 10, Adverse Channel Enhancements, which is designed to eke out the most data transfer performance from poor connections. MNP does not stand alone but works with modems that may conform to other standards. The MNP standards specify technologies rather than speeds. MNP Classes 2 through 4 deal with error control and are in the public domain. Classes 5 through 10 are licensed by Microcom and deal with a number of modem operating parameters.

MNP2 is designed to work with any modem that's capable of full duplex communications. It works by confirming each byte as it is sent by having the receiving modem check characters in blocks of 64, using 12 extra bytes so that the sending modem can compare what it sent out with what came back to see if any errors occurred during transmission. Of course, this two-way street of data cuts effective transmission rates to a theoretic maximum of 84 percent of what would otherwise be possible.

MNP3 improves on MNP2 by working synchronously instead of asynchronously. Consequently, no start and stop bits are required for each byte, trimming the data transfer overhead by 25 percent or more. Although MNP3 modems exchange data between themselves synchronously, they connect to PCs using asynchronous data links—which means they plug right into RS232 serial ports.

MNP4 is basically an error-correcting protocol, but also yields a bit of data compression. It incorporates two innovations. *Adaptive Packet Assembly* allows the modem to package data in blocks or packets that are sent and error-checked as a unit. The protocol is adaptive because it varies the size of each packet according to the quality of the connection. *Data Phase Optimization* eliminates repetitive control bits from the data traveling across the connection to streamline transmissions. Together, these techniques can increase the throughput of a modem by 120 percent at a given bit-rate. In other words, using MNP4 a 1,200-bit-per-second modem could achieve a 1,450-bit-per-second throughput. Many modems have MNP4 capabilities.

MNP5 is purely a data compression protocol that squeezes some kinds of data into a form that takes less time to transmit. MNP5 can compress some data by a factor up to two, effectively doubling the speed of data transmissions. On some forms of data, such as files that have been already compressed, however, MNP5 may actually increase the time required for transmission.

MNP6 is designed to help modems get the most out of telephone connections independent of data compression. Using a technique called *Universal Link Negotiation*, modems can start communicating at a low speed then, after evaluating the capabilities of the telephone line and each modem, switch to a higher speed. MNP6 also includes *Statistical Duplexing*, which allows a half-duplex modem to simulate full-duplex operation.

MNP7 is a more efficient data compression algorithm (Huffman encoding) than MNP5, which permits increases in data throughput by factor as high as three on some data.

MNP9 (there is no MNP8) is designed to reduce the transmission overhead required by certain common modem operations. The acknowledgment of each data packet is streamlined by combining the acknowledgment with the next data packet instead of sending a separate confirmation byte. In addition, MNP9 minimizes the amount of information that must be retransmitted when an error is detected by indicating where the error occurred. While some other error-correction schemes require all information transmitted after an error to be resent, an MNP9 modem only needs the data that were in error to be sent again.

MNP10 is a set of *Adverse Channel Enhancements* that help modems work better through poor telephone connections. Modems with MNP10 will make multiple attempts to set up a transmission link, adjust the size of data packets they transmit according to what works best over the connection, and adjust the speed at which they operate to the highest rate that can be reliably maintained. One use envisioned for this standard is cellular modem communications—the car phone for data.

V.22 is the CCITT equivalent of the Bell 212A standard that delivers a transfer rate of 1,200 bit per second at 600 baud. It actually uses the same form of modulation as Bell 212A, but is not compatible with the Bell standard because it uses a different protocol to set up the connection. In other words, although Bell 212A and v.22 modems speak the same language, they are unwilling to start a conversation with one another. Some modems support both standards and allow you to switch between them.

V.22bis was the first true world standard, adopted into general use in both the United States and Europe. It allows a transfer rate of 2,400 bits per second at 600 baud using a technique called *Trellis Modulation* that mixes two simple kinds of modulation, *quadrature* and *amplitude* modulation. Each baud has 16 states, enough to code any pattern of four bits. Each state is distinguished both by its phase relationship to the unaltered carrier and its amplitude (or strength) in relation to the carrier. There are four distinct phases and four distinct amplitudes under v.22bis, which, when multiplied together, yield the 16 available states.

V.32 is an international high speed standard that permits data transfer rates of 4800 and 9600 bits per second. At its lower speed, it uses quadrature amplitude modulation similar to Bell 212A but at a higher baud rate—2,400 baud. At 9,600 bits per second, it uses trellis modulation similar to v.22bis but at 2,400 baud and with a greater range of phases and amplitudes.

Note that while most Group III fax machines and modems operate at 9,600 bits per second, a fax modem with 9,600 bps capability is not necessarily compatible with the v.32 standard. Don't expect a fax modem to communicate with v.32 products.

V.32bis extends the v.32 standard to 14,400 bits per second while allowing intermediary speeds of 7,200 and 12,000 bits per second in addition to the 4,800 and 9,600 bit per second speeds of v.32. Note that all of these speeds are multiples of a basic 2400 baud rate. The additional operating speeds that v.32bis has, but v.32 does not, are generated by using different ranges of phases and amplitudes in the modulation.

At 14,400 bits per second, there are 128 potentially different phase/amplitude states for each baud under v.32bis, enough to encode seven data bits in each baud. Because there are so many phase and amplitude differences squeezed together, a small change in the characteristics of a telephone line might mimic such a change and cause transmission errors. Consequently, some way of detecting and eliminating such errors thus becomes increasingly important as transmission speed goes up.

V.42 is a world-wide error correction standard that is designed to help make v.32, v.32bis, and other modem communications more reliable. The v.42 incorporates MNP4 as an *alternative* protocol. That is, v.42 modems can communicate with MNP4 modems, but a connection between the two won't use the more sophisticated v.42 error-correction protocol. At the beginning of each call, as the connection is being negotiated between modems, a v.42 modem will determine whether MNP4 or full v.42 error-correction can be used by the other modem. The v.42 is preferred, MNP4 being the second choice. In other words, a v.42 will first try to set up a v.42 session; failing that, it will try MNP4; and failing that, it will set up a communications session without error-correction.

V.42bis is a data compression protocol endorsed by the CCITT. Different from and incompatible with MNP5 and MNP7, v.42bis is also more efficient. On some forms of data, it can yield compression factors up to four, potentially quadrupling the speed of modem transmissions. (With PCs, the effective maximum communication rate may be slower because of limitations on serial ports, typically 38,400 bits per second.) Note that a v.42bis-only modem cannot communicate with an MNP5-only modem. Unlike MNP5, a v.42 modem never increases the transmission time of *incompressible* data. Worst-case operation is the same speed as would be achieved without compression.

Other Modem Considerations

All of these modem standards support true duplex communication. That is, data can be transferred in two directions at the same speed simultaneously. Before the v.32 standard was adopted, however, the makers of high-speed modems used their own, proprietary modulation schemes, some of which were true full *duplex*, some which used different speeds for sending and receiving, and some could only operate in one direction at a time, switching the direction of the flow of data as communications needs changed. These modems, once state of the art, have been relegated to oddball status by the acceptance of v.32 and v.32bis standards. Newer half-duplex, 9,600 bps modems now conform to an international standard, v.29.

That's not to say products that don't conform to the full-duplex standards are totally unusable. As long as you control both ends of the conversation, you can use these other high-speed modems successfully—even economically. Because they currently cost less than v.32 modems, the high-speed but nonstandard systems can offer great savings. The key to using this strategy successfully is having business offices or coworkers and friends who agree to adopt the same model of modem. The problem with using these nonstandard modems is that they are nonstandard and thus can foreclose on access to online databases and bulletin boards, which are quickly moving to v.32 (if they haven't already).

Note that with the exceptions of v.42/MNP4 and v.32/v.32bis, the various modem standards are independent of one another. That is, getting a modem that uses one standard does not assure that the modem will work with other (particularly slower) standards. For example, nothing in the Bell 212A standard requires a Bell 212A modem to be able to communicate with a Bell 103 modem. While most modems do incorporate more than one communication standard, such backward compatibility is not guaranteed by the standards themselves. Should you buy a v.22bis modem to communicate at 2,400 bps, you may be surprised if it does not work at 1,200 bps and slower speeds. So it is important to check all the standards a modem supports.

Fallback describes a capability with which some modems are endowed that allows them to test the quality of a telephone connection and negotiate using the highest speed that the connection will allow with the other modem. If, for example, a bad telephone line won't allow a modem to use full 9,600 bps v.32 communications, it may negotiate to use Bell 212A instead, falling back from 9,600 bps to 1,200 bps.

Modems that support multiple standards are not automatically guaranteed to fallback. They may try the speed for which they are set and, failing that, simply give you a "No Carrier" error message when they can't make sense out of the data on the telephone line. You've got to make the call again at a different data rate. Of course, you may get a better (or worse) line on the second try, so your modem may never be operating optimally for the connection. Automatic fallback is thus important in any modem you buy if you want to extract as much communications potential as you can from every dial-up connection.

Note, too, that once a modem falls back, it may not leap forward again. Many modems may slow down when a burst of noise or other transient problem temporarily degrades the quality of connection, then continue to operate at that low speed even if the connection quality improves. Other modems, such as those that follow MNP10, adjust their speed both upward and downward to accommodate any change in connection quality.

Modem speed is the major factor in setting the price of a modem. Faster modems are more complex and more exacting, consequently, they cost more. If you don't need the fastest modem in the world, you can save big. If you rarely transfer files, you probably don't need high speed. But if you're moving dozens or hundreds of kilobytes every day, a 9,600-bit-per-second or faster modem can pay for itself in lower phone bills in a matter of months.

One final note on modem speed: Don't think for a moment that you'll always get throughput of 9,600 bits per second from a 9,600 bps modem. The modem world doesn't work quite that way. Modem standards indicate only what signals a modem can deal with under ideal conditions, but not every connection is ideal. Modems vary in their ability to accommodate noisy telephone lines, changing levels, and other signal problems. Check modem specification to determine how well the product can deal with noise, what its minimum signal is, and other signal recovery features like echo-cancellation.

Over a perfect telephone line, nearly all modems function perfectly—without errors. However, perfect telephone lines are impossible to find, and even getting an acceptable one nowadays seems to require bribing an operator. The performance differences between modems appear as line quality goes down. Better modems are better able to cope with bad connections. They work with worse circuits and can pull data through with fewer errors.

One result of newer standards and protocols is that the effective throughput of modems will vary with line quality depending on the technical adroitness of the design of each product. Although two modems may each follow the same standard, one may move data faster than the other because fewer blocks of data must be re-sent because of errors that sneak in the telephone line. Unfortunately, this difference does not show up on the specification sheets; it can only be judged with rigorous testing. If you need to find a modem with the best possible performance, you're forced to depend on test reports and the reputations of the modem manufacturers.

Don't forget hardware reliability. As with other computer peripherals, the more reliable modems are those with fewer components (because there's simply less to go wrong). Look for a modem that uses the latest electronics (VLSI and Surface-Mount Components). More compact modems, by necessity, use these space-saving (and reliability-increasing) technologies.

Rapidly becoming a nonissue in modem purchases is the command set used by a product. The command set is the assortment of instructions a modem understands that tell it to carry out different functions (for example, dial the telephone or hang up). No command set has received official sanction by the CCITT as the one and only worldwide standard. However, most modems today follow a *de facto* standard, the Hayes command set. Also known as AT commands because each command line begins with the "Attention" characters "AT," this standard was originally developed by Hayes Microcomputer Products for use with its line of Smartmodems.

The popularity of Hayes modems led many software companies to incorporate AT commands in their programs. Other manufacturers adapted their modems to AT commands so that they could work with all the same software as Hayes modems. More communications were written using AT commands because of the proliferation of compatible modems. And so on. The result is that a modem that recognizes the Hayes command set will work with the widest variety of software. Modems with Hayes compatibility are thus more versatile.

Note, however, that the Hayes standard is not immutable. As new modem features and capabilities are developed, the command set becomes richer. A program that takes advantage of a newer, more advanced Hayes command may be frustrated by an older modem with a more limited command set. Some modems only recognize the most rudimentary of commands, for instance using ATDT to initial the dialing sequence. Others more elaborately mimic the operation of Hayes products and incorporate the same registers as used by Smartmodems, which permit, for instance, setting the number of rings required before the modem answers.

Hayes actually holds a patent on modem control that covers part of the AT command set, specifically the way that a command can interrupt a communication session. Consequently, any modem that claims 100 percent Hayes compatibility must be licensed by Hayes.

Other modem command sets have been used in the past, and modems that use non-Hayes commands are still available. The commands used by a modem are significant only to the extent that your communications program must know what commands to use. The commands have no effect on the data exchanged between two modems. You can use a non-Hayes modem as long as your communications program knows the command set of your modem. Of course, most communications programs understand the Hayes command set best. Unless you have masochistic tendencies or software that is specifically designed for another modem command set, the safe bet is selecting a modem that's as Hayes compatible as possible.

The final consideration in selecting a modem is the features that are offered. "Features" is a broad term that is used to indicate all the other differences between modems.

For the most part, the features of a modem determine how easily and conveniently it can be used. Primeval no-frills modems once required that you dial or answer the telephone manually and physically connect the modem to it at the appropriate time, for instance when you hear the carrier tone of the modem at the other end of the line. Today, such manual modems are rare, mostly just leftovers of obsolete product lines. All the circuitry required for auto-dialing and auto-answering of your phone are incorporated into the standard integrated circuits used by nearly all modem makers. These features come essentially free to the modem manufacturer, so you should expect them to come free to you, too.

In today's competitive communications world, you'll find that nearly all current modems are equipped with a basic minimum of features far beyond the needs of the casual user. Specific applications may demand features that are out of the product mainstream (for instance, AutoSync to allow your modem to communicate synchronously with an asynchronous connection to your PC). If you need modem abilities beyond basic dialing and answering, you should carefully check the features offered by the products you're considering.

Selecting one modem from the hundreds of products currently available is no small task. However, it can be made more tractable by making four separate judgments about each particular modem's performance, compatibility, features, and price. Choose the performance level you need, compatibility with the standards used by the services you plan to regularly connect with, the features to match the needs of your software, and the price you can afford. Although the modem you choose won't likely lead your PC on a quest to take over the world, it will connect you and your PC with the world of data communications.

More than any other PC peripherals, modems are likely to come with software, typically a full-fledged communications program. This software can be more than just a free program—it can be a key to unlocking particular modem features (such as the ability to use higher-numbered serial ports). Be sure to ask what you get when you order—and make sure it comes in the box when you get the modem.

Choosing Between Internal and External Modems

In general, all modems, regardless of the standards they follow, fall into two classes—internal and external. The difference is, of course, where the modem is installed: inside an expansion slot of a PC (in a laptop, it may be a dedicated modem slot); or external to the computer, connected by cable to a serial port. On the surface, physical appeal may seem the best guiding factor because often exactly the same circuitry is available in either of the packages. Other considerations might lead you to preferring one style of modem over the other, however.

An external modem offers the advantage of portability—you can move external modems between different systems, even those of different architectures. The same external modem can serve a PC, Mac, or Amiga as easily as moving a plug and cable from one system to the other. Even if you have two or more identical PCs (or whatever), moving an external modem between them is easier than swapping an expansion board between different systems.

Another advantage of external modems is that most of them give you a good look at what they are doing, courtesy of front panel light-emitting diodes that monitor vital modem functions. You can see the state of modem control signals and whether data are actually being sent or received. While you can run some diagnostic programs that will put a semblance of these indicators on your monitor screen when you have an internal modem, this software tends to complicate things and can even slow down communications.

Another reason to look at external modems is that sometimes you might not even be able to find an internal modem for your computer. For example, you might be blessed with an odd, old, discontinued machine (say a Data General One laptop) for which internal modems are not readily available. Or your small footprint PC might already be stuffed to its maximum three-slot capacity with a network adapter, SCSI adapter, and GPIB board for your scanner. You might simply not have room for an internal modem.

The big advantage of internal modems is that they tend to be a few dollars cheaper than external units. Internal modem makers can cut costs because they don't need all the extra packaging or power supplies (although they need some extra signal circuitry) required to make external modems.

Internal modems aren't always cheaper, however. Special-purpose internal modems, such as those designed to fit particular notebook-style PCs, often demand a price premium. Typically, the original manufacturer of the computer is the only source for such modems, and because the manufacturer controls the whole market, it can control the price, too. Then again, with notebook or laptop PCs, the convenience of putting everything in one totable package may offset the price difference. In other words, the manufacturer can get away with a bigger profit because you are willing to pay more for convenience.

For portable applications, the pocket modem can be an ideal compromise that keeps your costs under control. Small enough to actually put in your pocket (or the pocket of a laptop computer's carrying case), pocket modems retain all the advantages of external modems—in particular, the ability to quickly shift them between different PCs. In addition, pocket modems can save laptop and notebook computer owners something more important than cash: battery power. Many of the internal modems of laptop PCs continue to consume power even when not in use, cutting the effective battery life of the computer. When operating, a modem inside a laptop PC may cut the duration of a charge on the system's battery by a quarter. A pocket modem, which draws no electricity from the battery reserves of the laptop, eliminates that kind of power drain.

All pocket modems are not the same when it comes to power, however. Some require their own batteries, typically a nine-volt transistor radio battery, giving you yet another diminishing resource to worry about while you travel. Line-powered pocket modems eliminate this hassle because they can get all the electricity they need from the telephone line itself, courtesy of the telephone company.

Power used to be an issue with internal modems in desktop PCs, but modern technology has mostly erased this concern. The only exception to the "Who cares?" rule about internal modem power is the combination of vintage modems and vintage PCs. If you have an original IBM PC with a 63.5 watt power supply, stay clear of old-technology internal modems, those that take a full-length expansion slot or multiple boards. These modems draw so much current that they can overly strain a PC that has been fully expanded with EMS memory and a hard disk. You're safe with a new modem, however. Most of today's inexpensive internal modems fit on short expansion boards (sometimes as little as five inches long) and draw negligible current from the computer.

An external modem somehow needs to connect to a serial port on your PC. While some pocket modems will plug directly into a port connector, most modems require a cable. Few modems come equipped with the necessary cable, so be sure to order a serial cable when you buy your modem. Almost universally you will require a straight-through serial cable, although the standard seven connections (rather than the full 25 of the serial connector) are generally sufficient. Pocket modems are so small that they can often plug directly into the serial port on the back of your PC or laptop. You'll just have to make sure that the modem and your PC use the same kind of serial connector—9- or 25-pin—and get an adapter if you need one.

A final factor to take into consideration in selecting between an internal and external modems is that the price difference between different manufacturers dwarfs the difference between the internal and external modems of any given manufacturer. Exactly how much you should spend depends on what you're looking for and what you're willing to settle for. As with any other PC product, you should carefully consider every aspect of your modem purchase before making your decision—select the one that you're absolutely sure you want, then settle for the one you can afford.

Fax Modems

Fax, short for *facsimile* transmissions, gives the power of Star Trek's tranporter system (but, one hopes, without the aliens and pyrotechnics) to anyone who needs to get a document somewhere else in the world at the speed of light. Although fax doesn't quite dematerialize paper, it does move the images and information a document contains across continents and reconstructs it at the end of its near-instantaneous travels. The recipient gets to hold in his own hands a nearly exact duplicate of the original, the infamous reasonable facsimile. From that angle, fax is a telecopier—a Xerox machine with a thousand miles of wire between where you slide the original in and the duplicate falls out. In fact, the now-aging telecopiers made by Xerox Corporation were the progenitors of today's fax machines.

Functionally, however, fax works like television for paper. Much as a television picture is broken into numerous scan lines, a fax machine scans images as a series of lines, one at a time, and strings all the lines scanned on a document into a continuous stream of information. At the receiving end, another fax machine converts the data stream into black and white dots on another sheet of paper, duplicating the pattern of the original.

In actual application, fax plays the role of a modem for pictures. While we in the West send our data across wires in digital bytes representing our alphabet of a handful of symbols, the fax machine serves the same purpose where pictograms rule. Squeezing kanji and katakana characters down an ASCII modem may have the same pleasant effect as swallowing a porcupine whole, but fax can digest the lot with nothing getting stuck in its throat and nary a burp. Quite understandably, the first growth spurt for fax occurred in Japan, a country with a combination of complicated typography and affection for technology.

Today, technology has blended the two wonder products of the 1980s, PCs and fax machines, into one. Add an adapter to your PC called a *fax modem* or fax board, and your PC can become a complete fax sending and receiving system. The allure is so great that digital fax systems are one of the favorite upgrades for PCs. One reason is that most PC-based fax systems are dual-purpose units. In one package and on one board you get both a conventional modem and fax power. Another reason is price. A fax board for your PC now costs less than just about any available fax machine. If you want fax capabilities, then, you will be sorely tempted to plug them into your PC.

On the downside, however, are a couple of as yet unresolved fax problems. While fax machines are no more complicated than a telephone to operate, PC-based fax requires computer knowledge and an ability to wade your way through software. Some people see the PC-ization of fax as an impediment to productivity rather than a convenience. Moreover, PC-based fax isn't fast. Many fax boards for PCs operate at half the normal fax rate. And you have to get those fax images out of your computer somehow. Typically you'll want to use a laser printer—but you won't get laser-like speeds. Printing a fax page may take several minutes.

When performance and ease of use count, most people still prefer stand-alone fax machines. However, the prices of fax boards are tempting. And, if you consider fax abilities as a free bonus on a modem (as they so often are), there's no reason not to upgrade to fax in your PC. Moreover, if you do a lot of fax sending rather than receiving, PC-based fax systems can deliver some powerful advantages. For example, you can print to fax as easily as to ordinary paper—if you have the right software. If you need to send a newsletter to 100 clients, you can create it in a desktop publishing program, then squirt it out to your fax board with your PC handling all the details of getting one copy to each person on your distribution list.

PC-based fax certainly isn't for everyone. But it can be a powerful tool. And it can be so affordable that you won't want to pass it up.

Fax Background

The concept of facsimile transmissions is hardly new. As early as 1842, Alexander Bain patented an electromechanical device that could translate wire-based signals into marks on paper. Newspaper wire photos, which are based on the same principles, have been used for generations.

The widespread use of fax in business is a more recent phenomenon, however, and its growth parallels that of the PC for much the same underlying reason. Desktop computers did not take off until the industry found a standard to follow—the IBM PC. Similarly, the explosive growth of fax began only after the CCITT adopted standards for the transmission of facsimile data. The first of these, now termed *Group 1*, was based on analog technology and used frequency shift keying, much like Bell 103 modems, to transmit a page of information in six minutes. *Group 2* improved that analog technology and doubled the speed of transmission, cutting transmission time down to three minutes per page.

The big break with the past and the breakthrough was the CCITT's adoption in 1980 of the *Group 3* fax standard, which is entirely digitally based. Using data compression and modems that operate at up to 9,600 bits per second, a full-page document can be transmitted in 30 to 60 seconds using the Group 3 standard. The data compression makes the speed of transmitting a page dependent on the amount of detail that it contains. In operation, the data compression algorithm reduces the amount of data that must be transferred by a factor of five to ten. Group 3 modems automatically fall back so a bad phone connection may slow fax transmissions to lower speeds to help cope with poor line quality.

Under the Group 3 standard, two degrees of resolution or on-paper sharpness, are possible (which also affects speed): *standard*, which allows 1,728 dots horizontally across the page (about 200 dots per inch) and 100 dots per inch vertically; and *fine*, which doubles the vertical resolution to achieve 200 × 200 dpi and requires about twice the transmission time.

In 1984 the CCITT approved a super-performance facsimile standard, *Group 4*, which allows resolutions of up to 400 × 400 dpi as well as higher-speed transmissions of lower resolutions. Although not quite typeset quality (phototypesetters are capable of resolutions of about 1,200 dpi), the best of Group 4 is about equal to the resolving ability of the human eye at normal reading distance. However, today's Group 4 fax machines require high-speed, dedicated lines and do not operate as dial-up devices. The ill-fated (now discontinued) Zap Mail services offered by Federal Express were based on Group 4 facsimile equipment.

All PC-to-fax modems that you can buy today use the Group 3 standard. But not all have the top speed the standard permits. Many plug-in PC fax modems top out at 4800 bps. While this lower ceiling makes for more secure communications and lower purchase prices, it also doubles the cost of every document you fax. In a few months, what you save in buying a slower fax modem with be devoured by telephone line charges—if you plan to use your fax modem a lot. If you look at fax as only a luxury that you'll use once or twice a month, however, you probably won't worry about slow-speed, 4,800 bps fax modems for your PC.

The PC-to-fax Connection

One of the first PC-to-fax connections was made by Xerox Corporation by tying an ordinary facsimile machine, their modem 895, to a PC. The fax machine functioned as a fax machine—scanning, transmitting, and regenerating documents. The PC took control. It sent commands to the fax machine to dial the phone and deliver transmissions to entire groups of recipients. The PC could also access the fax data stream, recording it on disk, storing documents, or previewing images before they were send or after they were received. A software utility could convert standard ASCII files into fax-compatible data.

Today's approach has refined the idea behind the Xerox creation but does away with the fax machine entirely. Instead, it subsitutes a fax-compatible, high-speed modem that installs in an expansion slot inside your PC. The PC itself creates the fax images—or they can be derived from a peripheral image scanner. The fax board converts the characters in your ASCII files into graphic images that can be received by distant fax machines. In effect, a fax board turns any fax machine into a nearly laser-quality printer.

At the other end of the connection, when a fax transmission is received it is displayed on the monitor screen, stored in a file, or printed using a standard dot-matrix or laser printer. Optical Character Recognition software can even turn the fax image into ASCII files for use with your word processor.

At both ends of the line, incoming and outgoing calls are managed much as they are in the linked fax-and-PC systems. The PC keeps making the calls, even to multiple recipients, logs them, and answers the phone when a fax comes in.

The primary advantage of putting a fax board into your PC is convenience. Without the connection, you'd have to print out a document made by your PC, then scan it into the fax machine. When you receive something without the PC-to-fax connection, you would have the paper copy as the starting ground for any manipulations you'd want to make. Unless you have a scanner, that means pulling out the scissors and rubber cement if you want to make changes. Link PC and fax, and you can work on the screen, editing with painting programs or electronic publishing editors. Going the other direction, you can create fax documents using your word processor or, with the appropriate conversion software, any other program. Instead of printing out the results, you send them out by fax.

Creating fax on the PC confers your work with an added advantage, an apparent increase in resolution. By their nature, scanners have to make do with whatever they are force fed. Unless the edge of a character or line perfectly matches the edge of a scanning cell, the question as to whether the corresponding dot should be black or white will be ambiguous. As a result, scanned characters can have fuzzy or jagged edges. When the character is made by a computer to be printed out using a fax machine, however, each dot can be optimally placed to give the sharpest apparent resolution. Fax text and graphics created on a PC thus look better than anything that's scanned in.

Selecting a Fax Modem

Standardization doesn't mean all fax modems for PCs are alike. Certainly they differ in speed abilities. More importantly, their control software differs. Two identical fax modems with different control software will act as unalike as a teenager solo or accompanied by a parent at the mall. The control software determines the speed of the modem (by how efficiently it compresses and decompresses files into fax format), what you can do with the modem, and how easy the modem is to operate. When buying a fax modem for your PC, then, you should consider not only its hardware features but those of the software that runs it.

You do have to consider the hardware, however. First, the speed: Faster is better, and 9,600 bps is best for a fax modem. Slower 4,800 bps products are only for people whose worlds don't revolve around fax or who have time to spare but little cash. Of course, you'll want a regular data modem on your fax board, too, so you don't have to waste two expansion slots on a single telephone connection. Consider the data section of a fax modem the same way you would any other modem: check the standards, the speeds, and the port compatibility it offers you. Even though your fax modem may ship out fax images at 9,600 bps, it probably will be limited to 2,400 bps when you want to make a standard modem connection. Don't expect more than that. Moreover, make sure that the data modem section of the fax board use the Hayes AT command set. You don't want to abandon your favorite communications software when you use your new modem. And ensure that you can electrically install the data modem section of the fax board at a port address unused by any other ports in your system. Remember, the data modem has an embedded serial port just like any other internal modem. It will need the same system resources as any serial port or modem.

When selecting a fax modem by the software accompanying it, you'll want to ensure you get all the features you need. Any fax modem will send files down the phone line, but you should check which graphic and text file formats the program will accept. You might not be able to transmit the files created by your graphics software.

One of the best feature of fax is that it standardizes the data format that's sent over your telephone. Any fax modem can cope with any Group 3 fax transmission without interpretation problems. However, this compatibility does not extend to the files that fax software stores on your disk. In general, each fax-board manufacturer's fax program uses its own on-disk storage format. Consequently, you cannot exchange disk files of fax transmissions with people who use a different fax system, even if both you and your partner follow the Group 3 standard to the letter.

Nearly all fax modems allow you to send the same message to a group of recipients, and to delay the sending of faxes to a later time, presumably when phone rates are lower. If you really need these features, however, you'll want to assure yourself that the modem you choose offers them. Speed is something that you can judge only by trying the software. The question you need to answer is not how fast the software works, but whether you can live with software that prints fax images so slowly.

Before you can install a fax board, you'll need to be sure that your PC is properly equipped to handle it. Most fax boards require at least a hard disk, DOS 3.1 or later, and a lot of memory. You'll also need a graphics adapter compatible with the fax program if you want to preview images before you send or print them. You'll also need to ensure the graphic adapter you choose is compatible with the software that controls the fax modem.

Installing a fax modem is like installing any other modem. You'll have to resolve any port conflicts before you start, slide the modem in, and connect up the phone line. The only additional complication is setting up the fax software.

Modem Support Issues

When you have a problem with a data or fax modem, you have two avenues of support. Most of the time, you'll first want to give a call to the vendor who sold you the modem. So check what the vendor offers for support before you buy any modem. A toll-free support line is ideal, particularly one that's attended 24 hours a day.

Before you buy, ask the salesman about his company's support policy. Ask whether the company has a support number at all. And make sure that the support line operates 24 hours a day—or at least into evening hours. You'll probably test your modem in the evening or late at night when telephone charges are lowest, so you'll want support to be there when you need it. Check whether the support line is toll-free. And ask whether there are enough people to answer your questions immediately or whether you'll have to wait—presumably forever—for someone to call you back. Technical support that depends only on the salesperson who wrote down your credit card number is usually as good as no support at all.

Modem manufacturers differ in their support policies. While many will try to help you with your problems (sometimes only after wending your way through the corporate hierarchy), others may not even be in business any more—or they may be located in some foreign land lacking telephone connections with the United States and the twentieth century. In that you may have to rely on the modem manufacturer for help when your pleas to the vendor go unanswered, you'll want the manufacturer of your modem to be at least reachable. A modem vendor with a consumer support line is a godsend, particularly if the line is toll-free. Technical support through a bulletin board service can be helpful, but remember, it will be difficult to connect to the BBS if you cannot make your modem work!

Product warranties are given by both the manufacturer and the vendor. However, the latter is usually more important because you'll get the most direct help with your modem from the vendor. The easy-to-quantify issue is the length of the warranty. A modem warranty should extend past the first connection to at least 90 days. You expect your modem to last much longer than that. So should its manufacturer. You'll find better products—and better vendors— will offer modem warranties measured in years. How that warranty is honored is also important. The easiest to deal with is a replacement policy under which the modem vendor will send you a replacement modem when you send yours back. If the vendor elects to repair your modem instead, you may be disconnected for weeks.

A return policy is also helpful if you cannot get your modem to work with your particular PC configuration. Subtle incompatibilities may make one modem unhappy in your system. If so, you'll want to be able to return the modem and try another model without suffering a restocking fee.

Manufacturers' warranties are trickier to get a handle on. In general, the warranty period starts when the product is sold to your vendor, not to you, so it may expire sooner than you think. Worse, a manufacturer may choose not to recognize its warranty if you don't buy from an authorized dealer. So it's important to clarify whether you get a manufacturer's warranty when you buy your drive. And of course, a manufacturer's warranty is meaningless if the modem manufacturer is out of business or beyond your reach in the depths of the Pacific Basin.

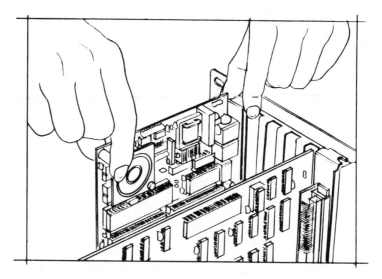

Figure 10.6 After you've assigned system resources to an internal modem, install the modem in any convenient expansion slots. Modems are so slow that fast 16-6:1 slots won't help them.

Preinstallation Considerations

One factor to which most people fail to pay attention when they install modems is port usage. While an external modem's need for a serial port is obvious, the needs of an internal or fax modem are more subtle. Even though an internal modem or a fax modem with ordinary data (Hayes-compatible) capabilities doesn't connect up to a serial port connector on your PC's back panel, it still needs a serial port to link its signals to your PC. The needed port is actually embedded in the circuitry of the internal modem or fax modem. While this circuitry eliminates your worries about the serial connections, you still need to be concerned with the usage of the port resources of your PC. (Fax modems that don't have the ability to work like ordinary data modems typically won't steal a serial port address from your PC, so you don't have to worry as much about port assignment with them.)

Every serial port in a PC—including the one embedded in an internal modem and the data section of a fax modem—must be

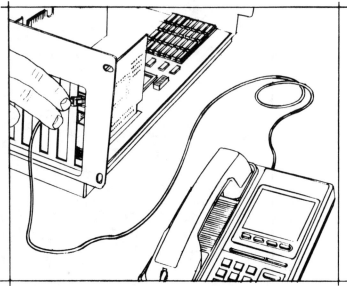

Figure 10.7 Once you've installed your internal modem, connect the jack that's labeled "phone" to your telephone. Make the same connection if you have an external modem.

assigned internal hardware I/O ports and an interrupt from your PC's innate resources. That means an internal or fax modem will steal one of the serial port names from DOS—COM1 to COM4— limiting the number of other serial ports you can install in your system.

Note, too, that not all internal modems can adapt to the full complement of serial addresses. Some internal modems, particularly older models, can only be set up as COM1 or COM2. A modem that can also be addressed as COM3 or COM4 will give you more serial port flexibility—providing your communications software can take advantage of a higher-numbered port (many older communications programs cannot).

When assigning a COM name to the serial port used by a modem—no matter whether it's an internal, fax, or external modem—you also need to be concerned about what your other serial ports are used for. Serial ports share interrupts in pairs. COM2 and COM3 both use hardware interrupt three, and COM1 and COM4 both use interrupt four.

If you connect a device that might issue an interrupt while your modem is in operation to the same interrupt line as is used by the

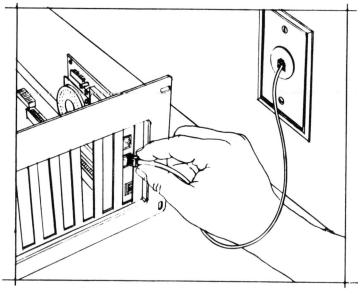

Figure 10.8 Connect the jack on the modem that's labeled "Line" to your telephone line. This also applies to external modems. With internal modems, your hardware installation is complete.

modem, the result can be an interrupt collision, which could interrupt your communications session or even crash your computer. This might happen when, for example, you have your modem assigned as COM4 and a mouse connected as COM1. Move the mouse while you're transferring a file, and your computer could lose its mind. The moral is to not share an interrupt between your mouse and modem by being careful what COM name you give each.

Modem Installation

An external modem is one of the easiest upgrades to install. You only need to make three, sometimes four, connections: plug the modem into your phone line, connect it to one of your PC's serial ports, and plug it into its necessary electrical supply. The optional connection is to your telephone.

The cables to use should not be a problem. The necessary power cable should come with the modem. In addition, most modems include a short telephone cable with modular connectors at either

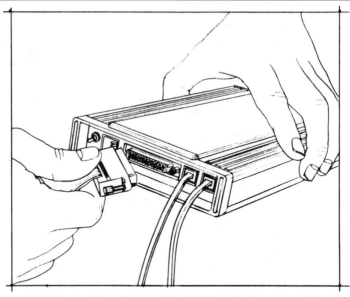

Figure 10.9 With external modems, your next step is to connect the serial jack on the modem to a serial port on your PC. Use a "straight-through" cable. Do *not* use a "mull modem" cable.

end for plugging into your telephone line. If you need to plug a telephone into the same line, get a two-jack adapter (which should be available in any store that sells telephones—drug store, electronics store, or discount store), plug the adapter into the jack for the telephone line, and plug both the modem and the telephone into the adapter. If your external modem has two jacks on its back, run a wire from the one marked "Line" to your telephone line jack. Connect the modem jack labeled "Phone" to your telephone.

You're expected to supply only the signal cable between your PC and the modem. Even this cable should not be a problem. You need a *straight-through* cable to make the connection. So-called *null-modem* or *cross-over* cables are unnecessary—they won't even work. For short distances (say six feet or so), a straight-through 25-pin ribbon cable will work just fine. If you choose to use a shielded cable, you'll only need the nine connections made on the small AT-style serial connectors (nine-pin, of course). Your modem cable normally should have a male connector on one end (to mate with the modem) and a female connector on the other end (to mate with your PC).

Internal modems and fax modems with direct data transmission abilities are hardly more difficult. Before you begin installing the

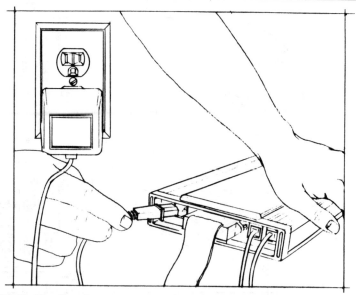

Figure 10.10 Finally, plug your external modem into an electrical supply. Most modems use external transformers that you first plug into a wall outlet and then into the modem.

internal modem, you should take stock of the serial ports already installed in your system so you can determine which unused port will be best for the internal modem. Assign the modem to an unused DOS name. To be safe, you'll want to avoid sharing an interrupt with your mouse or other pointing device. In other words, if your mouse is connected to COM2, don't define your modem as COM3. If your mouse is connected to COM1, don't define your modem as COM4. Once you've decided the port at which to locate your modem, you should set the modem hardware to use that port. Most internal modems have a switch or jumper to select the port value used. PS/2 modems and some more exotic new modems may make the port selection a software process.

Once you've set up your internal or fax modem's port assignment, you're ready for the hardware installation. First, you'll want to turn off your PC, unplug its power cord, and remove its lid from the case so you can locate a vacant expansion slot for your modem. In general, any slot will be fine. Nearly all modems use 8-bit bus connectors, so any ISA 8- or 16-bit slot or an EISA 32-bit slot should accommodate the modem. Any Micro Channel slot should accommodate any Micro Channel modem. Once you've located a slot, just slide the modem in. Screw down its retaining bracket.

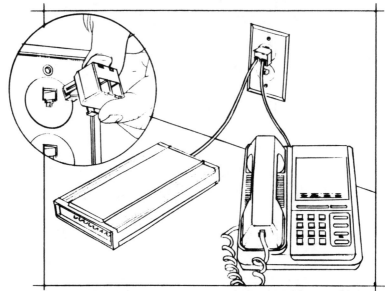

Figure 10.11 If your modem has only one jack and you want to share your modem line with a telephone, you'll need an adapter (inset). Plug the adapter into your telephone line, then plug both the modem and the phone into the adapter.

Next, test your modem before putting the top back on your PC. Connect the necessary cables. Typically, you'll need to plug in one or two modular telephone wires. If there is just one jack on the back of your internal modem, connect it to a standard modular jack to which you would plug in an ordinary telephone. If you need to plug a telephone in to the same jack, get a two-jack adapter, plug the adapter into the jack, and plug both the modem and the telephone into the adapter. If your internal modem has two jacks, run a wire from the one marked "Line" to your phone jack. Connect the modem jack labeled "Phone" to your telephone.

To test the modem, plug in your PC and boot it up. Use your communications program (or the one that came with the modem) to make a call. If it works, you know the internal modem or the data section of an internal fax modem is working. At this point, you may want to install the software that accompanied your fax modem so that you can test its fax abilities, too. Some fax modems come with software that tests and verifies proper operation without a telephone connection. Try that now, if you have it. Once your modem passes all the tests, you can safely button up your PC. Turn it off and replace the lid.

If the modem fails to operate with your communications program or its own self-test software, check to make sure that the modem's command set is compatible with your software. (You should expect that the software that came with the modem will use the right command set.) And be sure that the communications program and the modem are set to use the same DOS port. These simple verifications will solve most of your modem problems. In a few minutes, your PC will be communicating with the rest of the world.

11.

GRAPHICS: ADAPTERS, MONITORS, AND INPUT DEVICES

If the latest software is any indication (and it is) the future of personal computing is in graphics. Upgrading your PC to full graphic capability can be a multifront effort. You may need a new higher-resolution display adapter, a matching monitor, and even a new input device to give your system the power it needs to manipulate images—be they engineering drawings, multiple-font printouts, or presentation graphics.

WYSIWYG—what you see is what you get—has long been the loudest buzzword in computer graphics. It means image on the screen looks identical (or as close as possible) to what finally rolls out of your printer.

For most systems, however, what you see is what you have to suffer through. A poor image on your screen is more than merely bothersome in getting the details of a printout right. It can be a big headache, too, the kind caused by eye strain, squinting, and just plain frustration. A graphics upgrade means that you can work better, produce snazzier graphics in less time and with less heartache.

Depending on how you count, your PC's graphics system has two or three upgrade candidates—the display system and its input devices. The display system itself can be seen as two parts, a display adapter and the monitor. The display adapter converts the abstract thoughts of your PC into an electronic form of an image, a *memory-map*, in which every dot that will make up the final displayed picture is represented by one or more bits stored in RAM. The display adapter then takes apart that electronic image and sends a copy of each piece to the monitor. Under guidance from the display adapter about which piece goes where, the monitor rebuilds the map in glowing form that you can see. Each of these two parts of the display system plays a role in the quality of the image you see. Change one by itself, and the final image you see may improve only slightly.

Input devices give you control of the graphics of your PC, helping you convert your notions into images. You can select commands, scan or trace images, or draw from scratch. The selection of input devices is wide and includes keyboards, mice, trackballs, digitizing tablets, and scanners.

Together, these graphics upgrades will help you put a new face on the work you do on your PC. And put a new face on yourself as you work.

Display Adapters

If you want to see something on your monitor, your PC needs a display adapter of some sort. Without one, navigating through your programs would be as satisfying and successful as arranging a rendezvous in a black hole. You wouldn't know where everything is or when anything was happening (indeed, in a black hole there is no where or when). You wouldn't even be able to see the DOS prompt to know when you could issue the commands to start programs.

Just because a display adapter is a necessity doesn't mean that the display adapter in your PC is necessarily good. You have your choice of a wide variety of display adapters, and the range is from poor to acceptable. Really great display adapters—the kind that do everything you want them to—remain in the realm of the imagination.

All display adapters are limited by industry standards that set the ultimate resolution or sharpness of the image along with other quality-determining factors, such as the number of colors that can be displayed and how stable the image is. Standards are followed because they guarantee a good match between software, the display adapter, and the monitor at the lowest possible cost—in dollars when it comes to the monitor and in performance when it comes to the software.

Currently, the defining characteristic of the various display standards used in the IBM environment is resolution. All else being equal, a higher-resolution image appears sharper on the monitor screen. Resolution is generally measured by how many individual picture elements or *pixels* (sometimes termed *pels*), roughly corresponding to the dots in a halftone magazine or newspaper photograph, it takes to fill the screen horizontally and vertically. For example, the first display system used by PCs, the Monochrome Display Adapter, had a resolution termed 720 by 350 because the image was made from 720 pixels laid across the screen horizontally and 350 vertically.

The MDA standard, in fact, defines "poor" in the range of available display adapters, Developed in 1981 and showing signs of old age even then, it was IBM's first effort at giving you a look inside your PC. In any discussion of graphics, the MDA standard can readily be ignored. The only graphics it can handle are *block graphics*, chunky images made from groups of pixels arranged in a nine by fourteen matrix. Sharp, bit-image graphics—those in which an image is made from individual pixels similar to the dots in that halftone newspaper and magazine illustrations—are impossible with the MDA system. Color is, too.

Note that the MDA system differs from all other IBM-standard display adapters in another peculiar way. It alone has the middle character "D" in its acronym; all the others have a "G." The "G" stands for Graphics. By rights, all other display adapters—the ones that you are apt to upgrade to—are *graphics adapters* as well as being display adapters. An MDA board is not a graphics adapter.

Three graphics standards have been included as standard equipment in most PCs. As they have been developed over the years, they have added improved quality to the images generated by PC equipment. In fact, the history of PC graphics has been one of increasing resolution with each of these video standards as it was introduced. The first graphics adapter for the PC, introduced in 1982 as IBM's Color Graphics Adapter (or CGA), achieved resolutions up to 640 by 200 pixels but did most of its graphics work at 320 by 200. Even by the low standard set by home television, CGA graphics looked poor indeed. To improve on that, in 1984 IBM introduced its Enhanced Graphics Adapter (or EGA) which pushed resolution up to 640 by 350 pixels. Today, the standard in most PCs is 640 by 480 pixels achieved by the Video Graphic Array (or VGA), introduced in 1987. Increasingly, PCs are now coming with graphics adapters following the first non-IBM color display almost-standard to win wide acceptance, *SuperVGA*, an extension of the VGA system that pushes resolution to 800 by 600 pixels. IBM has also introduced two display standards that have won only modest acceptance among PC users, both of which are capable of 1024 by 768 resolution, *8514/A* (introduced in 1987) and the Extended Graphics Array or *XGA* (introduced in 1990).

Another graphics standard you may encounter is the Hercules Graphics Card or *HGC*. This is a monochrome graphics system based on the MDA text-only system. Hercules graphics has the same resolution as MDA and uses the same frequencies and monitors. It differs only in offering a standardized way of addressing individual pixels on the screen—if you have software that follows the HGC standard. Most inexpensive monochrome display adapters now offer MGC capabilities. Couple an HGC-compatible adapter and a matching monitor, and you'll have the least expensive way of adding graphics to most PCs—and one of the most out-of-date.

If your PC is not capable of generating SuperVGA or better images, you're a candidate for a display adapter upgrade. Even if you have SuperVGA circuitry, you still might want to upgrade to get more out of your PC. More means making any or all of the three improvements a display adapter upgrade can yield. A display adapter upgrade can raise the resolution of the images on your monitor screen. It can also increase the number of colors your PC can display, giving greater realism to its images and even increasing apparent sharpness. And a new display adapter can accelerate the rate at which changes appear on your monitor screen, making your system seem snappier. While some adapters excell at just one of these virtues, by proper adapter choice, you can improve all three aspects of your PC's display performance.

Resolution Issues

Since it was introduced, the VGA standard has gone from an expensive, complex proprietary system into the minimum expected from any PC. The circuitry has been simplified to a few chips, so inexpensive that many manufacturers build it into their computer system boards. Nearly all graphics software now expects a VGA board and will operate in that mode without further ado.

With VGA so simple (or supposed to be) and higher resolutions so complex, you may wonder why anyone would want to venture into the unknown territory beyond the VGA standard. Someone somewhere apparently thinks you'll want to—nearly every new VGA graphics adapter includes at least one SuperVGA mode with 800 by 600 pixel graphics.

The best reason to capitalize on SuperVGA is the simple one. The picture looks better, a lot better. SuperVGA images are discernibly sharper than VGA.

On the downside, you may not be able to take advantage of the sharpness of SuperVGA using the software you normally run. Not all programs can take advantage of 800 by 600 pixel displays. Although DOS is independent of the resolution of the display system because it operates in text mode, which can readily adapt to any display systems, most graphics adapters don't give you the option of booting and running DOS in 800 by 600 pixel mode. (You may wonder why graphics adapter makers don't allow you to set their boards to boot up in their high-resolution modes with a super-sharp 15 × 10 text font. So do a lot of people.) As a result, using high resolution means you're essentially limited to operating environments like Windows and GEM and a few CAD applications (notably AutoCAD, which every display adapter appears to support).

To achieve compatibility with these environments and software packages, display adapters that venture beyond the last IBM-sanctioned display standard to win popular acceptance, VGA, usually use *software drivers*. The software driver is a special translation program that tells your software about the special features of the hardware, in particular, how to access those features. You'll want to check what software drivers are included with or available for (there's sometimes an extra charge) any display adapter you consider.

Software drivers are used in different ways depending upon the application. For example, Windows 3.0 integrates the installation of software drivers for display adapters into its set-up procedures. AutoCAD requires you to execute the driver program (called an ADI driver) from the command line or a batch file before you run each AutoCAD session.

If you're committed to Windows or OS/2 Presentation Manager, however, a monitor with 800 by 600 pixel abilities is good news indeed. Windows looks great in 800 by 600 mode. Compared to VGA, it's like spraying on the Windex and wiping the dirty haze away. Jagged edges on images begin to disappear. You can see more detail, and even text in small typefaces is adequately clear for everyday work.

But if you spend most of your time staring at a graphics screen, 800 by 600 pixel resolution may not be enough. Most experts agree on a minimum acceptable resolution for Computer-Aided Drawing and related applications of 1,024 by 768 pixels. All the arguments in favor and against 800 by 600 resolution apply to 1,024 by 768—only more so. Anyone who has used a display operating at that resolution level will never want to go back to VGA. But such high resolutions generally require a commitment to an operating environment and poverty to get working. Still, three to five years from now you can expect 1,024 by 768 to be a primary display standard among PCs.

Going to still higher resolutions would seem the next logical step, and it is. But there will be a lot of trepidation before you put your foot down. Today, prices sprint far ahead of reality once you pass 1,024 by 768 pixel resolution. While some inexpensive display adapters are already making claims of 1,280 by 960 (or 1280 by 1024) resolution, you'll incur substantial penalties for crossing the threshold—even if you find an inexpensive display adapter that supports higher resolutions, you'll still need a high-quality (and high-priced) monitor to make all those dots visible. And the performance of even the fastest PCs will evaporate trying to run graphics at that level unassisted by some speed-up strategy.

If you plan to venture into high-resolution territory, one warning is in order. Higher resolutions demand better circuit components on display adapter boards to handle the increased amount of image information. In particular, memory and digital-to-analog conversion circuitry must be faster. To cut corners—and to accommodate less expensive monitors—some display adapters produce *interlaced signals* at their highest resolutions. Most display standards operate noninterlaced. In the computer industry, interlacing is viewed as inherently evil, something to avoid, because it compromises image quality on some monitors. The primary image defect with interlaced display systems is image flicker. For optimum viewing, noninterlaced signals are preferred—providing, of course, you have or acquire a monitor that can use them. Interlacing will be described more completely in the discussion of monitors, later in this chapter.

Color Issues

Resolution means nothing if the color on your display looks like your monitor got bruised in a blueberry pie fight with aliens—a few colors splattered about resembling nothing you'd see in the real world. But all too often high-resolution color images are mere caricatures of reality. The selection of colors can be so slight you might expect the screen to have been generated less by expensive graphics software than by a toddler with a budget box of eight Crayolas. All you get is a few basic colors (red, blue, green, maybe even orange and pink) but none of today's high-fashion in-between shades (taupe, berry, blush, hemorrhage, and contusion). The color limit is imposed not by the device you're most apt to blame—the monitor—because the analog-input monitors with which the latest graphics adapters work have essentially unlimited spectra. Rather, the short-hued rendition is a result of your choice of display adapter—and more particularly, its memory.

The color capabilities of display adapters are measured two ways, by the maximum *palette*, the range of colors that any particular on-screen pixels can be, and by the actual number of colors that can be simultaneously displayed. This duality arises from the way graphics boards deal with colors. A given number of bits (sometimes called *color-planes*) are assigned to code the color of each pixel in the storage system of the graphics adapter. A one-bit code can specify one of two colors, whether any given pixel is on or off. Two bits can specify four colors; eight bits, 256 colors. Memory is thus the limit on the number of colors that a graphics board can store. For a 1,024 by 768 pixel image in 256 colors (eight bits), a graphics board needs at least three-quarters of a million bytes of video memory. That's a lot of bytes and not much color. If a display system were limited solely to 256 predefined colors, its images would look artificial and cartoon-like. Getting realistic or photo-quality image would require even more megabytes. To achieve what computer people consider realistic color—16.7 million different hues—you need 24 bits of storage per pixel.

To broaden their color range without demanding more memory, graphics adapters use *color look-up tables*. Instead of defining a color, the board's video memory stores codes. Each code is matched to any one of a much wider-variety of colors that make up the board's palette.

In VGA-derived systems the palette stretches for 262,144 colors because the VGA system relies on a device called a Digital-to-Analog converter (DAC, also rendered as RAMDAC because it works with random-access memory) that can use 18-bit codes in its color map. The subtle variations allowed by such wide palettes can create reasonably realistic images under the VGA standard even though only 256 different colors may be displayed on the screen at a time.

(Most images are made from a limited number of tones, often all drawn from the same family, so often a small number of different hues can suffice.) In that a couple hundred thousand colors is close to the number of hues that the typical color picture tube can unambiguously generate, the VGA palette is a good compromise between color and cost.

But it's not good enough for some people. The human eye can distinguish millions of colors, and so they want the ability to store millions of colors to accommodate realistic tones in devices with better fidelity than a cheap computer monitor. In general, the computer industry has converged to a single high-end color standard: 24-bit color in which eight bits is used to store brightness information for each of the three primary colors.

The problem with 24-bit color is that it requires three bytes of storage for every pixel on the monitor screen. At high resolutions, that can be a prodigious amount of memory, over two million bytes (2,359,296 to be exact) at 1,024 by 768 pixel resolution. Manipulating that much memory dozens of time a second can slow your system down. It also can extract a cost, particularly for display adapters that use more expensive (but faster) video RAM or VRAM chips.

Some display adapters compromise and use DACs capable of handling full 24-bit color, but minimize memory down to the level for 256 on-screen colors. You get a realistic, wide palette but no way of displaying anything but a fraction of its potential. When 256 simultaneous on-screen colors is the limit for a display adapter, a palette wider than 256K is superfluous.

Better compromises are becoming available in the guise of new RAMDAC chips. Edsun Laboratories' (now part of Analog Devices) Color-Edge Graphics (CEG) and Sierra's Hi-Color RAMDACs finesse more colors onto the screen without needing more memory. These chips rely on expropriating part of the eight-bit code for storing 256 colors for a more refined method of encoding color transitions. The result is more on-screen colors with less memory—with the requirement of software drivers to bring the products into full bloom. They will work at normal VGA resolutions with VGA color capabilities without special software, but require special code to coax them to create their wider spectra. Because the exotic RAMDAC chips add little to the overall cost of a display adapter, they represent one of the better alternatives in upgrading to more color on your PC.

When you go shopping for a graphics board upgrade, you'll find that the color potential of the board can be described in several ways. Specifications may simply list the number of colors—that's simple. But the number of colors may be complicated by the wider selection that makes up the palette that those colors may be drawn from—for example, 256 colors from a palette of 262,144. Worse, the specifications may list only the number of color planes that the board can store.

The number of color planes is the same thing as the number of bits used to store color information for each on-screen pixel. One bit per pixel can code only whether a particular dot is on or off, white or black. Two bits per pixel allows four grey levels or colors, with two of the choices typically being black and white.

Figuring out the number of simultaneously displayable colors from the number of bit-planes or bits per pixel is easy. Just calculate two to the number of bit-planes (2^n where n = bit-planes). Sixteen bit-planes yields 65,536 colors; twenty-four yields the 16.7 million colors that the best display adapters aspire to.

Performance Issues

Slide two PCs side by side and the one that will feel faster is the one that blasts images on its screen quicker. After all, the screen is the essential human interface. It's what you *see* of what your computer does. You can't see the calculations being carried out inside your PC's microprocessor; you can't glimpse the head of its disk drive dashing back and forth; you can't see data scurrying down the network line. But you can see characters appear on the screen, lines being drawn, and minutes racing by. Although display speed may not accurately represent all the other invisible activities going on inside your system, it is the element by which their performance is judged.

Video performance is more than superficial, however. A slow display system can put the brakes on the rest of your PC. Many programs wait until the screen update caused by one task or operation is completed before going on to the next operation. For example, a graphics program might calculate a line, then actually draw the line before it's ready for the next calculation. The longer it takes to draw the line, the greater the period between the calculations, the longer the series of calculations takes to execute, and the longer you drum your fingers on your desk. The performance of the display system can thus severely limit the overall performance of your PC.

Two external factors can be the major performance limits on your PC's display abilities: your system's microprocessor and its memory. Your microprocessor must figure out where to put every dot of the display. Once those onerous calculations have been carried out and the answers saved in system memory, the information—potentially a megabyte or more of data—must be moved from system memory to video memory through the performance-slowing funnel that's called the expansion bus.

Were these the only speed-controlling factors, all video adapters would deliver exactly the same performance in a given PC. Of course, all adapters don't. Several additional factors in the design of display adapters result in the large performance differences observed between different boards.

One reason that display adapters work at different speeds is that each has its own electrical design. Some designs are simply better than others, better able to carry out their appointed operations. Put two display adapters side by side, and you can never tell which will be faster. But you can make some judgments about display adapter performance by looking at competing products, asking questions, and examining the specifications. Two of the most important factors to examine are the bus width used by the board and by its on-board BIOS.

Bus Width

Graphics display speed is also influenced by the width of the expansion bus linking your graphics board to the rest of your PC. Graphics boards that use a true 16-bit interface potentially can generate images twice as fast simply because they can accept data twice as fast as ordinary 8-bit display adapters. In fact, just upgrading your 8-bit display board to a 16-bit graphics adapter in itself may nearly double the snap of text and graphics displays on your PC if your PC has a 16-bit or wider expansion bus.

For higher-end graphics boards, in particular *coprocessed graphics adapters* that have their own, built-in graphics coprocessor chip to accelerate display speed, bus width is not a major issue. These boards do not require huge blocks of data to be transferred across the bus, so the width of the connection is not as important. However, nearly every modern coprocessed graphics adapter uses at least a 16-bit bus connection, making the interface of little concern when you shop for a graphics upgrade at the high end.

BIOS Issues

Display speed is also influenced by software and firmware. Every display adapter since IBM's now-archaic EGA adapter has included its own on-board BIOS to tell your system how to handle its advanced display modes. This BIOS affects the speed at which some programs can change your display. A more efficient BIOS will be faster.

The display BIOS also faces issues of bus width. Many graphics adapters—particularly older designs and cut-rate products—have 8-bit BIOSs; other use 16-bit. The former will, of course, execute more slowly in all but 8088-based systems (in which a purely 16-bit BIOS won't be a benefit at all).

BIOS shadowing will minimize the effects of narrow-width BIOS code on advanced graphics adapters. Some PCs have built-in provisions for automatically shadowing the video BIOS, no matter what its origin. Some graphics board manufacturers also include utilities to allow the BIOSs on their products to be shadowed on systems lacking their own shadowing abilities. In either case, you can gain a performance advantage by shifting to shadowing.

Note, however, that shadowing won't affect most graphics applications because most of these will either write directly to the memory on the graphics adapter or use one of the drivers supplied with the graphics adapter. Drivers automatically run in fast RAM memory, so shadowing won't have any effect on driver performance.

In other words, shadowing will be most important if you use your graphics adapter for text-mode work—not exactly what you're buying a graphics board for. Don't worry about shadowing or BIOS matters if you plan on doing most of your work in graphics mode, for instance using the Windows or OS/2 Presentation Manager environments.

Graphics Coprocessors and Coprocessed Adapters

While clever display adapter designs can accelerate performance somewhat, they don't break through the fundamental barriers imposed by the microprocessor overhead in calculating the image and the logistical overhead of moving picture data from system memory to display memory. A graphics coprocessor, however, can break both barriers.

The secret to the success of graphics coprocessors is how they communicate with your PC's microprocessor using a higher-level interface, a graphics language, instead of moving bytes at the hardware level. Traditional display adapters work by giving your system's microprocessor direct access to their on-board video memories. They are consequently called *direct-access* display adapters or *memory-mapped* display adapters (because the memory accessed by the microprocessor represents a map of the on-screen image). In contrast, a display adapter with a graphics coprocessor—called a coprocessed display adapter—works as an isolated subsystem that communicates with your microprocessor using a high-level interface, essentially a programming language. The graphics coprocessor, rather than your PC's microprocessor, carries out most of the instructions for calculating which dot goes where on the screen.

By using their higher-level interfaces, coprocessor boards lighten the display processing load on your microprocessor. Ordinary display adapters work fastest by direct memory writing using your system's microprocessor to calculate where each dot will appear on the screen and push it into memory. The high-level languages used by graphics coprocessors let your PC's microprocessor simply send out compact commands to create complex on-screen shapes—commands such as draw a line or circle, or fill in an area. Issuing a command to a graphics coprocessor involves transferring only a few bytes, compared to the millions required by direct memory access, making communications within your computer quicker. Moreover, the high-level command leaves the graphics coprocessor to do the actual computation work of generating a display, taking a load off your system's microprocessor and speeding up its overall operation.

Note that once the graphics coprocessor receives an instruction from your PC's microprocessor, it can go about its work while the microprocessor does something else. In effect, your system has two processors working at the same time, achieving a degree of parallel processing. But the graphics coprocessor and the coprocessed display adapters made from it earn their performance advantage not just by working in tandem with your microprocessor but actually doing its job better. Graphics coprocessors are specially designed for pixel work, and they can carry out the graphics computations many times faster than most general-purpose microprocessors.

Graphics coprocessors also know other tricks. For example, they can do *display-list processing*. That is, once they do the math to calculate an on-screen image, they save the results (as a "display list") so everything doesn't have to be recalculated to regenerate the screen image. The difference can reduce the waiting from a minute or more to zooming into and out of a screen detail to a few seconds. Although display list processing is not exclusively the province of the graphics coprocessor, coprocessors can use it very effectively.

Graphics coprocessors often have other special hardware features that can accelerate display speeds. For example, hardware zooming and panning relieve the need for recalculating pixels during many fundamental display operations.

Besides speed, coprocessed display adapters generally add higher resolution (usually significantly higher resolution) and greater color capabilities to your PC. Although these benefits are not a direct result of graphics coprocessor technology, coprocessors, color, and resolution go hand in hand. Every increase in sharpness adds to the amount of data that must be displayed on the screen, and as the information on the display becomes prodigious, a graphics coprocessor is the only way of handling it without sacrificing your patience or your sanity.

Graphics Languages

While the use of higher-level communications between microprocessor and graphics coprocessor increases display efficiency, it also results in the most troubling aspect of the graphics coprocessor— the Babel effect. Different brands of coprocessors have different designs and speak different languages. Moreover, DOS has no built-in support for graphics coprocessors. The challenge of communicating with the graphics coprocessor is thus left to your applications.

Not all applications know how to use graphics coprocessors, and even those that do probably don't understand the intricacies of all of the available coprocessors. Consequently, the first thing you should do when contemplating buying a graphics coprocessor is to determine whether it will work with your software.

Your coprocessor choices will be limited to those usable by your applications. The coprocessors that are compatible with a specific program are usually listed in the "Requirements" section of the manual that accompanies your software.

Some applications, like Microsoft Windows and AutoCAD, put the onus on the maker of graphics coprocessor boards to achieve compatibility. The publishers of such software tell coprocessor companies how to make their products work with their software. The coprocessor maker then provides a special software driver with its graphics coprocessor.

The drivers used to communicate these higher-level instructions can have a substantial effect on board performance, as can the board's own efficiency in translating its instructions. For example, many high-resolution graphics boards process the Application Interface instructions used by IBM's 8514/A adapter substantially faster than the official IBM product that defines the standard. In other words, the performance delivered by a graphics board on high-resolution images depends not only on the hardware, but also on the quality of the drivers supplied with it.

If you're fortunate, you'll have a choice of a number of graphics coprocessors that will work with your software. Choosing the right one is a matter of matching its resolution and frequencies of operation with the monitor you have or plan to buy.

Any monitor that you want to use must be able to synchronize with the horizontal and vertical scanning frequencies (measured in kilohertz and hertz, respectively) produced by the graphics coprocessor when running your applications software. Most graphics coprocessors require more expensive multiscanning monitors that accept a wide range of scanning frequencies. Just be sure that the output frequencies of the graphics coprocessor are within the range that your monitor can handle.

Coprocessor Chips

Strictly speaking, a graphics coprocessor is an integrated circuit chip or a collection of several. A coprocessed graphics board is made from the coprocessor chip, support circuitry, and video memory.

Today's most popular graphics coprocessor chips are those of the Texas Instruments TMS34010 family. The TMS34010 is a 32-bit microprocessor that's been optimized for manipulating graphics. The TMS34020 is a newer, higher-performance version. Sometimes other coprocessor chips are used, such as those from Hitachi and Motorola. The Intel i860 and i960 are a high-performance Reduced Instruction Set microprocessors that many manufacturers are adapting to graphics use, the latter being the newer, faster chip. IBM's 8514/A is an entire board that works like a graphics coprocessor but lacks a true coprocessor chip. The IBM XGA system uses what is essentially a proprietary IBM graphics coprocessor.

Coprocessed graphics adapter boards are almost complete computers in themselves, which means that there are many influences on their performance—not just which coprocessor chip is used, but also the speed at which it operates and how much memory is present on the board. Judge them as you would any computer. A board with more memory and a higher clock speed (assuming the same coprocessor chip) will deliver more performance and have greater capabilities than a lesser board. It will also likely cost more.

When considering any display adapter, carefully examine the amount of memory it offers and the amount to which you can expand it. The memory on the board is important because it is the primary factor in determining the maximum resolution and number of colors the board can display. More memory allows more of each.

Graphics experts argue over which of the various coprocessors is fastest and best. Leave those arguments to them. The important point is that a coprocessed display adapter can help the performance of some applications and that having a graphics coprocessor (one that can be used by the applications that you run most often) is immensely better than a high-resolution graphics board that lacks a coprocessor. To realize those performance gains, you need an application that supports the particular graphics coprocessor that you choose, and it must be an application that can take advantage of higher-level language instructions. A word processor, for example, won't speed up appreciably with a coprocessor. A computer-aided design program likely will. Operating environments like Windows and OS/2 PM will benefit from some graphics coprocessors more than others. (IBM's XGA, for example, was designed particularly to speed up the operation of windowing environments.)

Many so-called SuperVGA graphics adapters offer resolution capabilities up to 1,024 by 768 pixels—and they deliver it. But because they lack the higher-level language abilities of coprocessor boards, they cannot achieve the quick performance of a coprocessed board on complex drawings. On the other hand, noncoprocessed graphics boards are much less expensive than their coprocessor-based equivalents. In other words, you'll pay for coprocessor performance, but the difference is worth the price.

Monitor Matching

Perhaps the most important issue when shopping for a display adapter is that it match your monitor. In other words, you must ensure that the monitor you own or plan to buy as part of your graphics upgrade works with the display adapter you chose. You must make a match in three areas to guarantee success: frequencies, signal type, and color capability.

Frequencies

The signals produced by all display adapters are not the same. They have different characteristic frequencies that describe how often they update each full-screen image (a measure called the *frame rate*, vertical synchronizing frequency, or just vertical frequency) and how often each of the lines of the image is drawn on the screen (called the line rate, horizontal scanning frequency, horizontal synchronizing frequency, or just horizontal frequency). The frequencies produced by a display adapter must match those accepted by the monitor for successful operation.

Normally you can just match standards. A CGA board will work with a CGA monitor; an EGA board will work with an EGA monitor; and a VGA board will work with a VGA monitor. (You can also force a CGA monitor to work with an EGA board and an EGA monitor to work with a CGA monitor, if you are venturesome.) At the SuperVGA resolution levels and above, however, standards-matching falls apart because of the divergence of standards. For example, the Video Electronics Standards Association (or VESA) has two "manufacturers guidelines" and one "standard" for the frequencies to be used at the 800 by 600 resolution level. Consequently, a SuperVGA monitor, which could be called "VESA compatible" because it follows one of the guidelines, might not function with a VESA-compatible display adapter that only follows the standard.

Monitor manufacturers have tried to tiptoe around this issue by building so-called *multiscanning* monitors (discussed in depth later in this chapter) that can accommodate a range of frequencies. Of course, the range of each multiscanning monitor model is different. As a result of this confusion, you must count frequencies. The range of frequencies accommodated by the monitor you plan to use must include the frequencies produced by the display adapter in the mode that you want to use. Table 11.1 lists the frequencies your monitor must support to accommodate the various display standards.

Table 11.1 **Synchronizing frequency range required from a multiscanning display at given resolution levels under various display standards:**

Standard	Vertical Sync	Horiz. Sync	TTL or Analog
720 × 350 Resolution			
MDA	50 Hz.	18.3 kHz.	TTL (one color)
640 × 200 Resolution			
CGA	60 Hz.	15.75 kHz.	TTL (16 colors)
640 × 350 Resolution			
EGA	60 Hz.	21.5 kHz.	TTL (64 colors)
640 × 480 (nominal, also operate at 720 × 400, 640 × 400, and 640 × 350)			
MCGA	60 & 70 Hz.	31.5 kHz.	Analog
VGA	60 & 70 Hz.	31.5 kHz.	Analog
800 × 600 Resolution			
VESA guideline	56 Hz.	35.5 kHz.	Analog
VESA guideline	60 Hz.	37.8 kHz.	Analog
VESA standard	72 Hz.	48 kHz.	Analog

1024 × 768 Resolution

8514/A	87 Hz.*	35.5 kHz.	Analog
XGA	87 Hz.*	35.5 kHz.	Analog
VESA	60 Hz.	48 kHz.	Analog

*This is the field rate that 8514/A and XGA monitors must be able to synchronize to; because these signals are interlaced, the actual frame rate is one-half the field rate or 43.5 Hz.

Signal Type

The universe of electricity is divided into the *analog* and *digital* domains, depending on how signals encode information. Analog signals code data as a varying of the *strength* (*amplitude*) or *frequency* of the signal. Digital signals code information as *discrete* state changes. The two don't usually mix—at least not happily.

The difference between the two signal types in display systems is how color and brightness information is coded. Digital signals use a digital code. Colors and brightness levels are identified by a pattern of signals carried on several distinct connections between the display adapter and the monitor. One wire in the connecting cable is used to carry each connection and thereby each bit in the digital code. For example, IBM's original Color Graphics Adapter (CGA) standard used four digital signal connections; the Enhanced Graphics Adapter (EGA) standard required six, all tucked in a single connecting cable.

Analog signals code brightness levels in voltage levels. A higher voltage of the signal corresponds to (or is the analog of) a brighter on-screen image. In that a single wire can carry any voltage, a single analog connection suffices to transmit an infinity of brightness levels.

Color information can also be coded in analog signals. For example, the National Television Standards Committee (*NTSC*) video standard, usually termed "composite video," is designed to do exactly that. To distinguish color from brightness information on the signal NTSC connection, color information is encoded on a subcarrier—essentially a special radio signal, also analog—that is combined with the brightness voltages.

The NTSC system has a major drawback, however. The frequency of the subcarrier sets an upper limit on the detail that can be contained in the brightness information. Consequently, NTSC is unacceptable for use with computers, except for inexpensive 40-column systems, the kind that connect to television sets and deliver image quality on par with regular television programming. However, many new display adapters offer NTSC outputs so that you can create multimedia images that are compatible with traditional video systems—television-style monitors, videocassette recorders, and videodisc players.

Analog display adapters that follow the PC and proprietary standards separate three signals corresponding to the primary colors of light—red, green, and blue. One connection is assigned to each, and each carries a separate analog signal without limits imposed by subcarriers. The three color signals, each able to indicate an infinity of brightness levels, combine in various mixtures to produce an infinity of colors, at least potentially.

Most color graphics adapters are limited to far fewer colors than are possible in theory. (An infinity fewer, in fact, leaving the paradoxical result that an infinity subtracted from another infinity yields a nonzero number—we'll leave the philosophers to haggle over that one!) In analog systems, then, the number of displayable colors is determined by the display adapter that produces the signals rather than by the monitor that's connected to it. In digital systems, both the display adapter and the monitor may limit color potential.

With display adapters, a compatibility problem arises since some display standards use digital signals (these include MDA, CGA, and EGA) and others use analog signals (VGA, SuperVGA, XGA, and 8514/A). Your display adapter may produce one, the other, or both signal types. Analog outputs are preferred today because they allow a nearly infinite range of colors to be communicated to the monitor. But monitors that meet one of the digital standards cannot handle analog signals, even if the analog signals have the appropriate frequencies. So you must match the signal type produced by your display adapter to those accepted by your monitor.

Some display adapters have both analog and digital outputs, relying on the latter to help you gradually make the transition into higher resolution graphics. The digital output will run your old CGA or EGA display until you can afford a new VGA or better monitor. Of course, you won't get the full quality the display adapter is capable of until you shift to the higher-quality monitor.

Color Capability

All analog monitors can theoretically handle an infinity of colors. The same is not true of digital monitors. The various digital display standards use different codes for their color outputs. It's important that the digital display adapter you choose and the monitor that you plan to use follow the same color coding. The principal codes are termed 8-color, which was used by early Apple computers and can pretty much be ignored in the PC environment; 16-color, or RGBI, which is used by the CGA system; and 64-color, which is used by the EGA system.

One or Two Displays

Some display adapters give you the choice of viewing everything that your PC does on one screen or having two. In the latter case, your system will typically boot up on one screen and display high-resolution graphics on the other.

Using a single monitor gives you one big advantage—it's cheaper simply because you only have to buy one monitor. The alternative, connecting the high-resolution graphics board to a separate monitor, brings somewhat more versatility—for example, some programs can devote one screen strictly to graphics and the other to text-based control—but at a high cost in dollars and desk space. Then again, most single-board systems don't preclude you adding a second monitor later when you find the need, the desk space, and the cash.

To bring together DOS and super-pixelated graphics, single-monitor graphics boards either incorporate their high-resolution abilities into an otherwise ordinary VGA board or operate as *pass-through* graphics adapters. That is, they connect directly to your existing VGA board through its expansion connector and pass its VGA signals through to your monitor when not operating in their high-resolution modes.

A few display adapters also offer the option of adding VGA capabilities to the basic high-resolution graphics adapter by plugging in a daughter card. Although the daughter card may save a slot and bind display functions tightly together, it's not necessarily the lowest-cost solution. Note that these daughter cards often cost $300 or more, while you can purchase an entire VGA board (if your system doesn't have VGA built in) for under $100. On the other hand, the daughter card implies that the high-resolution board manufacturer tested the VGA daughter and is sure that it will work properly with the high-resolution section. When you mix and match VGA and high-resolution display adapters yourself, you can sometimes run into uncooperative combinations.

Connections and Connectors

At heart, the installation of a display adapter board of any type appears trivially easy. You only need to plug an expansion board into your PC. But display adapters, and particularly the coprocessed ones, are rarely so straightforward—installation only begins with getting the board into your system. You'll need to consider how many monitors you want to use and how to connect the display adapter boards to them.

Most coprocessed graphics boards now give you a choice of using one or two monitors in your system. With two monitors, one is connected to your computer's existing video circuitry and displays most DOS-based programs. The other connects to the coprocessed graphics board and shows only the applications compatible with the coprocessed board.

The single-monitor choice is obviously the least expensive, but it has its own requirements. Typically, you have to pass-through the video signal produced by your existing VGA adapter. With such coprocessed adapters, you'll need a special cable (most coprocessed board makers supply one gratis with their products) and a compatible VGA board. This cable connects between the VGA feature connector—an edge connector at the top of most VGA boards—to a similar connector on the coprocessed board. Its purpose is to send the video output of your VGA board to the coprocessor and thence to your monitor.

When installing a coprocessed display adapter in a PS/2 with VGA circuitry built into its system board, you ordinarily don't have to worry about such cables. Instead, you must be certain to plug the coprocessed board into the expansion slot in your system that has the video extension connector, which is identifiable by the connector on the system board that extends slightly further toward the rear of the system than the other expansion connectors.

Classic bus and EISA computers that have their VGA circuitry built into their system boards should (but don't always) have a VGA feature connector on their system boards for connecting with coprocessed display adapters. According to the IBM design, a VGA feature connector is an edge connector similar to those on the lower edges of expansion boards. Sometimes this feature jack is a header—two rows of square, gold-plated pins, instead of an edge connector. This is the format specified by VESA for video extension connections. If your PC has system-board VGA, examine it before you order your display adapter because the cable you need will depend on the connector that's on your system board. (Some graphics adapters now come with VESA feature connectors, too, so you should check your VGA board to determine the cable it requires.)

The cable at the other end of your display adapter—the one that links the board to your monitor—is also critical. Even at ordinary VGA resolution, monitor cables are far from standard. Certainly most monitors now accept the 15-pin high-density D-shell connector that IBM chose for VGA, but many monitors use 9-pin connectors—or different 15-pin D-shells (dare we call them ''low density''?), 25-pin D-shells, or even three to five BNC jacks more like you'd expect on an over-the-horizon radar set. Similarly, display adapters that venture beyond VGA may use different connectors. For example, some boards use a 9-pin D-shell like a CGA or EGA connector, but with an entirely different pin-out.

When you order a display adapter, you'll need to specify the connectors you'll require at both ends of the cable. If you have a choice of what to use, the separate BNC cable approach is the best because it better isolates the signals. Some monitor makers actually rate the BNC inputs of their products with higher bandwidths (and, thus, more resolution) than their all-in-one connectors.

Of course, with a multiple-BNC cable you're left with three to five identical-looking connectors for a matching number of jacks. Fortunately, most BNC cables meant for computer monitors are color coded (either with actual color bands near their connectors or with simple designations, such as R for Red, B for Blue, G for Green, H for Horizontal sync, V for Vertical sync, and C for Composite sync).

The number of connectors used is a function of the way the synchronizing signal is delivered to the monitor. Three cables are used for "sync-on-green"; four, "composite sync"; and five, "separate sync." Some all-in-one connector systems give you the same options. You'll have to match your monitor to the connections provided by your display adapter using the facilities the monitor provides (automatic sensing, a switch, or whatever), which you should find described in the manual accompanying your monitor.

Once you make the connections, you need to install the software accompanying your display adapter to match the applications you want to run. Today, this installation process is usually managed by automatic programs and you only need to make a few choices from menus. Once that's done, reboot your system, start your application, and prepare yourself for the speed, resolution, and colors of your new display adapter.

Installing Display Adapters

The hardware installation of a display adapter is usually the easiest part of the upgrade job. You merely need to slide the board into the appropriate slot of your PC. Of course, there are complicating issues, such as which slot to use.

The first step in the installation process is to open up your PC and scout out the slots that are available for the installation of a display adapter. If your system already has a display adapter that you want to replace inside it, the old display adapter slot is a likely candidate. Before you automatically steal the old slot, however, examine your new display adapter and the slot. Most of the latest display adapters use 16-bit interfaces. The performance of these boards will be compromised if they are installed in an 8-bit slot. Some 16-bit boards may not even work in an 8-bit slot. If your new display adapter is 16-bit and your old one was 8-bit, remove the old board and install the new one in some other slot, one that has a 16-bit interface. Sixteen-bit ISA display adapters will also work in 32-bit EISA expansion slots.

In Micro Channel computers, you should install any display enhancement product in the slot that has the VGA feature connector extension. The VGA feature connector extension is an added part of

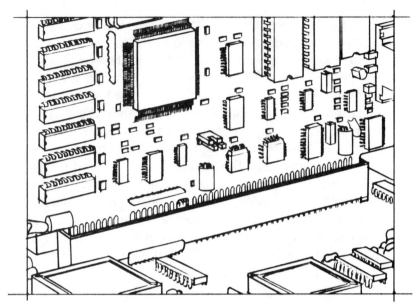

Figure 11.1 To get full performance from your display adapter, you must use the widest bus interface the board will accept. 16-bit display adapters should be installed in 16-bit expansion slots, as shown here.

a 16-bit slot connector that projects toward the rear of the computer's case.

If your PC does not have a display adapter in an expansion slot (because the circuitry is built into the system board) or if you are adding a second adapter (such as a coprocessed board), find a slot for the new board that matches the bus-width of its edge connector.

In any case, don't install the board yet. You have to set it up first. You may have to change jumpers or switch settings on the board or even on your system board.

The first adjustment to make is in the case when you have a 16-bit display adapter and no 16-bit slots available. Many display adapters have adjustments to allow you to use a 16-bit board in an 8-bit slot. If that's what you plan to do, make the adjustment.

Check the memory addresses used by your display adapter. If you're replacing your system board video circuitry or your old display adapter, you can use the default range of most upgrade display adapters, in general the range from A0000(Hex) to BFFFF(Hex) or a narrower selection within that range. Experiment with alternate addresses only if the default addresses don't work.

Many coprocessed display adapters require a second address range and sometimes an Input/Output port address. In general, you should first try the defaults recommended by the manufacturer of the display adapter. If your system does not properly boot up once the installation is complete, or if it crashes when you try to start a high-resolution mode, you should experiment with changing these addresses.

If your PC has system-board video circuitry that you want to replace, check your computer's owners' manual for your computer on how to switch it off. Some systems require that you move a jumper to turn off this circuitry. Others automatically sense the addition of another display adapter and make the appropriate switch themselves.

If you're installing a coprocessed display adapter that needs to link with your system's existing VGA circuitry, prepare the connection now, before you install the new board. PCs with system-board VGA circuitry typically provide a header or edge connector to which you can plug in the new coprocessed adapter. Most VGA and better primary display adapters have a VGA feature connector you can plug in to. In any case, you'll want to plug in one end of the VGA connecting cable before you slide in the display adapter so you have room in which to work.

Finally, you're ready. Slide the display adapter into the appropriate slot. Screw it into place. If you need to make a VGA feature connection, do that now. Then plug your monitor into the display adapter. Turn on the monitor and your PC and verify that the display adapter works properly.

If it does not, try resetting the jumpers or switches on the display adapter board to one of their alternate settings, then try again. Once your system boots properly and you determine that the higher-resolution modes work, you can reassemble you PC.

Monitors

Your monitor is simply the most important visual element of your PC. The image on its screen is all that you can see of what your computer does until (and if) your work is committed to paper. You continuously call upon your monitor to reveal your PC's innermost and tiniest thoughts. And the monitor's screen must be something that you're willing to look at for hours on end. If you're not happy with what you see, you'll want to upgrade your monitor.

If any rule dominates all your other cares and concerns in finding the right monitor upgrade for your PC, it is to please yourself. The best monitor is the one that yields the most pleasing image to your own eye. Maybe you don't require the utmost in resolution. Maybe you are so attuned to interlacing that to you a flicker-free frame rate dominates all other concerns. Maybe you like off-color, out-of-convergence displays because you suffer from sixties nostalgia and the creative color scheme gives you a drug-free high. Whatever the case, remember that your monitor is your portal into your personal computer. If you don't like what you see there—if you strain your eyes and credulity—you won't be happy with your work or your PC.

Finding the right monitor upgrade requires more than looking, however. You've got to match the monitor to your display adapter, to your PC, and to your software. The concerns are manifold.

Selecting a Monitor

As with other computer equipment or nearly anything else, a monitor is not difficult to buy. Write a check or read your bank-card number over the phone and await the delivery truck—it's easy. But getting the sharpest monitor, the one with the best color, the one that's the best value, and the one that will work best with your PC is more of a challenge. You have to match the monitor to your display adapter to ensure that it will work with your PC. Whatever standard or nonstandard you elect to follow, you must be certain that your software can take advantage of it. And your monitor choice must be agreeable to both your eyes and your purse.

You'll have a number of technical concerns in making these matches. But your first choice is philosophical. You must decide where your plans for your PC fit in with the designs of the monitor manufacturers.

Scanning Range

The philosophical starting place in considering a new monitor is with the three different kinds of monitors that you can connect to your PC. Monitors are a lot like people—some march in step with a common standard, some stroll in syncopation with their own drummers, and some just don't care either way, accepting a dance from whoever offers. The banners under which the common-standard monitors rally are the well-known display standards used by most display adapters—MDA, CGA, EGA, VGA, and XGA. The different drummers of the display world use their abilities to go beyond the common mien, linking up with their own proprietary display adapters to become complete video systems. And those that don't care are the uniquely adaptable multiscanning displays.

From these three major classes you must select your next monitor. The choice can be easy, even preordained, but you should consider all the alternatives before you commit your cash.

The common standard has a lot in its favor—safety in numbers and the low prices that come with near-commodity merchandising. Any VGA monitor you find should plug directly into a VGA display adapter and give you an image. You don't have to pore through manuals for timing specifications, mix and match frequencies, or tangle with adapter cables. And when you decide to follow one of the popular standards, you have an unbelievable range of monitors to select among, from tiny monochrome screens to 31-inch multi-hued monsters.

Pick any display standard, and you'll find the prices are unbeatable. For example, nearly every computer hardware company—seemingly anyone with the ability to write—puts its name on a VGA monitor of some kind. And this competition has driven prices down below the level where EGA had been lodged back at the time VGA was announced four years ago. Shop around and you'll discover monochrome VGA displays under $100, color under $250. Monitors that owe their allegiance to other standards are even cheaper—with close reading of the ads, you can probably find TTL monochrome displays for little more than $50.

The big drawback in selecting one of these systems is that standards are made for the masses, and for many people the popular choice means mediocrity. By selecting a monitor that transcends the mundane industry standards, you can get higher resolution, faster operation, more information on each screen, perhaps even a screen shape more commensurate with the vertically oriented letterheads and newsletters you spend most of your life dealing with.

The price you pay for the benefit beyond the common standards is, of course, measured in dollars. Not only are proprietary monitors themselves more expensive, but you also have to pay for the matching proprietary display adapter that makes a complete display system. When you do, you may suffer compatibility problems with some PCs and applications. Some proprietary display systems won't work with your favorite programs. Some even have difficulties with plain old DOS. Even when you find a proprietary display system that can function with DOS, you may find that your dearest investment doesn't deliver any greater quality on most of the work that you do. Often even the highest-resolution proprietary systems step back to the VGA standard—or worse, back to CGA—when DOS scrolls down the screen.

The flexibility of multiscanning monitors gives you possibly the best of both worlds: The ability to follow the standards when you must but also transcend them when you can. A multiscanning display can adapt to several standards as well as to some proprietary display modes that give you more colors and resolution than more commonplace monitors allow.

But multiscanning monitors have their limits, too. No multiscanning display will work with all possible display adapters. They may fall short at either the high or low end or may simply lack a special input capability required by an esoteric display adapter. Moreover, when you want to only make a modest improvement on today's standard, perhaps to boldly go forward to VESA, quality multiscanning displays often aren't the most affordable solution.

Which style of monitor is best to buy depends on what you have and what you want. If your concern is only the matter of matching a monitor to the display adapter that's already in your PC, you can probably play the standards game. If you want to hedge against future standards, however, the multiscanning display may be a better choice. And if you need high performance or high quality for a specialized application like desktop publishing or computer-aided design, the best bet is likely a proprietary display system, one that requires you to toss out your old display adapter and procure a complete system that includes both monitor and a matching board, probably a graphics coprocessor.

No matter which direction you choose, you need to know the signposts that will help point you on your way. All monitors have certain distinguishing characteristics that make some better than others and otherwise define the applications for which they are best suited.

Input Type

Once you've made your philosophical choice, you need to consider all the technical matters that separate monitors from one another. The best place to start is where monitors start—with the signal provided by your PC. Display adapters under different display standards, as well as proprietary display systems, produce signals that may use digital or analog signals. Correspondingly, monitors may accept one, the other, or both signal types.

Analog monitors just do what they are told. If they receive the right combination of signals, they can produce nearly any color you want. While analog signals offer a potential for coding an infinite number of colors, the monitor spectrum isn't quite infinite because of limitations in the phosphors in the tube and even the discrete number of electrons that must light each pixel. Even so, you can expect to get about 256,000 different colors from a good analog display according to monitor makers. Some makers claim even more. No one will argue that any monitor today can produce the 16.7 million individually distinguishable colors produced by a true 24-bit display adapter. But computer monitors still do as well in reproducing color as the primary gauge on civilization—the television set. In fact, computer monitors usually do better.

Digital monitors are more limited. Their spectrum is limited to the square of the number of connections provided for the digital signals. The four connections characteristic of the original CGA system allows 16 colors. The six connections of the EGA makes up to 64 colors possible. Today, the available selection of digital-only color monitors is primarily limited to units that conform to those two video standards. Beyond 64 colors, the number of connections required becomes ungainly at best.

Monitors with digital inputs may accept only one of these standards—CGA or EGA—or may have a switch that allows you to select either. The switch is best, particularly on multiscanning displays, because it allows you to use either 16-color or 64-color display adapters.

While digital signal coding is in some ways a special case of analog signaling—you could think of a digital signal as a special case of analog that uses only two of its infinity of potential voltages, *zero* and *full*—analog monitors are not innately digital-compatible. There's no easy way of translating the four- or six- (or whatever) wire digital code into analog signals. Many multiscanning monitors have built-in circuitry to handle the job, but unless this feature is explicitly mentioned in the specifications of a monitor—for instance, as a listing of both analog and digital inputs—you should not expect an analog multiscanning monitor to work properly with digital signals.

Going the other direction is even more difficult. Analog signals will not properly drive a digital display.

In other words, you must match the type of signal produced by your display adapter with the monitor that you buy. Proprietary video systems do this matching for you. After all, when you buy a complete package, you should expect the pieces to work together.

If you choose a monitor that matches a recognized display standard—TTL Monochrome, CGA, EGA, or VGA—you'll also be sure of getting a product that handles the right signal type. Multiscanning monitors are the only ones that will likely cause you problems, and you can avoid them by selecting one with both analog and digital inputs.

Required Frequencies

Like horsepower ratings in the days of muscle car, the number of hertz, kilohertz, and megahertz in the specifications of every monitor is important. These numbers describe the frequencies at which the monitor is designed to operate. Unlike horsepower ratings or even microprocessor speeds, however, bigger numbers here aren't necessarily better—or even necessary.

In fact, if you stick with industry display standards or a packaged proprietary display system, you need not worry about the irksome need to match frequencies. But when you step beyond the standards or try to connect up a multiscanning monitor, suddenly these frequencies will haunt your daydreams and nightmares with the same evil inevitability as your boss standing over you at work. There are just so many frequencies and so little sense to them.

Two frequencies determine what signals a monitor can recognize and work with: the *horizontal scanning frequency* and the *vertical scan-*

ning frequency. For brevity, "scanning" is often dropped from the names.

The first of these figures describes how often the lines of the video image are formed. For example, a horizontal frequency of 15 kilohertz (thousands of cycles per second) means that lines appear on the screen at a rate of 15,000 per second. Vertical frequency describes how often a complete full-screen image (or frame) is produced.

Sometimes these frequencies are referred to as *horizontal sync* and *vertical sync*—sync standing for synchronizing—because pulses at the beginning of each line and each frame are used to synchronize or lock the displayed image with the expectations of the display adapter. If the image cannot be locked, the result is akin to the rolling image of an old television with a misadjusted vertical hold control or a torn image that needs its horizontal hold adjusted. (Remember when televisions had vertical and horizontal hold knobs? Remember when televisions had knobs? Feeling old?) The important thing about these frequencies is that any monitor you buy must be rated to operate at the frequencies produced by the display adapter in your PC.

Monitors that can lock to only a single horizontal and vertical frequency are called *fixed-frequency displays*. Those that can lock to two or more sets of frequencies are termed, logically, *multiple fixed-frequency displays*.

A special case of the multiple fixed-frequency display are *dual-frequency displays*, which are designed to latch onto two fixed horizontal frequencies. The preeminent example is IBM's now-discontinued 8514 monitor, its model 8515 replacement, and other manufacturers' products compatible with the IBM units. These displays are capable of locking to VGA frequencies as well as the 1,024 by 768 interlaced images created by IBM's 8514/A and XGA graphics systems. Some of these dual-frequency displays can also lock into the SuperVGA signals defined by the VESA specifications. Newer multiple fixed-frequency displays may be aimed at making SuperVGA images under the more advanced versions of VESA.

Multiscanning monitors work with any frequency within a wide range so they can accept the signals of a variety of display adapters. The specifications of most multiscanning monitors list the frequencies of signals the products can accept. The lowest range of horizontal frequencies that should be of interest to you are those of CGA, about 15 kHz. The MDA system requires horizontal frequencies of about 18 kHz; EGA, 22 kHz; VGA, 31kHz; 8514/A, XGA, and some VESA systems, 35 kHz. High-resolution graphics coprocessor boards may require horizontal frequencies of 48 kHz and higher (check the manual of your graphics adapter). Proprietary display systems can push horizontal frequencies even higher. Note that if you have a VGA board that operates in its CGA and EGA modes, when it simulates those displays it maintains its own nominal 31 kHz horizontal frequency. You only need a monitor that dips down to 15 kHz if you have a CGA or EGA display adapter.

The range of vertical frequencies that monitors are required to handle is somewhat more modest. Few display systems are as slow as the 50 Hz used by MDA. Monitors that range down to 56 Hz will handle most color display standards, including SuperVGA under VESA, but not MDA. Most multi-scanning monitors easily adapt to frequencies in the range of 60 Hz (used by CGA, EGA, and some VGA and VESA modes) to 70 Hz (other VGA modes). But a higher top end is required for newer standards, such as the high-refresh VESA standard (72 Hz) and interlaced 8514/A signals (88 Hz). All of these frequencies are summarized in Table 11.1.

When buying a monitor, the scanning frequency rule is simple. The frequencies generated by the display adapter in your PC must either match those at which your monitor is designed to operate or they must be within the range accepted by your multiscanning monitor.

Autosizing

While multiscanning monitors can do wonders when you have to mate with odd signals, the matching frequencies may not be your only worry. The monitor must also be able to cope with varying image heights. Even within the VGA standard, the height of images displayed on the screen can vary when your software switches between display modes. Along with image height, the *aspect ratio*—the relationship between the height and width of the image—changes, making your graphics look out of shape. Squares become rectangles, and every circle will seem to have a slow leak.

The problem is that the VGA standard created by IBM is actually three separate standards, each one differing by the number of lines making up each image. The basic VGA graphics mode makes images 480 lines high. In text mode and the VGA's double-scanned

CGA-compatibility mode, images are built from 400 lines. EGA graphics on VGA monitors are drawn with 350 lines. All else being equal in a monitor, the greater the number of lines it displays, the taller the resulting image will look. If a VGA monitor does not have provisions for adjusting its image height to match the three different line counts, aspect ratio and image shape may go from fat to thin to fat again, like Oprah Winfrey trying a pure protein diet.

To avoid such endo- to ectomorphic (and back again) graphics, IBM endowed its VGA monitors with a unique system that automatically adjusts the heights of images to match the different modes of the threefold standard. The VGA graphics adapter in your PC tells your monitor how tall to make its image, indicating the number of lines that comprise each image by coding the polarity of its horizontal and vertical synchronizing signals. A truly VGA-compatible monitor detects the polarities of the two synchronizing signals and adjusts its internal electronics to maintain a constant height across all three VGA standards. The fourth possible sync signal coding is used by IBM to indicate interlaced 8514/A and XGA signals that are made from 768 lines.

Beyond VGA and 8514/A, this sync-indicated system falls apart. No additional codings of sync signals are available beyond the basic four. Even if there were, it would be hard to imagine the monitor industry deciding on an acceptable standard for them. Consequently, monitor makers must either develop their own broader-based autosizing method, stick with the VGA standard and only autosize for four image types, or just let the image height vary with the signal standard. Each of these three approaches has been adopted by a number of monitor makers.

The most desirable monitor is one that can autosize to match any standard. Least desirable is a monitor that entirely lacks autosizing. Most (if not all) VGA monitors can autosize for the three VGA signal types. Most multiscanning monitors make provisions for setting image height to match different standards. Before you buy, make sure that a prospective monitor can maintain a constant image height with all the graphics standards you plan to use.

Monitor Controls

Even when a monitor lacks autosizing, it need not be impossible to use—as long as its controls are located conveniently. When a monitor manufacturer puts the knobs that control the size of its on-screen image—typically, controls labeled horizontal size, gain, or width and vertical size, gain, or height—where you can readily reach them, then you can manually adjust any picture for the proper proportion.

If you often jump between operating modes—text and graphics— or occasionally leap back to EGA graphics, the manual method of image sizing will prove to be tedious and time-consuming, forcing you to twist the controls every time you shift between programs. But if you stick with a single standard—for example, running only Windows 3.0 programs or never exiting Lotus 1-2-3—you'll need to make image size adjustments but once.

With some monitors, you may discover that the manufacturer has worked hard to make all the important image controls difficult to find or impossible to adjust. They may put the image controls on the back of a big-screen set so you need gorilla arms to make an adjustment and caterpillar eyes to see the effect. You'll want to avoid such monitors.

On the other hand, some monitor manufacturers believe they know what you want far better than you do, so they seal all the image controls inside their products. Just to make things interesting, they usually emblazon the monitor with a warning to the effect that there are no user serviceable parts inside and that you will inevitably die if you try opening the case. If such a monitor maker has perfect aesthetic judgment—which means it agrees with your own—this simplification can work out. But if beauty to you is in the eyes of the beholder and you're beholden to your own views, you're out of luck. You'll be condemned to suffer with a picture from purgatory for the duration of your ownership of the monitor. In other words, make sure you get ready access to the size and positioning controls of any monitor you buy.

Besides location, you may also have your choice of the type of control used for image adjustments. For example, NEC has substituted digital push-buttons for the more conventional analog knobs or shafts for the size and positioning adjustments of many of its monitors. Pressing one button make the image larger; another makes it smaller. These digital controls are often coupled with memory so the monitor can recall the settings you've made for each frequency range at which it operates. That way the monitor can adjust the image to your own personal degree of perfection as you skip between display modes.

Push-button digital controls are not for everyone, particularly when they invade everyday functions like brightness and contrast. Push-button controls don't tell you how close to the middle or end of their range they are set, nor can you tell from the knob position approximately where the control is set. Before you buy a monitor with digital controls, you may want to try one and see if it works the way you do.

No matter whether a monitor has push-buttons or knobs, the range of the image size controls can also be important. You'll want a monitor with sufficient control range so you can fill the entire screen with image. If it doesn't, you won't get everything that you've paid for. Some monitors are parsimonious with their pictures and confine the active video area far within the margins of the picture tube face. You can lose as much as an inch all the way around the screen, making a 14-inch monitor the equivalent of a 12-inch display. If you pay for a big screen, *make sure* you get a big image area to go along with it.

Sharpness Versus Resolution

For most people, the most important characteristic of a monitor is its sharpness. On a sharp display, every character is clearly chiseled against the background like the lettering of the cornerstone of a new building. With an dull display, you can't tell the difference between a lowercase "m" and a gnat smashed against the screen. Dull characters tend toward formlessness and ambiguity, a definite disadvantage when you try to discern the values in cramped spreadsheet columns or the fine print in an on-screen contract you're construing.

Worse, a fuzzy screen can be bad for your eyesight and may sow seeds that blossom into a full-fledged migraine as your work day winds down. Working with a dull display can provoke eyestrain. It may cause you to unconsciously squint at the screen to try to make the display look sharper, which means you'll get a headache but not a sharper view. No amount of eyeball gymnastics can make up for sharpness that's not there.

Sharpness is the final product of the monitor—what you see on the screen—but it is affected by everything in your display system. If the signals sent to the picture tube lack detail, then the sharpness of the tube is wasted. Resolution is the figure familiar to those who want the sharpest possible image on the screen. But the figure that many monitor makers give as resolution in a product's specifications often does not reflect the actual amount of detail on the screen. That's because what many manufacturers call *resolution* actually amounts to a measure of another monitor parameter, one more properly termed *addressability*.

The difference between resolution and addressability is the difference between strolling across the rusty red surface of Mars and knowing that you could find Mars through your telescope as the fourth planet from the sun. Resolution is—or should be—the reality of the situation, the measure of actual image sharpness. Addressability is a promise or conception of what could be. It merely refers to a monitor's ability to light up a dot on the screen at a particular location.

Addressability is the ultimate limit on how sharp an image can be on the screen, but other factors in the design and manufacture of the monitor may limit its sharpness far below its addressability. For example, any monitor that claims to be VGA compatible has an addressability of 640 by 480 pixels. But the actual resolution of the display might be much less, perhaps more in line with the 320 by 200 pixels promised by medium-resolution CGA. In the case of better monitors, addressability and on-screen resolution converge and become the same figure. But with inexpensive monitors, the on-screen image may only aspire to be as sharp.

Addressability is determined by the signals generated by your display adapter. The board inside your PC sets exactly how many lines will sweep across each image frame and how many individual dots will be in each line. Your monitor needs only to be able to decode the signal sent by the video adapter to achieve that level of addressability. The resolution of a display is a function of its quality, the results of its electronics, mechanical construction, and the quality of its components.

One of the biggest influences on resolution is the cathode ray tube, the picture tube of the display. Because the picture tube is usually the most expensive part of a monitor, it's often the place where manufacturers cut corners when designing inexpensive displays. A cheap picture tube can easily tempt a monitor maker. The price difference between a good tube and a cheap one may amount to $100 or more—effectively a $200 price difference in the finished product. At current market prices, that's nearly enough to double your cost of a VGA display.

Among the most important factors in the price and quality of a picture tube is the *shadow mask* or slot mask that with current display technology is required between the electron guns and screen inside the tube. The shadow mask is a thin sheet of metal perforated with holes or slots. Its purpose is to assure the purity of the colors on the screen by preventing the electrons meant for the green phosphors from hitting the red and blue phosphors (and the red from blue and green, et cetera).

Most picture tubes in monitors have three color "guns," which shoot electrons at the screen to make it glow. The guns are arranged in a triangle, with one assigned to illuminate each color on the screen. The mask is designed so that unwanted phosphor colors fall into the shadow of the mask cast by the electron beam meant for the desired color. The holes in the shadow mask thus determine how closely spaced the dots of color can possibly be on the screen. Color dots of one hue must be spaced at the same distance apart as the holes in the mask. The term that describes this hole spacing—and thus the spacing of color dots on the screen—is *dot-pitch*.

A special kind of color picture tube, called the *Trinitron*, uses a different arrangement of its electron guns. Instead of a triangle, its three guns are aligned in a straight line or compressed into what is essentially a single-gun unit. Instead of circular holes in the shadow mask, the picture tube uses a series of vertically oriented slots to help control each electron beam. Rather than spacing between dots, the resolution limit on these tubes is set by the spacing between slots, the *slot pitch*. Note that in one dimension—along the axis of the slot—the electron beam in a Trinitron picture tube is essentially unlimited. Nothing mechanical need stand in the way of the color spacing except for one or two *tensioning wires*, which can sometimes be faintly seen running across the width of a Trinitron screen. To some people, the dark shadow of these tensioning wires is a grave image defect, one that is most apparent on light backgrounds such as the white that Windows uses as a default. Before you buy a Trinitron-based display, take a look at the screen with a light background and assure yourself that the thin horizontal shadows won't bother you when you use the monitor.

You're apt to see an increasing number of Trinitron-based monitors offered in coming years. Sony Corporation developed the technology and patented it. In 1991, the initial Trinitron patents expired, opening the market for other manufacturers.

For many monitors, the dot-pitch of the picture tube sets the ultimate limit on sharpness. Unlike resolutions, which are given in the number of lines or dots that can be discerned across the face of a monitor tube, dot-pitches are customarily given in terms of the spacing of holes in fractions of a millimeter. It's easy to convert these dot-pitch numbers into an equivalent resolution figure, however. All you need to do is divide the dot-pitch into the dimensions of the display area.

For example, a 14-inch VGA monitor might have an active image area that measures about ten inches wide by eight inches high. In metric, that's 254 millimeters by 203 millimeters. In this case, the minimum required dot-pitch would be just under 0.40 millimeter (that is, 254 mm. width divided by the 640 dots stretching across it). Most—but hardly all—VGA monitors in the 12 to 14-inch size have dot-pitches in the vicinity of .031 mm to comply with the rigors of this math.

A display with a finer dot-pitch will produce a sharper, more pleasing image. A display with a coarser dot pitch (higher numbers) will produce unacceptably fuzzy images.

Some manufacturers offer what they call VGA monitors with 0.50 millimeter or coarser dot-pitches. Although these displays accept VGA signals, they cannot produce the resolution required for VGA images. They are VGA displays solely because of their 640 by 480 addressability. They will work with your VGA adapter, but images they make will likely be unacceptable. Avoid them if you can.

The dot-pitch required by a given video standard is a function of monitor size. Large-screen displays don't need dot-pitches as fine as smaller screens at the same resolution level. However, because most larger monitors are designed to produce resolutions beyond VGA, they usually have dot-pitches comparable to those of smaller-screen displays.

Note that dot-pitch is important only for monitors that use multiple electron guns and shadow masks or slot masks. Monochrome displays use a single electron gun because they need to produce only a single image color. They do not need shadow masks. Consequently, monochrome monitors do not have dot-pitches. Any listing of a dot-pitch for a monochrome monitor is simply an error.

When buying a monitor that complies with a display standard, the required addressability is a given. The resolution will be anyone's guess. But the dot-pitch will tell you how sharp the monitor could possibly be. If the dot-pitch of a monitor is not high enough to support the standard under which the monitor is to operate, the monitor is likely to be unacceptable. Consequently, for most people dot-pitch is the most important figure when shopping for a monitor.

Convergence

But dot-pitch is not the only influence on the sharpness of the image on the screen. The three electron beams in the color tube must be properly aimed before they are shot at the screen—or they need some kind of midcourse correction to ensure that they arrive at the proper destination dots. If not, the beams may not line up properly. One color may be offset from the others and give any image a rainbow of outlines instead of a single bold color.

When the electron beams of a color display don't line up, every line drawn on the screen will become two or three lines of different colors. Every dot will become a cloverleaf or multicolor glob. The effect is worst with text. Reading becomes a guessing game with each letter a speckled, multicolored pox on the screen.

The term *convergence* defines how closely the three electron beams in a color monitor actually converge on a single point (actually, the correct dot in an individual pixel). When a display is badly converged, individual pixels are no longer sharply defined, but become two- or three-color blurs as one electron beam spills over onto the phosphors of another color. Monochrome monitors are inherently free from such convergence problems because they have but one electron beam.

Convergence problems are a symptom rather than a cause of monitor deficiencies. Convergence problems arise not only from the design of the display, but also from the construction and set-up of each individual monitor. They can vary widely from one display to the next and may be aggravated by damage during shipping.

The result of convergence problems is most noticeable at the screen periphery because that's where the electron beams are the most difficult to control. When bad, convergence problems can be the primary limit on the sharpness of a given display, having a greater negative effect than wide dot-pitch or low bandwidth (discussed below).

Many monitor makers will claim that their convergence is a given fraction of a millimeter at a particular place on the screen. If a figure is given for more than one screen location, the center of the screen will invariably have a lower figure—tighter, better convergence—than a corner of the screen. The number given is how far one color may spread from another at that location. Lower numbers are better. A typical monitor may claim convergence of about 0.5 (one-half) millimeter at one of the corners of the screen. That figure often rises 50 percent higher than the dot pitch of the tube, making the convergence the limit on sharpness for that particular monitor.

Note, however, that while dot-pitch is a global phenomenon across the screen, misconvergence is a localized problem. Moreover, misconvergence problems may be confined to individual monitors that have been jarred, jostled, or generally mistreated in shipping.

Unlike a coarse dot-pitch, misconvergence problems often can be corrected by adjustment of the monitor. Many monitors have internal convergence controls. A few, high-resolution (and high-cost) monitors even have external convergence adjustments. But adjusting monitor convergence is a job for the specialist—and that means getting a monitor converged can be expensive, as is any computer service call.

Monitor Bandwidth

Dot-pitch is purely a mechanical limit on monitor sharpness. Convergence is a combination of mechanical and electronic limits. Purely electronic factors also influence the sharpness of images appearing on a monitor's screen. Chief among these electronic factors is *bandwidth*.

The picture formed by your graphics adapter is sent to your monitor as an electrical signal in which each dot on the screen is represented by a tiny time segment. The duration of that time segment is a function of the horizontal and vertical scanning frequencies of your monitor. The shortest possible time segment that the electronics of your monitor can define clearly sets an upper limit on the resolution of your display system.

The length of this shortest time segment is measured in microseconds, but is more usually expressed as its reciprocal value, megahertz, as the bandwidth of the monitor. The more megahertz in a monitor's bandwidth, the shorter the time that can be devoted to each dot, and the sharper the image that the monitor can display (within the limits of its dot-pitch and the quality of its construction).

The quality of the electronics inside a monitor determine its bandwidth. Better monitors have bandwidths with higher megahertz ratings. In theory, you could compute the bandwidth required by any video standard from the resolution and frame rate of the standard. For example, VGA's 640 by 480 resolution and 70 Hz frame rate multiplied together yields 21,504,000 MHz. While that calculation gives a rough indication of required bandwidth, other factors must also be considered.

The resolution numbers apply only to the active viewing portion of the screen. A substantial fraction of the time, the video signal is not being displayed. At the end of each line of the image, the electron beam turns off, then races back to the other side of the screen to start the next line. This process is called *retracing*. At the end of each frame, the beam must retrace from the bottom of the screen back up to the top to begin the next frame. In addition, blank areas are left on each side of the screen, and the corresponding part of the video signal must also be left the equivalent of blank. All of these factors tend to increase the bandwidth required for properly processing a video signal.

Compensating in the other direction—reducing required bandwidth—is the actual on-screen pattern of pixels. The image that requires the highest resolution would be a pattern of alternating on and off pixels. But this toughest pattern actually has a frequency of one-half the product of resolution times frame rate. Thus, the actual demand for bandwidth is one-half the resolution times frame rate once the inactive video periods are added in. In other words, the actual bandwidth required by a video standard is approximately equal to the first rough resolution-times-frame rate calculation—and is one of those strange cases where you can come up with the right answer for the wrong reasons.

Interlacing

One way of circumventing the bandwidth limitations in the electronics of a monitor is to cut the vertical frequency or frame rate of the signal. However, frame rates cannot be arbitrarily reduced because high frame rates—generally above 60 Hz—are required to eliminate image *flicker* on the monitor screen.

Flicker arises when the on-screen image flashes at a rate below which your eye would blend the intermittent illumination of each pixel into the illusion of continuous light. Minimizing image flicker requires higher frame rates, and higher frame rates push up the bandwidth required in a monitor; this, in turn, pushes up the price.

Some video standards use a trick called *interlacing* to try to minimize the effect of a lower frame rate. Interlacing allows a higher frame rate to be simulated with a narrower bandwidth.

The idea behind interlacing is simple—slice the image in half and alternate showing each half, making the image flash at twice its actual frame rate. Rather than alternating sides of the screen, interlacing involves alternating scan lines. First the odd-numbered lines are scanned, creating a zebra-striped half-image called a *field*, then the even-numbered lines are scanned to fill in the dark places with the rest of the picture's detail. The two interwoven fields make up a single image *frame*, hence the derivation of the term *frame rate*.

Because the lines are so closely spaced, your eyes can sometimes be fooled into thinking that the whole image is refreshed at the rate of one field. Consequently, a high field rate suffices, instead of a high frame rate. Since the frame rate is effectively half of the field rate, the bandwidth required for the system is cut in half.

Interlaced displays suffer the free-lunch problem. In effect, interlacing appears to be giving you something for nothing, which should automatically lead you to believe that there must be some strings attached. There are. The illusion of a continuously lit image is often not successful. The image tends to flicker, a just-perceptible flashing of the screen that appears to travel down the screen as mysteriously as the aurora borealis. Worse, obtaining the full claimed resolution from an interlaced image requires that the alternately illuminated scan lines mesh perfectly together. Often they don't, resulting in a loss of up to half the detail in an image.

People vary in their ability to detect flicker and thus tolerate interlacing. Moreover, their susceptibilities may vary with the ambient lighting around the interlaced monitor and even how the individual viewer feels (are you having a good day?) when looking at the display. Flicker is most noticeable when you view the monitor screen out of the corner of your eye, rather than directly. It is also more apparent the larger the screen. Consequently, nearly everyone has different feelings about the effectiveness and palatability of interlacing.

The best rule is that a noninterlaced display will always appear better than an interlaced display. But a higher-resolution interlaced display may be more useful than a lower-resolution noninterlaced display, particularly when the former is substantially less expensive than the latter.

Whether a display is interlaced depends on the graphics adapter you use. Most monitors will handle both interlaced and noninterlaced images. However, a monitor must be able to synchronize to the high field rate (rather than frame rate) used by the interlaced system. Some multiscanning monitors do not have the range required to display interlaced 8514/A or XGA images. So if you plan on using interlaced signals, be sure that the monitor you choose explicitly supports them.

Monitor Colors and Phosphors

One way that monitors designed specifically for interlaced signals cope with flicker is through the use of long-persistence phosphors. *Persistence* is a term that describes how long the screen phosphors of a monitor glow after they have been struck by the beam from the electron gun. Ordinary screen phosphors are short-to-medium persistence. Long-persistence phosphors permit the glow of each pixel on the screen to linger a little longer, bridging over the low frame rate. However, long-persistence phosphors often cause image *lag*—ghostly afterimages that linger after screen changes—which can be more irritating than flicker.

Phosphor type can be an issue in buying a monitor for other reasons. Phosphor type also controls the color of the image and the brightness of the image displayed on a monitor.

With monochrome monitors, phosphor type will determine the overall color of the screen—typically green, amber, or white.

Green is the color of old-fashioned radar sets and oscilloscopes because it is believed to be easiest on the eyes in dark surroundings. Common wisdom holds that green is the preferred color for cave-dwelling monitor viewers, the kind who switch off every the light in their offices so every business meeting becomes a seance.

Amber, which actually ranges from yellow to nearly neon orange, is supposed to be better when the surroundings are bright. Against a dark screen, amber yields higher contrast than green and doesn't as easily wash out from splashes of sunlight.

The trend today, however, is to white screens. With graphics, white screen produce grey-scale images reminiscent of familiar black-and-white photographs and television—and, hence, more realistic in appearance to all of us in the television generation. White screens also mimic the paper on which so much of the world's work is carried out.

One white is not the same color as another, however. Each monochrome monitor manufacturer brews his own combination of faint shades into its nominally white screens. The result is that the white on monochrome screens ranges from bluish (like black-and-white television) to the yellowish of bleached white paper. The termed "paper white" is not critically defined, however, so one manufacturer's paper white monitor can be an entirely different shade of white than another's.

Phosphor color also is important in color displays, as you might expect. While most of today's color monitors use essentially similar blends of phosphors—the most popular is designated P22 (or B22)—you'll still find a range of colors cast to different manufacturers' products.

One of the variables is *color temperature*, which refers to the general cast of all the colors in the spectrum. White light is not a single color, but a mixture of all colors. And as with the whites of monochrome displays, whites on color monitors are not all the same. Some are richer in blue, some in yellow. The different shades of white are described by their color temperature, the number of kelvins (degrees Celsius above absolute zero) that a perfect luminescent body would need to be to emit that color. Like the incandescence of a hot iron horseshoe in the blacksmith's forge, as its temperature gets higher the hue of a glowing object shifts from red to orange, then yellow and on to blue-white. Color temperature simply assigns an absolute temperature rating to this spectrum of colors.

For example, ordinary lightbulbs range from 2,700 to 3,400 kelvins and are obviously orange. Most fluorescent lights have non-continuous color spectra rich in certain hues (notably green), while lacking others that makes assigning a true color temperature impossible. Other fluorescent lamps are designed to approximate daylight with color temperatures of about 5,000 kelvins, a yellowish to pure white. When the sun is obscured by clouds, the outdoor color temperature shifts dramatically higher towards blue, because the blue sky provides most of the brightness. The outdoor color temperature may rise to 10,000 kelvins.

Normally, your eyes automatically adjust to accommodate the temperature of available light. As a result trees, grass, and flesh tones look the same under the noonday sun and at sunset, in direct sunlight or in the shade, even though the color temperature may vary thousands of kelvins.

In theory, then, any color temperature would do for a monitor screen. And if the monitor were the only thing you ever looked at, that's true. You'd never have to worry about kelvins. But a problem related to color temperature arises when you do critical work such as color desktop publishing with your monitor—and you expect the ideal WYSIWYG. Screen colors don't look anything like what comes out of your color printer or film recorder.

The underlying problem has to do with forms of illumination and the perception of color. Monitor colors just aren't the same as colors on paper or film.

You've faced the underlying problem before, perhaps in elementary school. Once you were weaned from eating crayons to actually drawing with them, you learned about the primary colors—scribble enough wax on newsprint and you'll get a dark, dingy mess. With a little sophistication, you learned that red, blue, and yellow will do for a nice ugly mess teachers claimed was actually black. In high school physics, however, you had to unlearn those lessons because the exam answer for primary colors mysteriously becomes red, blue, and green, which, when mixed, yield white instead of black.

The difference is between two different kinds of primary colors, the *subtractive* and *additive*, the primary colors of pigment and light. The two are not the same. When you try to match monitor colors on paper, the difference becomes painfully obvious. Your monitor spews out light while your printer fuses down pigment. You cuss up a storm when the match is about as close as two socks slipped on in the dark.

Because pigments only reflect light, their actual color depends on the light illuminating them and its color temperature. On the other hand, your monitor screen emits light, so its color is independent of illumination. To get the best match between your display and your hard copy, you have to ensure that you view the output of your printer under light of the same color temperature as the light generated by your monitor.

The colors and blend of the phosphors used to make the picture tube screen and the relative strengths of the electron beams illuminating those phosphors determine the color temperature of a monitor. Originally, color television tubes were designed to reflect the perfect sunny day with a color temperature of about 6,000 kelvins. Evidently some engineers felt that the ideal day was actually rather soggy and overcast, suitable only to ducks, Englishmen, and ending Californian droughts. So an alternate color standard was developed with a color temperature of 9,300 kelvins, which is reflected in most commercial computer monitors.

For most purposes, this high color temperature is fine. Your eyes accommodate to it, and you never notice its overcast quality. For critical work like photographic retouching and color desktop publishing, however, color temperature may be crucial. You'll want to look for a monitor with a color temperature equivalent to your normal workplace surroundings or one that has an adjustable color temperature.

Monitor Brightness

Although rarely disclosed by specification sheets, other important differences mark a monitor as more suited to specific applications. Brightness is a particular example. Some monitors are capable of generating brighter images that others, making them more suited for use in environments with high illumination.

Sometimes brightness comes at a penalty. When brightness is increased on some monitors, the *spot size* (the footprint of the electron beam) increases. That is, as the monitor gets brighter, each pixel on the screen becomes a fuzzy glob instead of a sharp dot. A better monitor will preserve its fine spot size over a wide range of brightnesses.

When a monitor is operated at a brightness level lower than its maximum, other problems can show up. The relationships between colors can shift with different brightness levels. This problem arises from nonlinearities in the amplifiers that are used to increase the input voltage of the monitor to the level necessary to drive the electron beams inside the monitor. These amplifiers must be exactly matched and absolutely linear. That is, the input and output of each amplifier must be precisely proportional, and this linear relationship must be exactly the same for all three amplifiers in a color monitor. In other words, the three must precisely track one another.

If the relationship between the signal strengths of the individual colors varies, the hue of the on-screen image will shift as its intensity varies. At some level, one color will be more intense than the others, lending its cast to the screen. At other levels, another color may be dominant so the hue of the on-screen image varies with brightness. This shading effect is usually most pronounced in grey displays—each dominant color tinges the grey.

The effects of such poor color tracking in monitor amplifiers are all bad. You lose precision in your control of color. The screen can no longer hope to be an exact preview of what will eventually appear on paper or film. You may even lose a good fraction of the colors displayable by your video system. The end result is that the color of the image on the screen won't be what your software had in mind.

A similar problem can occur in monochrome monitors (which have but one video amplifier) and in color monitors when all three video amplifiers are exactly matched. If the input and output of each amplifier do not vary in a precisely linear relationship, the brightness of the image won't reflect the image that your software attempts to generate. The relationship between different grey levels will shift; some grey levels may even disappear from the monitor's repertory. In a perfect monitor, each grey level will exactly track the intensity of the input signal to the monitor. That is, a signal twice as strong should cause a grey level twice as bright.

Nothing on the specifications sheet of a monitor will reveal to you how well the colors and greys of a monitor track. You'll have to observe this with your own eyes. One general rule holds: If you can't see a problem, then don't worry about it. If you can see a problem, it will only bother you more as time goes on.

Tilt-swivel Base

While once an option, tilt-swivel bases should now be considered standard equipment in any monitor. The base elevates the monitor about two inches to a convenient viewing height and allows the easy adjustment of the screen for comfortable viewing. Some tilt-swivel bases are permanently attached. The better alternative is the removable base, which allows you the option of using the monitor without it. If a tilt-swivel base is not included with a monitor, figure an extra $20 to buy a universal tilt-swivel monitor stand from a mail-order vendor.

Monitor Connections

Installing a monitor upgrade is easy once you've found the right unit. Just plop it atop your PC (if it fits), plug it in (to the wall and to your display adapter) and turn everything on.

Plugging in may be the only challenge. The biggest problem you'll face is the cable, and with the many monitors the cable is not a simple matter. Some monitor manufacturers and vendors try to make things easier for you and include the necessary connecting cable with their displays. That's generally okay for single-standard monitors (CGA, EGA, or VGA displays) but can be limiting for multi-scanning units. The cable that comes packed with the monitor might not fit the obscure display standard you've chosen. Before you buy, check to ensure the proper type of cable accompanies your monitor choice. If the monitor cable requires a 9- to 15-pin adapter, ensure that one accompanies your purchase. There's nothing so frustrating as unpacking a new toy at 9 P.M. and discovering you have no way of plugging it in.

Some monitors come with cables permanently attached—a great idea if you're afraid of losing the cable, but worrisome should your cat confuse the cable with the licorice she's fond of chewing or should you break the connector on the end. The permanent connection can make a simple accident expensive. You'll have to take the whole monitor in for repair. The loose cable supplied with the monitor wins when you worry about such prospects—should your model train run over the monitor cable and cut it in half, you pay only for a new cable, not a technician's time to replace it.

Figure 11.2 Monitors use any of a variety of input connectors. Shown here are (from top left clockwise): a nine-pin D-shell; a 25-pin D-shell; a 15-pin high-density D-shell (VGA style); and a set of five BNC connectors. All connectors shown are male.

A few vendors make bargain-hunting more of a challenge by making the monitor-connecting cable an extra-cost option. When comparing monitors, be sure to factor in such incidentals.

If you have to buy a cable separately, or if you're subverting the reigning standards, you'll have to worry about the type of connectors on the cable. Display adapters matching the popular standards all use the same style of connector—9-pin D-shell connectors (female on the display adapter) for MDA, CGA, and EGA, and special high-density 15-pin D-shell connectors for VGA. But monitors are known to use anything from 9-pin connectors to full 25-pin connectors that you can confuse with serial and parallel ports. Some use three to five video-style BNC connectors. Even monitors with permanently attached cables may have odd connectors at the end; for example, some VGA displays may offer retro-mode 9-pin connectors.

Connect the cable between your monitor and your display adapter first. Then plug the power cable into the back of the monitor (if necessary), and finally plug the monitor power cable into a wall outlet. (If your monitor has a switch to select 115- or 230-volt operation, verify it is in the correct position before plugging in the monitor.)

If you're downgrading your display system instead of upgrading—or just trying to get by on the cheap with an MDA monochrome, a CGA or an EGA color system—take a thinking pause before you connect your new monitor. All three of these standards use 9-pin D-shell connectors on their display adapters, but the signals used by the color and monochrome systems are completely different. In fact, plugging an MDA monitor into a CGA or EGA display adapter can destroy the monitor (and plugging a CGA or EGA display into an MDA isn't advisable either). Verify the adapter type and display compatibility before you make the connection. Be vigilant when you turn one of these systems on for the first time, too. If you don't see a cursor flashing in the upper left hand of the monitor or hear a squealing noise come from the monitor when you turn it and your computer on, turn them both off immediately! Those symptoms warn of a mismatched display.

Once you've got your monitor plugged into your display adapter and wall, switch on your PC and let it start booting up. Again, check the upper left corner of the monitor for a cursor or some other indication that all is well—such as a memory count-up or copyright message.

When you're sure your monitor type and display adapter match, but you still don't see anything on the monitor when you switch on your computer, first make sure that both the monitor and computer are actually plugged in and turned on. Listen for signs of life inside your computer; check the power indicator on the monitor.

The next troubleshooting step is to adjust the brightness and contrast controls to their full speed (clockwise) positions. If the monitor screen doesn't light up at all, the monitor may be bad. If you see a mess of lines on the screen highlighted with bright dots, odds are your monitor can't cope with the signal produced by your display adapter. If you see a few zigzag lines tracing down the screen, suspect your display adapter or the connection between it and your monitor.

With color displays, one family of colors missing from the display indicates a loose or bad signal cable. Failure to display color on a color screen can also be the symptom of a bad cable or a monitor that doesn't support IBM's automatic sensing scheme. If the cable is good, you can often force your VGA monitor to work in color by issuing the command MODE CO80 to DOS.

Odds are, however, that your monitor upgrade will come to life immediately, rewarding you with a sharper, more colorful view of your computer's innermost thoughts.

Input Devices

Computers don't process data in general; they process the data that you give them. If you had no way of loading your PC with information, it could never give you answers that were relevant to what you do. Just as the monitor gives you a look at what the PC is doing, an input device tells your PC what you want and what to work with.

The classic input device is the keyboard. What you type on it gets entered into the computer's memory, to be analyzed, acted upon, or stored. Keyboards are ubiquitous and they are the most efficient way of sending your thoughts to your PC, but they have a drawback. They are lousy at handling graphics. Drawing a picture with a keyboard is cumbersome—you can either use a corner of the keyboard to scratch an image into loose sand (which won't help your PC understand it much) or you can type in a series of commands that tell the machine what to draw (which isn't how you think in images).

For handling graphics, you need a graphic input device, one that can translate shapes into computer-digestible form, one that can let you manipulate images naturally—by pointing. In the PC realm there are now several common pointing devices. Among the most used and most useful are the mouse, the trackball, and the digitizing tablet. When you need to convey a complete picture in its original form, the scanner is a handy addition to that trio. Optical character recognition will add the ability to read printed text to the scanner's otherwise autistic talents.

Each of these devices have its own strengths and features. And each is a subtly different upgrade to make.

Keyboards

Before you venture off into graphics territory, you almost always need to get started with a keyboard. Even if you configure your PC to boot up into a graphics environment, you must somehow first program the boot-up process. And that programming inevitably means plunking your fingers down on a keyboard.

Keyboards are tricky upgrades—but not because the upgrade process is difficult. In fact, it only requires you to unplug your old keyboard and plug the new one into its place. The real reason that keyboard upgrades can be mind-boggling is that the selection of a keyboard is not a technical issue. It's a matter of personal preference, and there's no accounting for tastes. After all, some people like liver. Others like IBM's 101-key enhanced layout. Others take the opposite view. Decisions about key layout have to be left to your own preferences.

Only two technical issues enter into your choice and installation of a keyboard change or upgrade. Any new keyboard must match the hardware and firmware standard used by your PC. And the keyboard needs to have the correct connector to mate with your system.

Currently, the world is plagued by only two PC keyboard electrical standards, the XT style and the AT style. The two styles use different internal firmware and they respond differently when your system tries to communicate with them. They cannot be interchanged.

An XT keyboard follows the original IBM keyboard standard laid down in 1981. On the surface, it has 83 keys and no illuminated indicators. The AT standard took over after 1984 with a new electrical design. Not incidentally, it added an additional key (bringing the total to 84) and illuminated indicators. The IBM Advanced Keyboard, the current 101-key model, follows the AT standard electrically and is interchangeable with it, but of course it brings along at least 17 changes, moving function keys to the top row, adding an additional cursor keypad, hiding the Ctrl key, and shrinking the Enter key.

The moral of this story is that if your system has an XT-style keyboard, you need an XT-style replacement to match it electrically. Most modern PC systems use the AT style of keyboard. The layout of the keys does not distinguish the two standards, so you can plug a 101-key keyboard into an XT if the keyboard follows the XT electrical standard.

A few replacement keyboards give you your choice of electrical standards—a switch (typically hidden on the bottom of the keyboard) allows you to select between the XT and AT electrical interface. All you have to do is be certain you have the switch properly set for your PC.

If a replacement keyboard does not work with your PC, the first thing to check is this switch. If you find a switch (typically labeled XT-AT), try sliding it to its alternate position to get the keyboard working.

The other difference between keyboards is the connector used to plug into your PC. Two connector styles are used by current keyboards. One follows in the tradition of the original PC and uses a large, 5-pin DIN connector. IBM abandoned that connector style with the introduction of its PS/2 series, which uses a smaller 6-pin miniature DIN connector. Compatible computer makers follow whichever standard they please.

The good news is that there is no electrical difference between the signals on these different connector types. A simple adapter will allow one type of keyboard to plug into the opposite kind of connector. The bad news is that such adapters can be difficult to find.

Once you match the connector on your PC to that of your keyboard replacement, you only need to plug in the replacement to get typing again. Be sure to turn your PC off before you plug in a new keyboard, however. To work properly, the keyboard must be initialized by signals from your PC, which are sent out while the machine is booting up. Besides, it's also good practice never to plug anything into your PC while its power is on.

Mice

Apple's Macintosh, the first personal computer with a graphic interface to make any real impression on the marketplace, introduced the *mouse*. The idea was a gem: People don't normally select items or operations by typing. Rather, they point. And the mouse was designed as a pointing device. (The only weakness in this argument is that people don't naturally point by rolling an odd-shaped plastic object around their desks, but that's another story entirely.)

The mouse was elegant in its conception. It was only a hand-holdable hunk of plastic that could measure how far you shoved it. Your PC could detect the motion you made, thanks to some kind of transducer hidden in the mouse. Based on the distance the mouse moved, the PC could move an on-screen cursor correspondingly. While difficult to explain, the mouse has proven effective. So effective that you need a mouse—or one of its kin—if you plan on moving to a graphics environment.

The problem is that mice come in different races—in different shapes and colors with differing numbers of buttons—and each works a little differently. Not all mice speak the same language. And not all will crawl into the same holes, because some require their own particular interfaces. Finding the right mouse requires you to take all of these issues into consideration.

Motion Detection

In that the entire purpose of a mouse is to detect movement, the motion detection mechanism is the most essential element of each product. Not all mice use the same technology to detect motion, however. Some are purely mechanical, others rely on optics. There's something to be said for each.

The most common form of mouse is the *mechanical mouse*. It features a small ball hanging down from its lower surface. As you push the mouse around, the ball spins. Two metal wheels inside the mouse contact the ball and spin as the ball rolls. A sensor inside the mouse detects how far each wheel spins. Because the two wheels are mounted at right angles to one another, they can detect motion in two directions—X- and Y-coordinates—anywhere across the plane surface.

The mechanical mouse design is reasonably simple. More importantly, it works on any surface that you can move the mouse across. In a pinch, you can pick up the mouse and spin its ball with your fingers. But the ball rubs against everything in its way—dirt, grease, leftovers from the pizza you ate sometime last year (that has decayed far beyond the grease or dirt stage). The mechanism can gum up. Fortunately, you can usually remove the ball from inside the mouse, wash it, and replace it. Most of the time the simplicity of the mechanism and the ability to clean it will prevent petrified pizza from gumming up the works.

The *optical mouse* is actually simpler mechanically than is a mechanical mouse. In fact, an optical mouse has no moving parts (if you don't count the mouse itself). Instead, the optical mouse relies on optical sensors and light-emitting diodes. The light from the diodes is bounced off a specially patterned surface called a *mouse pad*. As you move the mouse over the surface, the nature of the reflections changes, and these changes can be detected by the optical sensors.

The advantage of the optical mouse is that it doesn't collect grime like its mechanical cousin (providing you keep your pizza off its pad). And it has no mechanical parts to wear out. On the other hand, it requires its specially patterned surface to work. To some people, that need can be a disadvantage. To others, it's a blessing because it forces them to keep a clean area for their mice to run on. Even folks with mechanical mice often invest in special pads to run them on.

Mouse Buttons

Besides detecting motion, a mouse needs to have some way of determining when you've found a choice spot—for instance, when you've finally got the mouse positioned over an icon you want to select. For this indication, mice rely on push-buttons. Different mice may have one, two, or three push-buttons.

The purest form of the mouse—the prototype mouse used by the Macintosh—has only one button. One reason underlying this design was that you, the fallible human, are less likely to mistakenly press the wrong mouse button. Two mouse buttons, however, give you more flexibility. One button can select while the other deselects. A third button adds another option—and the chance for more confusion.

In truth, the number of buttons is important for only one reason: software. Some programs are written to use one button; some require two. Very few require three. Thankfully, most applications make allowances for other button counts than their primary preference (for example, by ignoring all but one button). Still, you're best advised to check the number of mouse buttons your application requires before you select a mouse. In general, a two-button mouse will work for most applications, often with one button to spare.

Mouse Protocols

Mice convert the motions they detect into a digital code that can be processed or analyzed by your PC. The only loose end is what code the mouse uses. A standard mouse code would help software writers craft their products to better take advantage of mice. A standard mouse code would be so useful, in fact, that the industry has come up with *four* distinct standards. Called *mouse protocols*, these standards were developed by four of the major forces in the mouse industry, and each bears its originator's name. These include: Microsoft, Mouse Systems Corporation (for a period known as MSC Corporation), Logitech, and IBM Corporation. The first three were designed for individual mouse products created by the respective companies. The IBM protocol was introduced with the PS/2 series of computers, which came equipped with a built-in jack that accepted a mouse.

In truth, you don't need to know the details of any of these protocols. You only need to know that they exist—and that they are different. You need to match the protocol used by your mouse to that used by your applications.

Today, the Microsoft mouse protocol is the most prevalent. Many applications have been written to directly accept code from Microsoft-compatible mice. For example, Windows 3.0 will make direct contact with any mouse that's compatible with the Microsoft mouse protocol. You can use other mice with these applications, although setting things up is a bit more difficult because other mice will require the use of software drivers to convert their protocols into a form that the applications will understand.

Note that PS/2 mouse ports are more hardware specific and require the use of mice that use the IBM protocol. A growing number of applications are being written to directly accept this protocol as well.

Most mice sold today are capable of emulating the Microsoft mouse protocol. Those that have this emulation built into their hardware can be directly substituted for a Microsoft mouse. Others require the use of drivers to make the match.

The important issue is to check your applications for what mouse protocols they will accept. You can then use any mouse that can match those protocols.

Mouse Interfaces

Your PC faces another barrier in understanding what your mouse has to say—your mouse must make hardware contact with your PC to transfer its signals. Mice connect with PCs in any of three ways: through a serial port, through a built-in dedicated mouse port; and through a special adapter that plugs into an expansion slot. Mice that use these methods are called, respectively, serial, proprietary, and bus mice.

From a performance standpoint, which style of mouse you choose makes little difference. All three kinds of mouse interfaces use the equivalent of a serial connection. The principal factors in choosing one over the other are the resources of your PC.

Obviously you will need a serial port if you want to attach a serial mouse that plugs into such a port. If you have a spare serial port, a serial mouse is the least expensive way of adding a pointing device to your PC.

Most people, however, have designs on all their serial ports and consequently don't want to tie them up with a mouse cable. The bus mouse provides an out. The bus mouse host adapter does not steal a COM port from DOS, nor does it necessarily share one of the serial port interrupts, the sharing of which often causes problems with modem communications. The only difficulty associated with using a bus mouse is finding a spare slot into which to slide the host adapter and finding the extra cash to pay for the additional hardware. A bus mouse and a serial mouse work effectively the same way. Which you choose makes no difference to your software.

If your system has a built-in mouse port, you may be stuck needing a proprietary mouse. While your source of supply may be more limited (and the mice consequently more costly), a proprietary mouse is the easiest of all to install. You only need to plug it in.

Mouse Resolution

Mice are sometimes rated by their resolution, the number of Counts Per Inch or *CPI* that they can detect. When a mouse is moved, it sends out a signal indicating each increment of motion it makes as a single count. The number of these increments in an inch of movement equals the mouse's CPI rating.

The higher the number of CPI, the finer the detail in the movement that the mouse can detect. Unless the mouse driver compensates, higher resolution translates into faster movement of the mouse pointer on the screen. That's because the screen pointer is controlled by the number of counts received from the mouse, not the actual distance the mouse is moved. Consequently, a higher-resolution mouse is a faster mouse, not necessarily a more precise mouse.

Mouse Installation

The installation procedure for a mouse depends on what kind of mouse you have. A dedicated mouse simply plugs into the appropriate jack on the back (or front) of your PC. A serial mouse, for example, is nearly as easy to install. Just plug the mouse into a vacant serial port. The only catch is that you may need to install a driver, in which case you may have to specify (as a command-line option) which port you have chosen. If you have more than two serial ports in your PC, you'll also want to be certain that you mouse doesn't share an interrupt with another device that may be operating at the same time, such as a modem port. That means if you attach your mouse to serial port one, then don't use serial port four for a modem; if you connect your mouse to serial port two, don't use serial port three for a modem.

Bus mice are the most difficult to install, but they are still easy enough so you need not fear them. Their host adapters slide into your PC exactly like any expansion board. Then the mouse simply plugs into the host adapter.

The first step in installing a bus mouse requires that you determine which of your system's resources you want to assign as the host adapter. In most cases, the host adapter will require one or more input/output ports as well as an interrupt. The instruction or installation manual accompanying the bus mouse should list the choices of resources that you can assign. In addition, the manual should also outline what the factory default values are, suggested alternatives, and how to change the defaults.

The first setting you should try is the factory defaults. You'll find that using the defaults is easier because you don't have to change anything. In addition, these are the settings that the manufacturer has found to work in the majority of PCs. If you find you need to alter the factory defaults, write down the changes you had to make in the instruction manual where the choices are listed so you can refer to them in the future. On most host adapters, you'll change these setting by altering DIP switches or jumpers.

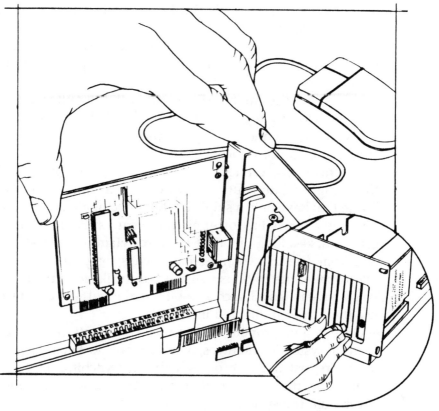

Figure 11.3 To install a bus mouse, set the configuration DIP switches or jumpers on the board (if you need to alter the default settings). Then simply slide the host adapter board into an expansion slot; screw it into place, and plug the mouse into the board.

Perhaps the most demanding part of installing a bus mouse is choosing which interrupt to use, particularly if you want or need to vary from the factory default. Your choices will vary with the kind of PC you have. If you have a computer with an 8-bit expansion bus, your choices will be limited because these machines have only eight hardware interrupts available to them. Of these, only three or four are available for expansion accessories, and these are typically already used in the average PC. Hardware interrupt 0 (computer people always start with zero, don't they?) is used by your system's timer; 1 is assigned to the keyboard; 2 is used by some display adapters and network adapters; 3 is used by the second serial port in your system; 4 is used by your first serial port; 5 by the hard disk; 6 by your floppy disk drives; and 7 by the printer port. The port used by your mouse cannot (or should not) be used by another peripheral. In 8-bit bussed machines, interrupt 2 is the most common choice.

Sixteen-bit PCs are more generous with their interrupts, having a total of 15 for input/output devices. The likely candidates are interrupts 10, 11, 12, and 15. A good choice is interrupt 11, the default choice of many bus mice.

In general, you can tell if your mouse's bus adapter board can use these higher interrupts by examining its expansion connector. Those that have only a single edge connector about four inches long can only address the lower eight interrupts. Boards with two edge connectors—a long one near the card-retaining bracket and a short one from one to two-and-a-half inches long—usually have all 15 interrupts of the 16-bit expansion bus available to them. Of course, you'll have to install such a 16-bit board in a 16-bit expansion slot to use the higher-numbered interrupts.

Once you've properly set up the host adapter to take advantage of your system's resources, you're ready to begin the rest of the hardware installation process. Start by switching off your PC, disconnecting the power cord for safety's sake, and removing the cover from the system.

Find a vacant expansion slot in which to install the host adapter. It is very important that you properly match the interface of the slot to the host adapter. Most bus mouse host adapters are designed to use 8- or 16-bit expansion slots, but some of their settings will be functional only in 16-bit slots. The reason is that 16-bit slots have more interrupt signals available on them. If you plan to use a higher-numbered interrupt (which you should to avoid conflicts with other serial ports in your system), you'll need to use a 16-bit expansion slot. Once you've firmly seated the host adapter in its expansion slot, be sure to screw the board securely in place.

After you've securely screwed the host adapter into your PC, you can attach the mouse cable to the host adapter. Just plug it in. Before you reassemble your PC, plug all the cables you removed from your PC back in again. Then switch your system back on with the case open. After it boots up, install the software that came with the mouse.

The typical software installation will require you to put a driver in your CONFIG.SYS file (or rely on the automatic installation procedure supplied with the software) and copy some files to your hard disk. Or you may be able to run a mouse driver from the DOS command line. Either way, once your mouse software is installed, test the mouse and be sure it works. If it does, switch off your PC and reassemble it. If your bus mouse does not operate properly, switch off your PC, remove the host adapter, and try setting it to use difference system resources. Once you're successful, reassemble your PC.

Trackballs

Just as Jinx the Cat hated meeses to pieces, so does anyone with a cluttered desktop. When there's no vacant spot on the Formica to give a mouse a good run, that premiere pointing device becomes, well, pointless. When the mouse is trapped by untidiness, the graphic operating environments that should help make PCs accessible to nontechnical users become nearly useless.

But the desk in disarray is only one of the problems faced by mouseketeers. The arm movements required to push a plastic rodent require clumsy, wasteful, and tiring whole-arm movements. They are inefficient and exhausting.

The leading mouse alternative, the trackball, eliminates these problems. Essentially a mouse turned upside down, the trackball is much like it sounds—a big ball that is rotated to cause a screen icon to move correspondingly. In addition, two or three push-buttons duplicate the selection functions of mouse buttons. Trackballs send out the same signals as mice and work with the same software. And, like most mice, trackballs are powered directly through the serial interface (or other connection that they use) so there's no need for an external power supply.

The species diversification of trackballs is nearly as wide as that in the Rodentia. In crafting a product, each trackball designer goes his own direction. Various products range in dimension from shooter-size to cue ball; the arrangement of push-buttons is confined only by the imagination (and definitely not by human dexterity); and the assembly itself can take on just about any shape or form. The ancillaries, too, go their separate ways—cable lengths, emulations, even data translations.

There's no definitive, perfect trackball because there's no standard way of holding and using one. Some trackballs appear designed for alien hands with 16 thumbs or fingers arranged in a full circle. Others seem like natural extensions of your own digits. Like beauty, the trackball depends on the beholder—the hand that's laid upon it, the way the hand holds it, even the way the user works.

There's even conflicting research on whether it's best to move a trackball with the thumb or fingers. According to a company that makes them, trackballs operates best with the fingers; the fingers are more agile, so they're more precise at spinning the ball. A competing company that makes a trackball designed for thumb control says that the thumb has more muscle control than the fingers. Some makers wisely don't take sides and make trackballs that can be used equally adeptly by the posed or opposed digit.

Some trackball deficiencies are obvious. One brand is decidedly handed one way or the other—you have to order the trackball for right- or left-handed operation. If you switch hands when you're tired from using one all day long, you won't want a product with definite handedness. Moreover, that natural hand for spinning a trackball may not be the one you use for writing. A right-handed trackball isn't always the best choice for a right-handed person. Before you order a one-handed trackball, be sure you know which hand you will favor in using it. To avoid such variables, most trackball manufacturers arrange their push-buttons symmetrically and offer hardware or software button redefinition to swap the functions of the two sides.

As with mice, trackballs are sometimes rated in resolution, the number of counts per inch of movement (CPI). As with mouse resolution, these numbers don't necessarily indicate precision. A higher number of counts per inch can actually make a trackball less precise to use. A trackball with a high number of counts per inch will move your on-screen pointer a greater distance for every degree of spin you give the ball. As a result, the high CPI trackball will make the on-screen cursor move faster, but with less control. A low number of counts per inch means you have to spin the ball further to move the cursor, giving you *greater precision* in your control.

Most trackball manufacturers now give you several choices for the effective resolution of their products so you can tailor its actions and reactions to match the way you work. In addition, most trackball makers offer *ballistic operation* in which the translation of ball movement to on-screen cursor change varies with the speed of the ball's spin. This yields fast positioning without loss of precision. The only problem is getting used to such nonlinear control in which the speed at which you spin the trackball has as much (sometimes more) effect as how far you spin it.

Probably the most important issue in a trackball is what software it works with. The great majority of trackballs emulate the most common mouse interface, that used by the Microsoft Mouse, in the PC environment. For PS/2s, they duplicate the protocol used by IBM's own mouse. Most trackballs also include menuing software to help the trackball take command of almost any software.

Unlike most other peripherals, there's no one trackball objectively better than the rest. Operating any of them is an acquired talent, like brain surgery, piano playing, or hair combing. Any judgment must be subjective, and which is better suited to a particular user depends most on personal preference and familiarity.

Trackball Installation

Trackballs are, for all intents and purposes, just mice turned upside down. They send out the same signal as mice do, using one of the familiar mice protocols. And they install exactly like mice. Often they use proprietary mouse ports like those on PS/2s. In that case, just plug your trackball into the appropriate port.

As with serial mice, serial trackballs simply plug into unused serial ports. If you have a free serial port, a serial trackball is a quick, easy, and cheap way of adding a pointing device to your PC.

Trackballs that use dedicated host adapters install just like bus mice. Their host adapters slide into your PC exactly like a bus mouse host adapter. The trackball then simply plugs into the host adapter.

When you install a trackball host adapter, your first step is to determine which of your system's resources you can dedicate to its use. As with a bus mouse host adapter, a trackball host adapter will require one or more input/output ports as well as an interrupt. You'll find the resources needed and a list of the assignments you can make in the instructions or installation manual accompanying the trackball. The trackball manual should also outline what the factory default values are, suggested alternatives, and how to change the defaults.

The factory settings are always the first choice because they are the ones that the manufacturer has determined work with the most PCs. Besides, you won't have to change anything. If you do decide to alter the factory settings, be sure to write down whatever changes you make. The best place to record this information is in the instruction manual where it documents the choices. Most of the time, you'll adjust the setting of a trackball host adapter by altering DIP switches or jumpers.

Once you've properly set up your trackball host adapter to take advantage of your system's resources, you're ready to begin the hardware installation process. Start by switching off your PC, disconnecting its power cord for safety's sake, and removing the cover from the system.

Find a vacant expansion slot in which to install the trackball host adapter, one that offers the proper interface. As with bus mouse host adapters, trackball host adapters are designed to use 8- or 16-bit expansion slots, but some of their settings will be functional only in 16-bit slots. If you plan to use a higher-numbered interrupt (which you should do to avoid conflicts with other serial ports in your system), you'll need to use a 16-bit expansion slot because only 16-bit slots have interrupts numbered higher than eight available to them. Once you've slid the trackball host adapter into the correct type of slot and firmly seated it, screw the board in place.

Next, plug the trackball cable into its host adapter. Before you reassemble your PC, plug all the cables you removed from your PC back in again so you can test your installation. Switch your system on with the case still open.

After your system boots up, install the software that came with the trackball. The typical software installation will require you to put a driver in your CONFIG.SYS file (or rely on the automatic installation procedure supplied with the software) and copy some files to your hard disk. Some trackball drivers are installed as programs that you run from the command line or inside your system's AUTOEXEC.BAT file. Either way, once your trackball software is installed, test your trackball and verify that it works properly. Once all seems well, switch off your PC and reassemble it.

Digitizing Tablets

Although they often resemble a deformed mouse coupled with a overdesigned pad and sometimes work the same way, a digitizing tablet represents an entirely different pointing technology. Digitizing tablets can be distinguished from a mouse in two ways. In its native mode of operation, the digitizing tablet indicates absolute locations; that is, you point to a particular location on the tablet. Later, by putting the pen or cursor back in the same location on the tablet surface, you can repeatedly identify the same point. In effect, the identified point is logically fixed to its location on the surface of the tablet. A mouse is a relative pointing device. It indicates displacements between locations rather than absolute locations. Roll a mouse across a pad, lift it up, and you have no guarantee that moving it back to its original location will identify the same on-screen point.

Whether absolute or relative positioning is preferable depends on how you work. If you draw with your eyes locked on the screen, relative locations may be all you need. If you want to trace an existing drawing, however, absolute positioning is a must. It's perfect when you need to make the on-screen (and in-file) digital image an exact analog of the on-paper artwork. Tape a blueprint to a digitizing tablet, and you can transfer every one of its lines into your favorite drafting program.

The absolute/relative distinction between tablets and mice is blurring, however, at least from the tablet perspective. Most of today's digitizing tablets include mouse drivers that allow them to emulate one or another mouse (Microsoft's mouse is the most popular emulation). Equipped with such an emulation, the digitizing tablet becomes more versatile than the mouse because it can deliver both absolute and relative positioning information, depending on what the application software requires.

Digitizing tablets also differ from mice in the way you use them. Typically, digitizing tablets give you a choice of using a *digitizer pen* (or stylus) or a *cursor*. Some manufacturers also call digitizer cursors pucks or tracers. A pen makes using a tablet almost indistinguishable from ordinary drawing. In fact, you can draw on paper with the ink with a digitizer pen as you digitize information for your applications. You hold the tablet pen the same way as you would a

Rapid-o-Graph or ballpoint. Only the long tail—the cable leading back to the tablet—will make you aware that you're connected to your computer. An increasing number of tablets even eliminate the need for this umbilical.

On the other hand, you manipulate tablet cursors the same way you would a mouse. A cursor is a hand-size pointing device with 1 to 16 buttons on top and a reticule with crosshairs that allows you to exactly identify a particular point to digitize. Compared to mice, cursors are more accurate (thanks to the advanced technologies used by tablets, the reticule, and absolute positioning) and less comfortable to use. While the latest and best mice are ergonomically designed so that you can rest your hand on them and relax most of the muscles in your forearm, cursors are generally gripped with your fingers extended as if you were picking up some kind of odious insect that threatened to crawl up your leg. Cursor design is perhaps one aspect of digitizing tablets that requires some rethinking.

"Digitizing tablet" is an amazingly straightforward term in the otherwise confusing corpus of computer cant. Digitization is the function, the process of converting positions on a plane (classic Cartesian X-Y coordinates) into digital values that can be used by applications such as Computer-Aided Design (CAD), drawing, and painting programs. The term "tablet" indicates the physical embodiment of the device and its metaphor. The digitizing tablet resembles the classic paper drawing tablet, a flat surface upon which you can sketch. The latest digitizing tablets are even close in size and heft to drawing tablets.

Underneath their simple, flat surfaces, however, the digitizing tablet is a complex electronic miracle that can pinpoint a specific location with an accuracy as fine as one-thousandth inch. Although as cheap as $499 or less retail, they use technologies as sophisticated as those that locate Soviet submarines or stealth bombers.

Digitizing Tablet Differences

Current digitizing tables range in size from the dimensions of a paperback book to a full drafting table. They differ in the accuracy and resolution they deliver, the speed at which they transmit information, and the freedom they afford you in using them. At heart, they use a variety of technologies to determine the coordinates of their pointing devices. And the pointing devices themselves have their own spectrum of differences.

Size is the most visible and perhaps the least important dimension to digitizing tablets. Many manufacturers offer tablets identical in all features except for the available drawing area. A given product line may embrace a range from 12 by 12 inches to 36 by 48 or more. This size difference is mostly a matter of preference. How much you need is guided by the application you plan to use, the images you wish to digitize, and how much you can afford. Bigger means bulkier and more expensive—and more expansive.

Big also means more precise because tablet precision is measured by the number of lines that can be resolved within a inch. A 48-inch tablet will resolve four times as many points as a similar 12-inch one. The bigger tablet will also be more tiring to use because you may have to stretch back and forth across the whole surface to draw what you want. Then again, applications often allow you to set the size of the digitizing area you want to use. You can do your coarse drawing on a small tablet section and work on details full size.

Size does not necessarily translate into working area, however. The useful space on a tablet varies with several outside factors. Both the application you run and the digitizing tablet driver you use with it control how much of the work surface is put to work. For example, AutoCAD provides its TABLET CFG command that allows you to shrink the tablet space actually devoted to screen manipulation and to define portions of the tablet as menu areas.

Resolution and Accuracy describe how well a given tablet can identify a point on its surface. Resolution indicates how far from one another two points must be to be individually distinguished. Accuracy indicates how closely the digitized data comes to the correct representation of the cursor position. The more lines of resolution per inch, the better. The smaller the accuracy specification—usually given in fractions of an inch—the better. In theory, at least. A larger variable is your own accuracy in positioning the cursor on the drawing you wish to trace. You'll need a steady hand and sharp eye to strain even the 0.025-inch accuracy of the worst of available digitizing tablets. Moreover, when precision counts, you may rely on the resolution of a tablet and the coordinate data supplied by your application (or a "snap-to-grid" facility) to zero in on the precise point you want to digitize.

Speed. If you're drawing freehand, speed may be the most important digitization issue to you. A tablet must be fast enough to follow the quickest motions of your hand. Most digitizing tables are rated in the number of points-per-second they can transmit back to your PC. This points-per-second speed is dependent on the communications rate of the connection between tablet and host. (You'll want to use the fastest data rate possible, serial speeds of 9,600 bits per second or quicker.) A slow tablet may not be able to keep up with fast freehand drawing. If you're merely sampling individual points from a blueprint, however, even a slow tablet will suffice.

Proximity indicates how far a pointing device can be lifted above the digitizing surface for a given tablet to recognize its location. The larger the proximity range of a tablet, the more freedom you have in drawing—and the thicker the art you can successfully trace through.

Software and Emulations. Two factors are important to determine if you can use a given tablet at all: software and emulations. The software included with a digitizing tablet may include specific drivers to allow the tablet to work with specific applications. For example, mouse support usually (but not always) takes the form of a driver.

Many applications already have built-in support for digitizing tablets. With these programs, it's important that the tablet you choose works like one that your favorite applications know. Most tablets can emulate one or another of the more popular data formats used by digitizing tablets. Make sure that the tablet you choose emulates something your software supports.

Cursors and Pens. The pointing devices that accompany digitizing tablets run a wide range—differing in size, shape, even color. From a usefulness and versatility standpoint, however, the most important distinguishing characteristic is cordlessness. Most pointing devices must be tethered to the tablet by a cable that is used in communicating position information to the tablet electronics. Some of the most recent tablet designs are now cordless. This can be a great convenience. Not only is there no cable to tangle, snarl, and resist your drawing efforts, but also cordless operation allows you to instantly switch between using a pen and a cursor. Moreover, a cordless pen can be as elegant to draw with as a Waterman fountain pen.

Of course, cordlessness can be a problem, too. Just as the life of a Bic pen in the corporate environment must average around 13 minutes—before it's pocketed and disappears from the known universe—cordless pens and cursors can travel just as quickly. Not that a cord will prevent a thief from liberating the pointing device (and at prices up to $250, the prospect may be tempting)—the cord serves only as a reminder not to put the pen in your pocket and stroll off. The umbilical can also prevent an expensive pen from dropping and self-destructing on the floor or from being trod upon. Some people actually tape strings to cordless digitizing pens to prevent them from traipsing off.

The shape and feel of a cursor or pen is the most subjective aspect of using a digitizing tablet. In general, a pen feels like using a bloated ballpoint, not unlike the typical technical pen. For the most part, the cursor is simply a hunk of plastic you can conveniently hold that provides a vehicle for push-button switches. While no cursor is as hand-pleasing as a Microsoft or KeyTronic mouse, they range from an okay grip to a cramp and a gripe about style over function.

The number of buttons you need on a cursor depends mostly on how many your favored applications support; pattern is a matter of preference. A 16-button cursor will mean that you might rarely have to go back to your keyboard to elicit functions. But you'll probably still have to squint at the cursor or scratch your head to remember which button does what.

Pens differ in the number of buttons they offer, too. In general, all pens give at least one switch that's activated by pressing down on the point, the *tip-switch*. A second button (and sometimes a third) on the side of the pen near the tip may also be available. How useful additional buttons are depends on the software you use.

Many digitizer pens have internal ink supplies so you can draw on paper as you transmit data back to your PC. Sometimes a manufacturer distinguishes its digitizer pens from a digitizer stylus in that the latter doesn't contain an ink supply. With few exceptions, pens can be equipped with dummy inkless cartridges to make them into styli.

A new kind of pen, the *pressure pen*, is rapidly becoming popular. Instead of merely indicating on or off, the pressure pen sends out a digital value corresponding to the effort applied to the pen tip. This force can then be used by an application to indicate the width, weight, or color of a line drawn in that application, a feature particularly useful in freehand sketching. Pressure pens vary in the range of forces they can detect and the number of pressure levels they can digitize, typically from 64 to 256.

Templates put menu-selectability on the tablet in the form of a usually laminated plastic sheet that defines and identifies areas on the tablet that will elicit particular functions in an application. Move the pen or cursor into an area, click a button, and a function is carried out.

Templates also have their drawbacks. Using one means that you end up watching the tablet and not the screen. Your head is apt to bob up and down as you work with your eyes shifting from template to screen. Templates also shrink the active area of the tablet that you can actually use for drawing, increasing speed and convenience but slighting on accuracy.

Still, templates can be useful. In fact, AutoCAD includes its own template for tablet users. Many tablet makers offer their own improvements on this or additional templates for commonly used applications like Windows.

Technology indicates the operating principal a tablet relies upon to find its pointing device. For the most part, the technology of a tablet is academic—as long as a tablet is accurate, it shouldn't matter to you whether it uses radar or telepathy. However, some technologies have some specific advantages and disadvantages. For example, the resistive decoding permits some tablets to be built as see-through sheets of glass. More exotic sonic technology allows some digitizers to turn virtually anything into a tablet.

Ergonomics. The importance of ergonomic issues depends on how you work. If you're the regimented engineer, you may prefer a heavy-duty tablet that stays put on your desk or drafting table (or even substitutes for a drafting table). Freewheeling artists may want the freedom of a lightweight tablet that can be cradled in your arms or on your lap. Moreover, some people like to suffer. Almost any tablet will do for them. For most people, however, a more comfortable tablet will make everyday work more pleasant—and every little bit helps.

All in all, you'll find more variety among digitizing tablets than just about any other input peripheral you can connect to your computer. Which is best depends not only on the quality of the product but your preferences and application.

Digitizer Installation

As with trackballs, digitizers are mouse variants. They install in much the same manner with two exceptions. There are currently no proprietary digitizers. And bus-style digitizers may use other interfaces besides serial-port derivatives. The only other difference is that many digitizing tablets require their own source of AC power, typically an external transformer.

For the most part, you only need to plug a serial-based digitizer into a vacant serial port, plug in its power cord, then run the software accompanying the digitizer.

The digitizers that use their own interface cards are installed exactly like bus mice. Their host adapters slide into your PC the same way as does any expansion board. Then the digitizer simply plugs into the host adapter.

With a digitizer host adapter, you'll again have to determine which of your system's resources you want to assign to the digitizing system. In most cases, the digitizer will require one or more input/output ports as well as an interrupt to control it. Check the instructions or installation manual that came with your digitizer to find out its needs. You'll set the resources used by the digitizer system using DIP switches or jumpers on its host adapter board. Most of the time, it makes the most sense to stick with the factory default settings. Change them only if you encounter an incompatibility with your PC (meaning that your digitizer doesn't work). And don't forget to write down the changes you make for future reference.

Once you've set the digitizer's host adapter to take advantage of your system's resources, begin the hardware installation process.

Switch off your PC, disconnect the power cord from your computer for safety's sake, and remove the cover from your system.

Find a vacant expansion slot in which to install the host adapter. Again, be sure to use an expansion slot with the same interface as the digitizer host adapter, an 8- or 16-bit slot as the board requires. Remember, a 16-bit slot is necessary if you want to exploit a higher interrupt. Once you've chosen a slot and firmly seated the host adapter in it, be sure to screw the board in place.

After the host adapter is installed inside your PC, attach the signal cable between the digitizer and its host adapter. Plug the digitizer into an AC outlet if it requires external power.

Before you reassemble your PC, plug all the cables you removed from your PC back in again. Then switch your system back on with the case open. After it boots up, install the software that came with your digitizer so you can test it out.

The typical software installation will require you to put a driver in your CONFIG.SYS file (or rely on the automatic installation procedure supplied with the software) and copy some files to your hard disk. Some applications, like AutoCAD, have built-in drivers for most digitizers, so in those cases you'll only need to run the set-up procedure for the application. Whatever is required, carry out the installation, then test the digitizer to be sure that it works. Once you're sure all is well, put your PC back together again and you're ready to use your digitizer.

Scanners

Getting great graphics from a PC is child's play—providing you let your child tinker with your PC. Getting those graphics into your PC is another matter. Professional artists hover over their monitors, pushing their mice around for hours and days crafting the images they want. If you're impatient, aesthetically impaired, or if phosphorous isn't your medium, you have hope, however, in the scanner.

With a scanner, you can capture as an electronic graphic image anything you have on paper—or, for that matter, anything reasonably flat. Dot by dot, a scanner can reproduce photos, line drawings, even collages in detail sharper than your laser printer can duplicate. Better yet, equip your PC with optical character recognition software and the images your scanner captures of typed or printed text can be converted into ASCII files for your word processor, database, or publishing system. Just as the PC opened a new world of information management to you, a scanner opens a new world of images and data to your PC.

The best part of today's scanners is that they are affordable. A hand scanner that can convert almost an infinity of graphic images into electronic form costs little more than a single disk of electronic clip art—prefabricated drawings in electronic form. Instead of buying an expensive mapping program (with layouts of cities you've never heard of, let alone need for your reports), you can draw your own on paper or copy an atlas (with the publisher's permission, of course) for a pittance.

Although they are technically sophisticated, scanners are operationally easy. If you can use a photocopier, you can master desktop scanning technique in a couple tries—and without wasting a sheet of paper. Hand scanners are nearly as easy.

In fact, the only problems you face in upgrading your PC with a scanner are selection and connection. You need to find the one right scanner from the wide variety of products available. Then you need to connect it to your PC so that its signals can be converted into files that will be accepted by your graphics or publishing software.

Of the two, the selection process is the one that will give your brain the biggest workout. Although all scanners accomplish basically the same task, the various scanning products are hardly identical. Not only do they work differently, they excell in different tasks. What you want to do with a scanner—capture simple drawings, duplicate color photos, or read printed text—is one of the chief factors in deciding which product is best for you.

To complicate things, you'll need to match a scanner technology with the way you work and what you can afford. You'll find that there's a scanner design for everyone except the miserly sort who won't begrudge $100 or so for the least expensive models.

Your first chore is getting a bit of technical background so you can discover what kind of scanner is best for you. Your PC will also need to be capable of using the scanner. In most cases, that means you'll need a hard disk drive to handle the huge files the scanner will create, a graphics-capable display systems to let you see what you've scanned, and often additional extended or expanded memory to speed up the scanner's operations.

Scanner Types

The essence of a scanner is elementary. It uses an array of light sensors that detect the brightness of the reflection off the image being scanned. In most cases, the scanner has a linear array of these sensors, typically charge-coupled devices (or CCDs), squeezed together hundreds per inch in a narrow strip that stretches across the full width of the largest image that can be scanned. The width of each scanning element determines the finest resolution the scanner can detect within a single line. The narrower the scanning element, the higher the resolution and the finer the detail that can be captured.

This lineup of sensors registers a single, thin line of the image at a time. Circuitry inside the scanner reads each sensing element in order to create a string of serial data representing the brightness of each point in the line being scanned. Once it has collected and arranged the data from each dot on the line, the sensing element can advance to read the next line.

How the scanning sensor moves to that following line is the fundamental design difference between scanners. Somehow the long line of sensing elements must shift their attention with extreme precision over the entire surface of the image to be captured. The scan typically involves a mechanical sweep of the sensors across the image. Two primary strategies have emerged in scanner technology. One requires the image sensor to move across a fixed original; the other moves the original in front of a fixed scanner.

Drum scanners exemplify the latter technology. They work like printing presses in reverse. You feed a piece of paper bearing the image to be scanned in, and it wraps around a rotating drum that spins it past the sensor string that's fixed in place inside the machine.

Two designs take the opposite tack and use the moving-sensor concept. The *flatbed scanner* is named for the flat glass surface upon which you place the item to be scanned, face down. The scanning sensors are mounted on a bar that moves under the glass, automatically sweeping across the image. The glass surface allows the sensors to see up to the image. *Hand scanners* make you the motivating force that propels the sensor over the image. You hold the T-shape hand scanner in the palm of your hand and drag it across the image you want to scan. The string of sensors peers through a plastic window in the bottom of the hand scanner.

Flatbed and drum scanners are designed with precision mechanisms that step the sensors or image a small increment at a time, each increment representing a single scan line. The movement of the mechanism, which is carefully controlled by the electronics of the scanner, determines the width of each line (and thus the resolution of the scanner in that direction).

Hand scanners present a problem. The sweep of your hand is not nearly as controlled as the movement of scanning mechanisms. If you move your hand at a speed other than that at which the scanner expects, lines will be scanned as too wide or too narrow, resulting in image distortion—at best the aspect ratio may be off; at worst, the scanned image will look as wavy as the Atlantic under the influence of an errant typhoon.

To keep track of the image, the hand scanner uses a feedback mechanism. For example, the Logitech ScanMan uses a rubber roller that senses how fast you drag the scanner along. The rate at which the roller spins gives the scanner's electronics the feedback it needs about scanning speed. From this information, the software that controls the hand scanner can give each scanned dot its proper place.

Each of these three technologies has its advantages and disadvantages. Some scanner designs are suited to some applications more than others.

For most people, the hand scanner is the most appealing simply because it is the least expensive. It needs no precision (and expensive) scanning mechanism. Moreover, the hand scanner is compact and easy to carry. You could plug one into a laptop PC (if your laptop has an expansion slot to accommodate the scanner's interface board or if you have an external adapter to match the scanner) and carry the complete system to the neighborhood library to scan from books in its collection. Hand scanners can also be quick because you can make quick sweeps of small images instead of waiting for the lumbering mechanism of another scanner type to cover a whole sheet. Hand scanners may also adapt to some nonflat surfaces and three-dimensional objects. For example, most will easily cope with the pages of an open atlas or gothic novel—although few can do a good job on a globe or watermelon.

The convenient size of the hand scanner can also be a disadvantage. To avoid being absolutely unwieldy, most will scan in a single pass areas only about four inches wide. Although that's enough for a column of text and most scanners offer a means of pasting together parallel scans of larger drawings and photos, the narrow strips of scan make dealing with large images inconvenient. Then again, because a hand scanner is not limited by a scanning mechanism, it can allow you to make absurdly long scans, typically limited only by the scanning software you use. Hand scanning is also a learned skill. You have to move the scanner at the right rate—very slowly at high resolutions—and doing so smoothly and reliably requires practice.

Drum scanners are moderate in price and compact in size because their mechanisms are relatively simple. However, that mechanism imposes a stiff penalty—only thin, flexible images can be scanned. In general, that means normal paper. Books (at least while intact) and solid objects are off limits. Only certain sizes of paper may be accepted. While this may be no disadvantage in a character-recognition application, it may be frustrating when you want to pull an image off a large sheet without resorting to scissors or a photocopier first.

Flatbed scanners are like copying machines in that anything that you can lay flat on their glass faces can be scanned—books, magazines, sections of poster, even posteriors and other part of your anatomy if you get imaginative, bored, or drunk. Of course, the scanned image can be no larger than the scanner bed. The big drawback of the flatbed scanner is price. Their precision mechanisms make them inherently expensive. While you might find a hand scanner for under $100, you'll be lucky to find a new flatbed scanner for less than ten times that—even more if you want color. But for regular graphics work, the flatbed is often the best choice.

Color Versus Grey Scale

Scanners also differ in how they perceive reality. Some see the world only in black and white, others have Technicolor vision, while most weigh matters in shades of grey. Which to get depends on what you do.

Color scanners are clearly the best. They can do anything a mon-ochrome scanner can, but with full spectral fidelity. A color scanner can make an amazingly good copy of any image—the results are breathtaking, and so are the prices. Prices of the least expensive color flatbed scanners start at about $1,000 through discount chan-nels; other models can work their way up to five or more times that price. Color hand scanners are also more expensive than their mo-nochromatic kin.

Because they are high-end engines, color scanners don't skimp when it comes to their abilities. Most can register anywhere from 256,000 to 16 million different hues. While that may be more than you or your software wants to manage, their palettes can easily be scaled back, either through hardware controls or through software. Some scanner programs even optimize the scanner output so that those hundreds of thousands of colors can be accurately repre-sented by a sampling as small as 256. Similarly, the color images are easily rendered in grey, again either in the scanner hardware dur-ing the scanning process or by software processing after the fact.

Many color flatbed scanners impose another penalty besides price. They can be slow, requiring a separate pass of their image sensors for each primary hue. On such machines, a complete color image takes three passes—three times as long as monochrome or as much as five minutes for a full-page image. Single-pass color scan-ners trim the waiting time.

Just as color scanners have different spectral ranges, grey-scale scanners differ in the number of shades they can detect. At the bottom are the plain black-and-white machines that recognize no intermediary tones. From there, the grey-scale range increases as powers of two. A few years ago, a scanner with a range of 16 greys was top of the line. Today, the figure is 256. That's a good place to be because 256 greys gives good results on most monitors (the VGA monochrome standard actually allows for only 64 greys) with a manageable amount of storage, one byte per dot in the image.

Most grey-scale scanners can also be set to recognize fewer grey tones; usually the selection is between 2 (black and white) 16, 64, and 256 greys. The more the greys you select, the larger the result-ing image file will be, but the more realistic the image will appear. A limited grey range is useful for text recognition and for capturing line drawings, but you'll want a wide range of greys to capture photographs.

Scanners also differ in the resolution that they support. All scanners have a maximum mechanical limit on their resolution. It's equal to the smallest step that their sensor can be advanced. Today you'll want at least 300 dots per inch as the minimum in your scanner.

As with colors and shades of grey, a scanner can easily be programmed to produce resolution lower than its maximum. Lower resolution is useful to minimize file size, to match your output device, or simply to make the scanned image fit on a single screen for convenient viewing. Many scanners shift their resolution in distinct increments—75, 150, and 300 dpi, for example—while others make resolution continuously variable.

Color can be an issue even with monochrome scanners. Most scanners provide their own sources of illumination for scanning images. (This eliminates one variable from the scanning process and makes for more uniform and repeatable scans.) Although the color of illumination might seem immaterial for a monochrome scanner, that's not necessarily true. Illumination color becomes important when you want to scan from color originals.

For example, some hand scanners use red light-emitting diodes (LEDs) for illumination. LEDs have long, trouble-free lives. But when colored objects are illuminated in their red light, the brightness reflected from the image does not correspond to the brightness the human eye would perceive in white light. Green illumination gives a better approximation of the human eye's perception of tones. Colored images captured by a scanner that uses red illumination may seem tonally incorrect. Flesh tones, in particular, scan too lightly. For line drawing and text recognition applications, however, red can sometimes be better. Red pencil or ink marks on an image won't reproduce, so you can sketch or comment in red and not have it show in your scans.

Optical Character Recognition

Scan a newspaper clipping into your PC and you can read it on the screen, paste it into other documents, and print it out just like any graphic image. But you can't edit it with your word processor. And when you press "Save," you might end up with a half megabyte file, even though the article in question only contains only a few dozen words.

The difference is data types. Your word processor uses text files in which each character is stored in a one-byte code called the American Standard Code for Information Interchange, or *ASCII*. Every letter is represented by a single distinctive byte value. When a page is scanned, characters are treated as graphics and stored as patterns of bits, the order of which corresponds to the dots found by your scanner. One character might require a hundred bytes to store.

You can translate text into graphic form and then into ASCII codes in two ways—by typing everything into your word processor or by optical character recognition. Add character recognition software to your scanner, and you can quickly convert almost anything you can read on your screen into word processor, database, or spreadsheet files.

Once the realm of mainframe computers and special hardware costing tens of thousands of dollars, optical character recognition is now within the reach of most PCs and budgets, available from direct vendors from $100 to $400. Just two years ago, a breakthrough—the introduction of feature-matching software—made fast, accurate character recognition possible with any PC scanner.

Previously, character recognition systems used a technique called *matrix matching*. The computer would compare small parts of each bit image it scanned to bit patterns it had stored in a library to find what character was the most similar to the bit pattern scanned. For example, a letter "A" would be recognized as a pointed tower 40 bits high with a 20-bit-wide crossbar.

The problem with matrix matching was that there's a world of variation to printing—different fonts, type sizes, and styles. For example, an Italic "A" has a completely different pattern signature from a Roman "A," even within the same size and type family. Consequently, a matrix-matching OCR system must have either an enormous library of bit patterns (requiring a time-consuming search for each match) or the system must be limited to matching a few type styles and fonts.

In the latter (and most common) case, you often have to tell the character recognition system what typeface you were trying to read for it to use the correct pattern library. Worse, most matrix-matching systems depended on regular spacing between characters to determine the size and shape of the character matrix, so these systems worked only with monospaced printing, such as that generated by a typewriter.

Feature-matching character recognition overcomes all of these problems by working smarter. Instead of just looking, it analyzes each bit pattern. When it sees the letter "A," it derives the essential features of the character from the pattern of bits—an upslope, a peak, and a downslope with a horizontal bar across. In that every letter "A" has the same characteristic features—if they didn't your eyes couldn't recognize each one as an "A," either—the feature-matching system doesn't need an elaborate library of bit patterns to match nearly any font and type size. In fact, feature-matching recognition software doesn't need to know the size or font of the characters it is to recognize beforehand. Even typeset text with variable character spacing is no problem. Feature-matching software can thus race through a scan very quickly while making few errors.

Although more straightforward than ever before, character recognition is still demanding when it comes to system resources. For example, the highly regarded OmniPage program from Caere Corporation requires Windows 3.0 and a wealth of memory—four megabytes of RAM and eight megabytes of hard disk space. You'll also need one of the scanners supported by the program to scan interactively or any scanner that can produce line art TIF files with a resolution of at least 200 dots per inch.

Today, the range of available recognition software is wide. Better programs use feature-matching algorithms and know how popular word processors, databases, and spreadsheets format text and data in their files. You'll want to be sure the recognition program you choose can generate files compatible with the other applications you use.

Character recognition programs work either interactively with your scanner or from standard bit image file formats. Some will even recognize text that your PC has received through fax transmissions. Be sure that the program you choose is compatible with your scanner or your scanner can generate the required file type. As with anything else, the best programs tend to be the most costly, but they more than pay for themselves in the time you save.

Scanner Connections

Getting acceptable performance from a scanner means using a high-speed connection because scanners generate prodigious quantities of data. For example, a full page scanned at 300 dpi with 256 shades

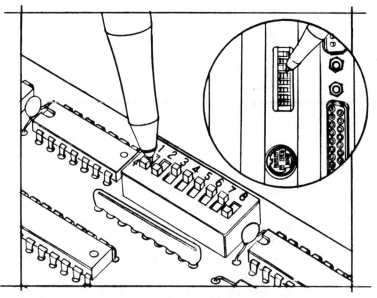

Figure 11.4 Scanners using proprietary interfaces require that you allocate system resources such as memory ranges and I/O ports to the host adapter. You'll need to make adjustments to DIP switches or jumpers on the board itself (main drawing) or through a cut-out in its retaining bracket (inset).

of grey requires over seven megabytes. You wouldn't want to move that through a standard serial port. At least three different interface designs are used by different scanners—*SCSI* (the *Small Computer System Interface*), *GPIB* (*General-Purpose Interface Bus*), and *proprietary*.

While some scanners do give you a serial option, in most cases you'll want to use a faster interface—one with substantially higher speed. For example, the Microtek MSF-300Z can move data 10 to 100 times faster through its proprietary interface as through a standard serial port. In hand scanners, the proprietary connections dominate because the tiny devices have neither the room nor the need for standardized interface circuitry. Desktop scanners often opt for one of the standard interfaces. These, too, are best treated as proprietary designs when you're connecting up a new scanner.

SCSI presents problems because the "standard" allows for so many variations that getting two SCSI products from different manufacturers to work together can be frustrating (at best). For example, you may have both an SCSI hard disk and a SCSI scanner, but the drive might not work when connected to the scanner's host adapter and the scanner might refuse to operate when connected to the drive's host adapter. You'll avoid some of these headaches if you just connect each device to its own host adapter, pretending that each SCSI board is actually a proprietary interface.

(If you *are* going to try to share a single SCSI host adapter between a disk and a scanner, use the disk's host adapter if you can. In general, the host adapters that come with SCSI hard disks give much faster performance than scanner host adapters.)

GPIB was originally developed by Hewlett-Packard Company (hence its original moniker, the Hewlett-Packard Interface Bus) for interconnecting its test and measurement equipment. It provides both a medium- to high-speed connection (fitting neatly between serial and SCSI) along with a structured control system. As with SCSI, multiple devices can be daisy-chained together using GPIB and only one host adapter in a PC. Although GPIB is used a lot in laboratory systems, it's not a common connection for PC peripherals. In that you're unlikely to hook up anything else to a GPIB host adapter, you'll end up connecting scanners that use GPIB as if they had proprietary interfaces.

When it comes to connecting up a scanner, there's nothing inherently bad about proprietary interfaces. Because each scanner is designed specifically to match its own interface and because other devices do not share it, your compatibility worries will be minimal. You should find the connection between the host adapter and scanner is quite straightforward—all you have to do is plug the scanner in.

But there's another place where you can run into compatibility problems—the connection between the host adapter and your PC. The host adapter has to share some of the resources of your PC with other expansion boards and even the system board, so it's possible (and often likely) that conflicts will occur.

Scanner host adapters often need to use input/output port, memory, and interrupt facilities of your PC just as other expansion boards do. For example, to deliver better performance some hand scanners are interrupt driven, which means they need to take exclusive control of one of the interrupts available in your system. Some desktop scanner host adapters use I/O ports to transfer data and instructions between the scanner and your PC. Some host adapters need to reserve an address range in which they will place their BIOS code. In each case, you must be certain that the facilities used by the host adapter don't conflict with the requirement of other accessories connected to your computer.

Choosing an interrupt to use if you have an 8-bit PC can be daunting because your choices will be limited. Eight-bit machines have only eight interrupts, of which only three are generally usable—and those are often put to work at other chores. As noted before interrupt 0 is used by your system's timer; 1 is assigned to the keyboard; 2 is used by some display adapters and network adapters; 3 is used by the second serial port in your system; 4 is used by your first serial port; 5 by the hard disk; 6 by your floppy disk drives; and 7 by the printer port. Your only choice is to use an interrupt that is not needed by another peripheral. Interrupt 2 is the most common choice.

Sixteen-bit PCs are more generous with their interrupts, having a total of 15 for input/output devices. The likely candidates are interrupts 10, 11, 12, and 15. A good choice is interrupt 11.

In general, you can tell if your scanner's host adapter can use these higher interrupts by looking closely at its expansion connector. If you see only a single edge connector about four inches long, then the board can only handle the lower eight interrupts. If the board has two edge connectors—a long one near the card-retaining bracket and a short one (which may be very short, perhaps only an inch long), the card likely can handle the 15 AT interrupts. In order to use interrupts higher than 7, you must install the scanner host adapter in a 16-bit (or 32-bit EISA) expansion socket, even though the board itself may look like an 8-bit short card.

I/O port addresses are more numerous than interrupts—in most systems you have a choice of 1,024 ports. But ports are more numerous because they are needed for more functions. Some expansion boards use several ports for their functions. For example, the Microtek scanner uses 16 ports and a Direct Memory Access (DMA) channel.

The trick is to find a range that other accessories in your system do not use. For the most part, common peripherals stick to certain well-defined values. For example, the first two serial ports in most systems use 3F8(Hex) and 2F8(Hex). In most cases, the default chosen by the scanner manufacturer should work fine. If you later discover your scanner doesn't work, changing the port address

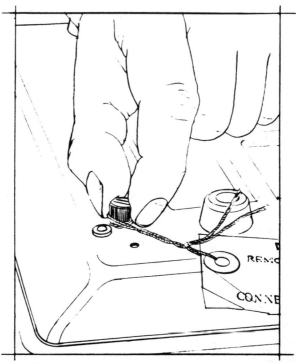

Figure 11.5 Many flatbed scanners have shipping screws or tape strips securing their mechanisms against transportation damage. Before you set up your scanner, be sure to remove these. In particular, check the bottom of the scanner for a shipping screw like the one shown here.

should be the first thing you try to get things going. The same is true for the memory addresses that may be used by host adapters.

Scanner Installation

The first step in installing a scanner is determining which of your system's resources it will need. The instructions or installation manual accompanying the scanner should tell you exactly what the product requires. The instructions should also outline what the factory default values are, suggested alternatives, and how to change the defaults.

Always try the factory default first. It's easier because you don't have to change anything. Moreover, these settings are those that have been found to work with most PCs.

If you find you need to alter the factory defaults, write down the changes you had to make in the instruction manual. That way you can always refer to them. (You'll find out how important this bit of forethought can be when you install the scanner software. It may demand to know the settings you made. If you didn't write them down, that may mean tearing apart your PC all over again.)

In most cases, these values will be set using DIP (dual in-line package) switches or jumpers on the host adapter board. In Micro Channel machines and more advanced host adapters, the required settings are made using the installation software accompanying the host adapter.

SCSI scanners may also require that you set a SCSI identification number on the scanner itself. The factory default is the best choice, but you should verify that the setting is proper and has not been jiggled, jostled, or manhandled to some other value.

Once you've properly set up the host adapter, you're ready to begin the hardware installation process. Start by switching off your PC, disconnecting the power cord for safety's sake, and removing the cover from the system.

Find a vacant expansion slot in which to install the host adapter. Be sure to properly match the interface—while 8-bit boards will fit in either 8- or 16-bit slots, 16-bit boards and 8-bit boards using higher interrupt numbers should only be used in 16-bit slots.

After you slide the expansion board in, you'll want to be sure to screw the board securely in place. Because scanners use large connectors (typically 25 pins or more) to plug into their host adapters, you can easily unseat the host adapter when you plug the scanner's cable in to it.

Most scanners can be plugged into their host adapter and into a wall outlet (if necessary) at this point. Simply connect the signal cable accompanying the scanner at both ends—one connector goes to the scanner, the other to the host adapter. Some scanners that use the GPIB connection may be an exception. These may require that you test out the GPIB host adapter before you connect the scanner. Check your instruction manual to be sure.

Next—before you reassemble your PC—plug your PC in again. Switch it back on; after it boots up, install the software that came with the scanner. If the installation procedure does not require you to have your scanner switched on, turn it on anyways so it can warm up.

The typical software installation will require you to put a driver in your CONFIG.SYS file (or rely on the automatic installation procedure supplied with the software) and copy some files to your hard disk.

Once you've installed the software, reboot your PC and try out the scanner with its control program or other scanning software. Your scanner should magically come to life. Typically, when you select the software command to scan, the scanner should light up as if by magic—that is, if you and the software have carried out all of the installation processes properly. Make a scan to verify all is well. If you're able to complete a scan and see an image on your PC, congratulate yourself on a job well done, switch off your PC, and reinstall its cover.

If the scanner doesn't work, you likely are suffering from a resource conflict of some kind. Switch off your PC, and try changing the port address, interrupt assignment, or memory address used by the scanner host adapter until the scanner works properly. Rather than trial and error, try the alternate suggestions listed in the instruction manual first.

Once your scanner is working, you'll find that it's definitely not child's play. Making a scan may take longer than your kid's attention span. But you'll cut the time and expense of getting good graphics and even text into your PC.

12.

TAPE SYSTEMS

A tape drive can add two important benefits to your PC—tape provides an excellent backup medium that helps keep your hard disk's data secure. And tape can be an exchange medium, letting you share information as conveniently as with floppy disks but in quantities measured in tens of megabytes. Unlike disks, a number of different tape systems are available, each with its own advantages. The right tape upgrade means not just installing a drive, but installing the right drive for your system and purposes.

Tape is rarely the first upgrade most people think of making. When you want to lavish some of your largess on your PC to make it better, primary in your mind probably is performance—a faster microprocessor, quicker disk, or more memory to speed the execution of a specific application. But lost somewhere in the dark reaches of your cranium is a faint voice reminding you of the fleetingness of mortal existence, the coquettishness of fate, and the vulnerability of important data stored on your hard disk. You need to do something to protect that information, and that something is a tape drive. As with medicines that taste akin to distillations of old socks, you probably recognize that a tape system will be good for you even if unpalatable. Tape is likely not something that you really want to buy, but something you really need that you have to pay for.

Like castor oil, tape has survived for an unbelievable number of years as one of the most unwanted items on the shopping list. It lacks fun, glamor, and sex appeal. It's simply a necessity—at least to some minds.

In truth, tape is no more a necessity than a personal biplane. What most people want is what tape does, not the tape drive itself. When you think tape, you think backup, a safety net for your hard disk. Tape is not the only backup system, nor is it always the best. After all, it is the oldest storage medium used by computers, and a number of better ideas have come along since (say, for instance, the Winchester hard disk). But even the backward biplane has its advantages in some applications—think of the barnstorming aerobatics that kept your eyes glued to the sky at the last air show you enjoyed. The ancient technology of tape has still to be topped in the applications it handles best.

Tape and computers go back a long time. In fact, they grew up together with magnetic recording and mainframe computers both teething through the '50s. But the association of tape and digital signals goes back further—punch tape, with holes popped out to signify the forerunner of ASCII, Morse code, for telegraphic transmissions. Long, thin ribbons of tape offer the perfect medium for recording long, single-file trains of data.

Magnetic tape was the first successful mass storage medium for mainframe computers—the one that kept computer operators hopping, lifting and mounting reel after reel of heavy tape, enough that even the most demure of technicians got enough of a workout to be able to challenge Arnold Schwarzenegger in arm wrestling. And tape keeps popping back into the personal computer industry. The original IBM PC succeeded in spite of being designed to use tape as a primary storage medium through the long-forgotten cassette port on the back of the machine. When toy manufacturer Coleco tried to break into the home computer market with its bargain-priced (and now unlamented) Adam computer, it relied on tape rather than disk storage. With all that going for it, you probably wonder why you should even bother thinking about upgrading your PC with a tape system.

But magnetic tape has a few virtues that keep it in the engineer's eye. In cartridges, tape is convenient and rugged. Most people still prefer cassette tapes to digital Compact Discs for music in their automobiles, for example. Tape has been around for a long time, so it is well understood and supported. You can buy tape drives (though perhaps not of computer quality) for a few dollars. And the tape itself, although a precision product, is cheap to make. In some widths, you can find it retail for under $20 per mile.

Tape has its weakness, too. While tape drives can write, read, and transfer information as quickly as disks, they are definitely handicapped when it comes to *finding* a random byte. That's because tape is strictly a sequential medium—the long ribbon stores information in a long stream with no shortcuts to find the one particular byte you need. In that most personal computer applications take a random approach to their data needs, tape just doesn't serve well, particularly when compared to the quick response of disk drives. What a disk can locate in a few thousandths of a second, a tape drive make take a few thousand seconds to find. Rely on tape as a primary mass storage system and you won't just have time to slow down and smell the roses. While you're waiting for a tape drive, you'll be able to stop and *grow* the roses.

Tape would be nothing more than a curious footnote in the history of personal computing were it not that two very important applications don't require random data storage or retrieval. These are system support functions that require simply copying large block of data and storing the results or sharing them with someone else. *Backup systems*—what you think of first when you think of tape—need to be able to make an exact copy of data stored on disk, maintaining the order laid onto the disk. Tape can make the one-for-one copy quickly and easily. *Exchanging data* also requires an exact copy of the contents of a disk to be transcribed byte for byte. Consequently, tape makes an excellent backup and data exchange medium.

Unlike other aged technologies, such as biplanes and buggy-making, tape isn't about to be pushed aside as a mere curiosity for the anachronistically inclined. As disk drives get ever bigger and faster, the value of a tape system thus increases rather than decreases. Tape can earn its keep because the more you depend on your hard disk, the bigger the threat the failure of your disk becomes. In effect, your disk is a time bomb, waiting to self-destruct and take your data along with it. A tape drive won't prevent the inevitable disk crash, but it will make recovering from disaster easier. Instead of a miracle, you'll just need some time to restore your files.

You don't need a complete disaster to show you the value of tape. Accidentally write over an important file—for example, copy an old version over a new version—and no file recovery program will help resurrect your data, but a tape backup will.

In addition, the same applications that demand huge hard disk drives also require some way of conveniently exchanging files. For example, say you're designing a new ocean liner, the QE3, and you need to send your preliminary CAD drawings for approval to the Royal Family. You can spend 15 days plotting them all out, invest in 12 cartons of floppy disks and a two-day backup session, or slide a single tape into your tape drive and issue a single command. Knighthood might never be so easy.

Certainly you have other technologies, such as optical disk cartridges, to choose for these same functions. But tape remains one of the least expensive (in terms of cost per megabyte stored) and most convenient backup media available.

Backup Philosophy

Viewed pragmatically, the primary application of the backup is indeed as insurance against the inevitable. All mechanical devices, as products of mortal toil, are subject to failure. When the cosmos aligns itself in a particularly malignant manner, even the best hard disk is apt to submit to the supernatural will, bow down—and break down—in submission. No measure of penance will earn you access to your data again.

If the gods don't get you, your own mortal spirit—or those of your coworkers—may. Even ignoring deliberate mischief and vandalism, your system is prey to human frailties and error. One errant keystroke and the command to rid your disk of garbage, DEL *.BAK, will wipe away your every batch file at DEL *.BAT. Whenever you write a program that POKEs or writes to your disk, you risk sending your system on a random seek-and-destroy mission, perhaps sliding extra little end-of-file markers every fifth byte on your hard disk or just dropping your bookkeeping records on top of both copies of its file allocation table.

A backup—and, in particular, a recently made backup—can protect you from such disasters and relieve you of contemplating suicide, swearing off computing forever, or simply swearing enough to earn your office an X rating. The backup gives you the security of knowing that you won't spend the next three months reconstructing your tax records or rewriting the canned report that you're scheduled to send to the boss each month to ignore.

In its most basic form, the backup is just a duplicate copy all the vulnerable data (and, often, programs) that you have. By keeping everything two places, you have a greater chance that one will survive when your most dreaded nightmares come true and a mutant starfish from Lawrence Livermore labs attacks your computer, cracks open your hard disk, and sucks the data out.

But the usefulness and protection of the backup system doesn't stop there. Multiple backups can give you multiple layers of security. Stored off-site, perhaps at a commercial data repository or simply in your bank safe deposit box, you can keep your most valuable files alive even when a conflagration or similar catastrophe strikes and annihilates your office and the surrounding neighborhood.

In addition to the extra measure of protection that they afford, some backup systems can also be used as data interchange systems. Once you've distilled your important files into a backup, you can send them anywhere in the world in a single small package for nothing more than the price of postage or a courier. Choose the right backup system, and you can even interchange data with different computer models and even different operating systems, from Macintoshes to minicomputers to mainframes.

If you're a PC manager or are foolish enough to volunteer for similar duties without pay in setting up systems for friends, the backup system can make your job a breeze. Once you've obtained the proper software licenses (or only use your own homegrown programs), you can save a whole hard disk environment on a cartridge, then transfer everything onto another system, setting up the most complex arrangement of files and directories as easily as plugging in the interface card and typing "restore."

All tape backup systems do not offer the same protections or potential, however. Some are faster, some offer more compatibility options, and some are cheaper. The first step in finding the right one to suit your own particular needs is to consider all the backup options and technologies that are available to you.

Sometimes backup systems, particularly older ones, allow you to choose among different backup methods. Typically your options are *image* or *file-by-file backups*. The image backup is a bit-for-bit copy of the original disk. Bytes are merely read from the disk and copied on tape without a glance to their content or structure. Because little processing overhead is involved, these image backups can be fast. File-by-file backups add structure to the information as it is backed up. Although processing overhead tends to slow down file-by-file systems, finding files within the structure (and, hence, individual file restoration) is easier.

In most current systems, these two techniques have merged or image backing up is totally ignored. Because file-by-file backups have become as fast as image backups, there's no incentive for putting up with the greater hassles of the image backup. Even systems that still offer image backup modes have smarter restoration software that can make sense of the inherent structure of image backups, so that individual file restorations can be made from them.

Consequently, if you buy a current backup system, you shouldn't have to worry about backup modes.

Backup Alternatives

When it comes to making a backup of your hard disk, tape is not the only choice. Nearly any medium that can hold data is a candidate as a backup system. Each one has its own strengths and weaknesses. Consequently, a look at all the various backup alternatives is in order before you commit your cash to a tape drive. The simple truth is that tape is not always the best choice.

For most people, tape is a single-purpose medium that serves to copy the contents of an active hard disk. For such simple copying, tape works well. Copying is a sequential operation—one file is transcribed at a time into the next blank area on the storage medium—and tape is by its nature a sequential medium. Its magnetic ribbon spools continuously pass its read/write head, ready to accept or disgorge information in sequence as it goes along. This single-minded purposefulness of tape is also tape's undoing. Other backup media can serve other functions besides simply backing up, potentially something important like primary storage. For example, cartridge-based disk systems offer the same data-exchange abilities of tape, but have an inherent speed advantage for many system functions.

Disk systems hold this advantage because they step beyond tape by providing random access to data. Disk read/write heads can quickly move tangent to normal data flow to get into the middle of things almost instantly. The heads of a disk drive can almost instantly scoot over to find a file, even when that file is part of a backup. Not only does such instant access benefit normal storage operations, it can be helpful even when using a disk as a backup system. For example, a disk system can compare an archived file with one you're thinking of backing up to see whether you even need to bother with making a copy of an unchanged file. The whole operation might take a second using a disk drive, while a tape system might have to scan the whole tape just to find the file. A file that's backed up to a disk is also usually faster and easier to recover than one on tape.

On the other hand, disk drive mechanisms are, by their nature, more complex—and consequently more expensive—than tape drives. The capacities of the typical cartridge-based disk system also pales in comparison with tape. Although cartridge disk systems allow virtually unlimited off-line storage, much like tape cartridges, disk cartridge capacity also tends to cost more per megabyte. Each disk cartridge generally holds less and costs more than a tape cartridge. For instance, while a $100 disk cartridge might hold 40 megabytes, a $20 tape can store 120.

Disk backup systems need not use cartridge-based media, however. In fact, simple redundancy ranks as the most straightforward disk backup method—just keep two disks spinning with the same files written on each. Odds are that one will survive the erroneous erasure or simple head crash. Most network operating systems support such built-in disk backup systems and use a technology called *disk mirroring* to automatically ensure that changes made to one disk are reflected in the contents of the other.

Even in a single-user PC, double-disk systems can be an excellent backup strategy, one that is surprisingly inexpensive. Because a second backup drive needs neither high performance nor an additional controller (most hard disk controllers can take care of two different disk drives), adding an extra 80-megabyte hard disk to your system can cost as little as $300–400.

Although effective in some situations, the double-disk technique affords no protection against the more wide-ranging disasters—tsunamis to tornadoes—nor does it give the convenience and security feature of removable media. The removable cartridge disk systems that eliminate these problems cost more. Moreover, cartridge capacity and the resultant amount of on-line data is also more limited than that available with conventional hard disks because most disk cartridges contain only a single platter. Most nonremovable hard disk systems use multiple platters. In addition, while removable cartridge hard disk systems are faster than most other backup systems, they are in general slower than conventional hard disks.

All multiple-megabyte magnetic disk cartridge systems suffer from standardization and compatibility problems. You cannot exchange information on disk cartridges between different manufacturers' systems. Even systems that use physically identical cartridges are often incompatible. Optical cartridges, both WORM and MO drives, suffer similar problems. Although tape used to be the same way, standards have emerged that allow some systems from different manufacturers to exchange tapes.

Tape is far from the lowest-cost backup system from a capital investment standpoint, however. As long as you're willing to put up with the inconvenience of shuffling floppies—stuffing your disk drive with a fresh floppy every 30 seconds to one minute—floppy disk backup can be a viable alternative, particularly when your equipment budget is tight. Floppy disk drives are the most affordable backup systems available simply because every PC already has a floppy disk drive of one sort or another. You only need to pay for the storage medium, not additional equipment.

Although scoffed at by equipment snobs, floppies (and particularly high density, 1.2- and 1.44-megabyte diskettes) can back up files faster than some more exotic streaming tape technologies when you use high-performance backup programs. And, of course, diskettes also remain the preferred file interchange medium for PCs. If you work on only a few short files at a time, your floppy disk drive may be the only backup system you need.

Compared to floppy disks, the big advantage of cartridge tape backup is that it's convenient. Instead of dealing with boxes of floppies (a complete uncompressed backup of a full 40-megabyte hard disk requires at least 28 high-density floppy disks), you can keep everything on one compact tape cartridge smaller—though thicker—than an audio tape cassette. More importantly, with tape you don't have to shuffle disks like an arthritic blackjack dealer, baby-sitting your system for half an hour or more while your hard disk slowly deals out its files.

Tape is also more reliable than floppy disk backup. Judged by the claimed error rates, backups kept on some cartridges actually are more secure than even the hard disk-based originals.

Moreover, the per-megabyte cost of tape typically is less than floppy-based backup. Even if you were to pay just a dollar per name-brand high-density disk—low even by mail-order standards—storing backups on tape cartridges can cut your costs by 50 to 75 percent. Figure $16 for 40 megabytes of tape; $20 for 120 megabytes. Indeed, tape is generally conceded to be the least expensive file archiving medium available.

Types of Tape Systems

A variety of tape systems are now available for use with PCs, and additional models will soon be offered as creative manufacturers and standards organizations dream up new products. Today your choices are indeed wide and include open reels of half-inch nine-track tape; cartridges using half-inch, quarter-inch, 150-mil, eight-millimeter tape; cassettes; videocassettes; and digital audio tape (DAT) cartridges. Each of these media has advantages and disadvantages that you should consider before zeroing in on a backup system.

Nine-track Tape

The grandparent and progenitor of all computer tape technologies is the nine-track open-reel system. Based on reels of tape half an inch wide and up to 3,600 feet long, the first of these systems were developed for mainframe computers in the fifties. No picture of the primordial computer was complete without a reel of tape jerking back and forth inside the closet-size tape drive of a computer that took control of the world—at least until the climax of the movie.

Open-reel tape and its associated drives have evolved through the years. First able to record 800 bytes of data on every linear inch of tape, the latest of these systems can squeeze nearly eight times more, 6,250 bytes, into the same space. Tape drives have shrunk to desktop size (not a size to fit on a desktop, but in some cases the size of the desktop itself).

Despite the evolution of the equipment, half-inch tape systems are remarkable in how little the tapes themselves have changed through the years and how standardized the data format they use has become. Twenty-year-old tapes that were made with mainframe computers can be read by drives attached to PCs today.

In many ways, open-reel tape is the only interchange medium available that is standard throughout all sizes and styles of computer. The recording format and data structure are essentially the same for open-reel systems no matter who makes them or where they are used. Connect a nine-track tape drive to your PC (no easy feat) and you'll be able to read and write tapes that can be exchanged with DEC minicomputers, IBM mainframes, even the most powerful supercomputers.

Open-reel computer tapes use nine tracks arranged laterally across the width of the half-inch tape. Eight of these tracks record data and one holds a parity-check bit. Each byte of information is written all at once, in parallel across the width of the tape, and successive bytes are written sequentially along the tape. The tape effectively has only one side and is written from one end to the other, then rewound. Flux reversals, the equivalent of data bits, are spaced anywhere from 800 to 6,250 per inch, with the most common density being 1,600 bits per inch.

The data density, reel size, tape thickness, and a parameter called inter-record gap (the distance between two blocks of data on the tape) all affect how much information will fit a single reel. Capacities around 60 megabytes are commonplace.

Software for nine-track systems can usually cope with the variables of recording format. For example, most nine-track control programs allow for various inter-record gaps and even convert the EBCDIC data coding method used by IBM mainframes into the ASCII code used by PCs. About the only nine-track format variable not completely under control of software is data recording density. Higher data densities are available only on nine-track transports that support them. Consequently, lower data densities are used for storage when data interchange is the goal. Lower-density tapes are readable on a wider variety of tape machines. The penalty of using lower densities is, of course, more tape must be devoted to store a given number of megabytes. For strictly making backups, using higher densities will lower storage costs.

Strictly for making backups, however, nine-track tape is a particularly poor choice. Compared to other technologies, open-reel tape is an ungainly backup medium. Tape reels can be over ten inches in diameter and nearly an inch thick (counting their flanges), yet that reel may store no more information than a two- by three-inch cartridge. Moreover, most open-reel tape drives themselves dwarf a PC system unit, both in size and price. The cost of an open-reel system designed for connection to a PC starts at $3,500 and can reach above $10,000—which may be more expensive than the computer you want to back up.

The flip side of nine-track backup issue is data integrity. Just as a battleship can suffer through storms on the high seas better than a rowboat, the large size of open-reel tapes earns them an extra measure of long-term security. Data are stored less densely and are less likely to degrade with time or through environmental effects.

The real value of the nine-track tape systems is in data interchange, however. Tape acts like "sneaker-net" taken to the nth degree. Although exchanging disks can operate as a rudimentary data-sharing network, nine-track tape moves megabytes as easily as disks move kilobytes. And while disks are forever linked to one operating system (except through the use of format conversion software), nine-track tapes know no such bounds.

The big tapes are often used to move databases between systems and distribute information, such as mailing lists. Connected to a PC, the open-reel system can function as both a backup and data interchange system. Factor in cost, however, and nine track is a curiosity for all but the wealthiest PC users.

3480 Cartridges

After more than 20 years of dominance in the mainframe world, open-reel tape is slowly being replaced (or augmented, depending on your point of view) by a new cartridge system developed by IBM. Usually referred to by the model number of the tape drive, 3480, these cartridges are little more than open reel tapes stuffed into a protective shell. The tape is still half an inch wide, and runs through the drive much like open-reel tapes. The drive mechanism pulls the tape out of the cartridge, winds it onto a tape up spool, and rewinds it back into the cartridge when it is done.

The difference is more than the convenience of cartridge loading, however. IBM has doubled the number of tracks (doubling them once or twice more is promised) and increased the data density so a single cartridge, less than a quarter the volume of an open-reel tape at $4\frac{3}{4} \times 4\frac{1}{4} \times \frac{3}{4}$ inches, can hold hundreds of megabytes. In addition, current implementations write two parallel sets of nine tracks simultaneously, doubling data throughput.

Packing more data on tape has its penalties, however, and with the 3480 system the price you pay is the price. Currently tape drives are big-ticket ($20,000-plus) products designed for the mainframe market.

Several companies are working at adapting the 3480-style cartridge into systems that would be practical (and affordable) for PC applications. However, these new 3480-style cartridge systems use different data formats than the true IBM 3480 tape drive. They lack the big advantage of open-reel tape—it ability to exchange information with mainframes. Although not currently available as products to attach to your PC, prices are expected to be in the $1,000–2,000 range.

DC6000-style cartridges

Cartridge tapes half the width of the half-inch that's popular among mainframes have become a top choice for backing up minicomputers and PCs. Among these, the first quarter-inch cartridges to gain any degree of notoriety were the predecessors to today's DC6000-style cartridge, named for the model numbers of the tapes that fit these drives. Originally created by 3M Company as a recording medium for data acquisition applications, such as transcribing seismological information in the laboratory, this style of cartridge has evolved to fit the needs of computer backup. The passing years have proved the cartridges—with their clear plastic shells, rugged aluminum bases, and clever internal belt-drive mechanism—to be a reliable and adaptable backup medium.

While drives using DC6000-style cartridges once operated at speeds of a few inches per second, had only a couple of tracks, and could pack only a few megabytes of data per tape, today's machines stream tape at 90 inches per second and can cram from 60 to 600 megabytes into each cartridge. Standards higher-capacity versions with 1.35 gigabytes of storage are being developed.

The DC6000-style of cartridge is clever enough to be patented. It's built around a thick, rigid aluminum baseplate that assures accurate alignment of the tape with the drive mechanism, with the tape driven by a friction band rather than the pressure roller used in audio tape systems. Only the read/write head touches the recording surface of the tape. A clear plastic shell with a hinged door over the head entrance protects the tape. In most older implementation of DC6000-based systems, information was written in nine tracks across the width of the tape. Newer systems use 18 or more tracks. Unlike the parallel recording used for half-inch tape, however, most DC6000 systems use serpentine serial recording. Data bits are written sequentially, in one direction, on one track at a time, continuing for the length of the tape. At the end of the tape,

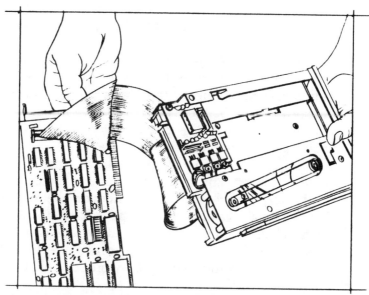

Figure 12.1 DC6000-style tape drives are two-piece systems comprising both a tape drive and a host adapter. You'll need to get them as a matched pair to insure easy installation and smooth integration with your PC.

the direction of its travel reverses, and recording moves down to the next track until all nine tracks are filled.

One of the biggest advantages of DC6000-style cartridge systems is that they are fast. Even early systems had data transfer rates identical to those of PC hard disks—five megahertz—and throughputs of ten megabytes per minute. Newer systems use a SCSI connection for even higher throughputs.

The one disadvantage of DC6000 systems is compatibility. Cartridges written on one manufacturer's DC6000-based system can rarely be read on a system sold by another manufacturer. Although an industry group, the Quarter-inch Cartridge or QIC committee, was formed with the aim of standardizing these systems, the group (which consists primarily of drive manufacturers who do not sell directly to the PC market) concerned itself chiefly with physical standardization. Data formats were left for system integrators to develop—and, in general, each one designed his own. In other words, don't count on DC6000 tapes as a data interchange medium unless you are certain that you and the person or organization with which you want to share uses the same make and model of tape drive.

Although DC6000 tape systems are necessarily more expensive than smaller tape drives (if only because DC6000 use their own dedicated host adapters), the big cartridges can be an economical storage system. In their larger-capacity formats, today's DC6000 cartridges can cost less per megabyte of backup capacity than smaller cartridges although the tapes themselves might be individually priced a few dollars higher. The big cartridges have also been available longer, and familiarity generally means a better understood, more reliable medium. Moreover, the less dense storage of older DC6000 systems also helps assure greater data integrity, much as half-inch tape does. Miniature tape cartridges compensate for their disadvantage by using error correction that, in theory, nearly eliminates the chance you won't be able to restore a backup you've made.

The most meaningful advantage of DC6000 systems is speed. They are able to move information at data transfer rates on par with some hard disks. More speed means less waiting, of course, and faster restoration when you need to recover after disaster strikes. On the downside, the higher speed of DC6000 systems also requires the use of a proprietary interface. That is, in addition to the tape drive itself, you'll have to buy and install an expansion board to run the drive. That means you lose an expansion slot in your PC—if you have one available to use.

DC2000-style Cartridges

Another shortcoming of the DC6000 cartridge and its drive units is more difficult to surmount—size. DC6000-style cartridges are almost the size of a paperback book, a full $6 \times 4 \times \frac{5}{8}$ inches. Squeezing a drive to handle those bulky cartridges into a $5\frac{1}{4}$ inch form factor PC drive bay, which is itself six inches wide, is a considerable engineering challenge; fitting a drive for those cartridges into the increasingly popular $3\frac{1}{2}$ inch form factor is simply impossible until the current physical laws are repealed.

The DC2000 cartridge represents an attempt to overcome both of those DC6000 limitations. Compact, at under $3\frac{1}{4} \times 2\frac{1}{2} \times \frac{5}{8}$ inches, the typical DC2000 cartridge holds 205 feet of quarter-inch-wide tape. Current systems can pack from 40 to 80 megabytes of raw data on one of these tiny cartridges. Using data compression, these same drives can effectively add 50 percent to their raw capacity with suitably squeezable data. Higher-capacity systems are being developed, both under the auspices of the QIC committee and in proprietary formats. For example, Irwin Magnetics has announced its own DC2000 tape drive that will pack about 320 megabytes on cartridges using special high-density tapes. The large capacities are achieved by packing data tighter and shoehorning more and more serial data tracks across the tape width—dozens—using a servo-tracking mechanism to ensure that the track and read/write head are correctly positioned and error correction to bridge over defects in the tape medium itself.

Among the most popular of the standards for DC2000 systems adopted by the QIC committee are QIC-40 and QIC-80. Among nonproprietary formats, these standards offer the least expensive access to tape that you can put into your PC. Complete systems capable of storing up to 120 megabytes (using data compression) are available for under $300. The secret of achieving these low prices is that both of these standards are designed to use a conventional floppy disk controller card as an interface to the tape drive. Although limited to floppy disk transfer speeds, when properly designed such systems can deliver adequate throughput.

The QIC-100 standard was developed to break through the floppy disk controller speed barrier, but it has proven unpopular in comparison to the other standards. Tapes made on QIC-100 systems are not compatible with other QIC standards, so this choice is not a good one for data interchange. The drives are now difficult to find and probably are not worth the effort.

A sidenote: Irwin Magnetics at one time sold about half the tape drives inside PCs and became an industry standard in itself. New Irwin systems are compatible with the QIC-80 standard (old drives are not, however, so be careful).

Perhaps the principal disadvantage of the QIC-40 and QIC-80 standards is that they require that the cartridges be formatted before they are used, much as you must format floppy disks. Although formatting is a small bother with floppy disks, it can be a hardship with QIC-40 tapes. Typically the process takes about one minute to format one megabyte of tape, up to 40 minutes for the full capacity of a single QIC-40 cartridge. (Some tape systems allow you to save time by formatting tapes for lower capacities.) While the formatting process can be time consuming, it has its upside. It adds flexibility and speed later on during backup and restoration. Moreover, it helps identify bad spots on tapes and assures that they won't be used for storing your valuable data.

To allow you to avoid the painfully long formatting wait, many tape manufacturers sell their DC2000 cartridges preformatted. If you opt for the laudable strategy of buying preformatted tapes, you'll want to take care to be sure that the tapes use the same format as does your tape drive.

If you've been turned off by DC2000 tape systems in the past because you read about them or tried them and discovered that they were quirky and slow, take another look at a newer drive. The technology has come a long way in the last few years. Today DC2000 tape drives rank as a top backup choice. Beside shirt-pocket physical size, DC2000 tape capacities now match the limits of the most popular PC hard disk sizes. You can even spread larger back-ups across several tapes if you have a hard disk measured in multiple hundreds of megabytes.

QIC-40 and QIC-80 offer a superlative advantage over the older standards used by DC6000-style tape systems. The new standards embrace not only the physical characteristics of the tapes, drives, and their connection with your PC but also the standard dictates how data are arranged on each tape. As a result, QIC-40 and QIC-80 tapes are much more interchangeable than are DC6000-style tapes. You're more likely to be able to exchange data on DC2000 cartridges with friends, coworkers, and coconspirators, even if each of you has a different make and model of tape drive. But you still must be careful and do your homework before you buy. There remain enough subtle differences between the data formats on tapes that you are still not guaranteed that one tape drive will read a tape made by another.

The one penalty of the low cost and high convenience of miniature tape cartridges is that their drives operate more slowly than DC6000 drives. Figure that your system will be able to transfer from one to three megabytes per minute to a DC2000 cartridge compared to three to ten megabytes per minute for a bigger DC6000 cartridge. The culprit that steals performance from DC2000 tape systems is the same floppy disk interface that makes the system affordable. This connection scheme limits the data transfer rate of DC2000 systems to about one-tenth the rate of hard disk drives. Your hard disk and your computer have to spin their wheels while waiting for the tape drive to catch up.

In practice, however, the performance penalty of miniature cartridges is not so severe, particularly because once you start the tape drive running, you can wander off and get into trouble some other place. In fact, most tape systems allow you to set a time (say, during your lunch hour or after 5 P.M.) to make backups unattended by your physical presence. When a tape drive operates without occupying your time, it shouldn't matter how long a backup takes.

Most modern miniature tape systems also take advantage of the otherwise wasted time your PC idles during the backup process by using it to compress your data before its stored on tape. Putting your PC to work in this way can actually speed up the backup process if your system is fast enough to handle the backup and compression at the same time. In general, you should notice a performance improvement with data compression if your system operates faster than 16 MHz.

DC1000 Cartridges

Out of the today's tape mainstream, but aiming at getting in, are several other tape formats. Some of these have already seen their short day in the sun; others are rising in prominence.

Among the former are DC1000 cartridges. About the same size as DC2000s, DC1000 cartridges use narrower tape measuring 150 mils (thousandths of an inch) wide. Each cartridge holds 10 to 20 megabytes.

As with DC2000 tape drives, the DC1000 systems typically interfaced through an extra channel in a PC's floppy disk controller. That, of course, made them slow. Figure in the modest capacities that were quickly dwarfed by fast-growing hard disks and the lack of the blessing of a standards organization, and you'll understand why DC1000 failed to catch on. Today, consider such a unit advertised at an unbelievably low price as a curiosity. Consider a unit installed in your PC as a liability.

Data Cassettes

Computer data cassettes have matured from a ungainly youth—as a slow, modem-speed, audio technology-based system for sequentially storing the outpourings of home computers—to high-speed competitors to more exotic cartridge systems. Using special high-grade computer cassettes and drives, the new systems can pack up to 60 megabytes on one tape at rates comparable to DC2000 and DC6000 cartridge technology. Although cassettes are not quite as compact as DC2000 cartridges, they are a familiar package that holds promise as a strong backup alternative.

Cassette-based systems are priced inexpensively. One reason is that they share their heritage with ordinary audio cassettes. The mechanisms are similar, although data-storing machines require greater precision in manufacturing and entirely different electronics. Nevertheless, economies of scale and common design make data cassette mechanisms among the least expensive tape drives that you can plug into your PC.

Cassette drives are relatively fast—on the order of DC2000 systems—and they are economical in their cost per megabyte of storage. All-plastic cassettes are cheaper to make than precision aluminum-based cartridges and they cost less, about $10 each. Even that relatively low (by computer standards) price might seem high compared to the $2 or so you probably pay for audio cassettes, which look pretty much identical to the digital variety. But data cassettes and audio cassettes are *not* interchangeable. Data cassettes use tape media with entirely different magnetic characteristics than the audio variety. Moreover, data cassettes have a special notch on their backbone to distinguish them from audio tapes. Audio cassettes lacking the notch won't even fit into a data cassette drive.

Two factors have prevented data cassettes from gaining greater acceptance. Today's data cassettes lack one virtue enjoyed by DC2000 systems—*standardization*. Data cassettes essentially are a proprietary storage system promoted primarily by Teac Corporation. In addition, makers of DC2000 tape systems don't view cassettes as being as reliable a medium as their own products. (Teac obviously feels otherwise.)

Video-based Tape Backup Systems

Of all media that can be directly recorded upon by consumers, videocassettes currently have the greatest capacity. A single two-hour movie requires storage space that would accommodate gigabytes of digital data. Capacity alone would make the VCR an intriguing backup device, but video tape has another advantage, *speed*. An ordinary, old-fashioned television picture requires a bandwidth of six megahertz, a pleasing rate for tape backup systems. Advanced video systems push transfer speeds even higher.

The problem with using a VCR for backing up your PC is that VCRs and computers don't get along well. VCRs are designed to handle analog information and computer data are in digital form. Intrigued by the potential of video media, backup system manufacturers have developed two strategies for converting video recording equipment to computer data. One strategy is to convert computer data into a video-compatible format. The other is to convert the video hardware to accommodate digital signals.

The former was the first to be tried for computer data storage. Digital data were used essentially to modulate a television signal. Much as a modem matches digital data to analog telephone lines, data can be converted to the standard television format using carrier frequencies. Once the data are converted to a video format, they can be stored—or even transmitted—as if they were ordinary television. Any standard videocassette recorder will then work as a backup system.

The potential capacity can be immense. If the full capacity of a two-hour videocassette could be exploited at the full television bandwidth, a single $5 tape could hold over five gigabytes of information. A dollar per gigabyte is cheap storage by any measure.

The primary problem faced by such digital-to-video systems is that analog recording systems are much more tolerant of some signal deficiencies than are digital system. In a video system, for example, a momentary lapse in the picture would be virtually undetectable to a casual observer. The same lapse would be fatal to a computer system. Videocassettes in particular are plagued with short-term signal lapses called *dropouts* that result from tiny bad spots on the tape. The one available VCR-based computer backup system compensated for the dropout problem with redundancy. It would write multiple copies of the data to be backed up onto the tape. This Band-Aid procedure was successful because it is statistically unlikely that each of the copies will suffer dropout degradation in the same place. According to the manufacturer of the data-to-video system, the redundant protection scheme lowered the error rate of the complete conversion and storage system to less than that suffered by ordinary hard disks. For further data security, videocassette-based systems also ensured data integrity by playing back the on-tape signal during the backup process, analyzing the playback to detect errors. In effect, each backup copy could be certified as correct before it was depended upon.

But redundancy is not a panacea. The duplication of information (combined with a conversion system that did not try to strain the signal-handling limits of the tape) trimmed the capacity of a two-hour videocassette to about 80 megabytes. Worse, the read-after-write verification process and the duplication of backups to eliminate dropouts severely slowed the speed of the backup process. The commercial data-to-video conversion VCR-based backup system was only able to creep along at a rate of about 13 megabytes every ten minutes, slower than the less-expensive DC2000-based tape systems.

The other video-based strategy has proven more useful. Instead of modifying the signals to act like video, manufacturers have adapted the electronics of videocassette machines to handle digital information more or less directly. For the most part, this strategy has been applied to video systems based on compact eight-millimeter tape cartridges, which use tape slightly wider than DC2000 and DC6000 systems.

Eight-millimeter tape systems deliver on much of the capacity potential of the video medium. Some systems pack two gigabytes (two thousand megabytes) of information on cartridges not much larger than standard audio cassettes. Because these systems use dedicated high-speed host adapters, they are fast. Some transfer data faster than the quickest DC6000-based backup systems.

Today, eight-millimeter cartridge backup is viewed as one of the better high-end backup systems. However, it is costly. (What do you expect at the high end?) Moreover, its huge capacities are unnecessary for most single-user PCs. Consequently, eight-millimeter backup is most suited for network servers and other commercial applications with huge hard disks.

Digital Audio Tape Systems

Closely allied to eight-millimeter video tape is the use of Digital Audio Tape (or DAT) recorders as computer backup systems. DAT machines hold the explicit advantage of being designed from the beginning as digital devices that store digital data. To convert an audio machine into a computer backup system about all that is required is reprogramming and repackaging.

DAT cartridges are amazingly compact, hardly a couple inches long, yet they can hold a gigabyte or two of computer data. Data transfer rates rival those of eight-millimeter systems.

The only disadvantage of DAT is that it's new. Not that the technology doesn't work, it works amazingly well. Rather, the cost of DAT is high on the development curve. Machines start at over $1,000. As (or if, depending on your point of view in such things) DAT is accepted as a consumer medium for sound recordings, prices of DAT-based backup systems are likely to fall substantially.

Until then, DAT is best regarded like eight-millimeter video tape, a system at its best for backing up the hard disk drives of network servers, overkill for individual PCs. By the time you need the capacity of a DAT machine to back up your hard disk, the price of DAT backup will likely have fallen to a level you can afford.

Choosing a Backup System

No one backup system rates as best for everyone. Each has its own combination of features that can recommend it for a given host PC environment. For most people, the most important factor in guiding their backup choice is cost. In general, more buys more—speed, capacity, compatibility, and convenience. But price isn't the only way to shop. Other considerations can overrule the price differences between systems. For instance, when you absolutely need access to mainframe tapes or want to interchange information, you'll have to bite the bullet and budget for an open-reel tape drive.

The best backup system is the one that you're most likely to use—and use routinely. No matter how good or expensive it may be, a backup system is worthless if you never bother to put it to work. The backup system that's easiest and most convenient to operate is the one least likely to be ignored—and the one most likely to help when disaster strikes.

No matter what backup hardware you choose, you still need a backup system. That system requires more than just hardware, even more than software. To make it work, you must adhere to a strict backup routine after you make one overall backup of all the files on your hard disk.

The absolute best backup system is one in which you make a duplicate copy of each file as soon as it is made. Finish a worksheet and immediately copy it to your backup medium. Without disk-mirroring software, this can also be the most bothersome to use because the onus is on you to do all the backup work. For the most part, software won't matter because you and not the PC will handle all the details of backing up.

For this kind of backup system, your best choice is a random access backup system—floppy disks, a duplicate hard disk, a cartridge disk, or a tape system that attempts to emulate a disk device. The last will be very slow — don't say you weren't warned. A device that's designed for random access—such as a disk drive—will speed the backup process so you can quickly make your copy and get on to something else. If you don't like the bother of constantly making copies, you may want to investigate disk-mirroring software.

The second major backup system is one with which you make file copies at regular intervals. For instance, every day at an appointed time you duplicate all the files that have changed that day by copying them onto the backup medium. This sort of routine is the backup choice in systems where data are really important—most mainframes are backed up on such a daily schedule.

Large-capacity media are often best for this kind of backup because the number of files to back up may be great and you won't want to stick around the whole time shuffling floppy disks in and out of the disk drive. Traditionally, tape systems have been the choice for these regular backups, although there is no reason that cartridge or duplicate hard disks can't be used. Removable cartridge media (tapes or disks) are usually preferred because they permit storing several copies of the entire system set-up for recovery when the worst disaster befalls you. Because of its price advantage and proven technology, however, streaming tape is the traditional medium of choice for this kind of backup system. For minicomputer systems and PC users with very large hard disks coupled with very little patience, the DC6000-style cartridge is particularly favored. Today, however, the majority of PCs will be best served by a DC2000-style cartridge system.

Backup Software Considerations

Backup software will determine how convenient the system is to use. The BACKUP command that comes with DOS will not control a tape backup system. It only works with floppy disks (and in some DOS versions, particularly those older than 3.3, it doesn't work very well). So you'll need control software for your backup system. Thankfully, most—but not all—backup hardware is accompanied by the software needed to operate it. You'll want to check when you order the hardware to be sure that the software you need is included.

But getting software may not be enough. You also want to be sure that the software does what you want it to. Most backup software packages give you a choice between command-driven and menu-driven modes. If you want to take direct control of your backup session, monitoring it every step of the way, or if you don't want to learn yet another set of commands, you should look for a backup system with the menu-driven software. If you want to automate your backups through batch files that you build yourself, a command-driven backup program is best. With the latest software, you don't have to give up ease of use for automating your backups. The best packages include a *batch mode* that allows you to use the menu system to automate your backups. In other words, the important issue is to be sure that the backup software that comes with whatever backup device you choose works the way you want it to. You'll probably want a set of command-driven backup utilities or a program that has its own batch mode. Ask when you order to be sure.

A few of the latest independent backup utility packages such as Norton Backup (from Symantec) and PC Tools Backup (from Central Point Software) are able to control some tape drives as well as floppy disk drives. You may prefer to use these programs because they are generally easier to use and more complete than the free programs that come with tape systems. If you choose to use such third-party software, make sure the hardware you buy will work with the software you want to use. Again, the best method to be sure is to ask the person who is selling—for your peace of mind ask both the software and the hardware vendor.

The most important selling point for backup software—and backup systems in general—is speed. After all, if you plan on overseeing all of your backups as they happen, the fastest backup system is always the more endurable. Even when you run in batch mode, a faster system will steal a smaller chunk of your working day. Some backup systems give you a better alternative: automatic backups made at an appointed time. If you don't mind leaving your PC running overnight (and have the faith that it will, indeed, continue to run overnight), you can take advantage of such programs to assure yourself of always having a recent backup without spending half your lifetime to make it. The automated backup systems have two key elements: the control software, which is often included in better backup programs; and backup hardware with sufficient capacity to hold all the backups to be made in the wee hours. After all, no one is going to be around to change tapes.

Remember the Golden Rule of backing up: The best backup system is the one that enforces the routine that you're most likely to follow. A backup system that does not get used (or used often) is not a backup system at all.

Media Considerations

In removable media systems, the price of tapes or disks can be a major factor in overall cost. Be sure to consider how many tapes you need and what they cost when investigating the price of backup systems. For instance, you may be able to buy an entire tape drive for the price of a couple Bernoulli cartridges.

For most backup scenarios, you will want sufficient media capacity to hold a minimum of three complete backups. For greater peace of mind or more elaborate backup rituals—such as keeping a separate backup for each day of the week—your media needs increase. Most people actively use between six and ten tapes in their regular backup routine.

Exactly how many tapes you'll require depends on how you want to carry out your backups. For the utmost in security, make a complete backup at the end of each business day. You'll need at least five tapes to cover such a scenario. That way, you'll have a week in which to discover you've accidentally erased something important. Some people advocate an even more complex strategy—one tape for each day of the week, with a separate tape for each Friday (or whatever) in the month (to add a month's worth of "What happened to that file?" security). You can even use a separate tape for every first Friday of the month for a year to have a snapshot of your system over a long period at regular intervals.

The alternative game plan is to make an overall backup and then at the end of each day append only the files that have changed to the tape. One tape could thus hold several weeks (even months) of backups. This also saves time because you have less data to back up in each session. The weakness of such a strategy is that you have only one backup of every file—perhaps enough—but then again, you bought your backup systems so you don't have to take such chances. You'll probably want to supplement such a system by making a new complete backup (on a different tape) once every couple of weeks. With such a system, you'll want at least four tapes.

Remember when figuring how many tapes you need to calculate the cost of periodically replacing any media that wear out. All tape media and all disks except for cartridge hard disks will eventually wear out because of the magnetic coating of the tape constantly rubbing against the head (or, in the case of flexible Bernoulli cartridges, the media constantly flexing around the head). The exact amount of life to expect from a particular medium depends on your own personal paranoia. According to one major media manufacturer, DC6000-style cartridges should last 5,000–6,000 passes across the read/write head. On the other hand, cautious mainframe managers may routinely replace open-reel tapes after they've been used as few as 50 times. A good compromise, according to the media manufacturer, would be annual replacement of your backup tapes.

Practical Backup Systems

Once you decide on the size of cartridge you want to use, you need to settle on a standard. Standards are important because they determine what software will work with your tape drive and whether you can exchange tapes.

If you have no plans to ever use your backup tapes to distribute data, if the tape drive you buy comes with its own software, and if you have great faith that the maker of the tape system you buy will support it until Gabriel blows his horn, you need not concern your-self with standards. Otherwise, you should ensure the tape drive you buy for your upgrade conforms to one or more of the industry standards.

Software compatibility is the reason standards are important when you shop for a tape backup upgrade. That's because adding a tape upgrade is different from adding a disk. A hard disk will work with DOS alone, but you'll always need some kind of special soft-ware for your tape drive. Remember, the BACKUP command that accompanies DOS doesn't know how to deal with tape.

It's not that the authors of DOS are stingy or retrograde in their thinking. It's just that there are so many different tape drives avail-able—many of them with their own particular commands and fea-tures—that accommodating them all through DOS would be about as easy as trying to speak a dozen languages at the same time.

Most—but hardly all—tape drives come complete with their own backup software. When you order a drive, make sure you ask about its software. Does the system include its own backup program? If it does not, you'll have to factor in the cost of backup software to the tape drive cost. Be sure to check what commercially available pro-grams will operate the drive. A discontinued drive without soft-ware that requires you to dream up your own backup program is not a bargain at any price.

If the tape drive follows one or more of the industry standards, you have a better chance that third-party software will be available for the drive. The standards you should be most concerned about are those agreed upon by the Quarter-Inch Cartridge (QIC) commit-tee. All of these standards are easily identified by the name of the group as their preface, such as QIC-40.

In mail-order advertisements, the two most popular standards you'll find are QIC-40 and QIC-80. The two are variations on the same theme. Both of these apply to DC2000 tape systems. Both include standardization all the way to the storage format on tape, which helps assure intercompatibility of tapes made on different systems. Both require that the tape drive work in essentially the same way, connected through your PC's floppy disk interface. QIC-80 just adds extra capacity through data compression.

The number indicates the primary storage capacity of a cartridge that follows the standard. These capacities are only nominal, how-ever. Some cartridges are stuffed with more tape to stretch QIC-40 drives to 60 megabytes, or QIC-80 to 120 megabytes. And, of course, tapes can be used to store less than their full capacities. Table 12.1 lists some of the different tape cartridges available.

Table 12.1 Data cartridge tape types

Model	Nominal Length (feet)	Tracks	Data Density (FTPI*)	Nominal Capacity (MB)
-- DC2000-STYLE --				
DC2000	205	24	12,500	40
DC2080	205	32	15,000	80
DC2110	205	32	20,000	86
DC2120	307.5	32	15,000	120
DC2165	307.5	32	20,000	128
-- DC6000-STYLE --				
DC300A	300	4	3,200	2.9
DC300XL/P	450	9	3,200-10,000	45
DC600A	600	16	10,000	60
DC615A	150	16	12,500	15
DC600HC	600	16	10,000	67
DC600HW	600	11	10,000	60
DC6150	620	32	12,500	150
DC6250	1020	32	12,500	250
DC6037	155	32	12,500	37
DC6320	620	26	20,000	320
DC6525	1020	26	20,000	525

Among DC6000 systems, most of the QIC standards don't specify the exact format to store data on tapes, so they don't guarantee that tapes can be exchanged between different makers' systems. However, the standards are worth looking for because they help to ensure software compatibility. That, in turn, helps you when you want to exchange tapes. Two tape systems that follow the same cartridge standards and use the same software are likely to be able to share tapes with one another. The most popular standards you'll see for DC6000 cartridge systems are QIC-02, QIC-36, and SCSI. Each of these standards is supported by a third-party software such as Sytron Corporation's SYTOS. Be careful when you buy. While nearly all currently manufactured tape drives follow one of these standards, closeout products do not. Drives that opt for proprietary standards may be insupportable without their manufacturers' software.

Bottom line: When you consider tape backup, you need to think of it not just as a drive unit, but as a complete system—you need both the hardware and software.

Shopping for a Tape Drive

When you start shopping for a DC2000-based tape upgrade, you'll find that the use of your PC's floppy disk interface adds another complication to the selection process. All floppy disk drives are not created equal and consequently all floppy disk controllers are not equal. Older floppy disks—those that use 360K-capacity, double-density disks—operate with a data transfer rate of 250K bits per second, while newer $5\frac{1}{4}$- and $3\frac{1}{2}$-inch high-density drives operate with transfer rates of 500K bps. (The latest 2.88MB floppies have a data transfer rate of 1 megabit/second.) Some floppy disk controllers were designed to operate at one or the other of these speeds. While newer DC2000-style tape drives can adjust themselves to operate at either speed, some older units were designed to operate solely at one or the other speed.

Unfortunately, you can't tell the difference simply by looking at the drive, so you must insist you get a tape system that's compatible with the speed of your floppy disk controller—or, if you're getting a new controller along with your tape drive, you must make sure that their speeds match. This speed difference is sometimes described in terms of host compatibility. A tape system that's only PC-compatible is probably rated at 250K bps. A tape system that's classed as AT-compatible but not PC-compatible operates at 500K bps.

A final consideration in selecting the cartridge type you want to use: The tape upgrade you select should fit inside your PC. Nearly all DC2000 tape drives are the same size as standard $3\frac{1}{2}$-inch floppy disk drives. They will fit anywhere a $3\frac{1}{2}$-inch floppy disk drive will, including in a $5\frac{1}{4}$-inch drive bay with the appropriate adapter.

Most of today's DC6000 tape drives are the same size as half-height $5\frac{1}{4}$-inch disk drives. While they will fit easily into a full-size computer, you may have difficulty squeezing one into a really compact machine, such as a desktop IBM PS/2 (except for the latest models that have $5\frac{1}{4}$-inch drive bays). Of course, drives that won't fit into your computer's chassis can be installed externally, but you'll need to buy an external unit (which is more expensive) or put together a case, power supply, and the proper cables to make a unmounted tape drive work. That will add to the cost and complexity of making the upgrade.

All things considered, you'll probably find a DC2000 tape cartridge system to be the best choice for backing up single-user computers with disk sizes up to 120 megabytes. Multiuser systems and PCs with larger disks are better served by the bigger DC6000 cartridges.

Physical Installation Considerations

Installation procedures for DC2000 and DC6000 cartridge systems differ because of the different size of the drives and different interfaces they use. Moreover, installation will vary with the system that you install them in. In particular, IBM's PS/2s used a novel floppy disk mounting scheme that simplifies tape drive installation. Each of the installation variations will be covered separately.

Before you begin *any* tape drive installation, however, prepare a place to work. Switch off the power to your PC and remove the power cable from your PC to ensure that you don't inadvertently switch the machine on while you're working. You'll also need to remove the cover from your system's case and, with some systems, the front fascia panel.

Installing a DC2000 system is invariably the easiest job because you need not tangle with odd adapters and complex system interactions. All that's usually required is plugging in a cable and screwing in the drive.

Because most DC2000 systems use the floppy disk interface of your PC, you've got to make electrical room for the drive before you can hope to install it. You need to have a free channel on your PC's floppy disk controller.

In most systems, that means you can have only one floppy disk drive in addition to your tape backup system because most floppy disk controllers can handle only two drives. There are exceptions, of course. For example, the original IBM PC floppy disk controller can handle four floppies—although you probably won't want to install a tape backup system in a PC because PCs don't have hard disks.

Some mail-order vendors offer work-arounds for people who need more than one floppy disk. You can add a special additional floppy disk controller that provides connections for a pair of extra drives, or you can replace your old floppy disk controller with one capable of operating four floppy disk drives. An elite few tape drives offer *disk multiplexing*, which allows the tape system to share a channel of your disk controller with a floppy disk drive.

Adding extra floppy disk control channels to your PC can be complicated. For example, if you have a PC with its floppy disk electronics built into its system board, you'll have to defeat your system's existing floppy disk control circuitry before you can install a four-drive controller. If you cannot defeat these circuits, you'll have to suffer with one floppy. Check your PC's instruction manual. Typically you'll find what you need to know where the instructions list jumper or DIP switch settings.

Outside of finding a free floppy controller channel, you shouldn't have any hardware worries with readying your system for a DC2000 drive. If the controller works for one floppy disk drive, odds are greatly in your favor that it will also work for the tape backup system.

In general, the only time you'll need to adjust your PC's set-up when installing a DC2000 tape system is when you replace an existing floppy disk drive with the tape drive. In that case, just run your computer's set-up program and inform your system of the number of floppy disk drives that are actually installed. Don't count your tape system as a floppy disk drive, even though it is connected to the floppy controller. If you do, your PC's power-on diagnostic will assume that the tape drive is a floppy disk drive—which, of course, it isn't—and report that the properly functioning tape drive looks like a broken floppy disk drive. To your system, your new tape drive should appear to not exist.

Installing DC2000 Drives in PS/2s

IBM's PS/2s make the addition of a DC2000 tape backup system easy. First, you'll need to prepare your second floppy disk bay for your new tape system. Simply remove the blank front panel from the bay. These panels snap into place, so you just snap it out.

Next, ready the drive. You'll need to attach the mounting sled to the bottom of the drive. The plastic sled has four places for screws

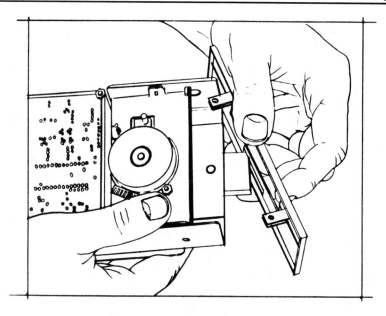

Figure 12.2 Most DC2000-style tape drives must be adapted to fit $5\frac{1}{4}$-inch drive bays. The first step is to install the proper bezel on the front of the drive to fit it to a $5\frac{1}{4}$-inch or $3\frac{1}{2}$-inch drive bay.

that match the mounting holes on $3\frac{1}{2}$-inch drives. Put a screw in each.

In PS/2s, you don't have to worry about cabling because the tape drive, like a second floppy disk drive, plugs directly into a waiting connector at the back of the drive bay. Some drives need adapters to match their electrical connections—the edge connectors on the backs of the drive—to the special connectors used by PS/2s. If your drive requires an adapter, install it before you put the drive in your computer.

Next, slide your new tape drive into the vacant floppy disk bay. At it reaches the end of its travel, you'll have to increase the force you apply to mate the connectors together. The sled will lock itself into place with a slight snap when the drive is fully inserted. Cover the drive with the new fascia that accompanied it, and you're finished.

If you've replaced a floppy disk drive in your PS/2 with the tape drive, you'll have to run the system set-up procedure on your computer's Reference Diskette to tell your PS/2 that you've cut down to

Figure 12.3 To make a $3\frac{1}{2}$-inch DC2000-style drive fit a $5\frac{1}{4}$-inch bay, you'll next need to install adapters (inset) to make the drive wide enough to secure in the bay. Simply screw the adapters to the sides of the drive, taking care that the adapters fit properly against the bezel.

only one floppy disk drive. Once set-up completes, you're ready to run your backup software on your new drive.

Installing DC2000 Drives in $3\frac{1}{2}$-inch Bays

Installing a DC2000 drive in systems with $3\frac{1}{2}$-inch drive bays is only a bit more complicated than PS/2 installation. First, you'll mount the appropriate fascia on the front of the tape drive or the front panel of your computer. Then, put the drive approximately in place and connect the cables to it. The drive will require both a power and signal connection (see below). Then, screw the tape drive into the drive bay. Depending on your computer, you'll either attach the drive by its side or its bottom. In either case, you'll want to use all four screws to ensure a secure mounting.

When your PC has only $5\frac{1}{4}$-inch drive bays, installation is complicated by one additional step, attaching a drive-bay adapter to the

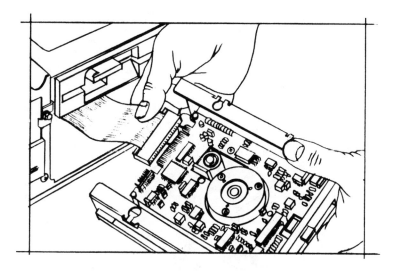

Figure 12.4 Before you slide the DC2000-style drive into its bay (or after you have it partly in place) plug the drive into the B: drive floppy disk connector. The B: drive connector will generally be in the middle of the floppy disk signal cable. Next, connect a power cable to the drive.

drive. These adapters are usually included with all DC2000 tape drives; to be sure that you get one, make certain that your source of supply knows what size bay your tape system must fit into.

The adapter typically comprises three pieces that fit together as a single assembly. Two of these are U-shaped metal channels that extend the width of the tape drive; the other piece is a front fascia panel to match the small drive to the larger $5\frac{1}{4}$-inch opening in your computer's front panel. Simply screw one of the adapter channels onto each side of the drive. Once the adapter is installed, the DC2000 drive is effectively a $5\frac{1}{4}$-inch half-height device that installs in a drive bay exactly like a DC6000 tape drive.

Installing DC6000 Drives

Physically installing a DC6000 tape drive or a DC2000 drive adapter to a $5\frac{1}{4}$-inch bay is as straightforward as installing a hard disk drive. The hardware you need depends on the mounting scheme used by

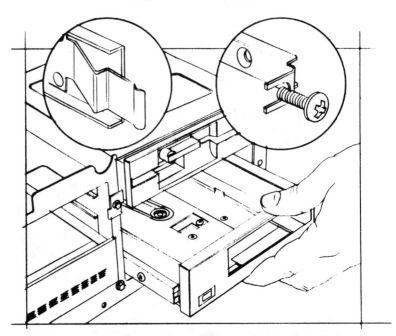

Figure 12.5 No matter the kind of drive you have, the final installation step is to slide it all the way into its bay. Check the connections, then screw the drive in place with AT-style brackets, one-piece brackets (right inset), or snap-in brackets (left inset) as required by your system.

your PC, but the mechanics are easy to figure out in any case. See the Appendix for drive-mounting details.

No matter what mounting hardware you use, the first step in mounting any tape drive is to put the drive approximately in place. Attach its cables to it before you screw the drive into place. This will give you more working room and save the skin on your knuckles. You need to plug in a power connector from your PC's power supply and the signal cable from the tape drive controller or, in the case of DC2000 drives, your floppy disk controller. One rule applies to the signal cable: The stripe on the edge of the cable goes to pin one on the tape drive connector.

What to do in the next step—securing your drive inside your computer—depends on the drive-mounting scheme used in your PC. The most straightforward is the direct-mounting method used by computers since the original PC. Drive units—disk or tape—are directly screwed into the disk bay using either of the sets of screw holes on the sides of the $5\frac{1}{4}$-inch device.

Mounting drives in IBM PCs and XTs and many clones using this direct approach has one disadvantage: The drives are held only on one side. For tape drives, this mounting method is particularly inadequate because of the high force require to insert a tape cartridge in the drive. This insertion force is high enough that you may bend the bay or break mounting screws when you try to cram a cartridge into the drive. Should your system provide access only to one side of the drive, you'll want to be certain your new tape unit is held as securely in place as its screws permit.

Better compatible computers (particularly tower-style cases) provide access to both sides of their $5\frac{1}{4}$-inch drive bays. Be sure to take advantage of the security offered by these computers and use all four screws to hold your tape drive in place, two on each side.

If you have an IBM AT or compatible computer with a case patterned after it, you'll find secure tape drive installation is easy. Standard $5\frac{1}{4}$-inch drives are installed using mounting rails attached to their sides that allow you to slide the drives into place. The rails fit into guide slots that hold the drive assembly securely on both sides. Many $5\frac{1}{4}$-inch tape drives—both DC6000 and DC2000 units with adapters already installed—come with AT-mounting kits or with the rails already installed on the sides of the drive.

Some AT-compatibles—notably Compaq Deskpros—use a similar mounting scheme with slightly wider rails that are incompatible with standard AT rails and the AT chassis. If you have one of these machines or a similar computer, you'll either have to scavenge rails from a device you'll be retiring from your system or attempt to get new rails to match your computer, which can sometimes be a challenge.

Another variety of AT-compatibles use drive-mounting rails that are narrower and, consequently, also incompatible with IBM rails. Most machines that use these narrow rails preinstall a set in each drive bay of the computer, even those without drives. In this case, you only need to detach the rails from the chassis, screw them to your disk, and slide the disk into place.

Rails are held in the computer chassis in one of two ways. IBM-style systems use small brackets that push the rails to the end of their travel in the bay. Some compatibles make the brackets part of the drive rails. In either case, one screw holds each bracket in place.

Just unscrew it to slide the old drive out and screw the bracket back in to hold your drive upgrade in place.

Tower-style IBM PS/2s use rails that are close enough to those used by the AT that AT rails will work in the internal $5\frac{1}{4}$-inch drive cages of these PS/2s. To loosen a drive in one of these computers so that you can slide it out of the chassis, press down on each of the large blue daisy-like knobs above the drive and turn it counterclockwise with the palm of your hand until the drive can slide out.

You must use the front bay in these computers so that the front of the drive is accessible through the fascia panel of your computer. You'll also have to remove the factory-installed blank panel from in front of the drive bay. To do this, pry off the entire fascia assembly (it should come off easily enough that putting your fingernails behind it will be sufficient). Once you've removed the fascia, just push the blank panel out through the back of the fascia.

If you have a DC6000 system, the next step is to install the tape controller. Put it in an expansion slot as close as possible to the tape drive. Most tape controllers use 8-bit interfaces so they will fit into any expansion slot that will physically accommodate the board. Usually, the best slot to use is the one adjacent to your hard disk controller. Once the board is in place, route the tape drive's signal cable to the controller as best you can and plug it in.

Using a DC6000 tape system with a modern small-footprint computer that has only $3\frac{1}{2}$-inch bays will require an external chassis. Some mail-order vendors offer drive units already installed in their own chassis with power supplies. Alternately, you can buy an internal drive and another vendor's case. Cases with room for two half-height $5\frac{1}{4}$-inch drives complete with their own power supply are available for under $50.

If you opt for the external system, ensure that the tape drive controller offers an external connector so that you can conveniently plug in the drive. You'll also want a cable with connectors at either end that match the drive and the controller.

Cabling Concerns

DC2000 tape drives follow the same cabling rules as floppy disk drives. That is, as with all devices, the red strip on the cable indicates the edge of the cable associated with pin one on the connector. Disk drive and tape drive signal cable-edge connectors have a small slot between their contact fingers, and this slot is always nearer the pin one edge of the connector.

In a system that has a floppy disk controller that handles two drives, tape drives must always be installed using the Drive B: cable connector. If you use the Drive A: connector, your computer would try to boot from the tape drive, which is generally impossible.

In the standard IBM-compatible cabling scheme, Drive B: is determined by the signal cable. Drive B: uses the connector in the middle of the two-drive daisy-chain floppy disk signal cable. Drive A: uses the connector at the end of the cable that has a twist in the cable right before the connector.

You'll also have to deal with the signal termination of your DC2000 tape drive. Tape terminations are handled as with floppy disk drives. When you install your tape drive using the Drive B: cable connector, you'll want to remove the termination resistor from the disk drive.

Each DC6000 interface standard uses slightly different cabling. With QIC-02 and QIC-36 systems, the only important issue is that you ensure that the red stripe on the connecting cable is on the same side of the connector as pin one on each end of the cable. Pin one is usually marked with a small "1" on the circuit board itself. With these interfaces, you don't have to worry about cable terminations.

SCSI drives require that you set a unique SCSI ID on the drive. The manual that comes with the software you will use with the tape drive will tell you what SCSI ID to use. In addition, you must terminate the first and last device in the SCSI daisy chain, but not the middle devices. Most SCSI devices have three terminating resistor packs, all three of which must be removed when a termination is not to be made. The Appendix includes more details about connecting SCSI devices.

Once your tape drive is in place and its cables are connected, and before you put the cover back on your PC, you should install your backup software. Most backup programs have built-in test procedures that will confirm that all went well with the installation of your new tape backup upgrade. After everything checks out, reassemble your PC. You can now make your first backup—and sleep easier.

13.

POWER SUPPLIES AND BACKUP POWER SYSTEMS

Computer circuits need a safe and steady supply of electricity to operate. A power supply gives its circuits safe power; a backup power system helps make it steady. Some PCs need more power than their power supplies offer and thus require a power supply upgrade when other parts of the system are upgraded. On the other hand, any PC—and PC user—can benefit from a backup power upgrade that makes work in progress invulnerable to power outages.

Electricity is the life blood of every PC. Every flip and flop of a computer's logic circuits requires a pulse of electricity. Not just any electricity will do, either. It must be pure DC, *direct current*, not the indecisive alternating current delivered on power lines.

And computer circuits are delicate, too, instantly destroyed by a direct shot from the 120 volts of the power line. Computer semiconductor circuits prefer their DC at a modest level of just five volts, although some disk drives need twelve to make their motors spin.

Not only do PCs require their own particular voltages to operate, they require them continuously. Interrupt the flow of electricity, and your PC will literally lose its mind. Every byte in its memory will evaporate faster than a tear in a hot skillet. The shortest interruption in utility power—a break no longer than the blink of your eye—and all you'll be staring at is the boot-up screen again, if you're lucky. If you're not especially blessed, however, your PC might never recover from a power failure, its circuits seared by the surge that often accompanies the restoration of power.

Delivering exactly the kind of electricity your computer needs is the job of its power supply. Assuring that there is a constant supply of electricity to run the power is the job of the backup power system. Of the two, the power supply has the simpler job. It only needs to transform the power line downward to the more sedate levels used by your PC's integrated circuits and rectify the line current, changing its AC into DC. Backup power systems have to detect power failures, generate the right kind of electricity to run your PC, and keep their own internal battery supply (where they get their electricity when your favorite utility decides not to provide it) fully charged. The power supply is mandatory; your PC won't run without it. The backup power system is optional; your PC will work without one, but you might not want to risk the consequences.

Power upgrades involve one of two changes: Getting more available electricity to run power-hungry peripherals like big internal hard disks and adding backup power to remove temptation from the Fates. The first means installing a power supply with greater capacity to your PC; the latter, plugging your PC into a backup power supply or sliding an internal power source inside your PC. This chapter will examine both upgrades.

The Purpose of the Power Supply

The electricity your PC demands from its power supply can be copious. For example, a 386 microprocessor alone is made from 375,000 or so transistors, each one thirsty for a few microwatts of electricity. As personal computers and the microprocessor they are built from become increasingly powerful, that need for power inside the PC increases as well. In fact, basic physical laws dictate that the faster a computer's circuitry operates, the more power it will consume— just as your car needs more gas for every mile-per-hour it travels over the 55 MPH limit.

And there's the problem and the reason you might consider the need for a power supply upgrade. No power supply can deliver unlimited amounts of DC. The components that make up the power supply face maximum limits beyond which they might overheat and melt down—literally. Fortunately, power supplies, like nuclear reactors, have safety shutdown circuits which turn the unit off, usually before any damage is done. That is, before any damage is done to the power supply itself. However, the simple act of shutting down is fatal to the data you're working on in your PC. That's what happens when your computer's power supply is inadequate to supply the needs of its circuitry. At some unpredictable time, the overworked power supply is liable to shut down on its own, leaving you in the dark and angry.

Today, most computers have power supplies that are able to handle 200 watts or more. That's generally more than enough to satisfy the needs of even a grandly expanded computer. But the power supply of the original IBM PC was rated at a modest 63.5 watts, and that's inadequate to run a typical hard disk in addition to the computer's own circuitry. Other computers, too, were designed and equipped with power supplies of less than 100 watts. Even the 135 watts of the IBM XT can be too small in some situations. If you're building your own PC—or have built one—the watts available from the power supply (and consumed by the PC's circuitry) will similarly be important to you. You, too, may be a candidate for an improved power supply.

Upgrading your computer's power supply if it is too small will give your machine the power potential it needs for reliable expansion. It may even help your machine run cooler—and that means longer, too. Even if your computer has an adequate power supply, there can be some good reasons for upgrading, and they involve keeping both you and your PC happy. In most desktop computers, all the cooling is entrusted to the fan inside the power supply. This one fan is charged not only with keeping the Fahrenheit inside the power supply under control, but also with circulating the air inside the entire chassis of your computer to keep its microprocessor, memory, and support circuitry from overheating. Moving too little air means insufficient circulation and heat build-up. That, in turn, can trim the life of your computer's internal components.

There's one more reason to contemplate a power supply upgrade. The fan in a computer's power supply is usually the noisiest element inside most computers. In fact, some systems sound as loud as a Hoover caught in a hurricane. Too many people put up with the caterwauling of their computers because they think they have no choice. But you do. Make the right power supply upgrade for your computer, and you can diminish the decibel output of a PC to the tolerable range.

Power Supply Upgrade Facts and Dangers

First things first—maintain your safety when dealing with devices that handle potentially fatal amounts of electricity. You want to be sure that the jolts put out by the power supply won't end up coursing through your body. Fortunately, when dealing with PC power supplies, most of your worries of electrocution are groundless. There's nothing dangerous in dealing with computer power supplies. They are sealed assemblies that have no exposed life-threatening voltages that you might accidentally touch. The likelihood that you might even get a shock during a power supply upgrade is about the same as the probability that a comet will crash down on your house tonight. Nor is there any danger to your computer's delicate electronic components if you're careful and follow the step-by-step procedure outlined here.

Moreover, no skill and (generally) only one tool—a screwdriver or nutdriver—is required to make a power supply upgrade. Changing a power supply is among the easiest things you can do to your PC. The entire operation usually can be completed in ten minutes.

And upgrading a power supply is cheap. Moving from 63.5 to 150 watts won't cost you much more than $50 from a reputable mail-order supplier. Premium power supplies—those with big fans for extra cooling or proprietary designs to keep things quiet—do cost substantially more, perhaps three times more than their more ordinary equivalents. Compared to the peace of mind and quiet operation they can bring, however, that's not at all much.

What a Power Supply Does

The design purpose of every computer power supply, no matter the watts it makes, is the same: Convert utility power into a carefully regulated source of the low DC voltages needed for operating computer circuitry. But that rated wattage does matter, and there are important differences you must consider when you select a power supply upgrade. You have your choice of rated output, the number and style of the connectors at which that power is delivered, the size and shape of the case in which the necessary power conversion electronics are packed, and the cooling that's provided to your system.

Computer power supplies are rated in the number of watts that they can deliver before overloading. In direct current circuits, like those of a computer, the number of watts is equal to the product of the volts and current (the amperage or number of amps) delivered. For example, a computer power supply might produce 5 volts at 20 amps and thus achieve an output of 100 watts.

The power supplies for practical PCs must deliver several voltages, however. In addition to a positive polarity 5 volts, they also need to produce -5 volts, 12 volts, and -12 volts. The rating of a power supply is the total of the output at each of these voltages.

Most of a circuitry in a personal computer uses positive five volts, so this potential usually has the highest rating of any of a power supply's output, typically 20 to 30 amperes. Disk drives typically use 12 volts to operate their motors, so the positive 12 volt supply is usually the next highest rated, usually from three to five amperes. The other two voltages are used by some specialized circuitry (for example, serial ports use both positive and negative voltages), but only in small amounts. Consequently, the negative outputs of computer power supplies are normally quite modest, often a fraction of an amp.

How Much Power You Need

The amount of power you need for your PC varies with what you want to do with it. Every PC is made with what its manufacturer considers to be an adequate power supply. But manufacturers rarely anticipate everything that you want to add to your PC. The original IBM PC, for example, was not designed to accept a hard disk drive, and consequently lacks sufficient power to operate one.

The power requirement of any computer system varies with the number of electronic components—expansion boards, disk drives, and the like—that you install inside it. External peripherals that plug in to wall outlets, of course, make no additional demands on your PC's power supply. The amount of power varies among expansion accessories. A short expansion board with just a serial and parallel port on it might consume as little as a watt. A big hard disk drive might need 50 or more. Table 13.1 gives some rough estimates of the amount of power required by various system components.

The power requirements of any computer system varies with the number of electronic components—expansion boards, disk drives, and the like—installed in it. Every system has different power demands. The chart below will help you estimate how much power your system may require.

Note none of these numbers is exact. Nor do they not apply to any particular products. Expansion boards differ substantially in the amount of circuitry from which they are made and their consequent power needs. Similarly, some disk drives operate more efficiently than others.

Table 13.1 **Typical power requirements in PCs:**

Expansion boards:

Packed AT-size board	15 watts
Full-length board	10 watts
Short Card	5 watts

Floppy disk drives (when running):

Old full-height 5.25 inch	15 watts
Half-height 5.25 inch	10 watts
3.5 inch	5 watts

Hard disk drives:

Full-height 5.25 inch	25 watts
Half-height 5.25 inch	15 watts
High-capacity 3.5 inch	10 watts
Low-power 3.5 inch	5 watts

System board:

PC or XT	20 watts
Older 286	40 watts
Newer 286	20 watts
Newer 386	25 watts
486	35 watts

In general, the values given are worst-case figures. Relying on these numbers will most often cause you to over estimate the power needs of your computer. That's the safest strategy because it helps assure that you'll have more than adequate power reserves.

When figuring power supply requirements, remember to start the tally with the system board. You'll need to add the requirements of one floppy disk system (DOS only allows one floppy disk drive to spin at a time), the hard disk (which constantly spins and thus has a constant need for power), and each of the expansion boards you've shoved into the system's slots.

Once you start adding up the needs of everything in the typical system, you see that 63.5 watts is clearly inadequate for any computer today, except laptop machines (which are not designed for extensive expansion, anyhow). One hundred watts is marginal for most PCs. Even the 135 watt rating of the original IBM XT is probably insufficient for a high-performance computer, particularly one that must handle a fast, high-capacity hard disk and multiple megabytes of fast memory. Today, 150 watts is probably the minimum you'll want in a desktop machine.

Power Supply Connections

How all those watts are delivered is also an important aspect of the power supply that you consider for your upgrade. The power supply must be able to connect to the system board of your PC and to all the disk and tape drives in its bays. For each device you attach to the power supply, you'll need one or more power connectors.

The connectors for the disk and tape drives are the easy part. All full-size disk (and tape) drives use the same style connector, and all commercially available power supplies use these connectors. About the only difference you'll find in drive power connectors is their number.

Quite simply, more is better. Four connectors are usually—but not always—standard on most power supplies. You probably won't want a power supply with fewer than four drive power connectors—that's enough for two floppies, one hard disk, and a tape drive or CD ROM player, or something that's still lurking in the back of a creative engineer's head.

Besides their number, how those connectors are attached to the power supply is also important to consider before you make a purchase. Some power supply makers put multiple connectors on a single set of wires from the power supply. This can be inconvenient because you may have to make odd twists in the cable—even stretch it—to connect multiple drives. The better arrangement is to give each drive power connector its own set of wires from the power supply box.

The connectors that plug into your PC's system board are another story. Every power supply and system board manufacturer seems to have its own standard. Pre-PS/2 IBM computers use two Burndy connectors for the system board link-up. PS/2s often (but, again, not always) combine the two connectors into one. While other manufacturers use Burndy connectors, many also use slightly different Molex connectors. The two are not 100 percent compatible.

One difference between the two connector types is that the pins of a Burndy are rectangular. Molex system board connectors use smaller, square pins. Only with great effort can you mate dissimilar connectors together. Before you order a power supply, take a close look at the connectors on the system board. You may want to disconnect one (with your PC switched off, of course) to examine the shape of its pins.

Most power supplies come equipped with Burndy connectors. Consequently, power supplies with Molex connectors are rare. You'll have to look harder to find them. Be sure to ask the vendor you order your power supply from what kind of connectors it uses.

Physical Considerations

In fitting a new power supply into your computer, the critical issue is whether the new unit will fit inside your system's existing case. In general, two standard sizes of power supply are available: those designed to fit the original IBM PC, XT and similar-sized chassis, and those made for the AT and its clones. AT power supplies are larger and, in keeping with their size, have higher power ratings. AT supplies generally start at 192 watts and are available in 250 watts and higher ratings. About 150 watts is tops for PC/XT power supplies.

The PC/XT power supply is a rectangular box that measures $4\frac{1}{2}$ × $8\frac{1}{2}$ × $5\frac{1}{2}$ inches (h × w × d). One side features a plastic extension that holds the big red paddle connected to an internal power switch. The jacks and cutouts on the rear panel are designed to mate with openings in the rear panel of the PC and XT chassis. Consequently, these locations have become somewhat standardized.

AT power supplies are vaguely L-shaped and measure $5\frac{1}{2}$ × $8\frac{1}{2}$ × 6 inches (h × w × d). Part of one corner is notched out to allow room underneath for the larger system boards in AT-size chassis. Again a big, red paddle is brought out from the power switch on the right side of the power supply, and the various jacks and fan openings on the rear panel have been standardized to match the corresponding holes in the AT rear panel.

Some power supply designs take liberties with the normal IBM component layout, however. In some cases, that's great. For example, adding a bigger fan or pair of fans and altering the shape of the power supply box can help give your PC better cooling abilities. But other modifications are undesirable. Rearranging the power switch and outlets are particularly problematic. Such an altered arrangement may make it impossible to install the power supply in your PC chassis. Consequently, when you order a power supply for

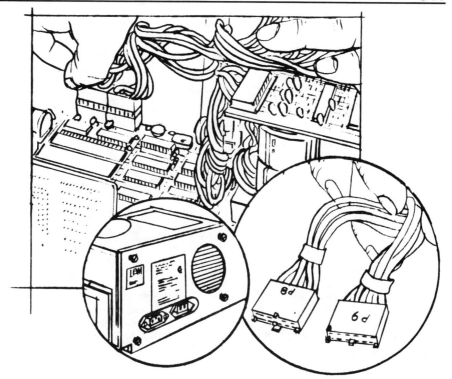

Figure 13.1 After you've disconnected all external cables from your PC, disconnect the internal cables to the power supply. In most cases, you'll find two, labeled P8 and P9 (right inset). Then remove the four screws that secure the power supply to your PC's chassis. The screws are located approximately in each of the four corners of the power supply (left inset).

your upgrade, ensure that it is an exact external match for the IBM design—and that the vendor will accept its return (without restocking charge) if it does not.

Personal computers that don't follow the IBM packaging scheme pose problems when you want to upgrade the power supply. You're likely to have a difficult time finding a power supply that will match the size and mounting requirements of a proprietary case, including those used by Compaq computers.

From an upgrade standpoint, that's hardly a dire situation. Most compatible computers (and even IBM machines) now have adequate power reserves for ordinary—and even extraordinary—system expansion. If you want to upgrade a non-IBM system for another reason (for example, to silence the turbo-charged wind-

Figure 13.2 Once the power supply screws are removed, push the power supply toward the front of your PC with firm, even pressure. It should be difficult to dislodge at first, but wil get easier to move the farther you press it forward.

machine noise of a late-model Compaq Deskpro), however, you may be out of luck. Should you want to replace the power supply in one of these nonstandard computers as a repair measure, you're likely to be stuck depending on the manufacturer of the computer to supply you with what you need.

Removing Old Power Supplies

The first step in any power supply upgrade is obvious—remove the old to make room for the new. But before you go wild with a screwdriver, you'll want to take a couple of preparatory steps to guard against complications caused by idiosyncrasies in the original manufacture of your PC. The design of the PC power system is supposed to be idiot-proof, but there is always some idiot in the factory willing to take up the challenge.

Begin by ensuring your safety and that of your computer. Remove all cables from all jacks on the rear panel of your PC. This will also give you the side benefit of flexibility—you'll be able to move

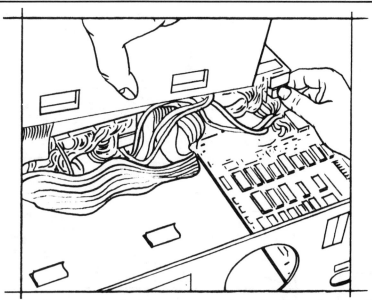

Figure 13.3 After you've pushed the power supply as far forward as it will go, you can lift it straight up and out of your PC. If it's still tethered by a cable or two, remove them now. Note the retaining tabs at the bottom of the chassis and matching holes in the power supply itself.

your PC anywhere you want, and turn it upside down if necessary, to make the removal and installation job easier.

Turn your PC off. Then unplug the power cord, the cord leading from the power supply to your monitor (if there is one), and all the cables attached to all of the expansion board-retaining brackets at the back of your computer. If you suspect age is taking a toll on your short-term memory, you may want to mark which connectors go into which jacks before you disconnect them all. Just for good measure, disconnect the keyboard cable and mouse.

Once you can freely move your PC around, remove the top of its case. The tops of most PCs, XTs, and ATs are held in place by five screws on the rear panel; the first PCs had only three screws. In any event, these will be the screws closest to the edges of the rear panel—one in the center; one in each of the lower corners; and, in machines using five screws, two in the upper corners. Put the screws in a safe place, then pull the top of the computer's case all the way forward, angle it upward, and lift it off.

Once you can peer inside your PC, the power supply will be easy to identify. It's the shiny chrome-plated box in the right-rear cor-

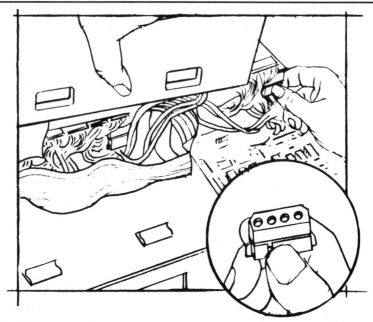

Figure 13.4 Before you drop the new power supply into place, you'll have an easier time reconnecting the power plugs to your disk drives. Hold the power supply with one hand and connect the power plugs with the other. The plugs are keyed to prevent you from inserting them improperly (insert), so if they don't fit, turn the plug over and try again.

ner. All of the power cables that you will need to deal with emerge from the left side of that box. You must disconnect all of these cables from the devices that they plug into. You cannot disconnect them from the power supply itself.

You'll find the job easier if you do the disconnecting in two stages. In the first stage, remove the one or two cables that connect the power supply to your system board. At this point, however, take a moment for one of those extra steps to ensure installing your new power supply will be trouble-free.

The connectors on these cables are supposed to be keyed so you cannot insert them improperly. However, sometimes the keys—tiny tabs that prevent you from inserting connectors in the wrong jacks—break off the connectors. Sometimes manufacturers remove all the keys themselves. In either case, it might be possible to plug the connectors of your new power supply upgrade in improperly.

To avoid dire consequences, take note of the colors of wires and the position of each color while the connectors are plugged into your system board. Write down the color scheme. Only then should you unplug the system board connectors.

You will find it helpful if you partly remove your existing power supply before you remove the power connectors from your disk drives. Consequently, the next step in this upgrade is to remove the four screws that hold the power supply in place. These screws are all located on the rear panel of your PC where they form a rectangle. Unscrew all four (in most cases a nutdriver is the best tool, though some manufacturers use Phillips screws), and put the screws in a safe place.

At this point, your old power supply might not feel the slightest bit loose. That's normal. It's still held in place by two tabs in its bottom. To free up the power supply, put your fingers around the edges of the chassis (taking care to not cut yourself on sharp edges—you may want to put on your mittens, just in case), and push the power supply toward the front of the computer with your thumbs. Don't jam it. Gradually increase the pressure with your thumbs until the power supply slides forward. The more it moves, the looser it will become.

When you finally push it far enough forward that it lightly touches the back of the disk drive bay, it will be free enough that you can lift it partly out of your computer's chassis. Because the drive cables are still attached, you'll probably have to rotate the power supply forward to lift it completely out.

While holding your old power supply with one hand, use the other hand to remove the power connectors from each of your disk and tape drives. Once these connectors are removed, nothing should be holding the old power supply to your PC anymore. Put the old power supply aside.

You may want to take advantage of this opportunity to clean up the inside of your PC. You can gently vacuum out the dust using a soft rubber attachment to your sweeper—one with a brush on the end will help dislodge the more reluctant dust bunnies.

Installing a New Power Supply

Installing the new power supply is pretty much the reverse of the removal process, but if you take a moment to familiarize yourself with the attachment scheme, the operation will go much easier.

Figure 13.5 Put the new power supply into your PC—lower it as far forward as it will go, then push it back into place, making sure it catches on the tabs in the bottom of the chassis. Then start each of the four screws that hold the power supply in place. After you've started all four, tighten each one down.

Examine the bottom of the power supply and you'll see two slots stamped into it. At the bottom of the chassis of your computer, you should be able to see two matching fingers stamped into the metal work. The fingers slide into the slots and hold the power supply down inside the chassis. When you put the power supply into the chassis, you'll have to make sure that those fingers properly engage.

Once you've completed the familiarization tour, hold the new power supply just above the vacant area in which it will be installed. The on/off switch should be on the right side, looking from the front of your PC.

Now plug one drive power connector into each of your disk drives. These connectors are keyed by two beveled corners so that you cannot insert them improperly. If a connector doesn't slide into the jack of one of your disk drives, turn the connector over and try again.

After all the drive power connectors are in place, lower the new power supply into the chassis.

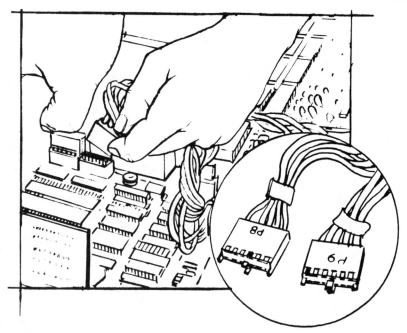

Figure 13.6 Finally, plug the two power supply plugs (P8 and P9) back into your system board. Note the keying tabs on the connectors. If the connectors on your power supply have more than one tab per plug, remove all but those shown in black in the inset.

When the power supply touches bottom, push it gently as far toward the front of your PC as you can. It should rest against the back of the drive bays. Now push down on the power supply to press it all the way into the chassis.

Gently slide the power supply toward the rear panel of your PC while you hold it down. The fingers in the chassis should engage the slots and make it progressively more difficult the farther back you push the power supply. You might not even get it to exactly touch the rear panel of the chassis. As long as it comes within about one-eighth of an inch of the rear panel, you don't need to worry. The screws will tighten it into place.

There's a trick to getting all the screws into your new power supply. First start one screw in the matching hole in the chassis and power supply. Make sure it turns freely, and spin it only one or two turns into place, *not* all the way. Then start the second screw, the third, and the fourth. Don't tighten any of the screws until they all have been started. That way you can shift the power supply around a little bit to get all the screws to fit properly. Once all four screws have been started, you can tighten them all in any order.

Finally, reconnect the power supply connectors to your system board. This simple task is the one place where you're likely to run into problems.

Many power supplies come with all of their plastic-tab keys in place on their system board power connectors. These tabs will prevent you from inserting either connector into the jacks on your system board. To make the connectors work, you'll have to trim off the excess tabs. Diagonal cutters are the best tool to use, but if you're careful you might cut the extra tabs off with a pen knife or nail clipper. You could even file them off.

The best model you have for getting the keying right is your old power supply. Compare the connectors of the old with the new, and make the new match the old.

With some computers, you'll find all the tabs have been trimmed off. You'll probably have to do likewise. But then you'll need to be very careful when you plug the connector in. Make sure that the connectors, when plugged in, match the color pattern you wrote down before removing the old power supply. *That's* why you wrote down all those colors.

Before you reattach all the external cables to your computer, you should make a safety check. Examine the voltage selector slide switch if your new power supply has one. It should be visible through the rear panel of your PC after the new power supply is installed. The switch will have two settings, typically 115 and 230, or 120 and 240. Standard line voltage in the United States is between 110 and 120 volts. You'll want to make certain that you can see a figure in that range visible on the voltage selector slide switch.

When you're certain the voltage is set properly, reconnect all the external cables to your PC and switch it back on. Your PC should come immediately to life. If it does not, check all the internal cables (and make sure you've plugged your system into a wall outlet). If you've followed all these installation instructions, double-checked your wiring, and your system still does not operate, chances are your new power supply may not be working. Contact your power supply vendor.

Once you're sure your system is operating properly, install whatever new options you've bought that required additional power. Switch your system back on and check it again before you put the top back on the case of your PC. When you're satisfied that all is well, reassemble your PC.

Your PC won't look any different, but you'll feel different—you'll have less to worry about. You'll know that with your new upgrade your PC won't suddenly run short of watts when it needs them most.

Backup Power Systems

If goblins and gremlins do exist, they live not in enchanted hollows or haunted houses but in power lines. The most mysterious of the dangers faced by any computer system are the vagaries of the utility-supplied electricity that runs them: the glitches, surges, sags, spikes, and—most dreaded of all—the blackout. The only weapon that gives protection from power outages is the backup power supply. Better backup power supplies will also ward off the rest of the evils that may be lurking in the electricity you feed your PC.

The protection afforded your PC by a backup power supply varies with the product you choose, however. The basic protection all backup power systems offer is reserve electricity to power PCs through utility failures. When the utility fails, the backup system takes over with its own electrical supply. Better backup units also protect against other power-related problems—*overvoltages*, when utility-supplied electricity inches dangerously above its nominal 120-volt level; *surges*, short bursts of even higher voltage; and *noise*, a potpourri of hitchhiking signals of various frequencies that can interfere with computer circuits. In effect, one upgrade can protect your PC from nearly everything that can sneak into it through its power connection.

To confuse issues, backup power supplies fall into three types, *off-line*, *on-line*, and *internal*. Off-line systems, more frequently called *standby power supplies*, do nothing until the power blacks out, then swing into action. On-line systems, usually called *uninterruptible power systems* (or UPSs), break the direct connection between power line and your computer, constantly conditioning the power that's routed to your PC. An internal system is a cross between standby and uninterruptible systems that installs inside your PC. If you have difficulty distinguishing these three flavors of power protection, you're not alone. The makers of standby supplies are rather indiscriminate (and misleading) in their labeling, often calling their off-line products UPSs. The standards and testing organization Underwriters Laboratories also uses this misleading nomenclature.

The words aren't nearly so important as what the different types of backup power supplies do. If you want to get the right kind of power protection upgrade for your PC, you'll need to know which type of backup device will give you the security you need. Each of the three types of backup system has its own strengths and weaknesses.

Standby Power Supplies

The primary purpose of any backup power system is to jump into action to fill the gaps in supply of electricity provided by your local utility. A standby power supply does exactly that—it stands watch over the utility power supplying your PC and, when the electric supply fails, it switches on to provide power from its internal batteries.

The operative word in that description is *switches*. Ordinarily, the battery current in the standby power supply is not connected to your PC. It switches into action. Making the switch—and even detecting that the utility power has failed at all—requires a short period, a time typically measured in milliseconds. Most PCs ignore such brief gaps in the power supplied to them, so the standby power system is able to create the illusion (to you and your PC) that electricity is continuously available even during a blackout.

The elements of a standby power supply are a set of rechargeable batteries to provide power when none is available from your electrical utility; an inverter, a battery charger that keeps power stockpiled in the batteries; and the switch for making the changeover. Better standby power supplies augment that minimum with spike and surge protection, sometimes even power control features such as multiple-switched outlets to which you can connect the various peripherals of your PC. You can't tell whether this protection is built into a standby power system just by looking. You'll need to check its specifications or ask the salesperson with whom you're negotiating.

The biggest advantage of the standby power system is that it offers affordable blackout protection that's easy to install. Models with surge arrestors will give you the most affordable blanket power protection available.

Uninterruptible Power Supplies

Exactly as its name implies, an uninterruptible power supply, or UPS, creates a constant flow of electricity that is never interrupted, even for the briefest fraction of a second. In its most elegant form, the UPS constantly generates the alternating current required by a PC from its internal batteries. All the while, the batteries are also being charged so the drain on the battery resources is continually replaced. When utility power fails, nothing happens to the output of the UPS because it merely continues to supply battery-backed electricity. The only alteration is that the batteries are no longer being charged, and their reserves slowly drain away.

The important part of this design is that the output and input of this kind of UPS are isolated from each other by the battery. All the evils of utility power are kept out of the supply going to the computer. So the UPS automatically protects against transient high voltages on your power line, the surges and spikes that might otherwise do damage to your PC's electronics. Not only are no additional surge arrestors necessary, the classic UPS yields better protection than just about any ordinary surge protector.

Other kinds of UPS, which are crosses between the classic UPS design and standby power systems, are becoming popular. For example, instead of the input being directly connected to the output of the backup power system (as it would in a pure standby supply), it can be connected through a transformer. The battery-backed part of the power system is connected to another winding of the transformer. When the utility power fails, the battery power section switches on. The reactance of the transformer—electrical energy stored in the magnetic field of the transformer—bridges over the brief gap caused by the switch. The output of the system can thus continue without interruption. Using this design, the battery-charging section of the power supply can be trimmed down in size because it never needs to carry the full output load of the power system.

The problem with UPSs is that they tend to be expensive for the amount of power they can provide. A UPS often costs about twice as much as a standby system with the same ratings. Although a true UPS gives the greatest possible power protection that can be afforded to a PC, a standby system coupled with spike and surge protection can be just as effective. Only a handful of first-generation PCs are so sensitive to brief power lapses that modern standby power supplies with quick switching won't work. (Only a fraction of IBM's original production of Personal Computers XT could not tolerate such quick switches.) If you want the best, opt for a UPS. Otherwise, you'll likely to be able to get along quite nicely with a standby power supply.

Internal Battery Supplies

Ask any criminal. An inside job is best, and that advice holds true even when it comes to a UPS. Putting a UPS inside your PC instead of outside offers some unique benefits that cannot be matched by any other power protection system—not just more safety but a lower price, too. But, of course, this design has its drawbacks as well.

Thanks to miniaturization and a better technological match, all the circuitry necessary to build a UPS—including the battery supply—today can be packed onto a single expansion card that plugs into one of your PC's expansion slots. And on the surface of it, putting a UPS inside a PC makes a lot of sense. The batteries used for backup power naturally produce direct current (DC), exactly the same variety of electricity that's produced by your PC's power supply and used by your computer's circuits. Unlike an external stand-alone UPS, a UPS-on-a-card approach doesn't require expensive circuitry to convert line power to battery power and back again. That saves both space and the cost of materials.

That's not to say building a UPS on an expansion card is trivial. The match between battery and computer current isn't all that perfect. Computer power supplies generate several voltages—plus and minus five volts as well as plus and minus twelve volts—and each would ordinarily require a separate pack of batteries. UPSs-on-a-card avoid the need for multiple battery supplies by incorporating DC conversion circuitry, which is nearly as complex as that required to build an external UPS.

The real problem with putting the UPS inside your PC is that the UPS won't be able to tell the difference between a real power outage and those caused by you flipping the big red power switch off.

The instant you turn off the power to your PC, an internal UPS will detect a power failure and swing into action.

With true computer industry adroitness, the UPS-on-a-card makers have turned this design flaw into a feature—one that can make a UPS-on-a-card an even more valuable product. All current internal UPS cards incorporate state-saving software, programs that automatically save the contents of your PC's memory and state of its microprocessor by copying all that data to the computer's hard disk when the power fails. Restore power to your PC, and the UPS's state-saving software will load everything back into memory so your system can resume from exactly the place it was when the computer was switched off. Taking advantage of this ability, the internal UPS adds an *auto-resume* to your PC—whenever you switch a system with an internal UPS, the state of your PC's RAM will be saved. Turn it back on, and its memory will be reloaded, and you can start your work from exactly where you stopped.

The biggest weakness of the internal UPS is that it offers only one kind of power protection—against total blackouts. Because it is located inside the PC after the power supply, the internal UPS is too far downstream to protect the computer's power supply from spikes and surges in utility power. You'll want to add a surge protection of some kind to your system even if you install an internal UPS. Moreover, the internal UPS won't keep a video monitor, external hard disk system, or external modem operating when utility power fails. You might want to keep a flashlight handy.

Backup Power Strategies

All backup power systems have a single purpose—providing electricity when utility current fails—but they don't have the same use. The difference is what you do with your PC and the kind of protection that you want. The classic case of the backup power system is the blackout bridge. The electricity from the backup system keeps your PC going throughout a power failure. Not only don't you lose your work, you won't even lose your train of thought.

In such an application, a backup power system has to be pretty hefty. Not only must it prop up your PC for the duration of the failure, it must also keep your monitor and other peripherals going. And if you want to see what you're doing, you might even need a lamp. Moreover, when used in this way, the backup power supply needs enough internal battery supply to carry the load across blackouts that stretch for ten minutes or more.

For the most part, relying on a backup system for completely uninterrupted operation of your PC doesn't make economic sense. Few blackouts stretch beyond a few seconds. In most cases, electrical power will return within a minute of a failure. Consequently, long battery life—enough to wait out the longest possible blackout—is not necessarily critical. Lower your goals, and you can get by with much less in the line of battery reserves. Most single-user systems can get along with just enough backup power that the computer can be properly shut down—all files saved, applications ended, and temporary files deleted. A minute or two will do. The best of both worlds, and perhaps the best compromise, is to couple enough backup power to carry a complete system through a short blackout—those lasting about a minute—with sufficient reserves for an orderly shutdown.

Server PCs need more. They cannot just switch off while a dozen or a hundred users are depending on the disks inside for storage. The server has to stay alive longer than any of the PCs that it services. Moreover, it must be able to signal the PCs it serves to let them know that the power has failed and that the system may be shutting down in a few minutes. Consequently, a server requires a special type of backup system—one with enough power to assure that all active files being used by all PCs connected to the server can be saved, and one with a built-in signaling system to notify the server of the power failure in a manner gentler than a total shutdown.

A final consideration is the unattended PC, be it a machine waiting to make a backup or waiting to service a telephone call or just waiting. A power failure will interrupt the wait. A backup supply can help keep the system going, but during a prolonged power outage an ordinary backup system is an invitation to trouble. Once the battery reserves in the backup supply run out, the unattended PC is on its own. If the failure occurs during a telephone transaction, the call will end and business being handled through it will have to be started anew, hardly a fatal error. But if caught in the middle of backing up a hard disk, a backup supply shutdown can be just as dangerous as an unprotected blackout. Files may be lost; worse, the disk being backed up could be corrupted. Once power returns, the unattended PC may not know how to return to its appointed business. It might just boot up and sit around wearing a DOS prompt until some unfortunate human is rooted from bed to ferret out the problem.

State-saving Software

The unattended PC needs a particular kind of backup system, one that can save the state of the PC being protected. Every register, every memory location, must be properly preserved so that it can be restored—automatically—when the unattended PC restarts as power is returned.

All the current internal UPS systems use state-saving software and operate similarly. The UPS instantly switches your PC over to battery operation whenever your PC's power supply kicks out because of a blackout or brownout. Battery electricity is supplied for a short period—a second or two—to bridge across brief service interruptions. After that short delay, the UPS assumes that the failure will be a long one, and the state-saving software swings into action, directing your PC to copy the contents of its RAM, video memory, and even microprocessor registers to disk memory.

If utility power returns during the period in which the operating state of your systems is being saved, the UPS control software returns normal control back to you once the state-saving operation is completed. You can resume exactly where you left off. But if utility power still has not been restored, the UPS-on-a-card system parks your hard disk and shuts down the system.

Turn your PC back on, and it will automatically restore itself to exactly the place it was when the power failed—the same software loaded into memory, the same image on the display, everything in place all the way up to the last keystroke. (Of course, since the computer may have been hung in an error condition when it was switched off—for example, for a warm boot—the UPS control software also allows sidestepping this automatic restoration.)

State-saving can be a perfect solution for keeping unattended PCs playing. For example, put an internal UPS in a network server, and it will pop back up after a power failure exactly where it left off.

As clever as this concept sounds, it has its drawbacks. As with all state-saving systems, each UPS-on-a-card requires the dedication of at least as much hard disk space as there is RAM to save. An eight-megabyte PC will lose eight megabytes from its disk plus sufficient disk space to store the contents of display memory. Moreover, saving a lot of memory to disk can be time consuming, taking as little as five or ten seconds or as long as several minutes, depending on the amount of memory to be backed up, the speed of your PC's microprocessor, and the performance of your hard disk. The profusion of memory types also complicates matters, particularly with 386 and 486 PCs. While all internal UPSs can automatically save the state of all standard types of memory (DOS, extended, and expanded), some have difficulty with the advanced memory-paging abilities of the latest microprocessors. If you have memory in your system managed under the XMS or VPCI protocols (the kind of extended memory used by DOS 5.0 and Windows 3.0, for example), you'll have to be more critical in your shopping. Be sure to verify that the internal UPS you buy can save the state of the memory in your system. Just like any terminate-and-stay-resident utility, state-saving software will steal some of your system's DOS memory from other programs. And it can be sensitive to the order in which it is loaded in relation to other TSR programs. For example, some state-saving software requires that it be loaded only after other software drivers.

Backup Power Supply Ratings

The fundamental difference among backup power supplies of a given type is capacity, how much electricity they can deliver. Capacity is not a single measure but two. You need to be concerned with how much power the backup system can deliver, that is, what is its maximum rating measured in watts or volt-amperes. In addition, you need to know how much energy the supply can provide, that is, how long it can back up your PC. Although energy is measured in ergs, joules, or (more familiarly) watt-hours, the principal measurement you'll want to tangle with is the time in minutes the supply will run your computer system.

Power

Nearly every backup power system is sold by its power rating. This figure helps you judge how much equipment you can protect with the backup system. Just as power supplies are limited in the amount of current they can handle by their designs and components, so are backup systems. Exceed the rating of the backup system and your protection device becomes an invitation to disaster. It will either fail as soon as you turn your system on or will gradually overload, failing right in the middle of some important calculation you're making.

Backup power supplies are rated in watts or volt-amperes. If you're familiar with Ohm's Law, a basic principle of electrical circuits, you know that power equals current times voltage, that is, watts equals amps times volts. With such an easy relationship between the watts, volts, and amps, you may wonder why the power protection industry needs two different measures. In truth they don't, but the reason is surprising. In alternating current (AC) systems, watts don't necessarily equal the product of volts and amps. In AC circuits, the voltage and current can be out of phase with one another—when voltage is at a maximum, the current in the circuit can be at an intermediary value. So the peak values of voltage and amperage may occur at different times. But power requires both voltage and current simultaneously. Consequently, the product of voltage and current (amperage) in an AC circuit is often higher than the actual power in the circuit. The ratio between these two values is called the *power factor* of the system.

What all of this means to you is that volt-amperes (VA) and watts are not the same thing. Most backup power systems will be rated in VA because it appears to be the higher figure because of the power factor. You must ensure that the total VA used by your computer equipment is less than the VA available from the backup power system. Alternately, you must ensure that the wattage used by your equipment is less than the wattage available from the backup power system. Don't indiscriminately mix the two. If necessary, you can change a VA rating to a watt rating by multiplying the VA by the power factor of the backup power supply. To go the other way, divide the wattage rating of a backup power system by its power factor to reach its VA rating. (You can do the same thing with the equipment you want to plug into the power supply, but you may have a difficult time discovering the power factor of each piece of equipment.)

Energy

The carefully controlled, continuous power created by a backup power system prevents power-line anomalies from harming computer systems. But even the best system can't guarantee an endless supply of pure electricity. When utility supply fails and the backup supply draws upon its internal battery reserves, the watt-hours are limited, typically to a fraction of an hour. As with all good things, the reserves of the backup supply must eventually come to an end. When the backup power supply runs out of backup power, the result is just as deadly to data as the utility failure the UPS is supposed to protect against.

Most manufacturers rate their backup systems for a given number of minutes of operation with a load of a particular size. For example, a backup system may be rated to run a 250 volt-ampere load for 20 minutes. These figures are useful for calculating how long you can expect your system to run on backup power and for comparing different products. If your PC and peripherals draw some other amount of power than that which is given in the duration ratings of a backup power system, how long your PC will run off batteries can be anyone's guess.

You can get an idea of the maximum possible time the backup supply will carry your system by the batteries it uses. After all, the only electricity is has available is hidden inside those batteries. Most batteries are rated in amp-hours, which describes how much current they can deliver for how long. You can convert that rating to a genuine energy rating by multiplying by the nominal battery voltage. For example, a twelve-volt, six amp-hour battery could, in theory, produce 72 watt-hours of electricity. That's a theoretical figure because the circuitry that converts the battery DC to AC will consume some of the power and because ratings are only nominal for new batteries. But the figure does give you a limit. If you have only 72 watt-hours of battery, you can't expect the system to run your 250 VA PC for an hour. At most, you could expect 17 minutes. Realistically you might expect 12 to 15.

If you want to add greater battery capacity to your backup system, these ratings become useful if not invaluable. You can calculate how much additional running time each battery will add to your system. You can even allow for the efficiency of the backup power supply by calculating how much life you get from the built-in battery of the system.

Buying a Backup Power Supply

The first step in locating the best backup power supply for your PC is to determine the type of protection that you need. If you want blackout protection that allows you to keep working when the power fails and to make the decision for yourself when to shut down your PC, a standby power supply is the inexpensive choice. An uninterruptible power supply will give you greater protection from electrical ills at a correspondingly greater price. If all you want is insurance against losing files and work to an unexpected outage, an internal power backup system will give you the least expensive solution, albeit one without surge protection. If you want automatic operation or have an unattended PC, the internal backup supply or an external power supply with state-saving software will be the best choice.

External Backup Supplies

If you choose to use an external backup power supply, your next step is to determine how much power you'll need. The amount required depends on the PC you have and whatever peripheral you would also like to protect. Many backup power supplies are sold in configurations designed for particular styles of PCs—XT-size, AT-size, server-size. In general, such systems make allowance for the connection of a monitor in addition to the PC, but for no other peripherals. About 250 volt-amperes of power is sufficient to safeguard the small-footprint PC, including ancient machines like the original PC and XT and desktop PS/2s (along with the typical 12- to 14-inch color VGA monitor). Move up to an AT or a high-performance desktop computer based on the 386 or 486 microprocessors and you'll want to get from 300 to 350 VA from a backup system. Tower computers, because of their larger power supplies and greater expansion potential, may require even larger backup systems, up to 500 VA.

Besides your monitor, the only other peripheral you'll want to connect to your backup systems is an external modem. In general, these draw a negligible amount of power so you probably won't have to make any allowance for one. Although you may be tempted to connect your printer to the backup system, that's not a good idea. Printers require a lot of power, which means you'll have to move up to a hefty (and expensive) backup system. Moreover, most impact printers use powerful electric motors that require a great deal of start-up power—so great, in fact, that they might overstrain an inexpensive backup system, either blowing the fuse or destroying some of its transistors. In other words, never, never connect a printer to a backup system.

When looking for an external backup power supply, you'll want to look at the indicators that are provided. Nearly every external backup supply includes warning bells, whistles, or Sonalerts to warn you that the system has switched over to backup power—just in case you hadn't noticed the lights went out. In addition, they give some warning to indicate when the supply is approaching the end of its electrical reserves. Some backup systems have more exotic arrays of indicators, such as thermometer or bar-graph style LEDs that show the discharge level of the batteries or a similar indication of the amount of current being drawn from the system. Whether these indicators are useful depends on how you intend to use the backup system. In most cases, an impending-doom indication is all that's necessary. Then again, having a full array of blinking lights, whistles, and meters may make you feel like the master of the universe.

Another difference among backup power systems is the waveform of their output power. Normal utility-supplied electricity comes in the form of smooth sine waves, and that's what backup power supplies should produce, too. Unfortunately, sine waves are expensive to make, so many backup systems skimp here. For standby power systems that will operate your PC for a few minutes at a time, you probably need not worry about the waveform. However, prolonged use of square waves may cause some equipment to overheat, so they should be avoided in uninterruptible systems.

Although waveform should be important, it tends to fall near the bottom of purchase criteria because few people understand what it means—and few backup systems deliver exactly what they promise. Part of this situation results from interaction between the backup power system and your PC. The waveform of any power system depends on the kind of load attached to it—highly reactive loads (for example, motors and transformers) cause the waveform to change shape, so you never know what's really getting to your equipment. Part of the discrepancy arises because there's no real standard for what a sine wave really is (at least in backup system brochures). You have to take the manufacturer's word for what kind of waveform its equipment produces, and you can bet most backup supply makers have engineers who squint their eyes to make themselves see sine waves in some strangely abstract shapes.

In some applications the output frequency of the backup system can be critical. Ideally, a backup system should produce power at exactly the 60 Hz that utilities supply. For PCs, anything close will work. Most PCs now have power supplies designed to work with a range of frequencies (typically, 50 to 60 Hz) so they will accept anything reasonable from a backup system. About the only devices sensitive to input power frequency are clocks. However, the clocks in most PCs don't rely on the line frequency to tell time. Instead they have their own crystal oscillators and thus function independently from power line frequency.

Internal Backup Supplies

If you choose to use an internal backup power supply, your purchasing criteria will be different from those for an external supply. For example, internal systems are more critical about the computers with which they are used. Because they connect directly to the output of your PC's power supply, the kind of connector used there is critical. Some internal backup systems are designed so that they will accept either Burndy or Molex power connectors. Others require that you get an adapter to match the kind of connector used by your PC's power supply and system board. When you buy an internal backup system, you'll want to specify the brand and model of computer you have so that your dealer can make the right match. Alternately, you can tell your dealer what kind of connector that you need. One look will tell you everything that you need to know.

Because internal backup supplies uniformly use state-saving software, in most cases you won't have to worry about the energy reserves of the backup supply. Most have enough battery power to save the state of all, except systems with extraordinarily large memories and extraordinarily slow hard disk drives. Other external backup power supply considerations are meaningless. You don't have to worry about output waveform or frequency because internal backup supplies deliver DC—the waveform of which is a flat line. Nor do you need to consider blinking lights—even if an internal backup supplies has them, you can't see them outside your PC.

With internal backup systems, the primary issue is the software packed with the hardware. The software must be compatible with your computer, its memory, and the applications that you use. Be especially critical in verifying that the internal power supply and its software that you want will be able to save all the memory in your system—including XMS if you use Windows 3.0. Saving only part of your PC's memory won't work.

Installing an External Backup Power Supply

An external backup power supply is almost trivial to electrically install. You need only plug the power supply into an ordinary wall outlet and plug the power cords from your PC and its monitor to the outlets on the back of the power supply. External backup systems that use state-saving software or link with network operating systems add another connection. These systems provide a signal output that is usually connected to a serial port. The backup supply uses this cable to indicate to its PC host when it has switched over to its battery power and when the battery power reserves are precariously low. The necessary cable should be supplied with the backup power system, but is often available only as an extra cost option. Backup systems from different manufacturers use their own connections and cable styles for this warning signal.

Where to put the power supply is the only loose end. With some units—those that are low, flat, and deep—the obvious place is to use the backup supply as a monitor stand. Those designed as power directors with multiple-switched outlets lend themselves to such installations, putting all of their power controls right at hand. If your monitor is on top of your PC, however, using a backup system to further increase its height is not a good idea. All backup systems are packed with heavy lead-based batteries. These can actually stress or bend the case of PCs with potentially deleterious consequences. If your monitor is located on a desktop and your PC next to your desk, however, sliding a backup system underneath the monitor should not be a problem.

Smaller external backup supplies are designed to be placed next to PC cases. There's no reason not to—unless it puts the backup supply too close to the edge of your desk. A heavy backup system can do substantial damage to itself, nearby equipment, and even you if it plummets to the floor. Be careful.

Bigger backup power supplies should be located as near as practicable to your normal operating position, your desk. You want the power supply within earshot so that you can hear its warning tones. And you want it close enough so that you can see and access it controls.

Check the manual that comes with your backup system to see how it recommends that you operate the system. In some cases, you'll want to leave the backup system on all the time and switch your PC on and off with its own power switch. Some backup systems prefer that you use its power switch to control the backup system, your PC, and your monitor together with the backup system's own on/off switch. Usually, using the backup supply's switch is best. That way, if the power fails during the evening or some other time you're not around, your backup system won't try to supply electricity to nothing. Working into such a no-load condition can damage some backup systems.

One additional hint: Most backup systems have several outlets on their rear panels. People who visit occasionally to clean your office typically look for the first outlet they can find to plug in their vacuum cleaners. And the first place to plug in is the back of the backup power system. They switch on the vacuum, and the initial surge its motor draws blows out half the circuitry inside the backup power system. The vacuum doesn't work, so they look for another outlet—and deny they had anything to do with the smoke curling out of the backup power system. Sound far-fetched? It isn't. Someone somewhere somehow will accidentally overload your backup power system if you're not careful. To avoid such problems, cover all unused outlets on the back of your backup power system with masking tape, an evil red color if you have it.

Installing an Internal Backup Power Supply

Conceptually, all internal backup power supplies are installed in the same manner. They intercept the output of your system's own power supply that is bound for the system board and substitute their own protected outputs. Only the connections and adapters used by various models of internal backup system vary.

In any case, the first step in installing an internal backup systems is to free up enough expansion slots into which to fit the backup system. These slots should be as close as possible to your system's power connections to ensure that the adapter or cables will stretch to accommodate the backup system. In some cases, you may get a better fit if you relocate your system's disk controller one slot further away from the power supply and slide the backup supply into the controller's old slot. Remember to keep 16-bit devices in 16-bit slots when you move expansion cards in systems with various slot interfaces.

Next, disconnect your system's power supply from the system board. In most PCs, you'll find two separate cable bundles, each going to its own connector on the system board. Often the connectors at the ends of these cables are labeled P8 and P9. To unplug these cables, you simply slide them up and out. Simple, perhaps, but not always easy. The connectors can fit tightly. You may need to rock them a little to get them loose. You might want to press down on the system board around the connectors as you try to pull each connector off so you don't stress the board too much. Although it's tempting to yank out the two connectors together by grabbing both bundles of wire at once, take your time and remove the connectors individually and carefully. Being too rash may destroy your system board, an expensive replacement proposition.

Next, connect the backup supply to your system's electrical system. Two basic methods are used by internal backup systems for this process.

One kind has two sets of jacks on the backup supply's expansion board. One set of jacks will match those in your system, be they Burndy or Molex. The other set will be another style of connector. Determine which set of connectors your PC's P8 and P9 cables (or whatever they are labeled) will fit into *but don't plug them in yet*. Now locate the second set of jacks on the backup card and the short adapter cable that came with the board. The adapter cable should have Burndy connectors on one end and Molex on the other. Plug one end of this cable into the backup supply using the jacks that did not match the connectors on the wires from your PC's power supply. Get the backup supply expansion board into position for installing inside your system, but don't slide it into place. Instead, first connect the free end of the adapter cable you just installed into the power supply jacks on your system board. Magically, the connectors at the other end of the adapter cable are guaranteed to match the jacks on your system board. Observe the keying and numbers of the jacks. The positions of the various colors of the new wires should match those of the old. Once that wire is in place, plug the wires from your PC's power supply into the matching jacks on the backup supply expansion board. Finally, slide the expansion board all the way into its slot and screw it into place.

The other style of internal backup supply uses a special three-connector adapter cable that's made to match the style of power connector in your PC, either Burndy or Molex. One end of this three-connector cable will fit into the system board power-supply jacks. Plug this connector into the system board jacks. In the center of the three-connector cable you'll find a jack that will accommodate the two power connectors that formerly plugged into your PC's system board. Plug these connectors into the central jack on the three-connector cable. Pull the cable out of the way and slide the backup supply into the expansion slot that you have prepared for it. Screw the board tightly into place. Finally, plug the remaining connector of the three-connector cable into the jack on the backup supply.

Once the backup hardware is installed, follow the software installation procedures accompanying the product. These will vary with the board you've chosen and even with the software version.

Check the technical manual accompanying the internal backup supply board to find out whether you must charge the board before you can rely on it. The only way to charge the board is to run your PC because the board draws its electrical supply from your PC's power supply (when it is turned on, of course). Once you're backup supply is fully charged, you can depend on complete protection against electrical blackouts for your PC.

Appendices

A.

Dealing With Your PC's Case

The real, physical work of upgrading is mechanical—the simple act of plugging in your new peripherals. In the ideal case, it's easy. But few PCs present you with an ideal case. Try installing an upgrade and you'll suspect your PC has the case from Hell. This section points out the more common complications and helps make the best of even the least ideal expansion situations.

Every expansion board and every external peripheral worth its salt includes a clever set of line drawings on cracking open the case of your PC and plugging in the board or whatever new miracle you've bought. In a perfect world, these illustrations should make this book entirely unnecessary. Tailored to the specific product, these instructions should provide you with all the guidance you need to get your upgrade going. Providing, of course, you own the one exact machine that the artist who drew the illustrations used as a model. And provided every step of the procedure goes by the book—no complications, no surprises, no bloody fingertips, no curses to make the rest of the family run for cover.

When you actually try to follow those instructions, however, you're likely to discover that cables sneak in the way like irascible sidewinders, screws miraculously migrate from the locations so carefully documented in the instructions, and Venus and Mercury align in such a way that tidal forces conspire against your new expansion board fitting into the slot you've chosen. Or you may breeze through the entire installation as if you've spent the last 15 years designing computer equipment and giving sage advice to Seymour Cray. Then, when you switch on your PC, a tiny wisp of smoke curls out of the power supply or, worse, nothing at all happens when you push up the big red powerswitch paddle on the side of your computer.

While the words below can't be guaranteed to cover every possible situation you could encounter while making an upgrade, they will point out many of the tribulations that the breezy instruction manuals choose to ignore. At the minimum, they'll confirm that it's not you, with your 13 thumbs and F-minus in high school shop class, who is botching the upgrade job, but rather the problems are the fault of some overeducated and underskilled engineer who never bothered to test out the results of his brazen design attempts.

Yes, indeed, you may be right and the world wrong. Sometimes we all need that reassurance.

Removing the Cover

The steps in removing the cover from the chassis of a PC, XT, or AT is probably the most documented PC procedure in existence. Remove the screws, pull the cover straight forward, then lift its front up and off. While these instructions sound simple, problems can arise in every step.

What can go wrong in removing screws? First, you have to find the screws and only remove the right ones. Then you've got to be able to thwart the efforts of the assembly gorillas and actually loosen and remove the screws. And you've got to be able to find the screws when you re-assemble your system.

For official IBM PCs, XTs, and ATs, locating the screws that need to be removed is fairly easy. All of these machines except the first batch of PCs (the so-called PC1s that allow only a total of 64K of RAM on the system board) use five screws—one located in each of the four corners of the rear panel and one more in the center of the top of the rear panel. PC1 use only three screws, omitting the two at the top corners. Remove more than five screws from the rear of one of these computers and something will be looser than it should be.

Clone computers make finding the screws more of a challenge. While most machines stick with the IBM screw arrangement, many others go off in their own directions. For example, Zenith puts four more screws at the lower edges of the side of the chassis. Others sneak screws under the lower lip of the chassis.

A couple of general rules will help you determine whether you should remove a screw. The screws that hold the lid on the case will, in general, be near an edge or corner. A screw in the exact middle of the rear panel—halfway between top and bottom and halfway from the right and left sides—is unlikely to be one of those that holds the lid in place. Second, you can generally see where a tab or edge of the chassis tucks under the lid of the case allowing the screw to fasten everything together.

A third rule: After you remove all the screws and the lid still doesn't come off, look again. Keep looking until you find out what's preventing the top from coming off. The first reaction—to force the lid off—is generally ill-advised.

There's a good reason why twisting a screw all the way into its hole is called driving it home. Many screws are like homebodies that love to nestle securely in their dwellings, unwilling to budge out of the warmth and security of their home come what may—including your best efforts with a screwdriver. Coaxing these screws out is never easy. But you can make the job easier by using the correct screwdriver and method of removal. Don't just twist the screwdriver. With a reluctant screw, doing that makes the screwdriver tip likely to pop up and mangle the head of the screw. Instead, press down when you want the screw to come up. Although that sounds counterintuitive, the added pressure will ensure that the screwdriver tip stays in the slot in the head of the screw. If the screws holding the top on have hexagonal heads that fit a nutdriver, by all means use a nutdriver to remove them. Since you can get a better grip while doing less damage to the head using a nutdriver, it's the better choice. Odds are the factory did, and that's why you have to spend four years pumping iron to get the strength to remove some of them.

If a screw resists your best efforts to break it free, you can encourage it along by giving it a gentle tap. Make sure your screwdriver is properly engaged in the head of the screw, then give the screwdriver a gentle downward rap.

Nevertheless, an unusually large number of PCs show an evil tendency to resist the removal of their lids even after all the screws have been properly removed. For example, my original PC snaps so tightly together that even without screws in place you might suspect someone had welded the top onto the chassis. This little bit of reluctance is rarely covered in the generic directions accompanying PC expansion products.

If you're certain that you've found and removed all the fasteners holding the top on your computer and the top does not easily slide off, it's time to gently force it off. Don't yank. Instead, put the palms of your hand on the top and right side of your system so that you can press on the front faces of the disk drives with your thumbs. Now apply firm pressure with your thumbs. Gradually increase the pressure until the top pops free.

As a last resort, grasp the two sides of the lid and give a quick, sharp yank forward—the same kind of quick motion that magician's use for pulling tablecloths out from under banquets. If that doesn't work, look again for a hidden screw. And assure yourself that your PC is supposed to disassemble in the same manner as a standard IBM PC.

The next step in the prefab instructions is to slide the top of the case forward. It should move smoothly. In some cases, however, you'll feel a bit of resistance. If you do, *stop*. In all too many PCs, the tab that holds the screw in the center of the rear panel dips down and catches on one of the flat ribbon cables running to the disk drives. If you don't pay attention to this, you can yank the cable off with the case lid, bend or break the matching contacts on the disk drive or its controller, or injure the cable itself by slicing it with a sharp edge of the tab. So if you feel the slightest resistance when sliding the lid forward, reach under the lid and determine whether a cable is caught on the central tab. If one is, push it down out of harm's way. Then continue to slide the lid off.

Once the rear end of the lid reaches the front panel, this central tab will stop against the back of the front panel or something else in the way (like a disk drive). At this point, lift the front of the lid up at about a 45-degree angle to the chassis. The bottom of the lid will come free from the case and allow you to lift the lid up so that the tab will clear the front panel. The lid should then be free, allowing you to set it aside and work peacefully on the components inside your system.

As computer manufacturers become more creative, they tend to go their own direction with the cases they wrap around their products. While many retain the early IBM slide-off-the-front configuration, a growing number have developed alternate designs. Some of these require a deft touch to successfully open.

The standard IBM design has several distinguishing characteristics. The back panel of the chassis is part of the chassis bottom, not the removable lid of the case. The screws that hold the system closed go through this back panel and attach to tabs at the sides of the lid and one tab at the center of the lid. The front of the case is a decorative plastic bezel that's permanently affixed to the lid (not the bottom of the chassis). And the sides of the case curl under both the right and left edge of the chassis, forming a lip about half an inch wide.

If the lid of the case does not curve around the chassis to form a lip, there's a good chance that the top of your computer will simply lift straight off. This style case also usually has two or three screws at the bottom edge of each of the two sides of the lid. After you remove these screws, try to lift the top of this style of PC straight up. You may have to flex the sides slightly to get it to release. If the front refuses to budge when you lift, but the back slides up relatively easily, the front of the lid may tuck under the front-panel bezel. Try pushing the lid slightly backwards before lifting again. You should only need to push it one-quarter to one-half an inch backwards before it frees itself from the front bezel. It should then lift straight up.

Some manufacturers make the very top of the case a separate piece. These systems reveal themselves with a seam or crack that runs across both sides of the case half an inch to an inch below the top edge of the case. These are typically held together by screws in the rear panel. The top has a lip that hangs down over the rear panel, and the screws that hold the top on go through this lip and fasten to holes threaded in the rear panel. The front edge of the lid is held down by tucking it under the front bezel. After you remove the rear panels screws from this style of case, you only need to slide the top backwards far enough that it clears the bezel, then lift it off.

Tower-style PS/2s of the Model 60, 65, and 80 series use a plastic version of this last case style, only the left side rather than the top of the case is removable. Instead of rear-panel screws, these machines use a pair of large captured-screws in the middle of the lid to hold the system together. These large screws are designed to be removed with a tool that's out of the standard PC repertory—a quarter (25¢ American). To open a tower-style PS/2 case, loosen the two large screws until they are free—but don't try to twist them out entirely and remove them. You can tell that they are free in their holes when they lean a bit to the side and you can press them in and they pop back out at you under spring pressure. Once these screws are free, you can pry around the edges to lift the lid off. The front of the lid tucks under the front panel of the system, but lifting the lid will force you to angle it in respect to the chassis. This angling will release the lid from the grasp of the bezel.

Other tower-style PCs use a variety of cabinetry schemes. Some are modifications of the traditional PC case. Some simply flop an ordinary PC cabinet on its side, making the bottom of the chassis one of its sides. Others modify the traditional case by switching the axis of the case—so that the lid is a tall inverted-U that nevertheless slides off rather conventionally.

Fitting Expansion Boards

Sliding an expansion board into a slot is an easy job, at least until you try to do it. By rights, all boards should fit all slots but more often than occasionally a board won't quite make it. The board may not seat in its socket, its retaining bracket may refuse to slide into place, or the board itself may not fit in the length of the slot.

A few expansion boardfitting problems are obvious. A board designed for an AT may not fit into smaller computers. The AT accepts boards nearly an inch taller than the cases of the PC and XT. Slide a tall board into a short computer, and you have a compelling reason to leave the top off the case. Similarly, long expansion boards won't fit into short slots, and the only people needing an explanation about why are probably the same folks who schedule rush-hour commuter trains.

Ordinary expansion boards not fitting in ordinary expansion slots are more difficult to explain. The causes are probably twofold—both the boards and the slots are too ordinary. The machine and expansion board makers may have taken a rather cavalier attitude to such exigencies as tolerances. As a result, either the length of the expansion board or the size of your PC's expansion slots vary somewhat from the agreed standard. For reasons known only to God and Mr. Murphy—the only man to correctly deduce the one true law of the Universe—expansion boards are invariably a fraction of an inch too long and slots a fraction too short.

The widely practiced method of coping with this problem of fit is to make the overgrown expansion board squeeze into the shrunken slot. Often the board can be bent or otherwise slightly curved to fit into the slot. Avoid this practice. Bending an expansion board is an invitation to danger, disaster, and an early demise to the product. Any time an expansion board is bent, both it and the components on it are stressed. The copper-foil printed circuit traces on the board can crack, breaking connections or making them intermittent. Worse, the cracks can occur within the inner layers of the board (many expansion boards are made from multiple layers glued together, though they appear no thicker than a single printed circuit

board), invisible to your eye but just as damaging to the function of
the board. Resistors and glass-clad diodes easily crack when
stressed. As a result, a single flex of an expansion board can leave it
bereft of life and your budget bereft of cash.

In truth, there is no entirely satisfactory way of dealing with this
problem other than returning the ill-fitting board for a replacement
of the proper dimension. Even then, you're betting that you got the
one board that was made too long, when it's more likely that only
the original prototype was the correct length. Although there's no
perfect solution, you can do several things to coax an oversize
board into an undersize slot. If the chassis of your computer is
flimsy, lightweight metal (and most too-small chassis appear to be),
you can slightly alter the size of an expansion slot by simply bending the metalwork. Don't be too ambitious or else you run the risk
of nothing fitting inside the chassis again. In some systems, you
can remove the plastic card guide at the front end of the expansion
slot, earning nearly one-eighth an inch of extra slot length. However, because it's not a good idea to leave an expansion board wavering loosely in its slot, you may want to try filing or sanding
down the card guide to make it thinner and replacing it. The slen-
derized card guide will still provide its essential function even after
the trim. Do not attempt to make an expansion board fit by sanding
or filing away at the board. Several problems could arise. You
might separate the various layers of a multilayer board or you may
get fine shavings of metal from the board mixed into a delicate
circuit or, worse, a disk drive.

Problems are apt to arise at the other end of the expansion slot,
too. Some card-retaining brackets will simply refuse to fit properly
in position. Most likely, they will stop about half an inch before
they are all the way into place. The problem in this case is usually a
failure to fit the tab at the bottom of the board into a matching slot.
Before attacking this problem, however, ensure that the reluctant
expansion board is actually engaging with the card-edge connector
at the bottom of the slot. If you don't get the board started in the
connector properly, there's no way that the card-retaining bracket
will fit. Should the board be started in the edge connector, but the
retaining bracket won't budge, the next step is to make the retaining bracket fit. Most of the time you can easily bend the bottom of
the bracket a fraction of an inch toward the rear of your system.
Sometimes a slight bend the other way works. One of these slight

bends is usually sufficient to make the tab on the retaining bracket find its designated slot.

Width as well as length is important with expansion boards. Except for the original PC, which had one-inch slot spacing, all IBM-standard personal computers space their expansion boards at 0.8-inch intervals. Some expansion boards come precariously close to that thickness. Multilevel boards—those with their own daughter-cards—often exceed that height. Scrunching too many boards too close together can lead to several problems.

Contact between expansion boards in adjacent slots is forbidden. Expansion boards should never touch one another. The biggest problem is the dreaded short circuit. When one of the printed circuit traces on the bottom of one board touches an uninsulated component at the top of another, odd things are apt to happen—and every one of them is likely to be bad. Inadvertent contact between expansion boards can send voltages onto the wrong circuits, causing data errors. Or it could route a supply voltage directly to ground, preventing the operation of the entire computer system.

Boards that touch can cause other problems, too. If there is any pressure put on one board by the other, the result is stress much like putting too long a board into too short a slot. The pressure may cause one or both of the boards to flex slightly, dramatically increasing the likelihood of failure.

Boards that are too close together may also cause heating problems. Certainly there's a cooling airflow inside your computer, but pack a number of boards closely together, and the airflow may be blocked, if only in a few small areas. Wherever the airflow is blocked, the result can be localized heating. And heat is the biggest threat to semiconductor circuits, shortening their lives as inevitably as death, taxes, and the obsolescence of your current PC.

If you have a choice, spread your expansion boards across the available expansion area. Don't start by filling slot one, then slot two, then slot three. Although there's something to be said for methodology, your system will be far happier if you first fill slot one, then slot six, then slot three. When you're gasping for life, you need air. So do your PC and its expansion boards.

Affixing the Cover

Getting all the screws into the back of a PC can sometimes be a headache. You may get three screws nicely seated, then the remaining two won't even start in their holes. You then end up trying to put the last screws in at odd angles and tapping new threads into the holes, a frustrating and undesirable alternative.

A neat trick will help assure that you can easily drive all the screws home. Instead of twisting each screw individually all the way into place, make the job a two-step process: First start all the screws, leaving them loose enough that you can nudge the cover in one direction or another; then, after you've got all the screws started, drive them home. This two-step process works because tightening any one screw locks the lid into an alignment that is optimal for only that one screw. Leaving the screws loose until you get them all started allows you to adjust the case lid as necessary to get each screw started. This technique works anywhere you have to put multiple screws into a single assembly.

One place three hands would be welcome is starting the two screws at the lower rear corners of the chassis. The flexible lid often flares out at the bottom so the holes in the rear of the chassis lead to blank metal instead of the tapped screw holes in the tabs in the lid. All you have to do is press the side of the lid of your PC against the chassis with one hand while you hold the screw in place at the hole with your other hand and rotate the screwdriver with your other hand. That's just another reason why nutdrivers are so helpful—they can hold the screw securely enough that you don't have to.

If you don't have a nutdriver, you can substitute ingenuity. Usually you can force the side of the PC into place with the palm of your hand and twist your fingers around to hold the screw in its starting position. How elegantly you manage this depends on your dexterity. You may have to lift the chassis to get your hand underneath. Of course, utility *not* elegance is the issue. No one will know the contortions you go through completing the assembly of your PC.

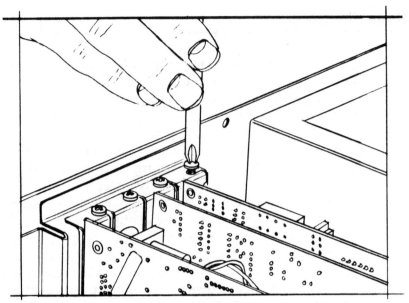

Figure A.1 It's vitally important to screw every expansion board into place. If you don't, you risk your own safety and that of your data.

The Case for Case Screws

While you have exactly one reason not to replace all the screws in your PC—and not a very good reason at that—you have several other motivations to tighten everything back up. The reason not to replace screws is simple laziness. Omit this step and you've save a couple of twists of the wrist and maybe a minute of effort. But you'll make your system vulnerable to a legion of disasters.

Not securing the retaining brackets of expansion boards to the rear panel of your PC is more than potentially dangerous. This omission has caused hundreds of thousands of dollars of damage in systems, one IBM engineer has confided to me. The only way that expansion boards can be electrically grounded to your PC's chassis is through the retaining bracket, and the screw at the top is the only part of the design that assures a firm mechanical and electrical connection. Certainly your PC will operate properly (or seem to) without this screw in place. But when disaster strikes in the form of a lightning bolt, you may be putting your life (and that of your PC) at stake.

According to a story related by an engineer at a large computer company (nameless because it's unlikely that the company will officially sanction a report of its product causing a conflagration), a production line was once stopped and engineers chained to their workstations when a report got back from a fire marshal that one of the company's computers had started a major business fire. After the company's engineers had studied the charred remains for nearly a week, they had found the true cause: lightning struck the power line, wandered through the computer, and tried to find its way to ground through the retaining bracket. The lack of a screw on this particular bracket caused a high-resistance connection that became so hot it started a fire. One screw, properly tightened in place, might have prevented the disaster. Okay, that's a rare occurrence, and an act of God, and besides you live in a tank at the bottom of the ocean and are thus immune to lightning. If you're lazy enough, you can come up with a million excuses. If you want to be safe, twist the screw into place.

The lack of a screw holding an expansion board in place also allows the board it's supposed to be holding still to shift. Move the computer, and the loose board can rattle out of its slot. Try to plug a connector into a loose board, and you're likely to push the board partly out of its socket. The board will stop working. Worse, you might angle the board so that some of the contacts on its edge connector cross the contacts on the socket connect with or, shorting two or more circuits together. In a fraction of a second, you could damage the expansion board or, more likely, your PC's system board.

If that's not a good enough reason to put the screws to your retaining brackets, here's one more incentive. Your mother always said that you should finish the jobs that you start. You wouldn't want to disappoint your mother, would you?

You should also replace all the screws that hold the top of your PC's case to its chassis. Certainly you should wait to replace them until you know your PC is operating properly after you've plugged in (or removed) an expansion board. But once you're certain the system is working, put every screw back in place.

There's no surprise more devastating—at least to your PC—than picking up your computer to move it, grasping it firmly on each side, only to have the chassis slide out of the case and crash to the floor. Potential victims include the PC itself (definitely not designed for such a plummet), the floor that it strikes, your feet that cushion the landing, and your shins that the whole mess is likely to bounce back up into. You won't know the real meaning of the word "sheepish" till the time you have to explain *that* accident to the repairman.

The screws that hold the lid on your PC's case also serve to electrically unify the system. This electrical connection helps to contain interference inside the computer, reducing the chance that signals emitted by your PC will creep into your or your neighbor's television pictures or radio programs or accidentally launch ICBMs from a nearby Air Force base.

People who review computer hardware (like this author) and those who must maintain a fleet of PCs for larger corporations are most tempted to forget the necessity of proper mechanical reassembly. Even I admit to not screwing in expansion boards when testing the dozen latest video expansion boards. But the system I depend on for writing is all snugged together, screws in place. Even the cable connectors are screwed into their jacks on the card-retaining brackets. After all, my livelihood depends on this machine, and I make every effort to ensure its reliability. You should do likewise with your own PC.

B.

DRIVE INSTALLATION

The easiest part of upgrading your disk device or anything that fits into a drive bay (such as a tape drive) is physically installing the drive in your computer. All the work is mechanical, and what you have to do is obvious. You can put a screwdriver to work and almost put your mind on hold.

The most complex issue is determining the means by which your drive should be secured to your computer's chassis. This should become obvious when you remove your old hard disk.

A number of mounting schemes are used by various computer makers. The most straightforward is the direct mounting scheme used by the IBM PC and a wide number of compatible manufacturers. The drive is directly screwed into the disk bay using either of the sets of screw holes on the sides or bottom of $5\frac{1}{4}$-inch and $3\frac{1}{2}$-inch drives. Simple, but not always effective as you'll see. Since then, IBM and most other manufacturers have developed exotic retaining schemes so complex they might make Rube Goldberg salivate (if he weren't dead, anyhow).

PC Disk Drives

The original PC and clones with the same style of case have two drive bays that accommodate only full-height drives—and don't do very well at that. They only accommodate full-height drives because their bays offer only two screws at the bottom, nothing halfway up to secure a second half-height drive in the bay. In fact, the sides of the bay don't even go up high enough to hold an upper drive.

The PC mounting scheme isn't very secure because drives are held in place only by one side. One side of the bay won't hold drives very securely. Should you install a tape drive using this mounting scheme, for example, and force a tape into the drive's slot, you are likely to bend the sides of the bay.

You can work around the full-height restriction of a PC bay by using *drive adapter plates*, thin sheets of metal that attach to either side of a pair of half-height drives and convert them into a single full-height stack. The plates work simply—they have four holes or slots to accommodate screws that fit two into one side of each drive, holding the drives together. You can even fabricate them yourself out of thin sheet metal (for instance, roof flashing or a piece of flat furnace duct). You can make your own template for the screw holds by stacking two half-height drives and measuring the distances between their holes—about $3\frac{1}{8}$-inch front to back, $2\frac{1}{8}$-inch top to bottom. You should make one plate for each side of a drive pair.

Installing these plates can be a problem because of the tight clearances in the PC chassis. Generally, you must use flathead or binder-head screws. Mount one side first, the side opposite the side of the drive bay into which you will put the retaining screws. Once you have one plate installed, slide the drive pair into the full-height bay. You may have to rock the drive to get the screw heads to clear. Once the drives are in the bay, slide the other plate between the drive and the side of the bay, lining it up so that you can put a screw through the side of the bay, through a hole in the plate, and into the lower disk drive. Screw in the front screw of the bottom drive loosely, then the rear screw all the way, then the front screw all the way. Then screw in the two screws to hold the top drive in place.

XT Disk Drives

The vintage XT series of computers showed that IBM could learn a bit from the mistakes in the original PC. While the first XTs would accommodate only two full-height drives, by the time the model was discontinued, it had learned to accept half-height devices as well by extending the sides of the bay upward. Moreover, even in its full-height configuration, the XT scheme provided slightly more secure mounting for one of its full-height devices.

The left bay of the XT was originally designed to accommodate a full-height, 10-megabyte hard disk drive, commodious in 1982, but paltry, indeed, by today's standards. If you want to replace an original XT hard disk—perhaps with a bigger, faster, half-height hard disk that can share its bay with a tape backup system—you're in for a surprise when you try to remove it from the XT chassis. Twist out the two screws on the left side of the drive, and it will not budge. That's because IBM added a third screw that goes through the bottom of the XT chassis into the drive. You must remove this screw to get the drive out of the computer. To access it, you'll have to turn the XT over. Remove this screw *before* you remove the two on the side of the drive so that the disk won't come crashing out of the chassis while you have it upside down. If the hole in the chassis of the XT for this screw matches one in the replacement drive you want to place in the computer, by all means use the screw.

Fitting half-height drives into all but the latest XT models requires the same ingenuity and adapter plate as putting them into a PC. In more recent XTs that allow for mounting holes for half-height drives in the sides of their drive bays, you'll still want to put an adapter plate on the blind side of the drive to hold the top drive more securely in place. The bottom of the drive tray will make the lower drive more secure. If your new drive choice has a hole on its underside matching the third screw-mounting hole in the XT chassis, you'll want to take advantage of it when installing your drive replacement. The extra screw will insure a solid mounting.

AT Disk Drives

IBM introduced a new, more secure mounting scheme in the AT, and many (if not the majority of) compatible computer manufacturers use the same scheme or a variation on it. The AT provides space for three drive units. On the left is an internal full-height drive bay designed for a full-height hard disk. The other two bays are on the right side of the chassis and are designed for half-height devices. IBM allows the bottom most bay to also hold a full-height hard disk or a special optical drive that requires front-panel access only to the top of its bezel. Most AT-compatible computers make the extra area below the lower of the two right-hand, half-height drive bays into a third half-height bay. Most also allow the full-height bay on the left to be split for two half-height devices. Some systems give all drive bays direct access through the front-panel bezel of the system, others restrict bays with front panel access to the three on the right.

In the AT, drives are not directly mounted to the sides of the drive bays. Instead they slide into place on mounting rails. The rails fit into guide slots that hold the drive assembly securely on both sides. The rails fit the guides tightly and hold the drive firmly in place from both sides. This mounting scheme has become so popular that many hard disks come with AT-mounting kits or with the rails already installed on the sides of the drive. These rails may be made from plastic or aluminum. Because both materials provide secure mountings, there's no particular advantage to choosing one material over the other.

The keys to the success of this mounting system are its solidity and the ease with which drives can be replaced. This mounting scheme is solid because the rails are held in place from four directions. The rail guides prevent up or down movement of the drive. A tapered stop at the end of the bay and a retaining bracket at the front of the bay not only lock the drive in laterally, they also press it solidly into place. Note that the pressure is applied to the rail and not the drive, preventing the force that secures the drive from mechanically distorting it.

The ease of using the rail system is obvious. You don't have to be double-jointed to install or remove a drive. All the hardware on the chassis you must monkey with is on the front panel. To mount the rails on the drive, you can put the drive on your workbench and twist and turn it any way you want to get the screws into their holes. You'll appreciate that ease should you acquire a disk or tape drive that comes without AT-mounting rails already attached.

If you have to install rails on a drive yourself, the most difficult part of the job is making certain that you have the rails oriented properly when you screw them into the drive. The vital consideration is that you put the tapered end of the rail at the rear of the drive. That is, when you slide the drive into your AT, the tapered end of the mounting rails should be first into the bay. Some rails are not tapered, however. If the rail you use lacks a taper at one end, it doesn't matter which end of the rail goes toward the rear of the drive. However, orientation may still be important to ensure that you mount drives at the proper height within the drive bay.

Although AT rails are a standard size, replacement rails have their own subtle variations. Many have four or eight holes punched in them instead of the two on genuine AT rails. The extra holes allow the identical rail to fit both the right and left sides of the drive. You have your choice of two heights to use with these rails, depending on whether you use the upper or lower set of holes. Which to use depends on your system. Put your new drive approximately in place in its drive bay and check where its drive-mounting holes line up in regard to the slot for the guide rail. Install the guide rail using the holes that put it at the appropriate height.

Because the holes are not in the center of genuine AT rails, these rails may lead you to think that your drive doesn't fit inside your PC—it may either mount too high or too low in the drive bay. If a drive does not properly fit into your AT, try reversing the rails. That is, turn them upside down while keeping the tapered end toward the back of the system. This will likely change the mounting height of the drive sufficiently to make it fit.

Another important consideration when choosing the screw holes to use when orienting the rails to your drive is to ensure that the rails fit so that they end about one inch inside the front of the drive itself. This allows the small brackets that secure the drive to poke slightly into the slots in the side of the bay to hold the rails in place while allowing the drive to project slightly through the bezel in the front of the case.

Securing a drive in an AT requires screwing in the small angular brackets at the front of each rail. The AT has three such brackets. Two are L-shaped; one is U-shaped. The odd bracket secures both the right side of the hard disk and the left side of the lower half-height bay.

AT-compatible Disk Drives

Some AT-compatibles—notably Compaq Deskpros—use a mounting scheme that's similar to that of the IBM AT, but for reasons of their own use differently shaped rails. For example, the rails of the Compaq line are slightly wider, making them incompatible with standard AT rails and the AT chassis. Compaq rails won't fit into IBM-size guides, and while IBM-size rails will fit Compaq guides they'll rattle around instead of yielding a secure mounting system. If you have a Compaq Deskpro or a similar computer, you'll either have to recycle your old rails (remove them from your old drive and switch them to the new drive) or attempt to get new rails to match your computer, which can sometimes be a challenge. Your best source of supply is the dealer who sold you the drive upgrade that you want to install. Or you can try the dealer who sold you your original computer.

Another variety of AT-compatibles uses drive-mounting rails that are narrower and, consequently, also incompatible with IBM rails. Most machines that use these narrow rails preinstall a set in each drive bay of the computer, even those without drives. In this case, you need only detach the rails from the chassis, screw them to your disk, and slide the disk into place.

Rails are held in the computer chassis in one of two ways. IBM-style systems use small brackets that push the rails to the end of their travel in the bay. Some compatibles make the brackets part of the drive rails. In either case, one screw holds each bracket in place. Just unscrew to slide the old drive out and screw the bracket back in to hold your drive upgrade in place.

PS/2 Disk Drives

For larger drives, tower-style IBM PS/2s use the same width mounting rails as those used in the AT, so AT rails will work in their internal $5\frac{1}{4}$-inch drive cages. To loosen a drive in one of these computers so that you can slide it out of the chassis, press down on each of the large blue daisy-like knobs above the drive and turn it counterclockwise with the palm of your hand until the drive can be slid out.

Special plastic mounting sleds are used to hold all drives in desktop PS/2s and $3\frac{1}{2}$-inch drives in tower-style models. The drive screws into the sled using the screw holes in its bottom, then the sled slides into place. A plastic tab at the end of the sled locks the whole assembly in place. To remove one of these drives, press down the wide tab under and at the front of the drive, then slide the sled forward.

These drives are sometimes reluctant to slide in or out. If a sled-mounted drive is reluctant when you try to remove it, be sure that you've released the latch. Be sure to hold the retaining tab in the center of the drive sled up when you try to slide the drive out. If you face resistance when you try sliding a drive in, ensure that the drive is properly mating with the connector at the back of its drive bay. Try wiggling the drive to get its edge connector to slide into the connector.

C.

THE PC TOOLKIT

Doing any job right depends on using the proper tools. Upgrading a PC is no different. Certainly the tools you'll require are commonplace—in most cases, a simple screwdriver is sufficient. Impatient people may even make do with a table knife levered into the screw slots. Using the right tools, however, will likely reduce the number and volume of Anglo-Saxon oaths you'll utter during the upgrade and help preserve the pristine condition of your PC's hardware so that the next upgrade goes equally smoothly.

One reason to rely on the right tools is that computer hardware can be notoriously difficult to manage. Many computer manufacturers apparently capitalize on the free labor available at the primate sections of their local zoos and use gorillas to twist the screws in place in their products. Or they use impact wrenches, Super Glue, and welding torches to assure that no screw will inadvertently—or purposely—be pulled from its hole. Try to remove one of these recalcitrant fasteners with the wrong tool and you'll grind and mangle the screwheads smooth, into impossible-to-extract shapes destined to haunt you every second you own the PC. Without the right tools, you may never get inside to install your upgrade—and if you do, you may never get in a second time when your upgrade needs a little extra aid.

The minimum in tools you'll need for working on your PC is a blunt-tip place knife, the kind you swipe from the kitchen to twist out a screw when you discover the tiny hands of children have taken your real tools to points unknown. In most cases, a knife and a lot of leverage will suffice because there's nothing complicated or delicate about removing or installing PC hardware. Just the same, using a knife for any chores described in this book is not recommended, and you take your personal safety into your own hands when you put a knife or any improper tool there.

To do the upgrade job right, you'll need a certain minimal set of tools. These include screwdrivers, nutdrivers, pliers, and, perhaps, a chip extractor. Often a single screwdriver will suffice for simple chores, such as installing an expansion board. However, computer manufacturers have not standardized on the fasteners they use for holding their products together. So if you want to be ready for any upgrade job, you best prepare yourself with a kit. Here's some specifics about what you should include:

Screwdrivers

All screwdrivers are not the same. While you may be familiar with the difference between Phillips and flat-blade screwdrivers, even ordinary flat-blade screwdrivers run a wide gamut. Using the right one is imperative if you want to ensure that you do your upgrade right.

Although most folks would consider one screwdriver to be interchangeable with any other, the blades can be distinctly different widths and thicknesses. Ideally, the width and thickness of the screwdriver's blade should exactly match that of the screw you want to extract or tighten into place. The proper fit assures that the screwdriver will have the maximum contact with the slot in the head of the screw and have the least amount of play. A blade that's too thick won't work at all—you can't get it into the slot in the screwhead. Too small a screwdriver won't allow you to put enough torque on the job to extract a reluctant screw. A blade that's too wide typically won't be a problem except in close quarters. Two sizes of screwdriver will normally suffice in a PC toolkit, $\frac{3}{16}$ and $\frac{1}{4}$ inch.

Phillips Screwdrivers

With other types of screwdrivers, the match between tool and fastener becomes even more important. For example, with the Torx screws used by Compaq and several other compatible computer makers, the wrong size of screw driver just won't work at all. With Phillips screws, the size match may seem less important, but is also critical. The wrong size of Phillips screwdriver—particularly one that is too small to properly fit a screwhead—is a guarantee that you will gouge and tear the head of the screw, potentially making the fastener impossible to extract.

Phillips screwdrivers come in a variety of sizes, the most common of which have the numerical designations of 0, 1, and 2. A higher number indicates a larger tool. In most cases, a larger Phillips screwdriver won't work on smaller screws. While you can sometimes make do with a smaller screwdriver for a large screw, don't risk it. The sharp crosses of the Phillips head will quickly turn into impossible circles, leaving you no choice but the ultimate solution in getting inside your PC, drilling out the screw.

Nutdrivers

Some computers, particularly the pre-PS/2 IBM machines, were assembled with hexagonal-headed screws that can be inserted with either a flat-bladed screwdriver or a nutdriver. Instead of a blade, a nutdriver has a hexagonal socket that firmly grips a matching fastener on all six sides. Using a nutdriver offers several advantages. The nutdriver socket more securely holds the fastener (as compared to a conventional screwdriver) so you can more easily start the fastener into its hole. And the nutdriver's better grip means that you can use more torque to tighten the fastener without damaging its head. That's how the gorillas at the computer assembly plant make PCs nearly impossible to disassemble.

Typically, two sizes of nutdriver are required for work on IBM and closely matched compatible computers. The screws holding the case covering the chassis require a $\frac{1}{4}$-inch nutdriver. The screws securing expansion board-retaining brackets use a $\frac{3}{16}$-inch nutdriver. Some tool manufacturers color code their nutdrivers for easy identification. Most commonly, the $\frac{1}{4}$-inch nutdriver is coded red; the $\frac{3}{16}$-inch nutdriver, black.

Torx Screwdrivers

The Torx screw is the better screw. Phillips improves on the standard slotted screw by giving a cross shape, four distinct surfaces of contact, to spread the force you apply. Torx does two better, giving you six points. That also makes it incompatible with standard screwdrivers. And makes Torx screws more choosey about the tool you use on them. Torx screwdrivers come in numerical sizes, and you must have the correct match between Torx screwdriver and screw to have any success at all.

From one perspective, that's good. You're much less likely to try to use a sharp knife or other ill-suited instrument to remove a Torx screw. It's also bad, because you probably don't have the right size

Torx screwdriver lying around. Even your corner hardware store might be challenged to find the right size for you. Worse, you probably won't know what size you need. And, because you cannot pull out the Torx screw without the right screwdriver, you obviously can't take a sample of the screws to the store with you to make a match.

If you are a harried technician in a large corporation charged with overseeing a flock of a thousand PCs, the drawbacks of Torx screws become an advantage. If everyone who has access to the PCs in your business could simply remove the lid and make changes (or liberate an expansion board or two), you'd have chaos on your hands. Put a little obstacle like a strange screwhead in the way, and you'll be able to sleep better nights (and afternoons, too).

Compaq is the one major manufacturer that has chosen to use Torx screws. Two sizes predominate, T-10 and T-15. Arm yourself with those, and you'll be able to handle nearly any upgrade in a full-size Compaq computer.

Long-nosed Pliers

For the most part, you won't need pliers, wrenches, or other such high-torque grippers for your work upgrading your PC. Normally you won't find anything to squeeze or any nuts to grab because, at worst, everything will simply screw together into threaded holes.

But there is one place where the tight, precision grip of long-nose pliers will be most welcome—when you have to change the jumpers that determine the settings of an expansion board or system board. With long-nosed pliers you'll be able to easily remove and relocate jumpers with little effort or frustration. Because of the devilish way that most board makers have of locating jumpers between other taller components, you will rarely be able to get a grip with your fingers alone. Tweezers may work, but long-nosed pliers will make the job much easier.

If you plan to exchange system boards, you'll need pliers to squeeze the mounting spacers together so that you can remove them. And if you drop a screw into the bowels of your PC, a pair of long-nosed pliers may seem a godsend.

Small electronic pliers are best. These are usually described by their overall length, from handle to tip. Even the tiniest, four-inch pliers will work satisfactorily for the typical upgrade job. If you have larger hands, five-inch pliers may be more to your liking, but six-inch pliers will probably prove too cumbersome for the delicate surgery involved in moving jumpers.

Chip Removal Tools

Some time or other you will be required to remove an integrated circuit in making an upgrade. That is, you'll have to pull an integrated circuit chip, such as a RAM chip or microprocessor, out of its socket so that you can put something else in its place. Sockets are designed to hold chips tenaciously. They have to. The chip must make perfect electrical contact with its socket if it is to work at all. Moreover, if chips were loose, they might rattle out of their sockets at some inopportune time, like when you're using the machine.

Chips are held in place so tightly that you're likely to be unable to remove them with your fingers. Moreover, the bigger the chip, the more pins it has friction-fitted into the socket and the more difficult it will be to remove. Typically, the biggest chips (microprocessors) are the ones you'll want to remove most.

Inserting chips, on the other hand, is relatively easy. One you have a chip in place with its leads directed into its socket, you can usually just press them in. Tools are rarely needed for ordinary insertion.

To make the removal process easier, you can invest in a aptly named chip removal tool. These come in a variety of configurations. The most common are designed for 16-, 18-, and 20-pin dual in-line package (DIP) integrated circuits. This tool looks like a giant, ill-formed tweezers. Simply a U-shaped piece of springy steel about six inches long, its jaws are separated by about the length of a chip. The tips of the jaws are bent at right angles so that you can maneuver them under the chip, squeeze the tool to lock them in place, and pull up.

Pulling large integrated circuits such as microprocessors in 28-, 40-, or 64-pin DIP cases or square pin-grid array case requires more effort than this simple tool can usually provide. A number of strange chip removal tool designs are used. All use a variation on the basic tool—a pair of grippers to slide under the chip and grab it—but add some kind of mechanical aid to pulling the chip. Typically this will be a screw that you twist to slowly lift the chip from its socket.

Chip removal tools are used rarely enough that most people prefer to improvise rather than buy one. Most commonly, they will use a flat-blade screwdriver to pry chips from their sockets. They hold the screwdriver parallel to the chip and slide its blade under one end of the chip. Then they either lever one end of the chip up by lifting the screwdriver or force the chip up by twisting the screwdriver blade. This process often works too well. One end of the chip lifts high while the other is still stuck in the socket, resulting in a steady progression of increasingly bent pins running from one end of the chip to the other. If you want to use this technique, you can minimize the number of bent pins by working from both ends of each chip. Either use two screwdrivers (which is ungainly) or use a single screwdriver to slowly work each chip from its socket. First lift one end slightly, then the other, back to the first, and so on until the chip is loose enough to remove with your fingers.

You can usually repair the damage of bent pins by using your long-nosed pliers to carefully bend them back. Don't be too vigorous. And don't plan on straightening the pins of a given IC more than once. Pins aren't designed to bend all that much, and they typically show their dislike for the procedure by sulkily letting go. A chip so crippled is worthless and will have to be replaced.

Using a screwdriver requires adequate space for prying, and space is usually at a premium inside your PC. You often cannot reach the chip you need to remove with a screwdriver. Fortunately, most PCs come already equipped with their own chip-removal tools—a blank expansion slot retaining bracket. Use the the L-shaped bracket as a lever, sliding the tip of its short arm under one end of the chip to pry up and loosen the chip. Just press back on the long arm, prying the end of the chip upward. As with using a screwdriver, you'll need to be careful to avoid bending the lead on the chip. Again, the best strategy is to pry up on one end slightly, then pry up slightly on the other, continuing the back-and-forth process until the chip is free.

D.

UNDERSTANDING SCSI

As its name says, SCSI—the Small Computer System Interface—is a "system" interface rather than a "device" interface like the more common connections used by hard disk drives. As a system interface, it works like an expansion bus. But more than that, SCSI is a smart expansion bus that has some of the advanced features of the EISA and Micro Channel buses used in PCs. For example, any SCSI device can take control of the connection and not depend on your computer to order data around. Moreover, SCSI has its own language by which the devices that are coupled together through it communicate.

One of the greatest promises of SCSI is its ability to serve as a high-speed, universal interface. Its design allows up to seven disparate devices to be connected to a single host adapter. Already, in addition to hard disks, SCSI-based CD-ROM, magneto-optical rewritable optical disk, tape drives, and scanners are available. Using SCSI, even a computer with a limited number of expansion slots could accommodate more peripherals that would be prudent. For some Apple Macintosh computers, for example, SCSI is the only expansion bus available.

However, SCSI has not been refined to the point that any mixture of peripherals attached to a single host adapter will plug and play. Some SCSI devices get along about as well as Eastern European ethnics fighting for their own homelands. The SCSI standard is partly to blame because in the past it has allowed for manufacturers to select the features to implement. All SCSI devices did not support all SCSI features, and those that did might take their own direction in how to do it.

Because of this situation, it's often a poor idea to try to chain multiple unmatched SCSI devices together. Rather, connect each SCSI device to its own host adapter if you can. (You will have to make sure that you can install multiple SCSI host adapters in your PC. Usually, you will have to relocate the SCSI BIOS code on some of the adapters to avoid conflicts.) The only way to assure that an SCSI system will work properly when you take it from the box is to buy a matched system—SCSI drive and matching host adapter. If you want to add a second SCSI hard disk to the SCSI system you already have installed, make it the same brand as the first. If you must mix and match SCSI drives and host adapters, get the assurance of the vendor selling both components that the two will work with one another.

SCSI now comes in different flavors—the two most important being ordinary SCSI and SCSI-2. The important difference between the two is that SCSI-2 is newer, bigger, better, faster, and more standardized. The original SCSI was designed with an 8-bit data path and a maximum speed of ten megahertz, which calculates to a theoretical ten megabyte-per-second throughput. SCSI-2 is a super-set of the original specification that allows designers to optionally incorporate data paths as wide as 32 bits and speeds up to 20 megahertz. A SCSI-2 system that takes advantage of all these pos-sibilities might possibly move information as quickly as 80 megabytes per second. More importantly, SCSI-2 makes more of the features of the SCSI connection mandatory—meaning that you should have fewer problems when connecting SCSI-2 components.

As this is written, SCSI-2 hard disks were just becoming avail-able, but none of them has taken advantage of all the performance options of SCSI-2. That's a forgivable sin because no drive mechan-ism made today can even approach the performance potential of SCSI-2.

You add SCSI to your PC using a *SCSI host adapter*, which is similar to a disk or tape controller but is much more complex. In the past (and even now in many cases) SCSI has not been an entirely satisfactory interface for PC hard disks because it was designed as a universal interface, one that serves not only different computer ar-chitectures but also operating systems and a variety of peripherals, from hard disks to scanners. The SCSI host adapter must match the signals designed for its universal bus to the particular requirements of the PC bus and DOS. The latter is the more challenging because SCSI structures information in the form of blocks and DOS thinks in terms of clusters. Early SCSI host adapters choked on the conver-sion process, and system throughput suffered. In a few years, how-ever, the efficiency of SCSI systems has improved immeasurably, although old, laggardly host adapters may turn up occasionally.

Because the host adapter can so severely limit the performance of a SCSI system, the choice of this adapter is as critical as your choice of hard disk or other peripherals you want to connect to it. A slow host adapter can be a roadblock to the performance of a fast hard disk or CD ROM player. Besides performance issues, your choice of SCSI host adapter will determine whether and how any hard disk you connect to it can boot your PC. It will also determine your flexibility in assigning device identifications and priorities to the peripherals you attach to it. In other words, when it comes to SCSI host adapters, you'll want to shop carefully.

You can attach SCSI-2 drives to an ordinary SCSI host adapter, but you won't realize all of their features or performance. Similarly, an ordinary SCSI drive will work when connected to a SCSI-2 host adapter. In either case, you can expect getting the system to work to be no easier or harder than working with a plain SCSI system.

Fortunately, if you're only going to use SCSI to connect up a hard disk or a CD ROM player and not chain seven odd devices together or design a SCSI peripheral from scratch, you don't have to worry about all the details of how the SCSI connection works. You only need to know the basics of what it takes to connect it to your PC. The following outline should help you no matter what kind of SCSI device you're installing.

Cabling

The mechanical aspects of SCSI are quite simple. A SCSI system consists of four essential parts. First is the aforementioned SCSI host adapter, which plugs into an expansion slot inside your PC and translates the signals on your PC's expansion bus into commands that can travel across the SCSI connection.

The second essential part of a SCSI system is a SCSI device. It can be a hard disk, CD ROM player, or any of a multitude of other peripherals that rely on an SCSI connection. Up to seven SCSI devices of any type or types can be connected together to a single SCSI host adapter. In theory, you should be able to mix hard disks, tape drives, CD ROMs, and scanners all on one SCSI connection. The reality of the situation isn't quite so rosy, as you'll see.

You also need an *SCSI cable* to link all the devices to the host adapter and software to link the SCSI system to your PC. Cables come in two types—flat, ribbon cables for internal installation of SCSI devices; and round, shielded cables for external devices. Internal cables usually use 50-pin connectors. External cables use 50-pin Amphenol-style connectors or, occasionally 25-pin D-shells. The former is preferred because each active SCSI wire is supposed to have its own ground, and 25 pins are insufficient for all the needed signals together with their grounds.

Finally, you need *SCSI driver software* to match your host adapter and SCSI devices with your PC. Often this software comes in two parts: a software driver that loads through your system's CONFIG.SYS file and BIOS code that's built into ROM chips on the SCSI host adapter.

Most of the time, SCSI devices for the PC market are sold as complete kits that include the drive, the host adapter, and the cable. Some vendors sell the various pieces separately, catering to people who want to design their own systems or add a second (third, fourth, whatever) device to the SCSI connection they already have. Avoid surprises and be sure you get everything you need—the drive player, host adapter, cable, and software—when you order.

Linking the different SCSI devices link together is easy—they connect as a single chain. That is, each external SCSI device usually has two physical connectors on it. You run the SCSI cable from the host adapter to one of the SCSI connectors on the first device you want to connect. It doesn't matter which of the two connectors on the SCSI device you attach to. Functionally, they are both the same.

Internal SCSI drives and some external units have a single SCSI connector. They still link together in chain but with multiple plugs on the cable that ties them together instead of duplicate drive connectors.

If you want to connect more than one external SCSI device to a single host adapter, you attach another cable to the second connector on the first device and run the cable to one of the two connectors on the second device. For three or more SCSI devices, you simply continue this procedure, running a new SCSI cable from device to device, chaining them all together.

Terminations

Once you've wired your SCSI devices together, you still have more work ahead of you. To prevent spurious signals bouncing back and forth across the SCSI cable chain, the SCSI standard requires that you properly terminate the entire SCSI system. A termination is a bank of resistors that absorb the excess signals on the SCSI line and prevent them from reflecting back across the cable.

According to the SCSI specification, the first and last device in a SCSI chain must be terminated. The first device is almost always the SCSI host adapter in your PC. The last device is the one that has a cable attached to only one of its two SCSI connectors.

The only time your host adapter might not be at the end of an SCSI chain is when you install both internal and external SCSI devices. This sort of connection typically puts the host adapter in the middle of the chain so the internal drive and not the host adapter should be terminated.

SCSI products are terminated in a variety of ways. The three most popular are internally with resistor packs, externally with dummy termination plugs, and using switches.

Resistor packs are components attached directly to circuit boards. Most PC-based SCSI host adapters come with termination resistors already installed. You can identify them as being three identical components near the SCSI connector about an inch long and one-quarter to three-eights an inch high and hardly an eighth of an inch thick. Most commonly, they are red, yellow, or black and shiny.

Typically these terminator resistors are removable—you can grab hold of one and pull it off the expansion board. There's normally no need to do that in the case of your SCSI host adapter because all three resistor packs need to be there except when you combine internal and external SCSI drives in a single chain.

You may also find these terminators on SCSI devices themselves. You're most likely to find them on an internal drive. Some external SCSI devices rely on the terminators on the drive inside their cases, requiring you to take apart the device to access the terminators.

External SCSI terminators are plugs that often look like short extensions to the SCSI jacks on the back of SCSI devices. One end of the terminator plugs into one of the jacks on your SCSI device, and the other end of the dummy plug yields another jack that could be attached to another SCSI cable. Some external terminators lack the second jack on the back. Generally, the absence of a second connector is no problem because the dummy plug should only be attached to the last device in the SCSI chain, the device that has an extra unused SCSI jack.

Switches, the third variety of termination, may be found on both external and internal drives. Sometimes a single switch handles the entire termination, but occasionally an SCSI drive will have three banks of Dip switches that all must be flipped to the same position to select whether the termination is active. These switches are sometimes found on the SCSI drive itself or on the case of an external unit.

Since the rule is that the first and last device in a SCSI chain needs to be terminated, in most cases you should ensure that only one SCSI device attached to a host adapter uses a terminator. Remove or switch off the terminators on all other devices except the last one in the chain. The termination on the host adapter takes care of the first device in the chain.

Identification

Because up to seven SCSI devices can be attached identically to a single chain, your system needs some method of distinguishing which device is which—like a name for each link in the chain.

In the SCSI system, this identification is carried out by assigning each SCSI device an SCSI ID number, zero to six (the number seven is usually reserved for the host adapter). The one important rule is that every SCSI device connected in a chain have its own, unambiguous SCSI ID number. In other words, never assign the same SCSI ID number to two or more devices in the same SCSI chain.

Most external SCSI devices are assigned their ID number by a switch on the rear panel of the equipment. Internal SCSI devices may have several jumpers or a switch on the drive itself that sets SCSI ID.

Some software drivers require that your SCSI device have a particular SCSI ID set. Other drivers are more accommodating, accepting any SCSI ID as long as you tell the software which you want to use. In any case, you should check the SCSI ID of your SCSI device when you install it, and write it down, should you need the number for future use.

If the driver software that comes with your SCSI device gives you a choice of SCSI ID numbers, you can give it any number when it is the only SCSI device connected to your system. However, higher-numbered SCSI devices have greater priority.

Often, SCSI hard disk drives are assigned an SCSI ID of six to make them the most important device connected to the system.

Some SCSI host adapters, however, require any device that's connected to the SCSI chain that needs to boot the computer host have an SCSI ID of zero. In general, a CD ROM player or scanner is not a high-priority device, so a lower number is appropriate for it, providing that number is not pre-empted by a hard disk drive.

Once you've taken care of the connection details, you're ready to try out your SCSI device. If it came with, or its host adapter came with, diagnostic software, check everything out. If you've paid attention to all the details, your SCSI system should work right off and deliver excellent performance.

INDEX

adapter plates, drive, 585–86
adaptive Packet Assembly, 376–77
addressability
  resolution versus, 440
  of memory. *See* memory,
    addressability of
Advanced Micro Devices coprocessors,
  154
Advanced RLL (ARLL) coding, 239
advanced set-up procedures, 107–8
Adverse Channel Enhancements, 378
ALL ChargeCard, 1056
analog signals, display adapters and,
  422–23
archive files, 74
archiving inactive files, 72–74
ARC program, 74
arrays, drive, 249–51
aspect ratio, 436
AT Attachment interface, 233–34
  host adapters and, 241, 242
AT command set, 382–83
AT computers, 95. *See also* 286 family
  of microprocessors
  increasing clock speed of, 103–5
  memory chip sizes, 203
AutoCAD, 47
  display list drivers and, 84
AUTOEXEC.BAT file, 54
AutoMate, 84
autosizing monitors, 436–37
average access time, 252–53

backing up a hard disk, 14, 262. *See
  also* Tape backup systems
  alternatives for, 498–500
  to another hard disk, 24546
  to floppy disks, 498–500

image or file-by-file backups, 497
  reasons for, 496–97
  software for, 515–16
backup power systems, 549–65
  buying, 559–62
  installation of, 562–65
  ratings of, 556–59
  standby, 549–51
  state-saving software and, 555–56
  strategies for using, 553–55
  types of, 549–50
  uninterruptible, 549, 551–52
BACKUP program, 66
bad clusters, 66
ballistic operation of trackballs, 467
bandwidth, monitor, 444–45
bank-switching, 182, 186–87
base memory, 183. *See also* memory,
  conventional
Bell 212A modem standard, 375
Bell 301 modem standard, 374
benchmarking programs, 444–5
bias field, 335
binary coded decimal (BCD) numbers,
  149
BIOS (Basic Input/Output System)
  conventional memory and, 183
  display adapters and, 415
  display performance and, 81–83
  display routines, 82
  floppy disk drives and, 287
    compatibility issues, 290, 296–98
bottlenecks, 23-49
  bus, 2931
  display system, 35–36, 41–42
  finding, 14–15, 25, 26, 40–45
    benchmarking programs, 44–45
    display system, 41–42

hard disk bottlenecks, 41
human interface, 43
microprocessor bottlenecks, 40–41
peripherals, 42–43
hard disk, 33–35, 41
human, 38–39
memory, 31–32
microprocessor, 23–24, 26–29, 40–41
modem, 42–43
network, 37–38
printing, 36–37, 42
recommendations for specific
  applications
    application development, 48
    computer-aided design (CAD),
      47–48
    databases, 46
    Microsoft Windows, 49
    OS/2, 48–49
    spreadsheets, 46–47
    word processors, 45–46
buffers
defined and explained, 54
look-ahead, 54
BUFFERS statement, 54–59
  disk caching and, 57–58
  expanded (EMS) memory and, 55–56
  HMA (High Memory Area) and, 55
  memory-hungry programs and, 58
  RAM disk and, 58
Burndy connectors, 539–40
bus
  as bottleneck, 29–31
  memory addressability limits and,
    181–82
bus mastering, 31
  hard disk controllers and, 237
bus mastering ports, 258
bus width, of display adapters, 414–15

cable connections
  floppy disk drive, 301–5
  hard disk, 265–69

for modems, 397–98
for monitors, 452–55
for power supplies, 539–40
cache controller, 191
cache memory, 109–10, 190–93
caching controllers, 235–37, 253–54
CAD (computer-aided design)
  programs, 409
    display list drivers and, 84
    math coprocessors and, 142
    recommendations for, 47–48
case screws, 580–82
CD ROM drives, 317–27
  audio CDs and, 320–21
  disks, 322–23
  installation of, 344–50
  standards for, 326–27
CGA (Color Graphics Adapter), 407
  memory addressing range of, 184
ChargeCard, 105–6
chip removal tools, 126, 597–98
CHKDSK utility, finding lost clusters
  with, 72
clock frequency, increasing, 103–5
clusters, 65
  bad, 66
  lost, 71–72
CMOS technology, 154, 156
Color-Edge Graphics (CEG), 412
colors, 12
  display adapters and, 410–13
  look-up tables, 411
  monitors and, 447–50
color scanners, 480–82
color temperature, 448–49
compilers, 48
composite video, 422
compression, file, 73–76
computer-aided design (CAD), 409
  display list drivers and, 84
  math coprocessors and, 142
  recommendations for, 47–48
CONFIG.SYS file, 54

BUFFERS statement in, 55–58
conventional memory. *See* memory, conventional
convergence problems, 443–44
Copaq Deskpros, replacement motherboards for, 121
coprocessed graphics adapters, 414–17
coprocessor chips, graphics, 419
coprocessors. *See* math coprocessors
cover of a computer
    affixing, 579
    removing, 572–73
crystal swapping, in AT computers, 104–5
Cubit, 76
Cyrix Corporation coprocessors, 157–59

databases, recommendations for, 46
data cassettes, 509–10
Data Phase Optimization, 377
data separator, 228
data transfer rate
    bus and, 29–31
    of hard disks, 33–34, 228, 254–55
    of networks, 38
DC1000 cartridges, 509–10
DC2000-style cartridges, 506–9
DC6000-style cartridges, 504–6
DEBUG program, port expansion boards and, 363–65
defragmenting a hard disk, 64–67
Digital Audio Tape (DAT) backup systems, 512–13
digital signals, display adapters and, 423
Digital-to Analog converter (DAC), 411, 412
digitizer cursors, 469
digitizer pens, 469, 473–74
digitizing tablets, 469–76
    cursors and pens for, 472–74
    ergonomic issues, 474–75

installation of, 475–76
    proximity of, 472
    resolution and accuracy of, 471–72
    size of, 471
    software and emulations, 472
    speed of, 472
    technology of, 474
    templates for, 474
DIPs (Dual In-Line Packages), 200
    installation of, 210–11
Direct Memory Access. *See* DMA
disk caching, 34–35
    BUFFERS statement and, 57–58
    compatibility problems, 69–70
    hardware-based, 35, 69. *See also* hard disk controllers, caching
    software-based, 34, 67–71
        caching hard disk controllers versus, 236
disk interface. *See* hard disk, interfaces of
Disk Manager, 262
disk mirroring, 499
display adapters, 406–29
    BIOS and, 415
    bus width of, 414–15
    CGA (Color Graphics Adapter), 407
    colors and, 410–13
    connections and connectors for, 425–27
    EGA (Extended Graphics Adapter), 407
    graphics languages and, 417–18
    installing, 427–29
    matching monitors to, 420–24
        color capability, 424
        frequencies, 420–21
        signal types, 422–23
    MDA (monochrome display adapter), 406–7
    for one or two displays, 424–25
    pass-through, 424
    performance issues, 413–15

resolutions of, 408–10
software drivers for, 409
standards for, 406–8
VGA (Video Graphics Array), 407
display-list processing, 417
display system, 9–13
as bottleneck, 25, 35–36, 41–42
CAD programs and, 47
improving performance of, 81–84
BIOS and, 81–83
display list drivers, 84
speed-up programs, 82–83
video shadowing, 83
list drivers, 84
DOS (Disk Operating System)
CD ROM extensions, 327
conventional memory and, 183–86
display routines, 82–83
driver software for floppy drives,
291–94
extended (XMS) memory and, 194
floppy disk formats and, 281–86
hard-disk performance and, 53–70
BUFFERS statement, 54–59
defragmenting your hard disk,
64–67
disk caching, 67–71
FASTOPEN command, 61–63
RAM disk, 59–61
search path, 63–64
memory addressability limits and,
179, 180
microprocessors and
80286 family, 95–96
80386 family, 96–99
8088 family, 93
DOS extenders, 180
DOSKEY, 87
dot-pitch, 441–43
DRAM chips, 205
drive adapter plates, 585–86
drive array, 249–51
DRIVER.SYS program, 292, 293

driver software, for floppy disk drives,
291–94
DRIVPARM.SYS program, 293–94
command options for different
versions of DOS, 284–86
drum scanners, 478–80
dual-frequency displays, 435
dye-polymer storage technology,
332–33

EEMS (Enhanced Expanded Memory
Specification), 189
EEPROM (Electrically Erasable PROM)
chips, 206
EGA (Extended Graphics Adapter),
407
8514/A display adapter, 407
EISA (Enhanced Industry Standard
Architecture), 31
EMC87 coprocessors, 158–59
EMS. *See* expanded (EMS) memory
Enhanced Expanded Memory
Specification (EEMS), 189
Enhanced Industry Standard
Architecture (EISA), 31
EPROM chips, 206
equipment flag, coprocessors and, 172
ergonomics, of digitizing tablets,
474–75
ESDI (Enhanced Standard Device
Interface), 231
ESDI controllers, 240
Excel, 47, 141
expanded (EMS) memory, 186–90
buffers and, 55–56
extended memory versus, 77–78
RAM disk in, 61
expanded memory emulation
programs, 187–88
expansion boards. *See also* memory
expansion boards
fitting, 576–78
for memory, 32

expansion bus. *See* bus
extended (XMS) memory, 190
   disk caching and, 69–70
   expanded memory versus, 77–78
   RAM disk in, 60–61
Extra, 81

fallback, 380–81
FASTOPEN command, 61–63
FAT (file allocation table), 65
   optical disks and, 335
fault-tolerant systems, 250
fax modems, 387–93
   connections for, 390–91
   selecting, 391–93
   standards for, 389–90
feature-matching, 484
file-by-file backups, 497–98
file compression, 73–76
Flash ROM chips, 206
flatbed scanner, 478–80
floating-point numbers, 138–39
floating-point units (FPUs). *See* math
 coprocessors
floppy disk controllers, 287–88,
 290–91, 294–95
floppy disk drive, 13, 275–312
   caching, 68
   compatibility with your PC, 277–78,
   283, 287–98
     adding a new BIOS, 290, 296–98
     floppy controller upgrade, 294–95
     software drivers, 291–94
   DOS considerations, 281–86
   installation of, 585–90
     AT-compatible, 589–90
     AT drives, 587–89
     PS/2 drives, 590
     XT drives, 586–87
   laptop computer compatibility,
   289–90
   mechanics of upgrading, 305–9
   physical considerations, 298–302

cables, 301–5
   internal versus external
   installation, 298–99
   mounting hardware, 299–300
   PS/2 considerations, 309–11
   set-up programs and procedures for,
   311–12
floppy disks
   as back-up medium, 498–500
   compatibility of, 279–81
   IBM standards for, 275–77
FontSpace, 75–76
formatting
   defragmenting a disk and, 66–67
   low-level, 270–71
486 family of microprocessors, 100–2
frame rate, 420, 446
FSK (Frequency Shift Keying), 374–78
full duplex, 380

GPIB (General-Purpose Interface Bus),
 485
graphics, 405–6. *See also* display
 adapters
   Color-Edge, 412
graphics adapters. *See* display adapters
graphics applications, 36
graphics coprocessor chips, 419–20
graphics coprocessors, 414–17
graphics languages, 417–18

hand scanners, 478–80
HardCard, 248
hard disks, 10, 11
   arrays, 249–51
   average access time of, 33, 34
   backing up, 262
     to another hard disk, 245–46
   as bottleneck, 24–25, 33–35, 41
   cable connections for, 265–69
   caching. *See* caching controllers; disk
   caching
   capacity of, 244–46

choosing a vendor of, 258–59
costs of, 259–62
databases and, 46
data transfer rate of, 33–34, 228
disk caching and, 34–35
finding lost clusters, 71–72
head crashes, 257
host adapters, 241–44
    IDE, 241–42
    SCSI, 242–44
    SCSI-2, 244
increasing capacity of, 71–76
    archiving inactive files, 72–74
    file compression, 73–76
interfaces of, 224, 226–234
    device-level interfaces, 227–31
of laptop and notebook PCs, 247–48
mounting schemes, 263–64
MTTR (mean time to repair), 258
performance of, 251–55
    average access time, 252–53
    caching controllers, 253–54
    data transfer rate, 254–55
physical installation of, 263–65
physical size of, 246–47
power supply and, 247
reliability of, 255–58
removing your old hard disk, 262–63
set-up program, 262
set-up programs, 261–62
software set-up of, 269–72
    AAA move set-up programs and
      procedures references here, 269
    DOS formatting, 272
    low-level formatting, 270–71
    partitioning, 271
    restoring files, 272
    system configuration, 270
speeding up, 53–54
    BUFFERS statement, 54–59
    defragmenting your hard disk,
      64–67
    disk caching, 67–71

FASTOPEN command, 61–63
    RAM disk, 59–61
    search path, 63–64
as a system, 224–25
system-level interfaces, 227–29,
    231–34
word processors and, 45–46
hard disk controllers, 224, 228, 234–40
    cable connections for, 267–68
    caching, 235–37, 253–54
        compatibility problems, 69
    ESDI, 240
    RLL, 238–39
    ST506, 237–38
hard disk utility packages, 66, 67
Hayes command set, 382–83
hdcs, 248–49
head actuator, 225, 252
Headroom, 81
Hercules Graphics Card (HGC), 407–8
high memory, 183
High Sierra format, 326–27
hit ratio, 192
HMA (High Memory Area)
    addressability of, 183–86
    buffers in, 55
horizontal scanning frequency, 434–36
host adapters, 229
    for scanners, 486–87
    SCSI, 233, 242–44, 602–3
    SCSI-2, 244

IDE (Integrated Drive Electronics),
    233. *See also* AT Attachment interface
    adding a second drive, 260–61
    cable connections for, 268
    translation mode, 270
IDE host adapters, 241–42
IEEE floating-point standard, 143–45
image backups, 497
input devices, 455–90. *See also*
    digitizing tablets; mouse; scanners;
    trackballs

keyboards, 455–57
input/output (I/O) bus, as bottleneck, 30
Integrated Information Technology coprocessors, 154–55, 160–61
interlacing, 410, 446–47
interleaved memory, 206–7
interleaving memory, 109
interposer board, 309
interrupts, modems and, 396–97
ISO 9660 specification, 326–27
ISO standard for magneto-optical (MO) drives, 340–41

Kerr effect, 334
keyboard macros, 86–87
keyboard quickeners, 86
keyboards, 455–57

LAPB modem standard, 375–76
LAPM modem standard, 376
laptop computers, floppy disk drive compatibility, 289–90
LCC (Leadless Chip Carrier), 114
Leadless Chip Carrier (LCC), 114
learn mode, of keyboard macro programs, 87
LIM memory. *See* expanded (EMS) memory
LIMulators, 187–88
list drivers, 84
long-nosed pliers, 596–97
look-ahead buffers, 54, 55. *See also* BUFFERS statement
lost clusters, 71–72 Lotus 123, 47, 141
low-level formatting, 270–71

macros, keyboard, 86–87
magneto-optical (MO) drives, 333–44. *See also* optical disks
  applications for, 343–44
  capacity of, 339–40
  cartridges for, 342
  coercivity of, 336–37
  drawback of, 337–39
  installation of, 344–50
  jukebox systems, 340
  method of operation of, 335–37
  standards for, 340–41
mass storage, 11–12. *See also* hard disks
math coprocessors (numeric coprocessors or floating-point units), 10, 28–29, 137–74
  applications that benefit from, 140–42
  basic understanding of, 138–40
  CAD programs and, 47
  8087, 150–51
  history of, 143–45
  Intel architecture, 149–50
  I/O-mapped, 145–47
  making the upgrade to, 164–74
    finding the right chip, 164–66
    orientation of chip, 168–72
    preparing a coprocessor, 167–68
    system preparation, 166–67
    system set-up procedure, 172–74
  memory-mapped, 145, 147–49
  spreadsheets and, 46–47
  387, 155–57
  387-compatible, 157–63
    Cyrix Corporation, 157–59
    487, 163–64
    Integrated Information Technology, 160–61
    ULSI, 161
    Weitek Corporation, 161–63
  387SX, 156–57
  287, 151–55
  287XL and 287XLT, 153–54
matrix matching, 483
MDA (monochrome display adapter), 406–7
  memory addressing range of, 184

mean time between failures (MTBF),
255–56
memory, 177–219. *See also* expanded
(EMS) memory; extended (XMS)
memory
  adding, 79–81
  addressability of, 178–82
    architectural limits, 181–82
    cache memory, 190–91
    conventional memory, 183–86
    expanded (EMS) memory, 186–90
    extended (XMS) memory, 190
    microprocessor limits, 181
    operating system limits, 180
    program limits, 179
  as bottleneck, 31–32
  for buffers, 55
  cache, 109–10, 190–93
  CAD programs and, 47
  choosing the type of, 193–99
    application considerations, 193–94
    hardware considerations, 1995-99
    performance considerations,
      194–95
  conventional, addressability of,
    183–86
  disk caching and, 70–71
  expansion boards for, 32
  high, 183–86. *See also* HMA (High
    Memory Area)
  improving speed of, 76–79, 106–10
    cache memory, 109–10
    eliminating wait states, 78–79
    extended versus expanded
      memory, 77–78
    interleaving, 109
    reducing wait states, 107–9
  installation of chips and modules,
    209–19
    inspecting your work, 218–19
    orientation of chips, 213–15
    plugging in modules, 215–18
    preparing chips, 210–12

    sockets, 212–13
    system set-up, 219
  interleaving memory, 109
  on motherboards, 123–24
  remapping, 97
  selecting chips and modules,
    199–209
    capacity, 202–4
    packaging, 200–2
    speed, 207–8
    technology, 205–7
  video, 81
  virtual, TSR management and, 80–81
memory caching, 32
memory expansion boards, 184,
  194–99. *See also* expanded (EMS)
  memory
  proprietary, 196–97
  640K DOS limit and, 184
memory management programs, with
  virtual memory capabilities, 80–81
memory remapping, 185
MFM (Modified Frequency
  Modulation), 239
Micro Channel Architecture, 31
Micro Channel computers. *See also*
  PS/2 computers
  floppy disk drives of, 295
  memory expansion boards for, 77–78
microcode, 139
microprocessors (chips), 10
  as bottleneck, 23–24, 26–29, 40–41
  bus speed and, 30–31
  8088 family of, 92–94
  memory addressability limits and,
    181
microprocessor upgrades, 91–133
  alternatives to, 103–11
    adding memory-management
      abilities, 105–6
    increasing clock speed of, 103–5
    memory speed-up tricks, 106–10
    replacing your entire PC, 110–11

choice of chip for
  8086 family, 94–95
  8088 family, 92–94
  80286 family, 95–96
  80386 family, 96–99
  80486 family, 100–2
method for, 111–12
  propietary upgrades, 124–25
  replacement motherboards, 118–24
  replacing the microprocessor,
    112–15
  turbo boards, 115–18
step-by-step guide to
  microprocessor replacement,
    125–27
  motherboard upgrades, 130–33
  turbo board upgrades, 127–30
Microsoft CD ROM extensions, 327
Microsoft Windows
  et and, 194
  recommendations for, 49
  software drivers for display
    adapters, 409
mirroring, disk, 499
MNP2 modem standard, 376
MNP3 modem standard, 376
MNP4 modem standard, 376–77
MNP5 modem standard, 377
MNP6 modem standard, 377
MNP7 modem standard, 377
MNP9 modem standard, 377
MNP10 modem standard, 378
modems, 370–401
  as bottleneck, 42–43
  duplex communication, 380
  fallback capability, 380–81
  fax, 387–93
    connections for, 390–91
    selecting, 391–93
    standards for, 389–90
  features of, 383–84
  function and purpose of, 371–73
  Hayes command set, 382–83

installation of, 397–401
internal versus external, 384–87
preinstallation considerations,
  395–97
reliability of, 382
speed of, 381
standards for, 373–79
support issues, 393–94
MO drives. *See* magneto-optical (MO)
drives
Molex connectors, 539–40
monitors, 429–55. *See also* display
system
  analog versus digital, 433–34
  autosizing, 436–37
  bandwidth fo, 444–45
  brightness of, 450–51
  colors and, 447–50
  color temperature and, 448–49
  connections for, 452–55
  controls of, 437–39
  convergence problems of, 443–44
  dot-pitch of, 441–43
  frequencies of, 434–36
  interlaced versus noninterlaced,
    446–47
  monochrome, phosphor type and,
    447–48
  phosphor type of, 447–48
  scanning range of, 430–33
  sharpness versus resolution of,
    439–43
  with tilt-swivel bases, 452
  Trinitron-based, 441–42
motherboards
  memory on, 196
  replacement, 118–24
  size of, 121
  step-by-step guide to installing,
    130–33
mouse, 457–65
  buttons, 459
  installation of, 462–65

interfaces, 460–61
mechanical, 458
optical, 458–59
protocols, 459–60
resolution, 461–62
MTBF (mean time between failures),
  255–56
multiscanning monitors, 421, 431, 432,
  435–36
multitasking, 96–7

National Television Standards
  Committee (NTSC)
  video standard, 422–23
navigating through menus, 86
network as bottleneck, 37–38
nine-track tape backup systems, 501–3
noise, 549
NTSC systems, 422–23
numeric coprocessors. *See* math
  coprocessors
nutdrivers, 595

optical character recognition (OCR),
  482–84
optical disks, 315–50. *See also* CD ROM
  drives; magneto-optical (MO) drives;
  WORM drives
  advantages of, 315
  disadvantages of, 316
  installation of, 344–50
  rewritable. *See also* magneto-optical
    (MO) drives
    dye-polymer technology, 332–33
    installation of, 344–50
    phase-change systems, 333
  technologies used for, 317–20
optimizing a hard disk, 66
OS/2, recommendations for, 48–49
overvoltages, 549

page frame, 187
page-mode memory chips, 205

page-remapping registers, 188–89
paletts, 411–12
parallel ports, 353, 357–70
  addresses of, 358–61
  connectors for, 361
  expansion boards, 362–70
    installation of, 366–70
    port preparation for installing,
      363–66
partitioning, hard disk, 271
pass-through graphics adapters, 424
PATH command, 64
PC-Kwik, 68, 69
PC-Kwik Power Pak, 86
  screen portion of, 83
PC Lab Benchmark Utilities, 44
PCs (personal computers), removing
  the cover of, 572–73
performance-measuring software,
  44–45
peripherals. *See also specific peripherals*
  as bottleneck, 42–43
Personal Measure, 44
PGA (Pin-Grid Array), 114, 172
phase-change storage, 333
Phillips screwdriver, 594–95
phosphors, 447
picture tubes, 440–41
Pin-Grid Array (PGA), 114
pixels, 406
PKZip program, 74
Plastic Leadless Chip Carrier (PLCC),
  114
PLCC (Plastic Leadless Chip Carrier),
  114, 154, 171, 172
pliers, long-nosed, 596–97
Power Meter, 44–45
power supplies, 533–49
  amount of power needed, 537–38
  backup. *See* backup power systems
  connections for, 539–40
  installation of, 545–49
  internal battery, 552–53

operation of, 536–37
physical considerations, 540–42
purpose of, 534–35
removing old, 542–45
safety considerations, 535–36
power supply, 13
hard disks and, 247
pressure pen, 474
print buffers, 37
printer spoolers, 84–85
printing, as bottleneck, 36–37, 42
print spoolers, 37
PROM chips, 206
protected mode, 95–96
PS/2 computers
disk drives for, 590
floppy disk drives for, 309–11
memory chip sizes, 203
pucks, 469

QIC-40 and QIC-80 standards, 507–8
Quattro Pro, 47, 141

RAM (random access memory). *See
also* memory
for buffers, 55, 57
insufficient, symptoms of, 58–59
video shadowing and, 83
RAMDAC, 411, 412
RAM disk, 59–61, 81
buffers and, 58
RAMDRIVE.SYS, 59–61
read/write head, 252
real mode, 95
real-mode memory, 183. *See also*
memory, conventional
reformatting, defragmenting a disk
and, 66–67
regeneration, 84
resolution, 12, 439–43
of digitizing tablets, 471–72
mouse, 461–62
restoring, to new hard disk, 272

retracing, 445
rewritable optical disks. *See* magneto-
optical (MO) drives
RISC (Reduced Instruction Set
Computing), 102
RLL coding, 239
RLL controllers, 238–39
ROM (read-only memory)
shadowing, 97
video shadowing and, 83
ROM chips, 206

scanners, 476–90
color versus grey scale, 480–81
connections of, 484–88
hand, 478–80
host adapters for, 486–87
installation of, 488–90
optical character recognition (OCR),
482–84
SCSI, 485–86
types of, 478–80
screwdrivers, 594–96
screws, case, 580–82
SCSI (Small Computer System
Interface), 231–34, 601–7
cable connections for, 268–69
cabling considerations, 603–4
CD ROM players, 327
identification of devices, 606–7
magneto-optical (MO) drives, 341–42
optical disks, installation of, 344–50
problems of, 232–33
scanners, 485–86
terminations, 604–6
SCSI host adapters, 242–44, 261, 602–3
SCSI-2 host adapters, 244
serial ports, 353–70
addresses of, 358–61
connectors for, 361
expansion boards, 362–70
installation of, 366–70

port preparation for installing, 363–66
set-up programs and procedures
  for floppy disk drives, 288–89, 311–12
  for hard disks, 261–62
shadow mask, 441
SIMMs (Single In-Line Memory Modules), 120, 202, 204
SIP (Single In-line Package), 200
  installation of, 211–12
SIPPs (Single In-line Pin Package), 202, 204
  installation of, 215, 217–18
slot mask, 441
slot pitch, 441
speed, as goal fo upgrading, 910
SPEEDISK.SYS, 68–70
SpeedStor, 262
spindle motor, 225
spoolers. *See* printer spoolers
spot size, 450
spreadsheets
  math coprocessors and, 141–42
  recommendations for, 46–47
Squish Plus, 76
SQZ Plus, 76
ST506 controllers, 237–38
ST506 device-level interface, 229
Stacker, 76
standby power supplies, 549–51. *See also* backup power systems
state-saving software, 555–56
static-column RAM chips, 205
static RAM (SRAM) chips, 110, 205
Statistical Duplexing, 377
straight-through cable, 398
SUBST command, 64
Super PC-Kwik, 68, 69
SuperVGA, 407–10
surges, 549
system boards. *See* motherboards

tape backup systems, 493–529
  alternatives to, 498–500
  backup philosophy and, 496–98
  choosing, 513–14
  as data exchange medium, 495
  installation of, 521–29
    cable connections, 528–29
    DC2000 drives in 31/2-inch bays, 524–25
    DC2000 drives in PS/2s, 522–24
    DC6000 drives, 525–28
    disk multiplexing and, 522
  media considerations, 516–17
  shopping for, 520–21
  software considerations, 515–16
  standards for, 517–20
  types of, 501–13
    data cassettes, 509–10
    DC1000 cartridges, 509–10
    DC2000-style cartridges, 506–9
    DC6000-style cartridges, 504–6
    Digital Audio Tape (DAT) systems, 512–13
    nine-track open-reel system, 501–3
    3480 cartridges, 503–4
    video-based systems, 510–12
templates, for digitizing tablets, 474
tensioning wires, 441
terminate-and-stay-resident programs. *See* TSRs
terminations, SCSI, 604–6
terminator, 306–7
3480 cartridges, 503–4
THOR system, 332–33
386 family of microprocessors, 96–99
386SL microprocessor, 99
386SX microprocessor, 98–99, 102
  for 286 sockets, 113–14
tools for working on your PC, 593–98
Torx screwdrivers, 595–96
tracers, 469
trackballs, 465–68
  installation of, 467–68

Trellis Modulation, 378
Trinitron picture tubes, 441–42
TSR management programs, 80–81
turbo boards, 115–18
    step-by-step guide to installing,
    127–30
286 family of microprocessors, 95–96
    adding memory-management
    abilities, 105–6
typematic rate, 86

UART chips, 356–57
ULSI(Ultra Larges Scale Integration)
  coprocessors, 161
UMBs (upper memory blocks), 185
uninterruptible power systems (UPSs),
  549, 551–52
Universal Link Negotiation, 377
upgrading, 3–20
    decisions about, 4–5
    exchanging information with other
    PCs, 13–14
    goals of, 8–14
        adding more mass storage, 11–12
        backup security, 14
        better performance, 9–10
        more colors and sharper images,
        12
        power reserves, improving, 13
        running particular applications,
        8–9
    installing the upgrade, 17–18
    plan for, 7–8
    reasons for, 5–6
    reasons for *not*, 18–20
    selecting an upgrade, 16–17
    simplicity and ease of, 3–4
upper memory blocks (UMBs), 185

V.22 modem standard, 378
V.22bis modem standard, 378
V.32 modem standard, 378
V.32bis modem standard, 379
V.42 modem standard, 379
V.42bis modem standard, 379
VDISK.SYS, 59–61
vertical scanning frequency, 434–36
VGA (Video Graphics Array), 407
video. *See* display system; monitors
video-based tape backup systems,
  510–12
video memory, 81
Video RAM (VRAM) chips, 205–6
video shadowing, 83
video system. *See* display system
Virtual 8086 Mode, 96–7
virtual memory system, 80–81
VLSI chips, 357

wait states, lowering number of,
  78–79, 107–9
Weitek Corporation coprocessors,
  161–63
word processors
    graphics-based, 45
    recommendations for, 45–46
WORM drives, 317–20, 327–32
    applications of, 331–32
    installation of, 344–50
    standards for, 329–30

XGA (Extended Graphics Array), 407
XMS memory. *See* extended (XMS)
  memory

ZIP (Zig-zag In-line Package), 200
    installation of, 211–12

About the Author

Winn L. Rosch has written about personal computers since 1981 and has penned nearly 1,000 published articles about them—a mixture of reviews, how-to guides, and background pieces explaining new technologies. One of these was selected by The Computer Press Association as the best feature article of the year for 1987; another was runner up for the same award in 1990. He has written six other books about computers, the most recent of which are *The Winn Rosch Hardware Bible* (Brady, 1989) and *The Micro Channel Architecture Handbook*, co-authored with Chet Heath (Brady, 1990). At present, he is a contributing editor to *PC Magazine, PC Week, PC Sources*, and *Computer Shopper*. His books and articles have been reprinted in several languages (French, Italian, German, Greek, and Portugese).

Besides writing, Rosch is an attorney licensed to practice in Ohio and holds a Juris Doctor degree. He was appointed to and currently serves on the Ohio State Bar Association's Computer Law committee.

In other lifetimes Rosch has worked as a photojournalist, electronic journalist, and broadcast engineer. For ten years he wrote regular columns for *The Cleveland Plain Dealer*, Ohio's largest daily newspaper, about stereo and video equipment, and regularly contributed lifestyle features and photographs. In Cleveland, where he still holds out, he has served as chief engineer for several radio stations. He has also worked on electronic journalism projects for the NBC and CBS networks.

In his spare time Rosch conducts experiments on spontaneous generation in his refrigerator and is researching a definitive study of Precambrian literature.